Dictionary *of* Word Origins

Attention Authors

'We Convert Fighters into Writers'. That's the motto of Manas Publications since more than four decades. Our message to the world is that India can win the battle not only by the bullet but also by the pen. There is no dearth of intellectuals in our country, but their knowledge is confined to them only. No sincere effort has been made by any other publisher to channelise their knowledge in national interest. That is why the talent of a large number of intellectuals remains latent. An author transforms his knowledge into a manuscript, and it is our job to spread his/her knowledge by converting it into a beautiful book. For over four decades, Manas has been motivating the intellectuals by publishing their manuscripts and would like to publish your manuscript too. So if you or your colleagues have any manuscript ready for publication or are working on it, kindly contact us with detailed synopsis and list of contents. We will transform your work into a valuable publication. If you wish, we can also suggest you the suitable subjects for writing the books related to your area of expertise. Manas is known for its publishing quality and commitments. We take utmost care in production and give wide publicity to the book as well as its author through our national and international distribution network.

Dictionary
of
Word Origins

by

Joseph T Shipley

Second Edition

Manas Publications
(We Convert Fighters into Writers)
New Delhi-110002 (India)

MANAS PUBLICATIONS

(Publishers for IAS, IPS, IFS, IRS, Defence, Press, Judges etc)

4402/5-A, Ansari Road (Opp HDFC Bank)
Darya Ganj, New Delhi-110 002 (India)
Off.: 23260783, 23265523, Fax: 011-23272766
E-mail: manaspublications@gmail.com
manaspublications@yahoo.com

2013

ISBN: 978-81-7049-462-1

Rs. 995/-

Printed in India at
Rajdhani Printers, Delhi
and published by Mrs Suman Lata for
Manas Publications, 4402/5-A,
Ansari Road (Opp HDFC Bank),
Darya Ganj, New Delhi-110 002 (INDIA)

TO

JAY R. AND JENNIE SHIPLEY

PREFACE

A WORD ABOUT WORDS

To know the origin of words is to know how men think, how they have fashioned their civilization. Word history traces the path of human fellowship, the bridges from mind to mind, from nation to nation.

And our language is truly international. The American speech, like the American people, comes from all over the world. Not two percent of our English words first rose in the British Isles. Somewhere in the Near East they seem to have started, in that Garden of Eden of earliest man. By one path they wandered up rivers, breasting the Danube into the heart of Europe, roaming westward with the Teutons and the Anglo-Saxon speech. On other journeys they took the water route of the great midland sea. Along the shores of the Mediterranean, they lingered in Greece, they built on the seven hills of Rome, and through the Romance language rejoined the Teuton strains to form our English. Twenty-five percent of our words migrated along the rivers; fifty percent, by the sea. The rest were gleaned from here, there, and the farthest corners—brought home by the three restless minglers, the soldier, the trader, and the priest.

Some of the words in our language can be traced to a remote past; some have histories that begin but yesterday. Many are members of large families, with intertwining legend and history; others, like Topsy, "just growed." Slow change, swift new coinage of science or slang, ancient or recent borrowing from many tongues: together they give flexibility, power, and beauty to English, the richest and most widespread language of all time. Of this great gathering of words, I have set down those that have origins at once interesting and enlightening.

Our word history is our race history. The basic democratic process is the shaping of speech. Every man has his tongue in it; the fool as surely as the sage, the peasant and the thief as richly as the robber-baron and the millionaire. The triumphant nobles of William the Conquerer, like the "fig-showers" of ancient Greece, are buried beneath the dust of time; but stories of both are caught in the words *silly* and *sycophant.*

An insight into man's growth; a fresh color and vividness of language; a quickened understanding of our words themselves: these are some of the by-products of a look into word origins. The present dictionary opens such a vista.

No effort has been made to include the slang of the moment — most of which dies with its hour. Some picturesque new words, however, have found their way into the volume, either as illustrating a constant language-process, or behind the skirts of more respectable relatives.

My thanks to the several friends that have made suggestions—and to any readers that may care to send further thoughts.

JOSEPH T. SHIPLEY

TERMS OFTEN USED

aphesis: the loss of an initial letter or syllable, as in *drawingroom*, from *withdrawing-room*. The word that remains is called aphetic.

assimilation: the shift of a sound to match its neighbor, *e.g.*, *assimilation*, from Latin *ad+simil*— . *Cp.* dissimilation.

augmentative: a form added to a word (or the new word) indicating something more than the original word, *e.g.* Italian *-elli*, *-one*; *trombone*.

back-formation: a word, or the creation of a word, from what is apparently a more complex form of the word; thus *grovel* is from *groveling*.

causal: a form indicating action to produce that named by another form of the word; thus *lay*, to make *lie; to fell* is the causal of *to fall*.

cognate: not immediately related, but from the same source. Italian and French are cognate languages, both from Latin; *fatherly* and *paternal* are cognates, the first via AS. through OHG, *fatar*, the second via L. through Gr. *pater*, both from a word akin to Sanskrit *pitar, father*.

dead metaphor: a figure of speech lost in the history of a word; what is now the normal sense was once a metaphorical application. Very many of our words are such tombs; *see, e.g. delirium; pluck*, in the main list.

degeneration: pejoration, *q.v.*

diminutive: a form added to a word (or the new word) indicating something less than the original word; *e.g.* Italian *-ini;* French *-ette;* English *-kin, -ling*: *duckling, darling*.

dissimilation: the shift of a sound so as not to repeat its neighbor; e.g. *angel* from Gr. *aggelos*. *Cp.* assimilation.

doublet: one word of two identical in origin. A list of these appears in Appendix I. There may also be triplets and quadruplets.

echoic: onomatopoetic, *q.v.*

elevation: melioration, *q.v.*

euphemism: a term employed to avoid direct mention of an unpleasant idea; *e.g.*, *gone west* for *died*.

frequentative: a verbal form indicating the repetition or rapid performance of the action of the simple verb, *e.g.*, *startle* from *start*.

ghost-word: a word produced by a misprint or other error, *e.g. tweed*.

Grimm's law: the principle of consonantal shift in words of Indo-European origin; explained at end of this list.

inceptive: a verbal form indicating the beginning, or the first stage, of an action: usually Latin *-escere*, French *iss*, English *-ish*. Thus *adolescent* is an inceptive, becoming *adult; vanish; coalesce*.

intensive: a form expressing increased force, as *splash* from *plash*. The prefix *com*, together, was used in Latin, sometimes, in the sense of altogether; this use survives in, *e.g.*, *commence, commend, conclude*.

melioration: improvement of meaning (during the history of a word), as with *bewitch*. Also called elevation.

metathesis: transposition of letters in a word, as *fringe* from Latin *fimbria*.

nonce-word: a word employed but once; either for a unique purpose, or as a new term that did not win acceptance; *e.g.*, manikins with *capkins* (little caps).

onomatopoetic: (Echoism is often used, today, for onomatopoeia.) imitative of a sound, as *bang, murmur*.

origin of speech, theories of: *See* end of this list.

pejoration: development of a worse meaning (during the history of a word), as with *villain, silly*. Also called degeneration.

TERMS OFTEN USED (Continued)

pejorative; lessening the value of: implying scorn, as the suffix in gang*ster*, racket*eer*, slugg*ard*.

pleonasm: unnecessary repetition—sometimes buried within a word, as in *darling*, which is a double diminutive, *-l* + *-ing*.

portmanteau-word: a word formed by pressing two together, *e.g. brunch* from *breakfast* and *lunch; chortle* from *chuckle* and *snort*. Also called telescoped.

reduplicated: formed through repetition of sound; *see scurry*, in the main list.

slide: the movement in meaning (during the history of a word) from the whole range of a scale to a specific point, usually one end, of that scale; *e.g., temper, humor*.

telescope: *See* portmanteau-word.

variant: a different form of a word, usually due to local peculiarities of dialect.

GRIMM'S LAW

The Grimm (Jakob, died 1863) that helped gather the fairy tales also produced Grimm's law of consonant shifting. Simplified to cover just the English field, it may be stated thus:

Group the consonants in three scales:

GUTTURALS: *g, k, kh* (Latin, *h*), *g*

DENTALS: *d, t, th* (Latin, *f*), *d*

LABIALS: *b, p, ph* (*f*), *b*.

Each Teutonic word begins one letter in its scale above the corresponding classical word. For instances:

GUTTURALS: *genus-kin, gelid-cold; circle, (h)ring; choler-gall, host-guest.*

DENTALS: *dual-two, dactyl-toe; trivial-three, theme-doom, fume-dust.*

LABIALS: *paternal-fatherly, putrid-foul; fertile-bear, fragile-break.*

THEORIES OF THE ORIGIN OF LANGUAGE

No primeval man has left a record of the way in which language started. It may have begun in individual cries, of pain or fear, or wonder, or triumph and joy; but it was soon brought to social ends, for the communication of these and other feelings and desires. None of the theories of origin of speech fully explains its complications; scientific opinion is indicated by some of their names. There is the *bow-wow* theory, which pictures language as springing from spontaneous animal cries. Or you may choose the *pooh-pooh* theory, which sees the start of words in emotional outbursts. Perhaps, instead, you prefer the *ding-dong* theory, which sees language arising from imitation of natural sounds. The word-stuff of the first theory still appears in the noises we use to say yes (uhhuh.), to indicate that we haven't heard (hmm?); to mark our hesitation (hmmm.) or our scorn (hn!). The second theory finds support today in exclamations (Ah!..Ow!) and calls (Ho!..Hey!) The third has the richest body of actual speech to favor it, in the many onomatopoetic, or echoic, words: *hum; thud; bump; boom; buzz; murmur; hiss.*

ABBREVIATIONS

AFr . . . Anglo-French
Arab . . . Arabic
Aram . . . Aramaic
AS . . . Anglo-Saxon
c . . . century, centuries
ca . . . about
Celt . . . Celtic
Chin . . . Chinese
cp . . . compare
d . . . died
Dan . . . Danish
Du . . . Dutch
e.g. . . . for example
Egyp . . . Egyptian
Eng . . . English
esp . . . especial, -ly
Fr . . . French
Flem . . . Flemish
G . . . German
Gael . . . Gaelic
Goth . . . Gothic
Gr . . . Greek
Heb . . . Hebrew
Hind . . . Hindi
Hung . . . Hungarian
Icel . . . Icelandic
i.e. . . . that is
Ir . . . Irish
It . . . Italian
Jap . . . Japanese
L . . . Latin
Lith . . . Lithuánian
LG . . . Low German
LL . . . Late Latin
M . . . Middle (before another abbrev.)
MDu . . . Middle Dutch
ME . . . Middle English
MHG . . . Middle High German
mod . . . modern
modL . . . modern Latin
NED. New English Dictionary (Oxford)
Norw . . . Norwegian
O . . . Old (before another abbreviation)
ODu . . . Old Dutch
OE . . . Old English
OHG . . . Old High German
OIr . . . Old Irish
ON . . , Old Norse
ONFr . . . Old Norman French
OTeut . . . Old Teutonic
Pers . . . Persian
Pol . . . Polish
Port . . . Portuguese
Prov . . . Provencal
q.v. . . . which see (plural qq.v.)
Rom . . . Romance, Romanic
Rum . . . Rumanian
S . . . Saxon
Sansk . . . Sanskrit
Sc . . . Scottish
Scand . . . Scandinavian
Slav . . . Slavic, Slavonic
Sp . . . Spanish
Sw . . . Swedish
Teut . . . Teutonic
Turk . . . Turkish
+ . . . combined with
?...origin questionable

DICTIONARY

of

WORD ORIGINS

A

A 1.
When we speak of a thing as *A1,* we mean that it is excellent in all respects. In Lloyd's ships' register, which records the condition of all vessels at all times, the condition of the ship's hull is indicated by letter; of its equipment, by number; hence the ship-shape quality of *A*1.

aard-vark.
This animal from South Africa has a name that has traveled, too. It is Du. *aarde,* earth+Du. *vark,* OE. *fearh,* from OHG. *farh,* cognate with L. *porc-,* pig (whence Eng. *pork*): earth-pig. There is also an *aard-wolf* in those parts.

abacinate.
A Broadway play of the 1944 season (*The Duke in Darkness,* by Patrick Hamilton, with Philip Merivale) brings this word to mind, from its threat to the main character. The word hides a much more sinister deed, being merely from L. *abacinare, abacinat-,* from *ab,* off, + *bacinus, basin.* The *basin* was used in medieval times when a man was blinded by holding hot metal in front of his eyes; to *abacinate* is to blind in this fashion. (For *basin, see basinet.*)

abacus.
See calculate.

abaft.
This word of five letters had originally four separate parts. The *a* is an OE. prefix or preposition, meaning on, at. The *b* is what is left (before a vowel) of *bi, be,* a preposition meaning about. The *aft* was OE. *aeftan,* from behind; this is from *af,* meaning off, away, + the superlative ending *ta.* Hence also *after,* more away, which was originally the comparative form of *af,* off, away. OE. *af* is cognate with L. *ab,* away; with Gr. *apo* (thus *apothecary* was first a storekeeper, from Gr. *apotheka,* store, from *apo,* away, + *tithenai,* to lay: to lay away), and Sans. *apa.* The L. and the Gr. prefixes, *ab* and *apo,* are frequent in Eng. words.

abandon.
See ban.

abash.
"Baa, baa, black sheep" begins with an imitative cry. The natural sound of the mouth opened wide in surprise or shame gives us *ba! See* abeyance.

abate.
The lessening accomplished in this word was evidently effected through no peaceful means. It is from Fr. *abaitre,* from LL. *abattere,* from *ab,* off, down + *battere,* from *battuere,* to *beat.* The same word pictures the old wall of felled trees, the *abattis;* also, the modern slaughter-house, the *abattoir.*

The same L. *battuere,* via Fr. *battre,* arrives at Eng. *batter;* and *battery,* at first the beating (assault, *q.v.,* and *battery*), then the means for delivering it. *The Battery,* New York, was the site of a fort. Via Fr. *bataille,* from LL. *battualis,* the adjective from *battuere,* come *battle* and *battlement; battalion* is, from Fr. *bataillon* via It. *battaglione,* diminutive of *battaglia,* from L. *battualia,* neuter plural of *battualis.* This may seem like *battology,* which is, from Gr. *battologos,* stammerer, from *Battos,* man mentioned in Herodotus, iv, 155, + *logia,* from *logos,* word, from *legein,* to speak. May the *battles abate!*

abattis, abattoir.
See abate.

abbot.
This word has traveled far, but a straight journey, from AS. *abbod,* from L. *abbas, abbat—,* from Gr. *abbas,* from Aram. *abba,* father. Beyond that, it is drawn from the calls of the *babe. Babe* and *baby* are likewise imitative of the sounds of the infant. So too are *papa* and *mamma;* whence L. *mamma,* breast

and the *mammals* all. (Note that *pap,* with its diminutive *papilla,* is also a term for the breast; whence possibly L. and Eng. *pabulum,* food, and L. *pascere, past*—to feed, whence Eng. *pasture,* the *pastor* of the flock; and Algonkin *papoose. Cp. congress.* We speak of the *paschal* lamb; but this is in celebration of the Hebrew holiday, from Gr. *pascha,* Heb. *pesakh,* from *pasakh,* to pass over, because the angels of the Lord, in smiting the first-born of the Egyptians, passed over the houses of the Israelites—who shortly thereafter passed over the Red Sea.) *Papal, papacy,* and *pope* are derived from *papa,* which was early used for bishop.

An early 20th c. art group, looking for a name, decided that, while the first emotional cry of the infant was *ma-ma,* its first groping toward intellectual expression was *da-da;* hence, *dadaism.*

abbreviate.
See abridge.

abdicate.
See verdict.

abdomen.
There are two suggestions as to the source of this word. As it is the pouch or paunch of the body, where things are stowed away, it may be from L. *abdere, abdit—,* to stow away, to hide, from *ab,* away, + *dare, dat—* (*see dice*), to give, to put. From this word there were early Eng. *abdite* and *abditive.* But the most visible part of the *abdomen* is its rounded outside; the first meaning of the word was the fat belly; and it may come from L. *adeps, adipem,* fat. This + the suffix *—osus,* full of, gives us Eng. *adipose. Adeps* is the scientific Eng. word for animal fat. *Adept,* however, is from L. *adipisci, adept—,* to attain, from *ad,* to + *ap—,* get.

There is an Eng. *abdite,* hidden. *Cp. recondite.*

abduction.
See duke.

abet.
See bait.

abeyance.
This word, indicating what you "hold" something in when you haven't yet received it, originally pictured the appearance of the expectant one. It is by way of the Fr. *a, at* + *béer,* from LL. *badare,* to gape. (Whence also the modern Fr. *aboyer,* to bark.) Through the Fr. *esbair, esbaiss—,* to make gape (L. *ex* + *ba!*) we have *abash,* and *bashful.* The simple noun (Fr. *baie,* from OFr. *baée, bayer,* to gape) has thus run two courses. As the sound of impatience (related to an original *ba,* the exclamation of surprise) it becomes the *baying* of hounds; thence, their pressing upon their quarry until it is forced to stand at *bay.* Hence also an obstacle, an embankment or dam. As the gap, the opening, it has come to refer to a space between two columns, and to such recesses as a horse-*bay* (stall), sick-*bay* on a ship, and *bay*-window. This meaning has intertwined with the body of water, *bay, q.v.*

abhor.
If something makes your hair stand on end, you *abhor* it, from L. *abhorrere,* to shrink back, from *ab,* away, + *horrere,* to stand on end (of hair). The noun *horror* is directly from the L.; the present participle of *abhorrere* is (Eng. also) *abhorrent. Horrible* and *horrid,* at first referring to the victim, have both been transferred to the cause, like the little girl with the curl in the middle of her forehead.

abide.
See bottle.

abigail.
This word for a servant girl grew into common use from several instances. *Abigail* (Heb., source of joy) was the wife of Nabal (*Bible, I Samuel* xxv); she introduced herself to David and later married him. Beaumont and Fletcher, shortly after the King James Version, 1611, of the *Bible,* used the name for a maid-servant in their play, *The Scornful Lady,* 1616. It was similarly used by Swift, Fielding, and others; then Queen Anne of England was attended by one *Abigail Hill* . . . thereafter the word could be spelled without the capital *A.*

ability.
This word was originally related to one's power to hold on to things; it is from the L. noun *habilitas,* from the adjective *habilis, habile,* from the verb *habere, habit-,* to have, to hold. Both *able* and *habile* come from this; *able* at first meant easy to handle; then possess-

ing ease in handling. The Fr. *habiller,* to make ready, then to dress, gives us Eng. *habiliment;* directly from the L. is *habit; see customer.* Many writers in the 16th and 17th c. wrote *hability,* trying to shift from the Fr. to the L. spelling; but by 1700 the form *ability* had prevailed.

These transformations—of *habit;* custom, costume; *habiliment*—suggest indeed that clothes make the man; the original sense, however, remains in *habilitate* and *rehabilitate.* The word *have* is from OE. *habben, haefde;* and a place that holds you (safely) is, via OE. *haefen,* a *haven.* This is common Teut., Dan. *havn,* transformed in the Eng. form of the name *Copenhagen.*

abject.
See subject.

ablative.
See suffer.

able.
See ability.

ablution.
See lotion.

abode.
See bottle.

abolish.
This is one of the few words that has grown stronger in meaning down the ages. The L. *ab,* away, + *olere,* to grow, from its inceptive form *abolescere,* led to Fr. *abolir, aboliss—,* to do away with; whence *abolish.* (An instance of a word that has grown weaker in meaning is *debate.*) The inceptive with prefix *ad,* to, L. *adolescere, adult—,* gives us *adolescent, adult; see world.*

abominable.
Omens, or signs of what is to come, were usually dreaded; most often, the sign was of evil. Hence the L. expression *absit omen*: May the omen be away. Hence an *abominable* thing was one to be away from, to be avoided; hence, a hateful or disgusting thing. In the 14th c., however, Wyclif (following the Fr.) spelled the word *abhominable,* as though it meant away from man (L. *homen,* man), inhuman, beastly. Shakespeare also uses this spelling, 14 times, *e.g. As You Like It,* IV, i, 6.

abortion.
An *abortive* effort, in the days of sun worship, might have meant one in which the striver turned from the east; *see orient.* Eng. *abort* is directly from L. *aboriri, abort—,* to miscarry, from *ab,* off, away, + *oriri,* to appear, arise, come into being. As an *aborted* child was usually deformed, the word was for a time spelled *abhorsion,* as though related to *abhor, q.v.*

abound.
See abundance.

about.
Like many other words that have come down from early Eng. (*e.g., abaft*), several small words have merged in this one. It is OE. *on, on + be, by,* near, + *utan,* outside: near by the outside of. Hence, near by; at first applied to position only, the word was soon used in many figurative ways, to mean nearly, around, etc.

aboveboard.
The first part of this word (for the second, *see board*) is twisted, from AS. *abufan,* from *bufan,* from *be ufan,* by upward, from *uf,* up. The whole word (this sounds like a charade!) draws its meaning, honest, from the suspicion that one might not be honest: It refers to the fact that one must shuffle cards *above the board, i.e.,* the table, so as to obviate the possibility of slipping in or changing cards. (*Charade* seems to come, from Prov. *charrada,* from *charrar,* to prattle; whence also *charlatan,* from It. *ciarlare,* to chatter. Similarly *quack,* an imitative word, is applied to a *quacksalver,* a doctor whose prattle sells his *salves.*)

abracadabra.
This word of medieval magic is traced to a mythical Persian sun god, summoned to the magician's aid. But also, its letters add (in numerology) to 365, so that it encompasses the entire year and the powers of the 365 attendant spirits of the Lord.

It is not a corruption of the Cabalistic Heb. *habraha dabar,* bless the object.

abrade, abrasion.
See rascal. (L. *ab,* off, + *radere, ras—.*)

abridge.
To make a bridge, or short cut, to something, is not the origin of this word. It comes through Fr. *abridgier,*

from *abrevier,* from L. *abbreviare,* to shorten, from *brevis,* short, whence Eng. *brief.* Related are Gr. *braxys* and Eng. *break.* Later on, directly from the L., came the doublet of *abridge, abbreviate.*

abscess.
See ancestor.

abscond.
See askance.

absent.
This is directly from the present participle, *absent—,* of L. *absum, abesse,* to be away. The Fr. pronounciation permits the well-known pun: when some one complained that a friend did not come around: *"Il s'absent trop";* another replied, in explanation: *"Il s'absinthe trop."* (He *absents* himself too much. He *absinthes* himself too much.) *Absinth, absinthe,* is from L. *absinthium,* wormwood, the plant from which the drink is made.

absinth, absinthe.
See absent.

absolute.
If you are *absolved* you are set free (from sin and guilt, in church use), from L. *absolvere, absolut—,* from *ab,* from, + *solvere, solut—,* to loosen. But if you are loose, free from ties, you are acting wholly by yourself; hence the sense of *absolute* monarchy and the like. The *solution* of a problem is that which loosens it—especially if it be a knotty one; then of course you have *solved* it. Chemical *solution* is aphetic for *dissolution,* a loosening apart (L. *dis,* away, apart); the verb still retains the full form, *dissolve.* The L. *solvere* is from L. *se,* apart [as in *segregate,* to set apart from the herd, L. *grex, greg—,* herd, whence also Eng. *aggregate* (*ag, ad,* to) and *gregarious*] + *luere,* to pay, to clear (of debt), to wash clean, from Gr. *louein,* to *lave.* Earlier is the Aryan root *lau,* to wash (whence Eng. *lather*); whence OE. *leag,* whence Eng. *lye.* On this trail, combining OE. *lafian,* to pour water, and L. *lavare, lavat—,* to wash, comes Eng. *lave; see lotion.*

absquatulate.
This humorous coinage of mid 19th c. United States has ancient antecedents. The *ab* is L. *ab,* from; the ending—*ulate,* an active verbal suffix, perhaps from L. *ferre, lat—,* to bear: hence, to carry away from a *squat.* *Squat* is from OFr. *esquatir, esquatiss—,* (whence also *squash*), from LL. *quatere, quass,* to press flat, to crouch; from LL. type *coactire,* from L. *cogere, coact—,* to squeeze, from *co,* together, + *agere,* to do, to make. The present participle of *cogere* is *cogens, cogent—,* whence Eng. *cogent,* pressing together, hence constraining, powerful. There was an uncompressed combination of L. *agere* and *co,* as well: *coagere,* whence the LL. frequentative *coagulare, coagulat—,* whence Eng. *coagulate*—not far in its fashioning from the word we began with!

abstain.
This is a word that came from the Fr.; then it was respelled to make it nearer the original L. OFr. *astenir* (whence early Eng. *asteine*) is from L. *abstinere,* from *abs,* off, + *tenere,* to hold. The simple verb gives us directly Eng. *tenant,* one holding; and, via the adjective, *tenacious. Cp. lieutenant.* The present participle of *abstinere* is *abstinens, abstinent—,* whence Eng. *abstinent.* The meaning of this word has influenced and made more general the sense of *abstemious, q.v.*

abstemious.
If liquor is too strong for you, you will choke on it. Sansk. *tam,* to choke, to be breathless, whence L. *temum,* strong drink, whence *temetum,* liquor, whence *temulentus,* drunk. If you keep away from this (L. *ab, abs,* away) you are *abstemious* (*-ous,* from L. *-osus,* full of, full of keeping away from strong drink)!

abstinent.
See abstain.

abstract.
See attract.

absurd.
The L. word *surdus* had several related senses. Originally meaning deaf, it was soon extended to mean mute also. We use it in that sense in phonetics, the *surds* being the *consonants* uttered without voice, as *p, t, k;* opposed to these are the *sonants b, d, g* (*sonant* is direct from the L., being present participle of *sonare, sonat—,* to *sound; consonant,* sounding together; *sonata,* etc.). Then the L. word *surdus* was used to translate Gr. *alogos,* in the tenth Book of Euclid's *Geometry* (*geo—,* earth, + *metron,* measure: first used in surveying; *geography,* writing about the earth; *cp. graft, sarcophagus*); hence it came to mean irrational (Gr. *a,* away from, + *logos,* word, reason). The same *surdus* also was used

to mean inaudible, or insufferable when heard (so that you wish you were deaf!); with *ab* as an intensive, this became Eng. *absurd.*

abuccinate.
See buccal.

abundance.
When fortune, or wealth, rolls upon you in waves (as may it often!) you enjoy things in *abundance* (L. *ab,* from + *unda,* wave). For a time in the middle ages, this was spelled *habundance,* as though from *habere,* have: to have in plenty. (For a similar misspelling, *see abominable.*) *Abound* is of course from the same word. When the sea comes in less pleasantly, we speak of an *inundation* (*in,* into + *unda*). The wavelike motion of a serpent, or the rise and dip of the countryside, is likewise a Latin figure of speech: *undulation.*

abuse.
See usury, urn. (from L. *abuti, abusus,* from *ab,* away + *uti, usus,* to *use*): the word meant to *use* up, then to *disuse,* then to *misuse.* (L. *dis,* away; *mis*— from OFr. *mes* from L. *minus,* wrongly, as in *mischance, miscarriage, mischief*: early Eng. *cheve,* from OFr. *chever,* from *chef,* head.)

abut.
See butt.

academy.
This name for a school, as many know, is carried over from the early days of Athens, when Plato taught in the grove called the *Academeia.* Not so many, however, know how the grove got its name.
A fateful young lady named Helen in her early days was carried from Sparta by the hero Theseus. Her brothers, Castor and Pollux (they are still to be seen in the sky: the constellation called *Gemini,* the twins) went in search of her, and a farmer named *Academus* put them on the right track. Since then, the grove on the farm of *Academus* was protected; the city grew around it, and it was in that grove, the *Academy,* that Plato spread his tables when he held his *symposiums* (*q.v.*). *Cp. Platonic.*

accent.
This word springs from a translation into Latin (*accentum,* from *ad,* to, + *cantus,* singing) of the Greek *prosodia* (from *pros,* added to, + *ode,* song). Syllables spoken with a grave *accent* were in a deep voice; those in an acute *accent* were a musical fifth higher; those with a circumflex (*circum,* around, + *flex,* from L. *flectere, flex,* to bend; whence Eng. *flexible, reflect*) began high and dropped a fifth while sounding.
With the shift from length and pitch to volume, in language sounds in the English tradition, the word has come to mean the stress; also, the sign that indicates any such emphasis.
By way of It. *canto* from L. *cantus* comes Eng. *canto,* a song, or a section of a poem (as Dante's *Divine Comedy*); via the Fr. comes *chant; cp. saunter.*

access.
See ancestor.

accident.
See cheat.

accolade.
See collar.

accommodate.
The word *mode* was anciently used (L. *modus,* measure) to indicate one of the scales in Greek music; then a tune; then a manner of singing; then the manner of doing anything. To *moderate* is thence, from L. *moderari, moderat-,* to give measure to. The diminutive of *modus, modulus,* similarly gives Eng. *modulate;* and, via It. *modello,* whence Fr. *modèle,* Eng. *model,* a little measure, criterion. A *modest* person is one whose ways are measured.
If things tune together well, they are attuned or *accommodated* to each other, (from L. *accommodatus,* from *ac,* from *ad,* to, with, + *com,* together, + *modus*). With L. *dis,* away from, we have *discommode. Commode* was at first an adjective, meaning convenient (measured together); in the 17th and 18th c. it became a noun, applied to various convenient things, from a headdress to a procuress, from a toilet to a chest of drawers; at the same time the intensive adjective *commodious* (L. *-osus,* full of, whence Eng. *-ous*) was introduced. A *commodity* was a convenience, then an opportunity, then advantage, then a thing to sell at an advantage, merchandise. Be *modest,* but not too *accommodating.*

accomplice.
See plot.

accord, accordion.
See prestige.

accost.
When you greet a person, you are (or were, before the telephone) likely to be at his side. *Accost* is from L. *ad*, at, to + *costa*, rib, then side. Thus the side of anything is also its *coast*, especially, today, the side of the ocean. To *coast* means to sail along the shore; then, to sail leisurely. However, from the side of a hill (which we no longer call its *coast*) we retain the meaning to *coast*, to slide downhill, as on a sled; thence, to ride without using power, as downhill on a bicycle to greet a friend at the station.

account.
See calculate.

accoutrement.
There are two stories suggested for this word. It may be from Fr. *accoustre*, from OFr. *cousteur*, the sacristan of a church, one of whose duties was to care for the sacred vestments, from L. *custos*, sacristan, whence *custodian*. Or it may be from L. *consutura*, a seam, from *consuere*, to sew together, whence Fr. *coudre* + *ac*, from *ad*, to. Either way, it covers the clothes.

accumulate.
L. *ad*, to + *cumulare*, from *cumulus*, a little pile, a mound. Thus when we say that a man has *accumulated* a fortune, we are putting into formal terms the thought that he has "made his pile."

accurate.
If you take pains, your work is likely to be *accurate*. Precisely; for its origin is L. *ad*, to + *cura*, pains, care (*curare*, *curatus* past participle, to take care). Hence a *curate* is one to whom is entrusted the care, or (the term is still thus used) the *cure* of souls. To *cure*, heal, is obviously the result of taking care. Make something with care (as *curiously* first indicated) and it will be well-wrought, worth taking note of. Hence the various meanings of *curious;* also, *curio*, *curiosity*. Something that has the power to heal is *curative;* one that takes care of a building or of a lunatic is a *curator*. Thus the one word has been applied to the agent (*curate; curious* person), the act (*cure*), and the product (*curious* object; *curio*). *Curiosity* is the quality in you; a *curiosity* is the thing at which you wonder. In applying your terms, be *accurate*. To *procure* (L. *pro*, in behalf of) originally meant to obtain with care, to *secure*—the first sense of which was in the adjective *secure* (L. *se*—, apart), remote from care; hence, safe. A *procurator* was a man in charge of the Emperor's treasury, in ancient Rome; it remains as an historical term, but for practical use has been contracted (and diminished in sense) to *proctor*. Similarly the old *procuracy*, which meant managing or acting for another, has dwindled into the common *proxy*.

acetic.
See acetylene.

acetylene.
It all began with wine that turned sour. Latin for *vinegar* (from Fr. *vin aigre*, sour wine) was *acetum*, from *acere*, *acet*—, to be sour. Hence, *acetic acid*, in more scientific term. Adding Gr. *yle*, substance, gives us Eng. *acetyl*, the basis of the *acetic* series of chemicals. Add to this the Greek ending that means female descendant (i.e., a weaker substance, from the "weaker" sex) and you have *acetylene*, from which organic compounds can be produced. From the same *acere*, via the adjective *acidus*, comes Eng. *acid*, etc. The root is not sour but sharp, L. *ac*—, as also in *acme*, *acumen*, *q.v.*, etc. From the same source is *acne*, or "the rosy-drop.".

ache.
Samuel Johnson, in his *Dictionary*, permanently confused us about this word. Deriving *ake* (A.S. *acan*, whence OE. *aece*) from Gr. *axos*, he said the spelling should be *ache*. Normally, in words of the sort, the verb in English has kept the *k* spelling and sound, the noun has taken the *ch* sound and spelling. Thus *bake*, *batch; break*, *breach; make*, *match; speak*, *speech; stick*, *stitch; wake*, *watch*. Here also, probably, belong *eat* and *etch*. Shakespeare distinguishes between the two forms; but we have given both of them the *ch* spelling and the *k* pronounciation. —Unless, of course, we use *ache* to mean the eighth letter of the English alphabet.

All the verbs above are common Teut. words: *bake* from AS. *bacan; break* (*see discuss*) from AS. *brecan; make* from AS. *macian* (the past tense, *made*, is telescoped from *makede*)*; speak* (*see unspeakable*) from AS. *sprecan*, *specan; stick* (*see attack*) from AS. *stician*, to pierce; *wake* (*see vegetable*) from AS.

wacian. A *batch* was, first, a *"baking"* of bread. A *match* was, first, one of a pair *made;* used esp. of animal and human mates; hence, to *match*. The *match* we light is via Fr. *mèche*, wick, and LL. *mysca*, from Gr. *myxa*, slime, snuff of a candle.

The *axos* from which Johnson thought *ache* to be derived is cognate with L. *agere, axi, actum*, to do, to drive, to move; whence *axis; action; see exact*. From *cum* (*com, co*) *together*, + *agere*, came LL. *coagulare, coagulat—*, to draw together, whence Eng. *coagulate*. The Gr. *myxa*, candle snuff or slime, is used as a prefix in Eng. technical words, *e.g., myxoma, myxomycetes*. But Gr. *mixo—* is the root from which comes also L. *miscere, mixtus*, to *mix;* whence Eng. *mix, promiscuous;* and directly from the Gr. such compounds as *mixolydian, mixogamous, mixtilinear*. Which *makes* quite a *mixture*, if not a *headache!*

achieve.

This word gives us a *headstart* for a long journey. Contracted from the Fr. *venir à chief*, to come to a head, from L. *ad caput venire*, it originally meant to come to a peak, to end. Death is the most significant end; thus Shakespeare says: (*Henry V*, IV,iii) "Bid them *atchieve* me, and then sell my bones." He also uses it to mean merely to bring to an end: (*Coriolanus*, IV, vii) "He does *atchieve* as soon As draw his sword." But the best end is a happy ending; in Shakespeare's time all three senses were employed: (*Twelfth Night*, V,i). "Some *atchieve* greatness, some have greatness thrust upon them." ME. had a *bonchief* (L. *bonus*, good) which we have lost, while preserving its more prevalent opposite, *mischief* (L. *minus*; Eng. *amiss*). Shakespeare coined the adj. *mischievous*.

Through the Fr. (ME. *chef*) also comes *chief*, the head person or, as an adj., the most important. The full noun is *chieftain*, an early form of which was *chevetaine*, which is closely allied to *captain*. *Captain* is indeed the same word, coming more directly from the L. *caput*, head. (*Head* itself is a widespread word: AS. *heafod*, G. *Haupt*, ON. *höfuth*, Goth. *haubith*, cognate with *caput*.) *Cp. cad*. There are many words from this source. *Capital* means relating to the *head*, as *capital* punishment; or standing at the *head*, as *capital* letter, *capital* (city), *capital* (property). To *capitalize* and *capitalist* follow from this use. Architecture still uses the word *capital* as the *head* or top of a column. *Capitol* was the temple of Jupiter, at the *head* (top) of the Saturnian hill in Rome, whence the hill was called the *capitoline;* now a *capitol* is an official state-house. To arrange items by *headings* was to *capitulate* them; whence the word was applied to stipulated or drawn up terms of a treaty; even in LL. a surrender is a *capitulation*. What men once, and boys still, put on their *heads*, is a *cap;* the middle ages (St. Isidor; Papias, ca. 1050) derived this from *capere, capt—*, to take: all men were taken beneath the *cap* of the church; but this is folk etymology. The French still picture *cape, chapel*, etc., from *capere*, quoting Isidor de Seville *"cape*, because it *captures* (*capiat*) the whole man."

From *capital*, property, whence ME. *chatel* (whence *chattel*-mortgage), *catel*, we derive what was long the most important property, *cattle;* thus to ask "How many head of cattle?" is to repeat oneself.

Cap-à-pie (the French now say *de pied en cap*) means from *head* to foot, as knights were fitted with armour, for soundest defense; hence they were in excellent shape, or (again folk etymology) in *applepie* order. *Cape*, meaning a cloak, originally a cloak with a hood, is also from *caput;* from it the LL. verb *caparo*, to put a cloak on, gives us the word *caparison*, to harness, to bedeck. More directly from *caput* is the same word *cape* as applied to a headland, earth jutting into the sea. The *biceps* (L. *bi*, two) seem to have two heads.

The word *cappa* had two medieval diminutives. *Capeline*, a skull-cap of iron worn by archers, survives in medicine as the bandage a surgeon makes (in the form of a sort of *cap*) for amputations or head-wounds. *Cappella*, a cloak, which has changed its form, has the more interesting history. For the cloak of St. Martin was preserved as a holy relic, and the guardian of this *cappella* (OFr. *chapele* ME. *chapele*) was the *chaplain;* the place where it was kept, the *chapel*. As this part of the church is not equipped with an organ, the It. *a capella*, from the *chapel*, has come to be the musical term for singing without accompaniment. *Chaplet*, another diminutive, is still used as a headdress of flowers. The hood worn by the Knights of the Garter (attendants on the Queen) was a *chaperon;* hence the application to any guide and protector. ME. *chapiter,* applied to a *heading,* then to a main division of a book, became *chapter;* in turn this was applied to the religious meetings where a *chapter* was read, then to those that met, and we have the *chapter* of a fraternity. Much more could be given on this *head;* but to *escape* monotony let us add only that often a man grasped by his cloak would slip out of it and flee—whence L. *ex cappa,* out of the *cape,* whence OFr. *escaper* (whence Fr. *échapper*), whence Eng. *escape.* Which in itself was an *achievement!*

Achilles tendon; Achilles' heel.
The tendon of your heel takes its name from the story, that *Achilles* at birth was dipped in the Styx to make him invulnerable. His mother, the Nereid Thetis, held him by the heel—during the Trojan War, Apollo revealed this to Paris, whose shot thus slew the Greek hero. Your *Achilles' heel* is your vulnerable spot. Siegfried (as *Samson* was betrayed by *Delilah,* who cut his hair: and his name symbolizes strength; hers, treachery) was seduced into marking his one vulnerable spot with a leaf; there an arrow pierced him.

acid, acme.
See acumen.

acne.
See acetylene.

acorn.
This word is common Teut., O.E. *aecern,* Goth. *akran,* fruit of the open fields and forests, from Goth, *akr,* OE. *aecer,* open field, akin to L. *ager,* Gr. *agros,* Sansk. *ajras,* whence Eng. *acre, q.v.* The Gr. word first means wild land, whence L. *agrestis,* wild, Gr. *agreus,* hunter; L. *peragrare,* to wander, whence (via the adjective *peregrinus*) Eng. *peregrination, cp. belfry.* Advancing civilization then changed the meaning to that which we associate with *agriculture,* from L. *agri cultura,* tilling the field, from *colere, cult,* to *cultivate* (*cultivating* the favor of the gods is to attend them, to worship them; hence *cult*). The most common "fruit of the forest" in northern Europe and England was that of the oak tree; hence the *aecern* by association with that tree was variously called *okecorne, okehorne, akern, accorne,* and finally *acorn.*

acoustics.
This word, a plural formed by analogy with *politics, mathematics, civics,* etc., comes via Fr. *acoustique* from Gr. *acoustikos,* relating to hearing, from Gr. *akouein,* to hear. Although we apply this word to *auditoriums* (from L. *audire, audit—,* to hear, + *—orium,* place where; *cp. audit*), there is an Eng. word, now obsolete, which neatly fits our radio talks; *acousmata* (plural of Gr. *acousma,* anything heard), things accepted on authority.

acquaint, acquaintance.
See quaint.

acquiesce.
See acquit.

acquit.
To *quit* is to leave a place *quiet* (L. *quietus*). LL. *acquietare,* to settle a claim (*ac,* from *ad,* to) meant that a man was thereafter left at peace; so, today, one can be tried but once for any crime. From the inceptive form of the verb, *acquiescere,* to rest, comes Eng. *acquiesce.*

acre.
This word is, from L. *ager,* fertile country, field, from Sumerian *agar,* a watered field, from *a,* water. *Potters' Field* (*Bible, Matthew* xxvii, 7: purchased with the thirty pieces of silver Judas threw away before killing himself) was once a field whence potters drew their clay; the soil rapidly decomposed the bodies . . . the free burial ground was later called *God's acre. Cp. saunter; goodbye; acorn.* A *wiseacre* has no relation to such fields, but is a combination of G. *Weissager,* know-sayer, prophet, and G. *Wahrsager,* truth-teller, soothsayer. On this path, via ON. *saga,* come *saga,* a saying, tale; and, via AS. *witig, wit; see* moot.

acrid, acrobat.
See acumen.

acrostic.
Two arrangements of Greek verse were: (1) in *strophes,* (from *strephein,* to turn; *cp. apostrophe*); and (2) *stichic,* (from *stichos,* row) or in continuous lines. (The former was used mainly in the drama; the latter, in the epic.) An *acrostic* (*cp. acumen*) is a row at the front, *i.e.,* the first letters of each line in succession spell a word

Originally, if this occurred at the end of the lines, the poem was a *telestich* (Gr. *tele,* far); now *acrostic* is used for both types—also if the significant letters criss-cross or run down the center. Note that there is also a rare adverb, *acrostic,* meaning slantwise, formed directly from the Eng. word *across.* *Cp: criss-cross.*

act.
See exact.

actinium.
See element.

action, active, actor, actual.
See exact.

acumen.
L. *acus,* needle, whence *acuere, acut—,* to sharpen. From these came the L. noun *acumen,* which we have taken directly, but use only in the figurative sense, as sharpness of mind. The adj. *acute* is used both figuratively (sharp-witted) and literally (*acute* angle, sound, accent). The same word, by aphesis, has become the familiar *cute.* Other forms appear in scientific use. The diminutive *aculeate* means equipped with a sting (insects) or with thorns (plants); *aculeolus,* a double diminutive, is used of cactus with many small prickles; and there are a dozen more such terms, as *aculeiform, acuminate, acupressure* (in medicine), *acupuncture, acutifoliate, acutonodose.*

The Gr. *akme,* point, gives us *acme,* highest point. Also, the *akropolis* (Gr. *akr—,* point + *polis,* city; *cp. police*) is on the highest point in Athens. *Acrobat* is from Gr. *akrobatein,* from *akros,* point (of toes) + *batos,* past participle of *bainein,* to go.

Through OFr. *ague,* whence Fr. *aigue,* from L. *acutus* comes Eng. *ague* (originally, *ague* fever), thus a doublet of *acute.* OE. *ecg,* from OFr. *ague,* (whence G. *Ecke,* corner) gives us *edge,* and *egg,* in to *egg on.* (Hen's *egg,* earlier *ey,* from AS. *aeg,* is common Teut.) By a slightly different route Gr. *akro,* comb, peak, whence L. *acer, acr—,* sharp, whence Fr. *aigre,* gives us Eng. *eager;* also directly *acid, acrid, acrimonious.* Be *eager* to sharpen your sense of word-values. But don't be *acrimonious.*

acute.
See acumen.

adamant.
See diamond.

Adam's apple.
According to folk physiology, the body of the first man was wiser than his soul. When Adam took from Eve his piece of the forbidden fruit, a bit of it, they tell us, stuck in his throat; hence, the lump now called the *Adam's apple. Adam's ale* and *Adam's wine* are humorously intended names for water.

add.
We often say Take away, instead of subtract; but instead of *add* we do not say Give to. Yet that is exactly what the word itself says, from L. *ad,* to + *dare,* to give—*dare, datum, see dice; addere, additum,* whence also Eng. *addition.* The gerundive (what ought to be) of *addere* is *addendum,* used directly in English; as is also the gerundive of *agere,* to do: *agendum,* plural *agenda; cp. ache.*

addendum.
See add.

adder.
See auction. Note that "mad as a *hatter*" (G. *natter,* adder) is not a slur upon the makers of our headgear, but really a reference to the snake. *Hat* (AS. *haett;* ON. *höttr,* hood), *hood* (AS. *hōd;* G. *Hut,* hat), *hut* (G. *Hutte*), *heed* (AS. *hedan;* G. *hüten*) are all common and related Teut. words, with the basic idea of protection of the *head* (AS. *heafod;* Du. *hoofd;* Goth. *haubith;* cognate with L. *caput; cp. achieve*).

addict.
See verdict.

addition.
See add.

addle.
This word has an *addled* history. In ancient Greece, an egg that did not hatch was called a wind-egg, Gr. *ourion oon.* Translated into L. as *ovum urinum,* this was confused with *ovum urinae,* egg of urine, rotten egg. The OE. word for urine was *adela;* hence the early expression *addle-egg.* The word was soon applied figuratively to persons; Shakespeare says (*Romeo and Juliet* III, i, 25) "Thy head hath been beaten as *addle* as an egg." *Addle-pate* and *addle-head* are frequent compounds; then the form

addled was used (before the verb, to *addle*). We may still call a man a bad, or a good, "egg".

Fuddle (earlier *fuzzle*, to make drunk) is perhaps coined on the analogy of *addle*, from *fudder*, a tun of wine.

adept.

This word (L. *adeptus*) was taken as a title by the alchemists that claimed to have attained the secret of the philosopher's stone. It is from L. *adipisci, adept—*, to attain, from *apisci*, to reach, inceptive of a root *ap—*, to get. An *adeptist* was a 17th c. term for an alchemist of repute. *See* abdomen.

adieu.

A person departing was wished "Fare well": good going; *cp. dollar.* And to the ones left behind, the journeyers said *"A Dieu"*—I commend you to God, from Fr. *à dieu*, to God. This is the Fr. equivalent of *goodbye, q.v.*

adipose.

See abdomen. This is but vaguely related to *avoirdupois*, which should be *avoirdepois*, from Fr. *avoir*, to have, + *de*, of, some + *pois*, weight. (The *de* was changed to *du* about 1650, through ignorant "correction"). The *avoir*, however, is originally the noun *aveir*, "havings," property, goods (hence, goods of weight); the *pois* is from OF. *peis*, from L. *pesum, pensum*, weight—related to *pensum*, thought; whence Eng. *pensive* Thus L. *pendere* meant to hang (Eng. *pendant*), to weigh, and to consider; *cp. aggravate.*

adjective.

See subject.

adjourn.

This originally meant to set a day for someone to appear; then, to put off until another day; then, just to put off. It is via OFr. *ajorner, ajourner* (Fr. *jour*, day) through LL. *adjornare, adiurnare*, from L. *ad*, to + *diurn—*, daily; whence also Eng. *diurnal; see jury*, which often is *adjourned.*

adjudicate.

See just, verdict.

adjure.

To swear or bind to a purpose; *see* conjure.

adjutant.

See youth.

admiral.

Perhaps it is the resplendent uniform of the sea-lord that put the *d* into his title, as though the word were related to *admire!* It is rather, from Arab. *amir*, prince, from Heb. *amir*, head, summit, and was first used of chieftains on either land or sea. In fact, the OFr. had a special word, *halmyrach*, for a sea-admiral; influenced by Gr. *halmyros*, briny sea. The suffix *—al* is from LL.*—aldus*, G.*—Wald*, as in *Reginald.* But *see emir.*

admire.

See admiral, emir.

admit.

See mess.

admonition.

See fee.

adolescent.

See abolish, world.

Adonis.

When we call someone an *Adonis*, we mean that he is handsome enough to be loved by Venus herself; for the goddess of love was enamoured of the youth *Adonis.* He was killed by a boar, while hunting. The Gr. verse supposedly first composed in laments for his death, is called *Adonic.*

Boar is common Teut., related to bear. To *bore*, to pierce (AS. *borian*) is also very common Teut. Its meaning of *boredom* may have come from the idea of *boring* the ears (G. *drillen*, to *drill*, also means to plague); since, also, slaves had to listen to their however prosy masters. Indeed, many a man since *Adonis* has been *"bored* to death"!

The name *Adonis* is from Phoenician *adon*, lord; related to Heb. *Adonai*, God.

adopt.

See pessimist.

adorable.

See inexorable.

adore.

This word is commonly derived from L.*adorare*, to pray to, from *ad*, to + *orare*, to pray. But it is so much stronger in its implications of the *adorable* one, that it is probably more directly from L. *ad*, to + *os, oris*: the same *adorare*, but meaning directly to put the mouth to, to kiss in worship. *See* inexorable.

adorn.
See augment.

adrogate.
See quaint.

adroit.
See dexterity.

adulation.
See wheedle.

adult, adulterate.
See world.

adumbrate.
To shadow forth (L. *ad,* to). *See* umbrage; *cp.* overture.

advance.
The 15th and 16th c. scholars reshaped many Eng. words after their supposed Latin originals. Thus OFr. *avouterie, avoutrie* had produced Eng. *avowtrie, avoutrie;* this was reshaped into *adultery,* as though directly from L. *adulterium; cp. world.* The Fr. *avant,* before, found Eng. forms in *avance, avantage.* And here the scholars made a mistake. Thinking these were traceable (as is the word *adventure*) to the prefix *ad,* to, they changed them to *advance* (to the *van*) and *advantage*—your benefit for getting there first. But *advance* is really from L. *ab,* away, + *ante,* before (LL. *abante,* whence the verb *abantiare,* whench Fr. *avancer*). To get away before meant rather to move forward than to get a head start; but the error is preserved in the spelling. *Van* itself, shortened from *vanguard,* Fr. *avantgarde* (*see vamp*) returns us to the same word.

adventure.
See dollar.

adversary, adverse.
See advertise.

advertise.
To *advert* is to turn to (L. *ad,* to + *vertere, vers—,* to turn. Hence also *adverse* and *adversary,* where the *ad* has the sense of warning. In fact, through Fr. *avertir, avertiss—,* the Eng. *advertise* (the *d* restored when L. was studied) originally meant to warn. Modern use has increased the need of the warning.

Avert and *averse* are from L. *ab,* from + *vertere, versus.* The abbreviation *vs.* is for L. *versus,* against, taken directly. *See* conversion.

advice, advise.
See improvised.

aegis.
See buck.

Aeolus.
See tycoon.

aerial.
See meteor.

aerie, aery.
See debonair.

aerônaut.
See debonair, nausea.

aesthetics.
See anaesthetic.

aestivation.
See hibernate.

affair.
See defeat.

affect.
This word is the result of two compounds of one L. word. The simple L. *facere, fact—,* to make, to do, is itself fertile in Eng. words, e.g., *faction,* (originally a making), *fact* (a thing done), *factitious* (made by human skill), *factor, factotum* (L. *totum,* everything). *Fiction* is from *fingere, fict—,* to shape, to fashion; hence *fictitious,* made up; earlier *fictive; cp. faint.*

In combinations, L. *facere* became *ficere;* hence *adficere, afficere, affect—,* to do to, act on, influence. The act of influencing or of being influenced—hence, of feeling—was *affection,* which from any mental state slid along the scale (*see* preface) to the kindly feelings. The result, when action on something is carried out (L. *ex,* out), is the *effect. Cp. defeat.*

The frequentative of L. *afficere, affect—,* is *affectare, affectat—,* to seek to do, to aim at. This has given us the same verb *affect,* but in the senses to aspire toward, to be fond of, hence, to assume as an air or as one's character . . . even as a false character; from this verb we have the noun *affectation.* With the words themselves thus intertangled it is little wonder that the schoolboy is similarly *affected!*

affectation, affection.
See affect.

affiance, affidavit.
See fiancée.

affinity.
See finance, para.

affirmative.
See infirmary. The first sense was of assuring someone, as still in the solemn statement I *affirm* . . .

affix.
See fix.

affliction.
When your spirits are cast down by adversity, *affliction* is indeed upon you. The word is the noun from *afflict,* from L. *affligere, afflict—,* to distress, from *af, ad,* to, upon + *fligere, flict—,* to dash. To dash upon someone was to *afflict* him. The word was earlier spelled *flight,* changing as did *delight, q.v.* This had of course no connection with *flight.* Note that this word, *flight,* combines in its spelling and meaning two unrelated words, both common Teut.: AS. *fleogan,* to fly; and AS. *fleon,* to flee; *cp. fleet.* The two verbs, however, were confused even in Anglo-Saxon. The *flea* is also from *fleon;* the *fly,* OE. *fleugon; cp. lobster.* A *fly* in the theatre is a (side) part of the scenery (usually plural, the *flies*) hoisted out of the way when not needed; or the space over the proscenium where such scenery is kept. Other combinations are clear . . . It is not easy to *flee* from *affliction.*

affluent.
To him that hath shall be given. Things just seem to *flow* toward him, until they *overflow,* and he is *affluent* (L. *ad,* towards + *fluens, flowing,* from *fluere,* to *flow*). From the L. adjective come *fluid* and *fluidity.* Easy *flowing* is *fluent;* hence *fluency.* The past tenses (L. *fluxi, fluctus*) are preserved in *flux, afflux, influx;* also (*fluctus* used as a noun, wave, whence *fluctuare,* to undulate) *fluctuation.* By way of the noun *flumen,* river, comes the *flume* we use of a channel, as for bearing logs down hill to a stream. And we speak of the *confluence* (L. *con,* from *com,* together) of two streams. *Influence* first was a term in astrology, the forces determined by the *flowing* in of the stars; so *accident* first meant the falling into place (*accidere,* present participle *accident—,* from *ad,* to + *cadere,* to fall; *cp. cheat*) of the stars—only unbelievers deemed it *chance!*

Fluorescent light is indirectly from this source. It (and the element *fluorine*) are named from *fluorspar. Spar,* from OE. *spaeren,* gypsum, is the name of several types of stone; one variety helps lower the melting point of other substances, is used as a *flux;* hence this was named *fluorspar, flow-stone.* Then it was observed that this substance, under certain conditions, began to glow; therefore the glowing was named *fluorescence* (*—esce* is the inceptive ending). Substances that continue to glow after the initiating cause has stopped are called *phosphorescent,* not from any relation to *phosphorus* other than that it also glows (*cp. focus*). Grimm's Law (*see* Preface) shows us that Eng. *flow,* from OE. *flōwan,* is related, not to L. *fluere,* but to L. *plorare,* to weep.

Spar is two other words, as well. A common Teut. word, ME. *sparre,* roof-rafter, gives us the nautical sense. The use in boxing is, from OE. *spierran,* to strike or thrust rapidly, (whence early Eng. *spar,* battle-ax), from OE. *spere,* from OHG. *sper,* whence Eng. *spear. Spare* and *sparse* are of different origin. The first is common Teut., from AS. *sparian,* from AS. *spaer,* from OHG. *spar,* frugal. *Sparse* is from L. *spargere, spars—,* to scatter. The odd noun *sparable,* the headless nail of the shoemaker, is named from its shape; the word is a corruption of *sparrow-bill.* A chipper, if not *affluent,* bird.

afflux.
See affluent.

affray.
See afraid.

affront.
See effontery.

afraid.
Punishment for breach of the peace must have been severe, since our word *afraid* comes from it. *Affray* (also shortened to *fray; cp. down*) is from OFr. *esfreier,* whence Fr. *effrayer;* it at first meant to threaten, to frighten, from LL. *exfridare,* from *ex,* out + OHG. *frithu,* peace. Then it meant a breaking of the peace. *Cp fear.*

Fray, to rub is from OFr. *frayer,*

from L. *fricare,* to rub. Its frequentative, *fricasser,* to tear, lingers in chicken *fricassé,* and (perhaps influenced by AS. *frenge,* fringe) to *frazzle.* The noun from *fricare,* L. *frictio, friction—,* shows us that rubbing is *friction.*

after.
See abaft.

aftermath.
However difficult the study of mathematics may be, this word does not derive from the feelings of a poor student *after math.* It is an *aftermowing* (AS. *maeth,* from *mawan,* to mow + *th,* a noun suffix), a gathering of hay for a second time; hence, any after-effects—especially after a cutting down, as in battle.

again, against.
Like many seemingly simple words, these have had a complicated history. The word *again* had many early forms, most frequent being *ayen, agen* (which is still the common pronunciation); it is from *on,* in + *gagn, gegn,* direct, straight ahead (whence also *gainly, ungainly*); hence opposite, meeting, coming to (repeating). The G. *gegen* means Eng. *against,* which was the early genitive of *again, agains, agens,* with a *t* added as though it were a superlative *—st*: the same thing had happened to *amidst* and *amongst.* (*Among* is from AS. *on gemang,* in the crowd; *cp. mongrel.*) *Against* first meant directly opposite, over against, or in contact with, *against* the wall; then opposed to. *Against* is sometimes written *'gainst;* as a prefix the root remains in Eng. *gainsay,* to speak *against.*

Gain itself is a most roundabout word. We have it directly from Fr. *gagner;* this was OFr. *gaaignier,* from LL. *gwadaniare,* borrowed in turn from the OHG. root *weidinjin,* to forage, from *weida,* pasture: from foraging, the sense shifted to obtaining that which one sought. If not, try *again.*

agaric.
See Appendix II.

agate.
See carnelian.

agenda, agent.
See add, exact.

agglutinate.
See clam.

aggravate.
The L. *gravis* means heavy; *ad* + *gravare,* to make heavy, to load, to put a burden upon. Used figuratively, it means to add to one's burdens or troubles; hence, to annoy one greatly. By way of OFr. *agrever,* the same L. word gives us *aggrieve,* to bear heavily upon, to offend. *Grievance* and *grievous* (full of *grief*) are from the same *gravis;* as are *grieve* and *grief,* heaviness of spirit; popular L. having changed the *gravare* to *grevare. Gravamen,* the burden of one's charge, or accusation, is directly from a LL. noun, *gravamen.* Directly from the classical L. adj. *gravis* is *grave,* in the sense of heavy, solemn, weighty, ponderous. (*Ponderous,* from L. *ponderare,* to weigh, from *pondus, ponder—,* weight, gives us also *preponderance—prae,* before—outweighing; and, taken figuratively, to *ponder,* to weigh, to consider).

Gravity (used both literally and figuratively), and *gravitate,* are also clearly from *gravis.* There are more exclusively scientific terms from this source: *gravid,* meaning heavy with child; *gravigrade,* walking heavily (as the elephant and the megatherium): *gravimeter; gravitation.* There are other origins and meanings of *grave, q.v.*

Close to L. *pondere* is *pendere, pensum;* from its sense, to weigh (the value of) came the meaning, to pay, whence Eng. *pension.* But *pendere* means to hang; whence *pendant; propensity* (L. *pro,* forward, toward: a leaning toward); *pendulum* (L. *pendulus,* hanging). The frequentative of *pendere* is *pensare,* to hang over, to dwell upon; hence, to think, whence Eng. *pensive, pansy. Dependent* (leaning upon, hanging from), *independent, independence,* are also from this source. The man that truly thinks is likely to be *independent.*

aggregate.
See absolute, caricature.

aggression.
See issue.

aggrieve.
See aggravate.

agitate.
See exact.

agnostic.

St. Paul (*Acts* xvii,23) speaks of the altar to "the unknown God," (Gr. *Agnosto Theo*). In early Christian days, there was a sect, the *Gnostics*, that claimed mystic knowledge. Huxley, wishing to indicate inability to have such knowledge, in 1869 coined the word *agnostic.* The term lacks the obloquy attached to *unbeliever*—which is all that is left in *miscreant* (OFr. *mescreire,* to disbelieve). *Obloquy* is simply *ob,* against + *loqui, locutus,* to speak; this verb gives us several words, *e.g., soliloquy,* from *solus,* alone; *loquacious; elocution,* speaking out, also *eloquent; circumlocution* (L. *circum,* around), of which the world has too much.

agony.

Pleasure rather than pain was the first intention of this word. From the Gr. *agein,* to lead, came the word *agon,* that into which men are led, an assembly. It came to be applied especially to the assemblies for watching the great Greek games, athletic and dramatic contests. (Many stories and plays have a hero and a villain, *q.v.;* but the great ones usually center the struggle within the soul of the main figure, the *protagonist,* from Gr. *protos,* first + *agonistes,* contender. A poem of Milton's is entitled "Samson Agonistes.") Thus *agonia* came to mean the contest, the struggle; applied as well to mental and moral struggles, it was extended to cover the physical and mental anguish one may have to endure. An *antagonist* is one against (Gr. *anti,* against) whom the struggle proceeds.

The *agonoclite* was an unbending person, esp. a 7th c. heretic who prayed standing; from Gr. *a*—not, + *gone,* knee, + *klitos,* bent, from *klinein,* to bend; *cp. climate.* From Gr. *gone* comes L. *genu,* knee, whence Eng. *genuflection* (L. *flectere, flex*—, to bend; *cp. accent*)

agriculture.

See acorn, saunter.

ague.

See acumen.

aisle.

See island.

ajar.

When is a door not a door? When it's *ajar. Ajar* is from AS. *achar,* from *a,* on + *char,* turn, from AS. *cierran,* to turn. Whence also *charwoman,* one who has a "turn" to do; and *chore. Charcoal* (though perhaps influenced by Fr. *charbon, charcoal,* from L. *carbo-n*—, whence Eng. *carbon*) is also wood turned coal; the verb to *char* was formed from *charcoal. Charivari,* gay turning about, with music expressing disapproval (now shortened to a "raspberry," or a "Bronx cheer"; *cp. Dutch*) is perhaps also a Fr. play on this meaning. *See jar.*

akimbo.

See camp.

Akropolis.

See acumen; *cp.* police.

Alabama.

See States.

alabamine.

See element.

alabaster.

Stemming from Gr. *alabastros, alabastos,* this substance is supposedly named from a town in Egypt. Used to make boxes for holding oils, it became the name of the box, then also a liquid measure.

In 16th c. Eng., the word was sometimes spelled *alablaster,* by confusion with *alblaster, arbalester, arblaster,* a cross-bowman, from *arbalest,* cross-bow. This word—spelled in a dozen ways—is from L. *arcus,* bow (whence Eng. *arc, arch;* but *see arctic*) + *ballista,* machine for hurling missiles, from Gr. *ballein,* to throw; *cp. ballot.*—Being delicately shaded, and translucent, *alabaster* became frequently used in comparisons, of the fair cheeks of fair maidens.

alack.

See alas.

alarm.

A frequent stage direction of Elizabethan plays calls for *"alarums* and excursions," meaning the dashing about and contending of armed forces. Fr. *à l'arme!* (literally, To the arm!), To arms! became in Eng. the word for the war cry or warning itself; thence, for anything, such as a special clock, that sounds a warning. The It. form, *all' arme!,* with the same meaning, was in the 17th c. mistaken for the command: All arm! As is often the case, the use of the word has been extended to include the emotion felt upon hearing a danger signal, the *alarm* or vague fear as at the approach of danger.

alas.
This exclamation of woe (Ah! woe is me) is a combination of an English sigh and a Roman fatigue: *ah* + L. *lassum,* weary, hence wretched; Eng. *lassitude; cp. last, let.* The poetic cry *"Alack and alas!"* draws the first word from *ah* + *lack,* defect, fault, shame; it was used as a term of reproach. Frequently used in the phrase *alack the day,* shame to the day (on which you were born?!!!), *alack-a-day,* the sort of person it was applied to came to be called *lackadaisical.* As the pallid poet sputtered: *"A lass? Alas! A lassitude* had crept upon me!" (The origin of *lass* is unknown, as are also the sources of *lad, girl, q.v.,* and *boy;* but this does not account for the story of the stork).

Alaska.
See States.

albatross.
This high-flying bird has given its name to a famous prison; it is from Port. *alcatraz.* The first part of the name is changed as though from L. *alba,* white. The name is a nickname, and was originally applied to the pelican, which was supposed to carry water for its young in its beak: from Arab. *al-qadus,* the water carrier.

albino.
See auburn.

Albion.
See auburn. Albion is also supposed to be of Irish origin.

album, albumen.
See auburn.

Alcatraz.
See albatross.

alchemist.
See chemistry.

alcohol.
When a happy drinker refers to his liquor as "eye wash," he little knows how exact his expression falls. *Alcohol* is from Arab. *al,* the + *koh'l* (Heb. *kakhal,* to stain, paint), a fine black powder (*collyrium*) for painting the eyelids. The word *kohl* is still used in this sense.

Applied later to any fine powder, the word *alcohol* was then used also of liquids extracted, distilled or "rectified"—that is, the spirit or quintessence of a substance. Since the most common of these was spirit of wine, the term came to be applied to the spirituous or intoxicating element in any liquor.

In 1834 Dumas and Péligot, in France, demonstrated the relation of spirit of wine with "wood-spirit" (wood *alcohol,* methyl *alcohol,* CH3); and the term came into its chemical use indicating a large group of related substances (CH3; C2H5; C3H7; etc. CH4; C2H6; C3H8; etc.) not all of which are liquid.

Intertangled in part of its history with the word *alcohol* is L. *collyrium,* from Gr. *kollyrion,* poultice, eye-salve, from diminutive of Gr. *kollyra,* a roll of coarse bread. (Country folk still make a little ball of the inside dough of a roll, to lay on a sore eye.) Ben Jonson (in *The Fortunate Isles,* 1624) uses *collyrium* for *alcohol,* as a coloring for the eyelids; this usc persists to the end of the 19th century. And truly *alcohol* has colored many an eye!

There is, of course, no connection between this *kohl* and *kohl-rabi,* which (via G. *kohl-rabi*) is from It. *cavoli rape,* cabbage-turnip. *Cabbage* is via Fr. *caboche,* big-head, chump, from It. *capocchia,* augmentative of It. *capo,* head, from L. *caput; cp. achieve.* This *rape* (for the *ravishing, see rapture*) is from L. *rapium,* turnip. *See turnip.*

Eng. *cole* (*kohl;* Scots *kale, kail,* as in the song about the "bonnie briar bush in our *kail* yard") is from AS. *cawel,* akin to L. *caulis,* Gr. *kaulos,* stalk. The familiar *cole slaw* (*slaugh*) is a United States shortening of *cole salade. Salad* comes via Fr. *salade* from a LL. form *salata, salted,* from *salare,* to *salt,* from L. *sal, salt; cp. salary.* It's still the same chopped cabbage!

alderman.
See world.

ale.
See drink.

alert.
Those that on hills or in high buildings watch for enemy planes are etymologically, as well as actually,

alert. OFr. *à l'erte,* from It. *all'erta, alla erta,* to the height, is from the L. *erectus,* from *erigere,* to set up, to build, as a watch tower, from *e,* out + *regere,* to rule, to make straight. (From this verb come *erect, erection;* by another path, *regal, regent; royal, q.v.*) It is easy to imagine how "on the watching place" came to mean "on the watch," vigilant; then lively, quick in action. Since the word itself contains the words *on the* watch, the expression "on the *alert*" is pleonastic.

In Fr. today, *alerte* means a military call; this sense has been borrowed to designate the signal for an air raid drill, or the drill itself. "Eternal *vigilance* is the price of liberty." *Vigil* is from another L. word, *vigil,* meaning watchful, *alert;* it is cognate with *vigere,* to thrive, from which we have *vigor* and *vigorous. Vigia* is a nautical term, from Sp. or Port.: a warning, on a sea chart, of a hidden danger.—A person who is on the *alert* is likely to be *vigorous,* and to thrive.

Alexandrine.
See Appendix II.

al fresco.
See fresco.

algebra.
Every high school lad knows this word; but few persons know that its first use in Eng. was in the sense of setting bones. It is from Arab. *al-jebr,* the reuniting, from Arab. *jabara,* to reunite. In the 16th c., when the word was used for a field of mathematics, writers thought that it came from Arab. *al,* the + *Geber,* the name of an Arabian chemist; it has no connection either with him or with gibber. The mathematical use is a shortening of the Arab. phrase *ilm al-jebr wa'l-muqabalah,* the science of reuniting and equating. In the middle ages, some writers used the last word, some used the first; in It. it became *algebra,* which has survived in Eng.

Those that think *algebra* difficult should note the remark in Blackwood's Magazine (1841): "When a child throws out his five fingers, he has *algebraized* before he can speak."

The standard Arab. work in the field was the *Algebra* of Abu Ja'far Mohammed Ben Musa, through which 9th c. study the use of Arabic numerals replaced the Roman, and made calculation less cumbersome. Hence calculation (*arithmetic*) was named in honor of this mathematician: from his native town of Khiva, Kharazm, he was known as *al-Khowarazmi,* which came into Eng. in 18 different forms, but finally crystallized as *algorism,* the technical term for *arithmetic. Arithmetic* (mistakenly called *arismetrik* in the Renaissance, as though from L. *ars metrica,* the art of measure) is from Gr. *arithmetike,* counting, from *arithmeein,* to number. *Geometry* is from Gr. *geo,* earth, + *metron,* measure. For *calculus, see calculate.* Mathematics has been called the mother of the sciences as Memory (*cp. amnesty*) is the mother of the arts. *See mathematics,* as some schoolboys never can.

algorism.
See algebra.

alias, alibi.
"Alias Jimmy Valentine" and *"Alibi Ike"* contain two Latin words. *Alias,* otherwise; *alibi,* (from *ali-ubi*) otherwhere. An *alibi* consists in showing that you were elsewhere, when a crime was committed somewhere.

Alice blue.
See Appendix II.

aliment, alimentary, alimentive.
See alimony; world.

alimony.
The L. *alere,* to nourish, produced the L. nouns *alimentum,* (LL.) *alimentatio,* and *alimonium.* All meant that which nourishes or sustains. From the first two we derive the *alimentary* canal, and *alimentation.* Phrenologists speak of *alimentiveness,* the animal urge to seek food. From the third form comes, *alimony,* which from its legal use has become limited to sustenance, or money for sustenance, allotted when a married couple is separated. *Cp. world.*

alkahest.
Not many words have been invented in recent years. Among them are *gas, q.v.,* and some trade names such as *kodak* (about 1890). Combinations are of course frequent, to express new substances or articles: *cellophane, phonograph,* etc.; *cp. Dora.* But in earlier times writers were freer with their fancies. Thus Paracelsus, out of the Arab. prefix *al,* the, built the word *alkahest* to mean the universal solvent the *alchemists* were seek-

ing. The last syllable may have been suggested by the common Teut. form, ME. *heste* (from *haitan,* to call by name, to summon; whence Eng. *hight*), a summons, a command to appear. (The *alchemists* certainly sought it ardently enough!) This word lingers in Eng. in the expression *at your behest.*

alkali.
For *acid, see acetylene. Litmus* may have been a lichen used for dyeing, from ON. *litr,* color, + *mosi,* moss; but *see litmus.* (*Moss* is common Teut., related to L. *muscus, moss;* AS. *mos.* meant bog, where the *moss* grew. Also *see peat.*) The ashes of the saltwort plant were early used to produce *alkali;* it owes its name to the process: Arab. *al-qaliy,* the ashes, from *qalay,* to fry.
See element: potassium.

all.
See alone.

allay, allege, allegiance, alliance.
See legible; *cp.* alligator.

allegory.
See amphigory.

alligator.
The shape and size of a lizard suggested an arm to the Romans; hence L. *lacertus,* upper arm, also was used for lizard. The Spanish took this to the New World, Sp. *al lagarto,* the lizard; whence Eng. *alligator.* This was also spelled *alligarter,* even *allegater*—whence the remark "I deny the *allegation* and defy the *allegater.*" *Allegation* is from L. *allegare, allegat—,* to declare on oath, from L. *al,* from *ad,* to + *lex, leg—,* law; via OFr. *alegier* this gives us *allege; cp. legible.*

allocate.
See couch, permit.

allow.
See permit.

alloy.
See legible; *cp.* alligator.

alluvial.
See lotion.

ally.
See legible.

alma mater.
See volume.

almanac.
This word, first used in the 13th c. by Roger Bacon, seems to have come from the Sp., and the Arab. *al,* the + *manakh;* but there is no such word in Arab. It has also been suggested that it is from the AS. *al-mon-aght,* all moon heed: from the records of the new and the full moon kept by the Saxons. AS. *mona, moon,* Goth. *mena,* are cognate with Gr. *mene.* Similarly *month,* the period of the moon, Goth. *menoths,* is cognate with L. *mensis,* Gr. *mene;* Sansk. *masa.*

almond.
The name of this kernel of the drupe of the *almond* tree is roundabout: L. *amandula,* from *amygdale,* Gr. *amygdale.* The *al* is probably from confusion with many words from the Arab. beginning with *al,* the. Similarly misunderstanding produced the *Jordan* almond, which has no relation to the Biblical Jordan, but comes from Fr. *jardin,* garden: the cultivated as opposed to the wild-growing variety.

almoner.
See alms.

alms.
This word has been curiously corrupted. An *almoner,* distributor of charity, is, from OFr. *almosnier,* which shows the halfway stage, from L. from Gr. *eleemosynia, alms,* from Gr. *eleein,* to pity. From Church Latin, AS. borrowed the word as *aelmaesse,* of three syllables; this was further shortened to two syllables, as *almes;* then to *alms.* Later, the original word gave us the Eng. *eleemosynary,* as offered by church-folk.

alone.
If you say "It's *all one* to me!" You mean "It makes no difference!"—which is the same thing. But when you are *alone* you are likewise *all one*: *alone* is, from *all* + *one,* meaning *all* by *one's* self. Aphetic from this is *lone;* whence *lonely.* The suffix *—ly* is from AS. *lic, like,* which first meant image, body. Thus *lonely* means that everything is *all like one*: just yourself. *Only* is, similarly, from AS. *anlic, one like*: there's but *one like* it. Hidden in *such* is the same ending, from earlier *swich,* from *swilch,* from AS. *swalic, like so.* This is a common Teut. form, AS. *swa, so;* Goth. *swa;* G. *so.* AS.

eall-swa, all so, became *also;* this (G. *also; als*) shortened into *as.* Now you may feel not *so lonely!*

aloof.
This word, from the Du. phrase *to loef,* to windward, is the same as *luff.* Originally it meant a device for changing a ship's course (OHG. *laffa,* oar-blade); then, bringing the head of the ship toward the wind. Thus one that holds himself *aloof* does not sail with the wind, but beats against the course.

alphabet.
See gamut.
One way of saying "from beginning to end" (English style, from soup to nuts) is from *alpha* to *omega,* these being the first and last letters of the Greek *alphabet.* This *alphabet* has the letter *o* twice: *omega* (big *O;* same prefix in *megaphone*) and *omicron* (little *o;* thus *microphone*).

also.
See alone.

altar.
Pious persons spoke of raising an *altar* unto the Lord; Milton says (*Paradise Lost,* xi, 323), "So many grateful *altars* I would rear." The center of worship was thus a place uplifted toward the heavens—as the word tells us, when we read to its past, from L. *altare,* from *altus,* high. *See world.*

alter, altitude, alumnus.
See world.

altruism.
The Fr. expression, *le bien d'autrui,* the right of another, was shortened in legal phrase to *l'autrui.* The philosopher Comte took this shorter term (possibly from the It. form *altrui,* from L. *alteri,* to another) and coined the noun *altruisme*—translated into Eng. as *altruism.* Comte opposed it to *egoism,* from L. *ego,* I. *Egoism* is the general philosophical point of view; *egotism* (the same word, with the *t* added to separate the vowels) has come to be used for a more personal selfishness, a conceit, a too frequent using of the word I. *"Ay, ay, sir!"*—with the same sound, meaning yes—may be another spelling of the pronoun I, as though one were answering a roll-call with an affirmative vote; it is sometimes spelled *aye.* On the other hand, *aye,* ever, is sometimes spelled *ay;* and the meaning yes may be from ever, used as an intensive "O.K." The *aye,* ever, is common Teut., AS. *a,* cognate with L. *aevum,* age. There is also a Madagascar animal *aye-aye,* named from its call.

alum, aluminum.
See element.

amalgam.
This word seems to be an *amalgam* of various sources. At least, three origins and a fourth route are suggested for it. It may be a medieval perversion of Gr. *malagma,* used by the doctors (Pliny) as a soothing plaster, from *malak,* stem of *malassein,* to soften (which might have influenced *molasses,* from LL. *mellaceum,* from *mell—,* honey. Eng. *mellifluous* is from L. *mell-* + *fluere,* to flow. This honey has probably altered the sense of *mellow,* from ME. *melwe,* ripe, related to AS. *melo, meal,* flour). Or this word may have journeyed into the Arabic, gotten an *al,* the, prefixed to it (*cp. alcohol; chemistry*), and returned as *amalgam.* Possibly it is directly from an Arab. word, *al-jamsa,* union, from *jamasa,* to unite. And who knows but that it is formed from Gr. *ama,* together, + *gamos,* marriage—whence *gamete; cp. monk!* The last thought, indeed, produced the rare noun *amalgamy.*

amateur, amatory.
See amethyst, ham.

amazon.
These warrior women of old were supposedly called *Amazons* because they cut off their right breasts, not to impede the drawing of the bow: Gr. *amazon,* from *a,* not, without + *mazos,* breast. This is in all probability a Gr. corruption, to make the word fit an apparent meaning, of the eastern moon-god *Mazu,* the moon being sacred to virgins. There is also a legend of a northern tribe of *Amazons;* this may have grown from the race of *Qvoens* (the Finns so called themselves), mistaken for *queans* or Swed. *Quinns,* women.

ambage.
See strategy.

ambassador.
This word, of one who frequents an *embassy,* is as devious as often the *ambassador's* dealings. It is traced to a LL. *ambaxiata, ambasciata,* from a supposed verb *ambactiare,* to go on a mission. Beyond this, the lines diverge, though

most of them go, via L. *ambactus*, servant, back into the Teut. or the Celt. Caesar (in the *Gallic War*, vi, 15) applies *ambactus* to the retainers of the Gallic chief; thus it is perhaps from OHG. *ambaht*, from *and*, towards, + *bak*, *back* (going and coming) or from *and*, towards + Sansk. *bkahta*, devoted. From the L., it may be *ambo*, about, to and fro, + *actiare*, a LL. frequentative from *act—; agere, act—*, to drive, to do. There are dozens of spellings of the words, *embassador, imbassator*, and the like; in any case, he is an *ambassador* extraordinary.

amber, ambergris.
See electricity.

ambidextrous.
See dexterity.

ambiguous.
When a sentence or an action makes you wonder, as though it were driving your mind in two directions, it is indeed *ambiguous* (L. *ambi*, around, on both sides + *iguus*, from *agere*, to drive + *—ous*, L. *—osus*, full of). L. *ambi* is cogn. with Gr. *amphi*, as in *amphitheatre*, one with seats all around; and *amphisbaena* (*cp. bane*, murder, evil), a snake with a head at each end. Such a snake, of course, lives only in mythology and inebriate fancies.

ambition.
From the Roman habit of going about (*ambo*, about, on both sides + *it—: eo, ire, itus*, go) to solicit votes. Thus an *ambitious* man is truly a "go-getter."

amble.
See ambulance.

ambrosia.
This was the food, as *nectar* was the drink, of the Greek and Roman gods. Some say *ambrosia* was the drink and *nectar* the food; but it makes little difference; both were a joy to the palate, and both conferred immortality: *ambrosia*, from Gr. *a*, not + *brotos*, mortal; *nectar*, from Gr. *nek*, death (thus *necropolis; cp. police*) + *—tar*, conquering. From its pleasant taste comes the *nectarine* peach, later just *nectarine*.

Gr. *brotos* is for *mbrotos*, from *mrotos* by metathesis from *mortos*, whence Eng. *mortal* and *immortality*. The root is *mor—*, to die, as in L. *mors, mort—*.

Dulce et decorum est pro patria mori.
It is sweet and fitting to die for one's country.

ambulance.
The early field hospital, for treatment of the wounded right in the battlefield, was called by the French *hospital ambulant*, walking hospital. From this, the noun *ambulance* was formed. World War II has produced the *ambucycle*, a sort of motorcycle *ambulance*. The L. *ambulare*, to walk, also gives us the adj. *ambulatory*, and the verb *amble*. With the prefix *per*, through, we have *perambulate*, to walk through (to inspect); then, to walk around. A *perambulator* was a person that walked about; then, a device for measuring the distance one walks, a "waywiser"—what we today call a *pedometer*, or "foot measure", *cp. pedagogue*; then, the carriage for a baby pushed before one as one walks around (this is often shortened, esp. in England, to *pram*). *See* hospital.

From the OFr. *ambler*, to go, came Fr. *aller, alleé*, which gives us Eng. *alley*. (The marble, *alley*, is short for *alabaster*, from Gr. *alabastros*, from the eastern word for the stone.) To *sally* forth, however, is not aphetic for L. *ex* + *aller*, but from Fr. *saillir, saille*, to rush, from L. *salire, saltus*, to leap, as in *insult* and *somersault*, *qq.v.* Many a leap leads to an *ambulance*.

ambulatory.
See ambulance.

ambuscade, ambush.
See strategy.

amen.
Despite the suggestion of a relation to the god Ammon, *amen* comes without change from the Heb., in which language it means certainty, truth. "Thus it is" was said when the thought was (at the end of a prayer) "Thus may it be." More profanely one might remark today, "Ain't it the truth!"

amenable, amenity.
See mean.

America.
See Appendix II.

Americanize.
See homo—.

amethyst.
This word was spelled *amatist* in the 16th c., as though it were the lovers' stone L. *amor,* love; *amare, amat*—, to love; whence *amatory; amorous*: *-ous* from *osus,* full of. The root *am*—is probably exclamatory in origin: baby-talk, like *yum-yum,* and the *mmm!* expressive of delight. Hence the one that works in love (the non-professional), the *amateur.* But earlier it was looked upon as a charm against drunkenness, thus was called by the Greeks *amethystos,* from *a,* not, + *methystos,* drunken, from *methyskein,* to intoxicate, from *methy,* wine. *Methyl,* as used in Eng., alone and as a prefix, is a back-formation from *methylene,* from Gr. *methy* + *hyle,* matter, wood—whence Eng. *hylic,* and many words with the prefix *hylo*—, as *hylobate,* woodwalker, *hylophagous, hylotheism. Cp. carnelian.*

amicable, amical.
See remnant.

ammonia.
Satires on medieval practices assert that even the excrement of saints was prized as a relic. But *sal ammoniac,* L. for *salt* of *Ammon,* is thus named because the substance was prepared from the dung of the camels near the temple of *Jupiter Ammon*—worshiped in Egypt as *Amun.* The gas obtained from this salt was later named *ammonia* ($NH3$). There may be some relation between the god and Gr. *ammos,* sand. The Romans were religiously hospitable, admitting to their pantheon gods of all the peoples they conquered. *Cp. vitamin.*

ammuntion.
See avalanche.

amnesia.
See amnesty.

amnesty.
A kind conqueror said he would forget the deeds of his enemies, and granted *amnesty,* (Gr. *amnestia,* oblivion, from *a*—, not + *mnasthai,* remember. Less grateful from the same root is *amnesia*). The adj. from the Gr. verb is *mnemon, mnemonikos,* whence Eng. *mnemonic.* The mother of the Muses was the goddess *Mnemosyne,* memory; in which connection we might note that both to the sages of India and to the wise men of Greece, wisdom is recollection. Thus today, after a quarrel, persons say "Let's forget it!"

amok.
See berserk.

among.
See mongrel.

amongst.
See again.

amorous.
See amethyst.
This is not related to *amoral,* which is Gr. *a*—, not + *moral; cp.* remorse.

amorphous.
See remorse.

ampere.
See moron; *Appendix II.*

ampersand.
When children were given the alphabet to copy, after the *z* was put the symbol &; this was called *"and per se, and"*: and by itself, and. Corrupted at first into *ampussy and,* it survived as *ampersand,* the name of the sign.

amphigory, amphigoury.
This hodge-podge of rigamarole (*q.v.*) or double-talk is double in its very name: from Gr. *amphi,* both, around, + *agoria,* speech (as in *paregoric, q.v.* and *category; cp. verdict*), or from *amphi,* around + *gyros,* circle; whence *gyrate, autogyro* (L. *auto,* by itself, as in *automobile* and many other forms, *autocrat, cp. democracy*). *Allegory,* a more sensible form of double-talk, is from Gr. *allos,* other + *agoria*: one story with another hidden inside. *Cp. ambiguous;* L. *ambi* is from Gr. *amphi.*
Hodge-podge is from earlier *hotchpotch,* from Fr. *hocher,* to shake; *cp. scurry.*

amphitheatre.
See ambiguous.

amplify.
See defeat.

amputation.
See curfew.

amuck.
See berserk.

amulet.

Especially about the necks of pretty babies, mothers hung *amulets*, to frighten away evil spirits. In the middle ages, infant mortality was much greater than now; the *amulet* was a charm, from L. *amuletum*, from *amolire letum*, to turn away death. An even older and more universal symbol is the *swastika; cp. monk.*

amuse.

The *Muses* were daughters of *memory*, q.v. To *muse*, however, now meaning to ponder, was first to stare (fixed gaze might be a sign of deep thought). The word is related to *muzzle* (keeping the head in a fixed position), which is OFr. *musel*, a diminutive of OFr. *muse*, perhaps from L. *morsus*, bite.

To *amuse* was, first, to cause to stare, to amaze. The sense gradually weakened: to hold the attention; then, to divert the attention (used thus, of miliary operations, to hide one's real intention; Marshal Saxe, mid 18th c., invented a light cannon called an *amusette*); then, to divert from any serious purpose, which is its present meaning. Queen Victoria (on receiving, as she had requested, the other books by the author of *Alice In Wonderland*) might have remarked: "The Queen is not *amused*," as she often did when her sense of decorum was disturbed.

an.

See number.

ana, —ana.

See psychoanalysis.

anabaptist.

See anacampserote.

anacampserote.

Xenophon wrote the *Anabasis* (379-371 B.C.) picturing the advance of Cyrus the Younger into Asia in 401-400 B.C.; the word has come to be applied to any military expedition of consequence; *anabasis* means to step forward, "the up-country march," from Gr. *ana* + *basis*, step; *see bazooka*. The prefix *ana* means again, over, back, and up; *cp. psychoanalysis.* An *anabaptist* is one that believes in *baptizing* more than once: Gr. *baptein*, to dip. An *anachronism* is something backwards in time (or out of time): an error such as the clock in Shakespeare's *Julius Caesar*. There is a word, once applied to an herb, now obsolete, that some would like restored to the language: *anacampserote*: Gr. *ana*, again, + *campserota* from *camptein*, to bend, + *eros, erot—*, love (whence also Eng. *erotic*): that which brings back departed love.

anachronism.

See anacampserote.

anaesthetic.

Things apprehended through the senses were to the Greeks *aistheta*, from the stem *aisthe—*, to feel; they were opposed to *noeta*, things thought, from *noein*, to perceive, from *nous*, mind. Eng. *noetic* and *nous* are philosophical words; but *aesthetics* has become (from its use by Baumgarten, 1750) the name for the general field of thinking about the arts—taken in through the senses, the "feelings"; and *anaesthetic* has become the term used in medicine for removing the senses (in local *anaesthesia*, only the feeling of the spot concerned).

anagram, analysis.

See psychoanalysis.

Ananias.

See Appendix II.

anapest.

See helicopter.

anarchist.

See annihilate.

anathema.

This word has come to mean its opposite. The Gr. *anathema*, from *ana*, up + *tithenai*, to set, was applied to something set aside as an offering to a god. It was devoted to the god; but since such things were usually to be sacrificed, the word came to mean doomed, accursed, and is used in that sense esp. by the Catholic Church. Note that in L. *consecrare, consecrat—*, from *con*, from *com*, together + *sacer*, holy, is a synonym of *desecrare, desecrat—*, from *de*, down, + *sacer*. In Eng. *consecrate* has kept the original sense of making holy, while *desecrate* has, like *anathema*, taken the opposite meaning. The expression *anathema maranatha* (Syr. *maran etha*: Let him be devoted; the Lord has come) is sometimes used as a very solemn curse.

anatomy.

The only way to discover the *anatomy* of a body is to cut it up. This the word itself tells us, from Gr. *ana,* up, back, again + *tome,* cutting, from *temnein,* to cut. Before electrons were suggested, the accepted theory of matter was *atomic,* the *atom* (Gr. *a—,* not + *tome,* cutting) being the smallest, indivisible particle, which could not be cut. (The term is still employed, as we still speak of the sunrise and sunset.) The ending *—tomy* (also *—tome;* and, from modern L., *—tomia*) is used in medicine to indicate a cutting instrument or operation. Thus *appendectomy.* There are eight spellings for removing the tonsils: *tonsillectome, tonsillectomy, tonsillotome, tonsillotomy* (double these by undoubling the *l*). The operation is not that complex. A "cutting" of the essence of something (Gr. *epi,* close upon) is an *epitome.* And a section (*cp. set*) of a book, bound separately, is a *tome.*

ancestor.

If something moves when you push it, you may say that it yields, hence L. *cedere, cess—,* to move, soon took the sense of to yield; whence Eng. *cede.* To move back is of course to *recede;* to move apart, *secede;* to move between (two quarrelers), to *intercede;* to move along with (another's will), to *concede* (L. *con, com,* with). To move under some one was L. *subcedere,* whence *succedere,* whence Eng. *succeed,* which first meant to come after —therefore, to replace, to win. From the past participle forms come *success* and *recess* (moved back; hence a space, hence an interval). The frequentative of *cedere, cess—,* to yield, was *cessare, cessat—,* to stop; whence Eng. *cessation* and, via. Fr. *cesser,* Eng. *cease.*

One who has come before is an *antecessor* (in L.); whence early Eng. *ancessour,* then via Fr. *ancestre,* Eng. *ancestor.* From the present participle comes Eng. *antecedent.*

To be able to move toward something is to have *access* to it (L. *ad,* toward, + *cedere, cess—*); also Eng. *accede.* The verb from the L. to move away has not continued in Eng. (L. *ab, abs,* away, + *cedere*) but the little hollow where flesh has moved away and pus forms is an *abscess.*

The *process* is the way of *proceeding;* the movement forward (*pro,* forward) may be in a *processional;* and the formal march out of an assembly is the *recessional.* The *deceased* is the one that has moved away—a euphemism, in the L., for the dead one . . . who has joined his *ancestors.*

(In general, the Eng. forms spelled *-cede* came early from the L.; those spelled *-ceed* came via the Fr. For *—sede, see subside.*)

anchor, anchorite.
See monk.

ancient.
See ancestor; *cp.* hold.

androgynous.
See banshee.

anecdote.

Originally (Gr. *an,* negative prefix + *ekdidonai,* to give out: *ex,* out +, *don,* give, as in *donation*) *anecdotes* were things kept secret, unpublished details of history. Since, however, these are precisely what most persons want to know, the meaning was soon changed to its present one, an interesting incident.

anemone.
See plant.

angel.
See evangelist.

angle.
See monk.

Anglo-Saxon.

Merry *England,* of course, is *Angleland;* but here agreement ends. We were long taught that the *Angles* came from *Anglia* (AS. *Angul;* ON. *Ongull,* a hook-shaped section of Holstein, Germany; the word itself—*cp. monk*—meaning hook). *Saxon* is from a tribe that inhabited *Saxony,* Germany, near the mouth of the Elbe; the word is OE. *Seaxan,* from AS. *seax,* ax. All this may be so; but more than Germanophobes point out that when the Teutons came to the British Islands, they found the *Gaels* (Celts) already there, and they used the Celtic term for them, *an-gael, the Gael;* whence the name of the land and the language.

We look from still another *angle* in music, being told that the *English horn* is a mistranslation from the French, for bent horn; Fr. *Anglais,* English, is pronounced like Fr. *anglé,* bent. For another such error, *see* bugle (slughorn). Yet if we have a French horn in English, why not an English horn in French? This may be folk etymology!

anguish.
See hangnail.

animadversion.
See conversion.

animal, animosity, animus.
See plant; *cp.* totem.

ankle.
See pylorus.

annal.
See anniversary.

annex.
See nexus.

Annie Oakley.
See Appendix II.

annihilate.
A child's frequent daydream gives him power to puff, and make his foes vanish, to wipe them away. This desire is caught in the word *annihilate,* from L. *an,* from *ad,* to + *nihil,* nothing: to turn into nothing. A *nihilist* is one that believes in no basic principles; specifically, the *Nihilists* were Russian revolutionaries in the 19th c. An *anarchist* is one that believes in no rulers, from Gr. *an,* not + *archos,* chief, from *archein,* to rule. Hence *arch—,* the prefix. Which brings us also to *nil,* a contraction of L. *nihil,* hence less than nothing.

anniversary.
The early church kept careful records, as the years rolled round, of the days of importance in its faith. These were the *anniversaria* (L. *annus,* year + *vertere, vers—,* turn) *dies,* days that had to be observed with especial ceremony. Since marriages were made in heaven, and birthdays were of great importance to noble families, the *anniversaries* of these occasions were also celebrated, as the years turned on and on.

The first half of this word is used to form many Eng. words, *e.g. semiannual,* every half year; *annual,* yearly; *biennial,* every two years; *perennial,* through the years; *sesquicentennial* (L. *sesqui,* from *semis,* half + *que,* and: a half in addition + *cent—,* one hundred) every hundred and fifty years, or the one hundred and fiftieth anniversary. *Annals* are events recorded year by year, or the records themselves. When we say that this is the year 1943 A. D. we are repeating ourselves, for A. D. represents L. *anno Domini,* in the year of the Lord, according to the Christian calendar. (For *Domini, see* dome.)

The second part of the word *anniversary* gives us even more Eng. words, for which *see* conversion.

We hope, however, than an *annuity* is not *annulled* (L. *annullare,* to reduce to naught, from *ad,* to, + *nullus,* none; whence Eng. *null* and void; *cp. annihilate*). *Annular* is from L. *annulus,* diminutive of *anus,* ring.

annoy.
When a Roman was disturbed by something, he might use the phrase *in odio habui,* I have it in hatred. There were a few such idioms, beginning *in odio* (whence Eng. *odious, odium*). The two words *in odio* were combined in OFr. as *anoi.* This was brought into Eng. in several forms: *noi* (whence *noisome*), *anoien, anuien;* it went into later Fr. as *anuier, enuier,* whence Fr. and Eng. *ennui;* also, from *anoien,* Eng. *annoy.* Notice that the cause and effect have been transposed: I hate it; it annoys me.

annual.
See anniversary.

anoint.
See lotion.

anomaly.
See homo—.

anonymous.
See pseudo—.

answer.
This is a mild word now; it once pictured a much stronger situation. It is, from ME. *andswerien,* from AS. *andswerian,* to swear in opposition to: *and,* against (cognate with Gr. *anti,* against) + *swerian,* to swear. The root of this word is *swar,* whence Sansk. *svri,* to sound, *svara,* voice, whence L. *susurrus,* whisper; Eng. *swarm,* that which hums. Hence also the song the *sirens* sang: *siren,* from L., from Gr. *seiren: seir—, sur—,* from root *swar,* to sound. Gr. *seira* is also a cord; and there is a symbol in the fact that the *siren* song tugged at the hearts of the mariners.

ant.
This little fellow was earlier called an *emmet,* properly. For the word, AS. *aemette,* is related to *a—,* off + ON. *meita,* to cut, from his nippers.
One's *aunt* is a survival of baby-talk, by way of OFr. *ante* (reduplicated in Fr. *tante*) from L. *amita,* from the mouths of infants.

ant—.
See ante—.

Antaean.
See giant.

antagonist.
See agony.

antarctic.
See arctic.

ante—.
This Eng. combining form is from L. *ante,* before. It occurs separately in *ante meridiem,* before midday, as 9 *a.m.* Also is such words as *antecedent; cp. ancestor.*
The combining form *anti—,* against, occurs as *ant—* before a vowel; thus *antarctic, cp. arctic; antichrist; antipathy, cp. osseous; antipodes, cp. pedagogue.*
Antediluvian is a late coinage (17th c.) from L. *ante* + *diluvium,* flood, from L. *diluere,* to wash away, from *de,* away, + *luere,* to loose, whence Eng. *lues,* medical word for a flow or discharge; also from L. *diluvium* via Fr. *déluge* comes Eng. *deluge.*
Antepast, now more often (directly from It.) *antipasto,* is a bite before the meal, from *ante* + *pascere, past—,* to feed; *cp. congress.*

Antean.
See giant.

antecedent.
See ancestor.

antediluvian.
See ante—.

antepenult.
See penult.

anthem.
There is a group of Eng. words from Gr. *anthos,* flower, *antheros,* flowery. Thus Eng. *anther; chrysanthemum* (Gr. *chrysos,* gold); *anthology, cp.* Athens; *anthemy.* But *anthem* comes from Gr. *antiphona,* reply, from *anti,* against + *phone,* sound. This gives us, directly, Eng. *antiphon;* and via OE. *antefne, antevne, antemne, antemn* it became the national *anthem.*

anthology.
See rosary; Athens.

anthracite, anthrax.
See uncle.

anthropoid, anthropology, anthropophagi.
See sarcophagus; *cp.* philander.

anti—.
See ante—.

anticipate.
See surrender.

antics.
When young folks cut *capers* (*q.v.*) we may say their *antics* are amusing. Such *antic* behavior is of *ancient* lineage; the word was first applied to fantastic designs and figures unearthed in Rome. These were *antique* (L. *antiquus,* from early *anticus;* Fr. *antique;* It. *antico*), but they were also ludicrous; hence the present meaning of *antic* There has been a similar transformation of *grotesque, q.v.*
Ancient, earlier Eng. *auncien,* is via OFr. *ancien* from LL. *antianus,* adjective formed, as was *anticus,* from *ante,* before.

antidote.
See dote.

antimacassar.
From *Macassar* (native *Mangkasara*), a district on the eastern island of Celebes, came the ingredients of a hair-oil, known by that name, which your grandfathers used when they were gay young blades. And your grandmother's mother, to keep the stain off her good chairs, put over the back of them the daintily laced pieces you still call *anti-* (L. *anti,* against) *macassars.* The unguents of our day are somewhat less staining . . . though we still need a good anti-lipstick.

antimony.
See element, pretzel.

antipasto.
See ante—.

antipathy.
See osseous.

antiphon.
See anthem.

antipodes.
See pedagogue.

antique.
See antics.

antiseptic.
See creosote.

antitoxin.
See intoxicate.

antler.
The stag at eve, dipping to drink his fill, has his lower *antler* before his eyes. To the Romans, this was the *ramum ante ocularis,* the branch before the eyes: the *ante ocular*— fused in OFr. to *antoillier,* whence early Eng. *antolier, auntelere,* and finally *antler.* When the word came to be applied the any of the branches of the horn, the low one was called the *brow-antler.*

Antwerp.
The shield of this city bears two hands, couped (cut off). The giant Antigonous, living there, cut off the right hands of passers-by who could not pay the toll, and tossed them into the river: *Antwerp,* from Flem. *handt,* hand + *werpen,* throwing. This is the story built to explain the name, and woven into the city's coat of arms. Actually, *Antwerp* is the city that grew up at the wharf, from Du. *aan,* at + *werf,* wharf.

anus.
See anniversary.

apathy.
This word prefixes Gr. *a-,* not, to Gr. *pathe,* from *pathos,* suffering; *cp. osseous.* Perhaps its sound helped give *bathos* its sense, as the opposite of *pathos* (*bathetic vs. pathetic*), as the ludricrous; it was first thus used by Alexander Pope, as a descent from the sublime to the ridiculous. The word is Gr. *bathos,* depth; not related to Eng. *bath* or *bathe,* which takes place in shallow water; these are common Teut. (The *Order of the Bath,* founded 1399, was thus named because the knights took a *bath* before the ceremony, apparently an unusual procedure in early days. *See garter.*) The word has kept its scientific sense in Eng. in such compounds as *bathysphere,* a diving bell, and *bathukolpian,* deep-bosomed. *Pathology* was, first, the study of suffering.

ape.
See monkey.

aperture.
See overture; month: April.

Aphrodite.
Hesiod tells us that the goddess of love was born of the foam of the sea: Gr. *aphros,* foam. The Phoenicians called their love-goddess *Ashtoreth;* the Gr. pronunciation of this would approximate *Aphtorethe*—which was then altered so as to hold an appropriate meaning, *Aphrodite,* foam-borne. The same word also survives as *Astarte,* and Assyrian *Ishtar.*

apiary.
See cell.

apocalypse.
This revelation is really an unveiling, from Gr. *apokalypsis,* from *apo*—, off + *kalyptein,* to cover. Calypso, in the *Odyssey,* gave Odysseus a magic veil.

apocrypha.
These books of doubtful authorship—hence not canonical, not accepted as part of the Bible, though the Catholics admit some books the Jews and the Protestants reject—draw their name from Gr. *apo,* away, + *kryptein,* to hide. *Cp. grotesque.*

apostle.
See pseudo—.

apostrophe.
Two forms and senses of one word have in this merged. The figure of turning aside to address someone, in the midst of a discourse, is the exact use, from Gr. *apo,* off, + *strophe,* from *strephein,* to turn. Eng. *strophe* (wherewith the chorus turned, in Greek tragedy) is from the same source. The Gr. phrase *he apostrophos prosodia* was used to indicate an omitted part of a word, as for the sake of rhythm; then the one word was used; later, for the sign that marks an omission (or, in Eng., a possessive case). Coming to Eng. via Fr. *apostrophe,* this second sense should be sounded as of three syllables; but it has borrowed the fourth from the other use.

apothecary.
See abaft.

apparatus.
See peep, sempiternal.

apparel, apparent, apparition, appear.
See month: April.

appease.
See propaganda.

appendectomy.
See anatomy.

appendicitis.
See subjugate.

appendix.
See penthouse.

applaud, applause.
See explode.

apple.
See peach.

applepie.
See achieve. The ***applepie bed,*** known to every boy in boarding school or camp, may take its name from the way the crust is turned back on itself (like the sheets folded over, halfway down, inside) on an apple ***turnover;*** but may be a corruption of Fr. ***nappe pliée,*** folded sheet.

application.
When you ***apply*** yourself to a task, you bring yourself into close contact with the job. This was the first Eng. meaning of the word, via Fr. ***applier*** from L. ***applicare, applicat—,*** from ***ap, ad,*** to + ***plicare,*** to fold. From the L. comes also ***application,*** the act of bringing things together. ***Complicate*** is of the same origin; ***see complexion.*** To fold under, as the legs in kneeling, gives us ***supplication, suppliant, supple.*** To ***supply,*** however, is from OFr. ***supplier, suppleier,*** from L. ***sub,*** under + ***plere,*** to fill; whence also ***supplement*** (with the noun ending); similarly ***complete*** and ***complement: cp. foil. Compliment*** is the same word, limited to the fulfilling of the requirements of courtesy.

apply.
See application.

apprehend, apprehensive.
See surrender.

apprentice.
See surprise.

apricot.
This word has come to us through many lands. It was once spelled ***apricock,*** from the Port. and Sp. form. By way of the Arab. ***al-burquq*** (***al,*** the)—the ***al*** being changed through the influence of the Fr. form, ***abricot***—it may be traced to a LGr. ***praekokion,*** thence to the L. ***praecox*** (***prae,*** before + ***cox,*** from ***coquere,*** to cook), early ripe. Thus a ***precocious*** child may well enjoy an ***apricot.***

April.
See month.

apron.
See suction.

apt, aptitude.
See lasso.

aquarium, aquatic, aqueduct.
See cell, duke.

arachnean.
See arachnid.

arachnid.
The spiders are the children of ***Arachne*** (Gr. ***Arachne*** + ***-ides,*** children of: ***Hesperides,*** children of the west; ***Atlantides, cp. atlas***). ***Arachne*** was a maiden whose weaving was so admired that she challenged Minerva. The goddess, though unsurpassed, praised ***Arachne's*** work, but the disconsolate maiden sought to hang herself—whereupon the goddess changed her into a spider. Anything fine as gossamer may be called ***arachnean.***
The Gr. ending ***-ides,*** offspring, has parallel in many tongues. Eng. ***-son;*** G. ***-sohn;*** Slavic ***-vitz, -witz, -vich; -sky.*** Others prefix the indication: Heb. and Arab. ***Ben: Benjamin,*** son of Yamin; Gaelic ***Mac*** and ***Mc.***

arbiter, arbitrate, arbitration.
See compromise.

arbor, arbour.
See neighbor.

arc, arch.
See alabaster.

arch-.
See annihilate.

arctic.
This region of the world antedates the drawing of ***arcs*** around a globe.

It applies to the north, from L. *arcticus,* northern, from Gr. *arktikos,* from *arktos,* a bear— from the appearance of the great bear as a constellation in the northern sky. *Arthur's Wain* (*wain,* cart, *waggon*) is an old Eng. name for the same star-cluster, by confusion of King Arthur with *Arcturus,* the *Bear-guard.* The Northern Lights were similarly called *Arthur's Host.* Legendary association of *King Arthur* and *Charlemagne* (*Charles magnus,* the great) has led to the constellation's also being called *Charles' Wain*—though it was hailed in Stuart times as for the English Charlies, and is probably from *churl's wain, farmer's waggon;* Gr. *hamaxa,* waggon; Heb. *as,* waggon, bier. . . . At the opposite side of the world, of course, is the *antarctic* (L. *anti,* against).

area.
See aureole.

arena.
As the butcher stores of yesterday used sawdust, so the older stores, kitchens, and amphitheatres, used sand, to soak up the blood. *Arena* (L. *harena*) means sand; the covering applied to the place.

areopagus.
See Appendix II.

argent.
The silver, or white, of a coat of arms. *See* argue.

argon, argonaut.
See element, argosy.

argosy.
From Gr. *argos,* swift, the ship *Argo* was named, in which Jason and his *argonauts* (Gr. *nautes,* sailors, whence *nautical; cp. nausea*) set sail for the *Hesperides* in search of the Golden Fleece. The gardens, *Hesperides,* took their name from the *Hesperides,* the nymphs that guarded it (with the aid of a dragon), daughters of *Hesperos* (L. *vesperus,* whence Eng. *vespers,* etc.), the evening star. *Hesperos* was the God of the west, of the sunset—the golden fleece? of the garden, in which grew the golden apples we call oranges (*cp. peach*), whence *hesperidene* and other scientific terms derived from or relating to the orange.

This story did not form, but doubtless influenced, the word *argosy,* a ship; earlier forms are *ragusye, ragosie*: the word meant (a ship) from *Ragusa* (It. *Ragusi*) in Dalmatia, where, in the 15th and 16th c., very large merchant ships were built.

(The magazine *Argosy* draws its name from the American publisher, *Frank Argosy Munsey,* who also used his last name for a title.)

argot.
See slang.

argue.
This word (from the Fr. and orig. the L. *arguere*) at first meant to prove. In the L. its various meanings, prove, reprove, come from a basic sense, to make white, *i.e.,* to make plain or clear. In the Gr. form it is related to *argent,* silver or white. It is in this sense that the South American land was named the *Argentine.* The chemical symbol for silver is *Ag. Cp. debate; discuss.*

Argus-eyed.
See Appendix II.

aristocracy.
See democracy.

arithmetic.
See algebra.

Arizona, Arkansas.
See States.

arm, armadillo, army, etc.
See art.

armistice.
See tank.

arquebus.
See blunderbus.

arrant.
See errand.

arras.
See Appendix II.

array.
See turmeric.

arrears.
Just as *advance* (*q.v.*) was formed, so there was an early verb in Eng., *arrear,* to the rear, from OFr. *arere,* from L. *ad retro,* to the rear. It was used as an adverb, and in the phrase *in arrear,* meaning behind, backward, in time, place, or

the fulfilment of obligations. *Arrearage* was also used in the last sense; but the simpler form (in the plural, because liabilities always seem multiplied) has survived, *in arrears.*

arrest.
See tank.

arrive.
See rival.

arrogant, arrogate.
See quaint.

arsenal.
Though the contents may throw one arsey-varsey (*cp. scurry*), this has no relation with the common Teut. *arse;* which indeed is in Gr. *arros,* from *arsos,* rump. *Arsenal* keeps in Sp. the sense of workshop that it had in the original; it is from Arab. *assinah,* from *al-sina'ah,* the art, from *sana-ah,* to make (*dar,* house, was used earlier: *dar assinah,* and remains in early Romance forms *darcena, taracena;* in Fr. and Eng. it was probably mistaken for *d',* of, and dropped)—hence, *arsenal,* a factory, a dock; then, from frequent military use, it was limited to a place for storing ammunition.

arsenic.
This name was given by the Greeks to yellow *orpiment* (L. *auripigmentum,* golden *pigment*); from Gr. *arsenikon,* from *arrenikon,* male—meaning strong: it is a strong poison. This story is the one the NED sticks to; but others label this folk-etymology, and journey to the Arab. *azzirnikh,* for *al-zirnikh,* from the Pers. *zarnikh, orpiment,* from *zar,* gold.
Pigment is from the noun form of L. *pingere, pict—,* to paint; whence *picture* and (L. *de,* down) *depict.* The same *pingere,* via OFr *peindre,* became Eng. *paint* . . . *Arsenic* was spelled in a dozen ways; the element forms many compounds; but any way you *picture* it, it's poison (*cp. intoxicate*). *See element.*

arsis.
See decay.

art.
See inertia. The root is *ar,* to fit, to join: in Gr. *harmos,* joint; whence also L. *arma, arms,* and the common Teut. word, AS. *earm,* whence Eng. *arm* of the body. *Cp. pylorus.* The L. *armare,* to *arm,* gives us *armor, armament, armada* (the *armored* one), *armadillo* (the little *armored* one), *army,* and more. *Cp. onion.*

artery.
See pylorus.

artesian well.
See Appendix II.

Arthur's Wain.
See arctic.

artichoke.
This choice vegetable was known to the Arabians, who called it *al* (the) *kharshuf.* In Spain this became *alkharsofa,* then *alcachofa.* Northern Italy borrowed the word, but turned its foreign ending into a more familiar form: by analogy with *ciocco,* stump, it became *articiocco*—whence Fr. *artichaut.* Eng. *artichoke* was probably also influenced by the sensation if you eat the wrong part. Note that *Jerusalem artichoke* has no connection with the Holy land, being a folk transformation of It. *-girasole,* turn (with the) sun. *Heliotrope* has exactly the same meaning (Gr. *helios,* sun + *tropos,* from *trepein,* to turn. *Cp. trophy*). *Cp. almond.*

artifice.
See defeat.

Aryan.
See Hibernia.

as.
See alone.

asbestos.
The more cold water poured upon quicklime, the more it steams; it is "the unquenchable stone," from Gr. *asbestos,* from *a,* not + *sbestos,* from *sbennynai,* to quench. Then the word was applied to a kind of flax that supposedly could not burn; finally, to the mineral we know as *asbestos,* often used for theatre curtains. The laughter of the gods (in Homer) is *asbestos,* unquenchable: the world to them is a source of endless comedy.

ascend.
See descend. The *ascent* is usually harder than the *descent;* but the *assent* is usually easier than the *dissent*—which, too, may cause *dissention* (disagreement leads to quarreling; thus the meaning changed). The *consensus* of opinion is

what leads to *consent;* though *consensus* first meant the harmonious working together of the parts of the body: from L. *con, com,* together, + *sentire, sens*—, to feel; then the agreeing of various persons. Thus *assent* is L. *as, ad,* toward; *dissent* is L. *dis,* away, + *sent*—. The feelings are involved in *presentiment,* also, not to mention the *senses* themselves through which we feel; the *sentiments* that we feel; *sensation; sensuous* (full of feeling); *sensual* (inclined to feeling, to the gratification of the *senses*); *sensible* (capable of feeling; hence, responsive); *sensitive* (the passive form, with feelings readily stirred). A *sentence* first was a brief expression of a feeling, an opinion; hence also *sententious;* then, a judicial decision; also, a grammatical unit of speech. But one (*cp. resent*) must hope not to rouse *resentment.*

ascetic.
This is from the Gr. adjective *asketikos,* from *asketes,* hermit. But the chief task of the hermit was to drive out the lusts of the flesh: the word is from Gr. *askeein,* to exercise (like athletes in training).

ascribe.
See shrine.

Asia.
See Europe.

askance.
This word may be from ME. *askoyne,* from Du. *schuin,* sidewise. But it more probably indicates the link between a candle holder and a fleeing banker: a *sconce* was a screened lamp or candle, from OFr. *esconse,* from L. *sconsa,* from *absconsa,* from *abscondere, abscons*—, to hide away. Hence also to *abscond.*

aspersion.
On a hot day, did you ever stand under a cold *aspersion?* Our use of this word is figurative; it is, from L. *aspergere, aspers*—, to sprinkle, to splash, from *ad,* on, to + *spargere, spars*— to scatter; *cp. affluent.* Since what is usually splashed is mud, the word has taken its present application.

asphodel.
See daffodil.

aspic.
The poisonous snake (L. *aspis*), the *asp* is also, esp. in poetry, called the *aspic,* which is its name in French. The French have a proverb *"froid comme un aspic",* cold as an asp: this common saying, applied with a humorous intent, gave its name to the frozen *gelatin* dessert, *aspic. Gelatin, gelatine,* via It. *gelata,* is itself *frozen,* from L. *gelare, gelat*—, to freeze, from *gelu,* frost. And *jelly* is the same word, via Fr. *geler,* to freeze (past participle, feminine, *gelée*). The earlier *aspic* was a *jelly* with meat or game frozen in; a delightful dish, despite Thackeray's having someone die (*Vanity Fair,* 62) "of an *aspic* of plovers' eggs" . . . which brings back thoughts of the *asp.* (Anticipating the American arch-realist Belasco, a French director provided Cleopatra with a mechanical *asp* that, before biting her, lifted its head and hissed. The final word rested with the critic that wrote: "I agree with the *asp.*")

aspire.
See trophy.

assail.
See insult.

assassin.
This murderer of one in high place was originally one of a band (our word comes from the plural form) of *Assassins* (Arab. *hashshashin,* hashish-eaters) who were organized as a secret society in Persia, in the 11th c. Their leader was supposedly the Old Man of the Mountains, who sent them forth to destroy the Christian leaders. The Christians retaliated by preserving their name to mark one that kills by treacherous violence, *assassinates.* (Through much of the east, hashish is called *bhang,* from Sansk. *bhanga,* hemp.)

assault.
See insult.

assent.
See ascent.

assets.
This word was first used of the money a dead man has left, to clear away his debts. It was spelled *aseth* in Piers Plowman (ca. 1370), from Goth. *saths,* full, cognate with L. *satis; see satisfy.* The early form, indeed, was supplanted by use of the Fr. *assez,* enough, from L. *ad* + *satis.* In case there are no *assets, liabilities* is from Fr. *liable,* from *lier,* from L. *ligare,* to bind, whence *ligament. Cp. legible.*

assignation.
See resign.

assimilate.
As the body takes in food, it changes all sorts of things (almost) into substances like the various parts of the body, each in its kind: blood, bone, tissue, nails, and hair, and all the rest. This process of changing unlike things to like is in the very word, from L. *assimilare, assimilat—*, to liken, from *ad*, to + *simil—*, like. Hence the figure of speech, *simile*, and things *similar*. There also developed the form L. *simulare, simulat—*, to be like, whence Eng. *simulate*. Thus also, *simultaneous*, from L. *simul*, applied to time.

assist.
See tank.

associate.
See sock.

assort, assorted.
See sorcerer.

assume, assumption.
See pr[illegible].

Astarte.
See A[illegible]ite.

aster.
See flower.

astonish.
The earlier form of this word was *astone* or *astun*. There are two theories as to its origin. It is traced through OFr. *estoner* (modern Fr. *étonner*), L. *ex*, out + *tonare*, thunder; as though struck by thunder. It thus meant to *stun*, to render senseless; later, the emphasis was laid on the mental rather than on the physical effect. But its development also suggests a stone: turned to stone. Thus there is repetition as well as hyperbole in the expression "I was *petrified* with *astonishment*!" *Petrified* (L. *petra*, rock + *fy*, from *fier*, from *ficare*, from *facere*, make) reminds one of the pun that established the Catholic Church: "On this rock (*Peter*) I shall stand."

astrachan.
See Appendix II.

astrolabe.
This measuring device is from Gr. *aster*, star, + *lambanein*, to take; *cp. disaster.*

astrology, astronomy.
See disaster.

asunder.
See sundry.

atavism.
See uncle.

atheism.
See monk.

atheist.
See theology.

Athens.
This city is rightly named: the flower of Greece—from the root *ath*, whence Gr. *anthos*, flower; whence, many Eng. words beginning *antho—*, *e.g. anthology*, a flower gathering (hence, book of selections) + Gr. *legein*, to gather.

athletics.
You are not really an *athlete* unless you have been in competition. The running, jumping, boxing, wrestling of the Greek youth in the Olympic games was rewarded with an *athlon*, prize; Gr. *athlos*, contest, *athleein*, to compete, *athletes*, a competitor. The adjective *athletikos*, with a plural formed by analogy with mathematics, politics, and the like, gives us Eng. *athletics*. The milder *callisthenics* are recommended for the fairer sex; from Gr. *callos*, beauty, + *sthenos*, strength; *cp. calibre.*

Atlantic, atlantides.
See atlas.

atlas.
The gods fought all who gave men power some day to equal the gods. From their deeds and punishments, various words have come into our language. The early *lucifer* match is from the fallen angel *Lucifer* (L. *lux*, *luci—*, light + *ferre*, to bring) who, just as *Prometheus*, tried to bring light, knowledge, to man. *Promethean* may refer to the desire, or the punishment, of *Prometheus*, who was chained to the rock with a vulture forever devouring his liver. *Sisyphus*, a king of Corinth, was punished by having to roll a heavy stone up a hill; just as it came to the top, back it rolled again: endless repetition of work thus forms a *Sisyphean* task,

like that of the motion picture publicity man. The giant sons of *Terra* (Earth) and *Titan* rebelled against the gods. Among them, *Tantalus* was placed in a pool to his chin, but the waters as he dipped toward them receded; fruit dangled over his head, but if he reached toward it drew away: to spread before one what one may not enjoy is to *tantalize*. *Atlas* was given the burden of holding up the world; he may be seen at the task in front of Radio City, New York, today. His name was also given to a mountain in Lybia supposed to support the heavens. *Atlantes* (Gr. *Atlas, Atlant—*) are stone figures, instead of columns, holding up a structure; so also are *atlantides* (Gr., daughters of *Atlas*). From Lybia westward the name *Atlantic, of Atlas,* was given to the ocean. Mercator, in 1636, used the name *atlas* of a book of maps, from the fact that the picture of *Atlas* holding the world was the usual frontispiece (*q.v.*). *Cp. tycoon.*

Note, however, that the first far-travelers came from the east, and that *atlas* is an eastern satin silk, from Arab. *atlas,* smooth, from *talasa,* to rub smooth: the early maps were painted on cloth.

atmosphere.
See trophy.

atom.
See anatomy.

atone.
A house divided against itself is as an evil man; to *atone* for one's sins is to find inner unity, to become *at one* with oneself once more. (Similarly, in OFr., to unite is *aduner, aüner, at one.*) In the same fashion, Joseph Smith, founding the *Mormon* sect (at Manchester, New York, in 1830), said that the Book of *Mormon* is from Eng. *more* + Egypt. *mon,* good. More frequently, such homemade combinations are slang or humorous compounds, *e.g. comeatable, come-at-able.*

The noun *atonement* was an earlier form than the verb, itself preceded by the expression "to make an *onement* with God."

For other fusings, *see Dora.*

atrophy.
See trophy (to which it is not related).

atropine.
See trophy.

attach.
See attack.

attack.
This word means literally to stick a *tack* into (OFr. *attaquer, attacher, ataquer,* from *ad,* to + Celtic *tak,* peg). *Attach* is its obvious doublet; to take the peg away is to *detach.* This is a common Teut. form: Goth. *tekan,* to touch; also L. *tangere, tact—,* whence *tangent, contact,* etc.; *cp. taste.* An initial *s,* however, has been dropped; the basic root is Aryan *stag,* to *stick;* whence Gr. and Eng. *stigma,* a *prick,* mark, sign; Gr. *stichein,* to prick; whence *instigate,* to prick into something; and A.S. *stician,* whence Eng. *sting* and *stick* (as, to *stick* a pig); Ir. *stang,* a pin. Thus the might of *attacking* armies, viewed down the ages, is as the *pricking* of a pin against the ribs of time. *Cp. etiquette.* But *see deck.*

In *prick* also an initial *s* has been lost: it is from the Aryan root *spark,* to scatter, *sprinkle,* whence L. *sparcere,* whence *spargere;* MHG. *sprengen,* to *scatter,* whence ME. *sprengen,* frequentative *sprenkle,* whence Eng. *sprinkle.* A *prick* was originally a mark, a dot, then a point, then the point's piercing. (*Pin* is from LL. *pinna,* from L. *penna,* a feather: *cp. vogue*: used as a stylus for writing on wax.) This group is linked with the Aryan root *sparg,* to crackle, to burst (after which, things scatter; whence, *spark* and *sparkle*: the little fire-burstings of stars), whence Teut. *sprak,* whence *sprank,* whence AS. *springen,* whence Eng. *spring, sprang.*

Water bursts from the ground in a *spring;* shoots burst from the ground in the *spring;* when planks split they are *sprung.* The children that burst from one are one's *offspring;* if you sit on a *tack* you *spring* off!

attain.
This is one end of the devious line of which later offshoots are probably *attach* and *attack* (*q.v.,* not found in Shakespeare). To *attain* is via Fr. *atteindre, atteign*—(whence also Eng. *attainder*), from L. *attingere, attact—,* from *ad,* to + *tangere, tact—,* to touch; *cp. taste.* But closely related to L. *tangere, tact—,* to touch, was L. *tingere, tinct—,* to steep; from which we have Eng. *tincture,* and via Fr. *teindre* and *teint,* Eng. *taint* and *tint.* The verb *taint,* perhaps, is an aphetic back-formation from *attaint,* which it-

self is a confusion of L. *attactum,* as though the past participle of L. *attingere* were *attinctum;* hence *attaint,* which was first the past tense of *attain,* to get at, to touch, became a seperate verb meaning to spoil, to convict. The senses are fused in the meaning to touch as with a disease, to *infect. Infection* is spread from L. *inficere, infect—,* from *in,* into + *facere,* to do, to make: to dip in, to subject or expose to. *Contagion* calls for actual *contact,* from L. *contingere, contact—,* from *con, com,* together, + *tangere. Cp. deck.* Let us hope that you *attain* without *attaint!*

attaint.
See attain.

attempt.
The L. *tener,* delicate, had a *d* slipped into it, in OFr. *tendre;* whence come Eng. *tender* and its compounds, *tenderloin* (*see sirloin*), *tenderfoot, tenderness;* directly from L., the *teneral* state of insects; etc. These must not be confused with the words L. *tendere, tens—, tent—,* to stretch: *tensile* strength, *tense* (the present and past *tense* are via OFr. *tens,* from L. *tempus,* time), *tendril,* and many more, for which *see tennis. Tent* is directly from *tendere, tent—,* but in its meaning of absorbent cloth to tuck in a wound, it is from the frequentative *temptare* (also *tentare*). To reach out toward something is to *attempt* it, from L. *attentare,* frequentative of *tendere* (whence the earlier Eng. form *attent; attend, attentive*), whence LL. *attemptare,* Eng. *attempt.*

attend.
See tennis.

attest.
See test.

attic.
One suggestion links this word with the countryside, *Attica,* the state in which Athens stood. From the manners of the city, *Attic* meant elegant. It was also applied to the style of architecture of that section; one feature of this was a small decorative row of columns atop a larger (as on the Pantheon at Athens); hence, *attic,* any top *storey.* But Sansk. *attaka* was the highest room of the Indian house, from *atta, lofty. Loft,* an upper chamber, and *lofty,* are both from AS. *lyft,* air, sky, from G. *Luft. Verandah* is from Sansk. *varanda,* a portico. *Storey, story,* floor of a house, is the same word as *story,* a tale (OFr. *estoire,* from L. *historia*), perhaps because of *"storied"* windows, a legend for each floor. Thus a *second-story man* just tells another tale!

A *store* (originally a verb, to *store*) is from OFr. *estorer,* from L. *instaurare,* to begin with, to repair, replenish. *Restore* is from OFr. *restorer,* from L. *restaurare,* to repair, the present participle of which *restaurans, restaurant—,* gives us *restaurant.*

attire.
See tire.

attorney.
The idea of *turning* is of course very old: from AS. *turnian,* from *tyrnan;* Fr. *tourner,* from L. *tornare, tornat—,* from *tornus,* lathe, from Gr. *tornos,* pair of compasses. From OFr. *tournoi* and *tournoiement* come *tourney* and *tournament,* at which the chief games were those in which knights rode away from one another, then *turned* and charged.

If you were in trouble, or were going away, you would select someone to *turn to* (Fr. *à,* to + *tourner, turn*), to represent you; this man was your *attorney.* Its first meaning was, one assigned to act for another; as still in the expression, *power of attorney.* When you take a *detour,* of course, you *turn away* from the main path (Fr. *dé,* from, + *tourner*). *Cp. torch.*

attract.
An *attractive* proposition is one that draws you to it. The first sense of *attract* was physical: to draw nourishment to oneself. It came into the language about 1550, formed by analogy with *contract* (*cp. distraction*) and *abstract,* used in Eng. a century and a half earlier. To *abstract* is to draw away (*trahere, tract—,* to draw; *at, ad,* to; *ab, abs,* away); hence, to draw away from the physical, hence, an *abstraction. Concrete* is from L. *concrescere, concret—,* from L. *con, com,* together, + *crescere,* to grow; whence *crescent* (*cp. excrement*) and (via OFr. *encresitre, encreiss—*) *increase.*

attribute.
See tribulation.

attrition.
See terse, tribulation.

auburn.

Here is a word that has changed color down the years. It is from L. *alburnus,* whitish, from *albus,* white. This gives us (directly from the L. neuter) *album,* a white tablet, book; *albino; albumen,* white of egg, and "perfidious *Albion,*" from the white cliffs of Dover. But Bishop Hall, speaking in his satires (ca. 1598) of *abron* locks, shows that the word was confused with Eng. brown. The spelling did not remain modified, but the color did. To put white down on something, L. *de + albare,* whence *dalbare,* whence F. *dauber,* to plaster, gives Eng. *dauber* and *daub.* The L. *albus* may be related to Hittite *alpash,* cloud, suggesting the color.

audacious.

It is one thing to hear a challenge, another to accept it. To the ancient Roman, however, no sooner heard than done. To hear is L. *audire* (*see audit*) ; to dare is L. *audere.* The adjective from this verb is *audax, audaci—,* bold; whence Eng. *audacious* (*—ous* from*—osus,* full of): full of *audacity.*

auction.

If you have ever had the joy of carrying off a desired object against the bid of others, you can see why *auction* comes directly from L. *auctionem,* from *augere, auxi—, auct—,* to increase, to add. (Thus an *auxiliary* is an added force.) But have you noted that a man who increases something, or increases the supply of things, is also an *auctor,* whence OFr. and OE. *autor,* whence Eng. *author!* An *augur* (promising blessed increase, as what fortune teller does not! and in this mood giving us the adj. *august,* the Emperor *Augustus,* and the eighth month) may be derived from this word, or from L. *auger,* from *avis,* bird + *gerere,* to handle, as interpreting the entrails or the flight of birds. Before starting an important project, it was customary to *inaugurate* it by consulting an *augur;* until *inauguration* was limited to the important public event of a new regime.

Auspicious is from L. *auspex, auspic—,* from *avis,* bird + *specere,* to see: *inspect,* to look at; *respect,* to look again, to heed; *speculate,* from L. *speculare,* to spy out, from *specere; conspicuous,* "full of looking together"; etc. (By dint of wishing, *auspicious* came to mean not merely full of *omen,* but full of good *omen.* Hence also *auspices.* Note that the ear, being a nocturnal sense, is more distrustful than the eye: *omen* and *ominous,* from L. *audire,* to hear,? imply evil impending.)

Auger, the tool, is from OE. *nafu, nave,* hub of a wheel, + *gar,* borer. (It lost the *n,* like *adder,* OE. *naddre,* serpent: *a naddre,* whence *an addre. Apron* is another familiar word showing this transfer: *a napron,* whence *an apron,* from OFr. *naperon,* diminutive of *nape, nappe,* from L. *mappa,* tablecloth. The Fr. gives us Eng. *napery,* and the Eng. diminutive *napkin.* The related MDu. *noppen* gives Eng. *nap,* rough hairs or thread on the surface of a cloth; hence ? the *nape* of the neck. Similarly *umpire* is ME. *noumper,* from OFr. *nomper,* from LL. *non pair,* from L. *non par,* not equal, an odd man called in when two parties disagree. *Cp. humble.* The reverse process appears in words like *newt*: *an ewt,* whence *a newt.* Thus *an eke-name* (Eng. *eke,* from AS. *ēcan,* to augment, a common Teut. word), an added name, became *a nekename,* whence a *nickname. Cp. map.*

audience.

See audit.

audit.

The earliest examining of accounts was done orally; the bookkeeper was given a hearing (L. *audire, audit—,* to hear). The present participle, the one hearing (L. *audiens*), gives us *audience.* Those seeking a radio job may be granted an *audition.* The voice of righteousness is too often *inaudible;* others require an *auditorium.*

audition, auditorium.

See audit.

auger.

See auction.

aught.

See nausea.

augment.

The L. ending *—mentum* (L. *mentum,* mind?) was added to the verbal form to name the action, or its result or means. Thus *fragment* (*cp. discuss*), *ornament* (L. *ornare, ornat—,* to *adorn;* whence also Eng. *ornate; adorn* is from L. *ad,* to + *ornare.* L. *ornare* is perhaps a contraction of *ordinare,* to set in order, from *ordo, ordin—*, order; *cp. orient.* From this we have Eng. *ordinance,* which meant first arrangement in *order; ordnance,* the arrangement of military supplies, then artillery in general; *ordonnance,* systematic arrangement; also *ordinary,* which first meant *orderly,* then regular, usual; and, via OFr. *ordener, ordeiner,* Eng. *ordain. Ordeal* is of other souıce, being AS. *ordel,* related to Eng. *deal*: a judicial test—which, from tests by fire, by throwing into a river, and the like, acquired its present meaning.). Sometimes the L *—mentum,* Eng. *—ment,* has been addded to a word not of L. origin, as *betterment, atonement.*

Thus *augment* was first an Eng. noun, then used as a verb, from L. *augere, auxi—, auct—,* to increase; *see auction.*

augur.
See auction.

august.
See auction; month.

aunt.
See ant.

aural.
See scourge.

aureole.
This is frequently understood as a crown of gold; thus John Donne refers to it as *coronam aureolam,* as a L. diminutive of *aurea,* golden circle, from *aurum,* gold. This notion has thrust the *u* into the original *areola,* from Fr. *areole,* from L. *areola,* diminutive of *area.* (L. *area* and Gr. *halos,* whence Eng. *halo,* have run through the same course of meanings: a plot of ground, whence Eng. *area;* a threshing-floor; a ring around a heavenly body.) De Quincey uses the word correctly when he speak of saints "born with a lambent circle of golden *areola* about their heads." Originally there was a disc, not just a ring; its purpose in all likelihood was not to indicate sanctity but to protect the figure from pigeon-droppings, which have not ceased to be a statuary pest.

aurora.
The Greeks and Romans made many gods, by putting a capital letter on the common name for a thing (unless the process went in the other direction, and the gods became the things.) Thus *Aurora* was the goddess of the dawn; whence Eng. *auroral. Boreas* was the North Wind, or the god thereof; the *aurora borealis* is the phenomenon otherwise known as the Northern Lights. At the antipodes, this is the *aurora australis,* from L. *auster, austr—,* south; whence Eng. *austral. Cp. stern.* "Beyond the north wind" is *hyperborean,* (Gr. *hyper,* beyond).

The southern continent of *Australia* was earlier L. *terra australis,* the southern land; but note that *Austria* is from G. *Oesterreich,* the eastern kingdom. *Austro—* is a combining form, as in *austromancy,* divining by the winds; *cp. necromancy.*

auscultation.
See scourge.

auspices, auspicious.
See auction.

austere.
See stern.

austral, Australia, Austria.
See aurora.

authentic.
The L. *sum, esse, fui, futurus,* to be, had a present participle, *sons, sont—,* used to mean the being, the one it was—hence, guilty. As it lapsed from association with the verb, two other present participles developed: (1) *essens, essent—;* this gives us Eng. *essence,* the *essential* thing, the being itself; for further emphasis the *quintessence, q.v.;* and (2) *ens, ent—,* from which we have Eng. *entity, nonentity.* The L. is related to Gr. *hentes,* being; this with Gr. *auto—,* self, gave Gr. *authentes,* one who acted for himself (hence did the job well); whence the adjective Gr. *authentikos,* Eng. *authentic.* Confused in the 14th c. with L. *auctor, author* (*cp. auction*), this was early spelled *auctentyke, autentyke;* from the first in Eng. it meant entitled to obedience or belief.

author.
See auction.

autochthonous.
See humble.

autocrat.
See amphigory.

autograph.
See graffito.

autogyro.
See amphigory.

auto-intoxication.
See intoxicate.

automobile.
See amphigory.

autopsy.
See pessimist.

autumn.
See equinox.

auxiliary.
See auction.

avail.
See infirmary.

avalanche.
This word has been traced, via Fr. *avaler,* to swallow, and Fr. *aval,* downward, to the L. *ad vallem,* to the valley —as L. *ad montem,* to the mountain, gave Fr. *amont,* upward. Others say that the first part of the word was shaped by association with this Fr. *aval;* but it is basically from L. *labi,* to slide, whence LL. *labina,* land-slide, whench Prov. *lavanca,* whence Fr. *lavanche.* Confusion of *la lavanche,* the landslide, gave *avalanche.* Similarly *la munition* became Fr. and Eng. *ammunition.* A number of words from the Arabic have kept the article *al,* the, as part of the Eng. word; *cp. alcohol;* and some Eng. words have lost or added an initial letter in the same fashion; *cp. auction. Munition* is, from L. *munire, munit—,* to fortify, from *mœnire,* to put a wall around, from *mœnia,* ramparts, from Sansk. root *mu,* to bind, to protect.

avaricious.
See harpoon. L. *avere,* to desire, had the adjective L. *avarus,* greedy. Hence also *avidity.*

avast.
The landlubber etymologists hunt around separate shores for this. Some claim it as from Du. *hou' vast,* for *houd vast,* hold fast. But the Portuguese were also great sailors: Port. *abasta,* enough (It. *basta*), supposedly from the Arabic of still earlier seafarers. *Cp. bazooka.*
The companion term, *belay,* also used to mean stop, more exactly is the order to tie up the running ropes of the ship: from an earlier *belage,* from Du. *bellegen,* to bind; *cp. legible.* When *belage* was used in English, *belay* meant to attack, to waylay, from OE. *bi*+ *lecgan,* to lay. But laziness and rough speech fused the two words, and with the passing of the highwayman as an English national institution, the nautical sense became supreme. *Avast,* my hearties!

avenge.
See vengeance.

average.
Appearing in 12th c. Fr. as *averie, average* came into use ca. 1490, meaning a day's work the King's tenants were required to give to the Sheriff, esp. with their beasts of burden. It is conjectured that the word is related, through Fr. *aver,* with L. *habere,* to have. The tenant must carry a certain amount of provisions (in war time) etc., according to his possessions, his "havings." The number of cattle he used might vary (a horse, *e.g.,* carries more than a mule), but the stipulated amount (the *average*) remains the same. The use of the word in this mathematical sense is found only in English.

Avernus.
See tavern.

averse, avert.
See advertise.

aviary.
See cell.

avidity.
See avaricious.

avigation.
See nausea.

avoid.
See vacuum.

avoidupois.
See adipose.

avouch, avow.
See vote.

avulsion.
Lamb speaks of eyes that come away "kindly, with no Oedipean *avulsion.*" The word is from L. *a, ab,* from + *vellere, vuls—,* to pull, to pluck. This is

more familiar in Eng. *revulsion,* a swift pulling back. A gentler drawing back provides a *revelation,* from L. *revelare, revelat—,* to draw back the *veil,* L. *velum.* By way of Fr. *révéler,* this gives us *reveal; cp. cloth: voile.* The morning summons in the army, *revelly, réveillé,* is the Fr. imperative, *réveillez,* of *se réveiller,* to wake up, to watch again, from *veiller,* to watch, to stay awake, from L. *vigilare; cp. alert.* Linked with this (via Fr. *réveillon,* a gay party, esp. at Christmas) is the boisterous *revel,* though via OFr. *reveler* it may also be connected with L. *rebellare,* to *rebel,* to fight back, from *re,* back + *bellum,* battle.

avuncular.
See uncle.

awash.
See Washington, *Appendix III.*

away.
This word is AS. *onweg,* on the way. It might also have been *ofweg,* off the way; that is what it was in *wayward,* from which initial *a* has dropped. It has dropped with more surprising consequence in *down.* The *downs* of England are the uplands, esp. the chalk hills, from AS. *dun,* whence Eng. *dune,* a doublet. *Adown,* meaning off the hill, lost its initial *a;* but *down,* the adverb, still carries one off the heights.

awe, awesome, awry.
A word sooner seen than heard is *awry;* perhaps my own childhood blunder leads me now to exaggerate the number of those that pronounce the word as though it were from *awe: aw ree.* The adjective from *awe* is, of course, *awesome* (*—some* usually means many would like it; as in *handsome,* originally pleasant to handle; *toothsome,* pleasant to eat. In origin the suffix is related to *seem,* as also in *lonesome*). *Awry* was in OE. *on wry,* as many call for ham.

All English words beginning with *wr* are of Teutonic origin; most of them have some sense of twisting. Thus *wrath,* twisting in rage; *wreath,* a twined garland (from OE. *writh,* a weak form of *writhan,* to *writhe, q.v.*). *Cp. pylorus* (wrist). *Wry* is directly from ME. *wrien,* to twist, from AS. *wrigian,* to turn aside; whence also ME. *wriggen,* to twist, and its frequentative Eng. *wriggle.* Many try to *wriggle* out when things go *awry.*

Wring is from AS. *wringan,* to twist. A *wrong* is something twisted; it is earlier *wrang,* from *wring.* And a *wrist* (*cp. pylorus*) is that with which we twist our hands.

ax, axe, axiom.
These are all words taken early into their present uses, though with many figurative applications widening since. *Ax* is earlier *aex,* OE. *ocs,* whence the early *ax-tree,* now replaced by *axle-tree* or *axle,* from OTeut. stem *ahsula,* diminutive of OTeut. *ahs-a, ax. Axiom* is via Fr. *axiome* from Gr. *axioma* (plural *axiomata;* Eng. *axiomatic*), that which is accepted, from Gr. *axios,* worthy. *Axis* is directly from L. *axis,* axle, pivot. The Gr. word for *ax* was *axine,* whence *axinite,* a stone with crystals shaped like an ax-head; and *axinomancy,* divination with a heated *ax; cp. necromancy. Axiolite* is a stone tending to crystallize along an *axis.* The foes of the United Nations in World War II are referred to as the *axis* powers, not because they were the pivot to turn the world, but because of their geographical position.

axis, axle.
See ache, ax. The *axis* is that around which something moves.

ay, aye, aye-aye.
See altruism.

azimuth.
The *summit,* highest point, is from Fr. *sommet,* diminutive of OFr. *som,* from L. *summus* (whence Eng. *sum*), replacing *supmus* as superlative of *super, superior,* above.

This is apparently unrelated to Arab. *samt,* way, direction, plural *sumut;* with the prefixed *al,* the, *al-summut, assumut,* this was used in astronomy and became Eng. *azimuth.* The same word, as applied in the phrase Arab. *samt al-ras, samt arras,* the direction up above, gives Eng. *zenith.* Then the Arab. *nazir,* opposite, used in *nazir assemt,* led to Eng. *nadir.*

azote.
See element: nitrogen.

azyme, azymite.
See zymurgy.

B

Baal.
See Beelzebub.

babbitt.
See Appendix II.

babble.
This is a mocking imitation of those that talk on and on, with little to say: *ba..ba..* + the intensive or frequentative ending *—le,* as in *trickle, startle,* etc. But the word was influenced by *babel,* the tower of confusion, which the Jews sought to erect as an entrance to heaven: from Heb. *Bab* + *el,* gate of God—a translation of the earlier Turanian *Ca-dimirra,* Gate of God. *Cp. bavardage.*

babe.
See abbot.

babel.
See babble.

baby.
See abbot.

baccalaureate.
See bachelor.

Bacchanals.
See Battersea.

bachelor.
This word has several stories hidden in its past. The Aryan root *wak,* to speak, whence Sansk. *vasa,* whence L. *vacca,* whence *bacca,* a cow (the lowing animal); a herd of cows is LL. *baccalia;* whence *baccalarius,* farm-servant. *Vassal* may be related to the Sanskrit root. (L. *vacca,* whence Eng. *vaccinate,* as Jenner in 1798 used the term *variolae vaccinae* for cow-pox.) In feudal days, he was subordinate to a *banneret,* a man that could lead retainers under a banner of his own. This is the most likely suggestion; there are more.
Being subordinate to the horsemen, these soldiers were OFr. *bas chevaliers,* corrupted to *bacheliers.* Having once fought in battle, they were entitled to the designation *battalarius,* corrupted to *baccalarius.* In the academic field, the *baccalaureus* is the recipient of the *bacca laureus,* the laurel berry; this is probably just an adaptation of the already existing word; thence, *baccalaureate.*
The Welsh had a word for it, too: *bacher,* a *vassal,* a youth, from *gwas,* boy, whence OFr. *bachelette,* young girl. His youth and service made it likely he was unmarried. Finally, via Ir. *bachlach,* peasant, shepherd, hence, man with a staff, from Ir. *bachall,* staff, it is traced to L. *baculum,* rod; *cp. bacteria.*

bacillus.
See bacteria.

bacteria.
When *bacteria* were first observed (ca. 1847) they looked under the microscope like little sticks—and were so called; but of course by a learned term: *bacterium* was coined from Gr. *bakterion,* diminutive of *baktron,* staff. Some time later (ca. 1883) another form of tiny vegetable organism—a bit larger than the *bacterium*—was discovered. For it a word was borrowed from medieval Latin: *bacillus,* from LL. *baculus,* a rod. There is an Eng. word, which died before the practice ended: *baculine,* referring to punishment with a stick. *Cp. imbecile.*

badge.
This word may be from L. *baga* (modFr. *bague*) ring, from *bacca,* link of a chain; or from AS. *beagh,* crown, ringlet. Thus it might stand as a sign of slavery or of high honor.

badger.

Sir Thomas More calls this animal a *bageard,* whence the suggestion that it is one with a *badge,* i.e., the white mark on its forehead. However, the name was applied late, to the animal known earlier as the brock or bawson, and is probably a nickname.

The Aryan root *tal,* to lift, formed the old L. verb, *tlao, tlatus* (surviving in classical L. only in the past participle of *ferre, tuli, latus,* to bring): *ablatus* was used of corn carried away (L. *ab,* away) from the field; whence *abladum,* whence LL. *bladum,* corn. (This is not related to *blade,* a leaf, or the leaflike flat of a sword, AS. *blaed,* leaf, from OHG. *plat,* whence Eng. *flat,* from Aryan root *bla,* blow, blossom, whence L. *florere,* whence Eng. *flower, flourish.*) LL. *bladger,* whence ME. *badger,* was a dealer in corn—a preoccupation of the animal given the name. In France the same animal was called Fr. *blaireau,* from *blé,* corn.

In many places the *badger* was a common pest (Wisconsin is thus the *Badger State*); hence grew the "sport" of putting a *badger* in a barrel and setting the dogs at it; this gives us the verb, to *badger;* also, the *badger-game. Badger* is still used in some localities for a dealer in grain, or a food peddler.

bag, bagatelle.

See baggage.

baggage.

There is a ME. *bagge,* whence Eng. *bag;* but this word is not frequent in Teut. But LL. *baga,* whence OFr. *baguer,* to tie up, whence *bagues,* bundles, and OFr. *bagage,* whence Eng. *baggage,* took the place of L. *impedimenta,* from *impedire,* to *impede,* from *im,* from *in* + *ped—,* foot; *cp. pedagogue* (Eng. *impede; impediment*) as the term for army packs. A little pack is a *bagatelle,* a trifle. The word *baggage,* at one time used for unimportant bundles, degenerated into meaning refuse; in this sense the Fr. used *bagasse,* which also was applied to a worthless woman, a camp-follower; hence the Elizabethan Eng. saucy *baggage.* The word gradually lost its bad implications, and is again applied to any lively girl, or to the supplies with which one travels. These two meanings were not in Shakespeare's mind, however, when he set forth with *bag* and *baggage.*

bail.

This word, (from L. *baiulare,* to carry, then to take care of) first meant in Eng. friendly custody of a person, guaranteeing to produce him when wanted. The man that gives *bail* was thus compared to the *baiulus,* Gr. *baioulos,* porter, trainer, nurse that carries a little thing (Gr. *baios*), a child. *Bajulus* is sometimes used in place of another word with a similar history, *pedagogue, q.v.*: the *Grand Bajulus* of the Greek Court. *Cp. villain.*

To *bail* out a boat came into use in the early 17th c.; but 150 years before, the word was used as a noun to indicate a scoop for pouring out water, from Fr. *baille,* bucket (Fr. *bailler,* to yawn), from LL. *bacula,* diminutive of L. *baca,* trough. A brewer's or distiller's trough is still called a *bac* or *back.*

bailiff, bailiwick.

See villain.

bait.

By two routes from the same origin (ON. *beita,* causal of *bita,* to bite; and the feminine *beita,* food) *bait* means to egg on, as to urge dogs (or rascals) to annoy and harass a person; and food—either given directly, as to *bait* a horse, or as a lure in fishing. From an OFr. form of the same word, *beter,* came *abeter,* to incite (*ad,* to + *beter*), whence our own word *abet* (one of those paired words, like "without let or hindrance:" "to aid and *abet*").

baize.

See bay.

bake.

See ache.

bakelite.

See Appendix II.

balaam.

In the *Bible* (*Numbers* XXII, 30) we are told that *Balaam* had an ass that spoke with the voice of a man. In newspaper offices, oddities kept in type, to be used when odd corners of space and columns' ends are unfilled, are called *balaam. Balaam's box,* at first the place where these were kept, was later used for the wastebasket.

bald.
See pie.

bale.
See bonfire.

balk.
See bulk.

ball.
See ballot.

balloon.
See blimp.

ballot.
This word (from It. *ballota, bullet,* diminutive of *balla, ball; bullet* is through the Fr. *boulette,* diminutive of *boule, ball;* the L. is from Gr. *ballein,* to throw; *see* devil) indicates the early method of secret voting, by placing white or black *balls* in a receptacle; hence, to reject something (now, especially a person from membership) is to *blackball* it. The opposite process is employed in a *lottery.* The L. word *sors,* a drawing, was translated in AS. as *hlot* Eng. *lot;* this term was borrowed by the Romance languages (Fr. *lot;* It. *lotto,* which gives us the game *lotto;* It. *lotteria,* Eng. *lottery*) and some of our uses are borrowed back from them. The AS. for casting lots is *weorpan hlot.* From *weorpan* comes Eng. *warp,* thrown across the *weft* or woof, to form the *web* or piece of cloth. Hence, something thrown crosswise, therefore distorted, is *warped.* AS. *webb* and AS. *wefan, weave,* are in one train of ideas and words. The drawing for order-numbers in the U. S. Army draft for World War II was made with balls. But *ballots* and *bullets* are closer in origin than in democratic employment.

ballyhoo.
Around 1885 the expression *bally* was substituted in Eng., for the oath Bloody! (*Cp. goodbye.*) A popular music hall song then used the refrain *"bloodyhooly truth,"* as an Irish phrase for *"the whole bloody truth."* It is also suggested that the term was influenced by the village of *Ballyhooly,* in County Cork, Ireland. What with the Irish reputation for *blarney* (Whoever hung out the window of *Blarney Castle,* near Cork, and kissed the magic stone, became a most cajoling speaker) the term *ballyhoo* was applied to the appeal made by the barker seeking customers for his show.

baluster, balustrade.
See banister.

ban.
Cognate with Gr. and L. *fa,* speak, *ban* was an edict, esp. the summons by proclamation, esp. of vassals called for military service. (In France, the *ban* is the part of the population liable for such service.) Since they did not always readily respond, *ban* came to mean the curse put upon the disobedient. In its form *banish* (Fr. *bannir, banniss—*), it meant to proclaim as an outlaw, whence (It. *bandito*) *bandit.* From the idea of the *ban* as that which was for general use (*e.g.* the *bannal* mill, the lord's mill, where all his serfs must grind), for everybody's use, came the sense of the adj. *banal,* commonplace, trite. The original sense is preserved in the expression marriage *banns.* To *abandon* is short for Fr. *mettre à bandon,* to put under (another's) control, hence, to give up.
In the early stages, when *ban* still meant an edict, a law, there developed (L. *contra,* against; Sp. *contrabando*) the adjective then noun *contraband.*
There is also a word *ban* (Pers., lord), title of the viceroy in certain east European countries: Croatia, districts of Hungary.

banal.
See ban.

banana.
See peach.

band.
See neighbor.

bandit, banish.
See ban.

bang.
See bhang.

banister.
This word is a corruption of *baluster,* influenced by OEng. *ban,* to stop, since it stops one from falling. *Baluster* is a roundabout word, commonly said to be drawn from the resemblance between the little columns of the *balustrade* and the flower of the pomegranate: from Gr. *balaustion,* pomegranate flower. But the rows of

portholes, or loopholes with pillars between, for the cross-bow archers on the medieval galleys, were LL. *balistariae,* whence It. *balestriera*—possibly from *balla, ball,* missile—but doubtless influencing the form of the word *baluster*. Remember this as you slide down the *banister!*

banjo.
See pan.

bank.
This word seems to have come from similar forms both north and south: AS. *banke,* from *benc;* and LL. *bancus.* Its original sense was something flat, like a shelf. Applied to earth, this gives us the *bank* of a stream, and *embankment*. Through carpentry, it became our *bench*. The Lombard money-changers (perhaps also those chased from an earlier temple) used to sit with the foreign moneys on a *bench* before them; hence a *bank* is a place where money is handled. If ruffians (or other causes) broke the changer's *bench* (It. *banca rotta,* broken, whence Fr. *banqueroutte*) it is likely that he is not solvent, but *bankrupt*. Note that Eng. restored the *p,* from L. *rumpere, rupt—,* break (*cp. discuss*)—which gives us many words, from *rupture* and *rumpus* to *interrupt* (L. *inter,* between); *eruption* (L. *e,* from *ex,* out); and *corruption* (L. *cor,* from *com,* altogether), originally a religious term. L. *rumpere,* to break, to burst, is echoic in origin, akin to the onomatopoetic *rumble;* the past participle, *rupt—,* captures in sound the completion of the act.

From the little *benches* spread for a feast (LL. *bancus,* whence It. diminutive *banchetta,* whence Fr. *banquette*) comes Eng. *banquet*. Eng. *bantling,* youngster, is via G. *Bankling,* bastard (*cp. coward*), from G. *Bank, bench:* conceived on a *bench.* (Perhaps the preliminary dallying gave us *banter.*) The quack that hawked his wares, with jokes and juggling, while standing on a *bench* was It. *montambanco,* from *monta in banco,* mount on *bench,* whence Eng. *mountebank*. *Cp. somersault.*

bankrupt.
See bank.

banns.
See ban.

banquet.
See bank.

banshee.
As one might expect, the word for woman (*q.v.*) was widespread in Aryan tongues: OHG. *quena;* Goth. *quino;* Gr. *gyne;* OIr. *ben;* Gael. *bean;* AS. *cwene*—whence Eng. *quean.* (AS. *cwēn,* wife, gives us the nobler *queen.*) The Gr. *gyne* gives us *gynecology,* and the words ending in *—gynous; e.g., androgynous; cp. sarcophagus.* From Ir. *bean sidhe,* woman of the fairies, we have *banshee.*

banter, bantling.
See bank.

baptize.
See anacampserote; Whitsunday.

barbarian.
This word may indicate urban scorn of bumpkins unshaved, from L. *barbarus,* bearded. The conservative Cato, however, attacked the Roman custom of shaving as foreign, and effeminate. We are told that Alexander the Great had his Greek soldiers shaved so that opponents could not grasp them by the beard. But the word *barbarian* may be a scornful imitation (*"bar-bar"*) of the sounds made by outlanders. Similarly *Hottentot* and *Tartar; cp. tatterdemalion.* The notion of stammering is related to these sounds; and perhaps the natives trying to learn the language of their conquerors hemmed and hawed.

A *barbarism* is an error in language, or a rudeness in speech, such as might characterize an outsider. In the middle ages, *barbary* meant heathendom; then, the *Barbary Coast* of North Africa (though this sense is influenced by the Arab. *Berber,* apparently from the old Phoenician name of the region).

barbarism.
See barbarian.

barbecue.
This pleasant festivity, also the verb for the kind of cooking, was originally an American Indian name for a stick set on two uprights, for spitting the animal to be roasted. The Spanish found it in Haiti, called it *barbacoa,* the Fr. spelled it *babracot* when they found it in Guiana. Since the entire animal is often hung to be cured or roasted, some French

(humorists, no doubt) derive the word from Fr. *barbe à queue,* beard to tail; this is, of course, the wrong *cue.*

The word *cue,* as in pigtail and billiard *cue,* is from Fr. *queue,* from L. *cauda,* the *caudal* appendage; *cp. bible; cue.*

bargain.

This is not, as the word might suggest, a compound, bar—gain. While it has been traced to a LL. *barcaniare,* to haggle, some think this word in turn is related to *barca;* a *bargain,* therefore, was originally something brought on a *bark,* or *vessel,* from far countries to your door.

barium.

See element.

bark.

See embargo. The *bark* of a tree is probably related to the *birch,* AS. *birce, beorc;* the *bark* of a dog is related to *barki,* windpipe, and probably via OE. *brecan,* to break, from the suddenness of the cry.

barley.

This word (? from Teut. *bara,* bread + *llys,* plant; though the suffix may be the more frequent *lic,* like), although originally an adjective, as in *barleycorn,* is cogn. with L. *far,* corn. The AS. *bara-ern,* barley-place, changing through *berern* and *bern,* became our modern *barn.* Perhaps related is AS. *beor,* our *beer.* To *corn,* as with *corned* beef, means to preserve with salt in large grains, the size of *corn* kernels. And *jerked* beef is not from to *jerk,* a variation of *yerk,* but from Sp., from South American *charqui,* dried in long strips. It was first in Eng. called *jerkin beef,* as though of leather.

Corn is from OTeut. *kurnom, grain,* from the Aryan form *grnom,* from the verb *ger, gr-,* to wear down. Hence a *grain* of sand, a worn down particle. The slang *corny* may be from the "Rube" greenhorn of the corn-belt (section of the U. S. A. where corn is grown); but Burton Rascoe suggests it is at least influenced by It. *carne,* flesh, in the sense of cheap meat.

barn.

See barley.

barnacle.

There are two different words hidden in this; neither can be traced farther back than the middle ages, where they take the same form: LL. *barnac* (masculine), *bernaca* (feminine), of which *bernacle, barnacle,* is a diminutive.

(1) The first *barnacle,* from the masculine form, was a bit, or a pinch placed on the nose of a restive horse, esp. to quiet it while it was being shoed. There was also an instrument of human torture in this wise; and some conjecture that this sense is derived from Saracen practices, from Pers. *baran-dan,* to squeeze. In a milder growth, *pince-nez* (Fr., pinch-nose) spectacles are called *barnacles.*

(2) The second, feminine *barnacle* is a wild goose; and with it etymologists have gone on a wild goose chase indeed. For there is the *barnacle* shell-fish, found esp. on logs along shore and on ships' bottoms (whence a man one cannot get rid of is called a *barnacle*). And this shell-fish thrusts from its valves long feathery appendages, so that through the middle ages and after (Campion in his *History of Ireland;* Florio, in the 16th c.) it was believed to give birth to a waterfowl, thence called the *barnacle* goose. Max Muller, an ardent chaser, suggests that the diminutive *bernacula* might be a variant of *pernacula,* from *perna,* a shellfish, and that this was confused and combined with *hibernicula,* the little (goose) from *Hibernia,* where the *barnacle* goose was found. There's a lot that's blamed on the Irish!

barnard.

Existing now only as a proper name (e.g., *Barnard College,* Columbia University, New York), this once labeled an important figure of the underworld, the decoy (*q.v.*). It existed also as *bernard,* and is from Eng. *berner,* feeder of the hounds, huntsman, from Celt. *brann, bran,* + the derogatory *-ard; cp. coward.* The *berner* was the hunter who waited along the track an animal was expected to take, with extra hounds; hence *barnard,* a lurking member of the gang. According to that expert on cozenage, Robert Greene, a gang required four members, a taker up, a verser, a *barnard,* and a rutter.

To *cozen* is from It. *cozzonare,* to train horses; hence (Florio) to act like a crafty knave; that the profession has changed little is shown by the similar shift in the meaning of *jockey.* (The word *jockey* was first a diminutive of *Jock,* the Scot. form of *Jack; cp. jackanapes.*)

barnstormer.

The popularity of theatrical road companies in the latter half of the 19th c. exhausted the halls; in England and America, the large *barns* of estates were used as playhouses. More recently, the summer theatre has revived the use of *barns,* usually permanently remodeled. *Barnstormer* was also applied, after World War I, to aviators that hired a *barn* near a smooth pasture-field, and took sightseers into the air.

baron.

From a LL. *baro* (of origin unknown) meaning man, *baron* was applied to the King's men, then to the Great *Barons,* or those men summoned to Parliament; hence, a lord. *Baronet* (dimin., a young or lesser *baron*) was applied to the gentlemen summoned to the House of Lords by Edward III. Fielding uses *baronet* for a *baron* of beef: *see* sirloin.

barricade.

See embargo.

bartlett.

See Appendix II.

base, baseball.

See bazooka.

It is suggested that *baseball* was carried over from the earlier (15th c.) game of *prisoners'-base.* This was originally *prisoners'-bars,* which through careless enunciation lost the *r* (similarly the fish *bass* was earlier *barse,* from AS *baers.* The musical *bass* is from It. *basso,* low, *base*).

bashful.

See abeyance.

basil, basilica, basilisk.

See bazooka, church.

basin.

See basinet.

basinet, basnet, bassinet, bassinette.

This abode of peace (except for crying spells!) has a warlike ancestry. OFr. *bassinet,* helmet, is a diminutive of Fr. *bassin, basin. Bassinette* is corrupted, as though from the same source, from Fr. *bercelonnette,* diminutive of Fr. *berceau,* cradle. This is from *bercer,* to rock, originally to swing like a battering-ram, from L. *berbex* from *vervex,* battering-ram. Rockabye baby, and don't bump your head against a wall!

Baby's cradle from helmet; helmet from bowl! But *basin* itself is probably from OFr. *bacin* from LL. *bacchinum,* bowl, from L. *bacca, baca, berry*—which it resembles. Thus words take shape!

basis, bas-relief, bass.

See bazooka.

bassinet, bassinette.

See basinet.

bassoon.

See bazooka.

bastard.

See coward.

baste, bastille, bastinado, bastion, bat, bate, baton.

See bazooka.

batch.

See ache.

bath, bathe, bathetic, bathos, bathysphere.

See apathy.

battalion, battle, battlement, batter.

See abate.

Battersea.

Whistler has made a painting of the *Battersea* Bridge. This does not lead to a place the *sea batters,* but to an island, once known as *Peter's Eye, Peter's Island,* from the adjacent *Abbey of St. Peter* at Westminster. This is one of many examples of folk-corruption; another is the old tavern *The Bag o' Nails,* from *The Bacchanals.*

battery, battology.

See abate.

bavardage.

This word, direct from the Fr., yields roundabout relations. It is from the verb *bavader* from OFr. *baver,* from *bave,* an imitative word that meant both *babble,* and the slobbery saliva that accompanies the *ba-ba-babble* of babes. The guard against this, a *bib* (from OFr. *biberon,* feeding-bottle, from L. *bibere,* to drink; whence also Eng. *imbibe*) was OFr. *baviere;* from this it was applied—

in Eng., as *beaver*—to the lower part of the face-guard of a helmet. Thus, speaking of the ghost, Horatio tells Hamlet (I,ii,230) they saw his face; "he wore his *beaver* up." L. *bibere* developed later noun forms, *bibera, biberaticum;* whence OFr. *beivre* and *buverage,* whence Eng. *bever,* surviving only in the dialect sense of a between-meals nibble, and the still widespread *beverage.*

The animal *beaver* is one of the commonest Aryan names: OE. *befor;* OTeut. *bebru;* L. *fiber;* OAryan *bhebhru,* reduplicated from *bhru, brown:* the brown animal.

bawl.
See brawl.

bay.
Several words of different origin have culminated in this English form. OFr. *baie,* from L. *baca,* berry; *cp. basinet;* gives us *bay*-tree, *bay*-rum, *bay*-berry (which is thus a reduplication). Applied to the berries of the laurel tree, this results in the *bays* of the conqueror: his wreath or garland, then, his fame. Shortened from *bay*-antler (the second branch of a stag's horn) *bay* is from OFr. *bes,* second; the French and Italians still cry *Bis!* when we call Encore! From OFr. *bai,* from L. *badius,* reddish brown, comes the *bay* horse; the feminine plural of this, *baies,* became the name of a coarse cloth, *baize.* From the LL. *baia,* an indentation of the sea; comes the *bay* of water; the *Bay* State (Massachusetts); the *bay*-window. This sense is mingled with that of the opened mouth, for which *see* abeyance. *Cp. antler.*

bayonet.
See Appendix II.

bazooka.
The rocket-projectile gun was named from its resemblance to the "musical" instrument, by Major Zeb Hastings of the U. S. Army, 1943; they both are made of straight tubing, open at both ends, and, adds Bob Burns in a letter to me, "both have a more or less devastating effect." Bob invented the *bazooka* in Arkansas in 1905, when he found two pieces of gas pipe that fit one over the other, and used them as a trombone. The name is a boy's ending tacked on to the slang word for loud talk, *bazoo;* they say of a boaster, "He blows his *bazoo* too much."

A toy noise-maker of the 1880's was called a *kazoo.*

There is probably, however, a suggestion of the old *bassoon,* of somewhat the same shape and depth of tone, from It. *bassone,* low, whence Eng. *base* and *basset;* from L. *bassus,* low, from L. and Gr. *basis,* pedestal, foot, whence Eng. *basis* and *base,* from Gr. *bainein,* to step. As being at the bottom, or to be stepped on, *base* is used in compounds such as *baseboard* and—originally *home base—baseball, q.v.*

In biology there are many compounds with *basi—;* but *basil,* the plant, is from Gr. *basilikos,* royal (sovereign remedy), from Gr. *basileus,* king. The Gr. *basilike stoa,* the royal portico where court was held, hence the court (or *basilika oikia,* royal dwelling), was shortened to Eng. *basilica.* The Gr. *basiliskos,* kinglet, diminutive of *basileus,* was applied to that imaginary king of the reptile world, the *basilisk,* pictured with a crown-like mark on its head.

From L. *bassus* via Fr. *bas,* low (as in Eng. *bas-relief;* It. *basso, low + relievo* from *rilievare,* to raise), meaning first low in place, then low in quality, comes Eng. *base,* mean. The faunal region of the deep sea is the *bassalia* (Gr. *halia,* assembly).

The fish *bass,* however, is common Teut., ME. *barse* from AS. *baest;* cognate with *bristle,* from ME. *brustel,* diminutive of AS. *byrst,* brush. The trees, *bass,* is a corruption of *baest,* inner bark, also common Teut., which has also given us Eng. *bast* and the verb *baste,* the inner bark fibers being used for this coarse sewing.

This leads us to another trail, being linked to OFr. *bastir,* to put together, to build; thence Fr. and Eng. *bastion,* the fortifications *bastiment* and *bastillion,* and the tower, *bastille,* later (from its use for the purpose) a prison. Best known of such places is the Paris prison, the *Bastille,* destroyed by the populace in 1789, on July 14th; thence the French Independence Day.

Baste, to beat, is probably originally imitative (of the sound of the blow, or of the breath with the effort), for it exists widely: Sw. *basa,* to beat with a stick; OFr. *batre;* Sp. *bastonada* whence Eng. *bastinado;* perhaps It. *basta,* Enough!; LL. *batere* from L. *batuere,* to beat. This is the same word as *baste* in cooking, from OFr. *basser,* to soak (note that *soak* also has the slang sense—to deal a less heavy blow being to *sock*). To *lambaste* adds OE. *lam* from ON. *lemja,* to *lame. Beat* itself is common Teut., AS. *beatan.* From this source are also Fr. and Eng. *baston* and Fr. and Eng. *baton,* with which to beat time, and via AS. *batt,* the *baseball bat.*

From L. *batuere* via OFr. *batre,* comes Eng. *bate,* to beat down, hold back (*bated* breath), hence reduce, deduct; whence also *rebate,* which first meant to beat back, then to beat dull, to blunt (as *rebated* spears in heraldry); hence to diminish or deduct; and *abate, q.v.* to beat down, hence hold back, lessen, as fans think Burns should never do with the *bazooka.*

be.
See fetus.

be—.
See rat.

beachcomber.
See inscrutable.

bead.
This word (aphetic for *ibed,* OE. *gebed*) meant prayer; to *tell one's beads* was to count one's prayers. Then it was transferred to the perforated balls strung together, the rosary, with which one kept track of the number of prayers. *Cp. forbid.*

beam.
Early in folk symbolism occurs the idea of the fire implicit in the wood (of which the world is made). Hence it is natural that the *Bible* pillar of fire (L. *columna*) should have been translated by AS. *beam,* tree, whence Eng. *beam*— at once the wood and the ray of light, *sunbeam. Beam* (Du. *boom;* G. *Baum,* tree) is a doublet of *boom,* of a ship. *Boom,* the sound, is an imitative word. A *boom* in business, *booming,* is probably a combination of the sound and the nautical phrase "to come *booming*", under full sail. "On the *beam*", just right, is a figure from the way in which a plane lands by light-control.

bear.
See berth.

beast.
The birds and the *beasts* were there. The current use of this word is to separate the four-footed kind from other members of the animal kingdom (as distinct from the vegetable and the mineral), from birds, fishes, insects, and men. But it has had its ups and downs. It is by way of OFr. *beste* from L. *bestia;* and first appeared in Eng. to translate L. *animal.* Before that, the general OE. word was *deor, deer,* which became restricted. Now, L. *animal* has come into Eng. in the general sense, and *beast* has been limited as indicated above, or still more narrowly to the wild and fierce varieties of animals; hence also *bestial,* which first was a general term for domestic animals, then figuratively was applied to men, attributing to them actions that slander the *beasts.*

beat.
See bazooka; beetle.

Beauchamp.
See Cambridge.

beauty.
Those that see a connection between *beauty* and goodness (*good* was once spelt *God*) may go beyond the usual dictionary, which traces the word, through ME. *bealte, beute,* to L. *bellus,* beautiful. For *bellus* is from *benulus,* dim. of *benus,* from *bonus,* good. Hence the *beautiful* and the *bene*ficial are etymologically linked. On the other hand, it should be remembered that the L. *bellum* means war. *Good* is from AS. *god, gath,* gather; hence it referred to that which was selected as fitting. What you gather are your *goods.*

beaver.
See bavardage.

bed.
This was a common Teut. idea, early used as a place to sleep; but also as a garden *bed.* Its L. cognate is *fod,* the root of L. *fodere,* to dig; whence the technical Eng. term *fodient,* a burrowing animal—as a *rodent* is a gnawing animal, from *rodere,* to gnaw; *cp. graze.* This suggests that early man made his *bed* in dug-out caves or lairs. The garden *bed* has probably no connection with this early sense of digging, but is figurative from the use or shape.

A *bedstead* is a (*steady*) place for the *bed,* from AS. *stede,* place. Thus *instead of* means in place of. The home*stead* was the home place, hence farm or village. This is common Teut., G. *Statt,* place, *Stadt,* town: cognate with ***stand;*** ***see tank.*** And ***steady, steadfast,*** mean keeping to one place.

bedeck.
See deck.

bedizen.
See distaff.

bedlam.
This is an Eng. corruption of *Bethlehem,* and before the 17th c. was used of the city in Jerusalem. But, particularly, it was a short name for the hospital of St. Mary of ***Bethlehem,*** in London, founded in 1247 but since 1547 used as a state lunatic asylum, a madhouse. Hence, the confusion and noise one might expect from a group of maniacs.

bedstead.
See bed.

bee.
See mealy-mouthed.

beef.
See mutton.

Beelzebub.
The Heb. *Baal, Bel,* means god. The *Bible* (2 *Kings*,i,2) speaks of a Lord of the dwelling, *Baalzebul.* In deliberate mockery of idols, this is corrupted (*Matthew*,x,25) into *Beelzebub,* Lord of Flies. *Belial,* esp. *sons of Belial,* (1 *Samuel*,ii,12) is retained in translation, as though a similar god; it is actually, from Heb. *beliyaal,* worthlessness, from *beli,* without + *yaal,* use.

beer.
See barley; drink.

beetle.
In case you do not know, there is an Eng. word *beetle,* meaning hammer, from OE. *bietel,* related to AS. *beatan,* to *beat, cp. baste.* The insect is, from AS. *bitela, biter,* from *bitan,* to *bite. Beetle-browed* means merely, browed like the *beetle* (with overhanging forehead).

befool, befoul.
See rat.

beg.
This verb reverses the usual time order, being formed from an earlier noun, *beggar.* Lambert le Bègue (the stammerer) was a pious monk; after him was established an order of nuns (in Liège, in the 12th c.) called *beguines.* Shortly afterwards, in the Netherlands, a male order was established (L. *begardus,* Fr. *begard*). As many of them were idle mendicants, the term took on its present meaning. *See bigot.*

begin.
See commence.

begonia.
See Appendix II.

beguine.
See bigot.

behalf.
See half.

behave, behavior.
See carry.

behemoth.
See leviathan.

behest.
See alkahest.

behold.
This word has gradually moved from a very active sense to a mere receptivity. It was common Teut., OE. *bihaldan,* to *hold by,* to restrain, retain, hold fast to. From this sense it came to mean to be attentive to, to consider. From this (in English alone) it developed the sense of to look at, to watch; finally it lapsed to its present usual sense, to take in through the eyes, to see. To be *beholden* has kept the earliest sense, of attached (by *obligation*) to a person. *Oblige, obligation,* and *obligatory* are themselves from L. *ob* (*ob,* in the way of; hence it may mean either towards or against) + *ligare, ligat—,* to bind; *cp. legible.*

beholden.
See behold.

belay.
See avast.

beldam.
This is one of the words that have degenerated. Literally, it is from Fr. *belle dame,* beautiful lady. It was used in early Eng. as a polite term for grandmother; but as politeness passed out of the language, it came to mean any old woman, then an ugly hag.

belfry.
Though it now means a bell tower, originally *belfry* had nothing to do with bells. It comes through OFr. *belfrei,* from *berfrei,* from OHG. *berg,* castle, guard (*cp.* Luther's hymn, ***Ein feste Burg ist unser Gott,*** A mighty fortress is our Lord) + *frid,* peace. To guard peace there was built, in medieval times, a siege tower, moved against the walls of a beleaguered town. As this grew out of use, the term was applied to any tower; since most towers have a bell, to a bell tower. Association with the word bell may have influenced the change from *r* to *l,* though such a shift (dissimilation) occurs elsewhere (*e.g. pilgrim,* from Fr. and Prov. *pelegrin; cp. saunter.* The *r* remains in Sp. *peregrino* and Eng. *peregrination; cp. "Peregrine* Pickle," by Tobias Smollett).

Belial.
See Beelzebub.

believe.
See furlough.

bell.
See foolscap.

bellarmine.
See demijohn.

belle.
See foolscap.

bellicose.
See supercilious.

belligerent.
See foolscap.

bellows, belly.
See pylorus.

bench.
See bank.

benedick, benedict, Benedictine, benediction.
Though the second spelling is more frequent, this name for a married man is from *Benedick,* in Shakespeare's *Much Ado About Nothing,* who begins the play by swearing never to get married, and spends the rest of it in the process of breaking that vow. The name *Benedict* is L. *bene,* well + *dicere, dict—,* to speak; *see win; cp.* verdict. The *Benedictine* order was founded by St. Benedictus, d. 543; *see drink.*

benefit.
See defeat.

benign.
See mal—.

benison.
See win.

berate.
See rat.

bereave.
Now used mainly in the passive (*bereaved*: "I was *robbed!*"), this means to snatch away: AS. *bereafian, be-, bi-,* a prefix making a verb active + *reafian,* to *rob,* whence Eng. *reave.* This is common Teut. Goth. (*bi*)*raubon* gives us Eng. *rob.* Du. *rooven,* whence *roover,* led to Eng. *rover,* who was first a pirate. The sense of wanderer (as pirates became fewer) developed from the quite different word Eng. *rove,* from OF. *rouer,* to prowl (Fr. *roué*) from L. *rotare, rotat-,* to *rotate,* go around; *cp. rodent.* There is also the influence of an obsolete *rave,* to wander, sometimes confused with the present Eng. *rave; cp. outrage.*

bergamask.
See Appendix II.

beriberi.
This is taken directly from Cingalese *beri,* weakness; the doubling makes it stronger—that is, indicates a greater degree of weakness.

berry.
See peach.

berserk.
The Scandinavian hero *Berserk* (ON. *berserkr, bear sark,* bearskin: Burns in *Tam O'Shanter* speaks of the *cutty sark*—short shirt—of the young witch) had twelve sons, *Berserkers,* whose violence terrified the land. Hence, to go *berserk;* akin to the running *amok* (*amuck*) of the Malay in frenzy.

berth.
Berth, earlier spelled *byrth* and *birth,* had the same origin as *birth,* the *bearing* of children; but the two words developed at different times. As might be expected, the *birth* of children came first. Toward the end of the 16th c., when commerce

grew active along the Thames and into the far seas, crowding ships had to be careful to "*bear* off" from one another—even more so, when suddenly grappling irons might swing out and foemen leap aboard; hence ships were required to give a wide *berth* to one another. From this probable source, and from the first meaning of sea-room, came the closer application to room to keep things aboard ship, then a place to keep the men, a *berth* for sleeping, as now also on other means of locomotion. The verb *bear,* to carry (a *burden;* a child: *borne* is now used for the first, *born* for the second: may it not be one!) is common Teut., cognate with L. *ferre,* which has the same two senses. Note also the intransitive use, to *bear* down on, to *bear* toward, to *bear* off. The NED has ten columns of senses, among which it is hard to get one's *bearings.* The animal *bear* is also common Teut.

beryl.
See brilliant.

beryllium.
See element.

besiege.
See subsidy.

bestial.
See beast.

beverage.
See bavardage.

bewitching.
See trance.

bhang.
See assassin. This is also spelled bang. To *bang,* to thump, is common Teut., imitative. Linotypers' cant says *bang* for exclamation point.

bib.
See bavardage.

bible.
"The *Book.*" Several of the terms for items used in writing show their origin in the raw material. Gr. *biblos,* the inner bark of the papyrus, whence the diminutive *biblion,* the rolled sheet used in writing. From the L. plural *biblia,* the *books,* comes our Eng. *bible,* which first meant any *volume,* then what was for many persons the only *volume,* the *Bible.* From the name for the plant itself, Gr. *papyros,* whence L. *papyrus,* whence Fr. *papier,* comes Eng. *paper. Book* (*q.v.*) itself is from AS. *bōc, boece,* the *beach* tree, boards of which were used for writing. Similarly, the stem or trunk of a tree in L. is *codex,* from *caudex* (whence It., and Eng. music term, *coda;* also the scientific terms *caudal* and *caudate,* pertaining to or having a tail), whence, from the wooden tablets on which they were written, Eng. *codex* and *code,* a system of laws. *See* liberty; volume.

biceps.
See achieve.

bid.
See forbid.

biennial.
See anniversary.

bigamy.
See monk.

bigot.
This word is suggested as a corruption of the exclamation *By God,* applied to those that often used it. But it is tangled in its history with the religious orders of the *Beguines* and the *Beghards* "and the *Bigutts*"—all of them originally terms of derision. The *Beguines* were women united in piety, in homes called *béguinages,* without the order of convents; their name is probably not from the word *beg,* but from dialect Fr. *bégui,* to stammer, with the feminine *—ne* or the masculine*—ard;* there is a LL. *begardus.* Thus they were referred to as stammerers, simpletons. Remember this when you "begin the *beguine!*" *Cp. beg.*

There is another suggestion. From Sp. *bigote,* whiskers, the word may have come to mean a fiery fellow, hence a zealot. *Cp. bizarre.*

bilious.
See complexion.

billiards.
This is a fairly old game; Spenser in the 16th c. spelled it *balliards,* as though it were named from the *balls.* It is from Fr. *billard,* curved stick. However, LL. *billard,* being derived from what it strikes, from L. *billa,* from *pila,* a *ball,* takes us back to Spenser.

billingsgate.
The spot along the Thames, in London, where the fishing boats bring their catch is called *Billingsgate*, earlier *Belin's gate*, from *Belin*, a king of Britain 23d (??) in line. The coarse language of the fishwives there was proverbial (Samuel Johnson was a victim of it); and abusive speech is known as *billingsgate*. It may have been influenced by O.E. *bellan*, to *bellow*.

billion.
See number.

biology.
See macrobian. (Gr. *logos*, word; then, ordered words: the usual suffix,—*logy*, for a systematized study).

birch.
See bark.

birth.
See berth.

biscuit.
(This has a different taste, in England, from that in America.) The word is Fr.—*bis*, twice + *cuit*, cooked, from *cuir*. Thus *Zwieback* is Du. from *zwie*, two + *backen*, to cook. And there is a trade name *Triscuit*, thrice baked. *Cp. cloth*: drill and twill.

bismuth.
See element.

bison.
See Appendix II.

bit.
See sarcophagus.

bite.
See beetle.

bitter.
The bad taste in your mouth is the result of a *bite;* and *bitter* is from AS. *biter*, related to *bite*. When you come to "the *bitter* end", however, there is another story. A *bitter* is a turn of the cable or ship's ropes about the *bitts*, the two posts for fastening them. Thus to be at the *bitter* end is to be at the end of one's rope—but the bad taste helped make the expression seem appropriate.

bizarre.
This word is via Fr. from Sp. and Port. *bizarro*, handsome, brave, perhaps from the Basque *bizarra*, beard, as a sign of a swashbuckler, "bearded like the pard" (*As You Like It*, II,vii,150). Note that Sp. *hombre de bigote*, bearded man, similarly meant a spirited fellow—though it was by foreigners turned into a term of derision; *cp. bigot*. From the roustabout, high-handed ways of such as Cyrano and "the three musketeers," the word *bizarre* shifted from dashing, courageous, to its present sense of extravagant, fantastic.

black.
Persons that say things are as different as *black* and *white* might be surprised at how alike these two are. Both were associated in the early mind with absence of color: *black* is AS. *blaec;* but AS. *blac* is *white*. Whence Eng. *bleach*, from AS. *blaecan*, to make white, from *blac*. Hence also *bleak*, pale. *Blanch, blank* (empty, white sheet), and *blanket* are of the same origin, via Fr. *blanc*, white, and *blanchir*, to whiten. The word *white* is also common Teut., AS. *hwit*, cognate with AS. *hwaete, wheat*.

blackball.
See ballot.

blackguard.
In the lord's retinue, after "the weavers and embroiderers" marched the *black guard* of the spits and iron pots and other kitchenry—so called from the color of their utensils, and their own. From the characteristics attributed to the brawny kitchen knaves by their cleaner fellows (Tennyson illustrates the tendency, in Sir Kay of his *Gareth and Lynette*) comes the present meaning, the pronunciation being shortened to *blaggard*.

blackmail.
See mail.

bladder.
See blatherskite.

blade.
See badger.

blame.
This first meant to scold, as often one chides before seeing who is really to *blame*. It is from OFr. *blasmer*, from L. *blasphemare*, from Gr. *blasphemein*, to speak ill, from Gr. *blapsis*, damage + *pheme*, speech. Its Eng. doublet is *blaspheme*, which came into

the language later and more directly, by way of religion.

blanch, blank, blanket.
See black.

blarney.
See ballyhoo.

blaspheme.
See blame.

blatherskite.
This Scottish word has become popular in the U. S., also as *bletherskate.* It is from ON. *blathr,* to talk nonsense, related to *blast* and *blow,* from AS. *blaeddre, bladder,* windbag, + *skite,* excrement. The first element, *blather, blether, blither,* has given us *blithering* idiot; the second has shortened into the slang cheap *skate.* (*Skate,* the fish, is from ON. *skata,* which also meant magpie—both from the long pointed tail. *Skate* on ice is, from earlier *scates,* from OFr. *escache,* stilts; Fr. *echasse,* wooden leg. Weekley says the first skates were shank-bones; whence Fr. *patin,* skate; *patte,* claw, whence Eng. *patten,* used for walking above mud.)

bleach, bleak.
See black.

bless.
This is a *bloody* word, directly from OE. *bledsian, blœdsian,* from AS. *blōd, blood;* it meant to consecrate with *blood,* in sacrifice to the gods. By a mistaken association with *bliss,* from AS. *bliths,* it was used when the English became Christians, to translate the L. *benedicere,* to speak well of, to praise; whence its present meanings. The Fr. word *blesser* still means to wound.

blimp.
This is a nonrigid or limp *dirigible* (short for *dirigible balloon;* the first balloons just drifted with the wind), smaller than the *Zeppelin* (named for *Graf von Zeppelin,* Count von Zeppelin, the designer, who died in 1917). There were two types of the small nonrigid balloon: the *A limp,* and the *B limp*: the *A limp* was unsuccessful; the *Blimp* survived.

First came the *balloon,* from It. *ballone,* augmentative of It. *balla, ball.* Then the *dirigible balloon* (L. *dirigere, direct*—, to *direct;* whence also Eng. *direction; cp. royal*); this might be either rigid or limp.

H. L. Mencken credits the word *blimp* to a man standing near the aircraft designer Horace Short, in 1914. They were trying to think of a name for the craft, when Short called for a *blunch* ("a drink half-way between *breakfast* and *lunch*") —whereupon the officer nearby said: "Call it a *blimp!*" Our word for a mid-morning meal is *brunch; cp. dismal.*

blind.
See sandblind.

blindfold, blind-man's-buff.
See buff.

bliss.
See bless.

blithering.
See blatherskite.

Blitzkrieg.
It used to be the thunderbolts of Zeus (or Jove, or of the Lord Jehovah) that wrought the damage; we know better now: if you hear the thunder, you are safe. Thus a swift descent from the sky is as a lightning flash; and the Germans called their swift attack, from earth and sky—bombers, paratroopers, etc.—a *Blitzkrieg,* lightning-war. When Santa Claus went through the sky on a jollier errand, his sleigh was drawn by reindeer, the first pair of which were named *Donner* and *Blitzen, Thunder* and *Lightning.*

bloat.
We think of a *bloated* person as puffed up, swollen, yet in the 17th c. it was remarked that "herrings shrink in *bloating.*" Two senses are closely intertwined. ME. *blote* is from ME. *blotne,* to soften by wetting. ME. *blout, blowt,* meant soft, flabby. But Hamlet looked upon "the *blowt* king"—and editors have spelled the word *bloat;* wherefrom all later users of the word (except for *bloated* herring, which is still steeped in brine: *marinated; cp. lapis lazuli*) have taken this turn, as swollen with self-indulgence.

bloody.
See bless; goodbye.

bloom.
See flower.

bloomers.
These baggy garments are always in the plural, like the more masculine *trousers.* They were made popular by Mrs. *Amelia Jenks Bloomer,* who was a strong supporter of Susan B. Anthony and the mid-19th c. American drive for women's rights. Her name is possibly connected with the *blossom* and *bloom* and *blowth* of a flower—all of which come from a common Teut. stem *blō,* to *blow.* From the beauty of flowers in *bloom,* the term came to be applied to the freshest, fairest moment of anything. (*Trousers* seems to come, by way of OE. *trouse,* from *trews,* from OFr. *trebus,* from LL. *tibraci,* which Isidore in the 7th c. said came from *tibia,* shin—we still call the shinbone the *tibia*—and *braccae, breeches.*)

blot, blotch.
Both of these words exist only in Eng., with no related forms outside. *Blot* was first used in the 14th c., it may have grown from *spot* (a rather common Teut. form, ON. *spotti,* speck, perhaps related to L. *spuere, sput*—, to spit; whence Eng. *sputum*). A number of Eng. words indicating force (or usually evil) begin with *bl;* e.g., blow, blast, blight (the origin of blight is also unknown), blemish. A *blotch,* which first appeared about the 17th c., may be related to patch or *botch* (ME. *bocchen,* to patch; the noun *botch,* at first unrelated, comes via OFr. *boce,* ulcer, from a common Romance root, It. *boccia,* Sp. *bocha,* LL. *bocia,* ball, whence Eng. *boss* took the sense of knob, as on a shield; Eng. *botch,* of pimple); it implies a more widespread stain or fault than *blot.*

blow.
See flower.

blue.
See red.

Bluebeard.
This story is not based on Henry VIII of England, though perhaps on Gilles de Retz, of Brittany, killed for his murder of six wives, in 1450. From the old tale, the name has been used generally; note that the secret room into which the wife must not look is in line with the notion of *taboo, q.v.*

bluestocking.
The famous French literary salons, decorated with women of beauty and wit, were copied in England, especially at Montagu House, London. There, about 1750, Benjamin Stillingfleet wore *blue* worsted *stockings* instead of the formal black silk. At once the persons attending these gatherings, especially the women with pretense to learning, were dubbed *bluestockings.* With the change in the status of women, the term has lapsed into history.

blunderbus.
This word is probably neither from *blunder,* in that it usually failed to hit the target, nor (as is more plausibly suggested) *thunder-box,* from G. *Donnerbuchse,* from *Donner,* thunder + *buchse,* box, gun. We may draw a cue from *arquebus,* or *harquebuss,* which is from MHG. *hakenbühse,* from *haken,* hook + *buschse,* so called because it was fixed on a hook when fired. (The spelling of *arquebus* is influenced by It. *archibuso,* from *arco,* bow + *buso,* hole, barrel.) *Blunderbus* is earlier *plantierbus,* from *L. plantare,* to fix: it was fixed on a rest before being discharged.

blurb.
This used to be called a *puff,* a gust of wind to help a book sail along; and sales were blown high by the gentle art of *puffery.* For these more vigorous days of gales for best sellers, Gelett Burgess, about 1914, invented the word *blurb.* He defined it as "a sound like a publisher;" perhaps it is echoic in origin.

blush.
See fourflusher.

boar.
See Adonis.

board.
This is a common Teut. word, meaning plank; hence, the side of a ship: AS. *bord;* from this source came LL. *bordura,* a margin, whence Eng. *border.* Hence *starboard* (*steer-board*) and *larboard* (left, ? from Swed. *ladda, load,* whence ? Eng. *lade*) refer to sides of the ship; as does *overboard.* To *board* a vessel first meant to come to her side—as was the method in sea-warfare: the two vessels came to one another's sides, hooked on the grappling-irons; then the soldiers leapt on *board! Cp. accost; cutlet.* A

boarder—a much later word—is one who gets his (bed and) *board* (table-*board;* hence, the food on it) at a place.

boarder.
See board.

bob.
This is a number of words. One meant a knob or cluster; hence, a short bunch or curl of hair, as on a *bob-tailed* horse, a *bob-wig,* or a *bob-haired* girl. Hence, anything short. Also, a blow and—perhaps as a result of the blow—a motion up and down. (The word is probably imitative in origin. A *bobbin* (Fr. *bobine,* origin unknown) was a kind of pin, then a cylinder, used in weaving; from it come *bobbin-lace* and *bobbinet. Bobby* pins for (*bobbed*) hair thus developed.

Bob is also by assimilation from *Rob,* short for *Robert; see bobby, Appendix II.*

A *bob-sled* is made of two short ones. The *bob-white and the bobolink* (sometimes *Bob o' Lincoln*) are named from their call.

bodice.
See bodkin.

bodkin.
This is another word with two backgrounds. In the sense in which Hamlet says a man could his own quietus make, with a mere *bodkin,* it is from Welsh *bidogyn,* diminutive of *biodog,* dagger. But it occurs in the phrase *Odds bodkins,* where it is euphemistic for *God's bodikins,* God's little body. In parts of England still, a thin person squeezed between two others (to make room at a table or in a cart) is called a *bodkin.* Body is a common Teut. word, AS. *bodig;* and *bodice* is just (a pair of) *bodies,* the word *body* being used in the 17 c. for the tight part of a dress, above the waistline.

body.
See bodkin.

bogus, bogy.
See insect.

bohemian.
See Appendix II.

boil.
See drink.

bolshevik.
This word referred to the party that took over power when the *Soviets* (*q.v.*) came into being. It is from Russ. *bolshinstvo,* majority, from *bolshe,* more. Opposed to the *bolsheviki* were the *mensheviki,* those in the minority.

bolster.
See poltroon.

bomb.
See bombardier.

bombardier.
This word, though reapplied to aviators, was used as early as 1560, of the man that fired the *bombard* or early cannon. It is derived from Eng. *bomb* (Fr. *bombe,* It. *bomba*), from L. *bombus,* from Gr. *bombos,* humming, in imitation of the sound it makes before going off. Both *bombilate* and *bombinate* (corrupted from L. *bombitare*) are Eng. sesquipedalian terms for to buzz. The same imitation gives us *bumblebee* and *bump; cp.* luncheon.

bombast.
When one is *bombastic,* one's discourse is "swollen full of wind"—what more recently was called "hot air," originally "stuffed with cotton padding." For *bombast* is from OFr. *bombace,* cotton padding, from L. *bombax,* from Gr. *bombyx,* silkworm. Similarly *fustian,* a common word (as the thing itself was common) in good Queen Bess's glorious days, originally referred to a coarse cloth of cotton and flax, from OFr. *fustaigne,* from LL. *fustaneus* (cloth) from *Fostat,* Cairo, where the cloth was made. *Farce* (LL. *farcire,* to stuff foods) drew its meaning not from inflated speeches, but from the interlude stuffed in between the acts of a serious drama.

Thus also *burlesque* is via the It. adjective *burlesco* from L. *burla,* mockery, from L. *burra,* puff of wool, used figuratively to mean nonsense.

bombilate, bombinate.
See bombardier.

bonanza.
This word (Sp *bonanza,* fair weather, from L. *bonus,* good) was applied to a pleasant calm after a difficult search—such as the finding of a gold mine, in the U. S. west—from the *Bible, Matthew* viii, which tells of the calm after

Christ rebukes the wind and sea; in Sp. *"una grande bonanza."* And down on the Stock Exchange, a good thing as a gift brought back the L. word *bonus.*

bonbon.
See bun.

bond, bondage.
See neighbor.

bonfire.
This jolly burning with which a holiday may be celebrated (as on Election Day, before Fire Department regulations intervened), or at which chops or frankfurters are roasted on picnickings, was originally a much more sombre affair. The word is a softening of *bone-fire;* it referred to the great pyres of bones of victims of the plagues that formerly swept over Europe, or of persons burned at the stake. In some country places, animal bones are still used for burning. Some claim, however, that the word is just what it seems: *bonfire,* from Fr. *bon,* good (cheer). There is also suggested as a source Dan. *baum,* beacon; Welsh *ban,* high. In any event, the word replaced an earlier AS. *bael fire,* from *bael,* burning, from Icel. *bal,* flame; whence Eng. *bale,* harm.

bonus.
See bonanza.

book.
See bible. The relation to *beech*-tree, however, is challenged by the fact that the earliest recorded uses are of *boks,* writing tablets.

boom.
See beam.

boondoggle
This seems first to have been a noun, an early word for gadget. When the New York Board of Estimate was investigating the use of relief money, 1935, Robert C. Marshal said the artists' project was making "leather crafts, three-ply carving, and *boondoggles."* It has been suggested that the word is related to Daniel *Boone's* whittling sticks to throw for his pet *dog;* however fanciful this may be, it is certain that to *boondoggle* means to be as busy as a puppy—doing nothing; and that the relief was a great *boon.* (In the 18th c., *tc boon* meant to repair public roads; and a *dogger* was a man that went fishing.)

boor.
See neighbor.

boot.
In the remark "He's a rascal, and a good one to *boot"* the last word is of uncertain origin; but *cp. butt.* If we put a comma after "one," however, the last word is from AS. *bōt,* profit, amends, related to Eng. *better* (the early positive, replaced by good). It can be traced to an early Aryan form, *bhud,* good.

There was an old Eng. game (Samuel Pepys learned it on Sept. 19, 1660), in which the players exchanged articles, with an umpire to tell how much each should get, to *boot.* The extra amount was contributed by all in advance, and kept in a cap, into which the umpire's hand was constantly dipping: the game was called *hand in cap.* From it comes our *handicap,* which from the allowance has also been applied to the weakness. From AS. *bōt,* advantage, whence *boot,* comes our *bootless* errands; *cp. sleeveless; bottle.* Related is the pirate's profit, his *booty.* The children's shoe, or *bootie,* is from the first word; there was an earlier *bottekin.* The Fr. *botte,* and the early Eng. forms *bute* and *botte,* from LL. *botta,* suggest that the footwear may be related to *butt.*

(Pronunciation of *booty* suggests that, though a pirate may confuse *booty* and *beauty,* not even the most insensitive soldier would mistake a *cutie* for a *cootie*—mispronunciation of *duty, New York,* and other such words is the result not of inability but of laziness or carelessness. The sound of the city may be influenced by the Yiddish *Nu?* —pronounced *noo*—meaning "What of it?" or "What next?" The former query indicates the state of mind that produces the mispronunciation.)

bootlegger.
Long before Prohibition became a national mockery, the *bootlegger* (in the mid 19th c.) plied his trade in Kentucky and other states. To escape the eye of the government agents, walking speak-easies of those early days used to carry the bottles of (corn) liquor between their legs and their knee-high boots; hence, *bootlegger.* In the days before the courts permitted the

sale of James Joyce's *Ulysses,* the purveyor of forbidden books came, by analogy, to be called a *booklegger.*

bootlicker.
See sycophant.

booty.
See boot.

borax, boron.
See element.

border.
See board.

bore.
See Adonis.

borealis.
See aurora.

born, borne.
See berth.

borough.
See dollar.

bosh.
There are three words here. One may come from G. *boschen,* to slope; it refers to the lowest, narrowing part of a blast-furnace. Then there is the use, perhaps from Fr. *ébauche,* rough sketch, used of a swaggering attitude, *to cut a bosh.* Finally there is the Pers. *bosh,* empty—hence as an exclamation, Eng. *bosh!,* worthless. This was spread through the popularity of the novel *Ayesha* (1834), by J. J. Morier (whose best-known book is *Hajji Baba,* 1824). Some persons think that most etymology is *fiddle-de-dee, q.v.*

bosky.
See strategy.

Bosphorus.
Macaulay protested against this spelling of the *Bosporus,* or *ox-ford* (Gr. *poros, ford;* cognate with L. *portus, port,* and Eng. *firth, forth, ford;* Norw. *fiord;* Gr. *bous, ox,* whence Eng. *bovine*)—the place where Jupiter as the divine bull swam away with *Europa;* whence *Europe, q.v.* The English *Oxford,* earlier *Oxenford,* is an easier crossing—though probably not from *ox* at all, being corrupted to the more familiar form from a still earlier *Ousenford,* from Celtic *uisge,* water + ford; *cp. drink*: whiskey. *Cp.* also *dollar* and *port.*

boss.
See blot. This word had several meanings, of different origins; the *boss* of a job is from Du. *baas,* master, earlier uncle (OHG. *basa,* aunt).

botany.
See plant.

botch.
See blot.

bottle.
This is glass today, but was once of the same material as your *boot, q.v.,* from L. *bota,* skin (thick hide). Via Fr. and It. *botte,* from LL. *butis, buttis,* comes Eng. *butt, q.v.,* in the sense of cask. A *buttery* is a place where *butts* are stored, not *butter, q.v.* The diminutive of *buttis,* LL. *butticula,* whence It. *bottiglia* and Fr. *bouteille,* led to Eng. *bottle,* first applied to wine-skins. There is no relation to the gallant practice of drinking from a lady's slipper.

There are three other paths by which *bottle* came into the language. Probably related to *butt,* as a bump or a lump, was OFr. *botte,* bundle; from its diminutive, *botel,* comes Eng. *bottle,* meaning bundle. In the 16th c. a foolish search was described as looking for a needle in a *bottle* of hay—the earlier form of hunting in a haystack. The *bottle,* a flower (also *bluebottle,* etc.) takes its name partly from its shape, and partly from an OE. *bothel,* whence also Eng. *buddle,* a marigold. Finally, a *bottle* used to the 13th c. but now surviving only in place-names, as *Harbottle,* comes from OE. *botl* from AS. *bodl,* from an old Teut. root *bu—, bo—,* to dwell. Up to the 14th c., *bold* meant a dwelling. This old *bo*—is not related to *abode,* which gets its meaning of dwelling from the sense of resting-place, from the verb *abide,* OE. *abidan,* to remain on, from *bide,* a common Teut. word, OE. *bidan,* to wait. There is also an obsolete *abode,* extended from *bode,* another common Teut. word (OE. *bod;* OHG. *gabot*) that first meant to command, to tell someone to do something. This lost its force, came to mean just to tell, hence to announce, to warn. It survives in *foreboding*—which many a woman has when her man takes to the *bottle.*

boudoir.
This was originally the room to which

milady might retire when offended her sulking or pouting room (Fr. *bouder,* to pout). It is, indeed, related to *pout* (OE. ? *putian;* Sw. *puta,* to be inflated), with the notion of swelling. Hence comes *pudding* (Fr. *boudin,* black-*pudding,* intestine), which meant *bowels,* then the entrails stuffed, a kind of sausage; the present sense is a shortening of *pudding*-pie. (The Eng. *p* is a shift from Rom. *b,* as in *purse,* from *bursa; see budget.* The word may be traced to L. *botulus,* sausage, the diminutive of which, *botellus,* pudding, whence OFr. *boel, bouel,* gives us *bowel.* A roundabout journey!)

bough.
See bow.

bounce.
This word, first pronounced *boons,* was used where the early G. used *bums,* Eng. *boom;* to represent the sound of a heavy object. Thus it meant the sound, or the blow, of an explosion; hence, the *bounding* away. (Similarly the verb *bound* until the 15th c. meant only to resound; then to recoil, then to leap. It is probably from L. *bombiare,* to hum, from L. *bombus,* a humming; *cp. bombardier.*) This effect of the sudden jump after a loud crash was carried into other meanings; hence to *bounce* (or *bound*) like a ball, to *bounce* it (as some women dance); to *bounce* a man (discharge him without warning or ceremony); and the sense of a *bouncing* fellow, meaning big, bragging, or other large implications (note that various words for striking have this figurative use: a *strapping* fellow; *spanking, thumping,* a *whopper,* a *bounder,* and the like, all imitative in origin, *whop* being a stronger form of the imitative *whip*). *Boundary,* the limits we set when we *bound* property, the *bourn:* That "undiscovered country from whose *bourne* no traveler returns," as Hamlet soliloquizes—these are traced through OFr. *bodne, bonne, bunde,* from LL. *bodna*—and there lost, though probably borrowed by the Romans from the Celts. The Eng. *bourne* is by a path that also brings Fr. *borne,* limit, perhaps related to bord, border, common Teut.

bound, boundary, bounder.
See bounce.

bourgeois.
This word first meant a citizen, in the exact sense of the inhabitant of a city: a freeman of a *burg* (Fr. *bourgeois,* from OFr. *burgeis,* whence also Eng. *burgess; see dollar*) as distinguished from a gentleman and likewise from a peasant. Hence, one of the middle class; hence one with the characteristics associated therewith. Note that these may be complimentary, as in the early associations of *urbane* (*see neighbor*) or the reverse, as the point of view alters.

bovine.
See Bosphorus.

bow.
Many of the simplest-seeming words have the hardest history to disentangle. *Bow* in all its senses was early, and common Teut. The first sense, from OE. *boga,* Da. *boug,* was anything bent; this was first applied to archways, and of course to the early weapon. From this, somewhat later, came the polite *bow* of greeting and departure; in this, the pronounciation has changed. But from one of the related forms came Eng. *bough;* the first sense of this word was the human shoulder (the curve or bend from the neck to the elbow); in this sense also the word was spelled *bow.* When the word shoulder (AS. *sculdor*) replaced this, *bough* was kept in its (at first figurative) application to the curve of a tree from the trunk; and *bow,* as the curve at the front of a ship. *Cp. branch.*

bowdlerize.
The *Rev. Thomas Bowdler* published *The Family Shakespeare* in 1818, expunging from it, as he observed, "Whatever is unfit to be read by a gentleman in a company of ladies." From his volume, popular but attacked by scholars, his name has become the verb for prudish expurgation.

bowel.
See pylorus, boudoir.

bower, Bowery.
See neighbor.

bowie.
See Appendix II.

bowl, bowling.
The early Eng. word, *boll,* OE. *bolla,* bud, small sphere, was common Teut. Cotton *bolls* are attacked by a *boll*-worm or *boll*-weevil. It is from the root *bul,* to swell (as in *bulbous* and *bulb,* though these hark back to Gr. *bolbos,* onion);

note also OHG. *bolon,* to roll. This word is retained in some of its senses; but in the sense of a spherical vessel it has been influenced in spelling by the course of Fr. *boule,* ball, which has become Eng. *bowl,* used in *bowling; cp. ball:* see *ninepins.* The game is in the plural, *bowls;* but the soup is in the *bowl.*

box.

This is another simple word with a complicated history. It seems to begin in Greece, where the *box* tree was called Gr. *pyxos,* in L. *buxus.* The church *pyx* is directly from this *pyxos;* the *box* was at first a small one, used for drugs or for valuables, named from the wood of which it was made. It has since been extended to any receptacle.

The sport of *boxing* may have arisen from a *box* on the ear, from the way in which the hand cups itself in striking; though it is also surmised that this *box* is imitative of the energy and sound. Note also that our *boxing* "ring" is shaped more like a *box.*

boy.

See alas. There were early names, such as AS. *Bofa,* OHG. *Buobo,* whence G. *Bube,* Eng. *booby, baby,? see abbot.*

boycott.

It is not so often owners that make trouble, as their agents. This was true of the tax-collectors before the French Revolution. It was true of *Captain Boycott,* agent for an Irish landlord, who asked such unreasonable rentals that in 1880 the Irish Land League, formed to handle such persons, subjected him to the treatment that has taken his name. In England, they spoke of *sending a person to Coventry* —for the soldiers were quite lonely there, with no intercourse permitted between the garrison and the townsfolk. (All eyes—save those of Peeping Tom, the tailor—were closed in Coventry, when, to make her husband, the cruel Earl Leofric of Mercia, cancel a heavy tax, Lady Godiva rode through the town, "clothed only with chastity." *Cp. taboo.*) It is, however, pointed out that *covent,* as in *Covent Garden,* the famous theatre, means *convent;* and suggested that, as folk say "go to Bedfordshire" when they mean retire for the night, *"send to Coventry"* may have been a folk term for relegating to seclusion.

brace, bracelet, bracer, brachial, brachiate, brachy-.

See brassiere.

braggadochio.

The first meaning of *brag* was the braying of a trumpet. *Braggart* is, from Fr. *bragard,* from *braguer,* to boast, but the simple form *brag* is earlier in Eng. than in Fr.; it was probably imitative in origin. By combining this with an It. ending, Spenser created a character in *The Faerie Queene* (II,iii) and a word in the language: *braggadochio, braggadocio.* The type is very frequent in literature, from the *miles gloriosus* (boastful soldier) of Roman comedy to characters in plays (Kelly, *The Show-Off,* 1924) and comic strips today.

But all things are not what they seem. This boastful figure, in Gr. drama, was called the *alazon;* he was usually outwitted by the underdog, a small and frail but sly and resourceful fellow, called the *eiron,* whose tricks were called Gr. *eironeia;* whence Eng. *irony.* The apparent innocence with which Socrates led his audience into traps has named his method of argument *Socratic irony.*

braille.

See Appendix II.

bran.

See barnard.

branch.

Just as *bough* originally meant shoulder (*see bow*), so *branch* first meant paw—from Fr. *branche* from LL. *branca,* paw. Thus, as the *bough* curves out of the *trunk* (body), so the *branch* comes out of the *bough* (limb). And out of the *branch* come the *twigs;* note that I use this in the plural, for it was AS. *twig,* related to *two* and *twice*: forking from the branch. The *trunk* of a tree draws its name from the fact that it was cut for use in building (L. *truncus,* from *truncare, truncat—,* to cut down; *cp. poltroon*); by extension, this was applied to the *trunk* of the body. The *trunk* for traveling was first hollowed from a tree-*trunk.* Athletic *trunks* are figurative, as though hollowed out and the legs stuck in; *cp. palliate*: *stocking.* And the elephant's *trunk,* that carries for him, is a folk-change from earlier *trump,* an imitative word, the object replacing the sound . . . We must not *branch* out too far!

brandy.
See drink.

brass.
See brassiere.

brassiere.
In the 18th c., a term popular for a drink to stiffen one up (the drink was popular much earlier) was a *bracer;* this is really asking someone to lend an arm. The word *brace* (with the diminutive *bracelet,* armlet) is, from OFr. *brace, brase* (Fr. *bras*), *brache,* from L. *brachia,* plural of *brachium,* arm. (From this plural, or dual, there being two arms, a *brace* came to refer to two of a kind.) To *embrace* is to take into one's arms. *Brassard* was armor for the upper arm. Scientific terms include, more directly from the L., *brachial,* of the arm; and *brachiate,* having arms. The word is related to Gr. *brachys,* short, used in many compounds, as *brachycephalic* (Gr. *kephale,* head); around 1600, *brachygraphy* was used for "shorthand."

Thus a *brassiere* (originally plural, Fr. *brassieres*) was first a support: the shirt worn to support a baby's body; it still is a support, as an arm around, but not for babies.

Brassiere is thus connected neither with *brass* nor with *breast. Breast* is common Teut., AS. *breost,* but not found elsewhere. The Fr. word is *sein,* from L. *sinus,* bend, curve; this gives us in Eng. *sinuous* (*sinus* + *-osus,* full of); also nasal *sinus* and mathematical *sine.* The L. and Gr. word for breast is *mamma,* a word from baby talk (like *mamma,* mother, in variations in many tongues); the adjective L. *mammalis,* pertaining to breasts, gives us the wide range of *mammals. Brass* is from OE. *braes,* not found elsewhere and its origin unknown; although AS. *brazian* means to harden metal; whence Eng. *brazen.* From the figurative *brazen-faced* comes the use of *brass* as impudence; suggested in Shakespeare's "Can any face of *brass* hold longer out?" (*Love's Labor's Lost,* V,ii,395), this sense was popularized by Defoe's verse satire *The True-Born Englishman,* 1701, of which 80,000 copies were sold on the streets, and which begins:

Whenever God erects a house of prayer
The devil always builds a chapel there;
And 'twill be found upon examination,
The latter has the larger congregation.

and which speaks of "a needful competence of English *brass.*" The use of *brass* for money is a sense it shares with several metals, from gold to tin.

brat.
See graft.

brawl.
This word for a noisy quarrel may have come from Fr. *brailler,* to shout around, frequentative of Fr. *braire,* to *bray;* Eng. *bray* is from this Fr. word. But the early Eng. sense seems not to have had the noise attached. Shakespeare uses *brawl* to mean contend; to *brawl* in church meant to do any talking outside of that required. Perhaps, therefore, *brawl* is a native Eng. word. To *bawl* is thus native, imitating the sound; it has parallels in other tongues: G. *bellen,* LL. *baulare,* to bark; Icel. *baula,* to low. A *brawl* is also low, though the noise be high.

brazen.
See brassiere.

breach.
See dollar. ME. *breche* is directly related to OE. *brecan, break,* common Teut.—but influenced by Fr. *breche.*
See ache.

bread.
The "staff of life" began as a "broken stick"—to show friendly intentions. The word is common Teut., OE. *bread,* OHG. *brot,* in the sense of piece, bit; then—from the most frequent practice with guests—it was applied to broken *bread.* Before this the word for *bread* was *hlaf,* whence Eng. *loaf; cp. lady.* For a time *loaf* and *bread* were used interchangeably; then *bread,* the word of friendship, came to be used for the food itself, and *loaf* grew limited to the whole thing as it comes from the oven.

break.
See ache, discuss; *cp.* abridge, breach.

breakfast.
See jejune.

breast.
See brassiere; but *cp.* nausea.

breath.
See inspiration.

breech, breeches.
This word, like the garment itself on a fat man, was most widespread. As OE. *brec, broec,* Celtic *bracca,* L. *braca, bracca,* it is linked with the Aryan root *bhrag—,* all meaning a covering for the loin and thighs, a loincloth. This developed until the garment came to the knees; whence *breeches* (in the plural, sometimes as *knee-breeches*) is applied to the knee-length article (*cp. knickers*) as opposed to the long *trousers.* (*Trousers* themselves are from that same L. *bracca,* plural *braccae; see bloomers.*) To say that a woman wears the *breeches* is of course to indicate that she is the boss of the family; the *breeches parts* in the theatre are those in which a woman wears man's clothes. About the 16th c., the *breech* came to be used for the part of the body encased in the garment; hence the *breech* is the "hinder part" of a gun; the early guns were *muzzle-*loading, the more recent ones, *breech-*loading. *Muzzle* is from OFr. *musel,* diminutive of OFr. *muse,* snout, possibly from L. *morsus,* bite—another diminutive of which gives us Eng. *morsel; cp. remorse.*
See bloomers; *cp.* leprechaun.

brekecoax.
See coagulate.

breviary.
See bull.

briar.
Smokers may be interested to note that their *briar* pipes have no connection with the thorny bush, the *briar* (OE. *braer*), but are drawn from the *heather* plant (OE. *bruyer,* from Fr. *bruyere,* from LL. *brugaria;* probably a Celtic word) from the roots of which the pipes are made. Hence comes *heathen; cp. pagan.*

bribe.
This gift-offering for favor was once for charity. The word is from OFr. *bribe,* crumb, piece, esp. a piece given to a beggar (OFr. *briber, brimber,* to beg). From beggar to thief to extortioner the meaning grew; from a gift begged to a gift demanded in exchange for a favor, or in order to keep one from harm.

bridal.
The *bride* (AS. *bryd;* note that in G. *Braut* is bride, and *brauen* is to brew) was first the betrothed, pledged but not yet married. The promise was sealed with a cup, the AS. *brydealu, bride ale,* whence Eng. *bridal. Bridegroom* is a folk substitution for *bridegome,* from AS. *brydguma,* from *bryd* + *guma,* man; cognate with Gr. *gametes,* husband, from *gamos,* marriage; and L. *homo,* man.

brie.
See Appendix II.

brief.
See bull.

Bright's disease.
See Appendix II.

brilliant.
This adjective, shining, is applied as a noun, a *brilliant,* to a diamond (*q.v.*) of the finest quality. Originally it was quite another stone; the word is from *beryl* (via Fr. *brilliant,* shining, from *briller,* to shine, from L. form *berillare,* from *berillus, beryllus, beryl*). This is from Gr. *beryllos,* from the lost oriental name.

bristle.
See bazooka.

Britain, British.
See Hibernia.

broach.
See broker.

brocade.
See cloth.

broccoli.
see broker.

brochure.
See pamphlet.

brogan, brogue.
See leprechaun.

broil.
See island.

broker.
After a deal, men were wont to *broach* a cask of wine. But the man that pricked it open was the first *broker* (ME. *brocour,* from L. *broccare,* to tap a cask). *Broach,* more com-

monly a verb, and *brooch,* the ornament stuck on with a pin, are variants of the same word. From wine merchant, the term was broadened to any retail dealer, such as the pawn*broker;* or to any middleman in a transaction.

The idea of piercing comes from L. *brocca,* spike; from the verb comes Fr. *brocher,* to stitch, *cp. pamphlet.* The diminutive of L. *brocca* is *broccola,* stalk, whence (It. plural) the vegetable *broccoli.*

bromide.

There is a Gr. *bromos,* oats, which gives us Eng. *brome,* a kind of grass. From this also, the learned word *bromatology,* the study of food. But there is also Gr. *bromos,* stink; whence *bromine* (from its foul and noxious smell) and its varieties, *bromide* and the *bromo—* compounds. *Bromo-seltzer* being used as a sedative, the magazine *Smart Set,* in April, 1906, suggested the word *bromide* for persons and expressions that tend to put one to sleep.

bromine.
See element.

bronco.

The cowboys in the U.S. southwest borrowed many Spanish terms from the Mexicans. Thus an untamed horse was a *bronco,* from Sp. *bronco,* rough; its tamer, a *bronco-buster.* This *bust* is slang for *burst,* itself slang (here) for break: to break the spirit of. Thus *to go on a bust* is to break loose (from moral restraint). A woman's *bust* was originally the entire torso; the origin of the word is unknown, but there is a Prov. *bust,* meaning the trunk of a tree. A *mustang* was at first a strayed horse, from Sp. *mestengo,* from (strayed from) Sp. *mesta,* the graziers' association

Bronx cheer.
See Dutch.

bronze.

Although *bronze* is confidently linked by some with *Brundisium* (via. It. *bronzo*), it has other associations. The word was first applied to ancient works of art, and may have had reference to the source (i.e. *Brundisium*) or to the color; later, it came to signify the material. As a color, it is linked with It. *bruno, brown,* of a common family, Aryan root *bhru; cp. beaver. Brown* is thus also common Teut. Via Fr. *brunir, bruniss—,* comes Eng. *burnish.*
See Appendix II.

brooch.
See broker.

broom.
See scrub.

brougham.
See Appendix II.

brow, browbeat.
See effrontery.

brown.
See bronco, beaver.

Brownian movement.
See Appendix II.

browse.

This word has come to be used interchangeably with graze, *q.v.;* it first meant that on which cattle fed when grass was scarce, from Fr. *broust, brout,* bud: they had to *nibble* the young shoots of the early spring trees. The early form *braugh* suggests a relation with *bragh, break; cp. discuss:* they had to *break* the twig-tips. A *browser* was a man that fed the royal deer in the wintertime. The sense shifted from the object to the action.

To *browse* in a library or a book keeps the sense of *nibbling* here and there. The word *nibble* is a frequentative of *nib, nip,* a small bite; whence also *nipple; see knick-knack.*

brummagem.

This is via *Bromwicham* and *Brimidgeham,* for *Birmingham,* England, long a center for the manufacture of cheap jewelry.

brunch.
See dismal.

brush.
See scrub.

bubble.
See bull.

buccal.

The *buccal* orifice is a fancy way of referring to the hole between your cheeks (L. *bucca,* cheek), where food goes in and words come out. The *buccinator* is the muscle in the cheek wall. In the days of chivalry, when the herald puffed his cheeks and blew the trumpet loud and long, from L. *abuccinare, abuccinat—,* to proclaim, from *a, ab,* from + *buccina,* trumpet, from *bucca,* cheek, there was an Eng. word *abuccinate,* to proclaim.

The strap of a helmet was usually fastened along the cheek; hence the fastening was called L. *buccula* (diminutive of *bucca*); this via Fr. *boucle* gave us Eng. *buckle,* which is now more often on a belt around the waist.

buccaneer, buccanier.
The French settlers in Haiti borrowed from the natives the habit of smoking meat over a *boucan* (Fr. form of the Caribbean word) or gridiron— whereon, said Cotgrave (1660): "the *canibals* broile pieces of men, and other flesh." From the typical occupation of these early settlers came the present meaning of the word. *Cp. cannibal.*

buck.
In the sense of animal, esp. male goat, this is a common Teut. word: Du. *bok,* Ger. *bock* (whence *bockbeer, buckbeer;* although *buckwheat* is from AS. *boc, beech; see* bible). From the verb *buck,* to behave like a goat, *i.e.,* to jump vertically, comes the idea expressed in *"Buck up!"* From AS. *buc,* trunk, comes *buck* meaning the body of a wagon, retained in *buckboard.* From AS. *buc,* (wooden ?) jug, comes the meaning, to wash clothes (MHG. *buchen;* Fr. *buer;* It. *bucare*). From Du. *zaag-boc* comes the meaning, a wooden frame for sawing, a *saw-buck* (horse is used in the same manner); whence, of course, comes *buck-saw.* (Similarly, *crane* the machine, from *crane* the bird; the artist's *easel*—in the 17th c., when the Dutch masters worked—from Du. *ezel,* donkey. We also have a *donkey-engine;* and a *monkey-wrench* is but one of the instruments named *monkeywise.*)

A killer of goats (Fr. *boucher,* from *bouc*) is a *butcher;* hence, a dealer in meats. Franz Werfel's play *Bockgesang, Goat Song* (1921), reminds us that *tragedy* is from Gr. *tragos,* from *aix, aig,* goat + *ode,* song; possibly from the origin of drama in the sacrifice of the scapegoat. The Latin for goat is *caper, capr—; cp. taxi; Capri.* The meaning of *aegis* is from the goat-skin shield of Zeus.

buckle.
This was originally on your cheek; *see* buccal.

buckram.
See cloth.

bud.
See puny. The *bud* from which come flower and fruit is traced no farther than to ME. *bodde;* but *see* butt.

budge.
See budget.

budget.
This word, like the matters concerned in it, has journeyed back and forth among the languages. OFr. *bougette,* wallet, is a diminutive of OFr. *bouge,* from L. *bulga,* leather bag. But the Romans borrowed the word from the Celts (who perhaps tanned the leather); it exists in OIr. as *bolg, bag.* When you make out your *budget,* you are organizing the contents of your *purse.* Indeed, *budge* was a 17th c. word for leather *bag;* but the verb *budge,* to stir, is from Fr. *bouger,* from L. *bullicare,* frequentative of *bullire,* to boil. But *purse* is closely associated with the first words; from AS. *purs;* LL. *bursa* (whence also *bursar* and Fr. *Bourse*), from Gr. *byrsa,* leather hide. Applied to a small bag closed by pulling a thong, it gives us the verb *purse* (the lips). *Cp. Bursa.*

buff.
This is from the color of the *buffalo,* from Fr. *buffle,* from Port. *bufalo,* from Gr. *boubalos,* from *bous,* ox. It meant first the animal, then the hide, then the color. *Buffing,* polishing metals, was first done with this hide.

The game of *blind-man's-buff,* earlier *blindman buff,* is from *buffet,* a blow, from OFr. *buffet,* diminutive of *buffe,* imitative of a dull blow; G. *puffen,* to jostle. Fr. *pouf* (Eng. *puff*) and *bouf* are used to imitate the sound produced by puffing the cheeks. Hence Eng. *buffet,* a blow, and a *buffer* that takes the blow; also *rebuff.* In these it is the sound that gave the sense; in Fr. and Eng. *buffet,* a sideboard, the idea of swelling out persists. Near the door of medieval castles and monasteries was a table laden with food, where the pilgrim might claim hospitality—and stuff himself; the stuffing-place, whence *buffet.* This derivation, however, is questioned. Another theory reminds us that the first *buffets* were chests on top of tables, which thus seemed puffed out. "Puffed out" with pride, according to a third theory, which says that the first *buffet* was a show-table, and the name originally slang.

To *blindfold* was first not to fold a cloth over the eyes but, from *blind-feld*, from *blind* + ME. *fellen*, to strike down, whence Eng. *fell;* the change to *fold* came by association. In the 16th c. Carlyle speaks of "government by *blind-man's buff.*" *See* bugle; *cp. fell.*

buffalo.
See bugle.

buffer, buffet.
See buff.

bug, bugaboo, bugbear.
See insect.

bugle.
Originally a *buffalo* (OFr. *bugle,* from L. *buculus,* diminutive of *bos, bovis,* ox—from which the Eng. *bovine,* oxlike, hence sluggish and enduring); the present meaning is just a shortening of *bugle-horn,* through which men blew. *Buffalo* is via Port. *bufalo,* from LL., from Gr. *boubalos,* from *bous,* ox, whence L. *bos;* the same animal was Fr. *buffle,* whence Eng. *buff,* which shifted from the animal to the hide to the color. (*Horn* is a common Teut. word, cognate with L. *cornu,* which gives us many scientific terms—*e.g. cornicle, cornify, cornute*—and the more familiar *horn* of plenty, the *cornucopia*: L. *copiae,* resources.) Note that the *slughorn* arose through an error of Chatterton's (1770): the battle-cry of the Gaels was the *sluagh-ghairm* (from *sluagh,* army + *gairm,* shout); although no horn is involved, this grew into our Eng. *slogan,* with which many a manufacturer blows his own horn. Browning copied the error from Chatterton, with it ending *Childe Roland to the Dark Tower Came.* Thus do words grow. *Cp. catchword.*

bulb, bulbous.
See bowl.

bulk.
The first sense of this word is retained in the nautical phrase, to break *bulk,* to unload: ON. *bulki,* cargo. By association with AS. *buc,* belly, it came to mean the trunk of the body. The two senses fused to its present meaning.

A *bulkhead* is not first a cargo-wall; the first part is from ME. *balk,* AS. *balca,* beam, ridge. To *balk* someone is to put a beam in his way; hence, to thwart.

bull.
This is another word that has acquired a host of meanings on its journey along the years. There seem to be two basic sources. (1) OE. *bole, bulle,* whence also Eng. *bullock,* the animal the *bull.* The *bull*-dog is named either from early use in *bull*-baiting, or from the shape of its head. From the potency of the animal came its use in the general sense of male; hence also, from the idea of strength in general, apparently, the stock market use of a purchase in expectation of a rise, then of the *bulls* that seek to increase market prices. (2) L. *bulla,* a bubble or other spherical object. This exists directly, as Eng. *bulla,* in physiology and medicine. As the papal *bull,* it referred first to the seal attached, then to the formal papal edict. [Less formal and full is the papal *brief* (from L. *brevis, breve,* short; whence also the Eng. adjective *brief*), extended to include legal *briefs* and other such documents.] The word *bull,* jest, nonsense,—for a time associated with Irish, and vulgarly linked as though from the animal—is also of quite early use; probably as a variation, via OFr. *bole, boule,* fraud, of L. *bulla,* bubble—prone, as many an investor has discovered too late, to burst into nothing. The *bubble* itself, earlier *burble,* like *gurgle, giggle, q.v.,* is imitative (of liquid *bubbling* up).

A *breviary* (L. *breviarium,* from *brevis*) was a summary or epitome; now it is used of the prayers of the Divine Office, the eight hours that sum up the day of the Catholic Church. These are: (1) *matins,* from L. *matutinus* (*matutinae vigiliae,* early watches). (2) *lauds,* from L. *laus, laud—,* praise; whence also *laudatory; cp. laudanum.* (3) *prime, q.v.,* from *prima hora,* first hour; sunrise, or six o'clock a.m. (4) *terce* or *tierce,* Fr. feminine of *tiers,* third, from L. *tertia hora*: the third hour of the canonical day, ending at 9 a.m. (5) *sext,* from L. *sexta hora,* sixth hour: 12 m. (6) *none* (the hour) or *nones* (the office), from L. *nonus,* ninth: 3 p.m. From saying the prayers at the beginning instead of the end of the three hour period, our *noon* came to be at 12 m.; *see luncheon.* (7) *vespers,* from L. *vesperus,* evening star, from Gr.

hesperos; cp. argosy. (8) *compline*, earlier *complin*, via OFr. from L. *completa hora*: the hour that *completes* (*cp. foil*) the services of the day.

bullet.
See ballot.

bullock.
See bull.

bumblebee, bump.
See bombardier.

bun.
The delicious *scone* comes from Du. *schoonbrot*, fine bread (G. *schön*, fine). Similarly *bun* seems to come from Fr. *bon*, good (a *bonbon* is a goody). It is probably not, as has been suggested, from OFr. *bugne*, a swelling; this word gives us *bunion*.

bunch.
See luncheon.

Bund.
See neighbor.

bunion.
See bun.

bunsen (burner).
See Appendix II.

bureaucracy.
See democracy.

burg.
See dollar.

burgess.
See bourgeois.

burglar.
Just as there is a town mouse distinct from the country mouse, so the town thief and the country thief are kept apart. The *highwayman* still tells us his habitat in his name; but the *burglar* is a city-practitioner. The common Teut. word for manorhouse is AS. *burg*, related to AS. *beorgan*, to protect. This gives us *borough, burg* (in slang, or as a frequent suffix in names); borrowed in LL. it entered the Romance tongues. But thievery was there too: LL. *burgaria, burglary*:—the L. word *latro*, thief, dropped out, but gave *l* to the *burglar*. It is also underneath the more technical term *larceny*, from Fr. *larcin*, from L. *latrocinium*, thievery, from *latro*, thief. But *cp. dollar.*

burgomaster.
See dollar.

burlesque.
See bombast.

burnish.
See bronze.

Bursa.
This is the Greek name for Carthage, from *byrsa*, hide. Legend tells us that Dido, arriving from Tyre, was granted by the natives all the land an ox-hide would cover, whereupon she cut it into thongs, and encircled the site of the city. *Thong Castle*, Kent, England, draws its name from a similar legend regarding Hengist. LL. *bursa*, hide, wallet, gives us Fr. *Bourse* (Rialto, Wall Street); Eng. *purse; reimburse*, to put back into the *purse* (L. *re*, back, again + *im*, from *in*, in). *Pursy*, fat, baggy, does not mean 'like a well-filled *purse*', but is from OFr. *pourcif*, from *poulsif*, from L. *pulsare, pulsat—*, to beat, and first meant 'out of breath'. *Cp. pelt.*

burst.
See nausea.

bush.
See strategy.

bust.
See bronco.

but.
See butt.

butcher.
See buck.

butt.
The protest *"But* me no *buts!"* is not from Shakespeare. H. L. Mencken's *New Dictionary of Quotations on Historical Principles* lists it as from Henry Fielding's *Rape Upon Rape*, II, ii, in 1730; but the same expression occurs in Mrs. Susannah Centlivre's *The Busybody* in 1708, and was probably current before. The *New English* (*Oxford*) *Dictionary* gives nine columns to *but; but* let that pass (Shakespeare, *Merry Wives of Windsor*, I, iv, 14). Over six columns are given to the uses of *butt*. Most of these seem related to the basic sense of a stump or lump or thick knob or end. Thus there is the *butt*, a flat fish, as also in the compounds *halibut* (*cp. holy*) and *turbot* (?, from L.

turbo, top: flat-top; or ?? from L. *turbo, turbin—,* something that spins, a whirlwind; whence Eng. *turbine; cp. trouble*—from the fact that the eye seems to turn from the side to the top of the fish). The wine cask *butt* is from L. *butta,* cask; It. *botte.* The *butt* of a gun is the thick end. *Butt* as a boundary mark or goal is confused between Fr. *bout,* end, and Fr. *but,* goal—both basically the same; in the sense of target, this has come to mean one that is the target for shafts of ridicule.

To *abut* is a similar fusion: to join at the end (Fr. *abouter,* the *a* from L. *ad,* at, to), and to reach the mark (Fr. *abuter*). The *début* (to down the goal) from Fr. *débuter,* to start off at bowling, became used figuratively for starting out at anything, then launching into the theatre or society—esp. (present participle feminine of *débuter*) of the *débutante.*

There is also a *butt,* meaning hillock, mound, which in the U. S. is more commonly used in the Fr. form, *butte.* The *butt,* used of the thick, *i.e.,* the hinder part, of a hide, also suggests the *buttocks. Bottom* (OE. *botm*) and *bottle, q.v.,* are in the same family. Similarly a *button* was originally a small knob, or a *bud* (listed as of unknown origin, *bud* may also be of this group). The Fr. *bout,* end, has the verb *bouter,* to thrust out; whence, via Fr. *bouterez,* supports, comes Eng. *buttress;* but *cp. parrot.*

The common word *but* has lost its original sense in English, *but* preserves it in Scottish. It is via earlier *bout, bute,* from OE. *buta,* from *be-utan,* by the outen, on the outside; hence, outside of, except for . . . As the Germans say, "This case has a *but* in it." *Cp. boot; bottle.*

Related to *butt* may be *bat,* from OE. *botte,* a heavy-ended club. The flying mammal, the *bat,* is a corruption of earlier *back,* from the Scandinavian, from Icel. *blacka,* to flutter. But *cp. bazooka.*

butte.
See butt.

butter.
This seems a luxury the Teutons did not know, for they have borrowed the word from south Europe: from L. *butyrum,* from Gr. *boutyron,* from *bous,* ox (whence ? Eng. *bossy*) + *turos,* cheese, related to *disturb,* from L. *turba,* tumult, whence Eng. *turbulence.* Eng. *buttery* is, however, a place where *butts* or barrels of liquor were stored; *cp. bottle.*

buttock, button.
See butt.

buttonhole.
This is corrupted, because of the usual method of fastening, from the earlier *buttonhold*—which perhaps better fits our own loops and other devices.

buttress.
See parrot; butt.

buxom.
Whether from the old saw, Handsome is as handsome does, or because those that do as they are told are rewarded with goodies and grow fat, *buxom* (earlier *bucksome,* from ME. *buhsam,* from AS. *bugan,* to bow) first meant obedient; then jolly, plump and good to look upon.

bycorne.
See chichevache. (L. *bi-cornu,* two horned; but the early pictures show the beast without horns—which, considering his nature, is wondrous strange.)

by-law.
This lingering word has no connection with what you can get by with. It is from ME. *bilaw,* from *byrlaw,* from AS. *baer,* village, farm, whence *boor; cp. neighbor* + *log,* law; and meant a local regulation. It may be related (through the root *bu,* to dwell) to *byre,* cowshed; and it remains at the end of place-names, *e.g. Derby* (which gave its name to a kind ot hat worn at the horse races).

C

cab.
See taxi.

cabal.
The mystic element in this word is preserved in Eng. *cabbala* and *cabbalistic.* It is by way of LL., from Heb. *qabbalah,* the received lore, from *qabal,* to receive. The word was popularized in Eng. during the reign of Charles II, from the fact that the initials of his 1671 ministers spelled the word: Clifford, Arlington, Buckingham, Ashley, Lauderdale. From this Privy Council came the modern *cabinet*: Fr., from It. *gabinetto,* diminutive of *gabbia, cage,* from L. *cavea, cage, cave,* from *cavus,* hollow. Hence *cavity, cavern, excavated. Cp. calf.* To *cajole* is to chatter (esp. to entice wild birds to be caught) like a bird in a cage, from OFr. *cageoler;* whence also *gaol;* from the 13th c. spelling *gaiole* comes Eng. *jail. Cabinet* is a diminutive of *cabin,* from ME. *caban,* perhaps taken directly from Welsh *caban,* hut, instead of from the Fr. One suggestion connects *gaberdine* with this word, as the diminutive of Sp. *gaban,* great cloak, from *cabana, cabin,* shelter; *cp. cloth.*

cabbage.
If you speak of a head of *cabbage,* you are repeating yourself; for *cabbage* means head. The name of the vegetable is Fr. *choux;* it is from Fr. *choux cabus,* headed *cabbage,* shortened to *cabus, cabbage.* By way of OFr. *cabuce,* from It. *capuccio,* a little head, it is from L. *caput,* head. *Caput, capit—* gives us *capital,* etc.; *cp. achieve.* There is a word in heraldry, *caboshed,* which means with the head full front, high. To *cabbage,* meaning to filch, may be from this source, figuratively (you put the leaves into a bag to make the vegetable come to a head; and the objects into a bag to slip away with them); or, from OFr. *cabasser,* to put into a basket, from OFr. *cabas,* basket —which may itself be from the same source.

cabin, cabinet.
See cabal.

caboose.
This is not related to *cab, q.v.,* but possibly (through the German) to *cabin,* being a *cabin aus,* or *cabaus*: originally a cook-room on the deck of a merchant ship (ca. 1760). It was not applied to the last (trainmen's) car of a train until ca. 1880, in the U. S.
The ending was perhaps fashioned as in *vamoose, q.v.,* and *hoosegow.* This is from Mexican Sp. *juzgado, huzgado,* past participle of *juzgar,* to judge: judged, therefore sentenced, therefore jailed.

cacao.
See vanilla.

cackle.
See laugh.

cad.
The military *cadet* was once the younger son, from Fr. *cadet,* from Gasc. *capdet,* diminutive of *cap,* head; *cp. achieve.* From this came the use, as *caddie* (Sc.), for errand boy; now limited to one that carries another's clubs on a golf course. Shortened to *cad,* this represents the English University opinion of an errand boy, applied to anyone of whom the students disapproved.

caddie.
See cad.

cadence, cadenza.
See decay.

cadet.
See cad.

cadmium.
See element.

caduceus.
Hermes (Roman, Mercury) messenger of the gods, carried a herald's wand, Gr. *kadukion, kedukeion,* from *kedux, keduk-,* herald (related? to L. *dux, duc-,* leader, *ducere,* to guide; *cp. duke*). This wand (an olive branch with two serpents twined) replaced the knotted staff, with one twined serpent, of Aesculapius, as the symbol of medicine: Eng., the *caduceus.* A snake brought Aesculapius an herb with healing powers; whereupon Pluto, lord of the underworld, asked Zeus to slay him. Far from being a spirit of evil (save to the gods; *cp. totem*), the snake, shedding its skin to renew itself, was a symbol of healing. The daughter of Aesculapius was *Hygeia* (Gr. *hygies,* healthy), whence Eng. *hygiene.*
The *caduceus* must not be confused with Eng. *caducity,* from L. *caducus,* infirm, from *cadere,* to fall; *cp. cheat.*

Caesarean.
See shed.

cage.
See cabal.

caitiff.
See manoeuvre.

cajole.
See cabal.

cake.
See cheesecake.

calamity.
In late 19th c. England there was a "cult of the *Calamus*"; Swinburne, W. M. Rossetti and others, in admiration of the American poet Walt Whitman, whose best known work is *Leaves of Grass.* Various grasses or reeds are called *calamus,* from L. *calamus,* from Gr. *kalamos,* reed. It was long supposed that the damage to cornstalks from hail or mildew produced the word *calamity.* The ancients assumed this derivation; and Bacon tells that drouth, when the corn cannot come out of the stalk, turns *calamus* into *calamitas* (L. *calamitas, calamitat—*). Today etymologists prefer to guess at an early L. *calamis,* hurt, which does not exist and has no known ancestors, but which seems to be present in the L. *incolumis,* safe,
The zinc ore, *calamine,* may be from *calamus,* because of the shape of lines in it; but is perhaps corrupted by alchemists from L. *cadmia,* from Gr. *kadmia. Calamint* was probably from LL. *calamentum, —mentum* the noun ending; but was corrupted by popular etymology as though from Gr. *kalos,* beautiful, + *minthe, mint, cp. fee.* For the Gr. prefix meaning beautiful, *see calibre.*

calcedony.
See cell.

calcium.
See element.

calculate.
The *abacus,* (L. from Gr. *abax, abak—,* slab), which since the 17th c. has brought to mind a frame with rows of little balls, for *counting* (*see below*), was originally a board covered with sand, in which the ancients traced figures, then erased them (as later, slates were used). They did their *calculating* with strings of little stones as *counters* (L. *calculus,* pebble, diminutive of *calx, calc—,* lime, limestone, which gives us *calcium* and many combinations in *calci—*). Thus Eng. *calculus* is both a medical term for a stony formation, and a mathematical term for a method of figuring. Thus *callus* is a bony growth; and *callous,* hardened skin.
Count (ME. *counten,* from OFr. *cunter, conter,* to tell, whence Fr. *conte,* tale, from L. *computare, compute,* from *com,* together + *putare,* to think, reckon) was in the 14th c., by a return to the L., spelled *compte,* from which, about 1500, came the spelling *comptroller,* still in use along with *controller* (L. *contra,* against + *rotulus,* register, *roll*: one that checks the *rolls; cp. rote*). There are many compounds from this stem: *account, accountable; recount; discount. Count,* as a title, came into Eng. in the 16th c. (much later than *countess*), at first only to represent Fr. *comte,* It. *conte.* It is from L. *comes, comit—,* one together, a *companion;* then esp. the *companion* of a king, hence a noble. (*Companion, company,* are from L. *com,* together, + *panis,* bread: men that have broken bread together. Note, however, that *comrade,* though its first two syllables became one under the influence of L. *com,* together, is really from Fr. *camarade,* Sp. *camarada,* from L. *camera,* box, room—our picture-taking machine is shortened from *camera obscura,* dark box—and meant a room-

mate. Likewise, *chum* is a late 17th c. abbreviation of *chamber-mate.*) The domain of a *count* is a *county.* A *counter,* as one who *counts,* or as a *calculating* device, must be distinguished from the many words that begin with *counter*— (ME. *countre,* from Fr. *contre,* from L. *contra,* against): *counteract, countermand, counterpart,* etc. But note that *country* is the place that lies *counter* your line of vision (against the city: LL. *contrata; cp.* G. *Gegend,* region, from *gegen, against*). Indeed the forms here are almost *countless!*

calculus.
See calculate.

caldron.
See chauffeur.

calendar, calender.
See dickey.

calendula.
See flower.

calf.
This is a common Teut. word, AS. *cealf.* The calf of the leg draws its name from resembling the *calf* before it has left the cow . . . Similarly, what we call a *cave-in* was first a *calve-in*: the mass of earth falling as a *calf* from a cow. *Cp. cabal.*

calibre, caliber.
This word (from Arab. *qalib,* mould, though possibly, from L. *qua libra,* of what weight: it was at one time spelled *qualibre*) seems to have been first used in Eng. with figurative application, as quality, rank. Then it was applied physically to the diameter of a cannonball, thence to the bore of the gun. A variation was *caliver,* a type of gun used in the 16th c. It is the same word as *calliper, caliper* (at first an adj.: *calliper* compasses; then used alone), instrument for measuring the bore, etc. These words must not be confused with others beginning *calli*—, from Gr. *kallos,* beautiful: *e.g., calligraphy,* beautiful writing; *Calliope,* she of the beautiful voice (now, in Barnum's pleasantly exaggerate way, the steam organ of the circus); *callisthenics,* exercise for beauty; Venus *Callipyge,* of the beautiful buttocks.

calico.
See cloth.

California.
See States.

caliper, calligraphy, Calliope, Callipyge, callisthenics.
See calibre.

calix.
See eucalyptus.

call.
See council.

callous, callus.
See calculate.

calm.
The Gr. *kaiein,* burn, whence *kaustos,* burnt, whence L. *causticus,* gives us *caustic,* both in chemistry (*caustic* potash and lime) and in manners. By way of Gr. *kauterion,* hot iron, whence L. *cauterizare,* comes *cauterize. Caution* is not related, coming from L. *cavere, caut*—, to take heed; as in *caveat emptor,* let the buyer beware. But by way of cognate L. *calere,* to heat + *facere,* to make, comes *calefaction,* with other such terms. Gr. *kauma,* heat, whence LL. *calma* ? (the change to *l* influenced by L. *calor,* heat, whence *caloric* and *calories*) gives us the present Eng. *calm.* The heat of midday in tropic countries calls for a cessation of labor (LL. ?*caumare,* whence Fr. *chomer,* to stop work) at about the sixth hour of the day (*sixth,* from L. *sexta,* whence Sp. *siesta,* adopted in Eng.); the word for heat was transferred to the idea of the rest, the *calm.*

calomel.
This white powder that becomes dark on exposure to light is named from this characteristic: Gr. *kalos,* fair + *melas,* black.

calories.
See chauffeur. L. *calor, calori*—, heat. *Cp.* calm.

calumny.
See challenge.

Calvary.
Many a mountain (*Breadloaf, e.g.*) is named from its shape. The hill near Jerusalem, on which Jesus was crucified, was called by the Hebrews *gulgolep,* skull. The Greeks transliterated this as *Golgotha;* then the Romans translated it into L. *cǎlvaria,* skull, whence *Mount*

Calvary, in Old English again translated into *Headpanstow.* The *calvaria* is the roof of the brain-case, in Eng. anatomy today.

calyx.
See eucalyptus.

cam.
See camp.

cambric.
See cloth.

Cambridge.
Today this may seem to be, clearly enough, the *bridge* over the *Cam.* But before there was a bridge, there was a ford, over the crooked river, from *cam,* crooked, (*Cameron,* crooked nose; *Campbell,* crooked mouth) + Celt. *rnyd,* ford. (*Campbell* has been modified as though from L. *campus bellus,* fair field, Fr. *Beauchamp.*)

camel.
See monk; dromedary.

camelia.
See Appendix II.

camembert.
See Appendix II.

camera.
See calculate.

Cameron.
See Cambridge.

camouflage.
This is the noun (Fr. *—age;* Eng. *act, —tion,* from L. *—ationem*), from Fr. *camoufler,* to disguise. Its first military use was in the form *camouflet,* a gas mine: from the sense of blowing smoke in the face. It is related to *muffle,* from Fr. *moufler,* to cover up, from *moufle,* a mitten, from LL. *mufula,* diminutive of G. *Muff, muff,* from OHG. *mouwe,* a sleeve. Note that the medieval Latin word is borrowed from the Teutonic; indeed, it may not be a diminutive, but from MLG. *mol,* soft + *vel,* skin, whence Eng. *fell,* cognate with *pelt, q.v.* From the idea of a woman's wide, hanging sleeve (separate in early days; a lady gave her sleeve to her knight when he went forth to win glory) came our winter *muff. Cp. copse, sleeveless.*

The *muff* of a player on a ball field is from another source, being an imitative word of OE. origin, to *muff,* to mumble; hence, a simpleton, an awkward fellow, a "butter-fingers." We have transferred the word from the person to the act.

camp.
This was first the field (L. *campus,* field, from Gr. *kepos,* garden) where an army might stay. Its wars would be waged upon a larger space (L. *campania,* plain); then the term for the place was applied to the activity; hence, an election *campaign,* which is usually bloodless. In ME., *camp* always means battle, like *Kampf* in German: Hitler's *Mein Kampf.* A college field is a *campus.*

The level ground near Naples was called *Campania;* similarly, a section of France is called by the Fr. derivative, *Champagne;* from this we take the name of the beverage. Shakespeare (*King Lear,* I, i) calls a large field a *champaign. See* champion.

The ridge, or cog, *cam,* is common Teut., Du. *ham,* Welsh *cam,* Eng. *comb; cp. quaint.* It is probably related to old Celtic *cambo,* bent back, crooked; whence Eng. arms *akimbo.*

campaign.
See camp.

campanula.
See flower.

Campbell.
See Cambridge.

canal.
See canon.

canary.
The color comes from the bird, and the bird comes from the islands. Shakespeare speaks of a dance, *canary* (*All's Well That Ends Well,* II, i) and of the wine (naturally, with Falstaff: *Merry Wives of Windsor,* III, ii). But the islands take their names from the dogs that abounded there: (L. *canaria,* from *canis,* dog, whence Eng. *canine.* The Gr. *kyne, kyn—,* dog, gives Eng. *cynic;* also *cynosure—cynos,* dog + *oura,* tail: name given to the tail of the constellation of the Lesser Bear, the last star of which is the pole-star, to which all mariners turned.) *Cannibal* is an error: Hakluyt, in his *Voy-*

ages (1598), says: "The *Caribes* I learned to be men-eaters or *canibals;*" Defoe in Robinson Crusoe follows him: the word *Caribal,* an inhabitant of the Caribbeans, was altered, from the idea that the *cannibals* ate like dogs.

The island of *Capri* is named from the many goats there; *cp. buck; taxi*: *Coney* Island, (*q.v.*) New York, from the great number of rabbits, or *coneys*—whose skins still provide many a fair lady with furs.

cancan.

This high-kicking dance of the Parisian cafés is named after the erudite discussions of the university scholars, whence also *dunce, q.v.* So many arguments began with the roundabout L. *quamquam,* although, that the word (pronounced, in Fr., *concon*) became the term for a piece of nonsense. By a bawdy pun on the sound of the word, among carousing students, it became the name of the skirt-lifting dance.

cancel.

In L., *cancer,* pl. *cancri* meant the shape of crossing bars; perhaps by dissimilation, from *carcer,* prison; *see* quarter. Because of his ten legs, the word was applied to the spread-out crab. Hence we have the Tropic of *Cancer, Cancer,* the fourth of the twelve signs of the Zodiac; *cancer* the disease, and (OE. *cancer, cancor*) the similar-seeming illness, *canker.* From the L. diminutive *cancelli,* crossbars (still used in Eng., *cancelli,* of the lattice between the choir and the rest of the church, whence *chancel, chancery,* and *chancellor,* from Fr. *chancelier*) came L. *cancellare,* whence Eng. *cancel,* to mark out with crossed lines. Fr. *canceler* means to swerve; Eng. *canceleer, cancelier,* a hawking term meaning the sudden turn of the bird before it strikes, came to mean to digress. So *crabbed* (from the crooked walk of the *crab*) cross-tempered, perverse. *Crab,* from OE. *crabba,* is related to LG. *krabben,* to claw, also to *crawl* and *crawfish.* While *crab* apple may be related to Sc. *scrab,* it is influenced by thought of twisted—the tree—and twisted mouth, wry—the effect of the fruit.

cancer.

See cancel.

candid, candidate.

Before election, those aspiring for office in ancient Rome wore togas that symbolized their purity (L. *candidatus,* garbed in white, from *candidus,* white). After a time, anyone running for office, no matter how double-dealing, was called a *candidate.* The word for the color, on the other hand, came to mean without deceit, frank, *candid.*

L. *candidus* is from *candere,* to shine; whence, with the noun diminutive, *candle,* a little shining (but: How far that little *candle* throws its beams!) The inceptive of the verb is *candescere,* the present participle of which, *candescens, candescent*—, gives us Eng. *candescent* and (with the intensive *in*) *incandescent* light.

candle.

See candid.

Candlewood means pine knots, which the early American settlers used for lighting.

candy.

Sweet-tooth down the ages shows how little man changes. *Candy* was first a verb in Eng.—its past tense spelled *candide* as though from L. *candidus,* white; *cp. candid*—but the word traveled much farther. The Italians say *zucchero candi,* as we say *sugar-candy;* but this is repetition: from Pers. *qand, sugar-candy;* Arab. *qandat, sugar-candy,* from *qandi, sugared,* made of *sugar.* It still is. The Sansk. *khanda,* lump *sugar,* is from *khand,* to break, as the crystalized sugar crumbled. *Cane,* however, is from Gr. *kanna,* reed, from Arab. *qanah. Sugar* itself is from OFr. *sucre,* from LL. *succarum,* from Arab. *sukkar;* connection is suggested (through bitter experience?) with Sansk. *carkara,* gravel.

cane.

See candy, canon.

canine.

See canary.

canker.

See cancel.

cannibal.

See canary.

cannon.

See canon.

canon.
Preceptors enforced their *canons* with a *cane;* countries use *cannon.* All three words are the same. The origin is probably oriental; there is Arab. *qanàt, cane;* Heb *qaneh,* reed. Thence Gr. *kanna, kanne,* reed; whence, from the straight hollow tube, *cannon.* But also Gr. *kanon,* whence L. *canon,* a rod; then a rule in the sense of a carpenter's rule or measure; thence, any rule or law. From the same source came Fr. *canne,* whence ME. *cane* (two syllables), whence Eng. *cane*—so that *cane, canon,* and *cannon* are triplets. But so also are *kennel* (a gutter), *channel,* and *canal,* from L. *canalis,* from the same Gr. *kanna,* reed, tube. The root is Aryan *skan,* from *ska,* to cut, whence Sansk. *khan,* to dig, whence *khani,* mine. *Kennel,* doghouse, is ME. *kenel,* from OFr. *chenil,* diminutive of *chen,* from L. *canem,* dog.

cant.
See saunter.

cantaloup.
See peach. Sometimes spelled *cantalope* (note the St. Valentine's day greeting: "We're too young, dear, we *can't elope."* . . . For *elope, see* subjugate.)

cantankerous.
This sounds like a coined word, a telescope of cant or canker and rancorous; but it really has a legitimate history. OFr. *contet* (whence Eng. *contest*) gave OE. *contekous,* quarrelsome, then *contekour,* quarreler; whence *cantankerous. Contest,* through the Fr. is from L. *contestari,* to call to witness against; *cp. test*: when witnesses are arrayed on both sides, there is indeed a *contest.*

cantata.
See incentive.

canteen.
The early shops were often just a corner of a room or of a cellar. *Canteen,* It. *cantina,* cellar, is a diminutive of *cant,* a corner, edge. (Thus Du. *winkel,* corner, also came to mean shop.) Applied first to a shop where drink and food were sold to soldiers, the meaning was extended to a chest for carrying bottles, then to the soldiers' water-holder.

canter.
See saunter.

canto.
See accent, saunter.

canvas, canvass.
See filter.

caoutchouc.
See latex.

cap.
See scourge, vamp.

capacity.
See discuss.

cap-a-pie, caparison, cape, Capeline.
See achieve.

cape.
See copse.

caper.
See taxi. There are two other meanings—and origins—of this word. From Du. *kaper,* from *kapen,* to take, plunder, it means a privateer, or the captain of such a vessel. From L. *capparis* (which was thought a plural, hence the Eng. without the *s*) it means a shrub (*Capparis spinosa*) the buds of which are used in seasoning and pickling.

capital, capitalist, capitalize, capitol, capitulate.
See achieve.

Capri.
See canary.

caprice, capricious.
See taxi.

capsize.
See capstan.

capstan.
There are several interlockings caught in this sailors' term. It seems to come via Port. *cabestan,* earlier *cabestran,* from the present participle (*capistrant—*) of a LL. *capistrare, capistrat—,* to fasten, varied from *capitrare,* frequentative of L. *capere, capt—,* to seize. But (like *capsize,* which began with the meaning "to come a header", to go down head first) it may be related to L. *caput,* head; *cp. achieve, manoeuvre.* But the *cap—* also suggested the origin in the word for goat; *cp. taxi*:—buck, *q.v.,* and

other animals have been used as names for machines. This leaves the latter half of the word to be explained; and the efforts to account for it remain in various spellings the word has had: *capstand, capstone, capstern,* and more. The mechanism, and also the rope that winding around it draws the anchor up, have likewise been called the *capstring.* Heave ho!

captain.
See achieve.

captivate, captive.
See manoeuvre.

capture.
See manoeuvre; purchase, achieve.

car.
See carouse. The L. *carrus, car,* from *currus, chariot,* from *currere, curs—,* to run, is from Sansk. *char, kar,* to move. *Cart* is the diminutive, from LL. *carreta. Cargo* (from LL. *carga,* burden, whence *carricare,* to load): that which is put on a *cart. Career* (Fr. *carrière,* from L. *carrus*) was first a road, a race-track; then, one's progress along it. *Cp. cutlet; hussar.*

carat.
The weight of a diamond is measured in beans. Little beans, being roughly of the same size and weight, made a convenient standard of measure in ancient times: *carat* traveled through Fr., It. and Gr., from Arab. *qirat,* from *qaura,* bean. The sign of omission, *caret,* is directly from L. *caret,* it is missing, from *carere,* to be lacking.

caravan.
See pan—.

carbon.
See ajar; element.

carboniferous.
See suffer.

carbuncle.
See uncle.

card.
See map.

cardigan.
See Appendix II.

cardinal.
The *cardinal* virtues are those on which salvation swings. The church similarly depends upon its *cardinals* (from L. *cardinalis,* essential, from *cardo, cardin—,* hinge, from Gr. *kardan,* to swing).
The color is named from that of the *cardinal's* gown; the bird, from the color.

care.
See chary.

career.
See car.

caress.
See charity

caret.
See carat.

cargo.
See car.

caricature.
This word is from It. *caricatura,* from *caricare,* from LL. *carricare,* to load a *car,* from *carrus, car, q.v.* One suggestion is that the picture is like an overladen *car, exaggerated* (L. *exaggerare, exaggeratus,* to heap up, from *agger,* mound, from *ad,* to + *gerere,* to bear; whence, *—igerous*). It is more likely that the word comes from the pictures' being borne about on a cart, on feast days, as the effigies of Guy Fawkes were carried in England.

caries.
See sincere.

carnage, carnal, carnation.
See sarcophagus.

carnelian.
This might have been so named, as the flesh-colored stone (from L. *carn—,* flesh); but it was earlier *cornelian*: from Fr. *cornaline,* from L. *cornu,* horn—being, like a horn, translucent. Similarly, *onyx* is from Gr. *onyx,* finger-nail; and perhaps *nacre,* mother-of-pearl, from It. *naccaro,* from Sansk. *nakhara,* nail. *Agate* is from Gr. *Achates,* a river in Sicily. *Chrysolite* is from Gr. *chrysos,* gold + *lithos,* stone (whence *lithography,* writing on stone). *Emerald* is an old word, from OFr. *esmeralde,* from Gr. *smaragdus* (whence Eng. *smaragdus*), from Sansk.

marakta. *Jacinth* is from L. *hyacinthus,* from the color of the blood of *Hyacinthus,* whom Apollo loved, and Zephyr slew in jealousy; the drops of blood from the dying youth formed the flower *hyacinth,* whose petals bear his name. *Jade* is from OFr. *ejade,* from Sp. (*piedra de*) *ijada,* stone of colic, from L. *ilia,* flank: it being supposed to cure a pain in the side. *Jasper* is from Gr. *iaspis,* from Arab. *yashp,* from Heb *yashpeh.* *Moonstone,* obviously dedicate, is a translation of Gr. *selenites* (*lithos*), stone of *Selene,* the moon; whence also Eng. *selenite.* *Pearl* is a common word, perhaps through the Sicilian *perna,* from L. *perna,* shell-fish. *Sapphire* is also old, from Gr. *sappheiros,* from Sansk. *sani-priya,* ? dear to the planet Saturn; Heb. *sappir.* *Sardonyx* is the *onyx* of *Sardis,* which place also gives us Eng. *sard.* *Topaz* is old, from ? Sansk. *tapas,* heat. *Zircon* is from Fr. *zircone,* from Arab. *zarqun,* from Pers. *zargun,* golden, from *zar,* gold. *Jewel* is of less price, being, from OFr. *joel, joiel,* from LL. *jocale,* diminutive of L. *jocus,* game, trifle, whence *jocular, joke.* *Precious* is via Fr. *précieux,* from L. *pretiosus,* valuable, from *pretium,* price. *Precious,* meaning affected, is from the Fr. application of *précieux,* in the 17th c., to the ladies, *Les précieuses,* (*the priceless ones,* ironically) who established the literary salons of Paris. And *stone* is a common Teut. word, AS. *stan.*

carnival.

This is generally explained through the Christian custom of feasts and frolics the day (or the week) before the Lenten fasting: *carnival,* from It. *carnevale,* from LL. *carnelevarium,* from L. *carnem levare,* to remove meat. Popular etymology points to L. *carnem vale,* farewell to meat. But the ancient Greek ship-cart ceremonies anticipated those of Christian Lent; the north-folk combined Celtic and Latin to call the ship-cart *carrus navalis;* hence perhaps the word *carnival.* *Cp. sarcophagus.*

carnivorous.

See sarcophagus.

carom, carrom.

This billiard shot has been corrupted to *cannon* (for which *see canon*). The word *carom* is a shortening of *carambole.* And the whole thing may have started with a golden-yellow fruit, which the Hindi call *karmal* (Malay *karambil,* coconut), the Portuguese *carambola;* and which Linnaeus in his botany took into modern Latin. (Linnaeus: Carl von Linné, 1707—78, founder of modern botany, not especially concerned with billiards.)

carotid.

The *carotid* arteries along the neck carry blood to the head; press them, and you presently drop into slumber. Hence the Greeks called them *karotides* (plural) from Gr. *karoun,* to stupefy. (The aforesaid consequence was known to the assassins, *q.v.*)

carouse.

The ancient Romans had goblets made in the shape of a crouched lion; the bowl was the belly, so that the only way to put down the goblet was by drinking down the wine. In the middle ages, the Germans used to lift their goblet, and cry *"Gar aus!"* (G. *gar,* completely + *aus, out*). Raleigh, who knew about tobacco as well, spoke of captains who "*garoused* of his wine till they were reasonably pliant." Hence, *carouse.*

Carousal and *carousel* are tangled in their history. But *carousel* (accented on the last syllable), with its horses and little carts, seems to be from It. *caroselle,* from *garosello,* a tournament, diminutive of *garoso,* quarrelsome, from *gara,* strife. This may be from L. *garrire,* to babble, which gives Eng. *garrulous;* or from L. *guerra,* war, from OHG. *werra,* whence Eng. *war.* The change from *g* to *c* was influenced by mixture with It. *carricello,* a little chariot, diminutive of *carro, car*—from the use of such carts in the merry-making. *Cp. car.*

carp.

See crop.

carpenter.

See harmony. *Carpentry* was as much an art, to the Greeks, as music and drama.

carpet.

The early floor and wall coverings were rude affairs, as the word indicates: *carpet* is from LL. *carpita,* from L. *carpere,* to pluck. At first it seems to have been applied to a monk's robe, then to the hangings—the best of which (as in *Hamlet,* where Polonius hides) were called *arras,* from the French city, *Arras,* where they were manufactured. To *carp* at someone, while directly from ON. *karpa,* to chatter, was changed in meaning by the influence of L. *carpere,* to pluck.

carriage.
By way of OFr. *cariage,* the action of *carrying,* this is from OFr. *carier,* to bear in a *cart,* whence also Eng. *carry, q.v.; cp. car.* The word has gone through a series of meanings, some of which persist—a charge for *carrying;* the *carrying* (capture) of a fort; the manner of *carrying,* hence, one's *carriage,* one's conduct; things that are *carried,* baggage, load—until it grew fixed in the sense of the means by which things and esp. persons are *carried,* a vehicle.

carrion.
This word is from ME. *caroine, caronye,* carcass, from OFr. *caronie* (also *charoigne,* whence Fr. *charogne,* title of a grim poem by Baudelaire); probably via a LL. form *caronia* it springs from L. *caro, carn—,* flesh; *cp. sarcophagus.* The northern Fr. form, *carogne,* applied figuratively to "a carcass of a woman", has come into Eng. as *crone.*

carry.
See carriage.
Among special uses: to *carry the day,* or the election, means to bear it (the victory) from the opponent; thus also to *carry a motion* in a legislative body. *Carry* was also, earlier, used alone where we now say *carried away,* to *carry on* a business—to *carry on* then came to mean to continue in a course of action, as a dying man may exhort his company, or just to *behave* (with the implication of *misbehavior*). To *behave* was formed as an intensive of *have*: the reminder *Behave yourself* meant *Have yourself* (Be self-possessed). The word *behavior* is the Eng. verbal noun (*behaver, behavor*) influenced by the Fr. *avoir,* to have. But don't be *carried away* (this is usually figurative!).

cart.
See car, carouse.

carton, cartoon.
See map.

carve.
This was the basic Teut. term for cutting. It was OE. *ceorfan;* but the form Icel. *kyrfa* shows that it is cognate with Gr. *graph*—as in *graphein,* to score (*q.v.*), to write; *cp. graft.* Early writing was always a *carving* or cutting; *cp. read.*

caryatid.
See Appendix II.

cascara, case.
See discuss, casement.

casein.
See cheesecake.

casement.
This is aphetic for *encasement,* that which holds together, from L. *en, in* + *capere, caps—,* whence *cass—,* to take, to hold. From this, also, Eng. *case* and by way of OFr. *chasse,* Eng. *chassis,* the *encasing* body, and *sash.* There is a mingling of this word with one that has dropped out of our language: *casemate,* a loophole. *Casemate,* though traced through Rabelais' Fr. *chasmata* to Gr. *chasma,* whence Eng. *chasm,* has closer forms. It seems to be applied to a loophole, whence the enemy may be slain, from It. *casamatta* (Sp. *casa,* house + *matar,* slaughter), from It. *mazzare,* from L. *mactare,* to slaughter. In Fr. *meutrière,* in G. *Mordkeller,* have the same double application.
L. *capsa,* It. *casa,* were general terms for a container, whether a box or a hut; as in Eng. book *case,* cigarette *case,* stair *case.* The It. diminutive *casino* was first a little summer house, then a public room, then a game played there. *Cp. cheat.*

cash, cashier.
See discuss.

cashmere.
See cloth.

cask, casket, casque.
See discuss.

Cassandra.
See Appendix II.

castanet.
This word, usually in the plural, as they are played in pairs, esp. by Spanish dancers, takes it name not from the color but from the form. (A sun-tanned maiden may be said to have a *castaneous* hue, from the color.) The Sp. *castanet,* Fr. *castagnette,* is a diminutive of Sp. *castaña,* from the L. *castanea, chestnut.* The Fr.

marron, chestnut, which we borrow for the delicious *marrons glacés,* iced *chestnuts,* has been associated with the family of the Roman *epic* poet Vergil (Virgilius *Maro*); but is perhaps from the Heb. *armon,* a tree translated as *chestnut.* (Speaking of *epics,* the Roman Martial deserves the ages' salvo for his cry, when it was suggested that he show his mettle by writing an *epic*: "What! Shall I write hexameters of wars, that pedants may spout me, and good boys and fair girls loathe my name!")

Epic is an adjective, Gr. *epikos,* from Gr. *epos,* which first meant word; but then, as one word leads to another, came to mean story, then the long narrative poem.

Chestnut itself is earlier *chesteine-nut,* via OFr. *chastaigne,* from that same L. *castanea.* This itself, however, may be via Gr. *kastanea* (short for *Castanian* nut) from (1) *Kastanaia* in ancient Pontus, (2) *Castana* in Thessaly, (3) the Armenian name for the tree, *kaskeni.*

Try biting into a *chestnut* that has grown old and dry, and you may guess the origin of the meaning, an old old story. Several accounts are given, of the origin of this sense, which is apparently American. According to one of the most favored, a travelliar was telling his tale: "—when suddenly out of a cork-tree—" "A *chestnut!*" interrupted a listener. The Captain insisted; but the man persisted: "A *chestnut,* a *chestnut;* I have heard you tell the story twenty times before!" From the tree, the fruit fell to the story.

caste.
See test.

castigate.
See purchase.

castrate.
See purchase.

casual, casualties.
See cheat.

cat.
See incinerator; catgut; cat-o'-nine-tails.

catalogue, catapult.
See paragraph. Note that Gr. *pallein,* to hurl, is the intensive (the first letter becoming explosive) of Gr. *ballein,* to throw; *cp. ball.*

cataract.
Keep your eye on this. A stream of water that dashes swiftly down was in Gr. *kataractes,* from *kata,* down, + *rassein,* to dash. But even in ancient times forts were equipped with a door that could be dashed down in the face of a sudden assault; the word took this sense in Greek, and the first English meaning of *cataract* was portcullis. And from this movement as of a door coming down (the idea of speed long lost) came the *cataract* we hope keeps out of the eye. *Portcullis* is a simpler term, from Fr. *porte,* door, + *coulissant,* sliding, from Fr. *couler,* to slide, from L. *colare,* to slide, to strain; *cp. dickey.*

The Gr. prefix *cata—,* down, back, against, occurs in a number of Eng. words, *e.g.*: *catachresis* (Gr. *kresthai,* to use); *cataclysm* (Gr. *klyzein,* to dash against, flood); *cataglottism* (Gr. *glotta,* variant of *glossa* tongue, whence—tongue in the sense of language—Eng. *gloss, glossary; glottis, epiglottis.* To *gloss* over is from MHG. *glos,* shining; whence also *glass; cp. electricity*); *catalogue* (*cp. paragraph*); *catalysis* (Gr. *lyein,* to loosen; *cp. lysol*); *catalepsy* (Gr. *cataleptos,* seized, from *lambanein,* to take). The raft *catamaran,* however, is directly from Tamil *katta-maram,* tied wood; *catamite* is from L. *catamitus,* corrupted from Jupiter's cup-hearer, *Ganymedes;* and *catamount* is short for *cat of the mountain.*

catarrh, catastrophe.
See paragraph.

catch.
See purchase.

catchpenny.
Catchpenny, potboiler, and *claptrap* all, when broken apart, reveal their origin. The first is general; the second refers to literature; the third is drawn from the theatre, but has become the most frequently applied to shoddy work done merely to win applause.

catchword.
Old books printed, under the last line of a page, the word that began the first line on the next page: this was the *catchword,* to hold the attention. The word was then applied to the last word (*i.e.,* the one that gave the cue) in an actor's speech; then, to any expression that holds the attention.

As the public grows informed, such expressions (as used by politicians and advertisers) are looked upon with suspicion; we suspect *catchwords*—and those that use them avoid the term, seek one less known and suspected, *e.g., slogan* (*q.v.*); similarly the users of *propaganda, q.v.,* now speak of the necessity of "indoctrination in education." *Cp. bugle.*

category.
See verdict.

caterer.
See incinerator.

caterpillar.
This "wyrm among frute," as the old English called it, draws its name from OFr. *chatte peleuse,* hairy cat. But its form and meaning were strengthened by two old Eng. words. A robber was a *piller,* whence Eng. *pillage*: Bishop Latimer refers to "extortioners, *caterpillers,* usurers." And a glutton was a *cater; cp. incinerate*: hence a *caterpillar* was a greedy plunderer. It still is.

Pillage is via Fr. *piller,* to plunder, from L. *piler,* to strip (the hide from), from L. *pilus,* hair. Whence also *plush* and *pile* (of velvet); *cp. cloth.*

catgut.
Since violin strings are made of metal, tennis rackets are strung with nylon, whence the name *catgut?* Originally it was sheep-gut, anyway.

The *cat* is accounted for through several resemblances. *Catlings,* small strings for instruments, may have been blended with *chitterlings,* guts. Shakespeare, in *Troilus and Cressida,* III, iii, says: "Unless the fidler Apollo get his sinews to make *catlings* on." Or it may have been *kitgut, kit* being a small violin as well as a *kitten* (G. *kitt,* lute; G. *kitze, cat*)

catholic.
When we speak of a man as having *catholic* taste, we mean that he likes most everything (or the best of every sort). Whistler said that such a man is not a man of taste at all, but an auctioneer. The word *catholic* comes via Fr. *catholique* (which shifted the accent to the first syllable, from the L. stress on the second) from L. *catholicus* from Gr. *katholikos,* general, from *kata—,* concerning, + *holos,* whole. (Thus also *holocaust* is from Gr. *holos,* whole, + *caustos,* burnt, from Gr. *kaiein,* to burn—which gives us *encaustic, cauterize, caustic. Caustic* is used literally of *caustic* lime, *caustic* potash, and figuratively, of *caustic* words, that make the victim smart. Note that *cauterize* is not related to *caution,* which is from *cavere, cau—,* to beware.) With the capital *C, Catholic* was early applied to the "church universal". At first it meant the entire body of Christian believers, as opposed to a single congregation; then it referred to the "universally" accepted orthodox doctrine and to the historic *Catholic Church.*

cat-o'-nine-tails.
It is suggested that this is from LL. *catonus,* a scourge loaded with lead—by a misunderstanding of Gr. *kat' omous,* upon the shoulders—mistaking the reception point for the weapon. But this skimps the problem.

The first scourges were made of thongs of cat's hide, seen in the hand of Osiris. The cat was a sacred animal among the Egyptians; striking is related to the belief that the strength (virtue) passed from the stick or hide to the person struck. (Remember that the cat is extremely lively; it has nine lives.) Akin to this is the laying on of the sword in knighting. The practice survived the belief: the use for playful striking of *ticklers,* sold at the medieval fairs, is a relic of this ritual striking, for fertility Note that Gr. *ticktein* means to beget; L. *titillare,* to tickle, whence Eng. *titillate. Tickle* and *kittle* are old alternate forms; *kitten, kid*: G. *Kitze,* youngling, *Kitzler, tickler.* As the years went by, the proverb grew:

A spaniel, a woman, a walnut tree,
The more they're beaten, the better
they be . . .

until the whole symbolic process degenerated into the schoolmaster's maxim: Spare the rod and spoil the child.

catsup.
See ketchup.

cattle.
See achieve.

caudal, caudate.
See bible.

cauldron.
See chauffeur.

causeway.
This is a road along a *causey,* which earlier term it has almost entirely replaced. A *causey* was a roadbed or a mound trodden down to make it hard, from OFr. *chaucie̋e* (Fr. *chausée*), from LL. *calceata, calciata,* as in *via calciata,* trodden way, from *calciare, calciat—,* to trample, from *calx, calc—,* heel; *cp. recalcitrant.*

caustic, cauterize, caution.
See catholic.

cavalier.
A medieval man on a horse (Fr., from It. *cavaliere, cavallero*—sometimes in Eng. *cavallero, cavaliero,* from Sp.—, from LL. *caballus,* horse) was likely to be a noble. But as he was on high, he was also likely to be *haughty* (Fr. *haut,* high; Fr. *hauteur* means both height and pride). Hence the noun *cavalier* means a knight; whereas the adj. means disdainful, *supercilious* (L. *super,* above + *cilium,* eyebrow). The same word, by way of the Fr. (*cheval,* horse; *chevalier*) is Eng. *chevalier.* In early Eng. this gave us the adj. *chivalrous,* which dropped out of use by 1600, but by the 19th c., under the influence of the romantic spirit, had been revived. *Chivalry* was long pronounced with the *ch* as in church; recently, the French sound as of *sh* has prevailed.

cave.
See cabal.

cave-in.
See calf.

caveat.
See show.

caveat emptor.
See quaint.

cavern, cavity.
See cabal.

cease.
See ancestor.

cedar.
See citron.

cede.
See ancestor.

ceiling, cieling.
This "sky of the room" was at times spelled as though it comes from Fr. *ciel,* from LL. *coelum,* sky—influenced, some say, by OFr. *cieller,* from L. *caelare,* to carve. But it was often spelled *seeling* from the early Eng. verb to *seel,* to close with boards. A combination is found in a sermon by Bishop Hacket, 1675: "Dost thou permit us to live in *sieled* houses?"

celandine. celidony.
See cell.

cell.
This word is from L. *cella* (from *celare, celat—,* to hide; *cp. helmet*). Used of a small compartment, such as the *cell* of a honeycomb, a store-room, slaves' quarters or prison; then of a hermit's quarters. A group of *cells* was L. *cellarium,* whence Eng. *cellar.* (Similar formations are *aquarium, aqua,* water; *solarium, sol,* sun; *apiary, apis,* bee; *aviary, avis,* bird). The diminutive of L. *cella,* L. *cellula,* is a frequent prefix (*cellulo—*) in Eng. scientific words; and gives us *cellulose,* full of little *cells.*

The Gr. for the bird, the swallow, was *chelidon.* This gives us the plant *celandine;* its juice was supposed to be a cure for bad eyes—used by the swallows to improve the sight of their young. Also, via Gr. *chelidonius lithos,* (*lithos,* stone, whence *lithography; see carnelian*) comes *celidony,* a stone supposedly found in the belly of a swallow, and cure for madness. *Calcedony,* also *chalcedony,* translates the Gr. *chalcedon,* the precious stone in the *Bible, Rev.* xxi, 19, named as one of the foundations of the New Jerusalem. This may be the swallow-stone, or from the city of *Chalcedon* in Asia Minor, or possibly—since some forms of the word are *carchedonia, carcedonia*—from Gr. *Karchedon,* Carthage. The Gr. word for brass was *chalkos,* which appears (often as the prefix *chalco—*) in a number of Eng. scientific words: *chalcopyrite* has nothing to do with books, but is a copper ore; a *chalcographer* is a man that engraves on copper. The *Chaldaic* language (of *Chaldea,* Babylon) was Aramaic, spoken by the Jews after the Captivity; but a *Chaldean* (from the practice there) is a soothsayer, an astrologer . . . If he charges for his "truths", in some places, these days, the *Chaldean* may find himself in a *cell.*

cellar.
See cell.

cellophane.
See focus.

cellulose.
See cell.

cement.
See shed.

cemetery.
See necromancy.

cent.
See dollar.

centaury.
See flower.

centigrade.
See congress.

cephalic, cephalo—.
See lent.

ceramic.
See crater.

cereal.
What you probably have had for breakfast this morning is named after the daughter of Saturn and Vesta, *Ceres,* the goddess of the harvest. The great Eleusinian mysteries celebrate the ravishing by Pluto, god of the underworld, of Ceres' daughter Proserpine. On Ceres' prayer, Jupiter granted Proserpine leave to spend part of the year above ground with her mother. The myth symbolizes the sowing of seed and the growing of corn.

cerebellum, cerebrum, cerecloth, cerement.
See crater.

ceremony.
It is well to behave according to thought-out procedure, when (according to the principle of *karma*) all one's acts have their inevitable consequence in one's own future. *Ceremony* is from Fr., from L. *caerimonia*: the noun ending (as in matrimony, harmony, etc.) + Sansk. *karma,* act, work, developed, in Hinduism and Buddhism, into the idea of the ethical consequence of one's acts.
It has also been, but less plausibly, suggested that L. *caerimonia* is from *Caere,* a chief city of ancient Etruria, whence the Romans derived many of their customs and rites.

cerium.
See element.

cesium.
See element.

cessation.
See ancestor.

chafe.
See chauffeur.

chagrin.
This was first the skin, or rough leather from a horse (from Turk. *saghri,* rump of a horse); in that sense it is usually spelled *shagreen.* But (as with the idea of *gooseflesh*) the figurative sense, as though one were rubbed with a rough hide, has prevailed.

chain.
See chignon.

chalcedony, Chaldea, chalco—.
See cell; *Appendix II.*

chalice.
See eucalyptus.

challenge.
This word has traveled, via OE. *chalenge, calenge,* OFr. *calonge,* OSp. *caloña,* from L. *calumnia,* false accusation. The original sense remains in Eng. *calumny;* but with the shifting forms came a shifting meaning. The first use in Eng. was an accusation; but since the old way of answering an accusation was to fight a duel, to accuse was the same as to summon to combat, to *challenge.*

chameleon.
It is easy to grasp the reason for the first half of this word, from Gr. *chamai,* on the ground, dwarf. It is harder to see why it was called Gr. *leon, lion* (whence also Eng. *leonine. Lion* is via Fr. and L., though the Gr. is probably from an Egyptian source.)
The *chameleon* can move its eyes independently. The color of its skin changes with its environment or mood; from this characteristic, the name is applied to changeable humans.

champ.
See champion.

champagne.
See camp; *cp.* drink.

champignon.
See champion.

champion.
In the days of chivalry, if a lady was offended, a knight at once took the field to defend her honor. By way of L. *campus,* field, whence LL. *campio, campion—,* fighter in the field (arena), the knight was called Fr. and Eng. *champion.* Since he remained in the field only if successful, the word took on its present meaning. The same locale for fighting is preserved in the term *field artillery. See camp.*

Champ, which is sometimes used as aphetic for *champion,* also means to chew. This word was earlier *cham,* and is probably imitative in origin. It is not related to *cham,* a variant of *khan,* from Turki and Tatar *khan,* prince. Samuel Johnson was called *the great Cham* of literature. (We may note that the Fr. and Eng. *champignon,* mushroom, is from the LL. *campinion—,* of the field.) For *chivalry, see cavalier.*

chance.
See cheat.

chancel, chancellor, chancery.
See cancel.

changeling.
Here is a word with a story invented to fit its sound. Obviously—said the superstitious English of Chaucer's day—this stupid child has been changed by the fairies; they've put one of their own instead. Everyone knows that the fairies' children seem at birth backward of speech, almost idiotic. *—ling,* of course, is the diminutive; *cp. gossip.* But it is the diminutive of OE. *change, chang,* a fool. The word, which occurs several times in the *Ancren Riwle* (*Rules for Anchoresses,* ca. 1225), was forgotten; then the story invented to explain what it seemed to mean, when a *fond* mother found that her child was a bit foolish. *See Thames; fond.*

channel.
See canon.

chant.
See canto, saunter. To *enchant* may mean either to sing a person into (a spell) or to sing against a person; *cp. trance.*

Eng. *oscines,* now a technical word for songbirds, earlier, those from whose song auguries were taken in ancient Rome, is from L. *oscen, oscin-,* from *ob-,* towards, + *canere,* to sing.

chaos.
See gas.

chap.
This is several words, mainly shortened from *chop; see color.* There is an old *chop,* to barter, AS. *ceapian,* whence Eng. *cheap,* and earlier *chapman,* dealer, whence Be a good *chap. Chop,* to cut, gives us *chip* and *chapped* (cracked) lips. Earlier *chapfallen* is now *chopfallen,* from *chap,* the lower jaw, which *chops* the food. The plural *chaps,* among cowboys, is short for Sp. *chaparejos,* leather breeches.

chapel, chaperon, chaplain, chaplet, chapter.
See achieve.

char.
See ajar.

character.
This first meant a distinctive mark or figure. (It was earlier *caracter,* the verb *caract,* from OFr. *caracter,* but L. *character* from Gr. *charakter,* an engraving instrument or the mark cut in by it. The Eng. word added the *h* in a later imitation of the Latin.) Then it was applied to a distinctive mark of the personality; gradually, to the sum total of such marks, each individual one being called a *characteristic,* from the Gr. adjective *charakteristikos.* Thus a *character-actor* is one that accentuates the distinctive or eccentric features of a figure, instead of giving a rounded portrait as of the whole man.

Reputation is from L. *reputare, reputat—,* to consider; from *re,* again + *putare, putat—,* to think—whence also *putative; cp. curfew.*

charade.
See aboveboard.

charcoal, charivari.
See ajar.

charity.
See whole. Charity was first an inner love; then a sign of this feeling; then an action or an act.

The L. *carus,* via Fr. via It. *carezza* from L. *caritia,* gives us Eng. *caress.*

Hence also (Gr. *charys*, thanks, grace; *eu-*, beautiful, well) the *eucharist*.

charlatan.
See aboveboard.

Charles' wain.
See arctic.

charm.
See trance.

charwoman.
See ajar.

chary.
The OE. noun *caru* gives us Eng. *care;* the adjective from this, OE. *cearig*, gives us *chary*. The words originally meant sorrow and sorry; from the meaning of sorrow, it shifted to trouble; then troubling yourself, taking trouble, hence taking *care*, being *careful*. The same shift is evident today in feeling *pains* in the side, and taking *pains*. The word *pain* shows the olden belief that our troubles are the result of our sins; we pay the *penalty*: *pain* is from Fr. *peine*, from L. *poena, penalty*. To *pine* is via AS. *pinian* from the same L. *poena;* its adjective, L. *penalis*, gives us *penal, penalty;* and, in close relation (from L. *paenitentia*, OFr. *peneance*, Eng. *penance;* and L. *paenitere*, present participle *paenitent*—, to be sorry, to *repent*) *penitent* and *penitentiary*, a place where you may *repent*. *See* also *trouble;* but be *chary* thereof.

chase.
See purchase.

chasm.
See casement.

chassis.
See casement, purchase. (*Chassis* is pronounced *shassy*.)

chaste, chasten, chastise.
See purchase, test.

chat.
See chatter.

chatter.
This is an imitative (echoic) word, like *twitter, jabber*. It is abbreviated in *chat*, which is also a milder word; and is reduplicated in *chit-chat*, a less consequential form of *chatting*.

chattel.
See achieve.

chauffeur.
This Fr. word for stoker was applied to the drivers of the early (esp. the steam-powered) automobiles. It comes by way of OFr. *chaufer*, from L. *calefícare*, from *calefacere*, to heat, from *calere*, to grow warm + *facere*, to make. The word *chafe* (as still, in *chafing* dish) at first meant to warm; then, to warm by rubbing, as the hands. Since often one might rub too hard, it came to mean to *chafe* the skin, to irritate. Similarly we caution someone, "Don't get hot!"

Caldron, cauldron, from ME. *caudron* is by way of OFr. *chaudron, caudron*, from L. *caldarium*, pot, from *caldus*, from *calidus*, hot. When you put things in a *cauldron*, watch your *calories!*

chauvinism.
Nicholas Chauvin, one of Napoleon's veterans, was so demonstrative in his patriotism that he became a bit laughable. Cogniard built a vaudeville around him (*La Cocarde Tricolore*, 1831), and the word slipped into the language. The use of *jingoism* in the same sense, and of a *jingo*, dates from a popular music-hall song of 1878:

We don't want to fight,
Yet by Jingo! if we do,
We've got the ships and we've got the men
And got the money too.

Hey Jingo! or *High Jingo!* had since the 16th c. been a conjurer's cry to make something appear; the opposite of *Hey presto!* Some suggest it was brought into Eng. by sailors, from *jinko*, the Basque word for God.

chaw.
See pylorus.

cheap.
See chap.

cheat.
In Eng. feudal law, if a man died without proper heirs, his possessions reverted to the lord. This transfer was called *escheat* (OFr. *escheoite*, from *escheoir*, from LL. *excadere*, to fall out, from *ex*, out + *cadere, casu*, fall Since all disappointed claimants know that they have been defrauded of their

just due, the word came to have its present meaning, *cheat.*

The L. *cadere, casu,* fall, gives us via LL. *cadentia,* whence OFr. *cheance,* Eng. *chance,* applied even by the ancients to the fall of dice (more honest, it seems, than the lord's lawyers!). Something of little concern, that can be left to the fall of the dice, is *casual;* those that fall in more serious battle are nonetheless *casualties.* An *occasion* (L. *ob,* whence *oc* + *cas*—) is that which falls in your path; from *occident*—, the present participle of *occidere,* we name the place where the sun falls at night, the *occident.* According to the position (falling together) of the stars, what befalls is (L. *ad,* to, whence *ac*) an *accident;* but *cp. affluent.* A *cheat* avoids taking *chances,* but may thank his lucky stars!

check, checkers, checkmate.

See exchequer.

cheese.

See cheesecake. The expression "He thinks he's the big *cheese*" seems to be Anglo-Indian, from Hindustani *chiz,* thing.

cheesecake.

Cake is an old Teut. word, ON. *kaka;* Du. *koek,* diminutive *koekje,* whence Eng. *cookie*—though the Eng. developed the delicacy by themselves; *cp. Dutch. Cheese* is even older, from AS. *ciese,* from L. *caseus,* whence Eng. *casein.* From the practice of the bright restaurants along Broadway, in New York's theatre district, of having a large cheesecake as the main window display, the word was transferred (in cinema and newspaper and theatre slang) to the main display in their publicity, *i.e.,* the lithe and lively legs of the actress. Rosamond Gilder (in the *Theatre Library Association Broadside*) reminds us that *cheesecake,* like little girls, is made of

> Sugar and spice
> And all things nice—

and points out that pretty Nell Gwyn, in the epilogue to a tragedy, protested:

> Nay, what's worse, to kill me in the prime
> Of Easter-term, in *Tart* and *Cheesecake* time!

Which perhaps kills two birds, but not to sing in a pie. First current use is credited to reporter Joe Marshland, of celebrities sitting cross-legged on a ship's rail.

Tart is three words. For the cake, from Fr. *tarte, see torch.* The adjective *tart,* sour, biting, bitter, is from OE. *teart.* The slang expression for a disreputable woman combines the sense of the bitter taste from the adjective with a shortening of *sweetheart* (a short *sweetheart* is a *tart*).

chemise.

See shimmy. The diminutive *chemisette* is also used.

chemistry.

The modern *chemist* prides himself on being scientific, on having cut off the mystic magic and mummery of the medieval *alchemist.* He has cut down but not escaped the golden taint; his name is aphetic for LL. *alchimista,* from Arab, *al kimiya.* Arab. *al* means the, as in *alcohol, algebra,* etc. The remainder of the word may be from Gr. *Chemia,* Egypt, from *Kym,* the Egyptian god of the Nile; it is at least influenced by Gr. *chein,* to pour, whence Gr. *cheimeia,* transmutation of metals, the goal of the *alchemist,* achieved by the *chemist.*

chenille.

See cloth.

cherry.

See peach.

cherrystone (clams).

See Appendix II.

chess.

See exchequer.

chestnut.

See castanet.

cheviot.

See cloth.

chew.

See pylorus.

Chianti.

See drink.

chiaroscuro.

(From the Italian, the first sound is k.)

Painting that presents high lights against deep shades; writing that contrasts quick joy with sudden sorrow, may be called *chiaroscuro*—from It. *chiaro* + *oscuro*, from L. *clarus* and *obscurus*. The L. *clarus*, bright, gives us *clarity;* and, via OFr. *cler;* Eng. *clear*. The L. *obscurus*, dark, remains in *obscurity*.

It. *chiaretto*, diminutive of *chiaro*, became in Fr. *claret*, diminutive of *clair*. The diminutive was applied (Fr. *vin claret*) to a wine neither white nor red, but yellowish or very pale red. Since the 17th c., however, it has been applied to red wines, and is the name of the color reddish-violet. *See red!*

chichevache.

This creature, destroyed (like the *dodo*) by a civilized world, was once. with its male mate, the *bycorne*, a popular *menagerie* figure. (Fr. *vache*, cow, came in by popular etymology; first it was *chichefache*, from Fr. *chincheface*, thin-face: a mythical creature with which to scare naughty children into being good.) Chaucer, in *The Clerk's Tale*, and Lydgate in a poem, ca. 1430, called *Bycorne and Chichevache*, give the true story. The *bycorne* was a monster fed only with patient husbands; hence he was always fat. The *chichevache*, his spouse, fed only on patient wives; she was always starving. [Note also that in the interlude of *The Four P's*, by Heywood, 1497?—1580?, the Palmer wins the prize for telling the biggest lie by declaring that he never knew, and in all his travels (a palmer is one that wears a palm as a sign that he has made the pilgrimage to the Holy Land) has never heard tell, of a woman out of patience. How times have changed!]

Dodo is from Port. *doudo*, stupid. *Menagerie* first meant the *management* of domestic animals. *Manage* meant to handle, from L. *manus*, hand, but was early influenced by *ménage*, from OFr. *mesnage*, from LL. form *mansionaticum*, *management* of the *mansion; cp. remnant.* And watch for the *chichevache!*

chide.

See child.

chief, chieftain.

See achieve.

chiffon, chiffonier.

This is directly from the Fr., meaning a place where women put away their odds and ends of cloth. *Chiffon* is also Fr., the diminutive of *chiffe*, rag—being originally an odd piece of cloth, esp. one used to add on a frill or other adornment to a dress. Hence, the present use for a very sheer cloth. *Cp.* cloth.

chignon.

This coil of hair at the nape of milady's neck, popular in various periods (1780, 1870, 1944) was worn in the 13th c. too, when it was Fr. *chaaignon*, a variant of *chainon*, link of a *chain*, from Fr., *chaine*, *chain*. (*Chain* is by that path from L. *catena, chain.*) The name is rather from its shape than from the fact that it is worn to bind the men.

child.

This word exists only in English; the other Teut. tongues use forms like G. *Kind; cp. racy. Child* is esp. the "fruit of the womb;" its direct source, OE. *cild*, is related to Goth. *kilpci*, womb; *inkilpo*, woman with child. Thus we have also *childbirth* (not babybirth); and while *child-wife* means a wife that is a *child*, *childwife* means a wife that's just had one. It is interesting, though *children* may not deem it relevant, to note that *chide* also exists only in English.

chill.

This word, early in Eng. (OE. *cele, ciele*) from the 9th to the 14th c. was the regular Eng word for *cold*. Then it dropped out of use for about two hundred years, replaced by *cold;* when it returned, it was applied esp. to the feeling of *cold* within the body, depressingly *cold*—though also in technical uses, as to *chill* cast-iron (note that in this application, it refers to the making of metals less hot, but also to the making of liquids less cold: Dickens' speaks of *chilling* beer at the fire.)

Chill, cool, and *cold* are really triplets. They come from the Teut. stem *kal*—. Via OE. *ciele* comes *chill;* via OE. *cald* come early *cauld* and *cold;* via the form *kol*— comes *cool*. The stem is cognate with L. *gel*—, whence Eng. *gelid; cp. aspic.*

Cold-blooded creatures are those whose temperature matches that of their atmosphere (fishes, reptiles); applied to persons, this means without passion, esp. of cruel or passionate acts performed without emotional stir, *in cold blood*. Thus of an angry man it is said (and was formerly believed) that his blood boils.

chimerical.

The terror has gone out of this word; its imaginary nature remains stressed. The *Chimera* (Gr. *chimaira*, she-goat) was a mythical monster, with three heads that darted flame, uniting the forms of the lion, the goat, and the dragon.

chimney.
The L. for a furnace or oven was *caminus*; a room equipped with one was *camera caminata.* This was abbreviated in LL. to *caminata,* which became OFr. *cheminee;* whence Eng. *chimney.* The word first meant a room with a fireplace; then (as the distinguishing feature of the room, the word was transferred) a fireplace; then by another transfer, the smoke-hole over the fireplace.

chin.
This was a widespread word: OE. *cin;* Gr. *genys;* Sansk. *hanus,* the lower jaw. Wagging the lower jaw is *chinning;* hence, talking a lot. *Chin-chin,* however, an oriental Eng. term for greeting, is from Chinese *ts'ing ts'ing.*

Chinaman's chance.
This is very indirectly related to the *Chinese.* Eng. *Chinaman* is a dealer in porcelain, *China* ware—which came to us via Pers. *chini.* The correlative expression, a bull in a *chinashop,* indicates the chance that a *Chinaman* has.

chink.
This word does not appear in Eng. before the 16th c. In the sense of a small crack or split, it replaced an earlier Eng. *chine,* with the same meaning, from OE. *cinu,* from the root *ki*—, to burst open. However, the *chink* of metal is an echoic word, and there may be some relation between the sound and the fissure—as the echoic word *crack* came also to mean a breaking, or the resultant split. *Cp. crunch; finance.*

chintz.
See cloth.

chip.
See color.

Chippendale.
See Appendix II.

chiropodist.
See pedagogue.

chisel.
See shed.

chit-chat.
See chatter. For reduplicated words, *see scurry.*

chivalry.
See cavalier.

chlorine, chlorophyll.
See element; yellow.

chocolate.
See vanilla.

choir.
See exquisite.

choleric.
See complexion.

choose.
See Valkyrie.

chop.
See color.

chord.
See prestige.

chore.
See ajar.

chorea, choreography.
See exquisite.

chortle.
See dismal.

chorus.
See exquisite.

chowder.
See clam.

Christ, christen, Christian, Christmas.
See cream.

chromatic, chromium.
See element.

chronometer.
See crony.

chrysanthemum.
See anthem.

chrysolite.
See carnelian.

chuckle.
See laugh.

chum.
See calculate.

church.
The Greeks had at least three words for this. One of them, *ekklesia,* first the general assembly of Athens, became Fr. *église,* church; in Eng. it abides in *ec-*

clesiastic, q.v. Another, *basilike,* gave us Eng. *basilica; cp. bazooka.* A third was Gr. *kuriakon doma,* house of the Lord (*kuriakon* is from *kurios,* lord. *Doma,* L. *domum,* gives us *domestic,* etc.; *cp. dome.*). From the first word of this, *kuriakon,* by a long trail over Teutonic Europe (the Romance and Celtic tongues took the word *ekklesia*) came Sc. *kirk* and Eng. *church.* The early spellings *chirche, circe,* made some think the word was from L. *circus;* it was first applied to the grounds and building, then (as a translation of *ekklesia*) to the members.

churlish.
See neighbor.

churn.
See cream.

chyle, chyme.
These two scientific terms are borrowed directly from the Greek, both from the root *ky—,* to pour. Both meant juice; Galen (Gr. physician of the 2d c. A.D.) used *chyme* of the raw juice, and *chyle* of the juice produced by digestion; we have followed his practice.

cicerone.
This word for a professional guide is drawn from the Roman orator, Marcus Tullius *Cicero,* because the constant flow of words of the guides reminded men of *Cicero's* eloquence (perhaps with tinge of satire). Cicero's eloquence led to his execution (43 B.C.) by the triumvirate that brought Julius Caesar to power.

cider.
You know the old story of the young man that saw a pretty girl, sat down beside her, and they sucked *cider* through a straw. And

Pretty soon the straw did slip;
I sucked sweet *cider* from her lip.
That's how I got me a mother-in-law,
From sucking *cider* through a straw.

Others achieve it in other fashions. If it drives you to strong drink, you are just going back to *cider,* which is from the Heb. *shekar,* strong drink, translated into Gr. *sikera,* then L. *sicera.* This became LL. *cisera,* and It. *sidro, cidro;* OSp. *sizra;* OE. *sither, sidre.* In references to the Vulgate, where it kept the meaning of strong drink, the form *sicer* was common in early Eng. (as *shicker* is slang for intoxicated); but the meaning softened very early to the fermented juice of apples, our *cider.*

The Heb. *shicker,* from which we borrow the word, is akin not only to *shekar* but to Heb. *shagah,* to go astray, to be intoxicated; whence also the Heb. word we have borrowed as the slang for one gone awry, *meshuga.*

cigar, cigarette.
See nicotine.

cilia, ciliary.
See supercilious.

cinch.
See precinct.

cinder, Cinderella.
See incinerator.

cinnamon.
See salary.

cipher.
This word is from Arab. *sifr,* empty, nil. When Arab. numerals came into European use, through Sp. *cifra,* whence Fr. *chiffre,* whence Eng. *cipher,* it came to mean to figure by use of the Arab. numerals; whence also *decipher,* to figure out. But the great addition to our earlier figures was precisely the *cipher,* O: from Arab. *sifr* came LL. *zephyrum;* Sp. *cero,* whence It. *zero,* whence Fr. *zéro,* whence Eng. *zero.* Thus *zero* is a doublet of *cipher.* *Zephyr,* a light breeze, is direct: Fr., from L., from Gr. *zephyros,* the west (mild) wind; hence, a light yarn.

circle.
See circus.

circuit.
See circus.

circumlocution.
See agnostic, refrain.

circumstance.
See state, tank.

circumvent.
See prevent.

circus.
The *Circus* (by which the Romans usually meant the *Circus Maximus,* largest ring, the great building at Rome) was first an oval or oblong building, encircled by rising tiers of seats; then (like the Greek theatre) an open arena; then

the company of performers. The word is L. *circus* (the accusative, *circum*, forms the L. prefix *circum—*, around, as in Eng. *circumference*: *ferre*, to carry, related to Eng. *fare* and AS. *ferian*, to carry, whence Eng. *ferry; cp. dollar*), from Gr. *kirkos, krikos*, ring—which remain in scientific Eng. in the *cricoid* (*krikos* + *-eides, -form*) cartilage and the prefix *crico—*. Thus a *"three-ring circus"* repeats itself.

A small ring was L. *circulus*, diminutive of *circus;* whence early Eng. *circul*, used of the heavenly courses in early astronomy. Through Fr. *cercle* (also from L. *circulus*) this shifted to ME. *sergle, cercle*, etc.; then the *i* was restored through Renaissance study of Latin, giving us the present spelling, *circle*. This is a rather *circuitous* course —though *circuit* comes from L. *circum—* + *ire, it—*, to go; *cp. obituary*.

Gr. *kuklos, kyklos*, circle, gives us Eng. *cycle*. But it also gives the name of the *Ku Klux Klan*, organized in Tennessee, 1867. *Clan* is *clann* in Gaelic, but *plant* in Welsh, springing from L. *planta*, sprout, stock, which of course directly gives us Eng. *plant, q.v.* Despite the secrecy, it is unrelated to *clandestine*, which via L. *clandestinus* comes from L. *clam*, secretly —which in turn is unrelated to the bivalve with tightly closed lips, Eng. *clam* (*q.v.*). But that's no *circus!*

cirrus.
See cloud.

citation, cite.
See exact.

citron.
See peach. The L. *citrus, citron*-tree, is from Gr. *kitron*, probably related to Gr. *kedron*, cedar (applied to a number of trees), and both probably of eastern origin. The *citron* seems to have come west from Media.

civet.
Shakespeare has Touchstone, teasing the country Corin in *As You Like It* (III, ii, 69), tell him that *"civet* is of a baser birth than tar—the very uncleanly flux of a cat." (Little did he anticipate that tar would supplant *civet* as a source of perfume!) The animal was probably named from the secretion (out of glands in the anal pouch); via Fr. *civette* from LL. *zibethum* and Gr. *zapetion*, from Arab. *zabad, zubad*. This is related to Arab. *zubd*, froth, *zubbard*, cream. The animal—and sometimes the person drenched in the perfume—was called a civet-cat.

civil, civilian, civility.
See police.

clack.
See cliché.

claim.
The simplest way of *claiming* what is your due is to cry out for it. And *claim* is (via OFr. *claimer*) from L. *clamare, clamat—*, to cry out, to declare aloud. Hence from the noun form, Eng. *clamor*. With the prefix *ex—*, out, we have also *exclaim* and *exclamation*. By transfer from the *claiming* to the thing *claimed*, the miner stakes his *claim*, his plot of ground.

clairvoyant.
See improvised.

clam.
If you've ever had a shellfish *clamp* down on your finger, you will understand that the word *clamp* is from a Teut. stem *klam—, klamb—*, to squeeze together. From the same source comes *clam*, which first meant anything that holds tight (as keeping one in bonds), then the bivalve, then a number of objects and instruments that resemble (in shape or in squeezing power) the *chowdery clam*.

The sound of striking the ground gives us several echoic words, *clamp, clump, stamp*. The *clump* of trees, which means a growth so close together as to seem one mass, is from ODu. *clompe, lump* (this shapeless mass is probably the origin of Eng. *lump*), ON. *klumba, klubba*, whence Eng. *club*: to *clump* is to tramp heavily and *clumsily* along (AS. *clum—* is related to *clam*, but *clumsy* is influenced also by ME. *clumsed*, from *clumsen*, to be numb), and Du. *klomp* is a wooden shoe made of a single lump of wood; also *clog*. To *stamp* on something was AS. *stempan*, to pound; whence also the milder *step*. Though this is of Teut. origin, it went into the Romance tongues, It. *stampare*, Sp. *estampar*, whence Sp. *estampida, stamping*, whence via its special use in Mexico our Eng. *stampede*. The Fr. form, *estamper*, to impress, came back to influence some meanings of the Teut., as in our postage *stamp* (which first was a note *stamped* on, as we now "cancel" the *stamp*).

Perhaps associated with the bivalve *clam* is OE. *clam*, mud; there was an early verb to *clamm,* to smear (also, from OE. *claeman,* to *cleam*); the interaction of these forms survives in the word *clammy,* like your hands when you are nervous. This seems to come from a root *kli—,* to stick: OE. *clam* and *claeg,* whence also Eng. *clay* and *cloam.* (Note that *loam* and *lime* are similarly related; and cognate with L. *limus,* mud, and L. *linere,* to smear, whence *liniment; cp. police.*) OTeut. *kli—* and *klaija—,* to stick, are cognate with Gr. *glia,* sticky; *kolla,* glue; *cp. crystal;* L. *glus, glut—,* bird-lime, whence Eng. *glue, gluten, agglutinate* (L. *agglutinare, agglutinat—,* to stick to: *ag, ad,* to). The process of sticking one simple word to another to form a compound (*e.g.,* pickpocket) is *agglutination.* Also see *clench; cp. cleave.*

Gr. *glia* may (through honey?) be related to Gr. *glykys,* sweet, which gives us many Eng. words: *glucose,* full of sweet; *glycerine; glycol* (*glycerine* telescoped with alcohol); and words combined with *glyco—* and *glycero—.*

Hot from the Fr. word for cauldron, *chaudière* (*cp. chauffeur*) we have *clam chowder.*

clamber.
See climate.

clammy, clamp.
See clam.

clamor.
See claim.

clan, clandestine.
See circus.

clang, clank.
See clench.

clap.
See clasp.

claptrap.
See catchpenny

claque.
See cliche.

claret.
See chiaroscuro.

clarity.
See chiaroscuro.

clash.
See clasp.

clasp.

This seems to be a corruption of *clapse,* an echoic word, like *clap, clash, smack, smash, splash.* The sound would be that of metal fitting together, as the *clasp* of a bracelet, or parts of armor. From the bracelet, the sense of embrace; *cp. brassiere.*

class, classic.

This word has shifted meaning many times, and has had various explanations. NED. traces it to L. *classicus,* of a *class*—then explains "of the highest *class.*" It adds that the word was later influenced by the sense of school *class,* referring to works taught in the *classes;* this meaning was dominant in the Renaissance. Later it was suggested that *classic* refers to anything representative of a *class,* that is, of a category, a generalization: the presentation of something universal.

Simply, it was used by the Romans (L. *classicus,* from Gr. *klesis,* division, from Gr. *kalein,* to summon) of the (six) divisions into which the Roman people were grouped; hence a *class* is a division, group, as in the school *classroom;* or as in the general *class* or category.

Aulus Gellius in the 2d c. A.D. used *scriptor classicus* as opposed to *scriptor proletarius* (*cp. world*); hence, *scriptor classicus, classical* writer, meant aristocratic. Later the sense was influenced by the idea "taught in the *classroom.*" Since the humanists thought only the Greek and Roman works were worth such study, we have the *classics.*

classification.
See defeat.

clause.
See close.

claustrophobia, clavicle, claw.
See pylorus.

Related to L. *claudere* is *clavis,* key; thus L. *conclave,* inner room, referred to persons locked together, as the cardinals when they name a pope. Hence, Eng. *conclave. See close.*

clay.
See clam.

clear.
See chiaroscuro.

cleave.

Considered as one, this is another word that means its own opposite. It is, however, really two distinct words: *cleave, clove, cloven, cleft;* and *cleave, cleaved.*

The former is OE. *cliofan,* from an OTeut. form *kleuth,* to cut with a blow (as wood along the grain); related to Gr. *glyphein,* to cut, carve; *cp. hieroglyphics.* The latter is OE. *clifan, clifian,* to cling, related to the OTeut. root *kli—,* to stick; *see clam.* This also developed an OTeut. *klimban,* to get up by grasping and clinging, whence Eng. *climb,* probably unrelated to *climax* and *climate, q.v.* But *klimban* had the noun forms *klith, cleofu, clifu,* whence Eng. *cliff* (sometimes *clift,* as it grew intertwined with *cleft,* from *cleave*).

cleft.
See cleave.

clench.
The basic Teut. root *kli—,* to stick (*see clam*) is prolific. By way of OE. *clinken* it gives us Eng. *clink,* to fasten; and through the OE. variant *clingen* a form now more common, *cling.* The Teut. causal form *klankjen* led to OHG. *chlankhan,* whence Eng. *clench,* a later variant of which is *clinch.* You *clench* your teeth but *clinch* a nail; *clench* your fists, then get in a *clinch.*

Clang, clank, clink, the sounds, are echoic words. The *Clink* was (first?) a notorious prison in Southwark, England; then *clink* was used of any hole of a jail; probably it combines the *clinking* sound and the *clinking* clutch of the chains.

clepsydra.
See drip.

clergy, clerk.
See shark.

clever.
One guess connects this word with ME. *cliver,* claw, as though it meant quick with the hands, handy. But earlier there was widely used Eng. *deliver* or *deliverly,* from LL. *deliberate,* freed from, therefore unhindered, adept. By pronunciation changes (? *d'liverly . . . gliverly . . . cleverly*) it reached the present form. This is perhaps more glibly than scientifically suggested; but to trace the history of many words one must indeed be *clever. Cp.* liberty.

clew.
See Europe.

cliché.
Used in Eng. to mean *stereotyped* (*cp. stern*), this word has a roundabout story. The three words used in English were first French. *Claque* imitates the sound of flat hands striking; then it was used of a group hired to applaud, in the theatre. The shorter sound, *clique,* was similarly later applied to a group of intriguers. (*Clic* and *clack,* in Eng., are used only for the sounds.) But Fr. *cliquer,* to strike, had a doublet *clicher;* then this was applied, as though a print were made with the flat of the hand, to the process of printing from a metal plate, of stereotyping. And the past participle, *cliché,* developed in Fr. and was thus borrowed in Eng., the sense of repeated time and again, hence trite.

click.
See cliché. *Clickety-clack* continues the imitation.

cliff.
See cleave.

climate.
Eng. *climb* (OE. *climban;* related to *cleave, q.v.*: *cp.* ON. *klifa,* to *clamber,* to stick) comes from the root *kli.* The same root is in the Gr. *klinein,* to slope, which led (Gr. *klima, klimat—*) to Eng. *climate,* as the Greeks thought that the earth sloped towards the north pole and that this affected the weather of the various regions. The relation between *climb* and *climate* is only by the root. However, the same Gr. word also led to (Gr. *klimax, ladder*) our *climax,* or ascending series—now often limited to the last rung, or the peak of the series. From the Gr. verb, by way of the L. *—clinare, —clinat—,* we have several words: *incline; decline; recline.* Also. from Gr. *proklitikos, pro,* toward + *klinein,* slope, we have Eng. *proclitic,* and via L. *clivus,* slope, the figurative *proclivity,* an *inclination,* tendency. *Declivity* has retained the literal sense.

climax, climb.
See cleave, climate.

clinch.
See clench.

cling.
See clench.

clinic.

This first meant a person confined to his bed, from Gr. *klinikos*, from *kline*, a bed, from *klinein*, to bend; whence also *incline, recline, decline* (to bend away, hence refuse). Then, from *clinic* baptism, it was used of a person that put off his conversion until his death-bed. As a namesake of mine remarks (O. Shipley, *Glossary of Ecclesiastical Terms*, 1872), "Aspersion was allowed of old in *clinic* baptism." (*See aspersion.*) The first use in medicine was in *clinic teaching*, the demonstration of the art of medicine at the bedside of the patient; thence, the current use.

Monoclinic crystals (e.g., mica, gypsum, borax, cane sugar) have one plane of symmetry. And *clino*— is a prefix, to mean sloping, as in *clinometer*, that measures *inclines;* but *clinoid* means shaped like a bed—on yours, I hope, "no pillow resigns and politely *declines* to remain at its usual angle!" *Cp.* climate.

clink.

See clench.

clipper.

This fast sailing ship (now used of airships as well) may be related to the common Teut. *clip*, to cut, as the boat cuts through the water. But it is pleasant to think that it may come down from *Cleopatra*. One of the early French ships of the type was called *Cleopatra-cum-Antonio*. Of course no one would keep a name like that; the sailors quickly shortened it to *Clipster;* then to *Clipper*—whence the name was given to the type.

clique.

See cliché.

cloak, clock.

See palliate.

clod.

See cloud.

clog.

See clam, log.

cloister.

See close.

close.

This word, in all its forms, is from L. *claudere, claus*—, to *close*. (The adjective has kept the *s* sound, as it has always been the final sound; the verb took on the *z* sound as it came from L. *clusa* via OE. *clusen, clysen*—then, through the influence of Fr. *clore, clos*, to Eng. *close*.) The diminutive of *close* (a confined place) is *closet*. Other derivatives are *closure, enclose, enclosure; include* (L. *includere* from *in, in* + *claudere*), *preclude* (L. *prae*, before; hence to shut off, shut out).

The first sense of the adjective was shut, hence also confined, (dungeon *close*); *secluded* (L. *se*— apart, + *claudere*); secret, stingy (*close*-fisted). Then, if all the spaces are *closed* up, things must be compact, or near; hence, *close* combat; cling *close;* and give your *close* attention.

A *recluse* is one *closed* away (L. *re*, back). To *close* altogether (L. *con, com*, together, used as an intensive; *cp. commence*) is to *conclude*. With which we do.

On second thought, let's look a little farther. Via LL. *claustrium* comes Eng. *cloister*. From L. *clavus*, nail (with which things are *closed*) because of its shape we name the spice *clove*. From L. *excludere, exclusus* (whence Eng. *exclude* and *exclusive*) via OFr. *escluse*, something that shuts out, comes Eng. *sluice*. To spike a gun, drive a nail in, was Fr. *enclouer;* coming into Eng. as *accloy*, this was used figuratively of stuffing so full the value was gone, that is, to *cloy*. And a *closed* section of a sentence is a *clause*. *See claustrophobia.*

closet, closure.

See close.

cloth.

This is an old Teut. word, AS. *clāthe*, though the vowel may be influenced by *Clotho*, one of the three Parcae, the Fates, that weave human destinies. *Lachesis*, (from Gr. *lagchanein*, to give by lot) spins the thread of life; *Clotho*, (from Gr. *clothein*, to wind thread) holds the distaff; and *Atropos*, (from Gr. *a*, not + *tropos*, turning: the unyielding) cuts off the thread and ends the life. The names of the types of *cloth* were more variously developed. Often the place from which the material came was added to the word *cloth*, then the latter dropped: thus *Calicut cloth*, whence *calico*. Similarly, *cambric*, from *Cambray*, in Flanders: there is a more recently developed cloth called *chambray*: *cashmere*, from *Kashmir; cheviot*, from the *Cheviot Hills; cretonne*, from *Creton*, Normandy; *damask*, from *Damascus* (whence also *damascene* or *damaskeen* steel and swords, the latter influenced by the idea of keen); *denim* is *cloth de Nimes*, France; *duffel*, whence *duffel bag*, from *Duffel*, near Antwerp; *frieze*, from *Friesland* (the architectural *frieze* is, from Fr. *frise*, from *Phrygia*): *gauze*, from *Gaza* in Palestine; *jersey* (the material and the garment made therefrom) from *Jersey*, England; *lawn*, from *Laon*, France; *lisle*, from *Lille*, France; *madras*, from *Madras*, India; *melton* (as in *melton* jacket) from *Melton Mowbray*, hunting place in Leicestershire, England; *muslin*, from It. *mussolina*, a diminutive, from *Mosul*, Mesopotamia; *nankeen*, from *Nankin*, China. *Silk* is via OE. *sioloc*, from L. *sericus*, from L. from Gr. *Seres*, the eastern race (Chinese?) that supplied the ancient Europeans; later, therefore without change from *r* to *l*, the same source via OFr. *sarge* gave us *serge*. Also, *sleazy*, from *Silesia; worsted*, from a parish in Norfolk, England; *poplin*, from Fr. *popeline*, from It. *papalino*, first made at Avignon, a *papal* seat; *tulle*, from *Tulle*, France.

So many *cloths* have been named from places that cities are suggested for some that have other origin: thus *buckram*, from *Bokhara*—but from Fr. *bougran*, from It. *bucherame*, from *bucherare*, to make holes in (Fr. *bouche*, mouth), from its coarseness; *satin* via Arab. *zaytuni* (Marco Polo called it *Zaitun*), from Chin. *Tzu-t'ing*, a great medieval seaport, now Chuanchow—but *satin*, from It. *setino panno*, bristly cloth, from L. *saeta*, bristle; *gingham* is not from *Guincamp*, France, but from Malay *gingan*, striped. *Dimity* is not from *Damietta*, Egypt, but, from It. *dimiti*, plural of LL. *dimitum*, from Gr. *dimitos*, of double thread, from *di*, two + *mitos*, thread. Here also *twill*, earlier *twilly* (AS. *twi*, two), translating L. *bilix*, from *bi*, two + *licium*, thread; *tweed* is a mistake for *tweel* (the Sc. sound of *twill*) influenced by the river *Tweed*, near which it was made. *Drill*, earlier *drilling*, from G. *drillich*, translates L. *trilix*, of triple thread. *Cp. biscuit.*

Baldachin, *baldaquin*, a rich embroidered stuff, LL. *baldakinus*, may be from *Baldacco*, Italian name for *Baghdad*. But it was also spelled *baudekin*, and is at least associated with Eng. *bauderia*, liveliness, and *bawdry*, finery, also (from *bawd*) loose bahavior.

Alpaca is the animal, Sp. *alpaco*, from *al*, the + Am. Indian *paco* ?, red. *Broacade* is from Sp. *brocado*, from *brocare*, to pick. *Chenille* is little caterpillar (*q.v.*), from L. *caniculum*, diminutive of *canis*, dog. *Chintz* is, from *chints*, plural of *chint*, from Sansk. *chitra*, pied (*cp. pie*). *Cotton* is just Sp. *qoton*, from Arab. *qutn*, the native name of the material. *Crape, crepe* is OFr. *crespe*, *crisp*, curled, from L. *crispus*, *crisp*, cognate with OHG. *rispen*, to curl. *Georgette* is from *Mme Georgette de la Plante*, a 19th c. French modiste. *Pile* is from L. *pilus*, hair, whence *pilosus*, hairy; from this via Fr. *peluche* comes *plush*. And *velvet* is from Fr. *veluet*, diminutive of *velu*, shaggy, from L. *villus*, nap; whence L. *villosus*, full of nap, whence Eng. *velours*. *Crinoline* is from L. *crinus*, mane + *linum*, *linen*, flax; thus Eng. *linen*. *Khaki* (first the *cloth*, then the color) is from Hind. *khākī*, dusty: the English Guide Corps in India, about 1850, dirtied their white uniforms to make them less visible. *Mohair* changed its last syllable from the hair in the cloth; it is from Arab. *mukhayyar*, the chosen, past participle of *khayyara*, to prefer, applied to a cloth of goat's hair. The same word, through OFr. *mouaire*, gives us *moire*. *Pongee* suggests a fine quality, from North Chinese *pun-chi*, own loom. *Taffeta* via OFr. *taffetas* is from Pers. *taftah*, woven, from *taftan*, to twist, to spin. *Voile* (pronounced *voyl*, from Fr. *voile*, pronounced *vwahl*) is the same word as *veil*, from L. *velum*, sail, curtain, covering; whence Eng. *reveal* (L. *re*, back). Other terms for *cloths* are more figurative. *Gabardine* is from *gaberdine*, pilgrim's cloak, from OFr. *galvardine*, from MHG. *wallevart*, whence G. *wallfahrt*, pilgrimage, from *wallen*, to wander + *fahren*, *fahrt*, to journey, to *fare* ("pilgrims" were often just wandering beggars); but *see* also *cabal*. *Nainsook* is from Hin. *nainsukh*, from *nain*, eye + *sukh*, from Sansk. *sukha*, delight: delight of the eye. *Seersucker* is from Pers. *shir u sukkar*, milk and sugar, said of a striped *cloth*. There is dispute as to the origin of *corduroy*. It might be, from Fr. *corde du roi*, the king's *cloth*, but it seems to have existed earlier in England than in France. It might be from the (ME.) proper name, *Corderoy*, king's heart. A final suggestion is that it is a shortening of *colourderoy*, from Fr. *couleur du roi*, the king's color. At any rate, it was early deemed a kingly *cloth*.

Among leathers, *Morocco* and *Cordovan* (*Cordova,* Spain) show their origin; both, while the Arabs flourished there. Of the great Umayyad prince *Attab,* however, from whom a quarter in Baghdad was named, and from that quarter came also *attabi,* whence *tabi,* a striped cloth, all that is left in Eng. is the *tabby* cat! *Cp. tabby.*

cloud.
Those floating masses of vapour in the sky were named for their most frequent or most pleasant shape, the *cumulus; cp. accumulate.* For the OE. *clud* meant a rock, or hill; basically, a mass of earth—from it comes also Eng. *clod.* Applied figuratively to the heaped mass in the sky, technically called *cumulus* (L. *cumulus,* mound,), it was used so commonly in this sense that it lost its first, literal meaning. The *cirrus* cloud is from *L. cirrus,* curl, fringe; the word is used also in botany, and gives us the combining prefix *cirr—, cirrh—* (the second being from the mistaken thought that the word was not Latin but Greek. Like the *calends—cp. dickey*—it does not exist in Greek.) The *nimbus* is probably a telescoping of L. *imber,* rain, and L. *nebula,* cloud, whence Eng. *nebular* and *nebulous.* For *stratus,* see trophy.

clove.
See salary, close.

cloven.
See cleave. From the Greek goat-foot gods (Pan and the satyrs) came the Christian demons, hence the devil betrayed by his *cloven* feet.

clover.
The poet Gay gaily pictures *clover* as "the *cloven* grass;" but its background is rather within-doors. It is (from the shape) OE. *claver,* from AS. *claefre,* the clubs at cards. Hence one that wins a good game is said to be *in clover!*

cloy.
See close.

club.
See clam.

cluck.
See laugh.

clue.
See Europe.

clump, clumsy.
See clam.

coach.
See vanilla. It now is accepted, however, that *coach* is via G. *Kutsche,* from Hung. *Koszi,* the town where the vehicle was first developed. A *coach* in studies or athletics is one who carries you along; the meaning is drawn by figure from the stage-*coach.*

coagulate.
See absquatulate. The past tenses of L. *coagulare, coaxi, coactus,* play no part in the college cry *Brekecoax coax coax!* This frequent roar from cheering squads at college games is from the chorus of the frogs, in Aristophanes' *Frogs,* 450 B.C.: *Brekekekex coax coax,* cries Dionysus, outcroaking the frogs as he is ferried over the Styx on his journey to bring Euripides back to earth. (The *coax* of the cry is in two syllables, even though the shouters are trying to *coax* the team along. Our verb *coax* was first a noun, *cokes,* a fool; then the verb, to make a *cokes* of. This is perhaps a shortening of *cokeney; see cockney;* or from Fr. *cocasse,* silly, which the French also derive from *coq, cock*: an echoic word; *cp. coquette.*) But just as a watched pot never boils, you can't *coax* a fluid to *coagulate. See ache.*

coalesce, coalition.
See world.

coast.
See accost.

coax.
See coagulate.

cobalt.
See element.

cobble.
See vamp.

cobra.
This is (via Port. *cobra de capello,* snake with hood; *cp. achieve*) from L. *coluber,* snake. Eng. uses *coluber* as the name of a genus of snakes; Cowper has a poem *Colubriad,* the epic of a snake. A snake-like object, or a cunning person, is *colubrine.* The Fr. form of this word, *couleuvrine,* applied figuratively to a long cannon, gives us Eng. *culverin;* the underground channel, *culvert,* may be another figurative use. The Eng. *culver,* pigeon, is from AS. *culfre,* without any further

known ancestry, even though snakes suck pigeons' eggs.

cobweb.
This is the *web* (*see ballot*) of a *cob,* or ME. *coppe,* spider. Sometimes the *web* was called *attercop,* by transfer: this is really the full name of the insect: OE. *attor,* poison + *cop,* top, head (or *cop,* cup). This may have influenced the name of the snake, *copperhead,* which is derived from its color. As this snake, unlike the rattler, strikes without warning, it became the symbol of a surprise blow, and was used, during the War between the States, of a Northerner that favored the South, a *Copperhead. Cp. copse.*

cock, cockade.
See coquette.

cockatrice.
See crocodile.

cockboat.
See vanilla.

cockney.
This term for the complacent city-dweller (Londoner) is traced in several directions. One derives it from Fr. *acoquiné,* to make a *coquin* of (*coquin* is a villain). Others play upon the townsman's ignorance of the country: a city lad, hearing a horse, said "The horse is barking." He was told "a horse neighs." Soon after, he cried "Oh! the *cock neighs!*" Winning admission to the NED is the suggestion that it comes from ME. *coken-ey,* cock's egg. This term was apparently applied to a dwarfed or malformed egg; then to a spoiled child; in the 19th c., to the citizens of London.

cocksure.
There are several stories behind this word. Weekley wonders whether it is not just a euphemism for *God sure!* There is an Irish *coc,* manifest, and indeed the Irish often are! The word *cog* is *coc* in Welsh; whence it is suggested that it means as sure as *cogs* fit into one another. But there is an older *cog,* or *cock* of a gun, from Fr. *coche,* still earlier meaning the notch of a bow for the arrow: only if the missile be set *"cocksure"* will it reach its target. One is reminded of the *Devil's Dictionary* definition of positive: mistaken at the top of one's voice.

cocktail.
Drinkers have it that this word is derived from its rousing effect, as of a horse ready for the race: it *cocks* up the tail. It is an American word, and perhaps from the racetrack. But back in the 18th c., Antoine Peuchaud of New Orleans concocted a drink he served in a wide bottomed cup, Fr. *coquetier,* whence Eng. *cocktay.* By transfer from the container to the thing contained, the *cocktail* is now transferred to the imbiber. Another story traces it to a Mexican girl, *Xochitl,* whose father sent her with the drink to the king; the king drank it, and married the girl, giving the drink her name.

cocoa, cocoanut, coconut.
See vanilla.

coda, code, codex.
See bible.

coel—, coeli—, coelo—.
These various suffixes, found in Eng. scientific words, are from two different sources. The more frequently used are from Kr. *koilos,* hollow; from this, we have *coeliac, coelenterata.* But L. *caelum,* sky, was long written *coelum;* whence *coelometer, coelonavigation* (not in the heavens but by the stars).

coffee.
See drink.

coffer, coffin.
See suffer.

cogent.
See absquatulate.

cogitation.
See exact.

cognate.
See exact.

cognition, cognizance, cognoscenti.
See quaint; science; knick-knack; scourge.

cohort.
See court.

coign.
See coin.

coin.

This word is borrowed from the French (Fr. *coin,* from L. *cuneum,* wedge). Originally, in French, it meant a wedge; in Eng. *quoin* means the wedge-shaped stone in an arch, and *coign* means a projecting corner: these are but different spellings of the word. But the word *coin* came to be used of the die for stamping money (from the shape of the die); in this sense it was taken into English. Then it was applied to the design stamped; finally, to the metal that was stamped, our *coin. Cp. sterling.*

colander.
See dickey.

cold, cold-blooded.
See chill.

cole.
See alcohol.

coliseum.
See colossal.

collage.
See remorse.

collar.

L. *collum* means neck; hence, *collere, collat—,* to neck, to embrace, whence OFr. *collier,* neckpiece, whence Eng. *collar.* When a man was knighted, it was the custom to strike him gently on the neck; hence L. *accolare* (*ac,* from *ad,* to), whence Eng. *accolade. See cat-o'-nine-tails.* Note that *collate,* to bring together, is *conferre, collat—,* from *con, col,* from *com* + *ferre, lat—,* to bring. The gathered Lives of the Fathers, read in the monastery, were the *collation;* the term was then applied also to the light meal that followed this. *Collateral* is from L. *com* + *latus, later—,* side; whence also *lateral* and (from the adjective *latus,* wide) *latitude.*

collate, collateral, collation.
See collar.

colleague.
See college.

collection.
See legible.

college.

By way of AS. *wis,* whence Eng. *wise,* we get *wisdom.* (The abstract suffix *—dom,* as also in *kingdom, halidom,* is from *do* + an earlier abstract suffix *—moz,* which in OE. became *—m,* as in *stream.*) For *intelligence* (from the present participle) and *intellect* (from the past), *see legible.* Though akin to this pair, a *college* cannot supply these qualities. L. *intel, inter,* among; L. *col, com,* together + *legere,* to choose: L. *collega* (whence Eng. *colleague*) was a partner in office; L. *collegium,* a partnership, an associated group. The word was first used for such associations, as the Apostolic *college,* the *college* of cardinals, the *college* of heralds, the electoral *college.* Then it was applied, at a *university,* to a group, founded to advance mutual study in a particular field, or to provide bettter lodgings, or to help indigent students. Thus a *university* usually had several *colleges.* From the fact that some *universities* had but one *college,* however, perhaps from the lapse of the others, the two words became interchangeable. Current use tends to limit *college* to an institution conferring the "undergraduate", bachelor, degrees; whereas a *university* will have more varied fields of instruction, professional schools; and will confer the "graduate", master and doctor, degrees. For *degree* and *graduate, see issue.* Our *university* is from L. *unum,* one + *vertere, versus,* turn; *cp. conversion.* L. *universum* gives us *universe,* turning as one; L. *universitat—,* Fr. *université,* whence Eng. *university,* was applied to the whole group associated in a task: *universitas magistrorum et scholarium,* the whole body of masters and students. From its early pronunciation (as the name *Clark* remains, and the word *clerk; cp. shark*) we have the resounding cheers for the *varsity* team. (Save through the antics of the cheer-leaders, there is no connection with *arsey-varsey,* for which *see scurry.*)

collodion, colloid.
See remorse.

collyrium.
See alcohol.

cologne.
See colonel.

Colombia.
See Appendix II.

colonel.
The man in charge of a *column* of soldiers. (Fr. *colonel,* from It. *colonnello,* from L. *colonna, columna,* Eng. *column*). The Eng. pronunciation is from OE. *coronel,* from Sp. by dissimilation. *Colony* is not land taken by a *colonel,* but comes from L.*colonus,* a tiller, from *colere, cultus,* to till—from which we also derive *cult, culture, cultivate.*
Yet a *colonel* may be a man of *culture.*
The L. *colonia, colony,* gave its name to the German city of *Cologne;* whence, from its manufacture there, our *cologne* (first, *eau de Cologne,* water of *Cologne.* We still speak of toilet water.)

colony.
See colonel.

colophon.
See Appendix II.

color.
L. *color* led to Fr. *couleur,* whence Eng. *colour;* the American *color* returns to the source.
Originally, there was a relation between *coloring* something and attempting to get it out of sight: L. *color* is akin to L. *celare,* to hide; *cp. cell.*
Color came into Eng. about the 14th c.; the earlier Eng. word was AS. *hiw,* Eng. *hue*—which first meant form (Goth. *hiwi,* form), then appearance (Sansk. *chhāvi,* skin, complexion), then *color.* Today we use *hue* of finer divisions of the primary *colors.*
To *hew* is common Teut., AS. *heawan,* cognate with L. *curtus; cp. cutlet; hay;* let the *chips* fall where they may! (A *chip* is a little *chop,* both imitative words, referring at first to wood. Then the lamb *chop. Chip* was used to mean a chessman, about 1650; the round *chips* came two centuries later.) The *hue and cry* is echoic. *See* chap.

Colorado.
See States.

colossal, colosseum, colossus.
Herodotus spoke of the statues of Egypt as Gr. *kollosos,* gigantic figure; whence Eng. *colossus* and the adjective *colossal.* From its size, the amphitheatre of Vespasian at Rome was called the *colosseum;* whence, any *coliseum.*

colt.
This first meant a young ass (Sw. *kult,* strong boy); in the *Bible,* it is used of a young camel. The origin is unknown. For the *colt* revolver, *see Appendix II.*

colubrine.
See cobra.

Columbia.
See States.

columbine.
See nasturtium.

columbium.
See element.

column.
See colonel.

comb.
See quaint.

combat.
See debate.

combustible, combustion.
See urn. (L. *com,* together, the *b* being added for easier sounding).

come.
See welcome.

come-at-able.
See atone.

comedy, comic.
See encomium.

comely.
A *comely* lass is good to look upon, but far from buxom, *q.v.* OHG. *chumig* meant weak, sickly; G. *kaum* means with difficulty; in Eng. the word early developed the sense of delicate; hence, pleasing.

comfit, comfort.
See confectionery.

comma.
See paragraph.

command.
To put something into one's hand (literally, a written order; figuratively, as a charge) was in L. *mandare,* from *manus,* hand, + *dare,* to give; *cp. date.* Hence also Eng. *mandate;* the *mandated* islands. With *com,* together, as an intensive (*see commence*), this early became L. *commendare, commendat—,* whence Eng. *commend, commendation;* also *recommend. Commend* first meant to give in trust, as a man *commends* his soul to

God—hence, to offer as worthy of acceptance, then, to praise. *Demand* (to take from the hand), *remand* (L. *re,* back), *command,* are later formations. To *reprimand* is influenced by these forms, Fr. *réprimander,* but from L. *reprimere, repress—,* to *press* back; whence also *repress.* L. *premere, press—* is the source of *press; express, cp. plot;* and, via Fr. *preindre, preinte* and *empreindre,* Eng. *print* and *imprint.* Also a cold *compress, compressed* air, and the clothes *press.*

commence.
When persons act together there is more power to them. Hence L. *com,* together, is sometimes used as an intensive (*cp. command*). Thus *commence* (with an extra *m* for good measure) is via OFr. *cumencer,* It. *cominciare,* LL. form *cominitiare,* from L. *initiare, initiat—,* to *begin.* Hence also *initiate;* and from the adjective L. *initialis, initial* (first, hence esp. the first letter). *Begin* is common Teut., AS. *beginnan;* this suggests an earlier *ginnan,* which has not been found; but later, *begin* sometimes lost its first syllable and was used (with or without an apostrophe) as *gin* and *gan.* To *start* was first to leap forward: AS. *styrtan;* its frequentative, AS. *steartlian,* gives us Eng. *startle.* The end of one's studies is the *commencement* of one's livelihood days.

commend.
See command.

commissary, commission, commit.
See mess. *Commission* meant, in succession: authority to act together for a prescribed purpose; the group thus authorized; the warrant for such an agent, as a *commission* in the army; the matter thus entrusted to an agent; the pro rata sum allowed to such an agent. *Commissary* is from LL. *commissarius,* one entrusted, from L. *commissus,* sent together.

commode, commodious, commodity.
See accommodate.

common.
See immunity.

commotion.
See mute.

community, commute.
See immunity.

compact.
See propaganda.

companion, company.
See calculate.

compel.
See pelt

competent.
See irrelevant.

complain.
See saxophone.

complement, complete.
See foil.

complex.
See complexion; *cp.* plot.

complexion.
This word has a *complex* history (L. *com,* together + *plectere, plexus,* to weave. Hence, a structure of fibres closely interwoven, as the solar *plexus.* Similarly L. *plicare, plicat—,* to fold, gives us *complicate, implicate,* and by way of OFr. *emplier* both *imply* and *employ,* to fold in, to involve. *Simplicity* is L. *sine,* without + *plica,* fold.). It was used of the weaving together of the characteristics of a person, in the personality. To the middle ages, these were:

(1) The four qualities: hot, cold, dry, and moist. Their mixture (L. *temperare,* to mix, *temper; cp. tattoo*) gives us a man's *temper,* or *temperament.* (Through the tendency of a word meaning a scale to slide to one end of that scale, *temper* usually today means a bad *temper.*) Of things, this gives us their *temperature.* L. *temperare* is related to *tempus,* time, whence *tempestas,* season—then esp. the stormy season, whence Eng. *tempest.*

(2) The four *humors, humours* (L. *humidus,* moist, *humid; humiditas, humidity*), or bodily fluids: blood (*sanguine,* from L. *sanguinis,* bloody, ruddy), phlegm, choler (yellow bile), and melancholy (black bile). Thus one may be of a *sanguine* disposition, or *phlegmatic,* or *bilious,* or *choleric,* or *melancholy* or *melancholic* even to *melancholia.* [And by the same scale-slide in the opposite direction, *humor* now usually means good *humor.* Note that *melancholy* is from Gr. *melan,* black + *chole,* (whence *choler, cholera*), bile. Thus the name of the reformer *Melanchthon* is a translation into Gr.

of his G. name, *Schwartzerde,* black earth. Thus Wolfgang Mozart changed his middle name from Gr. *Theophilus* to L. *Amadeus,* God-loving, G. *Gottlieb.*] Since a man's nature is often revealed by the color of his face, *complexion,* the individual weaving of these assorted possibilities, came to its present meaning. *Cp. element*: bismuth.

From L. *plicare, plicat—,* to fold, come a number of words, *e.g., explicit, implicit, duplicity* (*see diploma*); via Fr. *plier* come *pliant* and *pliable. Replica* is from L. and It.; from the Fr. comes *reply,* a figurative use of Fr. *replier,* to fold back. Thus *retort* first meant to twist back; *cp. torch.* (It is also suggested, however, that *simplicity* comes from L. *simplex* from *simplus,* whence Eng. *simple,* akin to *simul,* like, and *singuli,* one. By a humorous noun ending, we have Eng. *simpleton.*)

complicate.
See complexion; *cp.* plot.

compliment.
See application.

compline.
See bull.

complot.
See plot.

compose, composition.
See pose.

compound.
See pose. A *compound,* an enclosure, is from Malay *kampung,* enclosure—possibly prepared for by Port. *campo,* field, *campaign,* countryside, etc., from L. *campus,* field. *Cp. camp.*

comprehend, comprehensive.
See surrender.

compress.
See command.

compromise.
When persons (groups, nations) cannot come to terms, they may send a few men forward together, to act in their behalf: (L. *com,* together; *pro,* forward, in behalf of—whence *pro-ally,* etc.; *mittere, miss—,* to send—whence *missive, mission, missile*: L. *missilis,* adapted to sending or throwing; L. *mission—,* the act of sending, then the ones sent, then their establishment or their task; *missionary;* LL. *missivum,* something sent) *compromise* was, earlier, the *promise* together to abide by an agreement made by such *arbitration*; then, the agreement itself. Since the final action is always less than either side desires, to *compromise* (oneself, then by extension, anyone) is to put oneself to the risk of being lessened; hence, to put into a disadvantageous position. Your word sent forth (of a deed to follow) is your *promise.*

The *arbiter* is the one that goes to see what he can do, from L. *ad,* to + *bitere, betere,* to go, to seek; whence the verb *arbitrari, arbitrat—,* and Eng. *arbitrate.*

comptroller, compute, comrade.
See calculate, curfew.

conceal.
See helmet.

concede.
See ancestor.

conceit, conceive, concept, conception.
See recipe.

conch.
The Gr. *cogche,* mussel, was hard to pronounce. It came into Eng, as *cockle*-shells all in a row. In L. it became *concha;* in Fr. this became *conche* and later *conque;* in Eng. by this path was an early *conche,* then *conch*—used esp. of the spiral shell of the larger molluscs, and also of this shell used as a horn (as when we hear Old Triton blow his wreathed horn). From the shape of the *conch,* it is used in slang (*conk*) to mean head (in England, nose), or a blow thereon; *cp. vanilla.* Triton, son of Poseidon, Gr. god of the sea, may get his name from the *trident* he always carries (Gr. *tri— don;* L. *tri— dent—,* three toothed; *cp. east*). *Conch—* is a frequent combining form. For *mussel, see muscle.* The *honk-honk* of the automobile and the goose is echoic.

conclave.
See claustrophobia.

conclude.
See close.

concoct.
This word originally meant to digest (to cook together, from L. *con, com,* together, + *coquere, coct—,* to *cook.*

Cook came into Eng. first as a noun, AS. *coc,* from L. *coquus.*) *Concoction* first meant digestion: in the medieval physiology this had three stages: the first *concoction* was the extraction of the fluids from the food; the second, the turning of the chyme (*q.v.*) into blood; the third, secretion.

With the lapsing of such ideas, the other sense of the word grew prominent: the preparation together of a number of ingredients, as for a stew, or a medicine; then, figuratively, of an elaborately but artificially worked out scheme or play, etc.: a *concoction,* something "cooked up".

concord.
See prestige.

concrete.
The *creatures* all around come from L. *creare, creat—,* to *create; cp. creole.* The inceptive of this is L. *crescere, cret—,* to grow; *cp. excrement.* Things that have grown together (L. *con, com,* together) are Eng. *concrete;* this first meant connected in growth; then continuous (its opposite being *discrete*: L. *dis,* apart). The mixture of pebbles, gravel, sand, etc. with lime or cement (*see shed*) is called *concrete* because it grows together into a single mass; *cp. attract.* Then the word was used in logic of qualities considered as growing together with their things: red head as opposed to redness; redness, withdrawn from the *concrete* head, is *abstract* (for which, *see attract*).

concussion.
See discuss.

condemn.
See damage.

condiment.
See recondite.

condition.
See verdict.

conductor.
See duke.

cone.
See sterling.

Coney Island.
See canary.

But that story may be folk-etymology, as some say it was earlier *Conyn's* Island, after a person.

confectionery.
A *confection* is something specially prepared, from L. *conficere, confect—,* to prepare, from L. *con, com,* together, + *facere,* to make. The Fr. word was *confire, confiss—,* to preserve, to candy; whence a fancy *confectionery* proprietor may call himself a *confiseur.* By older English paths, OFr. *confits* changed to Eng. *comfit,* a sugar candy (usually with a nut enclosed). The word *comfit* is sometimes linked with *comfort,* which is from L. *confortare,* to strengthen, from *com + fortis,* strong. *See defeat.*

conference.
See suffer.

confine.
See finance.

confirm.
See infirmary.

conflagration.
See flamingo.

confluence.
See affluent.

conform.
See like.

confound.
See dumb, futile.

confront.
See effrontery.

confuse.
See dumb, futile.

confusion.
See dumb.

congenial.
See racy.

conglomeration.
See globe.

congregation.
See congress.

congress.
Gradual (L. *gradulis,* from *gradis,* step; *cp. centigrade,* by 100 steps) progress is the method of democracy, effected by *congress* (*gradior,* I step, whence *congredi, congressus,* to step together). From the group (L. *grex, gregis,* herd) that goes together came the noun (L. *congregation—*) *congrega-*

tion, retained in Eng. as a religious *flock*. Similarly L. *pascere, past—*, to feed, gives us *pastoral* in rural application, but *pastor* in the religious. Milton's *pastoral* poem "Lycidas" combines the two senses.

The *pastor* is related to Pan, god the feeder, god of the flocks and fields, hence nature everywhere. *Cp. diapason; pan.*

Our *flock* has a double origin. As a tuft of wool (ON. *floke*, OHG. *flohho*, Fr. *floc*, from L. *floccus*) it is related to *flake* (as in snow*flake*; other senses of *flake* relate it to *flay* and Du. *vlak, flat*, which, as a level place, came to mean floor, dwelling). As a *flock* of sheep, tended by the *pastor*, it is found only in the Scand. languages (ON. *flokkr*, Sw. *flock*, Dan. *flok*) and is a variation, by metathesis, of *folk*. A good place to observe the *folk*-ways is in the *Congressional* Record! *See issue.*

conject, conjecture.
See subject.

conjugal, conjunction, conjunctivitis.
See subjugate; *cp.* yokel.

conjure.
This was originally to swear together, from L. *con, com*, together, + *jurare*, to swear; *cp. jury*. A *conjuration* was thus a solemnly binding oath among several persons; hence, a conspiracy. But it was also used of a solemn call upon something sacred; hence of the summoning of spirits or other supernatural powers to do one's bidding; with the lapse of belief in this form of spiritualism, the word was applied to the performance of the *conjurer*. In early times, the pronounciation *cun'jer* was favored for every sense; when the sense of performing "magic" tricks became dominant, the sound *con joor* developed for the sense of binding by oath, or appealing strongly, to *adjure*. (Against appeals to the powers of darkness, pious Christians would keep their fingers crossed—the sign of the cross to ward off evil; or to imply that they don't mean it, the Lord should keep off the devil, as when telling a lie.)

conk.
See vanilla.

connect, connection, connexion.
See nexus.

Connecticut.
See States.

conscience.
See remorse.

conscript.
See shrine.

consecrate.
See anathema.

consecutive.
See pursue; *cp.* set.

consensus, consent.
See ascend.

consequence, consequential.
See pursue; *cp.* set.

consider.
Astrologers used to examine the stars, to see how their coming together (at a person's birth) indicated the future. Hence L. *considerare, considerat—*, to observe carefully, from *con*, from *com*, together + *sidus, sider—*, star. And one that has pondered well is likely to be *considerate* (which first meant giving thought, then more esp. giving thought for others). There is also the scientific term *sidereal*. *Cp. disaster.*

consist.
See tank.

consolation, console.
See insolent.

consommé.
See prompt.

consonant.
See absurd.

conspire.
See inspiration.

constable.
See marshal.

constant.
See tank.

constellation, consternation.
See disaster.

constituent, constitute.
See season.

constrain, constrict.
See prestige.

construct, construe.
See destroy.

consul, consult.
See council.

consume, consummate, consummation, consumption.
See prompt.

contact, contagion.
See attain; deck.

contain.
See tennis.

contamination.
See attain; deck.

contemplate.
See temple.

contemporary.
(L. *con, com,* together). *See* pylorus.

contend.
See temple, tennis.

content, contention, contentious, contentment.
See tennis.

contest.
See cantankerous.

context.
See text.

contiguous.
See deck.

continent.
See tennis.

contingency, contingent.
See deck. Contingent first meant coming together, thus happening (by chance); then, as a noun, one's lot, what comes to one when spoils etc. are divided; then, the due proportion of something, esp. of troops to be sent.

contort.
See torch.

contraband.
See ban.

contract.
See distraction.

contradiction.
See verdict.

contrast.
See tank. (LL. *contrastare,* to stand against).

contribute.
See tribulation.

contrite.
See terse.

controller.
See calculate.

convalescent.
The L. *con, com,* together, is an intensive here. The inceptive ending, L. *—escere,* to grow, makes this mean to grow *valid* again; *see infirmary; cp. verdict.*

convene, convenient, convent, convention.
See council; prevent.

converge, conversant, conversation.
See conversion.

converse.
See advertise; conversion. *Converse* the verb (whence *conversation*) is from L. *conversari,* to turn about with, hence to talk with; *converse* the adj. is directly from *convertere, conversus.*

conversion.
From L. *vertere, versi—,* turn, and its derivatives come a great number of Eng. words, of which *conversion* (L. *con,* together, among) has both a religious and a chemical application. A *convert* and a *pervert* (L. *per,* through, whence through and through, thoroughly, whence away entirely, to no good end: *per*dition, *per*ish) indicate further forms. *Conversation,* originally the act of living or being (turning about) among others, came to mean physical intimacy: the law still speaks of "criminal *conversation*"; only in the 17th c. did *converse* come to mean to talk together. *Verse* (influenced by AS. *fers* and Fr. *vers*) indicates the turning at the end of a line (in early writing, prose was written on and on without space between words until the width was filled; poetry—hence *verse,* turned—moved for its specified feet, then began a new line.) *Conversible* and *convertible* both were used until the 19th c.; today, we speak of a *convertible* sedan (*q.v.*). The

right hand side of a book is the *recto* (L. *right*); turn the page and you have the *verso*. From their position as axis of the body, we name the *vertebra*. The axis of the sky, then the tip of the pole (zenith) is the *vertex* (L. *vertex, vertici—*); hence a line drawn up to it is *vertical*. As it is on such a line that the earth, that all cosmic matter, spins (according to Descartes) a *vertex* or *vortex* came to mean a rapidly spinning body—whence the *vorticists* of modern art. The effect of such spinning is *vertigo*, which may also be felt on looking from a *vertiginous* height. A variation of *vertere*, to turn, is LL. *vergere*, to bend, from which we have *diverge, diversion; converge*. *Verge*, from this source, has blended in its history with *verge* (L. *virga*, rod; related ? to L. *virgo*, maiden), still used for the male organ of an invertebrate. This rod, perhaps originally a phallic symbol, was carried in procession as badge of authority, a mace; then "within the *verge*" was used as meaning within the (turning) boundary of the power of the Lord High Steward (12 miles around the King's court). It was gradually used of the limits or edges of that territory; then "on the *verge*" came to mean on the brink of a place or of an action.

The frequentative of *vertere* was *versare*, with adj. *versatilis*; from these forms we have *versatile*, rapidly changing, then adapting oneself to changing circumstances; also *versed; conversant*. There are many more, but to continue would *divert* (L. *di*, from *dis*, two ways, apart, away) us too long [*divers, diverse, diversion* and *divertissement*—that which turns us away—*diversified; advert* (*cp. advertise*); *animadversion*—L. *anima*, mind—etc.] from the main flow of this book.

convertible.
See conversion.

convex.
See vehicle.

convict, convince.
See victoria.

convolution.
See volume.

cook.
See concoct.

cool.
See chill.

cop, copper.
See copse, element.

copperhead.
See cobweb.

copse.
This word is made familiar in the semi-classical remark of Macbeth's sentry, on beholding Birnam Wood march toward Dunsinane: "Cheese it, the *copse!*" (Incidentally, the play marks an early use of camouflage.) The word is short for earlier *copys*, which is a variant of the still used *coppice*. Both *copse* and *coppice* first meant a grove of small trees grown esp. for cutting, from OFr. *copeiz, coupiez*, LL. type *colpaticium*, something cuttable, from LL. *colpare, colpat—*, to cut with a blow, from LL. *colpus*, earlier *colapus, colaphus*, from Gr. *colaphos*, blow, cuff.

There was also an early Eng. *cops, copse*, meaning fetters or hasps, whence (by Grimm's Law and popular etymology) probably *handcuffs*. Indeed, *cuff* on the sleeve may be from this source, or from LL. *cuphia*, a variant of *cappa*, a *cap, cape*, hood with cloak.

There is a *cop*, an early form of *cup*, earlier both *copp* and *cuppe;* from its shape this came to mean a top or summit. The *cop* on the street corner may be derived from *copper*, as in

Brass button, blue coat,
Couldn't catch a nanny-goat!

but *copper* in that sense seems to have come from *cop*. Its source is probably the verb *cop*, to catch, from an obsolete *cap*, from OFr. *cape* (The legal L. for a writ was *capias*: you may seize) from L. *capere, capt—*, to take *captive*, to seize; *cp. achieve, manœuvre*. The metal *copper* is from L. *cuprum* (which first occurs in 301 A.D.) from *Cyprium aes*, the Cyprian metal. *See cobweb*.

copulate, copulative.
L. *copula* is a bond, from *co—*, together + *apere, apt—*, to fit, whence Eng. *apt; cp. lasso*. Hence via L. *copulare, copulat—*, to join, come Eng. *copulate* and the *copulative* verb. Via Fr. *couple* this gives us our Eng. *couple* and the *coupling* devices on a train.

coquette.
The *rooster* (so called because he *roosts*, from AS. *hrost;* common Teut.)

is, by imitation of his favorite call, also named *cock*, as in L. *coccus*. From the shape of the *cock's* head (with the comb) come several words: the *cock* of a gun, a tap; the *cockade;* the *coxcomb*, fool—who was adorned with a *cock's* comb. The *cocker-spaniel* was trained to chase the wild variety, or *wood-cock* (note that this is a bird; not the *woodchuck*, from Am. Indian *wejack*, corrupted). A Fr. diminutive of *coq*, *cock*, is *coquet;* the feminine is *coquette*, a woman that displays herself like a strutting cock. (Among all animals save man, it is the male that preens and flirts.)

Flirt, used in the 16th and 17th c. of a slight jerk (to *flirt* a fan) has been traced to AS. *fleardian*, to trifle, whence AS. *fleard*, a bit of folly, whence *? fleer*. It was often spelled *flurt;* and has been associated with Fr. *fleureter*, from *fleur*, *flower*, to flit from flower to flower, as does the bee. Certainly the comparison is often made by the poets, *e.g.* Ben Jonson:

> I'll taste as lightly as the Bee
> That doth but touch his flower,
> and flies away.

cord.
See prestige.

cordial.
See prestige; drink.

Cordovan, corduroy.
See cloth.

core.
See scourge.

corn.
See barley.
A small *corn* (AS. *cyrnel*) is a *kernel*.

cornelian.
See carnelian.

corporal, corporeal, corps, corpse, corpulent, corpuscle.
See leprechaun.

correct.
See royal.

correspond.
See spouse.

corrode, corrosion.
See rodent.

corruption.
See rote.

corsair.
See hussar.

corset, corslet.
See leprechaun. Note that *body* was used in the 17th c. for the tight part of a dress; *cp. bodkin.*

corvette.
See curb.

corybantes, corymb, coryphée.
See exquisite.

cosmetics, cosmic, cosmopolitan.
See police.

costume.
See customer.

cotangent.
See deck.

cotton.
See cloth.

couch.
This was first a transitive verb, meaning to put in a place, to lay down, as to *couch* a lance; but by the 14th century it had acquired the intransitive sense, to lie in a place. It is via OFr. *coucher*, earlier *colchier*, from L. *collocare* from *col*, *com*, together (used intensively; *cp. commence*) + *locare*, *locat—*, to place; whence *location; cp. lieutenant; allocate* (L. *al*, *ad*, to); *dislocate*, to put out of place, etc. The literal sense can be seen behind such figurative phrases as *couching* his remarks in no uncertain language.

cough.
This word, from an AS. form *cohhian*, like *laugh* (*q.v.*), is of echoic origin. So is *hoot;* also *hoop* (Fr. *houper*), as a call to dogs and horses. This was later rendered as *whoop;* whence first *hooping-cough* and the now prevalent *whooping-cough*.

The *hoopoe* is named from its cry, more closely approximated in the L. name for the bird, L. *upupa*. The *hoop* that girls roll and their elder sisters wear in *hoopskirts* was common Teut., OE. *hop*. For the type of *hoop* used in the dress, *see furbelow*.

council.
This word was for a long time interchangeable with *counsel;* the differences

today are mainly from deliberate distinctions drawn in the legal field. *Council* is from L. *concilium*, an assembly, from *con, com*, together, + *calare*, to call. (*Call* is common Teut., ME. *kallen*, to cry loudly, to chatter; cognate with the Aryan root *gar—*, to chatter.) Counsel is from L. *consulere, consult—*, to deliberate; whence also *consul* and *consult*. There is also a L. *consilium* from this verb; which, however, is from L. *com*, together, + *salire*, to leap; hence, to get into a huddle; *cp. somersault*. This may be traced to a Sansk. root *gar—*, to go. Thus a gadabout is likely to be a chatterbox; and we can see why *counsel* and *councils* are often confused and confusing.

If those that have leapt together finally come together (L. *convenire, convent—*, from *venire*, to come) in a suitable fashion—from the present participle *conveniens, convenient—*, comes Eng. *convenient*, when the desire and the means come together—after they thus *convene*, they may come forth with a *covenant* [*convenant*, the earlier form, was lost, then revived; Emerson in his poem *The Visit*, ca. 1840, uses *convenance;* then lost again. A *convent*, first a (church) assembly, similarly lost the *n*—as still in place names like *Covent Garden*, the famous London playhouse; the restored form *convent* was for serious purposes retained], such as the two *covenants* the Jewish and Christian Lord God made with man.

counsel.
See council.

count, counter.
See calculate.

counterfeit.
See defeat.

countess, country, county.
See calculate.

courageous.
See supercilious.

course.
See cutlet.

court, courtesan, courtesy.
The young ladies of a *court* may not be chickens, but the *court* was once a poultry-yard. The word is from OFr. *court*, from L. *cors*, from *cohors, cohort—*, an enclosed space, from *co*, together + *hors, hort—*, garden, whence *horticulture*. Hence the body of men trained in one field, a *cohort*. Enclosed fields belonged to rulers; so that the word gradually came to refer to the seat of a king, or the place whence he dispensed (or dispensed with) justice. The woman of the *court* was a *courtesan;* her frequent behavior changed the meaning of this word. *Court plaster* (from LL. *plastrum*, from Gr. *emplastron*, from *emplassein*, to daub over, from *plassein*, to mold; *cp. plant*) was that from which the *court* ladies cut the little patches with which they adorned their faces and shoulders; sometimes these were decorative designs, sometimes they showed the family or political party. *Courtesy* is, of course, behavior such as should grace a *court*.

couvert.
See overture.

covenant, Covent Garden.
See council.

Coventry (to send to).
See boycott.
The word *Coventrized* is being used to mean almost wiped out, as *Coventry* by German bombs, November 15, 1940.

cover.
See curfew; overture.

covert.
See overture.

cow.
This word was very common Teut., OE. *cu*. The plural ME. *kun, kyn*, gives us *kine*, which is the general word for cattle of either sex; but outside the Teutonic forms the word was used for both cow and bull: Sansk. *gav—;* Gr. *bous;* L. *bos, bov—; cp. Bosphorus*. There is no etymological relation between the *cow* (*cu*) and its *cud*, which is from AS. *cwudu*, related to a Teut. root *kli—*, to stick; Gr. *glia*, sticky; *cp. clam*. And *see mutton*.

coward.
A turn-tail. The suffix *—ard* (OFr. *—ard, —art;* G. *hart*, bold) originally implying recklessness, came to indicate excess, or disrepute: *drunkard, laggard, bastard*. [OFr. *bast* is from LL. *bastum*, packsaddle, sometimes used as a bed. Thus the word is short for "son of a packsaddle", as one might say "son of a gun"—and should be a warning for *hitch-hiking* girls. *Hitch*, earlier also

hatch and *hotch,* first meant to jerk, as in Fr. *hocher la tête.* From moving jerkily ("*Hitch* your chair over a little") it came to mean to hobble; then, to fasten (a horse) with a hobble; then, to fasten; finally, to catch on something (as Miss Mitford says, in *Our Village,* "*hitching* our shawls in a bramble"). To ask for a *hitch* combines the newest and the oldest senses. By *hitching* his waggon to a star, Emerson meant that the farmer allied himself with the universal forces (*i.e.,* gravitation, when going downhill). *Hike* meant first to tramp; then, as any *hiker* will testify, to drag along. The word *hike* is cognate with *hitch,* so that to *hitch-hike* is in a sense reduplicated, *q.v.*]

The stem *cow—* in *coward* is not related to the animal, but from OFr. *coe—,* from L. *cauda,* tail; related thus to *caudex* whence *codex; see bible.* A *coward* is thus also one that does not keep the *code.* Note that the timid hare in the medieval beast tales (*cp. monkey*) was named *Coart.*

coxcomb.
See coquette.

coy.
See decoy. Fr. *coite,* earlier *quetus,* from L. *quietus, quiet.* This is the past participle of *quiescere, quiet—,* to grow still; whence also Eng. *quiescent.*

cozen.
See barnard.

crab, crabbed.
See cancel; penthouse.

crack.
See chink, crunch, swivel.

crackle.
See swivel.

craft.
This was a common Teut. word for strength, AS. *craeft,* G. *Kraft.* In English only it came to mean skill, then occupation (at which one was skilled), as in *craftsman, woodcraft.* From clever, *crafty* came to mean cunning. Boats of small *craft* (power) were called small *craft,* then just *craft.*

cram.
The word *crumb* was spelled *crum* until into the 19th c.; it seems to spring from a verb meaning to rub; thus a *crumb* is a tiny bit rubbed off. There is an OE. *crimman, cram, crummen,* to put in—which gives us Eng. *cram,* as when a hungry man *crams* his gullet; this is related to OHG. *krimman,* to press, to scratch; ON. *kremja,* to squeeze—hence to Eng. *cramp,* as in *cramped* quarters or in your stomach; *cp. luncheon.* There seems to have been the basic sense of to claw, also to squeeze, to strain; hence *cramp* also means a grappling-iron and other such instruments, and is linked with *clamp,* akin to *clench, q.v.* Other words in this group are *crimp,* (to put a *crimp* into something), *crump,* and its causal *crumple* (like *tramp,* also echoic, and *trample*). *Crump* meant first the sound of a blow; then the blow itself, then the doubling up or bending in as from a blow; hence, the cow with the *crumpled* horn. There is also a *crump* that is purely echoic, from the sound of pigs or horses *munching*—*munch* and *crunch* are similarly echoic words.

cramp.
See cram, luncheon.

crane.
See buck.

crank.
When you *crank* a car, you use a bent bar; there is something bent behind every use of the word. There was an old verb, *crankle,* to zig-zag; it survives in the variant form *crinkle.* About 1600 the word *crank* was used for a twist of speech, as in Milton's "Quips, and *cranks,* and wanton wiles" (*L'Allegro*); about 1850 it was used for an eccentric idea or act; about 1880, for a person with a mental twist. This use survives. Some of the meanings of the word have been influenced by G. *krank,* ill—which is probably of the same origin; one sign of illness is the body bent in pain.

crash.
See crunch.

crass.
See hard.

crater.
One conception of the volcano (*q.v.*) makes it the forge of the gods; the Roman blacksmith god Vulcan works at his fires there. Another picture presents it as cooking the devil's broth; this thought is preserved in the *crater,* from Gr. *krater,* bowl, mixing vessel, from Gr.

kera—, kra—, to mix. Closely allied is Gr. *keramos,* clay for the potter, whence our *ceramic* ware. L. *cera,* Gr. *keros,* is wax; whence Eng. *cerement* and *cerecloth* (waxed cloth for wrapping the dead). This has no connection, however, with *ceremony, q.v.,* nor with *cerebrum,* (related rather to Gr. *kara,* head) and its diminutive *cerebellum*—which have been called our inner *tweedledum* and *tweedledee.*

(*Tweedledum* and *tweedledee,* whom Lewis Carroll has made familiar—*Alice In Wonderland,* 1865; *Through the Looking-Glass,* 1871—were first derisive imitations of the sound of the flute, used in the rivalry between the musicians Bononcini and Handel, 1725.)

cratometer.
See hard.

cravat.
See Appendix II.

craven.
Here again, two explanations. The original word was *creaunt* or *cravant.* It is therefore not one that *craved* (AS. *crafian*) his life from the opposing soldier; but, from OFr. *cravante,* from L. *crepare,* present participle *crepans,* to break: one that was overcome and broken. In The *Ancren Riwle* (*Rules for Anchoresses,* ca. 1225) a person overcome is pictured as crying *"craven, craven"* in submission.

crayfish.
See penthouse.

cream.
This word had originally no connection with cows or milk. It is first, from AS. *crisma,* from OFr. *cresme,* from L. *chrisma,* consecrated oil, used in anointing, from Gr. *chrisma,* anointing, from *chriein,* to anoint. The *Christ* is the anointed one, Gr. *Christos* —whence *christen, Christian, Christmas* (*mass* is from L. *Ite, missa est,* Go, it is sent away: *dismissed*: the final words of the service). But L. *cremor* meant the juicy ooze of boiled corn (from L. *cremare, cremat—,* to burn, whence Eng. *cremation*); this became LL. *crema,* and was used in the term *cremor lactis, cream of milk,* then shortened to *cream.* The two developments merged in the modern word.

The common Teut. word for *cream* (surviving in G. dialect, *Kern*) changed, through AS. *cyrin,* into the Eng. *churn,* wherein *cream* is made butter.

There is also a Gr. *krema,* to hang, which through the Fr. may have given us the military term *crémaillière,* and directly gives us Eng. *cremasters,* the technical term for suspenders.

crease.
This word is a doublet of *crest,* from ME. *creaste,* from OFr. *creste,* from L. *crista,* ridge. And a *crease* or fold was originally spoken of in terms of its projection, like a ridge on a roof or a forehead, or the *crest* of a wave.

create, creature.
See creole.

credit.
See miscreant.

cremation.
See cream.

creole.
This term was at first applied to all West Indians whose fathers were white. They were usually raised for service in the household, and treated with more favor than the full-blooded natives. The word *creole* is Sp. *criollo,* diminutive of Sp. *criado,* foster-child, from L. *creare, creat—,* to *create, created.* Eng. *create* and *creature* (thing *created*) are thus of the same root; and the word in a way is the father's admission of his paternity.

creosote.
This liquid, when first discovered (by Reichenbach, 1832) was found to have strong *antiseptic* powers. It is named from this fact, by (an ungrammatical) coinage from the Gr. *kreo—,* from *kreas,* flesh, + *soter,* saviour. The doctrine of salvation is sometimes (not very often!) referred to as *soteriology.*

A *septic* tank is where things putrefy, from Gr. *septikos,* from *sepein,* to spoil; hence *antiseptics.* There is no relation to *September* (L. *septem,* seven); *cp. month;* nor to the division of an Irish clan, the *sept*—which is a fancy spelling of *sect; cp. set.*

crescent.
See excrement.

crest.
See crease.

cretin.
See nincompoop.

cretonne.
See cloth.

crib, cribbage, crime.
See garble.

cricket.
The insect, with the diminutive ending *—et*, draws its name from the sound, *krik*. The game draws its name from the bat that was used (originally curved like a hockey stick, with the ball bowled along the ground). Its origin is uncertain: not that of *crutch; cp. criss-cross;* perhaps via Du. *krick* from Fr. *criquet,* also *croquet* (our game), diminutive of Fr. *croc,* shepherd's staff, our *crook.* The whole is from a Teutonic stem meaning bent, or pronged—whence also *crooked,* and the man that does not go straight, the *crook.* Its first course may be echoic of the sound of prongs striking stone; there is thus Fr. *croquer,* to click the teeth, to chew; whence the *croquettes* (again the diminutive ending) that we eat.
Contrarywise, as the *crook* would feel, from the sportsmanship associated with the English game comes the reproving remark "That's not *cricket!*"

cricoid.
See circus.

crimp.
See cram, luncheon.

crinkle.
See crank.

crinoline.
See cloth.

crisis.
See garble.

crisp.
See cloth: crepe.

criss-cross.
The alphabet, in the medieval hornbook, was preceded by a *cross;* thus it made the *Christ-cross row.* The reduplicative tendency of tongues changed this to *criss-cross,* which no longer need be the religious *cross. Christ* is L. from Gr. *Christos; cp. cream.* Similarly *Messiah* is from Aram. *mshīhā,* from Heb. *māshīah,* from *māshah,* to anoint. *Cp. conjure.*
Cross is from AS. *cros,* from L. *crux, cruci,* whence Eng. *crucify,* to make into a *cross.* The meaning of the adjective is from the opposite directions of the two sticks; hence, also, *across,* from AS. *a,* on + *cross.* Hence, to be at *cross-purpose;* and *cross,* angry. L. *cruci—* also, gives us *crutch,* AS. *cryce,* from the shape of the top; the *Crutched Friars* wore a *cross,* as did the *Crusaders*: Prov. *crozada, crossed,* whence Fr. *croisade,* whence Eng. *crusade.*

critical, criticism.
See garble.

crocodile.
This word is directly from Gr. *crocodeilos,* gravel-worm, applied since Herodotus (5th c. B.C.) to the giant reptiles of the Nile. The word took many forms, among them *cockadrill*—which led to its being confused with its mortal enemy, the *cockatrice.*

While the *crocodile* still exists, the *cockatrice* died with medieval natural history. It is a translation of Gr. *ichneumon* (also used in Eng.) from *ichneuein,* to track, from *ichnos,* footstep; the animal seeks out and devours the eggs of the crocodile. And *cockatrice* is from L. *calcatrix,* similarly from L. *calcare,* to track, from *calx, calc—,* heel; *cp. recalcitrant.* Confused also with the *trochilus* (bird that picks the *crocodile's* teeth; *cp. troche*), this creature was in imagination bird, beast, then reptile; pictured as a water-snake, it came to be identified (from the first syllable of its Eng. name) with the *basilisk; cp. bazooka*: a monster born of a *cock's* egg, and which kills by its mere glance. By a figure of speech easily accepted, the *basilisk,* killing with a glance, was used of a woman, esp. a wanton woman; hence also the *cockatrice* (as in Dekker's *The Guls Hornebooke,* 1609, where, in the chapter "How a Gallant Should Behave Himself in a Play-house", a house by the waterside is recommended, the better "to shun shoulder-clapping and to ship away your cockatrice betimes in the morning". Thus the creature has come back to the water; and she probably sheds *crocodile tears.*) The term *crocodile tears,* for false semblance of sorrow, rises from the notion that the *crocodile* moaned to attract its victims, and shed tears while devouring them.

crone.
See carrion. The word is not related to *crony, q.v.*

crony.
This is 17th c. university slang. Samuel Pepys speaks of a *chrony* of his; the word is from Gr. *chronios,* contemporary, from *chronos,* time, whence *chronometer,* time-measurer: the fancy word for a watch, or the word for a fancy watch.

crook, crooked.
See cricket.

crop.
This is a common Teut. form, with the basic meaning of swelling, or lump, or bunch. In OE. *cropp* there were two meanings, the *crop* (lump in the throat) of a bird, and the top or head of a plant. The second of these has developed into the *crops* that are gathered at harvest. The *crop* of a whip is the thick handle. As a noun, there is also the echoic sense, of the sound *crop crop* of an animal *cropping* grass. The sense of *cropping* comes from the noun: to cut off the *crops* is to *crop.* This also has been extended in use, as to *crop* one's hair, cut it short on the head. Whence also—as may you not!—to come a *cropper.*

Harvest is AS. *haerfest,* autumn, picking time; cognate with L. *carpere,* to pick; Gr. *karpos,* fruit. To *carp* is thus to pick on someone, though this association may have altered an OE. word akin to ON. *karpa,* to talk loud, to boast. The boaster often comes a *cropper.*

croquet, croquette.
See cricket.

cross.
See criss-cross.

crouton.
See crust.

crowd.
This word, OE. *crudan,* not found early in the other Teut. tongues, was first a verb, meaning to press: Don't *crowd* me! From the idea of pressing or squeezing through came the present application to a *crowd,* as at any parade.

There is a medieval fiddle called a *rote* or a *crowd;* OFr. *rote,* from the Celtic: Ir. *cruit;* Welsh *crwth.* Sometimes this is referred to, in English also, as a *crwd*—a rare instance of *w* as a word's only vowel.

crozier.
See lacrosse.

crucifix.
See fix.

crucify.
See criss-cross.

cruise.
The Dutch (*q.v.*) were great mariners, rivals of the English upon the seas, which they frequently crossed. And the Du. for cross (*see criss-cross*) was *kruis,* which gives us Eng. *cruise.*

crumb, crump.
See cram.

crumpet, crumple.
See luncheon.

crunch.
This word, earlier *craunch,* is a nasal variation of *crash,* an echoic word, softer than the sharp split of *crack. See cram, knick-knack.*

crusade.
See criss-cross.

crust.
The hard outer part of the bread (as opposed to the crumb, which breaks off; *cp. cram*) was named *crust* from OFr. *croute, crouste* (the diminutive gives us the *crouton* we put in soup), from L. *crusta,* hard shell, whence the family of the *crustaceans.*

crustacean.
See crust.

crutch.
See criss-cross.

crwd.
See crowd.

crypt, cryptography.
See element: krypton; grotesque.

crysanthemum.
See flower.

crystal.
The ancients knew little of the structure of *crystals* (*cp. clinic*); they were impressed with their clarity. The word (gradually applied to other forms, as the structural similarity was recognized) was first applied to snow and frost: Gr. *kryos,* frost (whence the combining form Eng. *cryo—,* as in *cryolite*); Gr. *krystallos,*

clear ice, whence Eng. *crystal.* Contrasted to Gr. *krystallos* is Gr. *kryptos,* hidden, from *kryptein,* to hide; whence Eng. *cryptic, crypto—; cp. grotesque.*

The opposite of *crystalloid* is *colloid,* from Gr. *kolla,* glue, + *—eides,* —form; *cp. remorse. Collogue,* however, seems a corruption of Fr. *colloque,* from L. *col, com,* together, + *loqui,* to speak, whence also *colloquy; cp. agnostic.*

cucking-stool.
See ducking-stool.

cud.
See cow.

cue.
The L. *coda* (*cp. bible*) via OFr. *coe, keue, cue,* became Fr. *queue,* which in the sense of tail (pigtail, long braid of hair) is spelled *queue* also in English—but also *cue.* One suggestion as to the origin of *cue,* a hint, is that it is a word at the "tail" of one speech, suggestion to the next actor that it is his turn to begin. The word, however, is not thus used in French. Early Eng. prompt-books used *Q,* which has been explained as the abbreviation of L. *quando,* when (as we wait for the drinker to "say when"). In the game of billiards, *q.v.,* the stick was first called the billard, the tapering end or tail of it was the *cue.* We now apply the word to the whole stick.

Also *see* barbecue.

culpable.
See culprit.

culprit.
This word passed through the mouths of the law clerks, hence was strangely altered. In the medieval English court, if a prisoner pleaded "Not Guilty," the prosecutor would answer: *"Culpable: prest,"* meaning: "He is guilty; I am ready to prove it." (*Culpable* is from L. *culpa,* fault. *Prest, pret,* is from LL. *praestus,* ready, from *prae,* before + *esse,* to be.) In court records this was abbreviated *cul. pret.*—whence, *culprit,* the man to be tried.

cult, cultivate, culture.
See acorn; colonel; cutlet.

culverin, culvert.
See cobra.

cumulus.
See accumulate; cloud.

cunning.
See king.

cup.
See scourge.

cupidity.
See psychoanalysis.

curate, curative, curator.
See accurate.

curb.
The *curbstone* is not primarily to *curb* a horse; yet each is by roundabout from the same source: via. Fr. *courbe* from L. *curvus,* bent; L. *curvare, curvat-,* to bend; whence also Eng. *curve;* the diminutive *curvet;* and, via It., *corvetto.* The ship, *corvette,* however, is named because of its shape, from L. *corbis,* basket. The way to *curb* a horse was to *curb* (bend) his neck by means of a bit and bridle; hence the general use in the sense of checking. The *curbstone* (in England usually *kerb, kerbstone*) is both *curved* at the top and serving to check flow of water, etc., from roadway to sidewalk (the ancient Roman roads were raised in the center-path). The other senses of the word follow from these, as when you *curb* your impatience.

cure.
See quarry; *cp.* accurate.

curfew.
The line *"Curfew* shall not ring tonight" reminds us of a custom renewed in the World War II nightly dimout. Medieval lights had to be put out at the ringing of an evening signal bell, the order Cover fire! (Fr. *couvre-feu,* whence Eng. *curfew*) being brought to England by the Norman conquerors. (Fr. *couvrir,* from L. *cooperire,* from *co(m),* intensive + *operire,* to cover; *fire* (AS. *fyr,* G. *feuer,* Fr. *feu;* cognate with Gr. *pyr,* whence Eng. *pyromaniac;* L. *purus,* cleansed as by fire, *pure.*)

But *purity* is a complex matter, and may lead on strange paths. Thus L. *purus* came to mean clean, by whatever process. Trees and vines are cleaned by lopping off excess, by pruning (*cp. propaganda*); hence *putare, putat—,* to prune. But if you prune away excess you also arrange what's left; and you must plan the pruning. Thus *putare, putat—* came to mean to reckon, then to estimate (whence Eng. *compute,* to reckon together; *putative;*

imputation; reputation) to consider. The original meaning was not lost, however; combined with L. *am*, from *ambo*, both, around, it gives us Eng. *amputation*, a lopping off, often necessary to keep the body clean (as when gangrene sets in). Thus cleanliness, though next to godliness, is often next to filth.

Another common way of cleansing is by washing; whence L. *purgere*, Eng. *purge;* and L. *puteus* is a well. But let the water stand, or let something stay too long soaked in water, and it becomes L. *putidus*, stinking, or L. *puter, putrid—*, rotten, whence Eng. *putrid; cp. polecat.* To make or grow rotten is Eng. *putrefy* (L. *ficere* in compounds, from *facere*, to do, to make). The L. *putrere, putrid—*, to rot, has the inceptive form *putrescere, putui;* whence Eng. *putrescent*, which it would take fire and water to make *pure*.

curio, curiosity, curious.
See accurate.

curmudgeon.
Listed today as of origin unknown, this may have come from Fr. *coeur*, heart + *méchant*, wicked. At least, so Samuel Johnson was told; in his dictionary he listed it as from "*coeur méchant*, Fr. an unknown correspondent." A dictionary of 1775 recorded it as from Fr. *coeur*, unknown + *méchant*, correspondent. It is idle to speculate how many similar errors, less easy to detect, remain perpetuated.

currant.
See Appendix II; see current.

current.
Through OFr. *curant, courant*, this is from L. *currere, curs—*, to run; whence also *cursive, discourse; cp. hussar, cutlet.* The present participle, *currens, current—*, gives us the *current* of a stream, as well as the electric *current*, and *current* events, those that run along as we read. *Currency* once meant flowing; it is now applied to forms of exchange *currently* employed.

Though early Eng. *cursen* is a variant of *Christen*, *curse* is not related to *cross.* It is not found in Teut., Celtic, or Romance; the nearest form is OFr. *curuz, coroz* (Fr. *courroux*, wrath) which is from OFr. *corocier* from LL. *corruptiare*, from *com*, altogether + *rumpere, rupt—*, to break, whence also Eng. *rupture; see bank; rote.*

The *currant* is an abbreviation, via Fr. *raisin de Corinthe*, from *Corinth; cp. peach.*

curriculum.
See cutlet.

curry (sauce); curry favor.
See turmeric.

curse, cursive.
See current.

curt, curtail.
See cutlet.

custodian.
See accoutrement.

customer.
Every storekeeper hopes to make his *customers* his very own. That's what they are; from OFr. *coustume*, from L. *consuetudo*, from *consuere*, to make one's own, from *con*, from *com*, together + *suus*, one's own. Similarly a *custom* is that which one has made one's own, whether it be a way of acting or a thing to wear. *Costume*, via It. *costume*, is thus a doublet of *custom.* Note that *habit*, from L. *habere, habit—*, to have, has the same double sense (first in Eng., in the 13th c., as a way of dress).

cut.
See cutlet.

cutaneous.
See hide.

cute.
See acumen.

cuticle.
See hide.

cutler.
See cutlet.

cutlet.
This seems, of course, a little *cut* (of meat), considering usual portions. But the diminutive has been added, not to Eng. *cut*, but to Fr. *côte*, from OFr. *coste*, from L. *costa*, side, rib, Eng. *coast.* (It is, in truth, a double diminutive: *—el—* + *ette.*) A *cutler*, also, is not simply one that *cuts*, but—again a diminutive; just one—LL. *cutellarius*, a soldier armed with a knife, whence Eng. *cutlass*, from L. *cultellus*, knife, from

culter, a ploughshare, whence AS. *culter,* whence Eng. *coulter.* This is probably related to L. *colere, cultus,* to till; whence *cultivate; culture; cp. colonel. Cut* is from Fr. *écourter,* to *cut* short, from L. *curtus,* short, whence Eng. *curt.* Fr. *écourté* gives us *cutty,* short, as in the *cutty* sark which Burns' *Tam O' Shanter* saw the witch dancing in. *Curtail* is from OFr. *courtald,* from *court,* from *curtus,* linked with the idea of docking a horse's tail. A *course* is a runway, or something to run through, as a *course* of studies; its diminutive *curriculum,* from L. *currus,* chariot, race-*course. Cp. car; hussar.*

cutty.
See cutlet.

cyanide.
This is from Gr. *kyaneous,* dark-blue, from which we have the Eng. combining forms *cyan—* and *cyano—*. But these forms may be used in that simple sense, or else as meaning related to *cyanogen* (*—gen,* from L. *generare,* to *generate,* to *engender*). *Cyanogen* was named by Gay-Lussac, when isolated in 1815, because it helped produce Prussian blue. The suffix *—ide* is used of simple compounds of one element with another or with a radical; first, of *oxide,* from *oxygen; cp. racy.* Thus *cyanide* is a compound of *cyanogen* (CN; carbon and nitrogen; also represented as *Cy*) with a metal. Potassium cyanide (KCy) is a deadly poison, often referred to in crime plays and stories.
The word *oxide* was formed, in French, by telescoping *ox*ygène and ac*ide.*

cyanogen.
See cyanide.

cycle.
See circus.

cylinder.
See dickey.

cynic, cynosure.
See canary.

Czar.
See shad.

D

dactyl.
See date.

dadaism.
See abbot.

daedal.
A *daedal* hand is one as skilled as that of *Daedalus,* the builder of the ancient labyrinth of Crete, said also to have invented the saw and the axe. He was held as a prisoner in Crete; but fashioned wings for himself and his son *Icarus* (Gr. *Daidalos; Icaros*) to escape. Over-confidently flying too high, *Icarus* ventured too near the sun, which melted the wax by which his wings were attached; he fell into the sea thereafter called the *Icarian* —hence an *Icarian* venture is one over-rash.

daemon.
See demon.

daffodil.
The Greeks had a flower they called the *asphodel;* its blossoms covered the Elysian fields, the abode of the blessed; hence, Eng. *Elysian.* By way of LL. *affodillus* this became Eng. *affodill.* The Eng. for spotted (like an apple) was *appled,* later *dappled*: G. *apfelgrau* is Eng. *dapple-grey.* Similarly the flower became the *daffodil;* more playfully, the *daffydowndilly* of the poets' garlands.

daguerreotype.
See Appendix II.

dahlia.
See tuberose.

dainty.
This word has traveled a bit, via OFr. *dainté, deintié,* from L. *dignitatem,* worth, beauty—whence also Eng. *dignity; cp. supercilious.* A person of proper quality will be particular in his tastes; hence the word came to mean fastidious; then it was transferred from the person to the object of his delight, the present usual application. The word *nice* (*q.v.*) has had a converse journeying.

dairy.
See lady.

daisy.
See flower.

dale.
See dollar.

Daltonian.
While chemists use *Daltonian* to refer to the atomic theory, first set forth by *John Dalton* (1766—1844), doctors apply it to color-blindness; particularly, they call green-blindness *Daltonism,* from the fact that the English chemist was thus afflicted.

damage.
To inflict a loss upon, to cause or devote to harm, was in L. *dampnare, damnare;* whence Eng. *damn, damnation.* A LL. form *damnaticum,* via OFr. *damage, dommage* (Fr. *dommage* means loss, pity) led to Eng. *damage.* To *damn* and to *condemn* (L. *com,* altogether, as an intensive; *cp. commence*) were at first the same, then *condemn* was used for ecclesiastical and legal actions. To make clear of loss is to *indemnify* (L. *in,* not + *damn*— + *ficere,* from *facere,* to make; *cp. defeat.*) The French suggest that *danger* (*q.v.*) is via *damnarium* from L. *damnum*: that which leads to loss.

Damascus.
This famous city, which itself has given us some words (*cp. cloth*), is named from a story. It is supposedly the place where Cain slew Abel: the field of blood, from Heb. *dam,* blood. Doubtless, as with many other names, the story was applied after the name.

damask.
See cloth.

dame.
See damsel.

damn, damnation.
See damage. The *dam* across a stream is common Teut. Note that the expression of unconcern is not profanity but "I don't give a *dam*" or "*a tinker's dam*". The *tinker's dam* is the older expression: the little *dam* of dough to hold the solder in place until it hardened; then the *dam* was thrown away. A *dam* is also a small Indian coin, and the phrase seems to have grown independently as an Anglo-Indian phrase. These may be folk euphemisms.

Damoclean.
This term for a danger that may drop instanter upon the victim is from the sword of *Damocles*, who having flattered Dionysius of Syracuse was set at a feast by Dionysius, but over his head a sword hung by a hair—symbolic of the situation of the monarch.

damoiselle.
See damsel.

damp, dampen, damper.
See dump; wet blanket.

damsel.
The Roman lord of the house, *dominus* (*see dome*), had as his mate *domina*, the mistress, lady. In OFr. this was shortened via *damna* and *damme* to *dame*. The diminutive form was, variously, for the young lady, *dameisele, danzele, damaiselle,* then *damoiselle*—from which the Eng. variants grew—among them *damoiselle, damosel, damozel, damsel.* My lady is *madame;* her junior (now the unmarried miss), *madamoiselle.* The *damson* is a variety of plum, from *damasen, damascene,* from *Damascene,* from L. *Damascenum,* of *Damascus, q.v.* Stick in your thumb and pull out a *damsel.*

damson.
See damsel.

dance.
Hey ding a ding ding
Fair maids in a ring.
The origin of *dance* seems to have been the round *dance,* or ring: the word is first used in the Romance tongues, apparently borrowed from OHG. *dansôn,* to stretch out. In the sense in which we use the word, it was reborrowed from It. *danzare,* OFr. *danser,* into G. *tanzen* and our jolly Eng. *dance.*

dances.
See Appendix II.

dandelion.
See flower; *cp.* indenture.

danger, dangerous.
A charming lady named *Dangerose* once yielded to the importunities of Damase, the Lord of Asnieres; defying the curses of Thigh, 37th Bishop of Mans, they lived in love together. One day, as the Lord was crossing a stream, a violent storm arose; stricken by lightning and overwhelmed by the waters, the wicked Damase was half-burned, half-drowned, and passed to perdition. The distraught *Dangerose* threw herself at the Bishop's feet in penitence; she lived thereafter in strict retirement. But her story spread far; and, whenever anything drew peril after it, the French said "*Ceci sent la Dangerose.*" Hence arose Fr. *dangereuse,* whence Eng. *dangerous.*
This monitory tale seems only a little less credible than the accepted etymology of *danger,* from OFr. *dongier,* from LL. *dominiarium,* from *dominium,* rule, Eng. *dominion;* the early sense of *in danger of* being "subject to the jurisdiction of." (If true, this derivation shows how the subjects feared their overlords: power indeed spelled *danger* to those beneath it!) *Cp. damage, dome.*

dapper.
This word illustrates the triumph of brain over brawn. It is common Teut. meaning heavy, powerful (*tapfer* still means warlike in German). Then, as did the victory, the sense shifted to clever, smart, neat in operation, then neat in appearance, *dapper.*

dappled.
See daffodil.

dark, darken, darkle.
See swivel.

darling.
See gossip, Viking.

Darwinian.
This word jumped a generation. It was first applied to the poetic style of *Erasmus Darwin* (English, 1731—1802). But his importance dwindled as that of his grandson grew; and the word nowadays almost always refers to the evolutionary theories of *Charles Darwin* (1809

—1882), as in *The Origin of Species,* 1859, and *The Descent of Man,* 1871.

dash.
See flash.

data.
See date, sequin.

date.
When you make a *date* with someone, you set a time. This given time (L. *dare, dat—,* to give, whence Eng. *data*) is the *date.* In ancient Rome, letters began: *Data* Romae, given at Rome, + the time. Hence *data,* Eng. *date* came to be used of the indication of the time.
If, however, it is the sweet fruit of the palm-tree you desire, you have it in your finger. It is from OFr. *dacte,* from Gr. *daktylos,* finger, from the shape of the fruit. (The *—l,* mistaken for the Teut. diminutive, was dropped.) The *dactyl* as a foot in verse is also a finger: it consists of one long division and two short—like the finger itself. AS. for *date* was *fingeraepla,* finger-apple. (It is suggested, however, that the Gr. *dactyl* for the fruit is folk-etymology, corrupting the unfamiliar Arab. *daqal* or Aram. *dagla,* palm.) *See helicopter.*

daub, dauber.
See auburn.

daughter.
See son.

dauphin.
This was taken by early Fr. nobles as a title: L. *delphinus,* whence Eng. *dolphin* (Gr. *delphis, dolphin.*) The Eng. *delphin* is used to refer to things pertaining to the *Dauphin;* but also as a variant of *delphic,* referring to the oracle of *Delphi,* at the temple to Apollo in the town of *Delphi* on the slope of Mount Parnassus. Because of Apollo their leader—their mother was Mnemosyne, Memory; *cp. amnesty*—the mountain was devoted to the Muses; hence Eng. *Parnassian*). Humbert II yielded the province of *Dauphiné* to Philip of Valois, 1349, on condition that the title of *Dauphin* be always borne by the king's eldest son.
See Appendix II.

dawdle.
See dude. It may be a variant of earlier *dadde,* to walk unsteadily; related to *dodder* and *dither. Dither,* earlier *didder,* is a variant of *dodder,* imitative of hesitant nodding and nidding.

day.
See week.

deal.
See dole; *cp.* augment. The word *deal* is common Teut., both as a plank, and as a portion. To *deal* is to give a portion, a *lot* [note how desire has increased *lot* (common Teut., AS. *hlot,* portion) from a portion to *a lot,* a large portion]. From the frequency of cheating at cards (or from fate's foul *dealing*) comes the desire for a fair *deal* or a square *deal.*

dear.
This word (though not recorded in Gothic) is common Teut., OE. *deore, diore,* OHG. *tiuri,* glorious, worthy, costly. From these senses, there developed the meanings, desired; hence, beloved. Just as *wealth* (*q.v.*) comes from *weal,* so from *dear* comes *dearth,* which first meant high price, hence the current sense of scarcity.

dearth.
See dear.

debate.
Even in early days it was understood that the purpose of argument is not to determine the truth, but to beat down (L. *de,* down + *battuere,* beat) one's opponent. As society grew more polite, the word *debate* took on its present meaning. The sense of strife remains in *combat* (L. *com, con,* against) and *noncombatant. Cp. argue; discuss.*

debauch.
See strategy.

debonair.
If you know a little French, you may take this as *de bon air,* of good air, well-appearing. But a person of good breeding and race will look well; the word means of good race: it is drawn from falconry, and refers to a bird *de bon aire,* of good *aery.* But this *eyrie* or nest of the hawk, high in the air, is spelled *aerie, aery, eyrie,* or *eyry*: it is a combination of LL. *aeria,* whence *area,* an open space (Eng. *area; cp. aureole*) and Gr. *aer, air*—so that your guess in the first place

was partly right after all. *Aeronaut* is *aer* + *nauta,* sailor; *see nausea.*

debouch.
See strategy.

debunk.
The L. *de,* from (to knock the *bunk* out of) has been added to this useful word. It is short for *buncombe,* and arose during the debates on the Missouri Compromise. Felix Walker, the member from *Buncombe County,* North Carolina, refused to stop for a vote, declaring that he was talking not to the House but to his constituents in *Buncombe.*

debut, debutante.
See butt.

decade, decadence, decalogue, Decameron.
See decay, number.

decalogue.
See number.

decay.
The Greeks beat time with the foot; raising it (Gr. *arsis,* raising, from *aisein,* to lift; whence Eng. *arsis*) and putting it down (Gr. *thesis,* putting, from *tithenai,* to put; whence Eng. *thesis; cp. Spoonerism*). The Romans, however, used the term *arsis* for the raising of the voice with the first syllable of a foot of verse; hence the same word *arsis* meant 'unaccented' to the Greeks and 'accented' to the Romans. Gradually the Romans substituted their own word, from *cadere,* to fall, It. and Eng. *cadenza;* so that now we speak of the *cadence* of a passage, where Shakespeare, in the opening lines of *Twelfth Night,* asks for "that strain again; it had a dying *fall.*" The word is different, the meaning is the same. With prefix L. *de,* down, off, away, we have *decadence;* and, via OFr. *decair,* Eng. *decay.*

A *decade,* however, is from Gr. *dekas, dekad—,* a group of ten, from *deka,* ten. As a combining form, *deka—* or *deca—* is common in numbers. It also gives us *decalogue,* the ten commandments. In Florence, in 1348, there was a plague; Boccaccio tells us of a group that left the city to avoid the pestilence; for ten days they told one another stories, which it took Boccaccio ten years to set down, but which are preserved in the famous *Decameron,* from It. *Decamerone,* from Gr. *deca,* ten, + *hemera,* day. The *Decameron* has lasted far more than a *decade,* and yet is far from *decay.*

Things that occur upon a day, then pass, are *ephemeral* (Gr. *epi,* upon, + *hemera,* day), like the *ephemera.*

deceased.
See ancestor.

deceit, deceive.
See recipe.

December.
See month.

deception.
See recipe.

decide.
When *indecision* has come to an end, and thought must yield to action, we have *decided.* This was once a strong word of action, from L. *decidere, decis—,* from *de,* down + *caedere,* to cut. From the past participle comes the blow that cuts opposition down, the *decisive* action. *Cp.* shed.

decipher.
See cipher.

decisive.
See decide.

deck.
This was early a noun and a verb: Du. *dekken,* to cover, from an earlier Teut. stem *thek, thak;* whence also OE. *thaec,* Eng. *thatch.* To *deck* (emphatic, *bedeck*) is thus to cover, clothe, adorn. And a *deck,* as on a ship, was a roof over part of the vessel (first, the stern). When cards are stacked one on top of another, they form a *deck.* The diminutive of *deck* is *deckle;* this was used of a frame that covered the pulp, in paper-making, and set the size of the sheet; hence, *deckle-edge,* the rough edge made by this frame. It is not a man trying to prevent cheating at cards, however, that calls "All hands on *deck!*"

Cognate with the Teut. *thek* is L. *tegere, tect—,* to cover (related to *tangere, tact—,* to touch; whence *intact;* hence also, via Fr. *tacher,* come Eng. *detach* and *attach;* but *see attack* for the Teut. form—and also *texere, text—,* to weave; *cp. text*); whence Eng. *tegument* and *integument. Integer* and *integ-*

rity are influenced by L. *tegere,* but are primarily from L. *in,* not, + *tangere, tact—;* thus *intact* and *integral* are doublets. And, via Fr. *entier,* untouched, whole, Eng. *entire* is a doublet of *integer.* Hence also *contact* (L. *con, com,* together). From LL. *contaminare, contaminat—,* from *contagmen,* from *con,* together + *tangere,* comes Eng. *contamination,* hence a doublet of *contagion.* Via the adjective L. *contiguus* comes Eng. *contiguous; contiguity.* Hence as well *contingent* (also *cotangent*) and the accident or *contingency,* which brings things together (as an auto and a pedestrian). From L. *attingere,* to touch to, to reach, comes Eng. *attain, q.v.* The frequentative of *tangere, tact—,* to touch, is *tactare,* to handle (related to Gr. *taktika?,* from Gr. *tassein,* to arrange, whence *tactics, q.v.*) and its variant *taxare;* whence, via OFr. *tasche,* Eng. *task;* but also, changing meaning from handling to estimating what you handle, then setting a price on it, comes Eng. *tax; cp. taxi, taste.*

There is no Eng. verb from simple *tegere, tect—.* to cover; but to uncover something is to *detect* it (L. *de,* from); whence Hawkshaw, Sherlock Holmes, and the other descendants of C. Auguste Dupin, the first fictional *detective.*

deckle-edge.
See deck.

decline, declivity.
See climate.

decoy.
The dispute as to the source of this word has not yet ended. *Coy* is from L. *quietus,* whence *quiet,* shy, retiring. To *decoy* is therefore to win from (L. *de,* from) its quiet. There is an earlier Eng. *acoie, acoy.* But there is also a Du. *kooi,* a cage for entrapping wild fowl, ultimately from L. *cavea; cp. cabal.* The *de* is then explained either as the Du. article *de,* the; or as short for *duck*: *duck-kooi,* whence *decoy.* One proponent of the first theory suggests, then, that *acoy* is probably from *quack-kooi.* In parts of Eng. a live, tame duck, used to attract the wild ones, is called a *coy* duck. We may speak of a *coy* darling, but a *decoy* is a snare.

dedicate.
See verdict.

deduction.
See duke.

deem.
This is common Teut., OE. *doeman,* OHG. *tuomen,* related to *doom; cp. dome.* It first meant to give judgment; hence, to estimate, to judge, to form an opinion. *Doom* retains the awesome sense.

deep.
See turtle.

deer.
See treacle, *cp.* beast.

defalcate.
The scientific term *falculate,* sickle-shaped. (L. *falculus,* diminutive of *falx, falc—,* sickle) retains the literal sense of this word: L. *de,* down, + *falcare, falcat—,* to cut. Applied figuratively to a dishonest servant who "cuts down" his master's possessions, it has retained the meaning of one that takes others' money.

defeat.
This is literally to unmake, to destroy, from LL. *diffacere, diffeci, diffect—,* from L. *de,* away, + *facere, fact—,* to make. In its affirmative aspect, this is one of the most fertile of all words. A thing made is a *fact.* A *faction* was, first the act of doing; then applied in Rome to a company of contractors for the circus chariot races; hence by extension, a group or party (with implications, from the early days, of unscrupulus ways of seeking their ends). (For *fiction,* see *faint.*) What might be done was L. *facilis,* easy; hence, Eng. *facile* and *facility.* One who makes is a *factor;* hence, in business, one who tends to *affairs* for another; one of the circumstances that helps make something: a *factor* in his rise to power; a *factor* in arithmetic. The power to do something is the *faculty;* by extension, that which one can do, a field of knowledge; hence, the persons in that department.

Many compounds are formed from the word *facere, feci, fact—.* Hence, *e.g.,* Eng. *affect* (to do to, *q.v.*); *effect* (emphatic; what is done, the result); *confectionery* (*q.v.*); *defect; disinfect; efficient* (from present participle: that which is making out well); *infect; perfect* (to carry through); *prefect; refection* (to remake, restore). By way of Fr. *faire, fait,* from *facere* come other words: *suffice; profit; affair* (made toward); *benefit* (well made); *counterfeit; fit* (made, suited); *forfeit. Satisfaction* (L. *satis,* enough); *rarefaction,* and many more. The *fashion* is the manner of doing

(L. *faction—*); the *factotum* (L. *totum,* all) is the Jack-of-all-trades. *Malfeasance* (L. *mal,* ill) calls for the *pontiff, q.v.* L. *fabrica,* whence Eng. *fabric* and *fabricate,* is from L. *faber, fabr—,* smith, which is earlier *facber,* one that can make; via OFr. *fabrica, faurca,* this gives us *forge.*

To *forge* ahead is a corruption of *force,* which is via LL. form *fortia* from L. *fors, fort—,* strong; *cp. saxophone.*

With prefixes *facere* became *—ficare* or *—ficere*; whence all our words ending in *—fication;* and, via Fr. *—fier,* words ending in *—fy;* such as *amplify; vivify; classification* (*see class*); *vitrification;* and also through the Fr., words ending in *—fice* and *—fic* (*Fr. —fique*), such as *artifice; orifice* (L. *or—,* mouth; *cp. inexorable*); *soporific* (L. *sopor,* sleep); *honorific; office* (L. *opus,* work, plural *opera,* as at the Metropolitan, New York: *office* was, originally, the work to be done; then, the post, as the *office* of sheriff; then, the place, as the sheriff's *office*); *pacify* (L. *pax, paci—,* peace; *cp. propaganda*); and hundreds more. Which would be not only *sufficient* but *surfeit!* But this word, if not a *feature* (L. *factura,* thing to be made, hence shape; OFr. *faiture*), is a *feat* (thing done)!

defect.
See defeat.

defence.
See plot.

defer.
See suffer.

defile.
See fylfot.

define.
See finance.

deflate.
See flamingo.

deform.
See formula. (L. *de,* from).

defunct.
See sponge.

degauss.
See gauss.

degenerate.
See racy.

degrade, degree.
See issue.

deign.
See supercilious.

deist.
See theology.

dejected.
See wasp.

Delaware.
See States.

delay.
See suffer.

delectable.
See delight.

deliberate.
See liberty.

delicacy, delicious.
See delight.

delight.
The *gh* in this word is a mistaken addition, from the long *i* sound—and perhaps by association of that which brings joy with brightness. *Delight* is from OFr. *deliter, delitier,* from L. *delectare,* to please: the frequentative of *delicio, delect,* to taste, then to enjoy. From this we have *delectable;* also, (from Fr. *delice,* a *delicacy*) *delicious. Delicio* has been traced by two paths: (1) *de + lacio, lacere,* to snare, whence *laques,* a noose—from which, via L. *laceus,* we derive our *lasso,* and via LL. *lacium,* our *lace,* which first meant a snare, a net; and (2) *de + licio,* from *lingere, lictus,* to *lick.* From *lick* comes the idea of taste, hence to enjoy. Somewhere along these paths may be the origin of the *lacteal* fluid, the first that anyone tastes; and *lactic* acid. Hence the *lacteous* circle in the heavens, the Milky Way, the *Galaxy* (Gr. *galaxias,* from *galakt—,* from *gala,* milk; L. *lac, lact—,* milk). The *delect—* from this source is not to be confused with the compounds of *lego, lect—; see legible.*

Note that your *latch-key* is a recent acquisition; the earlier *latch* was a noose, its diminutive *latchet,* via OFr. from LL. *laciare* from L. *lacere,* to bind, snare.

Delilah.
See Achilles tendon.

delirium.

That which is strange is often feared, therefore hated; otherwise it may be called mad. In Sp. *novedad,* novelty, is commonly a synonym for danger. If a fellow doesn't follow the rut, he must be out of his mind—at least in the opinion of the Romans, who fashioned the word *delirium* from L. *de,* away from + *lira,* furrow. Herein lies one of the greatest obstacles to world peace. *Delirium tremens,* as in alcoholics, adds *tremens,* from L. *tremere,* to quake. The gerundive *tremendus,* whence Eng. *tremendous,* which at first meant fearsome, then was transferred from the emotion to its cause. The L. adj. *tremulus,* whence the noun *tremor* and (through It.) *tremolo,* led to L. *tremulare,* whence Fr. *trembler,* whence Eng. *tremble.* Though one may become almost *delirious* with joy, the word is not connected with *delight, q.v.*

delphic.

See dauphin.

deluge.

See ante—, lotion.

demagogue.

See pedagogue.

demand.

See command.

demean, demeanor, demesne.

See mean.

demi—.

See semi—.

demijohn.

This is not half a johnny, but a corruption of Fr. *dame-jeanne, Lady Jane.* The same word occurs in Sp. and It., among sailors, nor is it known in which language it came first. It may be a corruption of *Damaghan,* a Persian town where glassware was manufactured. Sailors had many words for liquors and the jugs in which they came; probably the shape of this one suggested a portly lady. In the 17th c. a drinking jug called *bellarmine* was a caricature of a cardinal by that name. The sailor's drink, *grog,* is from the nickname, *Old Grog* (from *grogram* cloak), of Admiral Vernon of the British navy, who (in August, 1740) ordered that the rum be diluted. Nonetheless, *groggy* means unsteady. *Grogram,* earlier *grograin* is from Fr. *gros grain,* coarse *grain* (of cloth).

democracy.

The suffix *—cracy* (Gr. *kratia,* power, rule, from *kratos,* strength, whence *kratein,* to rule) means government by, as in *aristocracy* (Gr. *aristos,* best), *plutocracy* (Gr. *ploutos,* wealth), *bureaucracy,* government by administrative officials. (*Bureau* is Fr. from *burel,* diminutive of *bure,* a coarse woolen cloth of reddish brown—with which early desks were covered—L. *burrus,* from Gr. *purros, purple,* red. Hence—but not etymologically—red tape, with which the decrees from the offices, *bureaus,* were bound.) Gr. *demos,* from Sansk. *de,* divide, point, originally meant the division of a country or tribe; thence, the people. *See pedagogue.*

Demogorgon.

See demon.

demon.

This word, from Gr. *daimon* or *daimonion,* was first used of a demi-god, a spirit ranking between gods and men, including the spirits of the dead Greek heroes. This is still often spelled *daemon* or *daimon,* to distinguish these creatures from their bedevilment; for to the Jews and the later Christians they were all *demons,* i.e., evil spirits. The word gives us a number of compounds, such as *demonology, demonomachy* (Gr. *machia,* battle), *demonifuge* (L. *—fuge,* to drive away, as *febrifuge;* also *fugitive; cp. devil.*) The monster *Demogorgon,* however, is rather from Gr. *demos,* people, + *gorgos,* terrible: the infernal being summoned in rites of magic (made popular through his listing in Boccaccio's genealogy of the gods). The *Gorgons* were snake-haired monsters (the head of one, Medusa, adorns Athene's shield).

demonstrate.

See monster.

den.

A *denizen* is not one that lives in a *den.* In early times, all unenclosed land was *forest.* Thus L. *fors,* outside, gives us *forest;* also, with the adjective ending L. *—aneus,* by way of Fr. *—ain,* Eng. *foreign.* The same ending, applied to one that dwells within (L. *de intus,* from within, whence OFr. *deinz,* Fr. *dans*) gives us *denizen. Cp. door.*

A *den,* from OE. *denn,* is the place where a wild beast dwells—which would be the opposite of the *denizen's* home. *Den* is related to the infrequent Eng. word *dean, dene,* meaning valley. The *dean* of a college or church (originally also, of an army) is from OFr. *deien* (whence Fr. *doyen*), from L. *decanum,* leader of ten, from L. *decem,* ten; *cp. decay.* The church *deacon,* however, is from Gr. *diakonos,* servant (of the Lord).

dent.
See indenture.

dentist.
See east.

dependent.
See aggravate.

depict.
See arsenic, painter.

depilatory.
See pluck.

deponent.
See posthumous.

deportment.
See port.

deprive.
See private.

derby.
See by-law.

deride.
That at which we can laugh is Eng. *risible,* from L. *ridere, ris—;* whence our *risibility.* But if we laugh something down, we *deride* it (L. *de,* down); hence also *derisive* and *derisory* (passive and active forms). From the diminutive, something that makes us laugh just a little is *ridiculous.*

The slang expression, to *ride* someone, has no relation to this *ridere;* it is figurative, as though one mounted and rode around on an ass. *Cp. riding.*

derivation, derive.
See rival.

derogatory.
This originally meant to ask for less, from L. *derogare, derogat—,* from *de,* down, + *rogare,* to ask; then to lessen (applied figuratively, to lessen in esteem). *See quaint.*

derrick.
This instrument for hoisting things was first applied to persons. About the beginning of the 17th c.—when the English should have forgotten their earlier scorn of the Dutch (*q.v.*), the hangman at Tyburn prison was named *Derrick.* Either he had an exceptionally large number of clients, or he was an exceptionally large man; at any rate, his name was transferred to the instrument; thence, to any machine for hoisting. A short form of the same name, *Dirk,* was applied to some of his victims—the sneak thief and the picklock; thence, to the short knife or *dirk* such a man might carry.

descend.
Meaning first literally to climb down, this word is also applied figuratively, as with one's *descendants.* To *ascend* is of course to climb up (L. *de,* down; *as, ad,* up, toward, + *scandere, scans—; cp. echelon*). *Facilis descensus Averni,* easy is the road to hell; *cp. tavern.*

describe.
See shrine.

desecrate.
See anathema.

desert, deserve.
See family.

desiderate.
See desire.

desire.
The stage-struck young that *moon* upon a star with vain *desire* are caught in the root of the word: L. *de,* from, + *sidus, sider—,* star. This is more readily noted in the formal word *desiderate,* from L. *desiderare,* to yearn for, to lack, *i.e.,* to be away from one's lucky star. From the same source, however, OFr. shaped *desidrer, desirrer,* whence Fr. *desirer* and Eng. *desire. Cp. consider.* Thus there is more than the attraction of light in "the *desire* of the moth for the star". (The use of *moon* in the sense above is a combination of *honeymoon* and the *moonstruck* swain; *cp. pants. Moon* is common Teut., AS. *mona; cp. month.*)

despair.
See desperado.

despatch.
See dispatch.

desperado.

A cornered rat fights; it cannot run away. We speak of the fury of *despair;* and *desperado* is the past participle of OSp. *desperar,* to *despair*: a *desperate* one, from L. *desperare, desperat—*, from *de,* without + *sper,* hope. It is a sad reflection on human hopes that the word *sper* has come to us only in its negative forms; *hope* itself is a late word, from AS. *hopian,* to *hope.* Note that in the expression *forlorn hope,* we have not the same word, but Du. *verloren hoop,* lost heap: the group of men that must make the breach and die.

despondent.
See spouse.

despot.
See husband.

dessert.
See family.

destine, destiny.
See season.

destitute.
See season; tank.

destroy.

To pile things up was L. *struere, struct—*. (Quite the opposite of the common Teut. *strew,* which meant to scatter things around: AS. *strewian,* closely related to the noun AS. *streow, streaw,* whence Eng. *straw,* which is *strewn* in stables.) To put things together is thus to *construct* something; but also (to put two and two together), to *construe* it. The reverse of this process leads to the *destruction* of what has been builded; via a LL. form *destrugere* and OFr. *destruire* the Eng. verb is *destroy,* as befell the ancient Troy. Besides the *structure* of our society, we have from this source *instruct, obstruct* (to pile in the way); *instrument* (that with which to build). And *industry* is from L. *indus,* within, + *struua, stria,* from *struere;* whence *industrialism,* which is not *indestructible.*

Instruction (piling in) grows from a theory of child training the converse of *education,* which is from L. *e, ex,* out + *ducere, duct—*, to lead; *cp. duke, doctor.* Pack the information in; or draw the talents out. The former does not spare the rod, but may *destroy* the *education.*

destruction.
See destroy.

desuetude.
See mastiff.

desultory.
See somersault.

detach.
See attack, deck.

detect, detective.
See deck.

deter, detergent.
See terse.

determine.

The *termination* is an ending, and a *term* is a period (that comes to an end). *Terminal* was first (and still may be) an adjective; the L. noun *terminus* has come directly into English: L. *terminare, terminat—*, to end; *terminus,* boundary. From the limit itself, as in *term* of office or imprisonment, *term* grew to mean the limiting conditions (the *terms* of an agreement); hence, the *defining* (L. *finis,* end; *cp. finance*) of the idea, as in a *term* of reproach; *terminology.* To *determine* is to set down limits or bounds to something, as when you *determine* to perform a task, or as *determinism* pictures limits set to man's freedom. *Predetermined* follows this sense; but *extermination* comes later. Otherwise, existence would be *interminable.*

detest.
See test.

detour.
See attorney.

detract.
See distraction.

detriment, detritus.
See terse.

deuce.

This is often an unlucky word (it is the lowest throw at dice; God did not look upon the work of his second day and find it good; many peoples and sects, *e.g.,* the Pythagoreans, regarded the *unit* as the principle of good, and the *duad* as the evil principle). The word, meaning two, from Fr. *deux,* from L. *duos,* thus came to be euphemistic for the devil. (Note that in Norm. Fr. god and the devil are thus joined, in the word *deus.*) *Deuce* at tennis is from the Fr. *à deux le jeu,* two to play.

devastate.
See waist.

develop.
Possibly from L. *volvere, volut—,* to roll, as in Eng. *revolve; cp. volume,* came a root *veloper,* to *wrap;* whence *develop,* to unfold—now used mainly figuratively, to unfold the possibilities of something. An *envelop* is for *wrapping* things in. The word *wrap* itself, earlier *wlap,* but with its ultimate origin unknown, may have had a part in this *development.*

deviate.
See vacuum.

device.
See improvised.

devil.
Apparently the greatest evil of old was slander; for *devil* is OE. *dēofol,* from Gr. *diabolos* (Eng. *diabolic*), traducer, slanderer, from *diaballein,* to slander, literally to throw across. Akin to the word *febrifuge,* something that makes a fever flee, Oliver Wendell Holmes coined the word *diabolifuge,* something that drives away the devil: from L. *fugare,* to put to flight. *Refuge* (L. *re,* back) and *fugitive* are from L. *fugere,* to flee; *refugee,* (from Fr. *réfugié*) was first applied to the Huguenots escaping after the revocation of the Edict of Nantes (1685), when the *devil* seemed let loose—a frequent opinion of *refugees,* who are likely to favor the suggested etymology of *devil* as a contraction of *do-evil! Cp.* demon, Satan.

devolve.
See volume.

devote.
See vote.

devour.
See sarcophagus.

dew.
This is a common Teut. word, OE. *deaw,* from an old Teut. form *dauwo—;* Sansk. *dhaw,* to flow. It is often used in puns for *do,* which is also common Teut.; *cp. dome*—as in the roadside invitation *"Dew Drop Inn." Cp.* inn.

dexterity.
Various reasons have been suggested for the preference of the right hand; esp., that in primitive times the left hand (with shield) guarded the heart, so that the right hand wielded the tools and the weapons. The right hand was favored, and a *dextrous* (or *dexterous*) person is one that can well use his right hand (L. *dexter, dextr—,* right; *dextra,* the right hand). The left hand was by consequence associated with ill-omen, whence *sinister* (L. *sinister, sinistr—,* left). *Dextr—* is a combining form in scientific words; mainly (as in *dextrin, dextrose,* grape sugar) of substances that cause the rays of polarized light to rotate to the right.
Adroit is from Fr. *à droit,* with the right hand; and in Fr. *le droit,* the right, also means, the law. We have *gauche, gawk,* and *gawky,* from Fr. *gauche,* left. We speak of our *right-hand* man, and of a *left-handed* compliment. *Ambidextrous* (L. *ambi—,* both) refers to someone gifted with two right hands . . . And yet one may praise the *dexterity* of a south-paw!
It is suggested that *dexter* is from an Aryan root *de,* pointing; and *left* from Aryan *le* (Gr. *laios;* L. *laevus*) bent, as to hold a shield. Note that in Hebrew, *jamin,* right; *smaul,* left; in Sansk. *dakshina, savya;* in Irish *deas, tuaidh;* right also means south; and left, north, as from the habit of facing east in prayer (to the sun?). The Greeks considered the home of the gods to be in the north; their word for right also meant east; for left, west.

dextrose, dextrous.
See dexterity.

di—; dia—.
See diabetes.

diabetes.
This word first meant a siphon. Then it was transferred (in ancient times) to the disease, which is marked by an excessive flow of urine. It is Gr. *diabetes,* from *diabanein,* to flow through; from *dia,* through, + *banein,* to go, to flow. An incessant downpour has been called a *celestial diabetes.* For its antidote, *see island.*
The prefix *dia—,* through, across, is frequent in Eng. words. Thus *dialect* is Gr. *dia—* + *legein, lek—,* to speak: speaking through the tongue of a special region. And *dialogue* is similarly *dia—* + *logos,*

speech: talk across and back. The *diameter* is measured across the circle. The *diapason* (Gr. *pason*, feminine plural, genitive, of *pan, pas*, all) goes all across the scale. The *diaphragm* (Gr. *phragma*, fence, from *phrassein*, to fence about) builds a fence across the middle of the body; by extension, similar partitions. *Diathermy* is a treatment that sends heat (Gr. *thermon*, heat; *cp. season*) through. The *systole* of the heart (Gr. *sy—, sym—*, together, + *stole*, from *stellein*, to put, to send) is balanced by the *diastole*.

There are two prefixes that might be confused with Gr. *dia—*. From the Gr. is *di—*, short for *dis*, twice, as in *disyllable, dichloride;* this corresponds to L. *bi—* as in *biceps; cp. achieve*. And from the L. is *di—*, short for *dis—*, away, apart, as full in *disappear* but short in *diminish, diploma, q.v., disection*, also *dissection;* but note *dichotomy* (L. *di—, dis—*, apart, + L. *sect—* cut; Gr. *di—*, two, *dicha—*, in two + *tomos*, from *temnein*, to cut; *cp. anatomy*).

diabolic.
See devil.

dial.
As a *water-dial* or a *sundial*, this marked the hours of the day; from L. *dialis* (from *diurnalis*) from *dies*, day. A frequent and pleasant motto on a sundial is

Nonnumero horas nisi serenas:
I count only the hours that are serene—

which is literally true of the *dial*, as we wish it might be, figuratively, of our selves. *Cp. jury.*

dialect, dialogue, diameter.
See diabetes.

diamond.
The jewel is named from its hardness, LL. *diamas, diamant—* being a corruption of *adamas*, from which we have the word *adamant*. *Adamas* is Gr., *a*, the negative prefix + *damaein*, tame. Spenser (*Faerie Queene* 1, 6, 4) and Milton (*Paradise Lost* VI, 364) speak of a "rock of diamond." The Eng. word *tame*, Goth. *tamjan*, is cognate with the L. *domare* (from which we have *indomitable*) and the Gr. *damaein*. Thus a diamond is a stone *untamed*. *Cp. dome.*

dianthus.
See flower.

diapason.
See diabetes.

diaphanous.
See focus.

diaphragm, diastole, diathermy.
See diabetes.

diatribe.
See tribulation.

dice.
Cp. ninepins. Dice is the plural of *die*, from ME. *de, dee, dey* (it was a popular game!), from L. *datum*, given, from *dare, dat—*, to give. *See sequin.*

dichotomy.
See diabetes.

dicker.
To *dicker* with some one sounds like slang today, but it is an old and widespread word. The Romans used, as a basis for bargaining with the tribes they met on all frontiers, a set of ten (hides), L. *decuria*, set of ten, from *decem*, ten. This term passed into most of the north European languages, and when the whites came to America they tried to *dicker* with the Indians.

dickey, dicky.
Etymologists are hard put to it to explain how names of persons come to be used for objects (*e.g., jack* for money). Thus they say that *dick*, meaning long words, is short for *dictionary;* and that *dick*, in "to make one's *dick*," is short for *declaration;* this still leaves a dozen standard and slang uses unaccounted for . . . even more for *jack*, not to mention *johnny*. A *dickey* is a piece of a shirt—the front part of a full-dress stiff-shirt, to give waiters expanse and save them expense—it seems to have no relation to the *dickey* bird; but this shirt front was earlier called *tommy*—perhaps by college slang, from Gr. *tome*, section; *cp. insect*. "In the reign of *Queen Dick*" was a way of saying "Never," like "at the *Greek Calends*"—these existed in the Roman calendar, but not in the Greek.

L. *calare*, to proclaim solemnly, gives strength to the theory of Karl Marx, that economics is at the base of our doings; for from it comes L. *calendae*, whence Eng. *calends*, the first of the Roman month; solemnly proclaimed: the days that accounts were reckoned and paid. The first meaning of L. *calendarium* was account-book; hence our *calendar.* To *intercalate* (from L. *inter,* between + *calare*) was to tuck an extra day between the months; as Augustus Caesar did with August, as we do with February in Leap Year. There are three words that might be confused with *calendar.* Two of them are spelled *calender:* one, from Pers. *qalander,* a begging dervish; one, from LL. *calundra,* from Gr. *cylindros* (whence Eng. *cylinder*) from *cylindrein,* to roll. And *colander* or *cullender,* from LL. *colatorium,* strainer, from *colare,* to strain. Watching the *calendar* often is a *strain.*

dictaphone, dictate.
See verdict.

diction.
See jury, verdict.

dictionary.
See verdict.

diddle.
See Appendix II.

die.
See sequin.

differ.
See suffer.

diffuse.
See futile.

digest.
The literal sense of this word is to carry apart, from L. *di,* from *dis,* apart + *gerere,* to carry. It was first used in the two senses of to scatter and to sort. The latter prevailed; in the mid-fifteenth century the word came to mean to sort out ideas in the mind; and a little later, to sort out the valuable parts of food (in the stomach, preparing it for assimilation). *See knick-knack; joke.*

digit, digitalis.
See flower; *cp.* prestige.

dignity.
See supercilious; under.

digress.
See issue.

dilapidated.
See lampoon.

dilate, dilatory.
See suffer.

dilemma.
See diploma.

diligent.
See sacrifice.

dim.
See meticulous.

dime.
See nickel.

diminish.
See meticulous.

dimity.
See cloth.

dine, dinner.
See jejune.

dinosaur.
When the secrets of prehistoric life were unearthed, scientists tried to picture the feelings of those confronted by the great monsters whose fossil bones were coming again to light. Sir Richard Owen (English, 1804—1892) named a few of these creatures, from Gr. words. Thus there was the terrible lizard (Gr. *deinos,* fearful, + *sauros,* lizard), which he christened (1841) the *dinosaur.* Years later he named the terrible bird, the *dinornis* (Gr. *ornis,* bird; whence also *ornithology; cp. tavern*). A decade earlier, the general term *deinothere, dinothere* (Gr. *therion,* wild animal), had been applied to an early species. (For *mastodon, see indenture.*)

dip.
See turtle.

diphtheria.
This word is from Gr. *diphthera,* skin; a pseudo-skin is formed in the throat during the disease. On the *diphthera* of the goat Amalthea, Jupiter wrote the destiny of mankind.

diploma.
Graduates today receive a single sheet (sometimes, still, of parchment); but it once was folded: Gr. *diploma,* folded sheet, from *diplous,* double. The official bearer of such a sheet was a *diplomat.*

The L. form, *duo*, two, whence *duplicare, duplicat—; duo + plicare*, to fold, gives us *duplicate, duplicity* (one's purpose doubled over) and the *duplex* apartment. *Double* is from L. *duplus*, from *duo + plere, plu—*, to fill, by way of the Fr. *double;* L. *dubium*, whence *doubt*, is also from *duo*, as the mind hesitates betwen two alternatives: what the Gr. would call a *dilemma*, Gr. *di*, two + *lemma*, assumption, from *lambanein*, to take. Perhaps it is when a *diplomat* is in a *dilemma* that he tries *duplicity*. (*Dupe*, however, has a quite different origin, being another form of OE. *huppe*, the *hoopoe*, from L. *upupa*, which was considered a stupid bird.)

diplomat.
See diploma.

dipsomania.
See drink; *cp.* mania.

direct, direction, directoire, directory.
See royal.

dirge.
See remnant.

dirk.
See derrick.

dirt.
Dirty and *soiled* are synonyms; but by different routes to the one meaning. *Dirt* is from ON. *drit*, excrement; thence it was applied to fertilizer, muck, mud; then earth—so that now we can hear the expression "good, clean *dirt*." *Soil* is two words. The first began where *dirt* ended: from OFr. *soul*, from L. *solum*, ground. The other meant to wallow in the ground, hence to stain oneself: from Fr. *souiller*, whence Eng. *sully*, from AS. *sylian*, whence AS. *sol*, wallow.

disabuse.
See urn.

disaster.
Consider (from L. *con*, from *com*, together + *sidus, sider—*, star) how the conjunction of *stars* affects your fortune, for if propitious planets are not at hand, you may meet *disaster* (from L. *dis*, away + *aster, star*). The star-shaped flower, the *aster*, bears this L. name; whence also the little sign we call an *asterisk*. In Shakespeare's *Julius Caesar*, Brutus is reminded that our fate lies "not in our stars, but in ourselves"—which becomes the central theme of Barrie's *Dear Brutus*.

The science of *stars* is *astronomy* (Gr. *nomia*, arrangement); at first this science was called *astrology* (Gr. *logos*, word, reason); but for the ancients the most important part was reading the future in the *stars*, which today seems rather superstition than science. The Romans paid considerable heed to the heavens, and had still a third word for *star*, L. *stella*. This gives us a girl's name; also *stellar; stellio*, the *star*-marked lizard; a group of *stars, constellation;* and *stellify*, to turn into a star, as happened to the *Gemini* (twins), Castor and Pollux.

Star is common Teut., AS. *steorra*, G. *Stern;* cognate with L. *stella*, from *sterla*. The L. *aster* is borrowed, from Gr. *aster;* Sank. *star*. *Consternation* is not directly related; its first Eng. meaning was dumbfounding amazement and terror, from L. *consternare, consternat—*, from *con*, intensive + *sternere*, to strew; but this in turn may be related to the strewn *stars*. Note that (reversing Eng. *star*, G. *Stern*) G. *starr*, stiff, is cognate with the Eng. adjective *stern*, *q.v.* *Cp.* *consider*.

disc.
See discus.

discern.
See garble.

disciple, discipline.
A leader or teacher sets down the *precepts* for his *disciples*. *Precept* is from L. *praecipere, praecept—*, to take before, to order, from *prae*, before + *capere, capt—*, to take; *cp.* *manoeuver*. Those who take away and spread the *precepts* are the *disciples*, from L. *discipulus*, the noun with diminutive ending (*cp.* *pupil*) from *discipere*, to take away. L. *disciplina*, from *discipulina*, instruction for *disciples*, gives us *discipline*. We still have the adjective Eng. *discipular*.

discommode.
See accommodate.

discord.
See prestige.

discount.
See calculate.

discourse.
See hussar.

discreet, discrete, discriminate.
See garble.

discursive.
See hussar.

discus.
This flat solid circular piece of stone or metal, heaved through the air in the ancient Greek games (Gr. *diskos*) has passed its name to various objects of similar shape. Directly it gives us *disk,* and through L. *discus* both *discus* and *disc.* Via AS. *disc,* G. *Tisch,* it gives us a goodly *dish.* Through the flat surface of It. *desco,* we have our *desk.* The Fr. *dais* gives us our Eng. *dais.* Altogether, quite a heave!

discuss.
As with *debate, q.v., discuss* was a violent word, until the coming of the Greek tyrants and Roman emperors made talk less potent in world affairs. It is from L. *dis,* apart + *quatere, quass,* to shake. From its frequentative, *quassare,* to shake to pieces, to shatter, comes Eng. *quash.*

A soldier puts on a helmet so that, though he be shaken, he will not break; hence *casque,* from It. *casco,* helmet, from L. *quassare,* to break (break the blow). This leads us on several journeys. From the sense of helmet, covering, come Port. *casca,* bark, and Sp. *cascara,* rind, whence Eng. *cascara,* used direct in medicines, as *cascara amarga* (Sp., bitter bark) and *cascara sagrada* (Sp., sacred bark: the buckthorn, used as a mild cathartic). A doublet of *casque* is *cask,* a tub. But the diminutive *casket* has another story. It is from the old word *cask,* a chest, so used by Shakespeare (II *Henry VI,* III, ii), from Fr. *cassette,* from L. *capsa,* chest, from *capere,* to hold, whence Eng. *capacity.* This *cask* has two other forms, triplets. *Case,* a receptacle, with the verb to *encase* (a *case,* an event—in *case*—is from L. *cadere, casu—,* to fall; *cp. cheat*). And *cash,* which at first meant the till, or box, where ready money is kept. Hence, one in charge of the *cash* is a *cashier.* But to *cashier* from the army comes directly from Fr. *casser,* to *break,* from L. *quassare.* Note that we also use *break* in both senses. But he that has *cash* is not likely to be *broke.* (*Break,* to snap, is from AS. *brecan,* common Teut.: Gael. *bragh,* a burst; L. *fragor,* a crash, from *frangere, fract—,* to break, whence *fracture, fragile, refraction, fraction; irrefragable,* that cannot be *broken* back; *fragment,* from L. *fragmentum,* a piece *broken* off.) *Cp. casement.*

Several compounds have this stem: *concussion* (*con,* from *com,* together); *percussion* (*per,* through); *repercussion* (through and back again). Similarly, *analyze* is from Gr. *ana,* apart, + *lyein,* to loosen. L. *quatere* is cognate with AS. *cwacian,* to shake; whence Eng. *quake* and the nickname of the Society of Friends.

A good *discussion* ought to end with a *punch,* for in the drink, *q.v.,* things are shaken together, as in the *discussion* they are shaken apart.

disdain.
See supercilious.

disease.
See ease. *Disease* first meant simply lack of *ease,* discomfort; but this feeling is usually caused by a more fundamental condition, to which the meaning shifted.

disect.
See diabetes, sext.

disinfect.
See defeat. (L. dis, away, + *in,* against).

dislocate.
See couch.

dismal.
This is two words *telescoped* into one: OFr. *dis mal,* from L. *dies mali,* unlucky days—also called *Egyptian days*: the term was first used of the Biblical story of the Jews' oppression. Chaucer says *in the dismal,* meaning, at an unlucky time.

Telescoping, as a deliberate process of word-formation (from the way the segments of a long hand-*telescope* slide into one another: the word is from Gr. *tele,* far + *scopein,* to look, whence Eng. *scope*) was practiced esp. in the nonsense works, *e.g. The Jabberwocky,* in *Alice in Wonderland,* by Lewis Carroll. One of his words that has entered the language is *chortle,* from *chuckle* telescoped with *snort.* A more recent folk coinage is *brunch,* from *breakfast* and *lunch. Cp. blimp.*

dismissed.
See cream, mess.

disparage, disparate, disparity.
See peep.

dispatch.
This word was in such a hurry that it swallowed another word. There was an early Eng. *depeach,* seen in Fr. as *depêcher.* This is from L. *depedicare,* from *de,* away from, off, + *pedicare,* to trip, from *pedica,* fetter, from *pes, ped—,* foot. From this source is Eng. *impede; see baggage.* There was an early Eng. *impeach,* meaning to hinder, also from this source.

Combining with, then replacing, this group is the term *dispatch* or *despatch,* from Sp. *despachar* from It. *dispacciare,* probably from a LL. *de,* from + *pactare,* to tangle, frequentative of *pangere, pact—,* to fasten (whence Eng. *pact,* etc. *See propaganda.*) Too often *dispatches* were tangled in red tape; *see red;* but to *dispatch* was to free from the tangles; hence, to expedite. And from this line of development, to fasten upon, (L. *im* from *in,* against) the word *impeach* came to have its present meaning.

disperse.
See aspersion. (L. *dis,* apart). It was emphatic in the cry *"Disperse,* ye rebels!", that foreran the shot heard round the world.

disport.
See plot.

disrespect.
See scourge.

dissect.
See diabetes.

disseminate.
See semi—.

dissent, dissention.
See ascend.

dissociate.
See sock.

dissolution, dissolve.
See absolute.

distaff.
When we speak of persons as related "on the *distaff* side," we mean of course, through the mothers: the women's side of the house. *Distaff* is from AS. *distaef,* from *diesse,* bunch of flax + *staef, staff.* The Eng. prefix *be—* is often used to denote the act of: *besmirch; belittle.* Thus to *bedizen* was originally to put the flax (*diesse*) on the staff; hence, to decorate profusely.

Staff is ultimately from Sansk, *stha,* stand; *see tank.* Its plural, *staves,* has given us another singular, *stave;* we *stave in* the *staves* of a barrel; we *stave off* an attack, with a *staff.* Erected as the sign of office, the *staff* was transferred from the sign to the officers, the general's *staff.*

distant.
See tank.

distemper.
See tattoo.

distil.
See instil.

distinct.
Attendance at chapel, in English colleges, is marked by the prick of a pin next the name of each man as he enters. The habit seems to be an old one. Thus *distinct* means pricked apart; *extinct,* pricked out; and *instinct,* pricked in: L. *instinguere, instinct—,* etc., from Gr. *stichein; cp. attack.* The first two also have forms from the present tense of the L. verb: *distinguish; extinguish;* the last has instead the form from L. *instigare, instigat—,* to prick on, *instigate.*

distort.
See torch.

distraction.
If you need something to draw you away from your daily concerns and worries, you'll find it in *distraction,* for this is from L. *dis,* away + *trahere, tract—,* to draw. (It is cognate with the common Teut. word, AS, *dragon,* G. *tragen,* to *draw.* Note that a *drawn* game is one in which the stakes are *withdrawn,* as there is no decision; also, our *drawingroom q.v.* has nothing to do with artists, but is a *withdrawingroom.*) *Extract* is to draw out—as every boy learns from the dentist. And *con-*

tract is to draw together, either thus growing smaller or thus coming to an understanding. To *detract* is to draw down, away (usually to draw credit or praise away). *Subtract* is to draw under, away from. A *tract* of ground (stretched out) is thus drawn; but a *tract* that is written is short for *tractate,* from L. *tractare, tractat—,* to handle, frequentative of *trahere, tract—*. And a *tractor* is that which draws things along. *Cp. attract.*

The almost wholly forgotten literal sense of *retract* (to draw back, hence to withdraw one's words) has come into use again: as they rise, airplanes *retract* their landing wheels.

distrain.
See prestige; plot.

distress.
See prestige.

distribute.
See tribulation.

district.
See prestige.

disturb.
See butter; trouble.

disuse.
See abuse.

dither.
See dawdle.

ditto.
See verdict.

diurnal.
See jury.

dive.
See turtle.

diverge, divers, diverse, diversified, diversion, divert, divertissement.
See conversion.

divide.
See improvised.

divine.
See witchhazel.

division.
See improvised.

dizzy.

This was originally one that made others' heads spin, being AS. *dysig,* foolish, akin to *giddy; see enthusiasm.* Like these words, it may first have meant, possessed by a god: Aryan *dhwes—,* Gr. *theos,* god. Your own head spins directly in *vertigo,* for which *see conversion.*

do.
See dome.

Dobbin.
See donkey.

docile.
See doctor.

doctor.

L. *docere, doct—,* meant to lead, to teach; hence (from the adjective L. *docilis,* easily led) Eng. *docile.* That which is taught is a *doctrine,* and *indoctrination* is a form of teaching opposed to education; *cp. destroy.* (For *induction, see duke.*)

The term L. *doctor,* learned, was used in the medieval universities as the title for their degrees; we still use it thus, esp. for *M.D.* (*doctor* of medicine) and *D.D.S.* (*doctor* of dental surgery). There are many more.

The *physician* draws his name from Gr. *physike,* knowledge of nature, from *physis,* nature, from *phyein,* to bring forth, cognate with Eng. *be; cp. onion.* The ending is *—ian,* one skilled in, after a word ending *—ica*: *mathematician; politician* (and other words by analogy).

Eng. *medicine* is from L. *medicina,* from *medicus,* healer, from *mederi,* to heal. The It. word for *doctor* is *medico.*

doctrine.
See doctor.

dodder.
See dawdle.

dodo.
See chichevache.

dog, doggerel.
See greyhound.

"Git along, little *dogie!*" refers not to a little *dog* (*doggie*) but to a stray (hence undernourished) calf. Their distended bellies look like "a batch of sourdough in a sack"; hence they were called *dough-bellies* or *dough-guts,* then *dogies.* The cowboy song is bringing the stray back to the herd.

dogma.

This word for an opinion firmly but baselessly held was more modest in its start. It is from Gr. *dogma, dogmat—*, what seems, from *dokein*, to seem. But so many persons have said "It seems to me" and as they continued have developed a positive tone and an assurance of certainty, that the *Devil's Dictionary* (Ambrose Bierce, 1906, 1911) is a wholesome remembrancer: positive—mistaken at the top of one's voice. One must keep in mind that things are not what they seem. Beware of the *dogmatic* man. A variant of Gr. *dogma* is Gr. *doxa*, opinion, also from *dokein*; the emphasis given to one's opinion made the word also mean glory, as in *doxology*, speaking glory to the Lord; *cp. paradox.*

doily.

See Appendix II.

dole.

This is two words that chime as one. There is OE. *dal*, a variant of OE. *dael*, which gives us *deal*. It first meant (as *deal* still does) to portion out; hence, what is *dealt* out to one in life, one's lot. The second sense died out as the other word grew strong: *dole* from L. *dolor*, grief; *cp. indolent.* And with the sense of sorrow or lamenting, the word took on again its sense of *dealing* out, but now esp. as charity to the needy—and also, from the nature of such charity, to *dole* out came to mean to give in tiny portions, niggardily. But a *doleful* person is not necessarily on the *dole.*

doleful.

See dole; indolent.

dolichocephalic.

See lent.

dollar.

About 1518, coins were minted from silver of *Joachimsthal* (Joachim's valley; G. *Thal*, whence Eng. *dale*); these were called *Joachimsthaler*—being coined by the counts of *Schlick*, they were sometimes referred to as *Schlickenthaler;* just as the *frankfurter* is the sausage (G. *Wurst*, sausage: *Wienerwurst*, from *Wien, Vienna*) from *Frankfort.* Similarly *hamburger* is the style of meat from *Hamburg;* it has no connection with ham, although *beefburger* and *cheeseburger* have appeared at *"hot dog"* stands. *Hot dog*, of course, is from the (I trust jocularly) supposed origin of the meat; in Eng. slang, a sausage is a *"mystery bag."* Both names of the coin were shortened into *Thaler;* whence Eng. (U.S.) *dollar.* A *cent* (L. *centum*, hundred) is one hundredth of a dollar; as a *mill* (L. *mille*, thousand) is one thousandth. *Cp. nickel.*

A *pound* is first a weight, from AS. *pund*, from L. *pondo, pound*, literally, by weight, from *pondus*, weight, from *pendere*, to weigh, to hang. *Shilling* (one-twentieth of a pound) has a double diminutive ending: from AS. *scylling*, from Teut. *skil*, divide + *—l— —ing*: as in *darling, duckling*, etc.; *cp. gossip*: a little little dividing, being a thin slice of the metal of a pound. There is an earlier Eng. verb *skill*, to divide; then, to make a difference: "What *skills* it?"; thence, to understand, to know how: this sense survives in the noun *skill*. *Penny, pence* (one-twelfth of a shilling) is from ME. *peni*, plural *penies* and *pens*, from AS. *pening*, from *pending* (which occurs in 835 A.D.); again the diminutive *—ing* + *pand*, pledge, a *pawn*, from L. *pannum*, cloth; *cp. pane. Farthing* (one-*fourth* of a penny) similarly means a little *fourth.*

Franc is from the name of the people, the French, *Franks*—which itself is from OHG. *franko*, from LL. *francus*, free, *q.v.* The city of *Frankfort* is the *Frank ford* (as in the Aryan root *per*, through, whence Teut. *far, fur*, to go; whence Eng. to *fare* and G. *Fahrt*, a journey. *Fare* first meant the going, as in *thoroughfare*, going through; then the rate of pay for the trip): *Frankfort-am-Main*, the *Frank ford* on the Main River; or else the sallying (*forth*) place of the *Franks*: OE. *forth*, whence also *fore*: *forth* is also an obsolete form of *ford; cp. Bosphorus. Hamburg* is the *home fort*: OE. *ham*, OHG. *haim*, home (common Teut.· also in *Hampstead, Hempstead, Oakham.* There is an obsolete diminutive *hamel*, from which survives the double diminutive *hamlet*) + OHG. *Burg*, fortress, walled town. *Ein' feste Burg ist unser Gott*, begins Luther's great hymn, A mighty fortress is our Lord. The term *burg* is used colloquially for city; but note that *burgh* (from OE. *burh*) is a variant of *borough*—somewhat as *through* and *thorough* are variants; even in OE., *thurh* with the variant *thuruh*. Hence *burgomaster* (Englished from the Du.

burgemeester); *burgrave*, from *Burg* + G. *Graf*, count. A *burglar*, *q.v.*, is a city thief. It is not, however, *burg* + *lar* from It. *larrone*, from L. *larron—*, thief; as the earlier forms are *burglator* and *burgulator*. These are Anglo-Latin formations, influenced by L. *ferre, lat—*, to carry (off), from the early Eng. *burg-breche*, town *breacher*—hence, still, our *breach* of the peace, which is one of the offences of the *burglar*. To *burgle* is a back-formation, at first intended humorously, from *burglar*, as in the policemen's song in Gilbert and Sullivan's *The Pirates of Penzance*.

Wien, Vienna, medieval *Vindobono*, is from L. *ventus bonus*, good wind—which perhaps indicates how early the city was known for its gay waltzes and spirited airs. But this leads us to one of the most complicated groups in the language. For L. *ventus*, the wind, is ultimately from the past participle of L. *venire, vent—*, to come; *see* also *prevent*. And Eng. to give *vent* to one's feelings follows this path (*vent*, air), but with other shadings. It is influenced also by *vent* via Fr. *ventre*, from L. *venter*, belly, paunch, womb (hence likewise related to *vent—*, come); whence *ventose, ventral; ventriloquist; cp. necromancy*. It is interesting to note the first method of *ventilation*, shown by the early meaning of the word: L. *ventilare, ventilat—*, to swing, to fan. OFr. *esventer*, from L. *ex* + *venter*, whence Fr. *eventer*, combines the two trails: out of the womb; and *ex* + *venire, vent—* to come, the *event* is the outcome. But there is also Eng. *vent*, a sale, from L. *vendire, vendit—*, via Sp. *venta*, sale. *Venture* is aphetic for *adventure*, from L. *ad* + *venire, vent—*, to come to (one), to happen. There is finally (linking its meaning with the first *vent*, above) *vent*, also *fent*, from Fr. *fendre*, from L. *findere, fiss—*, to cleave; whence Eng. *fissure; cp. finance*. Which brings us again toward the almighty *dollar!*

dolor, dolorous.
See indolent.

dolphin.
See dauphin.

Dom, domain.
See dome.

dome.
This word comes from such a mingling of two trails that it is impossible to separate the footsteps. The combination is most clearly seen in the Eng. *Domesday Book*, where the meaning is the Book of the Day of *Doom*. There are two Gr. words: ***themis***, **that which is set up, stem *the*, and *dema***, house-top, also *domos*, whence L. *domus*, house. The house most frequently referred to, for centuries, was the *domus Dei* (house of the Lord), which was often called just *domus;* its most outstanding feature came to be called the *dome*. From *domus* comes the L. *dominus*, master of the house, therefore the Lord. There is a lengthy list of words derived from this dual origin: *domain* (also, from Fr., *demesne*); *Dom* or *Don* as a Sp. or Port. title, originally applied to the Benedictines; through the LL., *domestic, domesticate; domicile;* the group of words implying acting like a lord: *dominant, dominate, domineer; dominical; dominie* (mainly Scottish), a teacher, a *don; dominion*. From the power (and the tower) of the lord, comes (LL. *domnionem*, a *dominating* tower, whence Fr. *donjon*) *donjon, dungeon*, at first a *dungeon* vault, or vault of the tower.

Domino, a hooded cloak worn by the servants of the Lord (priests), came to refer to a mask over the upper part of the face, which the hood might hide. (Thus to *hoodwink* is to cover the eyes with a hood or the like; to blindfold; to fool.) From the Fr. expression *"Faire domino,"* to make or put on the hood or cap, said when the last piece was set down, winning, *domino* came to be the name of a game.

Doom is a word of long Teutonic use, from *don*, to place, set—the verb *do* + the abstract ending *—moz*, OE. *—m*, as G.*—tum*. (This is a noun ending in Eng. words, such as *kingdom, wisdom;* by my *halidom*—OE. *hálig*, holy.) *Do* itself, OE. *don*, is one of the most persistent of Aryan stems, appearing in Sansk. *dha;* OPers. *da;* Gr. *the;* L. *—dere* in 3d declension verbs: *condere, dedere*, etc.

Domesday Book, domestic, domesticate, domicile, dominant, dominate, domineer, dominie.
See dome.

dominion.
See dangerous; *cp.* dome.

domino, don
See dome.

donation.
See anecdote.

donkey.
This is a rather recent word (late 18th c.) for what was explained as a "Dicky, or an ass". The word is probably from a proper noun, *Duncan;* as the name for a patient or old horse, *Dobbin* (which did not grow quite so general) is a form of *Robin, Robert.* Dicky-bird and Jenny wren, we use such names again and again.
Another variant of *Robin, Rob,* was *Hobin, Hob. Hob* was used as the common name for a clown; as *Robin Goodfellow* and *hobgoblin,* it was applied to a mischievous imp or a bogy; *cp. insect.* As *hob,* diminutive *hobby,* it was applied to a horse. A *hobby-horse* is a toy horse on which one rides and rides without getting anywhere; hence the use of *hobby* for an occupation engaged in just because one is having a good time.

donkey-engine.
See buck.

doom.
See deem, dome.

door.
This word, in the sense of gate also, is widespread: OHG. *tor;* Sansk. *dwar;* Gr. *thera;* L. *fores.* From the Gr. *therapeutikos,* from *therapenein,* to attend, from *theraps. therap—,* doorman, attendant, comes Eng. *therapeutic.* From the L. (*fors,* outside the door) come Eng. *foreign* and *forest.* The ending in *foreign* is by false analogy with *reign;* the word is from ME. *foreine,* from OFr. *forain,* from L. *foras,* from *fors;* in Eng. too it first meant out of doors; then outside, hence excluded (from court); hence, alien. *Forest* is short for LL. *forestem silvam,* the woods outside; *i.e.,* not fenced in. L. *fors* came to be Fr. *hors,* which comes into Eng. in two expressions: *hors de combat,* out of the fight, disabled; and *hors d'oeuvre,* out of the ordinary course, then esp. food as a first or extra course, at a meal.
As early as the 14th c. men were using the expression "dead as a *doornail*".

Dora.
As a girl's name, *Dora* might be short for Gr. *Theodora,* gift of God; or just Fr. *d'or,* golden. It was quite otherwise, however, when England declared War in August, 1914; being at once the name of the *Defence of the Realm Act*—drawn from its initials.
Initials have recently been a favorite way of referring to parties, bureaus, and other creations of human officialdom; when they can be formed into words, they have a chance of entering the language. Thus *Waac,* from *Women's Auxiliary Army Corps,* in the United States, 1942; the first *A* was dropped when the Corps became a regular part of the Army. This word was helped along by its resemblance to *whack,* a blow (imitative of the sound) and *whacky* (from Yorkshire dialect), a fool. The men in service (1943—4) have a favorite in *snafu,* spread by the film shorts in the Army-Navy Screen Magazine relating the misadventures of *Private Snafu*—whose name spells (in polite parlance) *"situation normal, all fouled up." Flak* is from the first letters of the component parts of G. *Fliegerabwehrkanone,* aircraft defence cannon (fire).
Syllables are also used in forming names, as *Nazi* (G. *Nationalsozialistiche*) and trade names like *Nabisco* (*National Biscuit Company*) and *Socony* (*Standard Oil Company of New York*: initials and syllable). And of course many existing words have been combined to create new ones, *e.g., killjoy, happy-go-lucky, daredevil, windbag, sobstuff, close-up, blackout, airplane, loudspeaker, sawbones, jawbreaker, makeshift, windbreaker, icebox, bathtub, skyscraper*—their new meaning easily seen.

dormant, dormer, dormitory.
See dormouse.

dormouse.
The L. *dormire, dormit—,* to sleep, characterizes this creature, the sleepy-mouse. *Mouse* is common Aryan, AS. *mus;* L. *mus, mur—;* Sansk, *mus; cp. muscle.* L. *dormitorium,* a place for sleeping, gives us Eng. *dormitory;* the window in such a room is a *dormer* window. Via Fr. *dormir,* to sleep, present participle *dormant,* comes Eng. *dormant,* like many potentialities.

dorsal.
See tergiversation.

dose.
When you swallow it, it's a *dose;* when doctors study it, it's *posology.* From the patient's point of view: *dose,* from Gr. *dosis,* from *didonai,* to give—and you have to take. From the physician's: *posology,* from Gr. *posos,* how much?

dotage, dotard.
See dote.

dote.
To *dote* on someone, or to be in one's *dotage,* may not be basically the same; but they show the same symptoms and are named from their appearance. OE. *doten, dotien,* meant to be silly; but MDu. *doten* (as MHG. *totzen,* to take a nap) meant to behave as though half asleep. This would apply to an old *dotard,* whereas a young lover might just seem in a trance.

Speaking of old lovers, when the Sheriff in De Koven's *Robin Hood* says "I *dote* on you," Annabel cries "Give me an *antidote!*" An *antidote* is precisely something given against, L. *anti,* against + Gr. *doton* from *didonai,* to give; *cp. anecdote* and *dose.*

double, doubt.
See diploma.

dough.
See lady. (The use of *dough* to mean money comes from the fact that it's what every woman kneads.)

doughboy.
Boy is not AS., but common Teut.: Du. *boef,* knave; a proper name in OHG. *Buobo.* For *dough, see lady.* The application of the term *doughboy* to soldiers seems directly from the pipeclay used to whiten uniforms, which became soggy in the rain. But it is also suggested that the name came from the shape of the large brass buttons, which resembled the good old dumplings called *doughboys.*

Another story has it that the word was first applied to the Light Division of the British regulars in the Peninsular War (in Spain under Wellington, 1812), because the soldiers themselves ground their wheat into flour.

dove.
See turtle.

down.
See away.

doxology.
See dogma.

doxy.
See paradox.

dragon.
See dragoon.

dragoon.
This word marks a transfer from the instrument to the operator. It is from Eng. *dragon,* from L. *draco, dracon—,* the fabulous monster; the word was applied to an early musket, from its belching fire; then to the soldier that fired it. The monster was earlier Gr. *drakon,* from *drakein,* to see—and it must have been a sight for St. George to behold!

drat.
See rat.

draw.
See distraction.

drawingroom.
This stately reminder of more formal days was the *withdrawing* room—shortened to *"'thdrawingroom . . . the drawingroom*—to which the women retired after dinner, while the men remained for some purely male conversation—politics and such. At a given point in every *"drawingroom* comedy" one gentleman puts aside his cigar and asks: "Shall we join the ladies?" *Cp. distraction.*

dream.
There is an OE. *dream,* meaning mirth and minstrelsy, which died in the 14th c. About the same time came into use another *dream,* related to OHG. *traum,* probably to Teut. *draugm—,* to deceive, whence ON. *draugr,* ghost: this is the one that still visits many folk by night, not to mention the vast if inactive army of those that have *daydreams.*

dreary.
This word has weakened down the years. It is the adjective from OE. *dreor,* gore, dripping blood. Its first meaning was bloody; thence, horrid; by further weakening it came to its present dull state.

drench.
See drink.

dribble.
See drivel.

drift.
See drive.

drill.
See nostril, cloth.

drink.

This is a common Teut. word: AS. *drincan.* It all depends on what you choose. *Water* seems equally widespread: AS. *waeter;* Du. *water;* G. *Wasser;* OSlav. *voda.* But *wine* is not only common Teut., AS. *win,* but also L. *vinum,* both wine and grape. From *vinum* + *demere,* remove, from *de,* from + *emere, emptum,* take, (whence Eng. *preempt,* take first, *cp. quaint*) came L. *vindemia,* whence Fr. *vendange,* whence Eng. *vendage, vintage.* If the *wine* turns sharp or sour, (from Fr. *aigre,* from L. *acer, acr—,* whence Eng. *acid, acrid, acrimonious*) it is *vinegar.*

Ale and *beer* (*cp. barley*) are common Teut. words; *mead,* earlier *meth,* ranges through Teut., Goth. *midus,* from Gr. *methy,* wine, from Sansk. *madhu,* honey. Also *hydromel,* from Gr. *hydro,* water + *meli,* honey. (Welsh *mead* is *metheglin,* from *meddyglyn,* medecine, from *meddyg,* healing, from L. *medicus* + *llyn,* liquor.

Benedictine (*cp. benedick*) is the drink prepared by the monks of the order of *St. Benedict;* as *chartreuse* is, by the monks of *La Grande Chartreuse,* Carthusian monastery near Grenoble. *Brandy* is short for *brandewine,* from Du. *brandewijn,* burnt wine. *Champagne* is from the province in France; *cp. camp. Chianti* is from a district in Tuscany. A *cordial* is a heartening drink, from L. *cordialis,* from *cor, cord—,* heart. *Gin* is short for *geneva,* from Fr. *genièvre,* from L. *juniperus,* whence *juniper,* the berries of which flavor it. *Julep* is from Arab. *julab,* from Pers. *gulab,* rose water. *Punch* is from Hind. *pānch,* five: alcohol, water, lemon, sugar, spice. For *vermouth, see wormwood. Rum* is short for *rumbullion*—which is a long story. The *bullion* is from Fr. *bouillon,* a hot drink, from L. *bullire,* whence Fr. *bouiller,* whence to *boil.* (The *boil* is OE. *byl,* from *bul,* blown up.) The word *rum* is borrowed from slang, from two sources. Romany (gypsy) *rom* means man; thence, odd fellow, as in "He's a *rum* 'un." But *Rome* was used as an adjective meaning fine, excellent (as a lady may exclaim "That's a *Paris* gown!"—even if made in Nipeekesaukee.); thus G. *Ruhm,* fame. (This is related to *rumor,* from the imitation of the sound of murmuring; but perhaps the name of the city itself is similarly derived.) Eric Partridge's *Dictionary of Slang,* 1938, gives five columns of words beginning with *rum,* mainly in the sense of good. Thus *rumbullion,* a good hot drink, whence *rum. Sack* is not from the drinks, *e.g.* Hippocras, that were strained through a *sack,* (from AS. *sacc,* from L. *saccus,* from Gr. *sakkos,* from Heb. *saq; sack,* to plunder, is from putting the booty in a *sack*) but from Sp. *Xeres seco,* dry *sherry,* whence Fr. *vin sec,* dry (not sweet) wine, whence Eng. *sack.*

Seltzer is from G. *selterser,* from *Selters,* a village with a mineral spring. *Sherbet* is from Arab. *sharbat,* a drink, sugar and water, from *shariba,* to drink; *sorbet* is a doublet; from the same source via L. *sirupus,* whence Fr. *sirop,* whence comes Eng. *syrup. Sherry* is older *sherris,* from Sp. *vino de Xeres,* from *Caesaris* (*Urbs Caesaris,* the city of Caesar), now *Jeres. Soda* is short for *soda water,* from L. *soda*: water + sodium bicarbonate; now more often carbon dioxide. L. *soda* is from Arab. *suda,* headache, which it sought to cure. Hot *toddy* is from earlier *tarrie,* from Hind. *tari,* from *tar,* a kind of palm. *Whiskey* is short for Celt. *usquebaugh,* water. Also from *water* are L. *aqua vitae, water* of life, the alchemists' term for alcohol; Fr. *eau-de-vie,* water of life, brandy; and Russ. *vodka,* diminutive of *voda,* water. From Gr. *dipsa,* thirst + *mania,* madness, comes *dipsomania.* And some persons need not be bitten by a mad dog to get *hydrophobia* [Gr. *hydro,* water (whence Eng. *hydra,* watersnake; *hydrant; hydraulic*: Gr. *aulos,* pipe; *hydrogen,* water - producing) + *phobia,* hatred].

Coffee is from Turk. *gahreh,* from Arab. *gahwah,* more basically, however, from *Caffa,* Ethiopia, where it still grows wild. *Tea* (earlier pronounced *tay*) is from mandarin Chin. *ch'a,* whence Arab. *shay,* Pers. *chā,* Russ. *chai,* Port. *cha.* The Eng. form comes from Du. *thee,* from Malay *teh,* from the Amoy Chin. dialect *t'e.* It's a long time between drinks. *Cp. intoxicate.*

By now you are probably *drenched.* The casual of *drink,* OTeut. form *drankjan,* gives us Eng. *drench.*

drip.

Drop, drip, and *droop* are various stems of the same echoic widespreading Teut. root; *cp. drivel. Dropsy* has no connection, save that there is water involved: it is aphetic for *hydropsy,* from Gr. *hydrops,* from *hydor, hydr—,* water—as also in *hydraulic; cp. drink.*

The *clepsydra* was the ancient water-clock (*cp. dial*), from Gr. *kleps—,* from *kleptein,* to steal (whence also Eng. *kleptomaniac; cp. mania*), + *hydor,* water, as the water and the moments stole away.

Also echoic in origin was the L. word for *drop,* L. *gutta* (still used in doctors' prescriptions). This, via OFr. *goute,* came into Eng. as *gout;* Shakespeare speaks of *gouts* of blood. From the medieval belief that the disease was caused by the *dripping* away of body humors, comes the wealthy man's ailment, *gout.*

Gutta-percha is of quite different origin (though the sap falls in *drops*): it is from Malay *getah percha,* gum of the *percha* tree.

drive.
This word is widespread, but found only in the Teut. tongues, OE. *drifan.* And that which is *driven* is the *drift,* whether it be a snow *drift,* or the *drift* (direction of the *drive*) of one's argument.

drivel.
Just as there is no relation between *shrivel* and *shrive* (*q.v.*), so there is none between *drivel* and *drive. Drivel* is earlier *drevel,* from A.S. *dreflian,* to slobber, hence, to utter meaningless sound. It is a variant of *dribble,* frequentative of early Eng. *drib,* an echoic word akin to *drip* (*q.v.*); *drop.*

Shovel, however, is related to *shove,* a common Teut. word, AS. *scufan,* to thrust. From this also came early Eng. *scuff,* to brush with the hand, or to drag the feet; whence the frequentative Eng. *scuffle;* also *shuffle.* The early game *shove-board* was later *shovel-board* and is now *shuffle-board.* To *shuffle* cards is to keep pushing them back and forth.

dromedary.
This was originally just a swift camel, from LL. *dromedarius camelus,* from Gr. *dromas, dromod—,* runner, from *dramein,* to run. Thus a *hippodrome* is a place for horse racing, from *hippos,* horse; *hippopotamus* is a water horse, from *potamos,* river; *cp. pot; intoxicate.* A *palindrome* is an expression that runs both ways, from Gr. *palin,* again: *e.g.,* Madam I'm Adam! And a parchment used again is a *palimpsest,* from Gr. *palimpsostos,* from *palin* + *pson,* to smooth.

droop, drop, dropsy.
See drip.

drosophila.
See philander.

druid.
See pay.

drunkard.
See coward.

ducat, duchess, duchy.
See duke.

duck.
See ducking-stool.

ducking-stool.
Scolds and other feminine offenders were in the 17th and 18th c. set in a *stool,* swung on a long pole (such as was used for drawing water from wells) and publicly shamed and *ducked.* Hence the name, by change from earlier *cucking-stool,* from the type of chair used, a close-stool, or toilet-seat, Teut. (ON.) *kuka,* L. *cacare,* to void excrement. They should have been ashamed!

Other suggested origins of the word, and the history of the custom, are traced in *Juridical Folklore,* by J. W. Spargo, 1944. Noting that the punishment of the *cucking-stool* is almost exclusively for female offenders, the book reminds us that three of the seven deadly sins (idolatry, blasphemy, false witness) are sins of the tongue. The *Epistle of St. James,* III, 6, says "the tongue is a fire"—hence put out the fire, check the sins of the tongue, by *ducking.*

The bird, *duck,* is from AS. *duce,* diver, from the verb form *ducan,* to dive, to *duck.* The cloth *duck* is found in Du. *doek,* linen; G. *Tuch,* cloth.

duckling.
See gossip.

duct, ductless.
See duke.

dude.
This, referring to a fellow all dressed up with no place to go—at least, no good reason for going . . . or being—is from G. *duden-kop,* drowsy head, from *dudden,* whence Eng. *dawdle.* Hence the appropriateness of the *dude-ranch.*

duffel.
See cloth.

dugs.
See son.

duke.
This noble was the leader of a troop, from L. *dux, duc—*, leader, from *ducere, duct—*, to lead. The slang use of *dukes* to mean fists is said to come from 19th c. rhyming slang: *Duke of Yorks* was used for forks, hence *dukes* were the hands that held them. It is more likely, however, that the word grew around the prize-ring, the battlers leading with their fists, hence *dukes*.

Many Eng. words have come from L. *duct—*. *Conductor* (L. *con*, from *com*, together); *viaduct* (L. *via*, road); *aqueduct* (L. *aqua*, water, whence *aquarium, aquatic*); *induction* (L. *in*, in); *deduction* (L. *de*, from); *reduction* (L. *re*, back); *production* (L. *pro*, forth); *abduction* (L. *ab*, away); *introduction* (L. *intra*, into, within); the *ducts* and the *ductless* glands.

Cognate are Eng. *tow*, from AS. *togian*, to draw; *tie*, from AS. *tigan*, ON. *taug*, rope; *tug*, from ME. *toggen*, AS. *teon*, to pull, whence also ME. *toght*, Eng. *taut*.

The *duchess*, who began as the wife of the *duke*, forms her name from LL. *ducissa*, from *duc* + the feminine ending. Similarly *duchy* is from LL. *ducatus*, whence It. *ducato;* Fr. *duché*, whence Eng. *duchy*. The Italian coin important to Antonio in *The Merchant of Venice* was first minted (in 1140) by Roger II of Sicily, in his *ducato* of Apulia; hence, *ducat*. Shylock learned that a man who has a bad debt sometimes can *duck* it.

dum-dum (bullet).
See Appendix II.

dumb.
Persons knowing that this word means incapable of articulate speech often assume that its use to mean stupid is colloquial; as a matter of fact, stupid was the earlier meaning of the word. A person that does not understand, does not know what to do, is likely to remain still and silent; hence the frequent exclamation of an impatient person: "Are you deaf!" "Have you lost your tongue?" And from stupid *dumb* came to mean speechless; even, occasionally (as in OHG.), deaf.

A *dumb show* (an Elizabethan stage term) is a pantomime. A *dumbwaiter* is a service (elevator) that—being mechanical—does not bother one with talk. *Dumb-bells* were originally the apparatus for ringing church bells, without the sound; they were used either in learning how to chime, or for exercise—hence, the later form of exercising *dumb-bell*. (The *dumb* belle is quite other, as every swain will know.) To *dumbfound* is to strike *dumb* (*-found*, from Fr. *-fondre*, from L. *fundere, fus-* to melt, to pour; whence also—*con*, together— Eng. *confound* and *confusion*). And the silent partner (imaginary player) in a card game is a *dumby*, now always *dummy*, like the silent partner of the ventriloquist.

dumb-bell, dumbfound, dumbwaiter, dummy.
See dumb.

dump.
See plunge. From the sound, the word moved to the action, to throw down heavily; hence also the town *dump*.

In the dumps is a different word, related to the Du. *damp*, haze; G. *dumpf*, close, oppressive, gloomy; *cp. wet blanket*. Don't let your spirits be *dampened*.

dunce.
"A fool unless he knows Latin is never a great fool." This Spanish saying indicates the scorn that came with the Renaissance, for the medieval hair-splitting; and all of it seemed to descend upon the bowed head of John *Duns* Scotus, d. 1308. (His name is a place name; either from *Dunse* in Berwickshire or from *Dunston* in Northumberland; in either case, it is now the name for a plain *dunce*.) It was the disciples of his rival Thomas Aquinas, d. 1274, that popularized the term. Aquinas was called by his schoolmates "The dumb ox." *Cp. can-can.*

Dundreary.
See Appendix II.

dune.
See away.

dungarees.
The clothes are named from the material, Hind. *dungri*, coarse calico.

dungeon.
See dome.

duodenum.
See pylorus.

dupe, duplex, duplicate, duplicity.
See diploma.

durable.
See suffer.

dust.
See February.

Dutch.
This word, once extended to all Germany (as still in Du. *duitsch* and G. *deutsch*), is now limited to the Netherlands. It is from OHG *diutisc,* popular, national. But just as *Slav,* which to the natives meant glory, became debased abroad into *slave,* so the popular *Dutch* at home were less liked across the Channel. The English didn't like the broom on the *Dutch* mastheads of the 16th and 17th c., indicating that these vessels "sweep the seas," and even after Britannia began to rule the waves, the *Dutch* were their chief colonial rivals. Thus—just as the English had earlier called venereal diseases *the French sickness* and the French called them *the Italian malady* —a score of scorn was turned upon the *Dutch.* Some of this survives: A *Dutch auction* is one in which the auctioneer gives a high figure, then gradually lowers it until someone buys. A *Dutch anchor* is something important that has been left behind, from a story of a Dutch captain that forgot his anchor and thus lost his ship. *Dutchman's breeches* is a small patch of blue ("enough to make a pair of breeches for a Dutchman") in a stormy sky.

A *Dutch bargain* is one clinched over liquor. *Dutch comfort*: Thank God it was no worse! *Dutch concert*: each plays a different tune. *Dutch courage*: induced by liquor (Holland gin?). *Dutch defence*: really a surrender. *Dutch feast*; whereat the host gets drunk before his guests. *Dutch gold*: an alloy of copper and zinc, for a cheap imitation of gold leaf. *Dutch luck*: undeserved good fortune. *Dutch nightingale*: a frog. *Dutch praise*: seeming praise that condemns. *Dutch reckoning*: a lump account, usually higher than if itemized. *Dutch treat*: each pays for himself. To talk like a *Dutch uncle* is not to mince words; usually to scold roundly. A *Dutch wife* is a pillow, esp. in the tropic colonies, of a man that takes no native woman. "If that's the truth, *I'm a Dutchman*": I'm damned—we might say: My name is mud. *Double Dutch* is what we call "double talk," gibberish. I'd better stop or I'll be *in Dutch* . . . Among the Cornish miners of Montana, U.S.A., an assessment (paying out instead of taking in) is called an *Irish dividend.* (*Ireland* is just an old Celtic name—no connection with *ire,* the angry isle!)

This *xenophobia* (Gr. *xeno,* stranger + *phobos,* fear) is found in many lands, and districts: townsman vs. gownsman; city vs. country; *cp. pagan.* Thus to the Romans the land of Carthage, Punica, was caught in the term *Punica fides, Punic faith,* treachery. What the English call taking *"French leave"* is to the French *"filer à l'Anglaise"*: the compliment returned! The *vandal* is from the sacking of Rome, 445 A.D., by Genseric, king of the *Vandals.* AS. *wealh,* foreigner (not a Saxon) was the term given to the earlier inhabitants: *Waelisc,* the *Welsh;* whence, to *welsh* on a deal. (*Walnut* is the foreign, or Welsh, nut, from AS. *wealhhnutu.*) And today, to the man of Manhattan (New York) "art is the quickest way out of the Bronx;" and the *pppht* of derision is called the *Bronx cheer.* The attitude is summed up in the old story of the two cockney urchins:

"Who's that?"
"Dunno."
"'Eave 'arf a brick at 'im!"

dwell.
This pleasant and now mainly poetical word has a grimmer history. Its first meaning was to stun, to make giddy, hence to mislead; as in Sansk. *dhwr,* to mislead. In OHG. it had reached the second stage: if you stun someone, you perforce delay him: OHG. *twellan,* to retard. Used also as an intransitive verb, it came thus to mean to delay, to linger; hence, to abide, to *dwell* in a place.

dye.
See sequin.

dynamic.
See dynamo.

dynamo.
This is a recent coinage, from Gr. *dynamis,* power, force, from *dynasthai,* to be able; hence Gr. *dynastes,* ruler, and Eng. *dynasty.* From this source we have

a large number of recent words, from *dynamic* and *dynamism* to *dyne,* the unit of force, and the combining form *dyna-mo-*.

dynasty.
See dynamo.

dysentery.
The Gr. *dys-*, meaning bad, ill (the opposite of *eu-*, good: *eulogistic* means speaking well of something; *dyslogistic,* speaking ill), is a frequent prefix, from *dysangelical* (opposite of *evangelical; cp. evangelist*) ; past *dyspepsia* (Gr. *dyspepsia,* indigestion, from *peps-, pept-; peptos,* cooked, digested; *peptikos* able to digest; whence also *pepsin* and the *peptic* juices). The bowels or "inners' were Gr. *entera;* hence an affliction there was Gr. *dysenteria,* Eng. *dysentery*.

dyspepsia.
See dysentery.

dysprosium.
See element.

E

eager.
See acumen.

ease.
If you don't know the answer, someone may call you a *goose;* he might have called you *anserine,* which means stupid (L. *anser,* goose), from the stupid notion that a goose is. An *anserate* cross, however, is quite another matter, being one with a bird or snake head at the extremities. This is from a LL. variant of L. *ansat-,* with handles, as in the *crux ansata,* more widely known as the swastika, *cp. monk.* But L. *ansatus* is used of a man with arms akimbo—a man "handled", as it were; certainly not one handling anything; and from this inactivity came a LL. form *asia;* whence Fr. *aise,* elbow-room; whence Eng. *ease.*

See answer. *Goose,* AS. *gas,* is common Aryan. The tailor's *goose* is named from the shape of its handle, like a *goose's* neck; whence the saying: Be the tailor never so poor, he'll still have a *goose* at the fire.

This word has several slang senses. To *goose* meant to hiss a play; hence the despondent players' remarks: The *goose* is in the house; hence also the expressions "to get the big bird"; "give him the bird"—which we use for a sound less like the *goose* hiss than like the *goose* honk, the Bronx cheer; *cp. Dutch.* From the story of the man that killed the *goose* that laid the golden eggs comes the expression "to cook one's *goose*"...Don't be *uneasy;* and keep clear of *disease.*

easel.
See buck.

east.
This word has been linked with *yeast,* that which makes rise, as meaning the rising-place; *Easter* is the season when the Lord ariseth. It seems rather to be from the Aryan root *us,* to burn, whence Sansk. *vas,* shine. *West,* similarly, has been called the place where the sun *wasteth;* it is probably rather the place where the sun abides at night, from Sansk. *vasta,* house; *vasati,* night. *South* is the *sunned* quarter, from OHG. *sunth,* the *n* dropping as in *tooth,* from *tanth,* from Sansk. *danta,* whence L. *dens, dent,* whence *dentist. North* is where the sun's course *narroweth,* and that's the only guess. All these words for the four corners of the earth are very old.

Easter.
This is from AS. *Eostre,* a pagan goddess whose festival came at the spring equinox. The festival was called *Eastron* (plural of *Eastre*). The Christian festival of the resurrection of Christ has in most European languages taken the name of the Jewish *Passover* (Fr. *Pacques,* It. *Pasqua,* from L. *pascha*—in Eng. the *Paschal lamb*—from Gr. *pascha,* from Heb. *pesach*); but in the Eng. the pagan word has remained for the Christian festival. *Passover* takes its name (the Hebrew has the same meaning, *pass over*) from the fact that the angel of the Lord, in smiting the first born of every Egyptian (before Moses led his people out of bondage), *passed over* the homes of the Israelites.

eat.
See indenture

ecclesiastic.
See church. The earliest assemblies had large elements of ritual in them, as even today ours begin with prayer. The Gr. *ekklesia,* before it meant church, meant the general assembly of the Athenians, from *ekkalein,* to call out. Hence also L. *ecce!,* Behold! esp. in *Ecce Homo,* Behold the Man, used in *John* xix, 5 of Christ with the crown of thorns.

echelon.
This arrangement of troops (in stag-

gered but parallel formation) has developed into the triangular pattern of aviation flight. It is Fr. *échelon,* rung of a ladder, diminutive of *échelle,* ladder, from OFr. *eschiele,* from L. *scala,* ladder—whence also Eng. *scale,* to measure (from the ladder-like divisions), or to climb (*scale* a wall). The *scale* of a balance is a common Teut. word: AS. *scealu,* cup, shell, whence Eng. *shale;* but OHG.*scala,* which word is also chip, husk, whence *scale* of a fish. The L. *scala* is cognate with *scandere, scans—* to climb, whence *scan* (to climb so as to observe; and to climb up the feet of a poem). *Scandal* is from Gr. *scandalon,* something that makes one stumble, *i.e.,* the spring of a trap, that sends one helplessly climbing in air.

echo.
See nuptials.

éclat.
See slate.

ecstasy.
See element (at end); tank.

ectoplasm.
See element (at end).

edge.
See acumen.

edible.
See indenture.

edict.
See verdict.

education.
See destroy.

effect.
See affect; defeat.

effete.
See fetus.

efficient.
See defeat.

effigy.
See faint.

effloresce.
See flower.

effrontery.
A bashful boy used to stand with lowered eyes; this attitude was associated with blushing. Thus in Latin, to be unblushing, unashamed, was to be "without brow", *ex + frons, front—, brow;* whence Eng. *effrontery.* There is an early Eng. *effront,* to free from bashfulness, to render bold, as a girl's encouraging smile.

This L. *frons, front—,* applied to the foremost part of anything, gives us Eng. *front* (which first meant forehead); *frontier; frontispiece, q.v.* A blow on the forehead was an *affront* (L. *ad,* to); then, figuratively, an insult. To bring face to face (L. *con,* against) is to *confront.*

These words may have influenced the form of Eng. *frown,* from OFr. *froignier, frongnier,* perhaps related to Teut. *frogna,* nostril—which a *frown* draws toward the *brow.*

Brow itself is common Teut., AS. *bru;* Sans. *bhru.* To *browbeat* is to overawe with stern and haughty *brow.* From folk association of brains with extent of forehead come—with some implication of mockery—our *lowbrow* and our *highbrow* —who is sometimes *supercilious, q.v.*

effusion.
See futile.

egg.
See acumen.

eggnogg.
See nugget.

egoism, egotism.
See altruism.

egregious.
This first meant outstanding, chosen from the flock, from L. *egregius,* from *ex— + grex, gregis,* herd; *see absolute.* But, in the cynical way of human nature, it came to be used mainly of those outstandingly bad.

egress.
See issue.

eight.
See number.

either.
See weather.

ejaculation.
See wasp.

eject.
See subject.

eke.
See auction.

-el.
See swivel.

elastic.
Those without study of physics think of an *elastic* (rubber) band; the word, earlier *elastical,* referred first to the property of expansion, as of gases; then, to the ability (the scientific use today) to return to the usual bulk after expansion or contraction. This "impulsive force" was named in the 17th c. from Gr. *elastikos,* driving, from *elaunein,* to drive. The property was at the same time called *elater,* then *elatery,* before the term *elasticity* supplanted it; now *elater* is retained (in Linnaeus' system, ca. 1740: Carl von Linné, Swedish naturalist, 1707-1778) for the family of beetles that can flip over from their back to land on their feet—at which a youngster would be *elated.* This *elation* is to be carried out of oneself, from L. *ef, ex,* out: *efferre, etuli, elatus,* to carry out; *cp. port.*

elation.
See elastic.

elbow.
See pylorus.

elder.
See world.

elected.
See legible.

electricity.
Resin, the sap of certain trees, sometimes with insects caught in it, and hardened through the centuries until turned to stone, has since early times been used as an adornment. It was often found in the ocean. We call it *amber;* the Greeks called it *elektron.* Then they discovered that, when rubbed, it has odd qualities: puff balls swing; things are attracted and repelled. This was (outside of lightning) man's first contact with *electricity.*

Among the uses man put this power to (formed by analogy with *execution*) is *electrocution.* When scientists saw in all matter only whirling *electric* energy, they took the original Gr. word to describe this basic whirl-stuff: *electron.* Amber adornments have been largely replaced by plastic ones; but *electricity* goes on.

The Gr. *elektron* is traced to Gr. *elektor,* sunglare, the ancient notion being that the glare of the sun hardened on striking the sea. Pliny the Elder, in his *Natural History,* ca. 70 A.D., knew its origin; he noted that the Germans called it *glaesum*—whence our *glass* and *glaze.*

In the meantime, the two substances found floating in the sea were both called *amber,* from *Arab. 'anbar.* One was Fr. *ambre gris,* gray *amber,* now Eng. *ambergris;* the other was *ambre jaune,* yellow *amber,* now Eng. *amber.*

electrocution.
See electricity, refrain.

electrolysis.
See lysol.

electron.
See electricity.

electuary.
See licorice.

eleemosynary.
See alms.

elegance, elegant.
See legible.

element.
This is directly from L. *elementum,* meaning basically the simplest form of matter. For a long time there were supposed to be four *elements:* earth, water, air, fire. Modern chemistry distinguishes ninety-two (some with variant forms, called *isotopes:* Gr. *isos,* equal + *topos,* place; they occupy the same place in the periodic table of elements). The ninety-two are listed here, each followed by its symbol and atomic number in the table of elements.

actinium. Ac. 89
Discovered by Debierne in 1899, this radioactive element is named from Gr. *aktis, aktin-,* ray.

alabamine. Ab. 85
Discovered in 1931 by chemists at the Alabama Polytechnic Institute, and named for the State. One of these chemists was Allison; *cp. virginium.*

aluminum. Al. 13
This was first called *alumium,* later (and sometimes still) *aluminium.* It is from L. *alumen,* a stringent substance, which also gives us *alum.* Although

the most abundant metal on the surface of the earth, *aluminum* was not isolated until the 19th century.

antimony. Sb. 51
The Gr. *stimmi* (also *stigm-*, whence Eng. *stigma*), mark, became L. *stibium*. A powdered mineral, *stibnite*, was used by the ancients as a pigment and for the eyes (it is the eastern *kohl*, *q.v.*). In the 11th century the metal was called *antimonia*, perhaps a L. form of Arab. *al-ithmid*. Also suggested as origin is the Gr. *anti monos*, against one, in the folk thought that the qualities of the substance are too many to be described by a single man. But *see pretzel*.

argon. A. 18
Discovered in the atmosphere in 1894, this gas was named from Gr. *argon*. *a—*, not, + *ergon*, work, as it does not readily combine with other elements. Also from Gr. *ergon* are Eng. *erg* and *energy*. Ramsay and Travers found this element, also the other inert gases *helium*, *krypton*, *neon*, *xenon*, *q.v.*

arsenic. As. 33
The mineral orpiment was called in Arab. *az-zirnikh*, the golden, from Persian *zarnikh*, from *zar*, gold; *cp. zirconium*. The Greeks also used the yellow pigment; but they knew its medicinal properties, and by folk etymology changed the Arab. name to *arsenikon*, akin to Gr. *assen*, potent (male).

barium. Ba. 56
This metal was isolated from an earth (discovered by Scheele in 1779) named *baryta*, from Gr. *barys*, heavy.

beryllium. Be. 4
Isolated in 1828, this element is named from the stone *beryl*, Gr. *beryllos*, in which it was first found. It is also called *glucinum*, Gl. (Gr. *glykeros*, sweet) from the taste of its salts. *Cp. glucose, glycerin.*

bismuth. Bi. 83
This was early G. *wismut*, later by folk etymology *Weissmuth*, white substance. Agricola gave it the L. form of *bisemutum*, whence our term. (*Agricola* Latinized many words, in his *De Re Metallica*, 1530. Incidentally, he translated his own name, which was German *Bauer*, farmer. Similarly *Melancthon*, 1497-1560, is the Greek of German *Schwarzert*, black earth; the first and last names of *Desiderius Erasmus* 1466?-1536, are L. and Gr. for *Gerhards*, strong in affection; Thomas *Erastus*, 1524-93, was really *Lieber*, loving one; and many others of the time made similar translations. *Cp complexion.*)

boron. B. 5
Long before the "twenty mule team" of the United States, *borax* was imported to Europe from Asia. The word is from Arab. *buraq*, Pers. *burah*, white. The element, drawn by Davy from *boric* (*boracic*) acid, was called *boracium*, then *boron*.

bromine. Br. 35
Isolated in 1825, this is from Gr. *bromos*, stink.

cadmium. Cd. 48
This word was applied to a brass dust in foundries, perhaps first in the neighborhood of Thebes, founded by *Kadmus*—who also is credited with the invention of letters. The element was found by Stromeyer in 1817.

calcium. Ca. 20
This metal was found in lime, L. *calx*, *calc—*; whence also *calculate*, q.v.

carbon. C. 6
The L. for charcoal and coal was *carbo*, *carbon—*. The element also exists as diamond, *q.v.*

cerium. Ce. 58
Discovered in 1803 by Hisinger and Berzelius, this element was named *cererium* after the asteroid *Ceres*, discovered by Piazzi in 1801. The name was soon changed to the simpler *cerium*. *Cp. uranium.*

cesium. Cs. 55
Found through the spectroscope in 1860, this metal was named for its color, L. *caesius*, blue gray. *Cp. rubidium; thallium.*

chlorine. Cl. 17
Named by Davy, 1811, from its color, Gr. *chloros*, yellowish green.

chromium. Cr. 24
We have *chrome* yellow, and *chromatic*, from Gr. *chroma*, color. The colored compounds of this element suggested its name.

cobalt. Co. 27
The medieval goblin that was supposed by the miners to keep ore from yielding metal was called *Kobold* (the name is from OHG. *Godbald,* bold in God); the name was given this element by Brandt, who isolated it in 1753.

columbium. Cb. 41
This element was found in England by Hatchett, in 1801, studying a mineral from the United States, sent by John Winthrop the Younger, governor of Connecticut, and put in the British Museum. Hatchett named it in honor of that country. Associated with the element *tantalum,* it is also called *niobium* (Nb.), after *Niobe,* daughter of *Tantalus.*

copper. Cu. 29
This is from L. *aes Cyprium,* bronze from *Cyprus.*

dysprosium. Dy. 66
The Gr. prefix *dys—*(opposite of *eu—* as in *eugenics*) means bad, hard; it destroys the good values of a word. Gr. *pros,* to, combined with this, makes a coined word indicating that the element was hard to reach. It was with difficulty separated from the element *holmium,* in 1886.

erbium. Er. 68
Various earths, from mines near the town of *Ytterby* in Sweden, were named by Mosander, who separated them in 1843, *erbia, terbia,* and *yttria,* from the name of the town. The first of these gives us the element *erbium.* Later two other elements were separated, *ytterbium* and *lutecium, q.v.* Others found with these earths are *gadolinium, holmium, scandium, thulium, thorium.*

europium. Eu. 63
The mineral *samarskite,* named after a Russian mine official *Samarski,* was found, about 1900, to contain two elements. One Boisbaudran named *samarium;* the other Demarcay named, after the continent, *europium.*

fluorine. F. 9
From L. *fluere,* to flow; used as a flux with metals because of its low melting point. A number of men died working with this element, finally isolated by Moissan in 1886.

gadolinium. Gd. 64
Several elements (*erbium, q.v.*) were extracted from the mineral *gadolinite,* which was discovered in 1794 by *Gadolin.* The element *gadolinium* was named after him.

gallium. Ga. 31
Lecoq de Boisbaudran, who discovered this element in 1875, named it for his country, France, the L. name for which is *Gallia. Cp. germanium; scandium*: nationalism in chemistry.

germanium. Ge. 32
This element, discovered in 1886 by Winkler, was named after his country, *Germany. Cp. gallium; scandium.*

gold. Au. 79
The L. *aurum,* gold, (akin to *Aurora,* goddess of the dawn) gives the symbol for this element; the name is common Teut., cognate with yellow (G. *Geld* gold; G. *gelb,* yellow).

hafnium. Hf. 72
Named after Copenhagen, formerly called *Hafnia.* It was discovered in 1923 by Coster and Hevesy; not recognized until then because of its likeness to *zirconium.*

helium. He. 2
This element was first observed in the spectrum of the sun, during an eclipse in India in 1868. The Gr. *helios* means sun.

holmium. Ho. 67
This element (found by Cleve in 1879, in *erbia* earth) is named after *Stockholm,* L. *Holmia.* It was isolated in 1911 by Holmberg.

hydrogen. H. 1
From Gr. *hydor, hydro—,* water, + *gen—,* to produce, as it formed water. Named bv Lavoisier.

illinium. Il. 61
Discovered by chemists at the University of *Illinois,* in 1926, this element was named after the State.

indium. In. 49
Named after the color of its lines in the spectrum, *indigo. Indigo* was earlier from L. *Indicum,* of *India.* The element was found in 1863. *Cp. cesium.*

iodine. I. 53
This element, discovered by Courtois in 1811, was named from the color of its vapor, after Gr. *iodes,* from *ion,* violet.

iridium. Ir. 77
From the colors of its salt solutions, Tennant, who discovered this element in 1803, named it after Gr. *iris, irid—,* rainbow.

iron. Fe. 26
The symbol is from L. *ferrum,* as also in Eng. *ferric* and *ferrous.* The name of the element is common Teut., but perhaps was borrowed from the Celts, who used *iron* before the Teutons: AS. *isern, iren;* Irish *iarann;* Welsh *haearn.*

krypton. Kr. 36
Found, in 1898, only after evaporating enormous amounts of liquid air, this element was named from Gr. *kryptos,* hidden; as also in *cryptography.*

lanthanum. La. 57
Mosander, in 1839, studying another substance, found this element, which he named from Gr. *lanthanein,* to lurk. Four years later he drew from it another element, which he called *didymium,* from Gr. *didymos,* twin. But in 1885 von Welsbach found that this was really two elements, which he called *neodidymia* (Gr. *neo—,* new) and *praseodidymia* (Gr. *prasios,* green). These names were shortened to *neodymium* and *praseodymium.*

lead. Pb. 82
This word is AS. *lead,* Du. *lood;* G. *Lot,* plummet; and *plummet* is from L. *plumbum,* the Roman name for the metal, which gives us the symbol of the element.

lithium. Li. 3
Gr. *lithos,* stone (as also in *lithography*) gives this element its name; when discovered by Arfvedson in 1817 it was thought to exist only in minerals.

lutecium. Lu. 71
This metal was named by Urbain, in 1907, after his native city of Paris, formerly *Lutetia.* It was found in *ytterbia; see erbium.*

magnesium. Mg. 12
Two substances found in the 18th c. in Gr. *Magnesia,* a district of Thessaly, were called *magnesia alba* and *magnesia nigra* (L. *alba,* white; *nigra,* black). To distinguish the elements, the first is called *magnesium;* the other, *manganese.* In the same district was found an oxide of iron with qualities now known as *magnetic.*

manganese. Mn. 25
See magnesium.

masurium. Ma. 43
Found in 1925, this element is named after the district of *Masuria,* in East Prussia, whence came the substance (platinum ore) from which it was extracted. It was found by Noddack and Tacke, along with *rhenium, q.v.*

mercury. Hg. 80
The symbol is from Gr. *hydor argyros,* water silver (*Gr. hydor, hydr—,* water, as in Eng. *hydrant, hydraulic,* + Gr. *argyros,* silver, cognate with *argos,* white, shining, speedy; whence Eng. *argent, argonaut*). The Romans gave the name of the god of merchants (and thieves, also messenger of the gods: *Mercury*) to a planet; then to a metal that seemed to possess some of the god's qualities.

molybdenum. Mo. 42
Gr. *molybdos,* lead, was applied to substances that left a mark, like graphite. From one of these, the element was extracted.

neodymium. Nd. 60
See lanthanum.

neon. Ne. 10
When found (in 1898), this was new, and was so named (Gr. *neos,* new).

nickel. Ni. 28
The miners called this *Kupfernickel,* because they couldn't get any copper from it; the "goblin" was interfering again (*cp. cobalt*): G. *Nickel,* goblin, is a form of the name *Niklaus, Nicholas.* In 1751 Cronstedt declared it an element and called it *nickel.*

nitrogen. N. 7
The Arab. *natrun,* which gives us Eng. *natron,* was taken into Gr. as *nitron,* whence Eng. *nitre.* Hence the element *nitrogen,* "*nitre*-born". It was

earlier called mephitic air; and, by Lavoisier, *azote,* from Gr. *a*—, without, + *zoon,* living thing.

osmium. Os. 76
This element is named from Gr. *osme,* odor—perhaps related to Gr. *osmos,* thrust; whence Eng. *osmosis.* It was found in 1803, by Tennant.

oxygen. O. 8
From Gr. *oxys,* sour (acid) + *gen*—, producting. Named by Lavoisier, but isolated by Scheels, in 1771 (published 1777) and Priestley, in 1774.

palladium. Pd. 46
The asteroid *Pallas* was discovered by Olbers in 1802; the element *palladium,* in 1803, by Wollaston. *Pallas Athene* was the goddess of Athens.

phosphorus. P. 15
From the Gr. *phos,* light, +*phoros,* bearing, this element was kept in the dark by Brandt, who discovered it in 1669, until it was also found by others. It glows in the dark.

platinum. Pt. 78
This was earlier *platina,* a Sp. diminutive of *plata,* silver; whence also our precious metal, *plate.*

polonium. Po. 84
When Mme. Curie first separated a radio-active element, in 1898, she named it for her native land, *Poland.*

potassium. K. 19
The symbol is from L. *kalium,* from the Arab. *al qali* (whence Eng. *alkali*), the ashes of a sea plant, from which sodium carbonate was obtained. This was long identified with potassium carbonate, from the ashes of land plants. These plants were burned in pots; hence, *pot ashes* (now Eng. *potash*); and the element derived from them, by Davy in 1807, was called *potassium.*

praseodymium. Pr. 59
See lanthanum.

protoactinium. Pa. 91
This element, if it loses an alpha particle, becomes *actinium, q.v.*; hence its name: Gr. *protos,* first. It was isolated in 1917.

radium. Ra. 88
This element was discovered by the Curies in 1898; its power of giving off rays gave it its name: L. *radius, ray.*

radon. Rn. 86
This element, discovered by Dorn in 1900, is given off by the element *radium;* hence its name. It is the heaviest gas known.

rhenium. Re. 75
Found in Germany in 1925, this element was named after *Rhenish Prussia* (along the *Rhine*). *Cp. masurium.*

rhodium. Rh. 45
Wollaston found this element in 1803. It is named from the color of its salt solution, Gr. *rhodon,* rose; whence also Eng. *rhododendron, q.v.*

rubidium. Rb. 37
This element gives red lines in the spectrum: hence its name, from L. *ruber, rubid*—, red; whence also Eng. *rubescent.* It was found through the spectroscope in 1861. *Cp. cesium.*

ruthenium. Ru. 44
A *Ruthene* is a Little Russian, from LL. *Rutheni* for *Russi.* Osann thus called an element he found in 1828, in ore from the Ural Mountains, Russia.

samarium. Sa. 62
See europium.

scandium. Sc. 21
The L. *Scandia* is Scandinavia; where this element comes from. It was found in 1879 by Nilson, in the *erbia group; cp. erbium; gallium.*

selenium. Se. 34
This element, found in 1817 by Berzelius, was first thought to be *tellurium,* to which it is akin. As *tellurium* is the earth element, this element was named after the moon: Gr. *selene,* moon. L. *tellus, tellur*—, earth, gives the name to *tellurium,* found in the late 18th century.

silicon. Si. 14
From L. *silex, silic*—, flint, comes Eng. *silica;* also the element. It was first named *silicium,* by Berzelius, in 1810, when he thought it was a metal.

silver. Ag. 47
This is a common Teut. word, AS. *seolfor,* a very ancient word. The symbol is from the Gr. *argyros,* shining; *cp. mercury.*

sodium. Na. 11
The symbol is from L. *natrium,* from *natron; cp. nitrogen. Sodium,* a L. form of *soda,* was coined by Davy, who obtained the element in 1808, using caustic *soda. Soda,* Fr. *soude,* is possibly from L. *solida,* solid.

strontium. Sr. 38
Isolated in 1808, by Davy, from a mineral from *Strontian,* in Argyll, Scotland.

sulfur, sulphur. S. 16
This is an old word, L. *sulfur, sulpur;* applied generally to substances that burned.

tantalum. Ta. 73
This element, found by Ekeberg in 1802, was hard to locate; its tracking down was a *tantalizing* (*q.v.*) task. Hence he named it *tantalum.* It was found with the element *columbium, q.v.*

tellurium. Te. 52
See selenium.

terbium. Tb. 65
See erbium.

thallium. Tl. 81
Found by Crookes in 1861, a green line in the spectrum, this element is named from Gr. *thallos,* green shoot, from *thallein,* to sprout. The same root gave us *Thalia,* the comic Muse. *Cp. cesium.*

thorium. Th. 90
Berzelius, in 1815, among the earths with *erbium, q.v.,* found what he thought was an element, and named it after the Scandinavian god *Thor.* He admitted in 1825 that he had been wrong; then gave the name to an element he found in 1828.

thulium. Tm. 69
Another of the elements found with *erbium, q.v.* (in 1879), this was also named for the part of the world where found: the Romans called the far north *Ultima Thule.*

tin. Sn. 50
It is natural that the Teut. term for this metal be used, for the ancient Romans secured *tin* from mines in Britain. The symbol stands for *stannum,* the earlier Roman name.

Titanium. Ti. 22
When Klaproth, in 1789, found an element in pitchblende (the emanations of which led later to the finding of *radium*), he named it after the Greek god of Heaven, *Uranus*—but directly from the planet *Uranus,* which Herschel has discovered in 1781. Six years later, he named another element (first called *menachanite,* because found by Gregor in *Menachan,* Cornwall, England) *titanium,* after the *Titans,* children of *Uranus* and Gaea (Earth).

tungsten. W. 74
This element is named (by Scheele, 1781) Sw. *tung* + *sten,* heavy stone. The symbol is for *Wolframium;* Agricola said that the mineral eats tin as a wolf eats sheep.

uranium. U. 92
See titanium.

vanadium. V. 23
One of the names of the Norse goddess Freya was *Vanadis;* this metal was named for her by Seftsröm and Berzelius, 1831.

virginium. Vi. 87
Named after Virginia, the native state of Allison, who found the element in 1930.

xenon. Xe. 54
Also found by evaporation of large quantities of liquid air (by Ramsay and Travers, in 1898), this is from Gr. *xenos* stranger, guest.

ytterbium. Yb. 70
See erbium.

yttrium. Y. 39
See erbium.

zinc. Zn. 30
This word, used by Agricola (L. *zincum*) is of unknown origin.

zirconium. Zr. 40
Drawn by Klaproth, in 1789, from the semi-precious *zircon,* this element was named from its source. *Zircon* is

via Arab *zarqun* from Pers. *zar*, gold; *cp. arsenic*. The element was not isolated until 1824, by Berzelius and not made, pure, until 1914.

Certain elements, when first found, were temporarily named for that from which they were extracted (or drawn from by prediction, before the finding). Thus *gallium* was called *eka-aluminum; alabamine, eka-iodine; germanium, eka-silicon; protoactinium, eka-tantalum; scandium, eka-boron; virginium, eka-cesium*. (The first of each of these pairs is two periods higher than the second, in the same element-group.)

The Gr. prefix *ek, eks* (L. *ex*), *ekto*, meant out of, outside. Thus we have also Eng. *ectoplasm*, a *plasma* (Gr. *plasma*, from *plassein*, to mould) outside the form; and *ecstasy*, which means literally a state of being beside oneself, from *ec*, out of, + *histani*, to cause to stand. The root of Gr. *histani* is *states*, whence many words like L. and Eng. *status; state; thermostat*, that makes the temperature stand still. *Cp. tank*.

elephant.
See focus.

eleven.
See number.

elf.
See incinerator.

eligible.
See legible.

eliminate.
See limen.

elixir.
See world.

elocution.
See agnostic.

elope.
See subjugate.

eloquent.
See agnostic.

Elysian.
See daffodil.

emancipate.
See manœuvre.

embankment.
See bank.

embarcation, embark.
See embargo.

embargo.
This was first an order shutting ships into a harbor (and not allowing others to enter) as when a war was expected. To *bar* was Fr. *barre*, a *barrier;* hence, a pole across something, and the *barre* for the ballet or the *bar* for the beer. With L. *in*, intensive, this via the Fr. *embarrer* gave us Eng. *embar;* and via LL. form *imbarricare, imbarricat-* came Sp. *embargar*, to arrest; whence Sp. and Eng. *embargo*. *Barricade* is directly from Fr. *barrique*, barrel, as *barricades* were thrown together of barrels filled with dirt and stones. Sp. and Port. *embarcar*, from L. *imbarcare, imbarcat-*, to go on board (whence Eng. *embarcation*), from L. *in*, into, +*barca*, boat, Eng. *bark*, give us *embark* . . . if there's no *embargo!*

embassy.
See ambassador.

emblem.
This is a picture within which is another idea, the object you see being a symbol. But this figurative use was preceded by a literal one; the word is from Gr. *emblema*, inlaid work, from *em*, in + *ballein*, to throw; *cp. ballot*. Thus the scales are an *emblem* of justice. Justice is blindfold so as to act without favor, equally for poor and rich. Similarly Zeus blinded *Plutus*, god of wealth (Gr. *ploutos*, wealth, stem Gr. *pleos*, more, whence L. *plus; cp. foil;* hence Eng. *plutocracy* — + Gr. *kratein*, to rule) so that he might distribute his gifts without regard to merit, like the rain, which falleth alike on the wicked and the good. *See parlor*.

embolism.
See parlor.

embrace.
See brassiere.

embroil.
See island.

emcee.
See refrain.

emerald.
See carnelian.

emigrate.
See immunity.

emir.

This word, from the Arab. *amir*, prince, from Arab. *amara*, to command, has also given us the more familiar word *admiral*, *q.v. Admire*, from L. *ad*, at, to + *mirari*, to wonder, meant first to marvel at, then to regard with pleased surprise, then just to look at with pleasure. From the same L. *mirari*, via L. *mirator-* and OFr. *mireor* comes the *admiring* glass, or looking-glass, the *mirror* at which milady makes her appearance *admirable*.

Another suggestion, more plausible, for the ending *-al* in *admiral* is that it was retained from the Arab., where it appears in very frequent combinations: *e.g.*, *amir-al-umara*, king of kings; *amir-al-muminin*, commander of the faithful.

emolument.

See salary.

emotion.

See mute.

emperor.

See empire.

emphasis.

See focus.

empire.

The L. *imperare, imperat-*, to command, gave L. *imperator*, commander, which was given as an honorary title (commander-in-chief) to the Caesars whence, via OFr. *emperere*, Eng. *emperor*. The L. *imperium*, rule, also via Fr. gives us *empire*; more directly, the adjective Eng. *imperial*. *Empiric* and *empirical*, however, are from the Gr. *enpeiros*, skilled, from *en*, in + *peira*, trial.

In early use, from an opposition between trial and study, the term *empiric* was applied to a trial-and-error doctor, a quack. It has been elevated into a philosophical attitude in *empiricism*. One that actually has tried things out is the *pragmatist*, from Gr. *pragma, pragmat—*, deed, from *prattein*, to do.

empiric, empirical, empiricism.

See empire.

employ.

See complexion.

emporium.

This is a place where merchants come together, Gr. *emporios* from *emporos*, merchant. Then, as recently, the merchant was a traveling salesman: Gr. *emporos* is from Gr. *en*, in + *por-*, *per-*, to travel (related, perhaps, to Gr. *pod*, foot; *cp. pedagogue;* L. *per*, through). *Perhaps* is a hybrid: L. *per*, through, + AS. *hap*, chance (perchance; *cp. cheat*), luck; whence *happen*. *Happy* first meant lucky; and if you were lucky you'd be *happy* too.

empyrean.

See pyre.

enamel.

See omelette.

encase.

See casement.

encaustic.

See catholic.

enchant.

See chant, trance.

enclose, enclosure.

See close, pylorus, *cp.* inclose.

encomium.

The *comic* spirit was borne, if not born, in the village revel in honor of Bacchus. From Gr. *kome*, village, came Gr. *komos*, revel; whence all our *comedy*. The song sung in this revel (Gr. *en*, in) was the *encomium*, in praise of the god of pleasure.

endocrine.

See garble.

endorse.

See tergiversation.

endure.

See suffer.

energy.

See element: argon; organ.

See zymurgy. Gr. *en*, with intensive force, + *ergon, ourgia*, working).

enfranchise.

See free.

engender.

See cyanide; racy.

engine.

This word shows the power transferred to its product. Pronounced with the accent on a long *i*, until mid 17th c., it meant mother wit, from L. *ingenium*, the powers inborn. Hence also *ingenious; see racy*.

England, English.
See Anglo-Saxon. *English* is a sound-shifting from *Anglish,* from *Angle-ish.*

engrave.
See grave.

enjoy.
See joy.

enmity.
See remnant.

ensign.
See sign.

ensilage.
See psilo-.

enslave.
See free.

enter.
See trance.

enterprise.
See surprise.

entertain.
This word had a long course to its present meaning. It is via Fr. *entretenir* from L. *inter,* among + *tenere,* to hold; *cp. tennis.* It first meant to keep things intertwined; then, applied to persons, to keep (to maintain). This also of ideas and things: to *entertain* an opinion. Then, to keep in good condition; again of persons, to keep occupied—which might mean either to keep busy or to keep amused. From the common preference in this regard, the current sense of *entertainment.*

enthrall.
See trance.

enthusiasm.
When anyone was really roused, it was assumed in the old times that a god (if not a demon) had possessed him. This possession, among the Greeks, was *enthusiasm,* from Gr. *enthousiasmos,* from *entheos,* a god within, from *en,* in + *theos,* god; *cp. month*: February. Similarly the Romans spoke of the temple-spirit; *cp. fanatic.* And the Anglo-Saxons, of the god-held man: AS. *gydig;* which we preserve as *giddy.*

entice.
Has a thing of beauty—a woman, a sunset — ever turned you from your busy thoughts? And set you suddenly afire? Then indeed you have been *enticed,* from OFr. *enticier,* from LL. *intitiare,* to set on fire, from *titio,* a firebrand. To *provoke* is to call forth, from L. *provocare,* from *pro,* forth + *vocare, vocat—,* to call, whence Eng. *vocation,* calling, from L. *vox, voc—,* voice, whence Eng. *vocal, vocable;* LL. *vocabularium,* whence *vocabulary;* Fr. *vois,* whence *voice. Lure* is from Fr. *leurre,* from OHG. *luoder,* bait. The siren's *voice* was a *lure* to *entice* sailors.

entire.
See deck.

entity.
See authentic.

entomology.
See insect.

entrance.
See trance.

entrepreneur.
See surprise.

entropy.
This term in the second law of thermodynamics, popularly construed as 'the universe is running down', was coined in 1865 by Rudolf J. E. Clausius (1822-88) after the word *energy, q.v.* It means the "transformation-contents" of a system, from Gr. *en-,* within + *trope,* transformation, from *trepein,* to change, to turn; *cp. trophy.*

entwine.
See prestige.

enumerate.
See number.

envelop.
See develop.

envisage, envy.
See improvised.

eohippus.
This is the dawn-horse, Gr. *eos,* dawn; *cp.* dromedary.

ephebic (oath).
Graduates of the College of the City of New York take the *ephebic* oath, of devotion to their city, as they enter manhood's years. An *ephebe* was a Greek of the age of 18 to 20: from Gr. *ephebos,* from *epi,* upon + *hebe,*

early manhood. Note that *Hebe* was the goddess of youth. Also, *hebetic*.

ephemeral.
See decay.

epic.
See castanet.

epicurean.
See Appendix II.

epidermis.
See propaganda.

epiglottis.
See laugh. (Gr. *epi-*, over, upon).

epitome.
(pronounced with four syllables). *See* anatomy.

equable.
The L. *aequus,* just, even, formed another adjective, *aequalis;* this came into Eng. as *equal.* From the verb L. *aequare, aequat-*, to make level or even, came Eng. *equation;* also L. *aequabilis,* that can be evened; hence smooth; from this we have Eng. *equable.* There was also L. *equus,* horse; Eng. *equine;* L. *eques,* horseman, L. *equestris,* relating to him; whence Eng. *equestrian.* From the Teutonic into this picture came OHG. *scur,* shed; MHG. *schiure,* barn; LL. *scuria,* stable: from the mistaken notion that this was related to L. *equus,* horse, came the forms that ended in Eng. *equerry,* the royal stables. And *esquire* (similarly shifting) is from OFr. *escuyer,* from L. *scutarius,* shield-bearer (Eng. *squire*), from L. *scutum,* shield. *Scutum* and its diminutives *scutellum* and *scutulum* are Eng. biological words; *scutellum* being a scientist's error; it is really L. *scutella,* platter. But actually from L. *scutum* via LL. form *escution*—comes Eng. *escutcheon,* as in the blot on the *'scutcheon.*

equal, equation, equestrian.
See equable.

equinox.
On March 20 and September 22, the sun's path crosses the equator; this is the *equinoctial* period, when day and night are of the same length (L. *aequus,* equal + *nox, noct*—, night). The *vernal equinox* is from the L. adjective from L. *ver,* spring; akin to L. *viridare,* to grow green, from *viridis,* green, whence Eng. *verdant, verdure. Cp. month; week.* *Autumn* and the *autumnal equinox* are from L. *autumnus,* from? *auctumnus,* the time of increase; *cp. auction.*

eradicate, erase.
See rascal.

Erasmus.
See complexion, element: bismuth.

erbium.
See element.

erect, erection.
See alert; royal.

erg.
See element: argon; organ.

ermine.
See Appendix II.

erosion.
See rodent.

erotic.
See anacampserote. Young Eros is the Greek Cupid; *see psychoanalysis; Appendix II.*

err.
See errand.

errand, errant.
The *knights-errant* sometimes had a specific *errand;* sometimes they just wandered about the countryside. This is caught in the history of the word, from Fr. *errant,* present particple of *errer.* This verb developed from L. *iterare,* to travel; *cp. obituary;* and also from L. *errare, errat*—, to go astray (whence lists of *errata; err; erratic,* etc.). *Knights-errant* kept their dignity; but the doublet *arrant* was so often associated with vagabond, knave, etc., that it became merely an intensive. *Errand* is a common Teut. word, from AS. *aerend,* mission; AS. *ār,* messenger, (For *knight, see lady.*)

errata, erratic.
See errand.

Ersatz.
See oleomargarine.

eruption.
See rote.

escape.
See achieve.

escarpment.
See scarf.

escutcheon.
See equable.

Eskimo.
See Hebrew.

especial.
See salary.

espouse.
See spouse.

espy.
See scourge.

esquire.
See equable.

essence, essential.
See authentic.

establish.
See tank.

estate.
See season. In political use, the *First Estate* is the body of Lords Spiritual; the second, of Lords Temporal; the third, the commons. While not represented in legislatures, the press has so much power in a nation that it has come to be referred to as the *fourth estate*.

estivation, estuary.
See hibernate.

etch.
See indenture.

Ethiopia.
This might well be—the Greeks thought so, too—*Aithiopia*, from *aithein*, to burn: the land of the sunburned. It is, however, an adaptation of the native Egyptian name, *Ethaush*.

etiquette.
This may have come natural to the ancients, for it is of Teut. origin. (Remember the story of the old man who walked through the crowded Athenian bleachers at a stadium; when he came to the Spartan section, the men rose as one, to offer him a seat—whereupon the Athenians applauded. When they were still again, a man from Thessaly observed: "The Athenians recognize virtue; the Spartans practice it.") *Etiquette* is from OFr. *estiquete;* whence also Eng. *ticket;* the Fr. is from G. *stecken*, to put, causal of *stechen*, to prick; whence Eng. *stitch; cp. attack*. The first meaning of *etiquette* was a label or *ticket* stuck on a post; such notices had the rules of the day, for army or court procedure; hence the present meaning.

To purchase things on *tick* is a (17th c.; *cp. mob*) shortening of *ticket;* sailors would use their pay-*tickets* for credit slips. A *ticket-of-leave* man was a convict released, under certain conditions, before his term expired; these terms were noted on his *ticket*. The insect *tick* is a Teut. word, related to G. *ziege*, goat, woodgoat. The bed *tick*, encasing the pillow feathers, is borrowed in Teut. tongues from L. *teca*, from *theca*, from Gr. *theke*, case. The slight blow, or sound, as the *tick* of a watch, is echoic. Whichever of these is involved, *etiquette* comes in; and the counsel to this generation is, like the watchful soldiers, to keep (Emily) posted.

eucalyptus.
The L. *calix*, plural *calices*, cup, is used in Eng. as a term in botany, together with derivatives such as *calicular*, *caliculate*, and the diminutive *calicle*. By way of OFr. it gives us Eng. *chalice*. But confused with this in many forms is L. *calyx*, plural *calyxes*, from Gr. *kalyx*, the outer cover of a fruit or flower, from Gr. *kalytein*, to cover. This also (*calyx*) is used in Eng. botany, with its derivatives *calycular, calyculate, calycle*. The one set of terms refers to cup-shaped forms; the second, to those that are covered (by hoods, pods, shells, etc.). There is one tree, the flower of which is covered by a sort of cap; hence (Gr. *eu-*, well, beautiful, + *calyptos*, covered) we call it the *eucalyptus*. *Cp. evangelist*.

eucharist.
See charity.

eugenics, euphemism.
See evangelist.

eulogistic.
See dysentery. (L. *logos*, speech; *cp. logistics*).

euphemism.
See evangelist.

Euphrates.

This river, named as if from Gr. *euphrasia,* delight, from *euphraino,* to gladden, is Hebraic in origin. It is from Heb. *parah,* to make fertile; possibly influenced by *Ephrath,* from *pharath,* to be sweet—the luscious valley.

euphuism.

For the Elizabethean ladies, an exuberant style of speech and writing developed, of which an outstanding example is in Lyly's *Euphues* (Gr. *euphues,* of good nature), 1759-80, which has given the *euphuistic* style its name. This should not be confused with *euphemism* (from Gr. *euphemizein,* to speak fair); *cp. evangelist.*

eureka.

The ancient king Hiero wanted to know whether the golden crown given him was all gold. While Archimedes was taking a bath, it occurred to him that a body must displace its own weight in water; this might be a way to test the crown. Without waiting to dress, he cried *Eureka!* (Gr. *heureka,* Found!, from *heuriskein,* to find) and hurried home to dry. The logical art of discovery is called *heuretic;* modern education is *heuristic,* in that the pupil is trained to discover things for himself.

Europe.

Assyrian monuments present *Asu,* land of the rising sun, and *Ereb,* "setting sun land." The Greeks carried these over as *Asia* and *Europe* (in the Homeric *Hymn to Apollo*). Europe then developed the legend of *Europa,* daughter of *Phœnix,* borne off by *Zeus* as a bull (*cp. Bosphorus*), and becoming the mother of *Minos* [whence, in Crete, the *Minotaur,* or bull of *Minos,* from L. *taurus,* bull, whence Sp. and Eng. *toreador.* This *Minotaur* lurked in the *Labyrinth* (from Gr. *labdys,* double-headed ax), the windings of which give us Eng. *labyrinthine. Theseus,* who slew the *Minotaur,* needed the *clue* (from AS. *cliwen,* ball of thread; also *clew*) supplied by *Ariadne.*] The suggestion has been made that Europe is from Gr. *euros,* black mould + *ops,* face, from *op,* visible, *i.e.,* fertile land; but this seems farther-fetched than *Europa* by *Zeus.*

europium.

See element.

evade.

See wade.

evangelist.

An *angel* is one of the messengers of the Lord; literally, one that brings word, from Gr. *aggelein,* to announce. If the tidings were especially good, they were brought by an *evangel,* from Gr. *eu—,* well, from *eus,* good. Hence one that hails the good tidings is an *evangelist.*

The prefix *eu—* appears in many Eng. words; *e.g. euphemism,* from Gr. *eupheme,* speaking well of; *eugenics,* from Gr. *eu—* + *gen—,* to produce. Sir Thomas More punned on the prefix in the title of his famous *Utopia,* 1516, which has given the word *utopian* to the language. For a *utopia* is a good place that is no place (Gr. *eu—,* well; *ou—,* not + *topos,* place; whence *topography—topos* + *graphein,* to write; and *topic,* from the title of a work by Aristotle, Gr. *ta topika,* On commonplaces). *See dysentery.*

event, eventuate.

See prevent; *cp. dollar.*

evident.

See improvised, vehicle.

ewe.

See mutton.

exact.

The original sense of this word survives in the verb: *exact,* from L. *exigere, exact—,* from *ex,* out + *agere, actum,* to drive. To force out came to be used as to force in the direction one desired, to insist upon. Hence the adj. *exact,* permitting no deviation. *Exigent* comes more directly from the same verb. Without the prefix, we derive *agent* from the participle, the *acting* one; from the gerundive (L. *agendum, —a,*) *agenda,* things to be done; and from the past participle (L. *actum*) *act,* a thing done, a performance. Hence *active, actor, action. Actual* meant done, completed, hence existing now. The opposite of *active* is *passive* (receiving the *action;* L. *pati—, pass—,* to suffer); the opposite of *agent* is *patient.* (Unless the *agent* is a first aid operator, in which case the recipient of the *action* is the *victim. Cp. trance.*)

The frequentative of L. *agere,* to drive, is L. *agitare, agitat—,* to move to and fro, whence Eng. *agitate.* From the *agi-*

tated stir comes the sense of *excitement.* *Excite* is via Fr. *exciter* from L. *excitare, excitat—*, to keep calling, to rouse (whence also Eng. *excitation*) frequentative of L. *exciere* to call forth, from *ex,* out + *ciere, cit—*, to call, to set in motion. The frequentative of *ciere,* L. *citare, citat—*, gives us Eng. *citation* and via Fr. *citer* Eng. *cite.* To move to and fro, gathering things together (mentally) is to ponder; thus L. *co—, com,* together + *agitare* gave L. *cogitare, cogitat—*, and *Eng. cogitation.* To think things out is thus Eng. *excogitate.*

(*Cognate* is from L. *co,* together, + *gnatus,* later *natus,* born, whence L. *natalis,* Eng. *natal.* And *cp. cognition.*)

The L. *exigere, exact—*, permitting no deviation, developed a noun form *exagmen,* the tongue of a balance, for weighing. Thence the verb, L. *examinare, examinat—*, and our Eng. *examine* and the often dreaded *examination.*

exaggerated.
See caricature.

exalt.
See world.

examine.
See exact.

example.
See quaint.

exchequer.
The game of *chess* (from OFr. *esches,* through Arab., from Pers. *shah,* king) was and is widespread. In that game, one must call *"Check!"* on putting one's opponent's king in danger; hence (from OFr. *eschec*) the meaning of holding someone in *check.* A bank *check* was originally a carbon of an order, for *checking* the deal. The board or table on which the game is played was OFr. *eschequier* (whence the game *checkers*); but the king's *counsellors* used such a table, with colored counters, in calculating the national revenues; hence, the *exchequer.* Finally, *checkmate* is from Arab *shah mat,* the king is dead . . . Wish me a good game!

excitation, excite, excitement.
See exact.

exclaim, exclamation.
See claim.

exclude, exclusive.
See close.

excogitate.
See exact.

excoriate.
See scourge.

excrement.
As bad money (the sociologists tell us) always chases out the good, here a less pleasant word has quite routed its harmless fellow. There was an early Eng. *excrement* (from L. *excrescere,* from *ex,* out + *crescere,* to grow—the present participle of which gives us *crescent*) which meant outgrowths of the body, *i.e.,* the hair and nails. Thus Shakespeare, *Comedy of Errors,* II,ii,79, exclaims:

"Why is time such a niggard of hair, being, as it is, so plentiful an *excrement?"* This has been supplanted by *excrement,* and *excrete,* from L. *excernere,* to sift out, from *ex,* out + *cernere, cret—*, sift. In the first sense, we still have the adjective *excrescent.* *Cp. concrete.*

excrescent.
See excrement.

excursion.
See hussar.

execute, executive, execution.
See refrain.

exemplary.
See prompt.

exempt.
See quaint.

exercise.
To *exorcise* is to chase out the demons, by the sacred word: from the Gr. *ex,* out, + *horkos,* oath.

To *exercise* is to let out the animals (hence, to keep them at work): from L. *ex,* out, + *arcere,* to confine. The original sense is seen in the expression "Don't *exercise* yourself" or "Don't get *exercised*"—meaning "all worked up". It was first transitive; you always *exercised* someone else. When the word grew more pleasant in its implications, a person might just take *exercise.*

exhibit, exhibitionism.
See expose.

exhume.
See humble.

exigent.
See exact.

exit.
See issue.

exorcise.
See exercise.

expatriate.
See zipper.

expect.
See auction.

expel.
See pelt.

expend.
From the sense of paying out (*see aggravate*) this came to mean, use up, as to *expend* one's energy. Hence, the supplies and men an army can afford to sacrifice for a certain gain are *expendable*, even though the victory is *expensive* (paying out; hence, costly).
To *spend* is aphetic from this word, or from OFr. *desprendre*: *ex—*, to pay out; *de—*, to pay down.

experience, experiment, expert.
See parlor.

expire.
See inspiration.

explain, explanation.
See saxophone.

explicit.
See complexion.

explode.
This word has been borrowed from more pleasant places, to fit a new notion. It is from L. *explodere, explo—* (whence Eng. *explosion*), to break into clapping, from L. *plaudere, plaus—*, to clap (at the theatre). To *applaud* is to clap at (L. *ap*, from *ad*, to). Something *plausible*, originally, was something that deserved *applause*—true or not, it was put across.
The original word was echoic of a sudden sound.

explosion.
See explode.

export.
See port.

expose, exposition.
See pose. To *exhibit* is to hold forth, from L. *exhibere, exhibit—*, to hold out (legally, to hold out to someone, to provide), from *ex*, out + *habere*, to *have*, to hold. *Psychanalysts* oppose *exhibitionism* and *inhibitions* (holding in; restraints).

expound.
See pose.

express.
See plot.

exquisite.
Things *exquisite* should be sought out —and are: from L. *exquirere, exquisit—*, from *ex*, out + *quaerere, quest—*, to ask, to seek. The meaning shifted from sought out to made with care, delicately done, therefore, exciting intense admiration. To seek into things is to *inquire*, from L. *inquirere* (*enquire* via OFr. *enquerre*); hence also *inquisition* (the noun ending, *—ion—*) and the adjective *inquisitive*. After the *Inquisition* came the *inquest*, which first meant any legal *inquiry*, then specifically the coroner's *inquest;* until the 17th c. this was pronounced with the accent on the second syllable; the *in* therefore dropped off, giving us the aphetic doublet *quest*, and the further noun *question*.

A *quire* of paper (though used to answer *questions*) is via OFr. *quaier* (Fr. *cahier*), from L. *quaterni*, set of four, from *quattuor*, four: now, 24 sheets (from four folded in six, as one folds a letter?). *Choir*, though sometimes spelled *quire*, is from ME. *quer*, from OFr. *cuer* (Fr. *chœur*), from L. *chorus*, from Gr. *choros*, the band of singers and dancers in the early religious festivals from which the drama sprang. Hence Eng. *chorus;* and the writing down of the dance pattern, *choreography*. *Chorea* is short for L. *chorea Sancti Viti*, Saint Vitus' dance. The small *choir* organ, however, is probably a corruption of 17th and 18th c. *chair organ*, attached to the back of the organist's seat. More directly from the Greek is *coryphée*, from Gr. *koryphaios*, leader of the dramatic chorus, from *koryphe*, head. The root indicates a group, as in *corybantes*, the orgiastic dancers; or in *corymb* in botany, from Gr. *corymbos*, cluster, head. Alas, not every *coryphée* is *exquisite!*

extant.
See tank.

extemporaneous.
See improvised.

extermination.
See determine.

extinct, extinguish.
See distinct.

extirpate.
See stipulate.

extort.
See torch.

extract.
See distraction.

extraneous.
See uncouth.

extricate.
See intrigue.

eyrie, eyry.
See debonair.

F

fabian.
See Appendix II.

fable.
See fib; *cp.* fate.

fabric, fabricate.
See defeat.

face.
Through Fr. *face* and Prov. *fassa, face* comes from L. *facies,* which first meant appearance, then visage. The schoolboy "with shining morning *face*" has the right of it: the word is from L. *fac-* as in *facem,* torch; hence, to shine, to appear. The *face* is that by which a thing shows itself; from this, the other meanings have developed, from *facing* an enemy to so behaving as to lose *face.*

The *facet* of a diamond is a little *face;* but *facetious* does not mean full of *facets* (*cp. supercilious*); it is from L. *facetus* (from ? *facere,* to do), graceful, pleasing; hence, pleasantly humorous. The *faucet* may be from L. *fauces,* throat; but it seems to have referred to the peg that stops the gap before it was extended to the tube through which the liquid flows.

facet, facetious.
See face.

facile, facility.
See defeat.

fact, faction, factitious, factor, factotum.
See affect; defeat.

faculty.
See defeat.

fade.
See wade.

Fahrenheit.
See Appendix II.

Faience.
See Appendix II.

fail.
See insult.

fain.
See turmeric, wheedle.

faint.
This is a doublet of *feint* (OFr. *faindre, feindre, faint, feint,* from L. *fingere,* to pretend). Its early sense, after pretending, was cowardice, which might lead one to pretend—but also might lead one to *faint* like the Victorian lady. From this flows the meaning of the adjective, weak. "*Faint* heart ne'er won fair lady."

The root of L. *fingere, fictus,* to fashion, to feign, is *fig,* whence *figment;* also *figure,* something fashioned; *effigy, cp. caricature; fiction.*

fair.
See profane.

fair maid.
See month: February.

fairy.
See incinerator.

fake.
See profane.

fall.
See fell.

Fallopian.
See Appendix II.

fallow.
See turmeric.

falsehood.
See livelihood.

fame.
See fate.

family.

There is history hidden in this word, from L. *familia,* household, from *famulus,* servant. At one time, the man was master, the woman probably seized in conquest, she and all her offspring the *servants* of the man. Indeed, the *servant,* which means one *serving,* was first one *preserved,* from L. *servare,* to *keep* (Eng. *preserve*), to protect; thus, one kept from the slaughter of the conquered race to work for the victor. A *familiar* was, in Shakespeare's time, a *servant* or a *serving* spirit.

From the frequent habit of eating, a popular form of *service* is the equipment on the table; to set the table, Fr. *servir;* to clear away, Fr. *desservir;* whence Eng. *dessert* (fruits and nuts brought in when all else is removed). Note that one's just *deserts* is, via OFr. *deservir,* from L. *deservire,* to serve well; hence, to *deserve.* The wide stretch of *desert,* and the verb to *desert,* are via Fr. *désert, déserter,* from L. *deserer, desert—,* to abandon, to unbind.

fan.

See fanatic.

fanatic.

Around a temple (L. *fanum,* whence Eng. *fane*) one is likely to find persons whose religious impulses make them seem overwrought. (Attend any revival meeting.) Such a person was called L. *fanaticus,* whence Eng. *fanatic.* (In baseball parlance, this has been shortened to *fan.*) The *fan* with which one blows (the heat away?) is from AS. *fann,* from L. *vannus,* a fan used in winnowing wheat. *Cp. profane.*

fancy.

See focus.

fane.

See fanatic.

fang.

See pylorus.

fantasy.

See focus.

faquir.

See profane.

farce.

See bombast.

fare.

See circus, dollar.

farm.

The theory of economic determinism might gather force from this word. In the middle ages, a tenant contracted to pay a specified rental (as who does not?) for his ground. This was called L. *firma* (L. *firmare,* to fix, from *firmus,* Eng. *firm*). By simple transfer, the name for the rent was given to the object for which the rent was paid: L. *firma,* whence Eng. *farm.* Note, however, that the *farmer* was originally the one that collected the rent; only in the 15th c. did *farmer* shift to the man that worked the land.

farthing.

See dollar; *cp.* furbelow.

farthingale.

See furbelow.

fasces, fascinate.

See Fascist.

Fascist.

When the Roman builders went forth on their work, they often carried their ax tied in the middle of a bundle of rods. L. *fascia,* band, with which this was tied, gave the name *fasces* to the bundles, which became the symbol of authority of the local Roman magistrates. *Fasces* is plural of L. *fascis,* a bundle; the diminutive of this is L. *fascina,* a bundle; whence L. *fascinare, fascinat—,* to bind, whence Eng. *fascinate,* to hold spell-bound. By obvious suggestion—remember the fable of the dying father who asked his sons to break a bundle of rods—the *Fasces* came to imply union; hence it was adopted by the *Fascist* party of 20th c. Italy, which did not succeed in *fascinating.*

The Romans developed the word L. *fascinum,* charm; and their term for the "evil eye" was *oculus fascinus.* We prefer to think of a more pleasant charm.

fashion.

See defeat.

fate.

There was no escaping, the ancients believed, the doom that the gods had spoken; this was your *fate* (L. *fas,* the divine word, from *fari, fatum,* to speak). Things not in accord with the divine word were *nefarious* (L. *ne,* not). Thus *fame* is the report spread of a person; if he is spoken of, but badly, he becomes *infamous* (which was formerly pronounced with the accent on the second syllable, *e.g.* in Spenser's *Faerie Queene,* I 12,27). A *fable* (L. *fabula*) is a little talk. (L. *fari,* to speak, is related, through Gr. *phemi, I say,* with Sansk. *bhash,* to speak; *bhan,* to resound, and thus intertwined with Eng. *ban, q.v.*) *Cp. incinerator.*

fathom.
This measure was first used on land. It is common Teut., AS. *faethm,* the outstretched arms. Used esp. of depth—

Full *fathom* five thy father lies,
Of his bones are coral made—

it came as a verb to mean to plumb the depths, to probe their mystery; hence, to make out the meaning of something obscure.

faucet.
See face.

fault.
See insult.

fawn.
See turmeric, wheedle.

fay.
See incinerator.

fear.
This word has been transferred from the cause to the feeling. It is cognate with Sansk. *per,* to go through; whence also Eng. *fare; cp. dollar.* Via. OE. *faer* it is from OS. *far,* ambush. The first sense in Eng. (in Beowulf) was of a disaster; from the thing undergone, the word shifted to the dread of the event. At first, it indicated a greater emotion than we now attach to the word, being the early Eng. equivalent of terror; *cp. terse.* The person that used to be *affeared, afeard* (from early *afear,* to frighten), is now (a wholly different word) *afraid, q.v.*

feat, feature.
See defeat.

feather.
See vogue.

febrifuge.
See devil.

February.
See month.

fee.
This is one of our earliest words, for it means *cattle* (*cp. achieve*), the primitive essential to community life, and the earliest instrument of barter—whence *money* (*see below*). In AS. *feoh* means both cattle and money; likewise Goth. *faihu;* Teut. *fehu;* L. *pecu,* cattle, and *pecunia, money* (Eng. *pecuniary*); Sansk. *pasu,* cattle. ME. *fee*-house is both a cattle-shed and a treasury. The OFr. form *fiu,* whence *fief;* LL. *feodum, feudum,* from *feu* + OHG *od,* wealth, whence *feud* as in the *feudal* system. *Pecu*— also gives us *peculiar,* which first meant one's own, private; and *peculate,* from *peculari; peculat—,* to take private property; not related to *speculate, q.v.,* from L. *speculari, speculat—,* to spy, from *specula,* watchtower.

Feud, a constant enmity, influenced in spelling by the above, is OFr. *faide,* OHG. *fehida,* AS. *faehth,* enmity, AS. *fah,* whence Eng. *foe.* The present participle of AS. *feogan,* to hate, is AS. *feond,* that which you hate, the enemy: G. *feind,* Eng. *fiend,* which in ME. meant any *foe,* but now means the arch-enemy, the devil. (This sense is not directly related to *money.*) The word *money* itself (OFr. *moneie,* from L. *moneta,* from *monere, monet—,* to warn: Eng. *admonition, monitor;* but also *monetary*) is derived from an epithet of Juno, as the goddess that gave warning; at her temple was established the first Roman *mint.* Originally *mint* (OE. *mynet,* from L. *moneta*) was a piece of *money;* then, *money* in general; then, the place where *money* is coined. *See coin.* (*Mint,* the aromatic plant, is from OE. *minte,* from L. *menta, mentha*—whence Eng. *menthol*—from Gr. *minthe.*) Thus the old expression "to hold in *fee* simple" (possessions held absolutely) came by a complex path.

feed.
See fodder.

feign, feint.
See faint.

felicity, felicitation.
See turmeric.

fell.
See buff. (As with other causal forms, this is the past tense of the simple verb: *fall,* to go down; *fell,* to

make go down: *lie*, to be down; *lay*, to make be down: *set*, *q.v.*; *sit*.) *Fall* is common Teut., AS. *feallan*. *Lie* is common Aryan, AS. *licgan;* Gr. *lexos*, bed—no relation to lexicographer. *Lie*, to tell an untruth (AS. *lēogan*), is commoner still. *See felon.*

fellow.
We often hear the term *Fellow-Workers!* but the first *fellows* were capitalists —even in the days of the feudal system. For the word is from OE. *feolaga*, from *feoh*, possessions, whence Eng. *fee*, *q.v.* + *lag* from OE. *lagjan*, to lay; and it meant a person that set down money in a cooperative enterprise. The use widened until it meant a member of the same company or group (*e.g.*, of a college, where the term *fellow* gradually grew restricted, as opposed to scholar, to the graduate members: now in the United States often short for *honorary fellow*); then even all our *fellow-men.*

felon.
This word has traveled in two paths. It is probably from L. *fel*, LL. *fellonem*, gall—this gives us also the adjective, *fell* chance. On the one side the word means an inflamed sore; on the other (first adjective, then noun) it refers to somebody full of bitterness at life; hence savage, striking back; hence the present sense of of the term; as also *felony*, *felonious*.

felt.
See filter.

feminine.
See marshal.

fence.
See plot. *Fend* is aphetic for *defend*, to beat away. *Offend* is to beat against; thus, to take the *offensive;* figuratively, to be *offensive*. The two are linked in Robert Frost's (unintentional) pun (*Mending Wall*):

Before I built a wall I'd want to know
What I was walling in and walling out
And to whom I was like to give *offence.*

fens.
See tag.

fent.
See dollar.

ferocious.
See painter.

ferris (wheel).
See Appendix II.

ferry.
See circus; *cp.* port.

fertile, fertilize.
See suffer, usury.

ferule.
See interfere. Of course the meaning was affected by the thought of a *rule* or *ruler* to measure length.

festival, festive.
See profane.

fetich.
Portuguese travelers along the Guinea shore bought little amulets from the natives, calling them *feitiço*, from L. *facticius*, manufactured. They were early called, in Eng., *fetisso*, directly from the Port.; the present form is via the Fr. *fétiche*. The meaning has shifted because of the native worship of such charms.

fetus.
See turmeric. The root *fe-*, to produce offspring, is akin to the Aryan form *bhwe-*, from *bheu-*, to come into being; whence Eng. *be*. An animal that has brought forth young, and can bear no more, was called Eng. *effete* (from L. *ef*, *ex*, out + *fetus*); the word is now used figuratively only, of persons, societies, etc., that have lost their vigor.

feud, feudal.
See fee.

fez.
See Appendix II.

fiancee.
The promise of fidelity given (or implied) at bethrothal is contained in the word *fiancé* (masculine), *fiancée* (feminine). The L. *fides*, trust, produced the adjective *fidelis*, faithful, the noun *fidelitat-*, whence Eng. *fidelity*, and the verb *fidare*, to trust, whence also *fiduciary*. To trust to, *ad* + *fidare*, became LL. *affidare* (whence Eng. *affidavit*, he has pledged his faith), whence OFr. *afier*, from which was fashioned the noun *afiance*, *affiance*, the act of confiding, of having trust. This was also an Eng. word; from it in turn was fashioned the Eng. verb *affiance*,

meaning to pledge, then to pledge in marriage. The Fr. forms developed also from the simple verb, *fidare,* Fr. *fier,* to trust, from the past participle of which, the one pledged, is *fiancé, fiancée.*

fiasco.

The word *flask* (for wine) is common in many tongues, AS. *flasce;* It. *fiasco;* LL. *flasco, flascon—;* whence also *flagon* via ME. *flakon.* Such an article was common, and cheap. When the Venetian glassmakers, famed for their fine glass, blew some glass with a flaw in it, they put it aside *far fiasco,* to make a bottle: hence *fiasco* came to represent the failure.

fiat.

See spouse.

fib.

This word, now used of a child's falsehood, is old and of obscured origin. It may be a back-formation from *fable,* as via *fibble-fabble,* nonsense. (*Fable* is from L. *fabula,* from *fari,* to speak.) Or it may be a shift from early Eng. *fob,* to cheat; Shakespeare uses *fob off,* to trick. This is a common word, from OFr. *forbe,* whence *fourbe,* cheat.

fiction.

See faint.

fictitious.

See affect.

fiddle-de-dee.

The word *Bosh!* meaning nonsense, has no connection with Gipsy *bosh,* a fiddle, being rather a natural exclamation of scorn; as the G. *Possen,* nonsense. *Fiddle-de-dee,* with the same dismissal of what the other person has said, has a more meaningful story. It is equivalent to an ironic "You don't say so!", being from It. *Fedidio, Fe di Dio,* by the Faith of God. *Fiddlesticks* is a further corruption, based on the sound of the first part of the word, but also nonsense.

fidelity, fiduciary.

See fiancée.

fiend.

See fee.

fierce.

See treacle.

fife.

See pipe.

fifth column.

Fifth columnists are sometimes the most dangerous soldiers of all. The term was first used in the Spanish Civil War, 1939, when a general of Franco's announced that he had *four columns* marching on Madrid, and a *fifth column* (spies, propagandists, saboteurs) already within its walls (For *column, see colonel.*)

fig.

See rap.

fight.

See fit.

figment, figure.

See faint.

file.

See fylfot.

filial.

See marshal.

filibuster.

Although practiced in Congress, this is a memory of the Spanish Main. The Eng. *flyboat* was a swift, light vessel—what the Eng. called a privateer but the Spanish, a pirate. In Sp., this became *flibote,* whence *filibote;* and the sailor a *filibuster.* From the man to the act; and from piracy to congressional privateering.

It is probably influenced by *freebooter,* Du. *vrijbuiter,* one that seeks *free booty.*

filter.

This word is taken from the substance used (OFr. *filtrer,* to sift through *felt,* from LL. *filtrum, feltrum, felt*). Whence comes the process of *infiltration.*

To *canvass* a neighborhood is derived, in the same way, from ME. *canevas,* from LL. *canabacius,* from L. from Gr. *kannabis,* hemp, canvas; the original sense was to sift through *canvas,* or hempen cloth.

final.

See finance.

finance.

This was originally a payment that settled matters, brought concern and accounts to an end (LL. *financia,* from *finare,* to pay a *fine,* from L. *finis,* a settled payment; also, the end, whence *fine,* in both senses; *final*). From *finitus,* ended, well-rounded, came *finite,* and the sense of *fine* as complete, exquisite. By way of Fr. *finir, finiss—* comes Eng. *finish.* Shakespeare seems to have coined *finical* (*King Lear,* II,ii,19). *Confine; define,* to mark the ends or limits; *refine; affinity,* the ends coming together; *infinite;* are also from this source. L. *finis* is *fidnis,* a boundary, end, from the root *fid,* whence *findere, fiss—* to cleave, whence Eng. *fissure,* from Sansk. *bhid,* to pierce, break, whence Eng. *bite; cp. sarcophagus.*

fine.
See finance.

finger.
See pylorus.

finical, finish, finite.
See finance.

fire.
This is most common Teut.; *cp. curfew.*

firm.
See farm, infirmary.

fissure.
See finance; dollar.

fit.
See defeat. When you have a *fit,* you *fight* against yourself—from AS. *fitt,* conflict, whence Eng. *fight.*

five.
See number.

fix.
The L. *fingere, fict-,* to fashion, had the root *fig-;* whence *figment, figure; cp. faint.* But L. *figere, fix-,* meant to fasten; whence Eng. *fix.* To *fix* is to make fast or stable; hence, to mend. To *affix* (L. *af, ad,* to), to *prefix* (L. *pre,* before), to *suffix* (L. *suf, sub,* under) are from this word. The chemist uses a *fixative;* the psychologist seeks the *fixation;* and the *Bible* has made us familiar (L. *crux, cruci-,* cross; *cp. criss-cross*) with the *crucifix.*

fixation, fixative.
See fix.

flagellation, flageolet.
See flamingo.

flagon.
See fiasco.

flagrant.
See flamingo.

flak.
See Dora.

flake.
See congress.

flamboyant, flame.
See flamingo.

flamingo.
The *flame* that soars from your fire is from L. *flamma*—either from the verb *flare, flat—,* to blow; or via an earlier L. *flagma* from *flagrare, flagrat—,* to blaze. From it we have Eng. *inflame; inflammation* (swollen and burning); *flamboyant,* with flame-like curves, hence showy.

The first of the L. verbs gives us Eng. *flare; inflation,* a blowing into, hence a swelling, an increase—and also to *deflate.* Via the diminutive OFr. *flageol, flajol,* Provencal *flaujol,* comes *flageolet;* and through OFr. *flaute* comes the *flautist* with his *flute.*

The second verb gives us (L. *con, com,* together, used as an intensive) *conflagration;* and *flagrant,* blazing, hence glaring, scandalous. It may be related to L. *flagrum,* scourge, with the diminutive L. *flagellum,* whip; whence Eng. *flagellation* and the botanical Eng. *flagellum.* The blazing bird (from its color) is Sp. *flamenco* (also a dance), and Port. and Eng. *flamingo.* But Port. *flamingo* also meant a *Fleming,* a man from Flanders; and the bird may have been named (*cp. Dutch*) in mockery of the bright clothes of the *Flemings.*

flapper.
This is an echoic word, from the verb *flap*—indicating a sound between a *flip* and a *flop.* It has been applied to the limbs of the seal; to the device used in *Gulliver's Travels* (on the isle of Laputa) to *flap* the absent-minded. Applied to the young wild duck and partridge, it made easy transfer to the human fledgling, trying her wings. We similarly speak of the *flip* behavior of an irresponsible miss; though more serious considerations cluster around the heavier sound of *flop.*

flare.
See flamingo.

flash.
This was first an echoic word (like *splash, smash, bash; cp. knick-knack*), of the sound of a sudden *dash* of water. Then used of the sudden sweep of a sword, it was later used of a sudden streak of light; then, of any sudden sweep, as, it came to me in a *flash.* The adjective *flashy* has traveled along the same path; it now means something that makes a bright appearance—for a short time.

To *dash,* as in to *dash* to pieces, is also echoic, with the sense of a sudden sweep.

flask.
See fiasco.

flat.
See flatter. (*Flatter* is of course also the comparative of *flat*: something even more *flat,* if that be possible. For note that such comparatives are, strictly, impossible; a thing is *flat* or it is not; it may be *nearly flat,* and *more nearly flat;* but it cannot, strictly, be *flatter*—however one may *flatten* it down! The same is true of *correct,* and many more.)
See badger; congress.

flatter.
Among the many Eng. echoic words were *flitter, flatter, flutter; cp. fleet.* To *flatter* meant to *flit* about. But its lightness influenced another word, from Eng. *flat,* a common Teut. word but probably from Fr. *plat,* from Gr. *platys, flat,* as in Eng. *platypus; cp. vessel.* The verb form, *flat,* to strike down or press down, developed the frequentative *flatter,* to press smooth; hence, to stroke; to caress; this soon took on the figurative sense of stroking with smooth words, as does an arrant *flatterer.*

flautist.
See flamingo.

flea.
See affliction, lobster.

fleece.
This is a common WG. form, MHG. *vlus,* sheepskin; cognate with L. *plu-* as in *pluma,* feather, whence Eng. *plume.* To *plume* oneself on something is to spread one's feathers, *i.e.,* to put on airs. From the patience with which the sheep stands while it is being *fleeced* comes the use of the verb in the sense of stripping someone of his belongings, to cheat.

fleer.
See coquette.

fleet.
The old saying still waters run deep has its converse in this word. For it comes through two forms of the same root: OE. *fleat,* from earlier *flaut,* meaning shallow (farmers still speak of plowing *fleet*); and via *fliotr,* (whence also via OE. *flyht,* Eng. *flight*) meaning swift. There was a verb, still preserved in poetry, as time *fleets* by, from OE. *fleotan* (whence also *float*), meaning first to rest on the surface of the water; hence, to *float* along, to glide away; the same word as a noun gives us that which *floats* on the water; quite early this was extended from a boat to a group of boats under one command, the *fleet.* A diminutive of Sp. *flota, fleet,* is *flotilla;* both these words—the second more frequently—are used in English.

A weak form of the verb *fleotan, flotan,* gives us Eng. *flit;* whence also *flitter;* an earlier frequentative (AS. *floterian,* from *fleotan*) gives us *flutter.* Similarly frequentative (from *flick,* a sudden movement with a light sound) is *flicker;* a noisier movement is *flacker,* now less used; these are all echoic. First meaning swift; then given to *flights;* then figuratively, as with a flash (*q.v.*) of fancy, came the adjective *flighty.*

The Aryan stem is *plu-,* to rain, whence *Jupiter Pluvius,* god of the rain, Eng. *pluvial;* and *plo-,* to drift, whence Eng. *flow* and via OHG. *fluot,* OE. *flod,* Eng. *flood.* Which is water enough for one root!

flexible.
See accent.

flick, flicker.
See fleet.

flies.
See affliction.

flight, flighty.
See affliction, fleet.

flim-flam, flimsy.
See whimsy.

flip.
See flapper.

flirt.
See coquette.

flit, flitter.
See fleet.

float.
See subject, fleet.

flock.
See congress.

flood.
See subject, fleet.

flop.
See flapper.

Florida.
See States.

flotilla, flotsam.
See subject, fleet.

flour.
See flower.

flourish.
See flower.

flow.
See affluent, fleet.

flower.
The verb, to *flower*, helps show the origin of this word, a doublet of *flourish*, from OFr. *florir, floriss—*, from L. *florere*, from L. *flos, flor, flower*. The Aryan root is *bhlo;* whence also to *blow* (which means both to puff with wind and to blossom): whence AS. *blowan, blawan;* ON. *blom,* whence Eng. *bloom.* The noun, a *blow,* is from the action of a sudden gust of wind. And *flour* is an alternate spelling, the thought being that it is the *flower,* or finest part, of the grain. *Flow* is not related; *see affluent.*

Several *flowers* draw their names from their medicinal virtue, real or fancied. *Sage* is from OFr. *sauge,* from L. *salvus,* saved. *Peony,* from *Paion,* healer of the gods. *Centaury* was discovered by *Chiron* the *centaur; hyacinth* sprang from the blood of *Hyacinthus,* beloved of Apollo Paion; *dianthus* is the flower of Zeus (Gr. *dios,* Zeus, god, + *anthos, anthus, anthemon,* flower).

The *aster* is from Gr. *aster,* star; the *calendula* supposedly bloomed at the *calends* (the first of the month, or perhaps "the little weather-glass;" *cp. dickey*); *campanula* is L. little bell; *crysanthemum* is the golden flower (Gr. *chrysos,* gold); the *daisy* is from AS. *daeges-eage,* day's eye; the *dandelion* is from Fr. *dent de lion,* lion's tooth; the *digitalis* is named from its finger-like corolla (hence also *digit*); *foxglove* is perhaps a double corruption: *fox,* from *folk* (little folk, the fairies) + *glofe,* from *gloche,* bell: fairy bell; the *geranium* has a seed like the bill of a crane (Gr. *geranos,* crane); the *gladiolus* is L. little sword (also in *gladiator,* swordsman); *helianthus* is the sunflower (Gr. *helios,* light, sun), as the *heliotrope* turns toward the sun (Gr. *trope,* turning; *cp. trophy*); *iris* is the L. rainbow; *phlox,* the Gr. flame. *Cp. nasturtium;* and visit the botanical garden.

The inceptive of L. *florere,* to *flower,* is *florescere, floruit,* whence Eng. *florescent* and via Fr. *florir, floriss—,* Eng. *flourish.* To blossom forth (L. *ef, ex,* out) is to *effloresce,* which must not be confused with *deflower.*

fluctuation, fluent.
See fourflusher.

fluid, fludity, flume.
See affluent.

fluorescent, fluorine, fluorspar.
See affluent; element.

flush, flux.
See fourflusher.

flute.
See flamingo.

flutter.
See fleet.

fly.
See affliction, lobster.

focus.
Home is where the heart lies. But also, where the hearth, the early center of home life. Hence, the center or common point of anything. (L. *focus,* hearth). The L. is from Gr. *phos,* from *phaos,* light, from *phainein,* to show, appear, which gives us many Eng. words. *Cellophane,* a recent commercial coinage. *Diaphanous* (Gr. *dia,* through). *Phosphorus* (*phos* + Gr. *phoros,* bringing, from *pherein,* to bring, bear). *Phantom, fantasy, fancy*: an appearance. *Hierophant,* one who shows the sacred mysteries (Gr. *hieros,* sacred), a priest; *cp. hieroglyphics. Phase,* an appearance, applied first to the *phases* of the moon. *Emphasis* (Gr.

em, en, in). '*Phaeton* (*Phaeton,* driver of the chariot of the sun), a kind of carriage. *Photograph* is a light-writing, as *telegraph* is far-writing (Gr. *tele—*, far: *telephone,* far-sounding; *phonograph,* sound-writing). The *elephant* is an ivory-shower: shifting as from Coptic *ebou* (L. *ebur*), ivory.

A *phenomenon* (earlier *phaenomenon,* from the passive Gr. *phainomai,* to be shown, to appear) was originally anything that was perceptible to the senses; its opposite is *noumenon,* a thing apprehended by the mind. But the sliding tendency—of a general term to approach one end of the scale; *cp. complexion*—has given *phenomenon* the meaning of an unusual or strange appearance.

fodder.

This first meant *food* in general: OE. *fodor, fodder;* OE. *foda, food;* gradually the first was used for cattle; the second, for men. The root is OTeut. *fothro-*, Aryan *pat-*, to feed. The form *food* has no analogues in the other Teut. tongues, which have, however, words from OTeut. *fodjan,* whence Eng. *feed.* From L. *pascere, past-*, to *feed,* comes Eng. *pasture; cp. abbot; pester.*

fodient.

See bed.

foe.

See fee.

foetus.

See turmeric; fetus.

foil.

This word has developed from two sources. From OFr. *fuler,* (whence Fr. *fouler*), from L. *fullo,* Eng. *fuller,* comes Eng. *full,* to tread or trample cloth. Combined with this came the force of Fr. *affoler,* (from Fr. *fol, fool, q.v.*) adding to the idea of trample that of defeat, thwart, *foil.* The name *fuller's earth* comes from the fact that the substance was used by *fullers* to clean cloth.

From OFr. *foil, foille,* (whence Fr. *feuille*), from L. *folium,* leaf (Eng. *folio,* a book made from a leaf or sheet folded once) come the senses of *foil* as a leaf; then the representation of a leaf in heraldry; then anything flat as a leaf (tin*foil*); then such a metal placed behind a jewel to set it off—whence, anything that heightens another by contrast. The Fr. *fleuret* (Eng. *floweret*) means a fencing *foil;* but the Eng. word may be an altered form of *foin,* to thrust, (from OFr. *foinne, foisne, fouisne,* from L. *fuscina* — cognate with *piscina,* from *pisces,* fish (Eng. *piscatory*)— a three-pronged fishing spear.

Full, the verb above, is not related to the adj. *full,* which is a widespread word: OE. *full;* OTeut. *fullo—*. Akin to Sansk. *puru;* Gr. *polys* (Eng. *poly—*, as in *polysyllabic,* etc.). Gr. *plethos, plethor—*, Eng. *plethora*), Gr. *pleres,* whence L. *plere, pletus,* to fill (Eng. *complete, complement, replete,* etc.), L. *plenus,* full (Eng. *plenitude*), L. *plus, plures,* more, (Eng. *plus, plural, plurality,* etc.) *Cp. police.* Which may easily be *fulsome* (abundant, plentiful; then plump, whence fat, coarse, offensive; now mainly of offensive affectation of affection).

foin.

See foil.

foliage.

See necromancy.

folio.

See foil, necromancy.

folk.

A common Teut. form. *See* congress.

fond.

When you are *fond* of something, you are likely to be a bit foolish over it—which is just what the word implies. It is from ME. *fonned,* past participle of *fonnen,* to be foolish, from *fon,* a fool. But originally *fonnen* meant to be insipid; Wyclif used it of salt that has lost its savor. Tracing *fon* back, we find that it meant first a virgin. From the usual opinion of housewives that have young girls working for them (not to mention the thoughts of impatient youths) the word came to mean a simple or stupid girl; thence, any fool. The verb was formed from the noun *fon.* Often the things we are *fond* of show we still merit the second sense of the word. From the simpleton's habit of sitting and holding something, the frequentative *fondle* shifted to its present sense.

fondle.

See fond, swivel.

food.
See fodder.

fool.
L. *follis,* literally a bellows, figuratively a "windbag," whence Fr. *fol, fou,* whence Eng. *fool.* But the slang sense came roundabout: *follis* also meant scrotum (as do L. *gerro,* from Sic.; and It. *coglione,* both also used to mean *fool*); so today we dismiss something as foolish by crying "Aw, nuts!" 'Nuts' and its forms (varying in meaning from 'crazy' to 'delightful': (to be 'nuts about' means quite other than 'Nuts to you!') has two and a half columns in Eric Partridge's "Dictionary of Slang," 1938. In the theatre, the 'nut' (that has to be cracked) is the initial sum required to produce a play. *Cp. dunce.*

foolscap.
This large paper draws its name from the design of the *fool's cap* it used to bear. Similar paper bore the coat of arms of Charles I of England; in 1642, Cromwell replaced this with the cap and belles of the fool.

[The linotyper's slip, by which Cromwell mocked the cavalier Charles with *belles* instead of *bells,* is too pat for correction. But indeed Eng. *bell* was OE. *belle,* from a common LG. word, probably from OE. *bellan,* to *bellow* (make a loud noise), perhaps related to *bellows,* for which *see pylorus. Beau* and *belle* are via Fr. from L. *bellus* and *bella,* beautiful. The middle ages derived L. *bellum,* war, from *bellus,* as a reminder that war is never beautiful. We draw from it Eng. *belligerent,* from *bellum* + *gerentem,* from *gerere,* to do, to wage.]

foot.
See pylorus.

forbid.
This word is from *bid,* related to *bead, q.v. Bid* is a combination of two earlier words. AS. *beodan* meant to announce, to offer, to command. AS. *biddan* meant to request, to press upon (G. *bitte,* please). The prefix *for-* had the sense of opposition or excess; *cp. indenture;* hence, to *forbid* is to *prohibit.*

To *prohibit* is from L. *pro-,* in front, + *habere,* to have, to hold. Its sense came somewhat as did that of *prevent, q.v.*

force.
See defeat.

forceps.
See manoeuver.

ford.
See port, dollar.

fore.
See indenture, dollar.

foreboding.
See bottle.

foreign, forest.
See den, door.

forfeit, forge.
See defeat.

forgive, forgo, forlorn.
See indenture.

form, formal, formaldehyde, formality, formication, formidable.
See formula.

formula.
This set of requirements to produce something is the diminutive of L. *forma,* shape, which directly gives us Eng. *form.* Hence, also *formal,* as in evening attire; *formality.* The chemical *formaldehyde,* on the other hand, is short for *formic alcohol dehydrogenatum* (alcohol with two atoms of hydrogen removed). The *formic* means related to ants, from L. *formica,* ant: the acid is in a fluid that ants emit. For other such *forms, see warm.* The *format* of a book is its shape, from the verb *formare, format-,* to shape. L. *formido,* dread, gives us the dreadful, *formidable* things; whereas something shapely is L. *formosa,* as the island. Compounds include *deform* and *reformation.*

forsaken.
See indenture.

forsythia.
See Appendix II.

fort.
See saxophone.

forth.
See dollar.

fortify, fortitude.
See saxophone.

fortnight.
See remnant.

forty.
See number.

fortuitous, fortunate.
See fortune.

fortune.
L. *fors, fort-,* meant chance, lot; whence Eng. *fortune.* The root is L. *ferre,* to bear; from it also came L. *fortis,* strong (able to bear), whence Eng. *fort; cp. saxophone.* The Roman god of luck was *Fortuna;* if Lady Luck was on your side, you were indeed *fortunate.* (If she favored the other fellow, it was *fortuitous*: *-ous,* full of...*cp. supercilious.*)

forward.
See indenture.

fosse.
See fossil.

fossil.
In the study of fortifications, the word *fosse* is used of a ditch or other excavation, fro[illegible] *fossa,* from *fodere, foss-,* to dig. [illegible]ljective L. *fossilis* gives us Eng. *foss*[illegible] This once was applied to anything d[illegible] from the earth, e.g., "that Irish *fossil* the potato"; but began in the 17th c.—when interest spread—to be limited to the remains of plants and animals of past ages. It is applied contemptuously to persons whose ideas seem out of past ages; widely, in other figurative ways. Emerson complains that "government has been a *fossil;* it should be a plant." He also says "language is *fossil* poetry"—this book, then, is a steam shovel.

foul.
See fylfot, polecat.

found, foundation, founder, foundry.
See futile.

four.
See number.

fourflusher.
Several of the senses of this word—*flush* of blood to cheeks (influenced by *blush,* from AS. *blyscan* to shine, from *blysa,* torch, fire); *flush* of victory (influenced by the idea of fleshing one's sword); *flush* with funds; and a *flush* of cards—are clear from its origin: from Fr. *flux,* from L. *fluxus,* flow, from *fluere, fluxi, fluct—* to flow; whence also Eng. *flux, fluent, fluctuation; cp. affluent.* Since, in the game of poker, it requires a flow of five cards of the same suit to make a *flush,* a *fourflusher* is one that cannot make good what he pretends.

fowl.
This is common Teut., OE. *fugel, fugol;* dissimilated from *fluglo-,* from the root *flug,* to fly; *cp. lobster.*

fox.
This is a common Teut. beast, MHG. *vuhs;* L. *vulpes; cp. vulpine.* The early Teut. root is *puk-,* probably related to Sansk. *puccha,* tail; the *fox* named from its flowing tail; *cp. squirrel.* But the reputation of the animal for trickery was early; ON. *fox* meant fraud; hence, *to fox,* and *foxy.*

foxglove.
See flower.

fraction, fracture, fragile, fragment.
See discuss.

franc.
See dollar.

France, franchise, frank.
See free.

Frankenstein.
See leviathan.

frankfurter.
See dollar.

frankincense.
See free.

fraternity, fratricide.
See shed.

fray, frazzle.
See afraid.

freak.
See inn.

free.
The man that calls himself heart-*free* is not talking in terms of origins. *Free* (OE. *fréon,* to love, cognate with Sansk. *priya,* dear: thus OE. *fréond,* whence Eng. *friend*) meant beloved. In the early home were those one loved, and the *slaves*—hence *free* came to mean, not *enslaved.* Note that *slave* (Fr. *esclave,*

from LL. *Sclavus*) is the name of the central European race, the *Slav* or *Slavic,* which in their own tongue means "glory;" but they had been conquered, and from them the Romans and even the *Franks* drew their servants. Hence *frank,* from the tribe that in the 6th c. conquered Gaul and gave its name to *France: free,* open. From this come *franchise* and *enfranchise* (Fr. *affranchir,* to set *free*); also the application of *frank* as the privilege of *free* mailing. *Frankincense* (OFr. *franc encens*: noble *incense* . . .) from *incendere, incensus,* to blaze, to set afire, from *in,* intensive + *candere,* to glow. The inceptive of this, *incandescere,* gives us *incandescent.* To *incense* is to set one's temper blazing.

French leave.
See Dutch.

fresco.
This It. word for *fresh* (*cp.* inn) is short for *in fresco*: in the *fresh* (plaster), hence a style of painting on plaster not quite dry, with water colors. The phrase *al fresco,* however, implies in the *fresh* air.

fresh.
See inn.

fret.
See indenture.

fricasse, friction.
See afraid.

Friday.
See week.

friend.
See free.

frieze.
See cloth.

frisky.
See inn.

front, frontier.
See effrontery.

frontispiece.
The end of this word is a sample of the power of association; it has no relation to *piece* (which, though found in Fr. *pièce,* is probably of Celtic origin, meaning a bit; cognate with Fr. *petit,* little). *Frontispiece* is from Fr. *frontispice,* from LL. *frontispicium,* looking at the brow, from *frons, front—,* brow + *spicium,* from *specere,* to look; *cp. auction.* At first it meant the front of a building, esp., a decorated entrance or the decoration over the door. From this, it was applied to the first or title page of a book; then to an initial illustration, or a preface. Milton, in *Paradise Lost,* III, 506, speaks of

The work as of a Kingly Palace Gate
With *frontispice* of Diamond and Gold.

frown.
See effrontery.

frugal, fruit.
See peach.

fuddle.
See addle.

fugitive.
See devil.

full, fuller's earth, fulsome.
See foil.

fume, fumigate.
See month: February.

fun.
See changeling.

funambulist.
You do have fun when near this fellow, for his main stay (if he can be said to stay) is the circus. He is, in more common parlance, a tightropewalker, from L. *funis,* rope + *ambulare,* to walk; *cp. ambulance. Fun, funny,* are related to ME. *fon; cp. fond. Funiculus,* a little rope, is used in several senses in Eng. A *funicular* railway is one in which the cars are tugged (as up a mountain) by a cable.

function.
See sponge.

fund.
See funeral.

fundament, fundamental.
See funeral, futile.

funeral.
L. *fundus* meant bottom; Eng. *fundus* is used in anatomy for the base of various structures; also, earlier, *fund.* But *fund* (now from the L. via Fr. *fond,*

fonds) developed the figurative sense of a basis to draw upon, a source of supply; this is the present meaning. Directly from the L. noun form *fundamentum* comes *fundament;* thence, the adjective *fundamental.* Possibly from this root came L. *funus, funer-*, ground for burial; hence (via the adjective, L. *funeralis,* Fr. *funerailles*), Eng. *funeral.* A further adjective form gives us *funereal,* gloomy as a burial; here, also, the now rare *funest* and *funestation. Insurance* makes safe—*en-sures*—a *fund* for a *funeral.*

Cp. futile.

fungus.

See sponge.

funicular.

See funambulist.

funny-bone.

If you hit the nerve that crosses the bone at your elbow, you will experience a sharp tingling. Why that is funny is not easy to see; but as the name for the bone is *humerus,* it does not take much change to reach the pun *humorous,* and the common name for the spot. L. *humerus,* shoulder, is from Gr. *amos,* shoulder, whence *omoplate,* (Gr. *plate,* broad surface, *blade,* whence *plateau*) *omosternum,* etc. For *humorous, cp. complexion.*

fur.

Here is a case of a thing's being named from its purpose. For *fur* is directly from OFr. *forre, fuerre,* sheath, case (possibly also Teut., OHG. *fuotar,* sheath; ON. *fothr,* lining). First it meant the lining of a garment; then, it was applied to the animal skins used for such lining. Note that *furacious* does not mean *furbearing,* but thievish, from L. *furax, furac-*, thief, from L. *furari,* to steal. Also *furious* means full of *fury,* from L. *furia,* from *furere,* to be mad. The first meaning was a tumult of mind approaching madness; this holds, except for figurative uses, like the *fury* of the gale.

furbelow.

That gay old sheet *The Spectator* rebuked the etymologists (No. 478, 1712) who suggest that "the *farthingale* was worn for cheapness, or the *furbelow* for warmth." Frills and *furbelows!* Garments gone by! This flighty flounce was earlier called a *falbala;* its origin is in some gay exclamation, such as *fal-lal-la. Farthingale,* the wide petticoat of your grandmothers' grandmothers, has a longer story. It is earlier *vardingale,* from Fr. *vertugalle, vertugadin;* there is an It. form *guardinfante.* From these comes the suggestion that the name is figurative: Fr. *vertu gardien,* guardian of virtue—the skirt being too stiff and wide for anyone to come nearer than arm's length! Fuller, in his *Worthies of England,* suggests it as from *Vertu* and *Gall,* as a wanton seeks to cover her shame with its wide protection. It is, actually, from Sp. *verdugado,* a hooped petticoat, from *verdugo,* a rod, from *verde,* a green twig. Green and therefore springy twigs made the best supports until whalebone was introduced.

furious.

See fur.

furlong.

This term is from farming, and means *long as a furrow.* But how long is a furrow? The answer is, forty poles. A pole is the width between two furrows, and was 5½ yards. The reason for these figures is that a legal acre was 40 poles long and 4 poles wide, so that the length of such an acre field (220 yards) was just an eighth of a mile. This made calculation easy for the early farmer. (For *acre, see saunter.*)

furlough.

We are careful to say that a private is granted a *furlough;* an officer takes a *leave.* But the two are the same word: *furlough* was earlier *furloff,* from Du. *ver lof, for leave;* OE. *leaf,* permission; by your *leave.* (*Leave,* as trees in spring, is from ME. *leve* from *lef, leaf.*) This is related to *lief,* from AS. *lief,* from AS. *leof,* dear, a common Teut. word; Goth *liufs;* L. *lubet,* it delights; AS. *lufu,* whence Eng. *love.* Sansk. *lubh,* to desire . . . But note that what we like, we think is just so; hence, OHG. *gilouban;* AS. *geliefan,* whence ME. *beleven,* whence Eng. *believe.* Thus we *believe* in what we *love.* L. *lubet* has a variant *libet,* it pleases, whence L. *libido, libidin—*, strong desire; from this come our Eng. *libidinous* and the Freudian *libido.*

The verb *leave* is from OE. *laefan,* to *leave* behind, to bequeath (causal of *belifan,* to remain). But if we *leave* something behind, we go away; hence the verb *leave* has both meanings. Thus when an officer's *leave* (noun: permission) has ended, he *leaves* (verb: goes away from, *leaves* behind) his family. He also *leaves* (bequeaths) them his fortune; hence the old saying, *love* 'em and *leave* 'em!

fuse, fusel, fuselage, fusil.
See futile.

fustian.
See bombast.

futile.
"The mouth of fools poureth forth folly." Bacon (6th essay) says: "As for talkers and *futile* persons, they are commonly vain." *Futile* first meant to pour forth; then was weighted with the observation that those who talk the most have the least worth saying. It is from L. *futilis,* pouring, from *fundere, fudi, fus—* to pour. (But note that even in L., *futilis* had come to mean leaky; thus the crew that went to sea in a sieve truly found their efforts *futile.*) The root is *fud,* pour. L. *fusilis,* able to pour, molten, gives us *fuse; confuse,* to pour together; *profuse* (L. *pro,* forth); *infuse; effusion, diffuse* (L. *dif,* away, apart); and a blood *transfusion* (L. *trans,* across).

Also from *fundere* come *foundry* (*found,* past of *find,* is from OHG. *finden, fand, funden. Found,* to establish, lay a *foundation,* is from OFr. *founder,* from L. *fundare,* from *fundus,* base, whence Eng. *fundamental;* from this source, also, come *profound;* and *founder,* to go to the bottom); *confound; refund,* to pour back—often a *futile* gesture. A *fuse,* as a tube with explosives, for setting off a charge, is short for earlier *fusee, fusel,* from LL. *focile,* a steel for kindling fire, from L. *focus,* hearth; *see focus.* The first use in Eng. was of the steel for the old flint-lock gun; *fusil* was then used of the gun itself, whence *fusillade,* rapid volley of gunfire; and *fuse* was used of the ignitor. *Fuse,* however, is influenced by *fusee, fuzee,* which (from OFr. *fusee,* a spindleful, from LL. *fusare—, fusat—,* to use a spindle, from L. *fusus,* spindle—probably related to Gr. *sphendone,* a sling and Sansk. *spandana,* quivering, throbbing, from Sansk. *spand,* to throb) has been applied to several spindle-shaped objects, from the *fusee* that sets off an explosion to an impregnated paper match and a "conoidal spirally grooved pulley" that helps your watch keep time. *Fuselage,* the spindle shaped (cigar-shaped) body of an airplane, is taken directly from the Fr., like *chauffeur, q.v.,* and *garage. Fusel* oil, obtained from liquor insufficiently distilled, is from G. *fusel,* bad liquor.

fylfot.
This early Eng. word for gammadion, swastika (*cp. monk*) may have been a combination, *fill foot,* from the pattern used to *fill* the *foot* of a painted window. It may, however, be *file-foot,* the *foot files* by (as does the leg in Eng. *triskele, triskelion,* from Gr. *tri.* three + *skelos,* leg: the pinwheel of three legs awhirl).

Eng. *file* is from two sources, one doubled. OE. *feol* gives us the *file* with the surface that is made rough to smooth other surfaces. L. *filum,* thread, moved into Fr. *fil;* whence the meaning thread, then a cord (later, iron spike; still later, *filing* cabinet) for keeping records in order; while it also moved into Fr. *file,* whence the meaning a succession, as of things in single *file.* (There is still another OE. *fylon,* earlier *fulo,* whence *foul;* this gives us Eng. *defile,* to render foul—not to be confused with *defile* from L. *de-* down, + *filum,* a place where one must move in single *file,* or such a column or motion. To *defile* a thing is interlinked with the notion of trampling on it; ME. *defoilen* being traced to OFr. *defouler; cp. foil.* But this sense is not related to *fylfot*).

G

gabble.
See gibberish.

gadget.
Here is a word that, though known for almost a century (recorded in 1886, but spoken earlier), has recently swung into wide use. Its origin is as obscure as the reason for its sudden prominence. It may be from Sc. *gadge,* a form of *gauge;* or from Fr. *gachette,* a small hook: apparently both words were used of various handy devices.

gadolinium.
See element.

gaga.
This may be a new slang term; but it is an old word: Norw. *gagga,* to bend backwards, as a bird might twist its neck, whence Icel. *gagr,* bent back. It is probably a reduplicated form of *ga, go,* meaning to keep *going* about, to bend from the course. It gives us the Eng. nautical term *yaw.*

gage.
See mortgage.

gain, gainly, gainsay.
See again.

gait.
See runagate.

gala.
See valentine.

Galahad.
See sangrail.

galaxy.
See delight.

gallant.
See valentine.

gallery, galley.
See galligaskins.

galligaskins.
The ship, *galley,* and the *gallery* are intertwined: Fr. *galère* means *galley;* It. *galera, galley,* It. *galleria,* L.L. *galeria, gallery.* The origin is G., probably from *kalon,* wood; thus *balcony* is It. *balcone, balco,* scaffold, OHG. *balcho,* Eng. *balk; cp. bulk.*
The Eng. *gallipot* is thus named because brought (from Italy) in *galleys. Gaskins, gascoynes,* were hose in the style of *Gascony.* Worn by the sailors of the *galleass* (a large *galley*) and the *galley,* they became known as *galligaskins.*

gallium.
See element.

gallon.
See quarter.

gallop.
The story of this word takes us to what Falstaff babbled of when he died. It appears also, in ME., as *walopen,* from OFr. *galoper, waloper.* Its source may be found in the ON. *wall-hopp,* a gallop, from *wall* (AS. *weald,* whence ME. *wald,* whence Eng. *wold,* a woods or a field), field + *hopp,* whence Eng. *hop*: thus, a field-*hopping* or bounding. The verb, to *gallop,* was formed from the noun. The word, however, may be imitative in origin, of the *clop-clop, glop-glop* beat of horse hoofs. Its MHG. form, *walop,* suggests as a possible source O Frankish *wala hlaupan,* to leap well. *Cp. lobster.*

gallows.
This was a common Teut. form, ME. *galwes;* also used in the singular, AS. *gealga.* The same instrument was used in France; the term applied to it, from Fr. *gibe,* a staff, was the diminutive *gibet,* a cross-handled staff; the shape suggested the transfer; hence, Eng. *gibbet.* The *jib* of a sailing-vessel was hung from the masthead; hence its name (though

some suggest its relation to Eng. *gybe,* to shift course, as then the *jib* swings—as does the *gallows*-pendant in the wind.)

galore.

Enough is as good as a feast. This sounds like an Irish proverb; and it is condensed into the one word (originally two) *galore*: from Ir. *go leor,* to suffiency.

galvanize.

See Appendix II.

gamb, gams (slang), gambit, gamble, gambol, game, gammadion, gammon.

See monk.

The swastika is called a *gammadion* because it is made of the Gr. letter *gamma* Γ used four times. *Cp.* fylfot.

gamut.

This word is formed like *alphabet* (Gr. *alpha,* a + *beta,* b) from two symbols: *gamma* was the sign for the note below A in the medieval scale, and *ut,* the first tone of the scale. Originally it corresponded to our G on the lowest bass stave. In the 11th c., it was applied to the whole scale; then, to the entire range of possible notes—or any range. The names for the notes of the scale are said to have been taken, by Guido d'Arezzo, from the accented syllables in the following hymn stanza:

Ut queant laxis *re*sonare fibris
*Mi*ra gestorum *fa*muli tuorum
*So*lve polluti *la*bii reatum,
*S*ancte *I*ohannes.

As the last note of the scale repeats the first, *do* (abbreviation for *ditto,* the same) was used, and replaced the uglier *ut.*

gang.

See yacht.

gangster.

A *gang* is a group that is going together, from OE. *gangan,* to go. It was first applied to a group of workmen, then to prisoners (chain *gang*); thence, to any group gathered for evil purposes. For the ending, *see spinster.*

gantlet.

See subjugate.

gaol.

See cabal.

garble.

Once on a time this verb meant merely to sift, esp. to sift spices. In Sp. *garbillo* is a sieve; apparently the word traveled through Arab. *gharbala,* to sift, from *ghirbal,* a sieve, from LL. *cribellum,* diminutive of *cribrum,* a sieve, related to *cernere, cret—,* to sift, whence Eng. *discern* (L. *dis,* apart). *Discrete* and *discreet* are doublets; the latter shifted its meaning from passive to active: not separate, but able to separate, to distinguish. *Crib,* a common Teut. word for box, hut, was first a manger where animals were fed, and may come from this source: where the sifted grain was put. But from sifting, or selecting parts, the word came (from frequent practice, no doubt) to mean the selecting of parts that suited one's own purpose, even though these were not fair or representative parts; hence the present meaning.

From the idea of using a *crib* (box, stall: the sheperd in the mystery play hides the stolen lamb in the infant Jesus' *crib*) as a place to hide things, came the meaning, to cheat, to steal; hence also, from the hidden store of cards, the game *cribbage.* The L. *cernere* is from Gr. *krinein,* to judge, whence Gr. *krisis,* the decisive moment, whence Eng. *crisis;* whence both a *critical* illness and a *critical* remark, and *criticism.* From the sense of judging, rendering a verdict, comes L. *crimen,* whence Eng. *crime;* also with the prefix *dis, discriminate.* You should try to *discern* what is *garbled.*

Gr. *krinein,* to sift, to separate, to judge, appears also in *Eng. endocrine glands* (Gr. *endon,* within). *Gland* is from OFr. *glandre* (which form reappears in the disease Eng. *glanders*) from L. *glandula,* diminutive of L. *glans, gland—,* acorn. The *pituitary gland* is direct from L. *pituita,* mucus. And *hormones* are named from their stimulating effect, directly from Gr. *hormon,* present participle of *horman,* to urge on.

gardenia.

See Appendix II.

gargantuan.

François Rabelais wrote *The Horrific Life of the Great Gargantua* in 1534, to be set before his *Pantagruel,* 1532. *Gargantua's* father's name, *Grandgousier,* means great gullet; and *Gargantua* may be related to *gargle* and *gargoyle;*

cp. giggle. Gargantua was originally a helpful giant in French folklore.

gargle.
See gorge; slang; giggle.

gargoyle.
See giggle.

garlic.
See onion.

garnet.
See pommel.

garnish.
This word first meant to fortify or to give warning, from OFr. *garnir, garniss—*, from *guarnir*, from *warnir*, from OE. *warnian*, to take warning; ME. *wernen*, to *warn*. Then it was applied to equipping with arms; and later was reserved for the more elaborate or fancy armour; hence, to deck out, to adorn. Hence *garniture* is still a fancy word for furnishings. In the sense of warning, to *garnish* was used for notice of the intended collection of a debt, whence the victim was the *garnishee;* this has since become a verb, to *garnishee* one's salary. May yours be spared!

garret.
Watch-towers on buildings came often to be just windows in the top storey. Hence OFr. *guerite*, watch-tower, from OFr. *guarir, warir*, to watch—of Teutonic origin, from OHG. form *warjan*, to *guard; cp. warrior*—led to OFr. *garite* and the Eng. *garret* of today. From the same Teut. form, through OFr. *warison* to *guerison* and *garison*, we have an Eng. *garrison*.

garrison.
See garret.

garrulous.
See carouse.

garter.
This was originally a shank-piece. A Celtic word, Welsh *garan*, shank, (related to gamb, ham, *q.v.*) was taken into the Fr. *jaret, garet*, a diminutive, meaning the bend of the knee. The band tied around there was OFr. *jartier*, whence Eng. *garter*. In the year 1344, King Edward II of England was dancing with the Countess of Salisbury (so the story runs), when her *garter* slipped off. The King lifted it, placed it on his own leg, saying *Honi soit qui mal y pense*, Shame upon whoso thinks ill of this; and founded the highest order of English knighthood, the *Order of the Garter. See apathy* (*Order of the Bath*).

gas.
This seems to be the only English word invented, made out of thin air. It was coined by the Dutch chemist, van Helmont, d. 1644. Possibly there was in his mind some sense of the word *chaos* (Gr. *chaos*, abyss), the primal emptiness out of which order (Gr. *cosmos*) was made. *Cp. police.*

gasconnade.
See Appendix II.

gastric.
See gastronomy, necromancy.

gastronomy.
Gr. *nomos* (*cp. number*) was the order or law; hence, *astronomy*, the ordering of the stars; *cp. disaster*. Put a *g* in front of Gr. *aster*, star, and you have Gr. *gaster, gastr—*, belly; hence *gastronomy*. The word was first used (in Fr. *gastronomie*) as the title of a poem, by Berchoux, 1801; but *gastric* fever came much earlier, as also Eng. *gastrimargy*, "belly-madness" (Gr. *margos*, raging), gluttony: Rabelais (Motteux' Eng. translation) speaks of *gastrolaters*. Also *cp. necromancy*. The scientific name of the large muscle of the calf of the leg, which makes it belly, is *gastrocnemius*, from Gr. *gastr—* + *kneme*, leg. (This is not related to *knee*, which is AS. *cneow*, the Gr. cognate of which is *gony;* Sansk. *janu;* L. *genu*, whence Eng. *genuflection; cp. accent—gnu* is native Kaffir *qnu*. Hence also AS. *cneowlian*, Eng. *kneel*.)

gate.
See runagate.

gauche.
See dexterity.

gaudeamus, gaudy.
See young.

gauntlet.
See subjugate.

gauss.
See Appendix II.
To *degauss* (World War II) is to equip a vessel with protection against magnetic mines.

gauze.
See cloth.

gavotte.
See Appendix II.

gawk, gawky.
See dexterity. *Gawk,* meaning to stare foolishly, is corrupted from *gowk,* from OE. *géac,* cuckoo, the bird being deemed foolish. *Cp. cuckold.*

gay.
See yacht.

gaze.
See gazebo.

gazebo, gazabo.
The peeping turret on an English 18th c. estate was given its name from a pseudo-Latin formation on the word *gaze,* a common Teut. word, Sw. *gasa,* to gape. The American slang *gazabo* is probably from Mex. *gazapo,* "smart guy."

gazette.
When folks first began to have coins to spend, they must have felt as though they were walking on air—they gave the coins the names of birds: eagle, raven; *cp. rap.* An Italian small coin was called *gazetta,* magpie. When newspapers were first printed, it seems folks were charged a *gazetta* for reading them; the word was transferred to the paper, and is now preserved in the *N. Y. Police Gazette.* Dickens calls a halfpenny a *magpie;* in 18th and 19th c. Eng. slang, it is a *mag.*

gelatin, gelatine.
See aspic.

gem.
Take a look at one. It derives its name from its appearance, L. *gemma,* bud. The original sense is retained in botany, Eng. *gemma, gemmation, gemmiferous* (L. *ferre,* to bear) and more.

general, generous, genius, genteel, gentile, gentle.
See racy.

genuflection.
See gastronomy.

genus.
See racy.

geography, geometry, geophagy.
See sarcophagus; absurd; algebra.

georgette.
See cloth.

Georgia.
See States.

geranium.
See flower.

germanium.
See element.

gerrymander.
One way of winning an election is to arrange the district limits so that your party has a majority living within it. This trick was managed by *Governor Elbridge Gerry,* of Massachusetts, U. S. A., about 1812. (It has been utilized since.) On the map, one such tortuous district looked like a *salamander,* whereupon came the happy suggestion of *gerrymander.*

Gestapo.
Short for G. *Ge*heime *Sta*ats*po*lizei, Secret State Police. *Cp.* Dora.

gesture.
See joke.

ghastly.
See ghost.

ghost.
The early use of this word was in the sense of a person's spirit, as still in giving up the *ghost;* hence, that spirit after it left the body, took a *ghostly* form, and —if there was unfinished business—came back in accord with the rules about not crossing running water, departing on the stroke of twelve, and the other laws ordained for *ghosts.* That it was commonly deemed a dangerous thing is shown by the origin of the word; OE. *gast* and *gaest* are from a root OTeut. *gaistjan,* to tear or to terrify. And that which terrifies is *ghastly.* In *ghostly* wise, the origin of *haunt* is hid in darkness. The *h* in *ghost* was added by Caxton (first Eng. printer, 1422?—91) but did not become fixed till about 1600. It belongs in *ghoul,* from Arab. *ghul,* from a root that means to seize.

ghoul.
See ghost.

giant.
Gaea (classical goddess of earth) and *Uranus* (*q.v.*, god of heaven) had sons called Gr. *gigantes* (one was Gr. *gigas*), who warred with the gods, and were finally overthrown, with Zeus (Jupiter) established on Mt. Olympus. Thus the *giant Antaeus* drew constant strength from his mother; Hercules had to lift him from the earth and hold him in the air, to overcome him; hence, one with *Antaean* (*Antean*) powers. After the war, the *giants* were punished in various ways; *see atlas.*

Our Eng. *gigantic* springs from this word; via OFr. *gaiant, geant,* it was shortened to Eng. *giant.* The *Bible* borrowed the classical word, in Latin, to apply to men of very great size and strength; hence, its widespread use in fairy tales (*Jack the Giant Killer*) and elsewhere today.

gibberish.
This word, earlier than the verb to *gibber,* is partly imitative of the sound of nonsense, but was influenced by the 11th c. Arabian alchemist, *Geber,* who, to avoid death on charge of dealing with the devil, wrote his treatises in apparent nonsense. Other imitative words of the same general mood are *jabber, gobble, giggle.*

Gibraltar.
This projection at the gateway to the middle sea was named from its Arabic conqueror, *Tarik*: *Jabalu't tarik,* Tarik's Mountain, whence *Jibal Tarik,* whence *Gibraltar.* The ending has been given an English sound; in It. it is *Gibilterrà* (from *terra,* land).

gibus.
See Appendix II.

giddy.
See enthusiasm.

gigantic.
See giant.

giggle.
See gibberish. There was also an early Eng. *gaggle;* not to mention *gargle* and *gurgle;* though note that L. *gurgulio* is windpipe. *Gargle* in Fr. is *gargouiller;* whence, from the sound and the distorted faces, Eng. *gargoyle,* the mouth of which was used as a spout to let rainwater off the roof.

Gilbertian.
See Appendix II.

gin.
See drink.

ginger.
The shape of the *ginger* root explains the word: from AS. *gingiber,* from LGr. *ziggiberis,* from Sansk. *srngavera,* antler body.

Gingerly is another word, from the gait of the lady, from OFr. *gensour,* comparative of *gent,* dainty, from L. *genitus,* born in the (noble) family, from *gens,* family; *cp. racy.*

gipsy.
See gyp.

girl.
You may guess freely here; Brewer lists several choices. There is *garrula,* a chatterbox (surely appropriate enough!), from L. *garrire,* to prattle. Then L. *gerula* is a nurse; AS. *ceorl,* a *churl;* Brewer himself suggests *girdle,* worn by maids and loosed at the marriage; also *gull* (impolitely!). The word is, we can at least say, a diminutive: perhaps of Gr. *koure,* lass; perhaps a corruption of *darling,* from AS. *deorling.* A *girl* can keep any boy guessing.

glabrous.
See glad.

glacier.
See graze.

glad.
L. *glaber, glabr—,* meant smooth; whence Eng. *glabrous,* smooth in the sense of hairless. The diminutive Eng. *glabella* is the spot between the eyebrows. The cognate OHG. *glat,* smooth, came into OE. as *glad.* As things smooth (look at any bald head) are shiny, the sense shining developed; this gradually took the place of the other. Then, applied figuratively, it meant persons of a shining disposition; hence the present application—as when Father Divine interrupts his speeches to cry out, apropos the general state of things: "Aren't you *glad!*"

gladiator, gladiolus.
See flower.

gladstone (bag).
See Appendix II.

glamour.
The *glamour* girl of today (always spell *glamour* with the *u*, because of its relation to *l'amour*) exercises her potent magic. Why not; that's the meaning of the word. But, with the second letter changed, pupils drone over it in school. Gr. *gramma,* letter, whence *graphein,* to write (thus *telegram* and *telegraph* are the same; *cp. focus*), was associated in the middle ages with the magic arts, *gramarye.* By dissimilation, this becomes *glamour.* In the prosaic range, it remained *grammar.* If you have the first, you little need the second.

gland.
See garble.

glass, glaze.
See electricity.

gloaming.
See globe.

globe.
L. *globus* meant sphere; L. *glomus,* ball. Both words (as *globe* and *glome*) have come into Eng., with their diminutives, *globule* and *glomerule;* but the second has been used in scientific combinations only, except for the compounds, as *conglomeration.* This carries an idea of rolled together into a coherent mass; a *conglomerate* gland is composed of several *conglobate* glands within one membrane. The tiny creatures whose ancient bony structure produced the chalk cliffs of England (Huxley—*cp. agnostic*—uses them as the basis of his famous lecture, "On a Piece of Chalk", 1868) are called *globigerinae;* they are an infinitesimal yet significant part of this great round ball we call the terrestrial *globe.*
To *gloam* was to *gleam* (AS. *glom* and *gleam;* AS. *glomung* gives us *gloaming*); it is related to *glow,* from AS. *glowan.* To *gloom* was to be sullen; a variant was to *glum;* both of these words were verbs before they were used as adjective and noun. There was then an adjective *glumpy,* akin to *grumpy*: this is echoic in origin, like *grumble* and *grunt* and the exclamations *humph* and *hrrmp!* It takes all sorts to cover a *globe.*

globigerinae, globule, glome, gloom.
See globe.

glossary.
There is a MHG. *glos,* sheen, related to *glare* and *glass; cp. electricity.* From this comes Eng. *gloss,* lustre, also as in to *gloss* over. But Gr. *glossa,* tongue (*cp. laugh*) came to be used in the sense of mother tongue, language. Hence a *gloss* to a text; and the wordbook, the *glossary.*

glow.
See globe.

glucose.
See clam.

glue.
See clam.

glum.
See globe.

glut, glutton.
See laugh.

glycerine, glycero—, glyco—, glycol.
See clam.

gnarled, gnash.
See knick-knack.

gnaw.
See pylorus, knick-knack.

gnu.
See gastronomy.

go.
See yacht.

Gobelin.
See Appendix II.

goblin.
See incinerator.

God.
See goodbye. (In ME. *god* was spelled without a capital letter.)

God's acre.
See acre.

goffer.
See gopher.

go-getter.
See whippersnapper.

goiter, goitre.
See gorge.

golf.
This game is older than any mention of Dutch games, but some say the word is

from Du. *kolf,* club (*cp. clam*). It may be named from the head of the stick, indirectly from L. *globus,* round mass, whence also *Eng. globe, q.v.*

gold.
See element.

gongorism.
See Appendix II.

good.
See goodbye, beauty.

goodbye.
This is a contraction of *God be with you.* A half-way stage appears in Shakespeare (*Twelfth Night,* IV,ii): *God buy you.* Religious words are often changed to less sacred forms, *e.g. By our Lady,* whence, *bloody,* the Eng. oath. The reverse process may have occurred with *gospel;* but this is more probably directly from AS. *god, God* + *spell,* saying, story—which gives us both the magic *spell* and the orthographical *spelling. God* and *good* are old but unrelated Teut. words. *God,* Goth. *guth,* may be traced to Aryan *ghut, god,* from *ghuto,* to implore: *God* is the one to whom we pray.

goof.
See yokel.

googol.
This word (we are told in *Mathematics and the Imagination,* by Edward Kasner and James Newman, New York, 1940) was invented by Dr. Kasner's nine year old nephew, asked to make up a name for a very big number, namely, 1 with a hundred zeros after it, ten to the hundreth power, 10^{100}. A footnote explains that the word is "not even approximately a Russian author"; but it is likely that the child created it from echoings of *coo,* a pleasant soothing sound, *ooh,* a sound expressing pleasant surprise, and *goo,* a sweet sticky mess of which a child would want a lot, with overtones of that character from what is comically called "the comics," *Barney Google.*
The child also seems to have invented the word *googolplex,* which is 1 followed by a *googol* zeros, $10^{10^{100}}$. This number is so big "that there would not be enough room to write it, if you went to the farthest star, touring all the nebulae, and putting down zeros every inch of the way." Yet it is a finite number, and no nearer infinity than 7. (The total of possible moves in a game of chess is $10^{10^{50}}$. The entire universe, with no blank space, filled with protons and electrons, would hold 10^{110}.) To reach an infinite (*q.v.*) number, you must journey to another sort of world. *Googol* is used seriously in mathematics. *Cp. myriad.*

gooseberry.
See yellow.

gopher.
From the Hebrew (*Genesis* vi, 14) this is the wood of which Noah's ark was builded (probably cypress, or pine). The animal is from Fr. *gaufre,* honeycomb, from the pattern of its burrowings. Then the Fr. made a thin cake stamped with a honeycomb design, whence also Eng. *goffer,* referring to the frilled design on dresses. This Fr. *gaufre,* in the north, became *waufre, wafre,* whence Eng. *wafer;* and in MLG. *wafel* and Du. *waefel,* whence Eng. *waffle.* Have it with maple syrup.

Gordian (knot).
See knot.

gorge.
Eng. *gargle* and *gurgle* are echoic words; similar forms are found in other languages; Fr. *gargouiller.* OFr. *gargate,* throat, probably suggested to Rabelais the name *Gargantua; cp. gargantuan.* L. *gargulio,* windpipe, developed a LL. *gorga,* throat. (Classical L. for throat was *guttur,* whence Eng. *guttural.*) From this L. *gorga,* used also of the whole neck, came OFr. and Eng. *gorge.* Applied first to the neck, this was later used of things shaped like a neck; hence, *gorge,* a ravine. Hence also to stuff the throat, to *gorge* oneself. Diminutives of *gorge* are Eng. *gorgelet, gorgeret, gorget;* the first two used in medicine, the third, in zoology and the army. There was also OFr. *gorgias,* a neckpiece, usually a gaudy one; this has survived in the adjective Eng. *gorgeous.*
Obviously from its protruberance in the neck came LL. *gutturiosum,* literally, full of neck, whence Eng. *goitre, goiter.*

gorgeous.
See gorge.

gorgon.
See demon.

gospel.
See goodbye.

gossamer.
What we call Indian summer—the spell of fine weather in late fall—was in England called *goose summer* (ME. *gossomer*); it was the season for eating the fatted goose. But in that season, fine spider-webs might glisten of a pleasant morn. In G. *sommer* is used both of the season and of *"summer-film"*; whence *gossamer* is applied to any very thin or delicate material. It was once guessed that the word came from *God-summer; cp. goodbye.* It is also suggested that the word is from *God's seam,* or thread, as legend tells this filmy substance is the ravelling of the winding-sheet of the Virgin Mary, which trailed back to earth as she ascended to heaven. And mention is made, too, of L. *gossipin—,* cotton. Enough to break the *gossamer* thread.

gossip.
Old folk are fond of talking. *Gossip* was originally *Godsip,* from AS. *God* + *sibb,* race: related through God, as Godmother or Godfather. (*Sib* + the diminutive suffix *—ling,* as in *darling, duckling,* gives us the modern Eng. social-science term for children of the same parents: *siblings.*) From the *gossip* that talks of the good old days, or more tartly of the bad young neighbors, the term was applied to the talk itself. A similar shift occurred in other tongues: the Scotch term for *gossip, cummer,* is from Fr. *commère,* fellow-mother, Godmother. And Eng. *compeer* (Fr. *com,* together + *pair,* from L. *par,* equal, on a *par*) in the sense of companion, was influenced by Fr. *compère,* fellow-father, Godfather. Old folk are fond of talking.

gothite.
See Appendix II.

gout.
See drip.

govern.
The comparison of a country's control with the steering of a ship is an old one: *govern,* from Fr. *gouverner,* from L. *gubernare,* to steer, whence *gubernatorial,* from Gr. *kybernan,* to steer. But if we go a step farther, the figure takes us back to land: Sansk. *kubara,* a carriage pole. Hence Lincoln's remark about not changing horses is in the ancient stream.

grade, gradual, graduated.
See issue.

graffito.
Writings or drawings scratched on the wall are often a public nuisance, though there are times (as with the appearance of . . . — V on walls all over Europe) when they are a factor in building morale. The practice is at least as old as Pompeii and ancient Rome, and they had a word for it: *graffito,* from L. *graffio,* a scratch, from Gr. *graphein,* to scratch, then to write. *Graph* is an element in many Eng. words, from *autograph* (Gr. *auto,* self) to *zymograph* (instrument for recording rate of fermentation, from Gr. *zyme,* leaven, ferment). *Cp. pasquinade.*

graft.
The cut shoots that are used in *grafting* trees looked to the ancients like the stylus or pen with which they wrote: (from. Eng. *graffe,* from Fr. *greffe,* from L. *graphium,* from Gr. *graphion,* stylus, from *graphein,* to write. This gives us *graph; graphite,* the substance in the pencil that does the writing; and the many words in which *graph* is either prefix or suffix). The suggestion is made that our slang word *graft* is from Eng. *graft,* work, from the obs. verb *grave,* to dig; but *grafters* avoid work: it seems more likely that the use is merely an extension of the other meaning: something added from outside. *Cp. carve.*

Imp also first meant a shoot, from AS. *impian,* to graft. Thence, a product or offspring, a child (*scion,* another AS. word for shoot, had the same shift of meaning). But *imp,* possibly because of the implications of the sound (which begins *impious, improper* and thus explosively starts many other words of unpleasant meaning) is most frequently employed in such a phrase as *imp of Satan. Brat* seems first to have meant a cloth; then, a pinafore; then, a discarded one, rubbish—whence it was applied contemptuously to a child. *Urchin* meant a hedgehog, from ME. *irchoun,* from ONFr. *herichun,* from L. *ericium,* hedgehog; then a goblin, then a little mischievous boy.

grain.
See **barley, pommel.**

Gramercy (Square, New York City).
This place, the site of the only pri-

vately owned park in New York City, owes its name to the crooked lake (*De Kromme Zee*) that used to be there—just as *Canal* Street used to have a *canal*, and *Wall* Street, now at the lower end of Manhattan's pavements, used to mark the city's outer wall. Shakespeare often uses *gramercy* as the Fr. *grand merci*, much thanks (*Titus Andronicus*, I,ii; *Taming of the Shrew*, I,i; etc.).

graminivorous.
See grass.

grammar.
From the root Gr. *gra—* in *graphein*, to write (*cp. graft*) came Gr. *gramma*, letter. The art of writing was Gr. *grammatike techne;* whence, via OFr. *gramaire*, Eng. *grammar*. Applied at first to the study of literature in all its aspects, this word was later restricted to the linguistic aspects, then to those structural elements to which the term is still applied. From the middle ages until the 19th c., *grammar* meant the study of Latin; hence, our *grammar schools*.
The association with Latin linked *grammar* with learning in general; in the popular mind (knowledge is power), learning meant association with the occult and hidden arts, for which *see glamour.*

granary.
See pommel.

grangerize.
To *bowdlerize* (*q.v.*) is to remove erotic elements from a book; to *grangerize* is to add sentimental. The Rev. J. *Granger* (d. 1776), in England, tucked into his books reviews, letters, pictures, anything he could gather relating to the work or its author. The name took hold with the practice.

grape.
See peach.

graph, graphite.
See graft.

grass.
When you say the grass grows green, you are using three words from one source. *Grass, grow,* and *green* all spring from a Teut. *grō,* apparently from an Aryan *ghra,* to grow. From the same root comes L. *gramen, graminis, grass,* which gives us several words, *e.g., graminivorous, grass*-eating. *See graze.*

A *grass widow* is not one that is free to gambol in new pastures, but a *grace widow,* from Fr. *veuve de grâce;* by *grace* or dispensation of the Pope, to allow divorce. It's easier nowadays, when women jaunt to Nevada to be *Renovated* (telescoped by Walter Winchell, from *Reno,* city that is the center of the divorce trade of Nevada, and *renovation,* renewal).
In India, however, a *grass widow* is not a woman freed by divorce, but a wife living in the cool *grassy* hill-country while her husband swelters at his job on the dusty plains.

grate.
See great, knick-knack.

gravamen.
See aggravate.

grave.
One source of this word is OE. *graef, grafan,* to dig. This probably has an earlier form, *ghrabh* (not related to Gr. *graphein,* to write). From this source comes the meaning: a place where a corpse is laid; also from this source are *engrave,* to mark by digging in; and *groove,* a line or mark dug in. Nor must we overlook the *graven* image.
Another source is akin to Du. *grave,* G. *Graf;* this survives in Eng. in the title *Landgrave.*
The nautical term *grave, graving-dock,* a place where a ship is beached to clean its bottom, is from Fr. *grève,* shore. The diminutive of this, as applied to the coarse sand of the shore, gives us (by way of the Celtic) *gravel.*
For *grave* from L. *gravis,* heavy, *see aggravate.*

gravel, graven.
See grave.

gravid, gravitate, gravitation, gravity.
See aggravate.

graze.
Several words have entangled in this form. When cattle *graze,* they feed on *grass,* and the word *graze* is a doublet of *grass,* from AS. *grasian.* But the word has also been affected by OFr. *graissier,* to make fat, from OFr. *graisse,* whence Eng. *grease,* from LL. *crassia,* from L. *crassa,* neuter plural of *crassus,* fat.

To *graze,* meaning to touch and glance off, is still more intertwined. It is from ME. *glacen,* from OFr. *glacier,* from LL. *glaciare,* to slip on ice, from L. *glacies,* ice, whence Eng. *glacier.* The change from *l* to *r* is through the influence of Fr. *raser,* to scrape (whence Eng. *raze, razor*), from L. *radere, ras—,* to scrape. But also—just as *radere* is related to *rodere,* to gnaw, whence Eng. *rodent*—this second *graze* is affected by the first, in the sense that cattle nibble off the grass but do not touch the fundament (as the *razor,* in turn, slices off the hair but—usually, we trust—not the skin).

grease.
See graze.

great.
See grit. The homonym, *grate,* is from LL. *grata* from L. *crates,* hurdle. (For something that *grates* on you, see *knick-knack*). The diminutive of L. *crates* was *craticulum,* whence by the same sort of change come Eng. *griddle* and *grill. Griddle* was earlier *gredile;* a variant of this, *gredire,* was changed by folk etymology (considering the material of which it's made) to *gridiron;* from the lines that mark the yards along the ground, this word is applied to a football field; *gridiron* is also shortened to *grid.*

The confusion of homonyms is used by Jonathan Swift (English satirist, 1667—1745) in his *Etymology in Earnest,* wherein he undertakes to demonstrate that the classical tongues were formed from English. He illustrates by showing the origins of a few well-known names. Thus, as we call a trouble-maker *a killjoy,* the Trojans called the Greek hero *a kill-case,* Achilles. One Greek ruler liked his eggs roasted on the coals; as soon as he woke every morning, the bedroom slaves called to the kitchen slaves: *"All eggs under the grate! All eggs under the grate!"* From being heralded that way every morning, he came to be known as *Alexander the Great.* (Serious etymology sometimes seems to use similar methods!)

greedy.
See issue.

green.
See grass.

greenhorn.
See yellow.

greengage.
See month; *Appendix II.*

Greenwich Village.
This place-name (from the so-called artists' quarter of New York City), used as an adjective to mean pseudo-artistic, with a suggestion of gay night life (as in the Paris *Latin Quarter*), doubles on itself. *Greenwich,* in England, is the center from which the time of the world radiates; it is earlier *Grenawic,* from AS. *grian-wic,* sun *village. Wic* and *village* are the same; *see villain.*

gregarious.
See absolute.

Gregorian.
See Appendix II.

gremlin.
This was apparently first used by a drunken pilot who blamed his crash into the sea on the *gremlins* (from bottles of *Fremlin* brand beer). It might be from OE. *greme,* to vex, with the diminutive noun ending. More likely is the thought of Ir. *gruaimin,* ill-tempered man + *goblin.* And there may have filtered in some prison-shudder of the *Kremlin!* Let them keep away!

grenade, grenadier, grenadine.
See pommel.

greyhound.
This dog is so swift that it has outrun its origin. *Hound* is common Teut., AS. *hund,* related to *hunt,* from AS. *huntian,* to *hunt.* The *grey* has no relation to color. One suggestion is that it is from AS. *grīg,* bitch; another, that it is a translation of L. *canis grae,* Greek hound. Other dogs are named from places: *dalmatian* (the "fire dog"); *spaniel* (from Spain); the *pekinese.*

The word *dog* (a rare *AS. docga,* mastiff) does not appear until the 11th c.; then it is the name of one large variety, usually elsewhere called *English dog.* As *hound* was widely used for varieties employed in hunting, it grew restricted in application, while *dog* gradually grew more general. Hence it came to be applied to *dogs* of indeterminate ancestry, and then in general scorn, as in *dog-Latin; dog-rhymes;* hence, perhaps, the diminutive *doggerel.*

grief, grievance, grieve, grievous.
See aggravate.

grind.
See ground.

gringo.
See Yankee.

grist.
See ground.

grit.
Two words here have kept separate, but have influenced one another. There is OE. *greot* from an early root form *ghreus*—, to pound, to crush; hence the *grit* that lingers in your spinach. There is also OE. *grytt,* earlier *greut*—, *graut*—, chaff, now used only in the plural as *grits* or *groats,* first a coarse form of oats, now applied to various other grains. The first *grit* came to be used of the texture of stone, as *all one grit, hard grit, clear grit.* Hence, of persons, *clear grit* came to mean of good hard quality: as, he showed his *grit.*

Probably from that OTeut. *graut*—, meaning coarse, big, came OE. and Eng. *great.* This first meant massive, stout (opposed to *small,* AS. *smael,* which first meant slender) ; hence also big with courage, and in other figurative ways, as in The day of our victory will be a *great* day!

groats.
See grit.

grocer.
See record.

grog, groggy.
See demijohn.

groove.
See grave.

gross.
See record.

grotesque.
This word means, like the figures on the walls of *grottoes,* which seemed outlandish to later critical eyes. *Grot,* earlier *grotta,* and *grotto,* are from LL. *grupta* (*crypt* is a doublet), from Gr. *krypte,* from *kryptos,* hidden, from *kryptein,* to hide. *Cryptography* is hidden, or secret, writing; the unabridged dictionary gives almost 120 words beginning with the prefix *crypt*— or *crypto*—, from *cryptaesthesia* to *cryptozygous.*

grotto.
See grotesque.

ground.
This is widespread in Teuton lands, but has no known cognates elsewhere. OE. *grund,* meaning the bottom; then, the earth as on the bottom of the heavens. All the other meanings rest on this *ground.*

The Eng. *grind,* on the contrary, is lacking in the other Teutonic tongues: OE. *grindan, grond, grundon* is perhaps cognate with L. *frendere,* to gnash the teeth; the first sense was the crushing between two surfaces (as the upper and the nether *grindstone*). Hence, all is *grist* (the noun, from OE. *grist* from *grinst*) that comes to the mill.

grouse.
See penguin; *cp.* pedigree.

grovel.
This verb is one of a group that have been formed by mistaking an adverb for a present participle. ME. —*ling* became later Eng. —*ly,* or —*long,* as in *headily* and *headlong.* Where the earlier form lingered, it led to the back-formation of a verb: *darkle* from *darkling; sidle* from *sidling; grovel* from *groveling.* The source here is AS. *groofling, along* the *groof,* belly.

grow.
See grass.

grumble, grumpy, grunt.
See globe.

guarantee, guard.
See warrior.

guide.
Here is another word that was *guided* back toward its origin. The L. *guidare,* to lead, had developed the OFr. *guie,* whence Eng. *guy* (*q.v.,* for another source), surviving in the ship's *guy rope.* But in the 14th c. the earlier form began to reassert itself, and by about 1500 the *guy* was replaced by the *guide.*

guile.
See warrior.

guillotine.
See Appendix II.

guinea-fowl.
See turkey.

gull.
See yellow. It is also suggested that the sense of *gull,* fool, may come from the bird's swallowing anything that is tossed to it. The bird name is common Teut. Hence also *gullible.*

gun.
Ships have names; so have trains. Men that work with them give names to engines, airplanes, guns. The list of munitions at Windsor Castle in 1330 mentions a "large ballista called *Lady Gunhilda.*" This, rather than the echo of its sound, gives us our *gun. Big Bertha* (G. *die dicke Bertha,* fat Bertha; from Bertha Krupp, whose husband owned the steel and munition works at Essen) was the most famous gun of World War I.

gurgle.
See giggle; gorge; slang.

guts.
See pluck.

gutta-percha.
See drip, gutter.

gutter.
L. *gutta,* a drop (*gutta percha* is modified to resemble this, from Malay *getah percha,* gum tree—the gum exuding drop by drop) became Fr. *goutte;* and a channel (on housetops) to collect the drops of rainwater was Fr. *gouttière,* whence Eng. *gutter. Cp.* drip.

From its use as a small channel along the side of a road, the word came to be associated with mud, mire, filth: hence the bird, the *gutter-snipe,* (picking at grains of food there) was contemptuously applied to persons whose career ended in the *gutter.*

guttural.
See gorge.

guy.
A god of the Baltic Slavs, *Svanto-Vid,* was adored with hysterical dances (such as accompany "revivals" in our time). With Christianity, his name (like other pagan names and institutions) was altered; they made *Sanctus Vitus, Saint Vitus,* out of him. Hence, *St. Vitus' dance.* Hence, also, the names: G. *Veit,* It. *Guido,* Fr. and Eng. *Guy.*

One of these *Guys, Guy Fawkes,* was caught (Nov. 5, 1605) in the "Gunpowder Plot" to blow up the Parliament. On the anniversary, effigies of him were carried through London streets; whence, *guy* came to mean any odd looking fellow, and as time made the memory mellow, any fellow at all. To *guy* still means to poke fun at, to fool. *See guide.*

gymnasium.
Though the college girl startled her parents by saying that she weighed 105 lbs. stripped for *"gym",* a *gymnast* is literally (Gr. *gymnos*) a naked person. *Gymnasium* (Gr. *gymnasion,* from *gymnazein,* to train: all exercise was in the nude) is a place for exercise. (Current practice at bathing beaches is re-approaching the Greek.) *Gymn—* and *gymno—* are Eng. combining forms for scientific words. Thus *gymnite* is a mineral (a hydrated silicate of magnesium) so named because found at Bare Hills, Maryland. *Gymnotus* is the electric eel (Gr. *noton,* back); it has no fins on its back. A score of such words are in the unabridged dictionary. There are also the *gymnosophists,* ancient Hindu philosophers ascetic of habits and scant of dress.

gynecology.
See banshee.

gyp.
An Arabian mantle (*jubbah*) came into the west as a *jibbah*—though on its trail it gave the Fr. *jupe* and *jupon,* skirt; and Eng. *jumper,* earlier *jump.* A short jacket, such as the servants wore at Cambridge, England, was called a *gippo,* still further shortened to *gyp.* Possibly influenced by *gipsy, gypsy* (earlier *gypcian,* from *Egyptian,* Egypt being their supposed home), it was applied to the servants themselves. It is easy, alas, to see how the word then came to mean a cheat! There is also the suggestion that the college boys may also have been thinking of *gyph,* a vulture—which was Greek to them. There is another sense of *gyp* in some localities: to handle roughly, to thrash, which may be related to *gee-up,* an order to a horse. *Gee-up* is really *geehup!,* commands to move ahead.

gypsy.
See gyp; tatterdemalion; island.

gyrate.
See amphigory.

H

haberdasher.
Learned references connect this word with Fr. *avoirdupois,* which in ME. is sometimes spelled *haberdupois;* but it is more probably connected with our freedom. That is, among the items determined by the first great document of liberty, the Magna Carta, was the width of a cloth called *hapertas.* A *hapertaser* or *haberdasher,* as it was easier to say, was originally a dealer in this cloth, from which men's garments were made.

habile, habiliment, habilitate.
See ability.

habit.
See customer.

hack.
See heckle.

Hades.
See tatterdemalion.

hadj.
See hegira.

hafnium.
See element.

hag, haggard.
See hedge.

hail.
See whole.

halcyon.
Popular mythology has altered this word. Gr. *alkyon,* kingfisher (L. *alcedo,* kingfisher; ON. *alka,* whence Eng. *auk*) was changed to *halcyon,* as though it came from Gr. *hals,* sea + *kyon,* conceiving: the story was that the bird made a nest that floated on the waters, and while the eggs were hatching the weather was clear and calm: the *halcyon* days.

hale.
See wealth, wassail, whole.

half.
When a man spoke of his better *half,* he was referring to the rib of Adam; for the first meaning of AS. *healf* (common Teut.) was side. If you worked in *behalf* of someone, you worked by his side. Since we have (in common consideration) two sides to our body, the word came to the present meaning of one *half.*

halibut.
See holy; *cp.* butt.

halo.
See aureole.

halogen.
See necromancy.

ham.
This word is from OTeut. *ham,* crooked, being first the part of the leg that crooks. The *ham* actor is a combination of cockney *hamateur* (*amateur,* via Fr. from L. *amatorem,* lover, from L. *amare, amat—,* to love, whence Eng. *amatory*) and *Hamlet,* the most frequently (mis)performed role. *Cp. monk.* From "the bend of the knee" (OE. *hamm,* crooked), this word was extended up the back of the thigh; *cp. garter.*

hamburger, hamlet.
See dollar.

hamper.
See harangue.

hand.
See pylorus.

handicap.
See boot.

handkerchief.
This was first a *bandanna* (Hind.

bāndhnū, knot-dyeing, batik, from Sansk. *bandhana,* binding), to use around the head, from OFr. *couvre-chef,* whence Eng. *kerchief, cover* head; *cp. achieve.* Thus a *pocket-handkerchief* is put in the pocket to carry in the hand to cover the head.

handle.
See thimble.

handsome.
See awry.

hangnail.
Most persons have been annoyed by a bit of skin that sometimes seems to *hang* from the fingernail. The *hangnail* drew only the *h* from its *hanging,* from AS. *hangian;* it is the much more important element of the pain involved: AS. *angnaegl,* from *ange,* pain, whence Eng. *anguish.* Isn't it so? *Cp.* nail.

happen, happy.
See emporium.

hara kiri.
This term for the Japanese suicide to "save one's face" was translated into English (probably by the Japanese) as "happy dispatch." It actually means belly cut. The N E D speaks of it as "formerly practiced"; but it seems recently to have been renewed.

harangue.
The G. initial *h* (or *ch*) was especially hard for the Romance tongue to sound before another consonant. (Thus OHG, *hnapf,* cup; AS. *hnaepp* became in OFr. *hanaps,* goblets, whence *hanapier,* a case to hold them. This was ME. *hanaper,* whence Eng. *hamper.*) OHG. *hring,* the circle (Eng. *ring*) in which an audience sat or stood, became *harangue;* the word itself was transferred from the group to the speech. The simpler process of droping the *h* (OFr. *renc,* whence *ranc*) gives Eng. *rank,* originally a circle of soldiers. Later, they marched and attacked in lines. And from this word, through Sp. *rancho,* the place for a *rank* of soldiers, then any row of huts, came Eng. *ranch.*

harass, harbinger, harbor.
See harum-scarum.

hard.
L. *crassus,* fat, coarse, came into Fr. as *cras,* then *gras,* with the meaning centering on the fat; *Mardi Gras,* fat Tuesday, Shrove Tuesday, day of celebration. In Eng. it came down with the emphasis on the coarse, giving us *crass* impudence. Gr. *cratos,* thick, strong, shifted trail also; but came via its Teut. cognate, from *kartus* and *hardus* to Eng. *hard.* Disagreeably *hard* was early *hardsk, hardsch,* MLG. *harsch,* Eng. *harsh.* An instrument for measuring power goes back to the Gr., *cratometer.*

harem.
See seraglio.

harlequinade.
Before he was a clown, *Harlequin* was a demon hunter, accompanied by his retinue of friends, his *meinie* (from OFr. *moynie,* from *mesnie,* from L. *mansionem,* household; whence Eng. *mansion; cp. remnant*). In OFr. he was *hennequin, hierlequin, hellequin;* in Dante's Inferno, *Alichino.* The English etymologists suggest that the name is a diminutive of a proper name, as Flem. *Han,* John. The French are more fertile. Recalling a *Judge Harley,* whom one of the medieval Italian comedians frequented in Paris, they suggest *"little Harley"—Harlequino*—as the nickname given this player, which stuck. They also suggest OHG. *Erle,* sprite, + *König, king*: *harlequin,* king of the spirits. Finally, accepting the diminutive, they suggest *hellequin,* from G. *Hell*: a little fiend from *hell.* From all this has descended the gay or madcap farce of the *harlequinade.*

harlot.
As furlough time in any war reveals, soldiers are reckless with their pay. Hence the horde of camp-followers. *Harlot* (first, of either sex, like *witch; cp. wicked*) is from OHG. *hari,* army, + AS. *loddere,* beggar. Since the camp-followers were mainly women, the sex and meaning grew limited accordingly.

harmony.
This was originally a term, not in music, but in carpentry, from Gr. *harmozein,* to fit together. *Harmony* is a basic principle in Greek and Oriental philosophy; note that both the Greeks and the Indians have a *carpenter* god; the Christian God is a mason, but his son was a *carpenter. Carpenter,* though directly from OFr. *carpentier,* from L. *carpentarius, cartwright,* from *carpentum,*

cart, is a Celt. word: from Gael. *carbad,* OIr. *carpat,* chariot.

The fact that wood is the primary lifestuff, "of which all things are made", shows it no historical accident but a mythical necessity that the god be referred to as a *carpenter.*

harp.
See harpoon The *harpsichord* is a variety of *harp* in which the *chords* are plucked when keys are struck; it was used from the 16th through the 18th c., before the pianoforte. The *s* has no etymological reason, but gives the word euphony.

Harpocrates.
The Gr. god of silence—his cult is forgotten today. His very existence is an error on the part of the Greeks, who saw the statues of the Egyptian Dawn God, *Har-(p)-chrot* (*Horus,* the sun) as a child with his finger to his lips. Dawn, the day's birth, was represented by an *infant* that cannot speak (L. *infans,* not speaking, from *in,* not + *fans,* present particple of *fari,* to speak); *cp. infantry.*

harpoon.
A *harpy* was one of the creatures the ancient Greeks and Romans had torturing their damned. The *harpies* snatched the food of those in Tartarus, just before it reached their mouth. Gr. *harpyiai,* snatcher, is related to Gr. *harpe,* claw, sickle, which gives us Eng. *harpoon.* The miser in Molière's *L'Avare* (*The Miser,* 1168; *avare,* whence Eng. *avaricious*) is named *Harpagon,* which is Gr. for grappling-hook.

The *harp* was a favorite instrument among the Teutons, OE. *hearpe,* whence the Romans borrowed the word as LL. *harpa.* Hence the figurative use, to keep on and on, as Polonius says of Hamlet "still *harping* on my daughter." One story has it that a medieval book says Nero could never get the burning of Rome out of his mind; he was constantly *harping* on it; the translator did not know the figurative use of the word—but he knew there were no *harps* in ancient Rome. He therefore "corrected" the instrument—and behold, Nero fiddled while Rome burned!

harpsichord.
See harp.

harpy.
See harpoon.

harry.
See harum-scarum.

harsh.
See hard.

harum-scarum.
This reduplicated word (*cp. scurry*) for a devil-may-care sort of fellow means what it seems to say: he is one that used to *scare 'em.* The first form, *harum,* is from an early Eng. *hare,* from OFr. *harer,* to set the dogs on, whence also *harass* (this has the accent on the first syllable), being from Fr. *harasser,* frequentative of *harer.* Related? is *harry,* from AS. *herian,* to make war, from the common Teut. and early Eng. *here,* army. Note that *harbor* was originally a shelter for the army, from *here* (OHG. *hari*) + *berg*: OE. *herebeorg.* And the *harbinger* was one that provided shelter, OE. *herberger; berg* (as in *burg,* city; *cp. dollar*) from *bergen,* to protect. The second part is from *scare,* which was intransitive, then transferred from the feeling to the arousal: *to scare* is from ME. *skerre,* a *scare,* from *skiarr,* timid. Hence the *harum-scarum.*

harvest.
See crop.

hashish.
See assassin.

hat.
See adder.

hatchet.
See heckle.

hatter (mad as a).
See adder.

haul.
See whole.

haunt.
Wyclif says "*Haunt* thyself to pity"—which is as odd to us as the early use of *prevent, q.v.* For *haunt* (from Fr. *hanter,* to frequent) first meant doing something frequently; then, going somewhere frequently, as to one's favorite *haunts.* Shakespeare used it of a ghost's returning to a place; and the practice spread.

have.
See expose.

havelock.
See Appendix II.

haven.
See ability.

havoc.
Cry *"Havoc"* and let slip the dogs of war. To us, this implies slaughter ahead; but to Shakespeare (*Julius Caesar,* III,i,273) and those before him, it meant plunder. The cry meant that the battle was won; the men could turn from butchery to booty. It is from OFr. *havot,* plunder. This is of Teut. origin; OFr. *havet,* hook, from G. *Haft,* a *clasp;* and (the G. guttural *h* or *ch* being like a *k*) akin to L. *capere, capt—,* to seize. It should be noted that the name for *hawk,* which was cried in hunting with that bird, was AS. *hafoc. Cp. manœuvre.*

Hawaii.
See States.

hawk.
See havoc.

hawthorn.
See hedge.

hay.
We strew straw (*cp. destroy*) and we *hew hay,* from AS. *hieg,* from OTeut. stem *hauw—,* whence *hew.* The word was naturally common Teut.; *cp. color.*
Many phrases employ the word. Look for a needle in a bottle (*q.v.*) of *hay;* make *hay* while the sun shines. To carry *hay* in one's horns (which is translated from L. of Horace) means to be dangerous; an ox that might gore had its horns wrapped with *hay. Hey nonny nonny* is not connected, being a phrase of jollity added for rhythm or rhyme, from *Hey!* a shout to call attention, which we still use. During the War between the States, illiterate soldiers were taught to march with bits of *hay* and of straw tucked in their boots: *"Hay* foot, Straw foot!"

hazard.
Roman soldiers tossed dice for the clothes of the crucified Jesus. The practice continued; at the time of the Crusades, William of Tyre tells us, a game of chance was played which the Sp. called *azar,* from the castle in Palestine called *Ain Zarba* or *Asart.* From the game, the word spread to anything *hazardous. See hold.*

head.
See adder.

heal, health.
See wealth, whole.

hearse.
The occasion that calls for a *hearse* is often harrowing; indeed, the word *hearse* comes from OFr. *herse,* from L. *hirpex,* a large rake or harrow. From the shape, the word was applied to a frame with iron points on which candles were stuck, used in the church. Put over coffins, the canopy borrowed the word, which was later applied to the bier, and even to the tomb. About the 17th c., it became restricted to the vehicle in which the coffin is borne to the grave. The word *rehearse,* referring usually to less solemn themes, literally means to rake over again.

heart.
This word is common Teut., cognate with L. *cor* (whence *core; cordial; cp. prestige*) and Gr. *kardia;* whence Eng. *cardiac* conditions. As the pumping organ, it was associated with the passions, esp. the tender passion, whence *sweetheart;* thence also with the feelings in general (my *heart* smote me); and the understanding, hence, to learn *by heart,* opposed to *by rote, q.v.* We say "His *heart's* in his mouth" of a man afraid; but Shakespeare said (*Coriolanus* III,i, 256):

> His *heart's* his mouth:
> What his breast forges, that his
> tongue must vent.

From its position and importance in the body, came its use as the center or *core* of a matter, as in the *heart* of the city. Take *heart.*

heath, heathen, heather.
See briar, pagan.

Heavyside (layer).
See Appendix II.

Hebe, hebetic.
See ephebic.

Hebrew.
By way of French, Latin, Greek, Aramaic, Hebrew, this word (referring to Abraham) is from *eber,* Aram. *ibri,* from the other side (of the river). All the names in the Bible—as indeed orig-

inally all names—have a specific meaning. The *Israelites* derive this name from *Israel,* from Heb. *isra* + *el,* wrestler with the Lord, descriptive of Jacob after his bout with the angel. The word *Jew* means one of the tribe of *Judah* or *Yehudah* (from which *Yud,* and *Yiddish*), called by his father Jacob, "lion." For *Christian, see cream.*

Names arise in various ways. A tribe's own name for itself may become the general word, *e.g. Slav,* meaning glory—which by their conquest became *slave; cp. free; Frank.* The Canadian Indians called the folk to the north *Eskimos,* eaters of raw meat.

heckle.

This word first meant an instrument for combing hemp. It is a variant of *hackle,* diminutive of *hack,* to cut. The noun *hack* meant a cutting instrument, like a pick-ax or hoe. A diminutive of this word, via Fr. *hache,* axe, is Eng. *hatchet.* As a verb, *heckle* meant to cut at, to cut roughly. Similarly *tease* first meant to pull apart the fibres of wool; it was common Teut., OHG. *zeisan,* to *tease* wool. The *teasel* or *teazle* was the thistle used for such purposes, then for pulling cloth to raise a nap on it. Both *heckle* and *tease* were early used figuratively, in their present senses; hence also *Sir Peter Teazle,* who is always *teasing* his Lady in Sheridan's *The School For Scandal* (1777). Cognate with *tease* was an early *touse,* to pull (whence the dogs named *Towser*); the frequentative of this is Eng. *tousle, tousled,* as formerly often my hair; and of course *tousling* often leads to *tussling—tussle* being just another form of the same word. An attempt to *heckle* often ends in a *tussle.*

A mere *hack,* originally a horse for hire, is short for *hackney,* from OFr. *haquenée,* a hired horse, esp. one easy for ladies to ride; hence, to *hackney* meant to break in, and *hackneyed,* easy to use, worn out.

hectic.

This first meant a habit, from Gr. *hektikos,* from *hexis,* habit, from *exein,* to have, to hold. Then it was applied to the habitual appearance, esp. of a consumptive. From the same verb, in the sense of to hold up, to support, came the name *Hector,* "the prop and stay of Troy," the son of Hecuba and Priam; from his boastful and domineering ways (in the late medieval drama) comes the verb to *hector.* The future of *exein,* to hold, is *skeso;* whence *schema,* form, whence Eng. *scheme.*

hector.

See hectic.

hedge.

This word is common Teut., AS. *hecg.* As *hedges* were grown to keep fields secure, to *hedge* on a bet is to surround it with counteractions. The *hawthorn* is ME. *hagathorn, hedge* thorn. A witch was a *hedge*-rider (OHG. *zunrita; cp. villain*); whence AS. *haegtesse,* witch, whence *hag.* This sense combined with the fierce eyes of the wild hawk, the *haggard,* the *hedge*-bird, waiting nearby to pounce upon the farmyard fowl—to give the adjective *haggard* its current meaning.

Behind the *hedge* is the OTeut. stem *hagja—,* whence also OE. *haja,* Eng. *hay.* This is akin to West G. *hakja,* whence Eng. *hatch* (gate) and the ship's *hatchway.* The origin of *hatching* birds is unknown. *Cp. heckle.*

hedonism.

See sweet.

heed.

See adder.

hegira.

This word, also *hijrah* and *hejira,* is from Arab. *hijrah,* flight. It refers specifically to the flight of Mohammed from Medina to Mecca—to which all Mohammedans turn in prayer; hence, the *Mecca* of one's striving. The Mohammedan calendar begins with the year of the *hegira,* 622 A.D.

Every Mohammedan seeks to make a pilgrimage to *Mecca* annually; but at least once during his life. This is called *hadj,* from Arab. *hajji;* the Hebrew pilgrimage to Jerusalem is Heb. *hag.*

heifer.

We sing songs of the bounding main; but the bounding kids and calves are preserved in the language. From L. *vitulari,* to skip, comes L. *vitulus,* calf. Related to Sansk. *cap, camp,* to go, to bound, are Gr. *kapros,* the bounding boar; L. *caper,* the goat—whence we cut *capers;* AS. *haefer,* a he-goat and *heafor,* whence Eng. *heifer.* This word was sometimes used as *heahfore,* from *heah,* high + *fore,* from *faran,* to go, whence Eng. *fare. Cp. taxi. Fare*well!

hejira.
See hegira.

helianthus.
See flower.

helicopter.
This airplane describes itself in its name, from Gr. *helix, helico—,* spiral (whence Eng. *helix*) + *pteron,* wing. It is not related to Gr. *helios,* sun, as in *heliography,* writing by (reflected) sun, and *heliotrope, q.v. Ptero—* is a frequent combining form, as in *pterodactyl,* wing-finger.

For *dactyl,* a foot in verse, *see date.* Reverse it (two short syllables followed by one long) and you have the *anapest,* from Gr. *anapaistos,* reversed, from *ana,* back + *paiein,* to strike. The *iamb, iambus,* or *iambic foot* (one short syllable followed by one long) is from Gr. *iambikos, iambos,* probably from *iaptein,* to assail, being first used (by Archilochus, 7th c. B.C.) for invective and satiric verses; or possibly from *ienai,* to go (as the feet amble along), with the ending as in *dithyramb,* the choric hymn to Dionysos. The *trochee* (*q.v.,* one long syllable followed by one short) gets its name from the patter of running feet.

heliotrope.
See artichoke, flower, trophy.

helix.
See helicopter.

helium.
See element.

hell.
See helmet.

Hellespont.
This word is figuratively used of a hopeless bar between lovers. It draws its name from Gr. *hellespontos,* sea of *Helle,* daughter of Athamas, who, flying on the golden ram from the wrath of her mother-in-law (even in those days!) Ino, fell into the sea. But the use is rather from the drowning of Leander, who nightly used to swim the Hellespont to meet his beloved Hero, a priestess of Venus. Many years later, the poet Byron swam the sea.

helmet.
The L. *celare,* to cover, to hide (L. *con,* together, used as intensive; *cp. commence*) gives us Eng. *conceal; cp. cell.* But the root *kel—* came into Teut. as *kelmos, helmos,* whence *helm* (also *heaume*), a large head-piece, the diminutive of which is *helmet.* There is an early Eng. verb, *hele,* to cover, to hide; and from this source comes the final hiding-place, *hell.* This was at first used of the abode of the dead, the underworld (which contained both the Elysian Fields of the blessed and Tartarus for the accursed); but its use to translate Gr. *gehenna,* in the *New Testament,* turned it into the haunt of the fiends and the devils, horrid *hell.*

helot.
See Appendix II.

helpmate.
This is a corruption of *helpmeet,* which is the product of a misunderstanding. The Lord God said (*Genesis* 2, 18): "It is not good that the man should be alone; I will make him an *help meet* for him." The word *meet,* suitable, was first attached to *help* with a hyphen, then used with it as one word. Feeling that this was somehow wrong, about half a century later (ca. 1715) the word *helpmate* was fashioned.

helpmeet.
See helpmate.

hemisphere.
See semi—.

hen.
See incentive.

henchman.
Sir Walter Scott revived many old English words; he had a keen sense for them, and a delight in their use. Occasionally, however, he made an error; for instance, he mistook this word as *haunchman,* therefore servant. It was ME. *henxtman,* from OE. *hengest man,* horse man, a groom or squire. *Hengest,* a stallion, is also a proper name; *Hengist* and *Horsa* (Eng. *horse*) were brothers who conquered Kent.

heptagon.
See number. (Swinburne entitled his seven poetic parodies *Heptalogia,* Seven Against Sense. One of the best is a self-parody.)

herb, herbarium, herbivorous.
See sarcophagus; neighbor.

herculean.
This adjective is from the tremendous tasks, or twelve labors, of *Hercules* (Gr. *Herakles*), which he performed for the goddess Hera—whence his name: *Hera* + Gr. *kleos*, glory. He was to: kill the Nemean lion, the Lernean hydra, the Erymanthian boar, the cannibal birds of Lake Stymphalis; capture the Arcadian stag, the Cretan bull, the horses of Diomedes, the oxen of Geryon, the girdle of Queen Hippolyte of the Amazons, the apples of Hesperides; bring the three-headed guardian dog Cerberus up from the underworld; and cleanse the Augean stables.

heresy.
This formidable crime consists really in thinking for oneself, from Gr. *hairesis*, choice, from *hairein*, to take. The *heretic* chose for himself, instead of following the given path.

hermaphrodite, hermeneutics.
See hermetically.

hermetically.
Hermes was the Greek god (Roman, *Mercury*) of science, commerce, thievery, eloquence. As messenger of the gods he bore the *caduceus*, or rod, and wore the *talaria*, or winged shoes. Gr. *eremites*, whence Eng. *hermit*, from Gr. *eremia*, desert, is probably not related; but *Hermes Trismegistus*, (from Gr. *Hermes tris megistos*, Hermes thrice-greatest) was identified with the Egyptian god Thoth, the founder of alchemy. Since melting metals was a principal method of the alchemist's quest, *hermetic* sealing came to mean sealing by fusion; hence *hermetically* is used of things tightly closed. *Hermeneutics*, the art of interpretation, draws its meaning from *Hermes* as the message-bearer of the gods, whence Gr. *hermeneus*, interpreter. The son of *Hermes* and *Aphrodite*, *q.v.*, growing together with the nymph Salmacis, who loved him so much she prayed they might become one flesh, gives us the *hermaphrodite*. *Cp.* caduceus.

hermit.
See hermetically.

hero.
This is another false singular (*cp.* *pea*), from Gr. *heros*, *hero;* the feminine is *heroine* (four syllables), whence Eng. *heroine*. The drug *heroin*, named to conceal its relation to morphium (*cp. remorse*), gives one a sense of grandeur, makes one think oneself a *hero.*

hesperides.
See argosy.

hetero—.
See homo—.

heterodox.
See paradox.

heterogeneous.
See paradox; *cp.* racy.

heuristic.
See eureka.

hew.
See color; hay.

hexagon.
See number.

hey.
See hay.

hibernate.
This habit of certain animals has probably nothing to do with the Irish; *cp.* *Hibernia*. The L. adjective *hibernus*, from *hiems*, winter, produced the verb *hibernare*, *hibernat—*, to spend the winter. Similarly, to spend the summer is *aestivation*, *estivation*, from L. *aestivare*, *aestivat—*, from *aestivus*, hot, from *aestus*, heat (also, tide, hence Eng. *estuary*). Bacon speaks of humans *estivating* in a grotto; but the word is applied also to creatures, *e.g.* the lung-fish, that lie torpid during the tropic dry season.
The L. *aestus*, tide and *aestas*, summer, are related to Gr. *aithein*, to burn; *cp.* *torrent*.

Hibernia.
The *Hibernian* race was to the Romans the wintry race, from L. *hibernus*, wintry, from the land of storms. It seems to spring, from Ir. *Ibh-erna*, from *ibh*, country + *er*, noble. The *er* is also in *Erin*, and akin to Sansk. *arya*, noble—*Aryan*, the noble race.
The same root, *er*, *yr*, noble, forms the first syllable of *Ireland* and the *Irish*. The *British* draw their name from another characteristic, *Britain* being earlier Celtic *brython*, tatooed.

hiddenite.
See Appendix II.

hide.
Three common Teut. words converge in this Eng. one. As a skin, ***hide*** is from OE. ***hyd.*** Pronounced with an initial *h* like clearing the throat, it is cognate with L. ***cutis,*** from Gr. ***kutos,*** whence Eng. ***cuticle, cutaneous.*** Linked by the story of Dido (granted as much land as she could cover with a bull's ***hide,*** she cut it into thin strips, and bounded the site of Carthage) is *hide,* a measure of land. This, via AS. *hid,* from ***higid,*** is related to AS. ***hig—,*** *hiw—,* family, household: G. *Heirat,* marriage; *Heimat,* home. The verb *to* **hide is from AS. *hydan,*** reminding us that one of the earliest disguises was an animal skin. Related also, via L. ***hispidus,*** bristly skin, whence OFr. ***hisdos,*** whence ***hidos,*** whence Fr. ***hideux,*** comes Eng. ***hideous.***

hideaway.
See oubliette.

hideous.
See hide.

hieroglyphics.
These words were carved by the ancient Egyptian priests (Gr. ***hieros,*** holy, + ***glyphein,*** to carve). A stone with ***hieroglyphs,*** with demotic (popular) Egyptian, and Greek lettering—inscribed in honor of Ptolemy Epiphanes, who in 195 B.C. had remitted the taxes of the clergy—was found in 1798 near *Rosetta,* Egypt, hence called the *Rosetta Stone.* Through this, the mystery of the meaning of *hieroglyphics* was solved. *Cp. focus.*

highbrow.
See effrontery.

hight.
See alkahest. Height is from AS. ***hiehthu,*** from ***high,*** common Teut., AS. ***heah.***

hijack.
See jackanapes.

hike, hiker.
See coward.

hippodrome, hippopotamus.
See dromedary, mess.

hireling.
See Viking. *Hire,* AS. ***hyr,*** is not known in most of the Teut. tongues; most work was performed on other bases.

history, histrionics.
See plot.

hitch, hitch-hike.
See coward.

hither.
See weather.

Hitlerism.
See Appendix II.

hoax.
See hocus-pocus.

hobby, hobgoblin.
See donkey.

hobnob.
When persons drank together, they used to remark: "Come what may." Or an early variation of the thought: ***hob and nob; hob a nob; hobnob,*** from ME. ***habnab,*** from ***habbe + nabbe,*** from AS. ***haebbe, to have + ne,*** not + *haebbe:* "Have and have not!" Thus to *hobnob* came to mean to associate familiarly. In grimmer guise, the phrase has been revived in "the haves and the have-nots," who seldom *hobnob.*

Hobson's choice.
See Appendix II.

hocus-pocus.
While the magician is babbling mock Latin ("double talk" of learned sound) before the transformation, he indulges in *hocus-pocus.* This term for foolery comes from the words he is supposed to utter, which themselves are a debasing of the Catholic sacrament, changing bread into the body of the Son of the Lord: *Hoc est corpus filii,* This is the body of the Son. When the formula is completed, the transformation is announced with a *Presto—Change-O!* (*Cp. prestige.*) Sometimes the magic formula is given as *hocus pocus filiocus;* it is shortened—Say *hocus* quickly!—to (what we now know it to be:) a *hoax. Cp. patter; scurry.*

hodge-podge.
See amphigory.

hold (of a ship).
This is the place that *holds* the cargo; but it used to seem more like

hell to those that worked on it. The word is earlier Eng. *hole,* from Du. *hol,* hollow, a common Teut. word, related to *hell,* from AS. *helan,* to hide.

There is still a tendency to add *d* or *t* to certain English words: "He was almost *drownded;*" "You *varmint*" (vermin) are colloquial samples; it has become affixed in many words, *e.g., hazard* (Sp. *azar*); *peasant* (Fr. *paysan*); *ancient* (= *ensign,* as in Shakespeare); *tyrant* (Fr. *tyran*).

hole.
See hold.

holiday, hollyhock.
See holy.

holmium.
See element.

holocaust.
See catholic.

holy.
See wealth. From the idea of excellent, then perfect, came the notion that it must have the protection of the Lord. Note that *holyday* and *holiday* are doublets (the first, solemn; the second, for rejoicing). *Hollyhock* is from *holyhock*: *hoc* (mallow) from the *Holy* Land. *Halibut* is from ME. *holibutte,* a *butte* (flounder) eaten on *holy* days: *cp. butt.*

holystone.
The common sandstone used for sailors to scrub their decks was soft and full of *holes;* hence, *holey* stone. The *e* dropped out of the word because those using it know no case; chiefly, because the sailors had to work with it kneeling—hence *holy.*

homage.
To pay *homage* to someone was once literal: a payment of fees and acknowledgement that you are his man, from LL. *homaticum,* from L. *homo,* man.

Note that Gr. *homos* means same; *cp. homo—; racy.*

home.
See dollar. Home is (as one might expect) a common Teut. word, OE. *ham.*

homeo-.
See homo-.

homestead.
See bed.

homicide.
See shed.

homio—.
See homo—.

homo—, homoeo—.
To many persons, the *I* seems most important; an *i* was once most important in Catholic doctrine. For the first *oecumenical* (Gr. *oikumene,* the inhabited earth, i.e., universal; from *oikos,* dwelling) council of the Church, called under Constantine the Great, at Nice in Asia Minor in 325, condemned the Arian heresy. Arius was a presbyter of Alexander in the 4th c., who maintained that Jesus the Son was of like essence or substance to the Father, but not the same. From Gr. *homos,* same, and Gr. *homoios,* like, + *ousia,* essence, come the names for the heresy, *homoiousian,* and for the accepted doctrine, *homoousian.*

As prefixes (with their opposite, *hetero—,* from Gr. *heteros,* other) these give us many English words. Among them are *heterogeneous, cp. racy; homologous* (Gr. *logos,* order); *homoeopathy, cp. apathy* (like cures like); *homonym, cp. pseudo—. Anomaly* is from Gr. *an,* not, + *homalos,* even, from *homos,* same.

When New York eliminated an extra charge for "Grade A" milk by ordaining just one quality, the companies found another more costly form: they spread the cream evenly throughout the milk, so that it is "made all one kind": *homogenized.* (*Homo* + *genus,* kind, + *-ize,* from Gr. *izein.* Via LL. *-izare,* this is a most frequent ending, in the sense of to make, to do: *monopolize,* Gr. *monos,* alone; *colonize, cp. colonel; oxidize; jeopardize, cp. jeopardy; Americanize; Bowdlerize.* It is still a live ending, and may be added to proper names, in the sense of to behave or to treat like.)

Note that L. *homo, homin—,* means man.

homogeneous.
See homo—; racy.

homunculus.
See uncle.

honey.
See mealy-mouthed.

honk-honk.
See conch.

honorific.
See defeat.

hood.
See adder.

-hood.
See shipshape.

hoop, hoopoe.
See cough.

hoosegow.
See caboose.

hop.
See gallop.

hope.
See desperado.

hopscotch.
Although earlier called *Scotch-hoppers,* this has nothing to do with men in kilts. It means simply line-leapers, as the game carries them over. The *scotch* is from OFr. *escoche,* from to cut, from *coche,* a notch, nick: the lines for the game were marked into the ground. Hence the use of *scotch* as a verb, to injure, to destroy.

hormone.
See garble.

horn.
See bugle.

horrible, horrid.
See abhor.

hors de combat; hors d'oeuvre.
See door.

horse.
See henchman.

horticulture.
See court.

hose.
See husk.

hospital.
Through OFr., from L. *hospitalis,* this was originally a place of rest and entertainment. Then it was applied especially to the establishments of the Knights *Hospitallers,* military monks whose order was founded in Jerusalem c. 1048, and who cared for poor pilgrims to the Holy Land. (At first they were known as the Knights of the *Hospital* of St. John of Jerusalem; then—having moved their headquarters —as the Knights of Malta.) From their use comes our modern sense of *hospital.* The L. *hospitare,* to receive as a guest, gives us the word *host. Hospitaller, hospitaler, hosteler,* and *ostler* are various forms of the one word: often the man who entertains or receives a guest must take care of his horses, and the last two spellings have been kept to designate the stableman at an inn. But the passive form *hospitari, hospitati—,* means to be a guest; and the word *host* for a time was used either for the man that entertains or the one that is entertained. From the more mundane form of entertainment the word *hostelry* continues; its Fr. form *ostelerie,* today *hôtellerie,* has given both Fr. *hôtel* and Eng. *hotel. Hospice* is another form, less frequent today. *Hospital,* by aphesis, became *spital;* since many Eng. words end in *le* or *el,* this was sometimes spelled *spittle*—whence, by association with another meaning of *spit* (OE. *spitu,* G. *spitzen,* onomatopoetic), *spittle*: a clot of saliva, *spital* came to be used for a shelter for the sick poor, hence a disgusting or loathsome place. *Hostage,* which early meant entertainment, became intertwined with OFr. *ôtage,* from L. *obsidatus,* from *obses, obsidis,* hostage, from *obsidere,* from *ob,* before, against, in the way of + *sidere,* to sit (from this word comes the verb *obsess,* originally to besiege; then *obsession,* a besieging; now the constant assailing of a fixed idea. *Obsidional* is still the military term, relating to a siege; also, the *obsidional* crown is the garland given a Roman general that raised a siege. The stone —volcanic rock— called *obsidian* is an error, in editions of Pliny, for L. *obsianus,* so called because it resembled a stone found in Ethiopia by a man named *Obsius.*) From this interfusion, *hostage* came to mean a pledge given for the fulfilment of a promise, then a person held as such security.

Host (Fr. *hôte,* from L. *hospitem*) has several senses. It means one that entertains, from the derivations given above. But also (OFr. *host, oost,* army, from L. *hostis,* stranger, enemy: note the one word for an outsider and a foe!) it means an armed force; then, any multitude. Related to the meaning of enemy, *hostile,* (OFr. *oiste,* from

L. *hostia*) is the meaning, victim for sacrifice; then, Christ in that aspect; then, the bread or wafer consecrated in the Eucharist. In this sense it also remains as *hostie* . . . Thus the man that extends *hospitality* to a *host* is not far from the injunction of Christ to love his enemies.

hospitaler, hospitaller, host, hostage, hosteler, hostelry, hostie, hostile, hotel.
See hospital; *cp.* inn.

Hottentot.
See tatterdemalion.

hound.
See greyhound.

hue.
See color.

huff.
See of.

huguenot.
This word was first political, applied to the members of the Swiss Confederation, 1518; then to the French reformers of 1560. It is a corruption (by association with the old Fr. name *Huguenot*, a double diminutive of *Hugues*) of dialect *eiguenot*, from G. *Eidgenoss*, oath-companion, from *Eid*, oath + *Genoss*, partner.

hum.
See ink.

human, humane, humanity.
See uncle. Note that until the 18th c., *human* and *humane* were interchangeable; then *humane* grew restricted to such qualities as become a man: *humanity* may thus be associated with *human*, and mean mankind in general; or it may be linked with *humane*, and apply to kindness, consideration, courtesy, charity (love of one's fellows) and the like.

humble.
A recent book on gardening is called "A Sense of *Humus*" (L. *humus*, ground, soil; cognate with Gr. *chthon*, as in Eng. *autochthonous*, on its own soil, native). To *exhume* is to take out of the ground. The L. adj. *humilis*, on the ground, lowly, became Fr. *humble*, whence Eng. *humble*, mainly in the figurative sense. *Humiliate* is the verbal form. "To eat *humble-pie*," meaning to submit to *humiliation*, is a transfer because of the sound, from *umble-pie*, a pie made of *umbles*, from *numbles*, the entrails of deer (OFr. *nombles*, by dissimilation from *lombles*, from L. *lumbulus*, diminutive of *lumbus*, loin, whence Eng. *lumbar* and *lumbago*). For the way in which the *n* gets lost, *cp. auction*.

humbug.
In several tongues, the idea of *humming* (an imitative word) is linked with jesting: *e.g.*, Sp. *zumbar*, to *hum*, to joke; Fr. *bourde*, *humbug*, *bourdon*, drone bee. The story is told of the students that carefully put together the legs of a grasshopper, the body of a beetle, the head of an ant, and asked their professor what sort of *bug* this might be. "Did you catch it alive?" he asked them. "Yessir." "Did it *hum?*" "Yessir." "Then," said the professor, "it must have been a *humbug*." It is also suggested that the name is corrupted from *Hamburg*, which during the Franco-Prussian War was the center of German propaganda; but the transfer is probably the other way. Another suggestion traces the word to Ir. *uim bog*, soft copper, referring to the worthless money with which King James II of England flooded the land, from the Dublin mint . . . *Bug*, in the slang sense, to cheat, means to sting as does an insect; the man was *stung*. *See attack*.

humdrum.
This has but vague memories of *humming* and of *drumming*, being a reduplicative sound imitative of boredom; *cp.* knick-knack.

humid, humidity.
See complexion.

humiliate.
See humble.

humor.
See complexion.

hump.
See luncheon.

humph.
See globe.

humus.
See humble; posthumous

hunch.
See luncheon.

hundred.
See number.

hunt.
See greyhound.

hurry.
See scurry.

husband.
Wives, attention! *Husband* is the master of the house: AS. *hūs,* house + *bōnda,* freeholder; *cp. neighbor.* Later was added the idea that he had a *wife.* (*Wife,* AS. *wīf,* first meant just woman.) For a time *husband* also implied one that cultivates the soil; but that sense was taken over by *husbandman* (one that *husbands,* manages thriftily). A *despot* is also the master of the house, from Gr. *despotes,* from *dems,* of a house or tribe + *pot,* from *potere,* to be able, whence *potent, potentate;* whence Gr. *demein,* L. *domus,* house. (Note the relation of *despot* and *democracy, q.v.*: government of the people but not by the people.)

husk.
It is pleasing to think of each ear of corn, cosy in its little house. And that is just the way it is, for *husk* is the diminutive of house, from Du. *huisken,* a little house, a case in which a thing is hidden. AS. *hosa,* a case, whence Eng. *hose,* stockings (then, flexible tube), influenced the shortening of the word. The *husky,* dog, is probably just a shortening, *Eski,* of *Eskimo.* A *husky* throat is a dry one, as though from the dust after *husking* corn (and you kiss the girl with the red ear). The one that has *husked* the most (in the frequent *husking* bees) is therefore a *husky* (strong) fellow.

hussar.
This word comes through East European sources, from Hung. *huszar* via LGr. *koursarios,* from LL. *cursarius,* from *cursus,* raid, from L. *currere, curs—,* run. By the Romance route, from LL. *cursarius* come It. *corsaro,* whence *corsare,* whence Fr. *corsaire,* whence Eng. *corsair.* An *excursion* was first a sallying out, from L. *excurrere,* from *ex,* out + *currere. Discourse* was first a running to and fro; then, the process of reasoning; then, its communication, from L. *discurrere,* as still in *discursive* and *scurry, q.v.*—perhaps related to *scour* (the countryside), from earlier noun *scour,* rush. *Cp. car; cutlet; quarry; scourge.*

hut.
See adder.

hyacinth.
See flower; carnelian.

hybrid.
See otter.

hydra, hydrant, hydraulic.
See drink, otter, wash; element: mercury.

hydrogen.
See element, racy.

hydrophobia.
See drink.

hygiene.
See caduceus.

hyper-.
See overture.

hyperbole.
See parlor; overture.

hyperborean.
See aurora.

hypnosis.
See psychoanalysis.

hypochondria.
See overture.

hypocrite.
See overture; cp. garble. The idea being that if you answer a person back you must be (from that person's point of view) insincere. It seems hard to believe that your opponent believes in his point of view.

hypothesis.
See Spoonerism.

hysteria.
If not *hysteria* in general, at least that form we know as *hysterics* is more common among women than among men; it was earlier called mother-sickness. The Greeks named it similarly: from *hysterikos,* from *hystera,* womb, whence L. and Eng. *uterus.*

I

iambic.
See helicopter.

Icarian.
See daedal. *Icarian* is also used of the communist communities founded by the followers of Etienne Cabet, 1788—1856, whose *Voyage en Icarie* (1840) pictured such a community.

ice.
See iron.

ichneumon.
See crocodile.

Idaho.
See States.

—ide.
See cyanide.

idea.
This word is Gr. *idea,* look, from *idein,* to see. In Plato (Gr. philosopher named Aristocles, 427?—347; called *Plato* from his broad shoulders; *cp. vessel*) the word shifted to most of its present meanings. From look grew the sense of conception of what is to come (look it over and see); hence, a pattern in the mind, an *ideal* (i.e., not real) picture. From this sense of *ideal*—since the mental picture is usually better than reality—came the *ideal* toward which we strive. *Cp. Platonic.*

ideal.
See idea.

idiom, idiosyncrasy.
See idiot.

idiot.
When Jeremy Taylor says "Humility is a duty in great ones, as well as in *idiots,*" he is using the word in its early Eng. sense, directly from Gr. *idiotes,* private persons, from *idios,* own, peculiar. (Note that peculiar, once meaning individual, unique, now means odd, queer.) Private persons were those that held no public office; gradually, those unfit or unable to hold public office; hence, mentally deficient. From the same word we have *idiom,* an expression peculiar to one language. *Idio—* is used as a combining form, a prefix, in a number of words, the most common perhaps being *idiosyncrasy*: *idio,* peculiar + *syn,* together + *crasis,* mixture, combination.

if.
Problems in the mathematics class often start with the word *Given.* This sounds more formal than a mere *If*—yet the two are one. *If* is aphetic for AS. *gif, given*: granted that, assuming. Thence to the beggars on horseback.

ignite.
See meteor.

ignoramus.
An *ignorant* person (from L. *ignorare,* present participle *ignorant—,* not to know, from *ig,* from *in,* not + *gnorare,* to know) is an *ignoramus.* This is taken directly from Latin, being the first person plural of the present tense: we do not know. It was that word which the Grand Jury used to write on the back of indictments they could not hold for trial; but when they came to be called the "*ignoramus* jury," they changed the wording to "No true bill." To *ignore* meant first, not to know; socially, if you do not (care to) know a person, you *ignore* him.

ignorant, ignore.
See ignoramus; *cp.* knick-knack.

illinium.
See element.

Illinois.
See States.

illuminate, illustrate, illustration, illustrious.
See limn.

imbecile.
This word, though it means without stick (from L. *im,* from *in,* not + *bacillum,* walking-stick, from *baculus,* staff; *cp. bacteria*) has no reference to sparing the rod and spoiling the child. It first referred to bodily strength, and meant one that needed a staff to support himself; without it, he was helpless.

imbibe.
See bavardage.

imbroglio.
See island.

immaculate.
See mail; trammel.

immaterial.
See irrelevant.

immediate, immigrate.
See immunity.

immolate.
The teeth that grind are the *molars,* from L. *molaris,* from *mola, millstone.* The Aryan root *mal,* to grind, spread widely, as hunting tribes took up agriculture: Gr. *mele, mill;* AS. *melo,* whence Eng. *meal;* Du. *maal;* L. *molere,* to grind. Thus *mill* has antecedents in AS. *myln* and L. *molinum;* since grain was often ground by pounding, to *mill* (as in boxing) may mean to pound around. The *maelstrom* is from Du. *maalstroom,* from *malen,* to grind, + *stroom,* stream. To sprinkle with *meal* in preparation for sacrifice was L. *immolare, immolat—,* whence, Eng. *immolate.*

immoral.
See remorse.

immortal, immortelle.
See remorse.

immunity.
In olden times, public service was rather an obligation than something sought; but after a time certain persons or classes were granted *immunity*—whence the term came to mean exemption from any inconvenience; then, from disease. L. *in, im,* not + *munia,* services, gifts; *munus, muner—,* gift, from *munerare, munerat—* meaning both to give and to discharge the duties of an office; in the first sense L. *re,* back, in return for, gives *remunerate.* The basic idea is of mutual exchange; the group that together is bound for mutual service is the *community,* from L. *communis,* whence Eng. *common;* through AS. *gemaene,* whence Eng. *mean, q.v., common,* general. From the sense of general this word came to mean *vulgar* (L. *vulgus,* the common people, similarly deteriorating), thence base—whence some tend to attribute it to (as it may be influenced by) Icel. *meinn,* base, hurtful, from the Aryan root *mi,* to lessen, whence *minish, diminish; cp. meticulous.*

Mean, in the sense of intend, is a common Teut. form, from OHG. *meina,* thought, from OHG. *minni,* whence Eng. *mind.* In the sense of intermediate—the golden *mean*—it is from L. *medianus,* whence Eng. *median,* its doublet, from L. *medius,* middle; whence also *mediate*: *immediate* means with nothing between. To stick oneself in the *middle* is to *meddle,* though influenced by OFr. *mesler,* from LL. *misculare,* from L. *miscere, mixtus,* to *mix,* whence *promiscuous.*

Municipal is from L. *municipalis,* pertaining to a town (L. *municipium*) that had been granted rights of Roman citizenship: *municeps, municipi—,* a free citizen, one that takes office, from *munia,* offices + *capere, capt—,* to take, whence Eng. *capture; cp. manœuvre. Munificent* is likewise from L. *muni—,* gifts + *ficare,* from *facere,* to make.

The root of this word is in Sansk. *mayate,* he exchanges, which leads also to other forms. L. *meare, meat—,* to go, whence Eng. *permeate* (L. *per,* through): if she be made of *permeable* stuff, as Hamlet remarks of his mother. The frequentative of *meare* is *migrare, migrat—,* to wander; whence *migrate, emigration, immigration.* Another form from the same root is *mutare, mutat—,* to change: whence *mutable; commute* (which first meant to exchange, as from a severe to a lighter penalty: "her sentence," says Macaulay, "was *commuted* from burning to beheading;" then to permit a lump payment instead of smaller sums: by such a lump payment one might buy a *commutation* ticket, such as a *commuter* uses on daily trips between city and suburbs, when he *commutes*); *permutation;* and the goal of the middle ages, recently attained: *transmutation* of the elements (not the only reason for believing we are still in the dark ages of mankind's development).

In similar fashion *leisure* gets its meaning: through Fr. *loisir,* from OFr. *leisir,* it is from L. *licere,* to be permitted, *i.e.,* to be permitted to refrain from giving service. One that thus refrains is probably *lazy;* but *lazy* is just a shortening of earlier *layserly, leisurely.* From the present participle of *licere, licens, licent—,* comes *licentia,* whence Eng. *license,* permission, freedom. Since this was frequently carried too far, there soon came the meaning held also in the adjective *licentious.* A *licentiate* was a friar authorized to hear confessions; then, a person granted a university *license* to practice a profession. A *lycée,* however, is Fr. for *lyceum; cp. Platonic.*

imp.
See graft.

impact.
See propaganda.

impair.
See pessimist.

impale.
See palace.

impassable, impassible.
See pass.

impeach.
See dispatch.

impeccable.
Here is a word that remains only in the negative. *Sinning* is so general that the word *sinful* is most frequent; hence *sin,* very common Teut., from the present participle of the root *es,* to be: to exist is to be a *sinner.* "In Adam's fall, We *sinned* all." But to be exempt from *sin* is so rare that we have kept the L. negative form, Eng. *impeccable,* from L. *in,* not, + *peccare, to sin*—which has otherwise lapsed through the It. into a mere *peccadillo.*

impede, impediment.
See baggage.

impel.
See pelt.

imperial.
See empire.

implicate.
See plagiarism.

implicit, imply.
See complexion.

import, important, importunate, importune.
See port.

imposition.
See pose.

impost, imposter.
From L. *imponere, impositum,* then *impostum,* to place upon or against, come literal and figurative uses; *cp. pose.* The literal pervades *impost,* a pillar upon which an arch is placed—or a levy that taxes your merchandise; the figurative controls the *imposter,* who taxes your patience.

imprecation.
See precarious.

imprimatur.
See spouse.

imprint.
See command.

impromptu.
See improvised.

improvised.
The man that, saying he had not expected to be called upon to speak, draws four pages of notes from his pocket, has a talk neither *impromptu* (L. *im,* from *in,* not + *promere, promptus,* to put forth, from *pro,* forward + *emere, emptus,* to take, to buy. Hence also *preempt,* to take before; *cp. ransom.*) nor *extemporaneous* (L. *ex,* out + *tempus, tempor—,* time: on the spur of the moment. Hence also *temporary; cp. pylorus*) nor *improvised* (L. *im,* from *in,* not + *pro,* before + *videre, visu—,* to see; not seen ahead).

The L. *videre, visu—* has a long train. "The way I see it," I *advise* you (L. *ad,* to + *visu—*); the shift in spelling—*advice;* prophecy, prophesy —is artificial; as also in *devise* and *device* (L. *de,* down: things seen down; the first meaning was, a detail). To distinguish, to see apart, is to *divide;* hence also *division.* (*Vision* is of course more directly beholden.) A unity, not divided, is an *individual*. *Provide* and *provident* are from L. *providere*, to see before; *revise*, to see anew; *evident*, seen out, clearly. To see into, to fix the eyes on, was L. *invidere;* why one gazed in this fashion we learn from the noun, L. *invidia*, whence Eng. *envy*. This is via the Fr., whence also *envious;* directly from the L. comes the doublet *invidious; cp. supercilious.*

Visual, visible, invisible, are other words from the L. *visus*, face, or *videre, visu—*, to see. But *see widow.*

By way of the French come still more: L. *visus*, whence OFr. *vis* (surviving in *vis-à-vis*, face to face) gives Fr. and Eng. *visage; envisage.* L. *visitare*, a double frequentative, from *visere, visit—*, from *vis—*, yields Eng. *visit*, to see often. The verb *videre* became OFr. *veier*, whence Fr. *voir, vu;* whence *clairvoyant* (Fr. *clair*, clear); *view; interview* (Fr. *entrevue*); *revue* (a satiric seeing again); *review. Providens* was shortened to *prudens*, whence *prudent*, seeing ahead—and Fr. and Eng. *prude* (*q.v.*), which originally meant wise. The wisdom of the law is crystallized in *jurisprudence* (L. *jus, juris*, law). Audiences like a *preview;* but actors in a *revue* should *improvise* only when the police pay them a *visit.*

impugn.
See pygmy.

impulse.
See pelt.

imputation.
See curfew.

in.
See inn (the same word).

inaudible.
See audit.

inauguration.
See auction.

incandescent.
See candid; free.

incantation.
See trance.

incarcerate.
See cancel.

incarnation.
See sarcophagus.

incense.
See free.

incentive.
Songs have many moods. One may hum a song, with not a care in the world. Or one may sing a sailors' *shanty*, to help him at his work. Or yell out a *chant* as a summons to war, almost a battle-cry. If you strike up the tune for someone, you are starting him on his way—perhaps even suggesting the direction. You are giving him an *incentive;* for *incentive* is from L. *incentivus*, setting the tune, from *incinere*, to begin, from *canere*, to sing. The frequentative of *canere* is *cantare, cantat—*, whence *cantata;* via Fr. *chanter, chant* and *shanty*. (*Shanty*, a hovel, is from Fr. *chantier*, a workshop, possibly from Gr. *cantherios*, pack-ass, but more probably the same *canere*, from singing at one's work.) The Aryan root is *han, chan;* whence both *chant* and AS. *hanna*, rooster, *hen*, whence Eng. *hen*. *Cp. saunter.*

inceptive.
See manoeuver.

inch.
See uncle.

incinerator.
This represents a modern method of waste disposal, but in connection with war and death it is an olden word, from LL. *incinerare, incinerat—*, to reduce to ashes, from L. *in + cinis, ciner—*, ashes, whence Fr. *cendre*, whence Eng. *cinder*—though also AS. *sinder*, dross, slag. The diminutive, Fr. *cendrillon*, gives us our *Cinderella.*

Cinderella's story exemplifies the fate of forgotten words: they change into known ones. Thus *Cinderella* wore—and lost—*une petite pantoufle de vair* . . . a little slipper of fur (*vair*, sable, weasel; still the Eng. word, *vair*, corrupted in some localities to *fairy*, weasel). But the scribe or translator, not knowing this dying word, instead of *vair* used *verre* (with the same sound): *verre*, glass. Hence the odd little slipper of glass for Prince Charming. Sable was worn by royalty, as in *Hamlet* III,2.

Another instance is that of Dick Whittington, the first great trader of

London, who furnished the cloth of gold for the bridal of Henry IV's daughter, in 1401. He was an *acatour,* now *caterer.* The old verb was *acat,* from OFr. *achat,* whence Fr. *acheter,* to buy; but the word was lost, leaving little Dick with *a cat!*

There are two lost words in the remark about never setting the *Thames* on fire: one masculine, and one feminine. The *tems* was an old word for a cake—such as Alfred the Great let burn when affairs of state were on his mind: He'll never set the *tems* on fire means he'll never have serious thoughts. But the *temse* was the wooden tube in which the piston of the old spinning wheel ran up and down; if one worked hard, this might begin to smoke; and She'll never set the *temse* on fire means she is not industrious. Both these words lapsed from the language, leaving the river *Thames* to take the conflagration . . . I have at least seen the Gowanus Canal on fire! (The same expression is used of many other streams, without such stories, which are probably folk-etymology.)

Fairy—not the weasel—first meant, the land of the *fay,* from Fr. *faerie,* from *fée,* from L. *fata,* one of the *fates. Elf,* a subordinate (and more malignant) variety of *fairy,* is from AS. *aelf,* from OHG. *alp,* nightmare; *cp. marshal. Kobold* was a proper name; also, *goblin,* diminutive of *Gobel,* from OHG. *Godbald, God-bold.* It is suggested that the immediate cause of *goblin* was the manufacture, by Jean Gobelin (d. 1467) of such a fine scarlet dye for his tapestries, folks thought he must be in league with the devil. *Cp. insect.*

incipient.
See manoeuver.

incision, incisive, incisor.
See shed.

incline.
See climate.

inclose.
See pylorus. *Enclose* is through the French; *inclose* has a closer tie to the Latin.

include.
See close. This is a doublet of *inclose.*

incompetent.
See irrelevant.

incorrigible.
See royal.

increase.
See attract.

incubate, incubation, incubator, incubus.
See marshal.

indemnify.
See damage.

indent.
See indenture.

indenture.
The *indentured* servant that came to the American colonies, exchanging some years' work for his passage, his keep and then his freedom in the New World, bore with him a duplicate of his master's agreement. To prevent trickery, the two copies were *dented,* or simply written on one sheet and torn, so that they must match. *Indent* is from L. *in,* in + *dens, dent—,* tooth, whence Eng. *dentist.* The *dandelion* is by way of Fr. *dent; cp. flower. Tooth* itself is from AS. *toth,* from OHG. *zand;* closely related to L. *dens, dent—,* from Gr. *odon, odont—,* whence Eng. *odontology; mastodon* (Gr. *mast—,* breast: from the nipple-like projections on the teeth); *trident* (L. *tri,* three). Sansk. *danta, tooth; adana,* food, from *admi, I eat,* whence Gr. *edein,* to *eat,* whence L. *edere;* AS. *etan,* whence Eng. *eat. Edible* comes directly from the L. The OHG. *ezzen,* whence MHG. *etzen* (G. *essen*) gives us *etch,* to *eat* with acid. The intensive form, OHG. *frezzan,* to consume, whence AS. *fretan,* whence Eng. *fret,* which first meant literally to *eat* away; then, to be gnawed with care. L. *obedere, obes—,* to devour (*ob,* intensive, + *edere,* to eat) has worked both ways. At first it was applied to a person eaten away, very lean; then, to one that devoured all he could, and became very fat. The fat meaning of *obese* has devoured the lean one. *Cp. ache.*

From the intensive *fr*—came G. *ver—,* a frequent prefix in G., *e.g., lassen,* to leave; *verlassen,* to abandon, *leben,* to live; *verlebt,* played out, decrepit. It is cognate with L. *per* (*see Grimm's Law* in the Preface) and is intensive from its meaning of forth or through or thorough: compare *perjure* and *forswear.* In Eng. it became the prefix *for—*, as in many obsolete words like *fordone, fordrunken, forwandered* (weary with wandering), *forfrighted, fordread.* It is no longer a living prefix (that is, no new words are formed with it); but it survives in *forbid, forgo, forgive, forlorn, forsaken.* Note that *forward* is really an older *fore* + *ward,* toward the front. *Fore, before* (with L. cognate *pre, prae, pro,* and Gr. *pro, para, pari: see Grimm's Law;* compare *predict* and *forecast*) is also a frequent prefix, as in *forebear* (but not *forbear*). *Forewarned* is *forearmed.*

independence, independent.
See aggravate.

indestructible.
See destroy.

index.
This is the noun. L. *index, indic—,* from *indicare,* to make known, to point out, whence *indicate; see verdict.* Its first meaning was the forefinger, the pointer. As a table of contents, pointing out what is in a book, the plural is *indexes* (Eng. form); for most other uses, the L. plural is retained, *indices.*
The L. *indicare* is from L. *in,* against, + *dicere, dict-,* to speak against, to single out. Hence also (ME. *enditen,* via Fr. *enditer;* hence the pronunciation) Eng. *indict* and *indictment.*

Indiana.
See States.

indicate.
See teach, index, verdict.

indifferent.
See suffer.

indigenous.
See racy.

indignant.
See supercilious.

indigo.
See red.

indium.
See element.

individual.
See improvised.

indoctrination.
See doctor.

indolent.
Doleful is a hybrid word, the AS. suffix *—ful* on OFr. *dol, doel,* whence Fr. *deuil,* grief, from L. *dolor,* grief, from *dolere,* to grieve, perhaps related to Aryan *dar,* to tear. The L. suffix for 'full of,' *—osus,* whence Fr. *—eux,* whence Eng. *—ous,* gives us Eng. *dolorous; cp. supercilious.* We have taken the L. noun directly, as *dolour, dolor.* But a man that does not grieve is probably at ease; hence, *indolent* (L. *in,* not) came to its present meaning. *Cp. dole.*

indomitable.
See diamond.

induction.
See duke.

indulgent.
See lent.

industry.
See destroy.

inebriate.
See intoxicate.

ineffable.
See nefarious.

inept.
See lasso.

inertia.
This word first meant lack of skill or power (from L. *in,* not + *ars, art—, art*), then the sluggishness that follows such lack. Hence, the scientific use, as meaning resistance to change.

inevitable.
See vacuum.

inexorable.
An *oration* is something that comes out of the mouth, from L. *os, or—,* mouth, whence *orare, orat—,* to speak, to pray. Hence *oral; orator; oratorio* (originally, service in the *oratory,* from L. *oratorium,* prayer room). Something you should pray to is *adorable; adore,* from L. *ad,* to + *orare,* to pray. An *oracle* (let no dogs bark!) is from L. *oraculum,* a little mouth—producing the still, small voice of destiny. But something out of which you cannot pray

yourself (L. *in*, not + *ex*, out of) is indeed *inexorable*.

infamous.
See fate.

infant.
See infantry.

infantry.
An *infant* is, quite naturally, one that is unable to speak (L. *in*, not, + *fans*, speaking, from *fari*, to speak. Thus *nefarious*, from L. *nefas*, wrongly spoken; and *multifarious*, originally, speaking many tongues). The It. *infante*, youngster, led to *infanteria*, those too inexperienced or otherwise unqualified for cavalry; hence, Eng. *infantry*. The *Infanta* is the Sp. princess, not heir to the throne.

infect, infection.
See attain, defeat.

infer.
See suffer.

inferior, infernal, Inferno.
See under.

infinite.
See finance. The *in* of course means not; but the difference between the *finite* and the *infinite* that is of concern is that, in the range of the *infinite*, the whole is no greater than some of its parts. *Infinity* plus whatever number you please, plus or times or minus *infinity* itself, is still *infinity*. *See* googol.

infirmary.
This is a place where you get fixed; but literally, a place for those not solid: L. *in*, not + *firmus*, solid; *cp. farm* + *arium*, a place ending, as in *aquarium*. L. *firmare, firmat—*, to make solid, to *confirm* (*con* is intensive; *cp. commence*), gave us not only *confirm* but the business *firm*: not that it is always well-established; but the word *firm* first meant a *confirmation;* hence, a signature; hence, the trade name of the company; hence, the company. With L. *af, ad*, to, the answer is in the *affirmative*.

A synonym of L. *firmus* was L. *validus*, strong, worthy, from *valere, valid—*, to be strong, to have worth. In addition to Eng. *valid* and *value* (*see verdict*), this gives us Eng. *valor, invalid* (not worth anything); *invalid* (a sick person; from the Fr. accent); and to no *avail*.

inflame, inflammation, inflation.
See flamingo.

influence, influx.
See affluent.

infra—, infrared.
See under.

infuse.
See futile.

ingenious.
See racy.

ingot.
See nugget.

inhibition.
See expose.

inimical.
See remnant.

initial, initiate.
See commence. The L. *initium* is from *in*, into, + *ire, it—* to go; hence the use of *initiation* as the ceremony of going into, or beginning in a special group or society.

injection.
See subject.

ink.
This word (from OFr. *enque*, from L. *encaustum*, from Gr. *enkaustos*, burnt in) was, in its L. form, the name of the purple-red fluid with which the official documents of the later Roman Emperors were signed. The L. accent varied; our word is from an accent on the first syllable; accent on the second syllable produced It. *inchiostro*, ink. From the original Gr. meaning come our Eng. words *caustic* and *encaustic*. If you use just a little *ink*—give just an intimation of the subject—you offer an *inkling;* but the word is derived from an older verb, to *inkle*, related to a root AS. *ink*, from *imt*, to murmur, mutter, like old Teut. *um—*, Eng. *hum* etc. The imitative sound *hum* was early used, also, in the sense of to joke, to trick, as in humbug (OE. *hum*, to joke + *bug*, ghost, as in *bugaboo; cp. insect*).

inkling.
See ink.

inmost.
See inn.

inn.

The pleasant places that pun their invitation: *Dew Drop Inn*, have etymology on their side; for *inn* is merely AS. *inn*, from *inne*, within, inside (whence *in*, *inner* and *inmost*); it was a sign used to indicate rest and *refreshment* within. *Refreshment* (*re*, again) is from AS. *fersc*, not salt, combined with the more general sense of *fresh* in Fr. *frais* and OHG. *frisc;* whence also *frisky*. The *fresh* you want to slap is from OHG. *frech*, whence AS. *frec;* whence *freak*: to get *fresh* is to be *freakish*—or to want too much, for AS. *frec* means eager, akin to ON. *frekr*, greedy; as also G. *fressen*, to gobble, from *essen*, to eat.

Refreshment is *re-creation*, from L. *creare, creat—*, *see creole*. But since all work and no play makes Jack (*see jackanapes*) a dull boy; *re-creation* has come to include *recreation* (that's why we need the hyphen to indicate the original sense). Similarly *restaurant* (which might seem to be from *rest au errant*, rest to the wandering) is the present participle of OFr. *restaurer*, from L. *restaurare*, to repair, from *re*, back, again + Gr. *stauros*, stake: to fix the fence. In its other OFr. form, *restorer*, it gives us *restore* and *restoration*. *Cp. errand, attic.*

Hotel, from Fr. *hôtel*, from OFr. *hostel*, is the place to find the L. *hospes*, which means both host and guest; *see hospital*. *Tavern* is from L. *taberna*, hut: its diminutive, L. *tabernaculum*, booth, gives us *tabernacle*. This is related to L. *tabula*, plank, whence Eng. *table;* its diminutive via Fr. *tablette* gives us *tablet*. Directly from the L. is *tabula rasa*, scraped *tablet*, clean slate, Fr. *carte blanche*, white card. Whereon we could start all over.

inner.

See inn.

innocent, innocuous, inoculate.

See nuisance.

inquest, inquire, inquisition.

See exquisite.

inscription.

See shrine.

inscrutable.

You may have seen the men at the popular beaches, in late fall or early winter when the crowds are gone, combing for treasure-trove; hence *beachcomber*. Or looking through the town dump . . . or the city garbage cans. The practice is an ancient one: L. *scrutari*, to examine, is from *scruta*, trash, refuse. The L. noun *scrutinium*, inspection, gives us Eng. *scrutiny*. *Inscrutable*: that which cannot be looked into.

insect.

Look at a few *bugs;* the first thing you notice is that they are all notched or cut in, towards the middle. *Insect* is short for L. *animal insectum* (*insecare, insect—*, to cut into) which itself is a translation from the Gr. *entomon* (*entos*, within + *temnein*, to cut. *See anatomy*), which gives us *entomology*. The word *bug* is of unknown origin; save that Welsh *bwg*, ghost, gives us the *bug* in *bugbear, bugaboo* (Boo!); also the hobgoblin variously spelled *bogy, bogie, bogey*, and (north Eng.) *bogle*. The fact that such a thing is pretended has led to the suggestion that it is the origin of the U. S. term *bogus*.

insidious.

See strategy.

insipid.

See sap.

insolent.

Conduct to which one is unaccustomed seems rude; *cp. uncouth*. If some one came up to you and began to rub his nose against yours, you would think him at least *insolent*. He would be, literally: from L. *insolere*, present participle *insolent—*, from *in*, not + *solere*, to be accustomed. L. *solari*, to soothe, gives us *solace* (as from the touch of an accustomed hand) and *console* (*con*, from *com*, together). Thus *company* brings *consolation*. A *solecism*, however, is an error in speech, a provincialism, such as might be found in the Greek spoken in *Soloi*, by the Athenian colonists in this town of Cilicia.

inspect.

See auction; scourge.

inspiration.

Plato says that when the poet functions properly, he is divinely *inspired*, possessed (*cp. enthusiasm*). He is breathed into by the god: (L. *in*, into + *spirare, spirat—*, to breathe). *Breathing* is a frequent process: *conspire*, to *breathe* together; *respiration, breathing* again and again—as in living; *perspire,* to *breathe* through; *transpire,* to *breathe* across (which means both to come to the attention, and to sweat); *aspire,* to *breathe* towards; *expire,* to *breathe* out (finally). *Breath* is an old word, but referred first to the steam or vapor of heated objects, or the visible air exhaled in cold weather, from Ayran root *bhre—,* to burn. (There is an old Eng. word *brede* from this root, OE. *braede,* to heat, meaning roast meat, whence our food, *sweetbread.*)

instantaneous.
See tank.

instep.
See pylorus.

instigate.
See attack; distinct.

instil.
The proper course of education goes little by little, as the ancients knew. They sealed their knowledge into the word *instil,* from L. *in,* into + *stillare,* to drop. Similarly, to *distil* (L. *de,* down + *stillare*) is to flow down drop by drop, as in a *still*—which noun is aphetic for *distil.* The *still,* small voice is common Teut., related to *stall,* a *standing*-place for cattle; *see tank.*

instinct.
See distinct.

institution.
See season.

instruct, instrument.
See destroy.

insulate, insulin.
See island.

insult.
Those that cry the boyhood jingle:—

> Sticks and stones may break my bones
> But words will never hurt me—

are probably unaware that *insult* and *assault* were originally the same. L. *salire, salt—,* to leap, whence *insilire, insult—,* with its frequentative *insultare,* to leap upon. Originally the word meant to attack physically; gradually the figurative sense of *insult* prevailed. L. *ad, to,* toward + *salire,* led to OFr. *asalir,* whence *assaillir,* whence ME. *asaile,* which in the 15th c. added another *s* and became Eng. *assail.* In both Fr. and Eng. a back-formation toward the L. produced OFr. *asaut,* whence ME. *asaut,* whence Eng. *assault.* (Similarly, *fault* is a restored spelling from ME. *faut,* from Fr. *faute,* but from L. *fallita,* a coming short:—OFr. *faillir,* to be wanting, whence Eng. *fail:* L. *fallere,* to deceive.) *Cp. somersault.*

insurance.
See funeral.

insurrection.
See sorcerer.

intact.
See deck.

intangible.
See taste.

integer, integral, integrity, integument.
See deck.

intellectual, intelligence, intelligentsia.
See legible.

intend, intense, intensify, intentional.
See tennis.

inter—.
See under.

intercalate.
See dickey.

intercede, interest.
See ancestor, under.

interfere.
The noun *interference* was formed as though from L. *ferre,* to bear, like *conference, difference; cp. suffer.* But while this might *refer* to bearing or bringing between, note that the verb ends in *e,* unlike *differ, suffer,* and the rest from *ferre.* It may rather be from L. *inter,* between, + *ferire,* to strike. Thus OFr. *s'entreférir,* first used of the shoe of a horse striking the fetlock of the other leg. Perhaps from the same source is the *ferule,* a rod; L. *ferula* meant a rod, and was also applied to the giant fennel plant, of which whipping rods were made.
See suffer.

interjection.
See subject.

interlocutor.
See refrain.

interloper.
See subjugate.

interlude.
See tennis.

interminable.
See determine.

international.
See under.

interrogation.
See quaint.

interrupt.
See bank.

interstice.
See tank.

interval.
See villain.

interview.
See improvised.

intestate.
See test.

intestine.
See pylorus.

intimidate.
See meticulous.

intoxicate.
The Gr. word for bow is *toxon*. Ascham in 1545 wrote a book entitled *Toxophilus*, lover of the bow. Then Gr. used *toxikon* for the poison in which the arrow was dipped; hence Eng. *toxin, toxic, antitoxin*. LL. used *intoxicare, intoxicat—*, as to *poison;* but just as today when a man says "Name your *poison*" he is using *"poison"* to mean "liquor", so the word *intoxicate* was gradually, from its figurative application, limited to the temporarily *poisonous* effects of too much liquor. *Auto-intoxication* is another medical term that keeps the stronger meaning. *Inebriate* comes directly from L. *inebriare*, from *ebrius*, drunken, *bria*, cup; *sober* is the opposite of "in his cups", from L. *so*, apart from + *bria*. *Poison* was originally a harmless draught (OFr. *poison*, from L. *potionem*, from *potare, potum*, to drink; whence also *potion, potable*, and *potation*, and possibly *pot*, from which one may drink), but with the medieval practice of lethal beverages it took on its fatal sense. One man's *potion* is another man's *poison*. For *tocsin, see touch. Cp. drink.*

intrench.
See retrench.

intrepid.
See terse.

intricate.
See intrigue.

intrigue.
Delilah caught Sampson by his hair; but many more women have made snares of their locks, to entangle a man. *Intricate* is from L. *intricare, intricat—*, to entangle, from L. *tricae*, hairs, trifles, from Gr. *thrix*, hair. From the It. form *intrigare*, whence Fr. *intriguer*, comes the plot to entangle, *intrigue*. To get out of such a tangle is to *extricate* oneself, not always easy.

introduction.
See duke.

inure.
See manœuvre.

invade.
See wade.

invalid.
See infirmary.

invective, inveigh.
See vehicle.

inveigle.
To *inveigle* someone, you must put (mental) blinders on him, as the word itself declares. It is earlier *envegle*, from F. *enveogler*, from *eveugler*, to make blind. This is from the Latin, but there is a lost step. A LL. form *aboculus* may have come from *alba oculus*, white eye (which was used to mean blind), or from *ab oculis*, eyeless, from L. *oculus*, eye; *cp. monk*.

inverse, invert.
See advertise.

invest.
The practice of fitting out the young man in smart clothes before he went forth to make his fortune led to the early

figurative use (It. *investire*, 13th c.) of *invest*, to clothe, in the sense of putting money into something with the hope of profit. While *investment* retains both senses, *investiture* has only the physical. Both *vestment* and *vestiment* are good Eng. forms; the *e* dropped from OFr. *vestement*; but there is also OFr. *vestiment*, as the word is from L. *vestire, vestit-*, to clothe, from *vestis*, clothing. It is from the Gr. *hesthes*, Sansk. *vastra*, garment. Thus a *vest* (though its first use was of the loose outer garment worn by men in the east, and thus applied for a time to similar garments as worn by women in the west) has no relation to the *vestal* virgins, who were the servitors of L. *Vesta*, the goddess of the hearth; as her Gr. form is *Hestia*. Without the capital, Gr. *hestia* means hearth, household. From the duty of the four (later, six) *vestal* virgins to tend the sacred fire of *Vesta* in her temple at Rome, an early type of wax match was called a *vesta*.

To *vest* a person with power is to clothe him therein; hence, the *vested* interests. There may be some connection between *vesta*, household, and the diminutive *vestibule*, *q.v.* for other suggestions.

investigate.

Hunters on the trail of escaped slave or other quarry *investigated* the flight (L. *in* + *vestigare*, to track, from *vestigium*, footprint, mark left behind). From this, Fr. *vestige* gives us Eng. *vestige;* but *vestigium* is also used in Eng., of a *vestigial* organ, a trace of a part once larger and more fully used (as the vermiform appendix in humans, and the projection—once a rest—on the bowl of a pipe).

Samuel Butler mentions other mechanical *vestigia* in his satiric *Erewhon* (read this title backwards; *cp. Utopia*), 1872.

investiture, investment.
See invest.

inveterate.
See mutton.

invidious.
See improvised.

invincible.
See victoria.

invisible.
See improvised.

involve.
See volume.

iodine.

You think of an antiseptic; the Greeks thought of a flower. *Iodine* is from Gr. *iodes*, like a violet, from *ion*, violet—named after the color of its vapor. The *ion* in physics is from Gr. *ion*, present particple of *ienai*, to go.
See element.

ion.
See iodine.

iota.
See jot.

Iowa.
See States.

irascible.
See ire.

ire.

The *Irish* are not etymologically the angry race (*Ir-* seems to be from *Eire; cp. Hibernia*), though *ire* is from L. *ira*, wrath. Hence also L. *iratus*, whence Eng. *irate;* and the inceptive L. *irasci*, to grow angry, whence *irascible*.

Ireland.
See Hibernia.

iridium.
See element.

iris.
See flower.

Irish.
See Hibernia.

iron.

After the rough utensils of the stone age, *iron* must have seemed smooth indeed to those that changed from the more primitive type of tool and weapon. The Sansk. root *is*, to glide(as on a smooth surface) may thus be behind both common Teut. forms: AS. *is*, G. *eis*, *ice;* and OHG. *isarn*, whence G. *eisen;* AS. *isen*, *iren*, whence *iron*. Thus *iron* is as smooth as *ice*.
See element.

irony.
See braggadochio.

irrefragable.
See discuss.

irrelevant.
See relief.
Lawyers often move to have testimony stricken out, as *"irrelevant, incompetent* and *immaterial."* The prefixes *ir—, in—,* and *im—* are, of course, all *in,* not, changing to suit the letter that follows.
Relevant is from L. *relevare,* present particple *relevant,* lifting up, from *re,* again + *levare,* rise, raise (Eng. *levant,* place of the rising sun; *cp. orient*), hence, to assist, to be pertinent.
Competent is from L. *com,* from *cum,* with + *petere, petit—,* to fly to, to seek, from Gr. *petomai,* I fly. To *compete* is to seek together; hence, *competitor.* But L. *competere* (present participle *competens, competent—*) meant also to solicit; hence (it was assumed), to be suitable for.
Material, from L. adjective *materialis,* from *materia, matter,* the basic substance, is from Sansk. *ma,* to measure, to produce (*mater, mother*) + the Aryan suffix *—tar,* indicating the agent.

Ishtar.
See Aphrodite.

isinglass.
The old Dutch fishermen knew that the sturgeon bladder (*huysenblas*) was iridescent, and partly let light through; when they found a kind of stone with the same qualities, they just transferred the name. (Metaphor gives rise to many meanings.) The *b* changed to *g* because you can see through glass. *Mica* is named from its crumbling (L. *mica,* crumb, perhaps related to Gr. *micron,* particle, bit). *Cp. remorse.*

Islam.
The Mohammedan world takes its name from its devotion: *islam* is the Arab. verbal noun from *aslama,* to surrender. Though they spread in conquest widely over the world, the *Moslem* or *Mussulman* (*muslim* is the present participle of the same verb) surrendered himself to the Lord. Once one has made such surrender, one is at peace; the *salaam* of the Arab is from Arab. *salam,* peace; a greeting also used by the Jew, from Heb. *shalōm.*

island.
The little word *isle* (from OFr. *isle,* from L. *insula, island*) has been a strong influence. It has, first, changed the unrelated word *island,* which earlier was *iland,* from AS. *iegland,* from *ieg,* watery land. The *land* is redundant, added as the basic meaning of *ieg* dropped from the people's minds. Secondly, *isle* has reached across into an entirely different field, to change the spelling of *aisle,* from Fr. *aile,* from L. *ala,* wing (applied to a building).
The original L. word survives in Eng. *peninsula,* almost an *island* (L. *pen,* from *paene,* almost). It is indeed a bright little, tight little *isle!*
Here is the home of the *isolationist.*
To make something an *island* is to *insulate* it, or, via It. *isolare* and Fr. *isoler,* to *isolate* it from other things. The drug *insulin* (first *isolated* in 1922 by Dr. F. G. Banting of the University of Toronto) was thus named because it comes from an *island*: the smaller glands of the pancreas, called, after their discoverer, the *islands of Langerhans.* (An *island* in the body is a group of cells or bit of tissue entirely surrounded by material of a different structure; thus, the central lobe of the cerebrum is the *Island of Reil.*) Don't let this *rile* you . . . To *rile* is a form of *roil,* to make a liquid thick by stirring up the sediment; hence, figuratively, to stir, to disturb, to annoy; the origin is unknown but the action is frequent. One suggestion links *roil* with OFr. *rouil,* mud, rust, from a LL. type *rubiculare,* to rust, from L. *rubigo,* rust. Another shortens *roil* from *broil,* to quarrel, from Fr. *brouiller,* to mix confusedly; whence also *embroil* (*em,* in) and It. and Eng. *imbroglio.* The cooking *broil* first meant to char; an earlier form was *brule;* it is from Fr. *bruler,* to burn, from OFr. *brusler*—also of unknown origin. If you let nothing *rile* you, you may lead the life of *Riley.* [It is suggested that this phrase is from the easy ways not of an Irish gentleman, but of a Gypsy lord, from the Gypsy word *rye,* gentleman, changed by folk-etymology to a man's name. The word was made popular by the book *The Romany Rye* (*The Gypsy Gentleman,* 1857) by George Borrow. It is from Sansk. *raj, raya,* lord, whence *rajah.* The *maharajah* is Hindu *maha,* great + *raj.* The feminine is *maharanee.*
H. L. Mencken writes me that "the life of Reilly"—an expression more widespread in the U. S. than in England—grew popular after 1898, when Charlie Lawlor and James W. Blake (authors of the well-remembered "The

Sidewalks of New York:" East Side, West Side, All Around the Town) wrote "The Best In the House Is None Too Good For Reilly." Edward B. Marks tells me that in 1899 his firm published the song "Everything at Reilly's must be done in Irish style;" but he inclines to attribute the spread of the expression to its use in the Harrigan and Hart plays, which pictured the Irish rising through police jobs and politics to prosperity.]

isolate, isolationist.
See island.

isotope.
See element.

issue.
This consequence first referred to anything that came out, esp. offspring. It is by way of OFr. *issir,* from L. *exire, exitus,* from *ex,* out + *ire,* to go. Thus *exit* is its doublet. "This way to the *egress*"—which Barnum's barkers cried when the sideshows were too crowded—takes us to L. *e, ex,* out + *gradire, gress—,* to step—whence many words, from *grade* to *progress.* L. *gradualis,* step by step, gives us *gradual; graduated* means marked off by degrees, like a thermometer or a bachelor of arts; *degree* itself is a step (marked) down, akin to *degrade,* to put down a step. *Digress* is to step aside; *transgress,* to step across (the proper bounds); *aggression* is stepping to (what's not yours). The basic root (through Sansk. *griddhra,* greedy), is Aryan *gardh,* to desire, hence, to step toward. And, of course, *progress* is the forward march of mankind down the ages! *Cp. congress.*

—ist.
See spinster.

item, itinerary.
See obituary.

—ize.
See homo-.

J

jabber.
See chatter, gibberish.

jacinth.
See carnelian.

Jack and Jill.
See tag.

Jack Ketch.
See Appendix II.

Jack Tar.
See Appendix II.

jackanapes.
This word for a conceited upstart was a nickname of William de la Pole, Duke of Suffolk, murdered at sea in 1450; his arms bore the clog and chain of a trained monkey. Possibly the ending means, *of Naples;* it is so used of other imports from that city-state; and there are records that through the early 15th c. *apes* were brought to England from Italy. The word *ape* itself is linked in, however; *jack* was a common name, frequently attached to other terms: *jackrabbit, jackass, jack-of-all-trades, jumping-jack, jackboot, jackdaw, jack-in-the-box, jackstraw* (there was a *Jack Straw,* led the English common people's rising in 1381) *jacktar, jack-knife, jack-o'-lantern.* Brewer gives a list of seventy-four terms, from *Jack Adams* (a fool) to *yellow jack,* saying that *Jack* is used "always depreciatingly," whereas *Tom* implies friendliness, *Hijack,* of recent slang, is from *jack,* a hoist.

jactation, jactitation.
See wasp.

jade.
See carnelian.

jail.
See cabal.

janitor.
See month: January.

January.
See month.

jar.
There is an *ajar, q.v.,* that means on the turn; another that means at odds with the world. The latter is from earlier *at jar; jar,* discord, being an imitative word (earlier *charr, chirr*) for harsh sound. The *jar* for holding things is via Sp. *jarro* from Arab. *jarrah,* earthen *jar.*

jargon.
See slang.

jasper.
See carnelian.

jaw.
See pylorus.

jazz.
Some students of the modern dance declare that this is an African word meaning hurry, brought into Eng. through the Creole. The more likely origin is in the name of the man that, down in Vicksburg around 1910, became world-famous through the song asking everyone to "come on an' hear, Alexander's Ragtime Band." Alexander's first name was Charles, always abbreviated *Chas.* and pronounced *Chazz;* at the "hot" moments they called "Come on, *Jazz!*" whence, *jazz* music. Other sources have also been suggested: Arab *jazib,* one that allures; Hind. *jazba,* ardent desire (Eng. *jazzbo*); and an African *jaiza,* rumble of distant drums.

jeep.
The name of this car is as American as its manufacture. The government, early in World War II, ordered a *General Purpose car.* The initials sound like a childish diminutive, *G. P., jeepie;*

but *jeep* seems to fit the machine. The word swept into the language as swiftly as the car into use.

jejune.
The implication of childishness some feel in this word is an echo of Fr. *jeune* (from L. *juvenis*), young. The word is really from L. *jejunus,* fasting (Fr. *jeûne,* fast). It came to be applied to food that lacked nourishing qualities; hence to things unsatisfactory (to the mind or spirit). The *jejunum* is the second part of the small intestine, which (as was noted in the year 1398) "is alwaye voyde of mete and drynke", seems always empty.
To *break* the night's *fast* is Eng. *breakfast;* but it is *dinner* too. This was the meal at which the lord *broke* his *fast,* probably about noon, the biggest meal of the day; now often at eventide. For *dinner* is by way of Fr. *diner* (whence also Eng. *dine*) from LL. form *disjunare* from *disjejunare,* from *dis-,* away + *jejunum,* fast. *Déjeuner* is still *breakfast* in French. Meals at all hours serve the one end!

jelly.
See aspic.

jeopardy.
When there was a drawn game, the Romans called it (LL.) *jocus partitus,* divided game, as they divided the wager. The term came into French as *jeu parti.* Then it was applied also to evenly matched opponents, so that the result was uncertain and the stakes (or the lives) were in danger; hence, Eng. *jeopardy.* For *jeopardize, cp. homo—.*

jerboa.
See muscle.

jeremiad.
See Appendix II.

jerk, jerked (beef).
See barley.

jersey.
See cloth.

Jerusalem artichoke.
See artichoke.

jesse.
This is a church word, used of a large branched candlestick; or of a genealogical tree on a church window, showing the family (symbolized by the flourishing tree) from *Jesse* through his son David to Jesus. Thus in the *Bible, Isaiah* 11, i—x, we are told "And in that day there shall be a root of *Jesse,* which shall stand for an ensign of the people." (Incidentally, this illustrates the earlier use of *ensign, q.v.*).

jest.
See joke.

jet, jetsam, jettison.
See subject.

jewel.
See carnelian.

jezebel.
This daughter of the King of Tyre, and wife of a wicked king of Israel (*Ahab*), has given her name for all time to a fierce old woman. The *Bible* (*II Kings*) tells how, as Elijah prophesied, she was devoured by dogs.

jingo, jingoism.
See chauvinism.

jitterbug.
The double meaning of *bug* (*see insect*) has led to its being used for the fixed idea of a fanatic or a maniac ("He has bees in his bonnet;" "He has a *bug* in his cap;" "He's *bugs!*"): hence the end of this word. As for the first part, rhyming slang and *Spoonerisms, q.v.,* were very popular sources of words in the last century; thus the victim of *gin and bitters* had the first letters transposed; he's been and got the *jitters.* From the similar spasmodic jerking of the devotees of the new dancing, the term was applied to them, the *jitterbugs.*

jobation.
See Appendix II.

jockey.
See barnard.

jocular.
See carnelian.

John Bull.
See Yankee.

Johnny cake.
See jury.

join, joint, jointure.
See subjugate.

joke.
Probably via It. *gioco* this is from L. *jocus,* game, from *jovius,* whence Eng. *jovial,* from *Jove,* the great player of practical jokes among the gods. His L. name is akin to Gr. *Zeus; Jupiter,* from *Zeus* + *pater,* father; *dios* (Heb. *Jehovah*?); related to Sansk *div,* to shine, to play; whence ultimately also L. *divus,* god, whence Eng. *divine.* From L. *joculator,* jester, came OFr. *jogleur,* whence *jongleur,* minstrel, who was also a *juggler. Cp. carnelian; witch-hazel.*
Jest was originally any deed, from L. *gerere, gest—,* to do, whence *gesture; digest,* from L. *digerere,* to put apart, to arrange (*digerere cibum,* to digest food). Used in such titles as *"The Merrie Gestes of . . .",* the word came to be limited to the humorous meaning.

jolly.
See Yule.

Jonah.
This term for bringer of bad luck has even become a verb: "Don't you *jonah* me!" In the *Bible* (*Jonah*), we are told that *Jonah* fled when the Lord bade him protest the evils of Nineveh; he took ship for Tarshish. A storm overtook the ship; the frightened sailors, learning of *Jonah's* flight, cast him overboard—whereupon all was calm. *Jonah,* as you know, spent the next three days in the belly of a whale; then went upon the Lord's errand.

jongleur.
See joke.

jonquil.
See junket.

Jordan almond.
See almond.

jot.
This is a variant and contraction of *iota* (*jota*), the smallest letter in the Gr. alphabet. Hence, to *jot* down is to make a very brief note of. *Iota* is sometimes called the Lacedemonian letter, because the inhabitants of this section of Greece (*Laconia*) were frugal of words; *see laconic.*

journal, journey, journeyman.
See jury.

jovial.
See joke, saturnine (from Jupiter).

joy.
This exuberance is associated with the *young, q.v.* And *joy* itself is via Fr. *joie,* It. *gioia,* from L. *gaudia, rejoicing.* To *rejoice* came on the same path, via OFr. *rejoir, rejoiss—,* from LL. *re,* again, + *gaudire,* to be glad. To *enjoy* something is to take *joy* in it. *Jewel* may be via OFr. *joel* from *gaudiellum, gaudia;* but *see carnelian.*

jubilation.
See jubilee.

jubilee.
L. *jubilare, jubilat—,* whence Eng. *jubilation,* is found in the imperative in the first word of the 100th Psalm: *Jubilate Deo,* Shout unto the Lord. The influence of this changed the first vowel in *jubilee,* from LL. *jubilaeus annus,* year of rejoicing, from Gr. *iobelos,* from Heb. *jobel,* ram; then, ram's horn used as trumpet. The year after seven periods of seven years each was set as a time of rejoicing, a *sabbatical* (Heb. *shabbath,* from *shabath,* to rest) year. This is the fiftieth year; hence *jubilee* and golden anniversary coincide. Since fields should lie fallow and slaves be set free, the *jubilee* became a term of great rejoicing among the Negroes.

judge.
See verdict.

judicial, judicious.
See just.

juggler.
See joke.

jugular.
See pylorus.

juke (box).
In the mountains of southern United States, many Elizabethan words, that have died out in England, are preserved. Thus *jouk,* to dodge, to move quickly, was applied to the places where liquor was sold, in prohibition times; hence, any cheap drinking place. When the automatic phonograph swept to popularity in such shops, it came to be called a *juke* box.

Julian (calendar).
See Appendix II.

July.
See month.

jump.
See plunge; also gyp. (The sound of feet landing).

jumper.
See gyp.

junction.
See yokel.

June.
See month.

junior.
See pigeon.

junk.
See yeoman.

Junker.
See yeoman.

junket.
The dessert is named from its having been first prepared in little reed baskets L. *juncus,* rush — the diminutive of which, Fr. *jonquille,* gives us the flower *jonquil,* from its leaves. The picnic, *junket,* is named from the practice of spreading rushes to sit upon; they are woven into little pillows, at outdoor stone-seated stadia, today.

Jupiter.
See joke.

jurisdiction.
See jury.

jurisprudence.
See improvised.

jury.
This body of sworn men gets its name, from OFr. *jurée,* sworn, from L. *jurare, jurat—,* to swear, from *jus, jur—,* law. *Jurisdiction* is from L. *juris + dictio, diction—,* declaration. But the word *jury,* in such combinations as *jury-mast* and *jury-leg,* temporary (a wooden leg), is for the day?, from OFr. *jornal, jurnal, journal,* daily, from LL. *diurnal—* from L. *diurnus,* from *dies,* day. Thus a *journey* was originally a day's march; a *journeyman,* a worker by the day; a *journal,* a daily record. *Journal* was first an adjective; ca. 1500 the noun (account, record, register, etc.) was dropped; by the end of the 16th c. its doublet *diurnal* (coming into use ca. 1550, meaning the list of religious services for the day) had replaced *journal* as the more formal adjective for daily. *Johnny* cake is a folk change from *journey* cake.
A *ledger* is (first) a book fastened in one place in the church, for records of births, marriages, etc., from ME. *liggen,* to *lie; leggen,* to *lay;* hence also MHG. *legge,* layer, whence Eng. *ledge. Cp. just.*

just.
Here again two older words have merged. *Just,* fair-dealing, is from L. *justus,* from *jus,* law, right, whence Eng. *justice.* But when we say that it is *just* ten o'clock, this is via Fr. *jouste,* hard by, next to, from OFr. *jouxte,* from L. *juxta,* near, whence Eng. *juxtaposition,* from *juxta + ponere, posit—,* to place. The L. form *jus,* law, had two stems, *jur—,* as in Eng. *jurisprudence, jury;* and *jud—,* whence *judicare, judicat,* to *judge,* as in Eng. *adjudicate, judicial,* pertaining to *judgment,* and *judicious* (L. *—osus,* whence Eng. *—ous,* full of), full of *judgment.*

justice.
See just; emblem.

juvenile.
See youth.

juxtaposition.
See just.

K

kail.
See alcohol

Kaiser.
See shed.

kaleidoscope.
A *trapezoid* (as also the flying *trapeze*) is named from its shape: Gr. *oidos, eidos,* form + *trapezion,* diminutive of *trapeza,* table, from *tetra,* four + *peza,* foot. A frequent suffix meaning shaped like is —*oid,* as in *spheroid; anthropoid* (Gr. *anthropos,* man).

Gr. *skopos,* watcher, then his target, then aim, range, gives us Eng. *scope; cp. dismal.*

Gr. *kalos,* beauty, *kallos,* beautiful, are pleasant thoughts; *cp. calibre.*

Put these all together, and you have a range of beautiful form, Eng. *kaleidoscope.*

Kampf.
See camp.

kangaroo.
When Captain Cook came to Queensland, Australia, in 1770, he naturally asked about the strange leaping animal. He then called it the *kangaroo.* There is no such native name; the native words, also used in Eng., are *wallaby* for the small species and *wallaroo* for the large —perhaps, originally, expressions of surprise. It is suggested that the Captain's word, *kangaroo,* is a misunderstanding and corruption of the native words for "I don't understand you."

Kansas.
See States.

karma.
See ceremony.

keg.
This apparently was first a tree-stump, AS. *kaak.* From the shape, it was applied to a barrel (Du. *kaak,* barrel) or basket; then esp. the stool on which offenders were exposed to public view, whence (esp. in Scandinavia) the sense of pillory; *cp. ducking-stool.* It kept the other meaning in OE. *cag,* whence Eng. *keg.*

ken.
See king.

kennel.
See canon.

Kentucky.
See States.

kerchief.
See handkerchief.

kernel.
See corn.

kerplunk.
See plunge.

ketchup.
Sometimes spelled *catsup,* this word has no relation to milk: it is an oriental word: Malay *kechap;* Chin. *ketsiap;* Jap. *kitjap;* meaning a sauce, as the brine of pickled fish. Our most familiar form is *tomato ketchup.*

kettle.
This is common Teut. but from a LL. source: *catillus,* a diminutive of *catinus,* a food vessel. "A pretty *kettle* of fish," the ironic expression, is corrupted from a pretty *kittle, kiddle,* a dam with fish nets, OFr. *quidel,* Fr. *guideau,* related to *guide,* as the fish are led in.

kewpie (doll).
See pupil.

khaki.
See cloth.

kickshaw.
Possibly influenced by *Pshaw!* in the sense of nonsense (as the G. form be-

came *Geckchoserie,* from *Geck,* a simpleton), this word is from Fr. *quelques choses,* some things. Dryden, in *The Kind Keeper,* gives us two stages of the shift:

Limberham: Some foolish French *quelquechose,* I warrant you.

Brainsick: *Quelquechose!* O ignorance in supreme perfection! He means a *keckshose!*

The ending was thought to be plural, thence changed to *kickshaw,* a trifle.

kid.

Originally the young of a goat, then the skin of that animal (*kid* gloves) this word is from ON. *kith,* being *kid* in the Scandinavian tongues. *Kith* and *kin* are from AS. *cyththu,* related to *cuth,* past participle of *cunnan,* to know; *cp. uncouth;* and from AS. *cynn,* (one's own) *kind,* common Teut., related to G. *Kind,* child and L. *genus.* The G. *Kind* has helped produce the slang sense of *kid,* child—whence the verb *to kid,* to treat as a child. (For *kin* and *kind, cp. racy.*)

kidnap.

See knick-knack; kid.

kidney.

From the shape and position of this gland, it derives its name: belly-egg. In ME. it is sometimes spelled *kidneer, kidnere;* and *neer* and *nere* are used alone to mean the *kidney;* but it is also spelled *kidenei,* from ME. *ey,* egg. The first syllable, *kid,* is a corruption of *quid,* from AS. *cwid,* belly, womb. Thus when Falstaff says (*Merry Wives of Windsor,* III,v,116) "Think of that, a man of my *kidney,* that am as subject to heat as butter; a man of continual dissolution and thaw" (which today's weather makes one realize!), he was referring to his fatness; but by extension from Shakespeare, the phrase "of his *kidney*" has come to mean "of his sort."

kin, kind.

See racy.

kine.

See cow.

king.

The divine right of kings was worked into the etymology of this word. It is AS. *cyning,* head (son) of the *cyn,* or tribe. But from early times we find forms like AS. *kuning,* as though from Goth. *kunnan,* from AS. *cunnan,* whence Eng. *cunning* and *ken*: king because he has wisdom. Carlyle several times emphasizes this origin. (*On Heroes and Hero-Worship,* VI; *Sartor Resartus,* III, 7).

kirk.

See church. (There is an old German saying that *Kinde, Küche, Kirche,* children, kitchen, church, are the woman's concern.)

kleptomaniac.

See mania.

knack.

See knick-knack.

knapsack.

The most important item in a soldier's kit is the food—which too often during war he must snap down quickly. Hence the pack he carries, the *sack,* to hold his victuals, is no more than a *knapsack* (LG. *knappen,* whence Eng. *knap,* to bite, to snap). Though sometimes used as a pillow, it has no other connection with *nap* (AS. *hnappian,* to take a short sleep. . . . Some suggest that these AS. and LG. words are related, both meaning basically to snap, as to snap the eyes closed, when there's chance for a minute's rest.) *Cp. knick-knack.*

knave.

See lady; knick-knack.

knee, kneel.

See gastronomy.

knick-knack.

This reduplicated word (*cp. scurry*) is from *knack.* The word imitates its meaning, the sound of a sharp short blow, a *snap.* Then it meant a trick, a device, a toy; then, the adroitness in performing the trick. (Thus we say "That's a *snap!*") *Knack* is a member of a fertile family. Many of the words in it are now obsolete; but the *kn—, gn—, n—,* initial sounds are found in words common in the Teuton tongues, and linked with Latin and Greek, back to far-off Aryan sources, meaning biting, breaking, or swelling (a protuberance, a *knuckle* to *knock* with, a head). Interlocked are the ideas of to eat and to know: ME. *gnawen,* to *gnaw;* AS. *cnawan,* to *know;* L. *gnoscere,* to know, whence Eng. *cognition; ignorant;* Gr. *gignoskein,* to *know;* Sansk. *jna,* to *know.* The idea of absorbing is common to both food and knowledge. Thus L. *rumen,* the first stomach of a cud-chewing animal, gives us both *ruminant,* chewing cud, and *ruminate,* to think over; Shakespeare says "Chew upon this" (*Julius Caesar,* I,ii,171) meaning ponder. To *digest, q.v.,* has the same double use; and since *digestion* absorbs only the good, a *digest* gives us (to continue the food figure) the meat of an item, leaving the shell. *Cp. strike.*

Some idea of this complex family of words may be gathered from the listing that follows. *Knab* is an old spelling of *nab; knabble,* an early form of *nibble. Knag* is a protuberant *knot* in wood. *Knap* (AS. *cnaep*), a mound; also, (Du. *knappen*), to break short; to bite off; whence *knapsack, q.v. Knar* is a *knot* (of wood); whence *knarled,* now more commonly *gnarled*—though *gnarl* is a diminutive of *gnar,* earlier *knarre, knar.* The *gn*— and the *sn*— words are akin: early *knaw* became *gnaw* (Gr. *gnathos,* jaw); *gnash;* Dan. *knaske,* to grind the teeth; *snap, snip, snarl, snatch, snob, snub.* Perhaps it is the influence of the *kn*— sound that changed *knave,* which first meant just boy, to the sense of rascal, as in *knavery. Knight* was spared the same fate by becoming a term in history; the G. form, *Knecht,* has come to mean menial. *Knicker,* a boy's marble, is from D. *knikken,* to knock—which itself (AS. *cnucian*) is an imitative word, like most of these. *See knickers.* For *knit, knot,* and *knout, see knot. Knob* is a later form of *knop,* still earlier *knoppe,* a bud; its form *knosp* (Gr. *knospe,* bud) is used as a term in architecture. *Knoll* (AS. *cnoll*) via Welsh *cnol* is a diminutive of Gael. *cnoc,* mound. *Knub* is a variant of *knob,* a bump; as a verb this meant to strike with the *knuckles;* and *knuckle* is a later form of *knockel,* with which we *knock. Knur,* also *nur,* is a *knot* or lump in wood; and *knurl* is wood *knotted* in the grain; to *nurl* is to give a fluted edge, as to a coin. *Knick-knack* itself is also spelled *nick-nack.*

The forms without the initial *k* are as common. *Nab* is of two sources: Ice. *nabbi,* a knob; and Dan. *nappe,* to catch. The second of these gives us *kidnap; cp. kid.* From ME. *nap,* a protuberance, comes the *nape* of the neck. (There are also *nap,* from AS. *hnappian,* to slumber; *nap,* from AS. *hnoppa,* the *nap* of cloth; and *nap,* a card game, short for *Napoleon.*) AS. *neb,* beak, cognate with *snap,* gives us the *nib* of a pen. *Nib* also meant to take a small bite; its frequentative is *nibble.* (*Snap,* and *snip,* as related to *nip,* earlier *knip,* to pinch, to bite, remind us that *s*— is often prefixed as an intensive: *splash* from *plash; smash* from *mash; squash* from *quash; scrunch* from *crunch; scratch* is paralleled by G. *kratzen* and Fr. *gratter;* whence Eng. *grate.* Mrs. Gamp, in Dickens' *Martin Chuzzlewit,* says *scroud* for *crowd.*) *Knip,* later *nip,* pinch, has the frequentative *nipple.* Also *nob,* to strike and *nob,* the head; *nobble,* to stun—though slang *nob,* whence *nobby,* is short for *nobleman;* and *nod* (OHG. *hnoton,* to shake); also slang *noddle,* the head, corrupted to *noodle.*

Nick (Du. *knik,* a nod) as in the *nick* of time; also (G. *knicken;* ODu. *nocke*) a slight cut, a *notch;* also a *nock. Nock* was first the horn end of a long bow; then the *notch* for the arrow (L. *nux, nuc*—, *nut,* was used with the same meaning). *Nick* is also an abbreviation of the devil, *the Old Nick;* contrariwise *St. Nick* (*Nikolaus*) is *Santa Claus,* patron of travelers. *See nickel. Niche,* the (originally shell-shaped) recess in a wall, is from It. *nicchia,* perhaps from LL. *nidiculare,* to nestle, from *nidicare,* to nest, from *nidus,* nest— but most probably from It. *nicchio,* shell, shellfish, from L. *mytilus,* mussel. *Notch* was earlier *otch,* perhaps by joining of the article, *an* + *otch,* whence *a notch. Cp. auction.* It is probably softened from *nock;* but also suggested is Fr. *osche,* from *oschier,* to cut, from L. *absecare,* to cut away, from L. *ab,* away, + *secare,* the present participle of which gives us *secant.* What we *gnaw,* we cannot *ignore;* we are what we eat. Which indeed is food for thought.

knickers.

A *knicker* or *nicker* is a marble of baked clay. In old New York, the man that made them was called a (Du.) *knickerbacker, knicker baker.* Like Smith, Baker, and many more, this became a proper name—chosen by Washington Irving as that of the supposed author of *Diedrich Knickerbocker's History of New York.* In Cruikshank's illustrations to this, the old citizens wore short wide pants caught in at the knees; these have since been called *knickerbockers,* or *knickers. See knick-knack.*

knight.
See lady, errand, knick-knack.

knit.
See knot.

knob, knock, knoll.
See knick-knack.

knot.
This is a common Teut. word, AS. *cnotta;* ON. *knutr, knot, knöttr,* ball. The cognate AS. *cnyttan* gives us *knit.* The *knots* a ship travels in an hour are measured by a log-line divided by *knots* into 120 parts, each the same part of a nautical mile as a half-minute is of an hour; hence the speed may be timed by the *knots.* A *Gordian knot* is like the one tied by Gordius (a peasant made king of Phrygia, who dedicated his wagon to Jupiter and tied it to the temple. It was tied so ingeniously as to defy all efforts to open it; but it was prophesied that whoever untied the *knot* would reign over the whole East. Alexander opened it), cut in twain by the sword. A *knout* (Sw. *knut* ? or Tartar *knout, knot*) is a lash of *knotted* thongs. *Cp. knick-knack.*

knout.
See knot.

know.
See quaint; knick-knack.

knuckle.
See knick-knack.

kobold.
See incinerator.

kohinoor.
The diamond has drawn its name well, from Pers. *kuh-i-nur,* mountain of light.

kohl.
See alcohol.

kohl-rabi.
See alcohol.

kopeck.
See sterling.

krypton.
See element.

Ku Klux Klan.
See circus.

kuomintang.
When I was a boy, scary tales of *tong* warfare in Chinatown used to supply some of the senseless thrill now provided by what are called the comics. But Chin. *tang* merely means society, or party. *Kuo,* nationalist; *min,* people: The nationalist people's party, the *Kuomintang.*

L

labor, laboratory.
See lotion.

labyrinth.
See Europe.

lace.
See delight.

lackadaisical.
See alas.

laconic.
The Spartans were parsimonious of patter. When they refused Athenian terms, on one occasion, the herald declared: "If we come to your city, we will raze it to the ground." The Spartan answer was the one word "If." From the name of the land of which Sparta was capital, *Laconia*, comes *laconic*.

lacquer.
See litmus.

la crosse.
The Indians used to play this game, with sometimes hundreds on a side. The French reduced the number, organized rules, and gave it the name—from the stick used, which they thought resembles a *crozier's* staff (OFr. *crossier*, bearer of the *crosse*, bishop's crook); hence the *jeu de la crosse*, game with the crook. The Indians did not care; for instance, on June 4, 1763, Pontiac arranged a game outside the fort at Michillimackinac; the whites watched; the ball went over the palisade; the Indians rushed in after it, took out their tomahawks, and massacred the whites. It has always been a rough game.

lacteal, lacteous, lactic.
See delight.

lad.
See alas.

lade.
See board.

lady.
A *lady* may seem removed from kitchen tasks, but in the days when she was just the head farmer's wife (as any farmer's wife today will tell) she had quite a job baking bread for all the helpers. In truth, that occupation gave her her name (OE. *hlaefdige*, from *hlaf*, loaf + *dig*, to knead). *Dough* is from the same source (AS. *dag;* ON. *deig*), which also gives us *dairy* (ME. *deyerie*, from ME. *dey*, woman, from AS. *daege*, from *dig*, to knead). By equal right, the *lord* is the *loaf-ward* (OE. *hlaford*, from *hlafweard;* OE. *weard*, whence End. *ward, warden. Reward*, however, is from OFr. *reguarder*, to *regard*, heed, hence repay). And the servant was the loaf-eater (OE. *hlafaeta*, servant)! A *steward* was originally a keeper of the pigs (AS. *stigu, sty* + *weard*). A *knight* was originally a youth (AS. *cniht*), then a servant, then a servant of a noble. A *knave* (AS. *cnafa;* Ger. *Knabe*) was at first a boy, then it became a term of scorn.

In *Lady-bug, Lady-Day*, and other combinations, there lingers the AS. use of *Lady* to mean the Virgin Mary.

laggard.
See coward.

lair.
See litter.

lamb.
See mutton.

lambert.
See Appendix II.

lame.
See lumber; *cp.* bazooka.

lamp.

Eng. *lamp* and *lantern* were once the same word, Gr. *lampas*, from *lampein*, to shine. The early *lamp* was a basin with a wick floating in oil; the Romans developed the type where the wick comes up within a horn (now glass) case for protection. But the Romans used the word *lux, luc—*, light. From this came the verb *lucere*, to shine, the present participle of which, *lucens, lucent—*, gives us Eng. *lucent;* came also the adjective *lucidus*, whence Eng. *lucid;* and the noun *lucerna*, lamp, whence Eng. *lucernal*, as the *lucernal* microscope; *cp. atlas*. And the influence of L. *lucerna* gave us, as a doublet to *lamp*, the Eng. *lantern*. Folk-etymology (as in Shakespeare's *A Midsummer Night's Dream*, V,i, 233, 237) from the *horn* case derived the spelling: "This *lanthorn* does the horned moon present."

lampoon.

OFr. *lamper*, to guzzle, is a nasal formation from *laper*, to *lap*, from AS. *lapian;* L. *lambere*, to lick. The imperative of the OFr. *lamper, lampons*, let's drink, was the refrain of an old drinking song. From the usual nature of the stanzas of such songs came the word *lampoon*.

Lap, a fold of a garment (hence, of the body when you sit) is a common Teut. word (AS. *lappa*, ON. *leppr*, clout), with diminutive *lappet* and *lapel*. From it comes the verb *lap*, to surround with cloth, (whence *overlap*); hence, more generally, to surround or encircle, as a *lap* of a race-course. A *lapidary* is from L. *lapidarius*, from *lapis, lapid—*, stone, whence *lapis lazuli*, azure stone; *dilapidated* means with the stones thrown apart, from *di, dis*, apart + *lapidare, lapidat—*. *Lapse* is L. *lapsus*, from *labi, laps—*, to slip, whence *lapsus linguae*, slip of the tongue. *Cp. luncheon*.

lance.
See launch.

land.
See lawn.

landau.
See Appendix II.

Landgrave.
See grave.

landlubber.
See luncheon.

lantern.
See lamp.

lanthanum.
See element.

lap.
See lampoon, luncheon.

lapel, lapidary.
See lampoon.

lapis lazuli.

See lampoon. *Ultramarine*, the color, was named not from the sea (L. *ultra*, beyond + *marin—*, of the sea) but because the *lapis lazuli* came from beyond the sea, from Persia.

Ultra gives us *ultraism*, beyond the surface of things, beyond comprehension. L. *mare*, sea, whence *marinus*, of the sea, gives us *marine;* whence *maritimus*, near the sea, whence *maritime;* whence *marinare, marinat—*, whence *marinated* herring: pickled in brine. Tell that to the *Marines! Marital* is not from this source; but from *mas, mar—, male* (the diminutive *masculus*, whence *masculine*) whence *maritalis*, of the male; whence L. *maritare*, whence Fr. *marier*, whence Eng. *marry*. This has no connection with the common Teut. word, *merry* (OE. *myrige*, from Teut. *murjo*, whence *mirth*.)

lapse, lapsus linguae.
See lampoon.

Laputan.
See Appendix II.

larboard.

See board. Two other suggestions are advanced. The helmsman always stood on the steer-side, *starboard;* hence, this side was empty, ME. *lere*, empty. The early form *leereboard* exists—but nobody then knew how to spell. Also, Du. *laager*, lower, is used to mean left; *lar* may be short for *laager*. Etymologists often go completely *overboard*.

lariat.
See lasso.

lark.
See rote, sky lark.

larva.

This word is directly from the L. *larva*, ghost. But as folks learned that ghosties were usually hidden humans, the word came to mean mask. It was applied in natural history to the grub state of an insect, which masks its true, final, appearance. Linnaeus (Carl von Linné, Swedish naturalist, 1707—78) gave currency to the technical sense.

lass, lassitude.
See alas, let, last.

lasso.
See delight. *Lariat* is a doublet of *reata* or *riata,* from Sp. *reata,* from *reatar,* to tie, from L. *re, back* + *aptare,* to fasten, intensive of *apere, apt—,* to fit; whence Eng. *apt, aptitude, inept.* Our more familiar form combines the article and the noun; *la reata,* whence Eng. *lariat.* Cowboys are seldom *inept* with the *lasso. Cp. copulate.*

last.
The *last* that the cobbler should stick to is from OE. *laeste,* shoemaker's *last,* from OE. *laest,* boot; OE. *last,* footstep; from an earlier root *lais—,* to follow a track, cognate with L. *lira,* furrow; *cp. delirium.*

The *last* that's best of all the game is from OE. *latost,* superlative of OE. *lat,* tired, whence Eng. *late; latost* became *latst,* thence *last.* The Aryan root was *lad—,* seen also (*ladtus*) in L. *lassus,* weary, whence *lassitude; cp. let.* To *let* seems first to have meant to abandon through weariness; in the same family is L. *laxus,* loose, *relaxed; cp. talc . . .* Somewhat *later,* the doublet *latest* was refashioned.

The verb *last* first meant to follow; hence, to continue, then to hold out, to *last.*

latch.
See delight.

late, later, latest.
See last.

lateral.
See collar.

latex.
Perhaps akin to L. *liquere,* Eng. *liquid* (*cp. world*) and to L. *lac,* an oozing gum (*cp. litmus*) was L. *latex,* fluid. This was applied in Renaissance medicine to the fluids of the body, esp. to the watery part of the blood; then, to an ooze from the cut stems of plants. Since 1909 it has been used of this fluid from the *siphonia elastica,* or Brazilian rubber tree; the native name for *latex, cahuchu,* via Fr. gives us Eng. *caoutchouc.*

lather.
See absolute.

latitude.
See collar.

latrine.
See lotion.

laudable.
See laudanum.

laudanum.
This is a folk-formation from L. *labdanum, ladanum,* from Gr. *ladanon,* from *ledon,* resin. The change came from association with L. *laus, laud—,* praise, because its effects were *laudable.*

lauds.
See bull.

laugh.
Laughter, seen by some as the distinguishing sign of man, was widespread, OE. *hlaehhan.* The root *hlah, hlag, klak, klok,* is probably echoic, as are *cluck* (earlier *clock,* AS. *cloccian*); *chuckle; cackle; cp. cliché.* The same root appears in Gr. *klossein,* to *cluck;* this is akin to Gr. *glotta,* a variant of *glossa;* Eng. *glottis; epiglottis;* prefix *glosso—* for things pertaining to the tongue; but *see glossary.* This too is basically echoic; as also Eng. *glut* and *gulp;* originally *glut* was a swallow; then, all that could be eaten in a swallow (L. has the same root, *glutire,* to swallow; the noun form gives us Eng. *glutton*). *Gluten* is directly from L. *gluten, glue* (*glue* is from a variant, LL. *glus, glut—; see clam*).

launch.
There was a L. *lancea,* perhaps itself of Celtic origin, which as the name for the hurled spear passed into all the Teut. tongues, Eng. *lance;* also used as a verb, as to *lance* a wound. From the OFr. *lance* was also formed a verb, OFr. *lancier,* ONFr. *lanchier,* whence Eng. *launch;* this first meant to thrust, then to drive forth, to leap forward. The swift little boat, however, is from Malay *lancharan,* from *lanchar,* quick; via Port. *lanchara,* Sp. *lancha,* this gives us Eng. *launch.* The *launch* that is *launched* is a different word from its *launching.*

laundress, lava.
See lotion.

lavaliere.
See Appendix II.

lavatory, lavender, lavish.
See lotion.

-law (mother-in-law, etc.).
This is not at all a legal relationship, as the name might imply. It is not from Fr. *loi,* from L. *lex, leg—,* which gives us all our *legal* entanglements, *cp. legible*; but good old Saxon, from AS. *lage,* Goth. *liuga,* marriage; related to AS. *licgan,* to lie down; *leger,* a bed, *legerteam,* matrimony. In Gr. *lektron* means both bed and marriage.

lawn.
See cloth. The *lawn* on which you *lounge* or play *lawn* tennis is earlier Eng. *laund,* from Fr. *lande,* moor, and is a doublet of *land,* a common Teut. word. (The soldier that pierced Christ's side with a spear fell into a "dreaming luske, a drowsie gangrill"; his name is passed down as *Longinus* or *Longius,* from which the early Eng. *lungis,* whence *lounge.*)

lax.
See talc.

laxative.
See luscious.

lay.
See fell.

lay (song).
See rote.

layette.
This word has no (etymological) relation to *lying in;* but is from OFr. *laie,* box; the diminutive is *layette,* even though nowadays some are big.

lazar.
See Appendix II.

lazy.
See immunity.

—le.
See swivel.

lead.
See element, livelihood.

leaf.
See furlough.

league.
See legible.

leap.
See lobster.

least.
See little.

leather-stocking.
See Appendix II.

leave.
See furlough.

leaven.
See yeast.

Lebensraum.
See rummage.

lecherous.
See licorice.

ledge, ledger.
See jury.

leek.
See onion.

left.
Those of *leftist* ideas—along with their *rightist* opponents, who expect violence from the *left*—will probably be surprised to learn that the word *left* is originally from AS. *lyft,* weak, worthless. It was applied to the hand that was usually the weaker, as opposed to the *right*: from AS. *riht, reht,* straight, just; cognate with L. *rectus; cp. royal. See* also *dexterity.*

The place of honor, in any formal meeting, is at the host's *right.* Hence, at the French National Assembly of 1789, the nobles took their seats at the *right* of the President, leaving the seats on the *left* for the "third estate" (*see estate*). From a position of ceremony, this took on a political significance: the nobles were naturally conservative; the moderates were in the center (the assembly-room was shaped like an amphitheatre), and the radicals were on the *left.* Carlyle, in *The French Revolution,* 1847, speaks of "the extreme *Left*". The warning "Don't get *left*" has of course no reference to radical ideas: *left* is here the past participle of *leave*: Don't let them *leave* you behind; *cp. furlough.*

The terms *leftism, leftist,* and *left-wing* all came into use ca. 1920, after the Russian Revolution. The "wing" is borrowed from military use, the *wing* of an army. For the word *wing, see vogue.*

legal, legate, legation, legato, legend.
See legible.

legerdemain.
See yeast.

legible.

Teachers that warn of spelling confusion between *legible* and *eligible* may not tell you (or know) that the two words are from the same source: L. *legere, lectum,* to choose, to pick. From the ability to choose the proper letters came the derived meaning of *legere,* to read: what is *legible* is what can be picked out. *Eligible* and *elected* (L. *e,* out of + *legere*) are what can be, and what have been, chosen. What ought to be read is a *legend* (L. gerundive, *legenda*): until the 16th c. this meant a saint's life, but with the Reformation and the hostility to the Catholic Church the meaning changed to "something told as history that is really made up."

Few words have more ramifications in Eng. that this L. one. A group of men picked out for military service is a *legion;* then, any large number; men chosen may be a *legation,* or *legates.* That which is chosen tends to become imposed, hence, *legal,* lawful: and through OFr. *leiel,* from L. *legalis* comes its doublet, Eng. *loyal.* (Similarly fashioned were *royal, q. v.* and *regal.*) To choose together is to make a *collection* (L. *col,* from *com,* together). To choose among, to discriminate, is to show *intelligence* (L. *intelligere, intellectum,* from *intellegere,* from *inter,* between + *legere*), or to be *intellectual. Intelligentsia* is from Russ., indicating first those that opposed the Tsar's regime. Such persons would probably have joined the early Romans in using L. *elegans, elegant—,* (present participle of *elegare,* a variant of *eligere,* to pick out) to mean choosy, finical; but with the decline of the Romans such choice came to be approved, as tastefully refined; hence, Eng. *elegance* and the *elegant.* Also *see college.*

Diligent came to its meaning by a series of shifts. If you choose one from a group, it is probably because you delight in it (thus L. *diligere, dilectum,* to delight in, from *dis,* among + *legere*). But if you enjoy something you will be active at it; therefore the present participle *diligens, diligent—,* enjoying, came to mean "constant in application". (*Delectable* comes by another path; *see delight.*)

Closely bound with this verb—for what you choose, you seek to hold, to bind—is L. *ligare,* whence It. *legare,* to bind, which gives us the *League* of Nations. Direct from L. come *ligament, ligature, ligation* (cp. *legation*); through It., the musical term *legato.* Another pair of doublets arises: L. *alligare,* from *ad,* to + *ligare,* whence Fr. *aloyer* (*cp. loyal*), whence Eng. *alloy,* a binding of two metals; but *alligare* also, whence Fr. *allier,* whence Eng. *ally, alliance.*

The word *liege* has a twisted story. One's *liege* lord is the lord chosen "freely" (Fr. *lige, G. ledig,* free), as on baptism one "freely" chose one's faith. However, to all practical purposes one was "bound" to serve one's *liege* lord; hence LL. *ligius* was popularly connected with *ligare,* to bind. By this path (OFr. *lige,* whence *ligeance,* whence ME. *legaunce*) comes *allegiance.* The confusion becomes worse with *allege* (Fr. *alléguer,* from L. *allegare,* from *ad,* to + *legare,* to read, to name), but entangled with OFr. *eslegier,* from LL.? *exledigare,* from G. *ledig;* also tangled with OFr. *alegier,* to lighten, from LL. *alleviare,* from *ad,* to + *levis,* light. In turn, this word, mixed with AS. *alecgan,* to put down, from *lecgan,* to lay (a common Teut. word) produced Eng. *allay,* to lighten. For a penultimate sample of the roundabout offspring of this root, a lawgiver is a *legislator* (L. *legis,* of the law + *lator,* from *ferre, tuli, latum,* to bring). But speaking of roots, note that from *legere,* to select, to pick, come the *leguminous* plants; *legumes* are the vegetables most easily and most frequently picked, those that grow in pods. *Soy,* by the way (Chin. *sho-yu,* from *shi-yu,* from *shi,* salted beans + *yu,* oil) has been used since 1696 of the sauce, but only since 1880 of the most useful bean (*soya* sauce dates from 1679).

legion, legislator, legume, leguminous.
See legible.

leisure.
See immunity.

length, lengthen.
See lent.

lenient.
See lent.

Leninism.
See Appendix II.

lens.
See lent.

lent.
This is two very different words.

A *loan* is OE. *laen* (OE. *laenan, lend, lent;* the present tense borrowed the *d* from the past tense in Middle English, and never gave it back); the Aryan root is *leiq—*, whence also Gr. *leipein,* to leave.

The other trail starts with the root *dlongho—*, slow, *long;* its Gr. form is *dolichos, long,* as in Eng. *dolichocephalic* (Gr. *kephale,* head; whence Eng. *cephalic* and the *cephalo—* compounds. The *cephalization* of man produced his civilization.); L. *longus,* hence Eng. *long.* But note that the verb is *lengthen,* the noun is *length;* also, via It. we have Eng. *lentamente,* a direction in music. OHG. *lanzig* grew into OE. *lencten;* whence *lenten*—the season when the days grow *long. Lenten* was originally a noun, meaning spring; and English is the only language in which it has developed a religious application. Some suggest that the *ten* (though sufficiently accounted for in the other growth) also represents the OTeut. root *tino—*, day; Sansk. *dina,* day: the season of the longer day. At any rate, the word itself was shortened, to *Lent;* when this became the usual word, *Lenten* was looked upon as an adjective formed from *Lent,* instead of the original word.

Note that L. *lens, lent—*, a seed, is used now in Eng. of the *lens* of glass (from the shape); while the seeds are named from the diminutive, LL. *lenticula,* whence OFr. *lentille,* whence Eng. *lentil.* L. *lentus* meant slow; whence Eng. *lentitude.* L. *lenis* meant mild; whence Eng. *lenient, lenify, lenitude.* Some persons are *lenient* even if it takes *long* to collect what they have *lent.*

If it seems *long* before something comes to you, you *long* for it; the first form was *me longs,* it is to slow to me. Also *see so-long. So-long!*

The root form *dlongho, dlgha,* Sansk. *dirgha,* may be related to L. *indulgere,* to be long-suffering toward; whence Eng. *indulgent*—as one must be to all lexicographers!

lentil.
See lent.

leonine.
See chameleon.

leprechaun.
This Irish gnome, the shoemaker of the fairies, has been said to derive his name from his trade, from Erse *leith,* one + *brog,* shoe (whence Eng. *brogan, brogue;* the *brogue* in speech is ?, from Ir. *barrog,* cramp, influenced by the word above); but the little fellow in all likelihood gets his name from OIr. *luchorpan,* from *lu,* little + *corpān,* diminutive of *corp,* body. This is related to ME. and OFr. *cors,* from L. *corpus, corpor—*, body; whence *corporal, corporeal, corps, corpse.* The L. adjective *corpulentus* leads to Eng. *corpulent;* the L. diminutive gives us *corpuscle;* the Fr. diminutive gives us *corset; corslet* is a double diminutive—which the Irish supplies for the *leprechaun!*

The O Irish *broc,* shoe, is akin to OTeut. *brok,* thigh-covering; *cp. breech.*

less, lessen, lesson.
See little.

let.
AS. *lettan* meant to hinder, to make *late* (AS. *laet* tardy, from G. *lass,* from L. *lassus,* weary, whence Eng. *lassitude*). But AS. *laetan* meant to allow. The first word survives in "without *let* or hindrance" and in a *let* ball (often erroneously called a *net* ball) in tennis, *q.v.* The dominant meaning, to permit, is thus the antonym of the other sense. Several Eng. words are their own antonyms, *e.g., fast, unbending, q.v.*

lethal.
See lethargy.

lethargy.
Here is another word that developed a story. Gr. *lethe,* oblivion, is from *lanthanein,* to be unseen; whence also Gr. *lethargos,* forgetful, whence Eng. *lethargy.* And we learn that one of the rivers in the land of the dead is the *Lethe,* in which the spirits bathe to win forgetfulness of their days on earth. The *Styx,* from Gr. *stygein,* to loathe, Gr. *stygos,* hatred (*Styx, Styg—*) is the river over which Charon must ferry them to the Elysian Fields (they hoped) or Tartarus; hence the *Stygian* crossing is into the next world. Gr. *lethe* is cognate with L. *letum,* death,

whence Eng. *lethal; cp. amulet.* The three other rivers of Hades are: *Acheron,* flowing with grief; *Cocytus,* weeping; and *Phlegethon,* from *phlegein,* to burn—from heat may come a clammy humor, hence Gr. *phlegma,* whence Eng. *phlegm; cp. complexion.*

letter.
See obliterate.

levant, leven, lever.
See yeast.

leviathan.
This word from Hebrew poetry (e.g., 103*d Psalm*) is from Heb. *livyathan,* from ? *lavah,* to twine. Used by Thomas Hobbes, *Leviathan,* 1651, as a symbol of the commonwealth, it has often (being, in the *Bible,* a sea monster) been used as the name of a large ship. Hobbes also wrote *Behemoth,* 1680, a suppressed study of the English Civil War, from Heb. *b'hemoth,* plural of *b'hemah,* beast, probably from Egypt. *p-ehe-mau,* water-ox —used of an animal even greater than the *leviathan,* as Milton calls it (*Paradise Lost* VII,471) "biggest born of earth." While in the field, we might think of *Frankenstein's monster* (novel, 1818, by Mary Wollstonecraft Shelley, the poet's wife) which slays its creator. Note that the term *a Frankenstein* is usually misapplied; that is the man, not the monster. For such creatures wholesale, *cp. robot.*

levigate, levirate, levitation, Levitical, levity.
See yeast.

lewd.
See uncouth.

libel, liberal, liberate, libertine.
See liberty.

liberty.
The L. word for free is *liber;* the noun, *libertas* (whence Eng. *liberty*), the adj., *liberalis.* Thus the *liberal* arts are those befitting a free man. But Latin *liber, libr—,* originally the bark of a tree, came to mean *book* (*see Bible*); whence L. *librarius,* whence Fr. *libraire, librarie,* whence Eng. *librarian, library.* The diminutive of L. *liber,* book, is *libellus,* little book, whence Eng. *libel;* but since pamphlets, from Elizabethan England on, were full of scurrilous attacks, the name was transferred from the booklet to its contents. *Liberty* does not permit *libel*—though from the freed man, L. *libertinus,* comes Eng. *libertine.* (The 17th and 18th c. Fr. *libertine* was unrestrained in politics and religion rather than in morals.) But L. *libra* also means balance, scales; whence the sign of the Zodiac, *Libra.* Hence also the use of L. *libra* as a measure, 12 ounces, one pound, and our abbreviation, 1 *lb.* The term *libration* is used in astronomy to mean oscillation, as a balance might tremble. *Liberate* means to set free; but *deliberate* is from L. *de,* down — *liberare,* to balance, weigh in one's mind.

libido.
See furlough.

Libra, library.
See liberty.

licence, license, licentious.
See immunity.

lich-gate.
See like.

lichen.
See licorice.

lick.
See delight, licorice.

licorice, liquorice.
This plant is named from its pleasant root: from *glykyrrhiza,* from *glykys,* sweet, whence *glucose, glycerin* + *rhiza,* root, Eng. *rhizome,* and dozens of words in botany with prefix *rhizo—.*
Lickerish, liquorish, earlier *lickerous,* meaning gluttonous, lustful, is a doublet of *lecherous,* which comes via Fr. *lécher,* to *lick. Lick* is a common Teut. word, AS. *liccian,* from L. *lingere, lict—,* from Gr. *leichein,* from Sansk. *lih,* to *lick. Cp. delight.* The *lichen* plant is so named because it seems to *lick* its way along. A medicine of powders made into a paste with honey, to be *licked* up, is an *electuary* (Gr. *ek, e,* out + *leichein,* to lick). I'd rather have the *licorice.*

lie.
See fell.

lief.
See furlough.

liege.
See legible.

lieutenant.
This word is directly from Fr. *lieu* + *tenant,* from L. *locum tenens,* holding place, from *tenere,* to hold, whence *tenacious.* He is thus acting in place of his captain, or head; *cp. achieve.* In mathematics we use the word *locus* to mean just what it did in L., place: whence *location.*

Vice (L. *vicem, vice,* turn) also means in place of, as in *viceroy* (OFr. *roy,* king); *vicepresident,* etc. Earlier, it changed to *vis,* or *vi,* as in *viscount* and *vicar* (Fr. *vicaire,* from L. *vicarius,* from *vicem,* whence *vicarious*). The tool *vice, vise,* is from Fr. *vis,* screw, from L. *vitis,* vine, from the spiral shape of the tendrils. (The jaws of the *vice* are worked by a screw.) *Vice* the fault is from Fr. *vice,* from L. *vitium;* whence *vicious* and (L. *vitiare, vitiat—,* to make faulty) *vitiate.*

life.
This naturally is very common, Du. *lijf,* G. *Leib,* body. Thought of as the body to which the spirit is attached, it is cognate with Sansk. *lepam,* glue, *lip,* to smear, to stick. But also there is the sense renewed in the expression "Stick to it!"; Aryan *lip,* to continue; thus *life* is cognate with Eng. *leave,* AS. *lifan,* to remain (be *left*). The ideas combine when you are "stuck on" someone. Then it's not a dull life!

Sansk *lip,* to smear, L. *linere* (*cp. clam*) are related to Eng. *lime* (as bird-*lime*) and its emphatic *slime* (AS. *slim,* L. *limus;* as *mash, smash* and the like; *cp. knick-knack*) and to the *slimy* animal, the snail, slug; Fr. *limaçon* (Eng. *limaçon* is a military manoeuvre and a mathematical curve, from the shape of the snail shell) and Eng. *limaceous.* The slug's path may look like silver, but it's still *slime.* For *snail, see thief.*

ligament, ligation, ligature.
See legible.

light.
See pylorus.

like.
This word has a devious story. It was originally OE. *lic,* a noun that came down into Eng. as *lich,* form, body, corpse, surviving in architecture in the *lich-gate,* an arch-covered gate to a cemetery where the corpse is set to await the clergyman. From its foreboding hoot, the owl was often called the *lich-owl.*

But this early *lic,* body, formed a compound, AS. *gelic,* having the form of (shaped together: the prefic *ga—* is cognate with L. *com,* together; and L. *conformis*—whence Eng. *conform*—had the same sense-shifting); in time this compound lost the prefix, and gave us Eng. *like,* similar, suitable.

The verb *like,* early *it likes me,* meant to be suitable; *if you like* (if it is suitable to you, if it please you) and such uses developed the present sense, as in *I like you very much.*

The same word was used; AS. *—lic, —lice,* to form adjectives and adverbs, meaning in the form or manner of. (Sometimes the whole word *like* was used, *e.g., childlike.*) In both cases, it became the suffix Eng. *—ly.* Since the adverb is usually formed by adding *—ly* to the adjective, there developed doubled forms: *kindly, kindlily; statelily; sillily;* these are now avoided. Sometimes two forms have developed, as *godly* and *godlike,* in which the *—like* form has more of the basic sense, formed *like.* The word *likely,* from meaning similar, suited to, came to mean pleasant or capable in appearance, as a *likely* lass.

lilliputian.
Gulliver made several voyages to queer lands (in the book *Gulliver's Travels,* 1726, by Jonathan Swift; really a satire on conditions in England in his day, but read now as pure adventure and fantasy). There are four journeys: to *Lilliput,* land of folk not more than six inches high; to *Brobdingnag,* where the dwarfs tower over our church steeples; to the floating land of *Laputa,* inhabited by scientists, "up in the air"; and to the home of the *Houyhnhnms,* noble horses served by beastly manlike *Yahoos.* The first of these is the best known—so much that motion pictures called *Gulliver's Travels* present *Lilliput* only. And it has given our language a word for something tiny.

lime.
See clam, life.

limelight.
To be *in the limelight* was to be what we now call in the spotlight: the earlier theatrical concentrating lights were produced by an oxyhydrogen flame

heating a piece of *lime*. Today various electric devices are used.

limen.
The L. word *limen, liminis,* threshold, was used in Herbart's *Psychology,* 1824, to mean the limit at which a stimulus ceases to be perceptible. Modern psychology speaks often of *subliminal* (L. *sub,* under) phenomena. But the word appeared much earlier in Eng., in other forms. *Eliminate* (L. *e,* out, beyond), meaning to put out of doors, expel, came to mean to get rid of (applied in several senses, from physiology to algebra). *Preliminary* activity occurs before (L. *pre,* before) you reach the doorway to the main action. *Postliminy* (L. *post,* after) is a term in International Military Law, referring to the return to their former state, after a war, of persons or things taken during the conflict. But L. *limen* might also mean the upper edge of the door, the lintel, whence (L. *sub,* under, up to) *sublime* —which first meant raised aloft; and *sublimation,* of something raised to a higher state—in chemistry, or in psychology. The word *limit,* boundary (L. *limes, limit—*) is cognate with *limen;* and leaves us with a feeling that this is but the *threshold* of the subject. (*Threshold* itself is from AS. *thersc,* to tread—*cp. thresh, thrash,* to tread corn— + *old, wald, wold,* ? wood of the doorway.)

limit.
See limen.

limn.
This word is a compromise between the Saxon and the Romance traditions. AS. *lim,* a limb, used as a verb, meant to draw a picture of. But this merged with old *lumine,* from OFr. *luminer,* whence Eng. *illuminate* (applied to manuscripts), from L. *lumen, lumin—,* light. Note that *illustrate, illustration,* originally meant (as in DuBellay's *Defence and Illustration of the French Language,* 1549) to add *lustre* to: *illustrious* is from earlier *illustre,* from L. *illustris; illustrare,* to shine upon, make glow, from *in* + *lustrate, lustrat—;* akin to L. *lux,* light.

limousine.
See sedan.

limpid.
This word, apparently from an early L. form, *limpa,* clear water, has had odd ranging. For *nymphs* inhabited the waters of ancient times; by association with Gr. and L. *nymphe* (bride as well as sprite; *cp. nuptials*), the L. word became *lymph,* still used in Eng. as a body fluid. But even in classical Latin the association was closer; Gr. *nymphian* meant maddened; hence L. *lymphaticus,* Eng. *lymphatic,* pertaining both to frenzy and to the secretion of *lymph,* as from the *lymphatic* glands.
To *limp,* and *limp* fingers, are related to one another; but their ancestry is lost; though the adjective may be shortened from *limber,* which in turn may be cognate with L. *lentis; cp. lent.*

line, lineage, lineament, linear.
See obliterate.

linen.
See cloth.

linguistics.
See tongue.

liniment.
See police.

linoleum.
Frederick Walton found, in 1863, that burlap and linseed oil formed a good basis for fixing patterns on lasting material. From L. *linum,* flax + *oleum,* oil, he called the result *linoleum.*

lion.
See chameleon.

liquid, liquidate, liquor.
See world.

liquorice.
See licorice.

lisle.
See cloth.

Lister (Listerine).
See litmus.

litany.
This word has doubled on itself. Gr. *lite,* prayer, developed the personal noun Gr. *litanos,* suppliant. Hence came the verb *litaneuein,* to pray; from which the further noun *litaneia,* prayer. Through L. this came into Eng. *litany,* a public prayer —often sung, and in procession.

literal, literate, literati, literature.
See obliterate.

lithium, lithography.
See carnelian, element.

litmus.
Litmus paper, by which acids may be tested, was originally *lakmose,* from Du. *lakmoes,* from *lak, lac* (Pers. *lacca,* red gum, from Sansk. *laksha,* animal dye, from *rakta,* past participle of *ranji,* to dye; whence Eng. *lacquer*) + *moes,* pulp. This was altered by the sense of OE. *lytyn,* to dye. From this came the early Eng. *litster,* a dyer, which produced the proper name *Lister,* and thence *Listerine,* from Sir Joseph Lister's early work on antiseptics. But *see alkali.*

litter.
The ancient *litters* of the queens, such as that of Cleopatra, were elaborate and gorgeous affairs. The word is from OFr. *litiere,* from LL. *lectaria,* from L. *lectus,* bed, from Gr. *lektron,* bed; *lexos,* couch, from root *lagh,* to lie.

In the middle ages, most persons were content with something less splendid; some strewn straw, *e.g.,* might suffice; hence *litter* came to mean something strewn for a bed and—what with careless habits—anything strewn about: refuse.

Litter, meaning a brood, though influenced by the forms above, is from Icel. *lattr,* breeding-place, from *leggja,* to lay, from *liggja,* to lie. It is connected with AS. *leger,* couch, whence ME. *layere,* place for lying, camp, whence ME. *leir,* whence Eng. *lair.*

little.
This was OE. *lytel,* from OS. *luttel,* related to OE. *lutan,* to bow down, whence an early Eng. *lout,* to bow down. The lowly, then clumsy, *lout* is probably from this verb, influenced by *lewd; cp. uncouth.*

The OTeut. root *laiso—,* small (with the comparative suffix *—iz*) gave us Eng. *less, lesser;* whence *least;* there are also used, *less* frequently, *littler, littlest.* The verb to *lessen* is from this source; but *lesson* is from OFr. *lecon* from L. *lection—,* reading, from *legere, lec—,* to choose, to read; *cp. legible.* To *lesson* some one is to "read" him a *lesson;* hence, to admonish, perhaps to *lessen* his pride. Let that be a *lesson* to you.

Little Red Riding Hood.
See tag.

livelihood.
It may be possible to put on a *falsehood* and hide from what truth might bring; but *livelihood* has no such idea of shelter. It is a corruption of earlier *lifelode,* from AS. *liflad,* life-course, related to *lead,* and *lode* in a mine; *lodestar,* guiding star; *lodestone.* There was also an earlier word *livelihood,* from OE. *lyvelyhede,* which meant liveliness; this form survived, and the other meaning. (*Falsehood* is from L. *fallere, fals—,* to deceive + *—hood,* from AS. *hād,* condition. *Lead* is from AS. *laedan,* casual form of *lithan,* to travel. Hence also *laden.* The OTeut. form *laida* gives us Eng. *load.*) The metal *lead* is from OE *lead,* MHG. *lot,* plummet; *see plunge.*

loaf.
See lady.

loafer.
This word might well have been an early Eng. word for servant (*see lady*); but it seems to have developed in the U.S., perhaps by a leisurely interpretation of G. *Laufer,* runner, from *laufen,* to run. *Cp. scamp.* Thus *presently,* which first meant immediatley, at the *present* instant, now means in a little while, don't hurry. The word *present* is from the *present* participle of L. (*pre*) *praeesse, praesens, praesent—,* to be before: in the sense of to be before one, at hand. The frequentative of this, *praesentare, praesentat—,* to place before, gives us Eng. *presentation* and the Christmas *present.* A *presentiment,* however, is from L. *prae, pre,* before + *sentire, sens—,* to feel—whence Eng. *sensitive; see ascend.*

loam.
See clam.

lobster.
This fine fish is really a *lopster* or *leapster,* from AS. *hleapan,* to *leap.* Thus OE. *loppe,* a flea (AS. *fleogan, fleah,* to fly. The Aryan root is *plu,* whence L. *pluec,* whence *pulex, pulec—, flea;* Sansk. *pulaka,* insect, from *plu,* to swim, *fly.*) and OE. *hleapestre,* a dancer. The shellfish derives more directly, however, from L. *lopusta,* from *locusta,* a leaping creature (on land or in the water; hence, Eng. *locust*). There is also a Sansk. root *langh,* to leap, related to AS. *leax,* and G. *lox,* the salmon, which *leaps* upstream to spawn.

Leap is from a common Teut. family; Goth. *hlaupan;* G. *laufen,* to run; OFr.

aloper; ME. *lopen,* to run, whence Eng. *lope.* Eng. *gantlet* is from *gat lop; see subjugate.* Hence also *interloper,* first a sea *poacher.*

Poach was earlier *potch,* from Fr. *pocher,* to *pocket,* from Fr. *poche, pouch.* To *poach* an egg is to hold it in a *pouch* while cooking. The Norman Fr. for *poche* was *poque,* the diminutive of which was *pokete,* whence Eng. *pocket.* Hence also is *pock,* used of a *pocket* in the skin, plural *pox* as in *small pox. A pox on you!*

The *orlop* deck, or cover of the hold of a ship, is short for *overlop,* from Du. *overloopen,* to run over. The wings of the *lapwing* may *overlap* (for *lap, see lampoon*), but the word is corrupted by folk etymology from AS. *hleapan,* to leap, + a type *winc,* to waver; OE. *wincian,* Eng. *wink* (*Winken,* Blinken, and Nod) related to *wince,* first meaning to turn aside, as to dodge a blow; and to *winch,* from AS. *wince,* a pulley, a thing that turns. Antelope seems to be unrelated, though its origin is unknown; nor is there any connection with cantaloup, *q.v.*

Leap Year is so called because (after February 29) each date jumps two days in the week, from the previous year. Thus, if your wife's birthday is July 4, in 1970 it will fall on a Saturday; in 1971, on a Sunday; but it *leaps* to a Tuesday in 1972. *Cp. fowl.*

locate, location.
See lieutenant, permit.

loco.
See yokel.

locomotion, locomotive.
See mute.

locus.
See lieutenant.

locust.
See lobster.

lodestar, lodestone.
See livelihood.

lodge.
See logistics.

loft, lofty.
See attic.

log.
This word, like *clog* (which was at first a synonym) is onomatopoetic in origin, suggesting cumbersome, bulky, clumsy movement; also *lug.*

The rate of motion of a ship was determined (15th—17th c.) by floating a piece of wood with a measuring device; this was called a *log.* The record of speed thus maintained was kept in a *log-book;* this has been shortened to the ship's *log;* hence, the *log* of any journey.

loganberry.
See Appendix II.

loge.
See logistics.

loggerhead.
A short heavy piece of wood (a *log, q.v.,* or *clog*) fastened to a man's leg, or a horse's, to check its movements, was also called a *logger.* By figure from this block of wood, a "blockhead" (stupid person) was also called a *loggerhead.* But the word was also applied literally. It was used of a long iron rod, with a big ball at one end; the ball was heated, then used to melt pitch, to thrust at an enemy. Heavy-headed creatures, including the snap turtle, were also called *loggerheads.* From these last two meanings came the expression "to be at *loggerheads*", meaning to quarrel sharply.

logic.
See logistics.

logistics.
This is two entirely different words in one. As applied to the art of arithmetical calculation, it is one use of the many words from Gr. *logos,* word, from *legein,* to say. In Greek, *logos* shifted its meaning from 'word' to 'reason'; hence, *logic.* In the sense of ordered knowledge, the suffix *—ology* or *—logy* is very common, from *acology* and *apology* through the many *'ologies'* Carlyle complained even maid-servants are being taught, to *zoology* and *zymology.* Army practice has brought to attention the other *logistics,* from Fr. *logistique,* from *loger,* to quarter; whence also Eng. *lodge* and the theatre *loge.*

logrolling.
When a new family came to a settlement, in American pioneer days, those already there, on a set day, joined in *rolling down logs* for the newcomers'

home. Then, on the principle of "You scratch my back and I'll scratch yourn", *logrolling* took its present meaning.

lone, lonely.
See alone.

lonesome.
See awry.

long.
See lent.

looney.
See pants.

lope.
See subjugate.

loquacious.
See necromancy; agnostic.

lord.
See lady.

lot.
See ballot, deal.

Lothario.
Despite the frequency with which this word is used, it is not from a play by Shakespeare. Massinger and Field wrote a tragedy, *The Fatal Dowry*, printed in 1632. In 1703, Nicholas Rowe produced his tragedy, *The Fair Penitent*, based on the earlier play. It was very popular for a century; from *Lothario* in it, Richardson drew the figure of Lovelace, in his *Clarissa Harlowe*, 1747-8, which suggested the theme for Rousseau's *Nouvelle Héloïse*, 1761. From Rowe's play, the "haughty, gallant, gay *Lothario*" has given his name to the type.

lotion.
Roman baths were large and popular; professional masseurs worked with *unguents* (L. *ungere, unguent—*, to anoint) and *lotions.* The word wash in L., though it took the form *lavare, lot—* (*lotion*), has the root *lu,* from Gr. *louein,* to wash. Hence, to wash down is to *deluge;* to wash to a place (as a river does earth) gives us *alluvial* deposits. The water plant par excellence is the *lotus.* In L. a man who *laved* himself was a *lavator,* the vessel or room for his washing was a *lavatorium;* hence, Eng. *lavatory.* By way of It. *lavatrina,* we have *latrine.* (*Laboratory,* of course, is a place where you *labor,* from L. *labos,* from *rabos,* strength: Sansk. *labh,* to get, perform, *rabh,* to seize). The delicate *lavender* (ME. *lavendre,* from Fr. *lavande,* from LL. *lavendula*) drew its name from its use in washing; from early times it was laid on fresh-washed linen to make it fragrant. LL. *lavanderia,* whence OFr. *lavandière,* with the feminine suffix *—ess,* gave us *launderess,* then *laundress. Lava* was first the name of a flow of water down a hill after a heavy rain. *Lavish* seems to be from OE. *lave,* to pour out, confused with the other flow we have been following. When George Gissing in his Grub Street days as a poor journalist used the British Museum *lavatory* too extensively, the authorities posted a sign: "For casual *ablutions* only" (L. *ab,* off: washing off). *See absolute.*

To *anoint,* first meaning to smear with an *unguent,* comes via OFr.. *enoindre, enoint,* from L. *inungere, inunct—,* from *in,* on, + *ungere,* to oil; by the same path (without the prefix) came Eng. *ointment;* more directly, extreme *unction.*

lottery.
See ballot.

lotus.
See lotion.

Louisiana.
See States.

lounge.
See lawn.

lout.
See little.

louvre.
See vulpine.

love.
See furlough.

lowbrow.
See effrontery.

loyal.
See legible.

lozenge.
This word would seem to be an ancient telescope of L. *lapis,* stone, and L. *laus,* praise, from the words placed on a tombstone. The tombstone was of *lozenge* shape; and the Prov. *lauza,* tombstone, slab, whence OFr. *lauze,* roofing slate (of the same shape), became Fr. *losange.* This has been applied to a de-

sign in heraldry; then (from the diamond-shape coat-of-arms of widow or unmarried woman that adorned it) to the *lozenge coach;* then, to the medicinal candy, our *lozenge,* to help preserve us from its earliest meaning.

lucent, lucid.
See lamp.

lucifer.
See atlas.

Lucifer.
See Prometheus.

lug.
See log. (Thus *lug* is used in slang for a heavy, clumsy person.)

lumbago, lumbar.
See humble.

lumber.
We speak of the *lumbering* gait of an awkward person; this is from ME. *lomeren,* to walk clumsily, from ME. *lome,* from AS. *lama,* whence Eng. *lame.* But the *lumberyard* has a longer story. Caesar speaks of the tribe of the *Langobardi* (Longbeards); these became the It. *Lombardi,* who dwelled in *Lombardy.* In 16th c. Eng. they were the moneylenders (hence *Lombard* Street, which Pepys spells *Lumber* St.). The storeroom for their pledges was called the *Lombard-room;* it would contain mainly discarded household goods, which came to be called *lumber,* as in England it still is. In American pioneer days, when the land was cleared for farming, there were many felled trees lying around; these, being discarded material, were *lumber*—which later was put to good use. *Timber* is common Teut., meaning first house (G. *Zimmer,* room), then the material for building; Goth *timrjan,* to build; Gr. *domos,* house, from *demein,* to build—whence, via L. and Fr., *domain; demesne; cp. dome.*

luminous.
See meteor.

lump.
See clam, luncheon.

lunatic.
See pants.

luncheon.
Lunch was originally a variant of *lump* (as *bunch* of *bump,* and *hunch* of *hump*), referring to a *lump* or chunk of bread. There is an 18th c. letter that mentions "a huge *lunshin* of bread"; *luncheon,* also spelled *lunchion,* is perhaps *lunching,* eating a slight meal. But there are other thoughts.

The first use of *lunch* is as a translation of Sp. *lonja,* a *noon* meal—which may therefore be the source. Certainly the form if not the meaning of *luncheon* (as it changed from a large *lump* of bread to a meal) is influenced by *nuncheon,* the much earlier word for *noon* meal. It is fancifully suggested that this is the *"noon shun",* resting and having a bite, in the shade, away from the heat of *noon,* like Sp. *siesta.* But *nuncheon* is from ME. *noneschench,* a *noon* draught, from AS. *scencan,* to pour out; OE. *skinker,* drawer of ale; Shakespeare (*I Henry* IV, II,iv,26) uses *"underskinker".* The verb is AS. *sceanc,* from *scanc,* whence Eng. *shank* —the *shank*-bone being used as a hollow pipe to stick in a bung-hole. Note that *nuncheon,* whence *luncheon,* was first an afternoon meal: *noon,* from L. *nona* (*hora*) the ninth hour, three p.m. *Siesta* is Sp., from L. *sexta* (*hora*), the sixth hour, twelve *noon.* Similarly, a *matinee* performance was first given in the morning, from Fr. *matinée,* from *matin,* morning; when the hour was changed, the name was kept. Church *matins* are from L. *matutinae vigiliae,* morning watches. *Matuta,* goddess of dawn (whence Eng. *matutinal*), from L. *maturus,* early, ripened, whence Eng. *mature. Cp. breviary.*

Lump is common Teut., from *lup, lub,* slow, heavy, whence *landlubber,* from *lap, to droop,* whence Eng. *lap. Cp. lampoon.*

Bump is imitative of the sound of a dull blow, then applied to the consequence. *Bunch* was first used of a *hump* (back), which is LG. *Humpel,* hillock, camel's *hump;* this replaced an earlier *crump*-backed (*crumpet,* a twisted cake, from AS. *crump,* crooked: "cow with the *crumpled* horn"; all *crumpled* up; whence the Eng. triplets *crump; crimp:* put a *crimp* in it; *cramp,* that doubles you up). Later, *bunch*-backed was replaced by 17th c. *hulch—, huck—, huckle—, hutch—,* finally *hunch*-backed. *Humped,* meaning downcast, is from the slump of a dispirited person (look at a camel's expression). To have a *hunch,* a lucky notion, is to have your back up: it was considered lucky to rub a person's *hunch*—streeet urchins still try to do it, before a fight.

lu[illegible].
See pylorus.

lurch.
See talc.

lure.
See entice.

lurk.
See talc.

luscious.
This word has grown roundabout. There was a ME. *licious,* aphetic for *delicious; cp. delight.* (Sometimes speech today shortens *delicious* to *'licious.*) But there was also Eng. *lush,* juicy, succulent; under the spell of this thought, the sense and sound of the other word moved along to *luscious.*

Lush itself is a variant of *lash,* loose, watery, via OFr. *lasche* from L. *laxus,* loose; whence our Eng. *laxative; cp. talc.* Often what's *luscious* must be followed by what's *laxative.*

lush.
See luscious.

lustre.
See limn.

lutecium.
See element.

—ly.
See like.

lyceum.
See Platonic.

lynch.
This is short for *Lynch* law, or *Lynch's* law. There are several claimants for the dubious honor of the origin. A Capt. *William Lynch* was said to have taken matters into his own hands, in 1776; a justice of the peace *Charles Lynch* is accused of the same procedure, about 1780. Both these men were Virginians; South Carolina enters the contest with *Lynch's Creek,* where ca. 1770 the "Regulators" used to meet. It is high time that the word became purely historical.

lysol.
This was originally coined as a trade name, from Gr. *lysis,* a loosening (L. *laxus;* Eng. *lax; cp. talc*) + *—ol,* a suffix, pertaining to *oil.* Eng. *lysis* is used as a technical term in architecture and medicine; and *—lysis* is a combining form in scientific terms, as *electrolysis,* loosening or decomposing by *electricity.*

M

macabre.

This word, most often used of the *dance macabre*, may be (as the NED suggests) from OFr. *macabré*, from *Maccabé*: the dance of the *Maccabees*. If so, the mood would rise not from *Judas Maccabeus* but from his distant descendants of the Herod line. Herodias, you may remember, had married her uncle; then her brother-in-law, another Herod, already married, put aside his wife and took Herodias; to all of this John the Baptist vehemently objected. Therefore, when upon Herod's birthday Herodias' daughter (by the first Herod) danced before her step-father, and he in his delight promised her whatever she wished, at her mother's instigation Salome said (*St. Mark*, 6, *St. Matthew*, 14): "Give me here John Baptist's head in a charger."

Since the notion is that the word *macabre* is from the Hebrew, note however that Heb. *kaber* meant to bury; and that Heb. *m'*— is a prefix with the sense, pertaining to. There is nonetheless something *macabre* in the result of Salome's dance of the seven veils.

There are, however, many medieval representations of the *chorea Machabaeorum*, the dance of the seven martyred Maccabee brothers in *Maccabees II* of the *Apocrypha;* this, more soberly, is the likely source of the word. (Note also that, in Arabic, *magbarah* means cemetery).

macadamize.

See Appendix II.

macaroni.

The It. *maccheroni* (*maccaroni*) was a mixture of meal, eggs, and cheese. Hence *macaronic* verse, that written in a mixture of a modern tongue and Latin, or in a vernacular with Latin endings; the form and the name were first used in 1517, by Teofilo Folengo, called Merlinus Coccaius. In the late 18th c., some Eng. fops formed the *Macaroni Club*, affecting to despise native cooking; hence, the *macaroni* of Yankee Doodle Dandy. The familiar *spaghetti* is a diminutive of It. *spago*, cord. *Vermicelli* is the diminutive ending to L. *vermis*, worm. Hence also *vermilion*, applied to the little cochineal, the source of the dye.

Macaroni, hence also the cake *macaroon*, of a crushed paste, may come from It. *maccare*, to pound—possibly related to Gr. *makaris*, barley broth.

macaroon.

See macaroni.

Machiavellian.

This term for cynical and shrewd seeking of one's end by any helpful means is from *Niccolo di Bernardo dei Machiavelli*, d. 1527, who enunciated such principles in his famous book *The Prince*, 1513. Many from his day to ours have sought to apply them.

mackinaw.

See Appendix II.

mackintosh.

See Appendix II. The apple is *Mc Intosh*, in the same *Appendix*.

macrobian.

The prefix Gr. and Eng. *macro*—, long, large, is used in a number of Eng. words. Thus *macrocosm* is sometimes used of the entire ordered universe (Gr. *cosmos*, order; *cp. police*), as opposed to its epitome in the *microcosm*, man. Also *macrometer;* and *macroscope*, vs. *microscope; cp. microphone*—which, however, is balanced by a word using another Gr. and Eng. prefix, *mega*—, as also in *megalithic* (Gr. *lithos*, stone); *megalo*— is likewise used, as in *megalosaur* (Gr. *sauros*, lizard; *cp. dinosaur*); *megavolt*.

From Gr. *bios*, life, whence Eng. *biology*, is formed *macrobian*, relating to long life. May you be *macrobian!*

macrocosm.

See macrobian.

madame, madamoiselle.
See damsel.

made.
See ache.

madras.
See cloth.

maelstrom.
See immolate.

magazine.
This word, meaning a storehouse (Fr. *magasin*, from OSp. *magacen*, from Arab. *makhāzin*, plural of *makhzan*, from *khazana*, to store up) as in powder *magazine*, was a frequent title of 18th c. books, as a storehouse of information. By midcentury it was applied to periodicals, which gradually monopolized the term. (Many words from Arab. retain the article *al*, the: this word does in the Sp. form *almacén* and the Port. *armazem*.)

magistrate.
See month: May.

magnate.
See tycoon; month: May.

magnesium, magnet, magnetic.
See element; *Appendix II*.

magnolia.
See Appendix II.

magpie.
See pie.

maharajah.
See island.

mail.
This one word is from at least four sources. As in *blackmail* it is from OE. *mael*, speech, agreement. "White rent" was paid in silver; *blackmail* was paid in labor or cattle, for an agreement not to plunder (esp. along the Scottish border). As in coat of *mail*, it comes from Fr. *maille*, from L. *macula*, spot (Eng. *immaculate*, spotless), then mesh of a net. As in the postman's bag, it is from OFr. *male* (Fr. *malle*, trunk) OHG. *malaha*, leather pouch. In the 17th c., one spoke of a *mail* of letters; gradually the one term stood for the whole.
An older Eng. *mail* (17th c., as The *Mail*, now The *Mall*, London) is from Fr. *mail*, from L. *malleus*, hammer (Eng. *mallet*, also *mall*, whence *maul*), applied as the name of a game, also called *pall-mall* (It. *pallamaglio*, from *palla*, from *balla*, *ball* + *maglio*, from *malleus*). This was pronounced *pell-mell* in 17th c. England; the name was transferred from the game to the alley in which it was played, then to the street in London (*cp. Bowling Green*, New York City). The pleasant confusion of the popular game (and of the street, the hub of London club life) led to the sense of confusion, everything *pell-mell* —though some trace this, by a rhyming repetition (as in pitter-patter, helter-skelter, etc.) to Fr. *meler*, to mix, mingle. Certainly the meanings of *mail* have mingled!

Maine.
See States.

majesty, major, majority.
See month: May.

make.
See ache.

mal—.
The L. word *male*, ill (Fr. *mal*) came into English as a prefix. Obvious in such words as *maladjustment*, *maladroit*, *malcontent*, it is present also in such words as *malady* and *malign*.
Malady is via Fr. *maladie* from L. *male habens*, the translation of Gr. *kakos exon*; thus Eng. *cachexy*, from Gr. *kakos* bad, + *exis*, condition, from *exein*, to have.
Malign, and *malignant* are formed like the antonym *benign*: L. *bene*, well + *genus*, variety, kind, from *gignere*, *gen*, to beget.

malapropism.
See Appendix II.

male.
See marshal.

malediction.
See verdict.

malfeasance.
See defeat.

malign, malignant.
See mal—.

mallet.
See mail.

mamma, mammal.
See abbot; *cp.* brassiere.

manage.
See chichevache.

—mancy.
For varieties of divination, *see* necromancy.

mandate.
See command.

manganese.
See element.

mania.
See necromancy. From one divinely inspired, this word has lapsed to indicate any frenzy, especially a mad desire. It is combined in such forms as *dipsomania* (Gr. *dipso—*, from *dipsa,* thirst) and *kleptomaniac* (Gr. *kleptes,* thief).

manilla.
See Appendix II.

manipulation.
See manœuvre.

manna.
When the Israelites looked upon the food that the Lord had dropped from the heavens, they said (*Exodus,* xvi,15) "What is this?"—for they wist not what it was. In Aram. *man hu,* what is it? And the early Eng. bibles kept the original words, thus creating it *manna.* But note that the sap of the tamarisk plant is Gr. *manna,* from Heb. *man,* from Arab. *mann.*

manner.
See manœuvre.

manoeuvre.
Military *manœuvres* may include many operations; the term has become general by extension from one class of operation: that performed by hand (from Fr., from LL. *manoperare,* from L. *manu operari,* to work by hand). Much earlier into the language, applied to farming, the chief type of hand-work, the same word came in the form of *manure,* which from tillage in general came to refer to fertilizing, mixing by hand. (The same ending is in the word *inure,* from *in,* into + OE. *ure,* work, from OFr. *uevre,* from L. *opera,* work.) *Manipulation* is from L. *manipulus,* handful, from *manus,* hand + *plere, plet—,* to fill; *cp. foil.* (The verb *manipulate* was formed from the noun.) The *manner* of doing something is via Fr. *manière,* from LL. *manuarius,* belonging to the hand. *Manual,* both as a handbook, and in *manual* labor, is from the same source. *Emancipate* is a bit more roundabout, dating from the days when the parent had power over the son: only the head of the family could acquire property: L. *manceps, mancip—,* one that acquires property, from *manu* + *capere, capt—,* to take by hand (whence also *capture, captivate,* etc. *Captive* and *caitiff* are doublets, from L. *captivus,* from *capt—. Captain* is from quite other source; *see achieve.*): *ex,* out, whence *emancipare, emancipat—,* to take from the property holder.

The tongs with which (first) the smith picked up hot metals were L. *forceps,* from *formus,* hot + *capere,* to take; also thence Eng. *forceps.* The L. *incipere, incept—* was equivalent to Eng. undertake, to begin; hence Eng. *incipient* and *inceptive;* for *recipient* and more, *see recipe.*

mansard (roof).
See Appendix II.

mansion.
See remnant.

mantel.
This word is a variant of *mantle, q.v.*

mantis.
See necromancy.

mantle.
There was probably some early L. word for cloak, surviving or reformed in the Sp. *manto,* cloak; in L. this appears only in the diminutive *mantelum, mantellum,* cloak, cover. This came into OE. *mantel,* whence Eng. *mantle.* It traveled also via the Romance tongues, and in the 12th c. was reborrowed from Fr. into Eng. as *mantel.* The word meant a cloak, but also a wooden shelter, as for men-at-arms attacking a walled place; the Fr. form has kept the second sense, as also in *mantelshelf, mantelpiece.* There also developed the further diminutives *mantelet, mantlet;* and the later Fr. *manteau* was used as an Eng. word in the 17th c. There also developed the form *mantua,* by connection with the city in north Italy; there are likewise a *mantua* gown, *mantua* silk; and *Mantuan* may mean relating to the classical poet Virgil, who was

born in *Mantua*. The word *mantle* came to mean any cover, as in the verb: a blush *mantled* her face.

mantua.
See mantle.

manual.
See manœuvre.

manufacture.
See mastiff.

manure.
See manœuvre.

manuscript.
See shrine.

map.
Just as a *cartoon* (from Fr. *carton*, from It. *cartone*, augmentative of *carta*, *card*; whence both *card* and *carton*) was first something drawn on a *card*, so a *map* was something drawn on cloth, from L. *mappa*, loincloth. Made from clout-rags was the *mop*, a doublet of *map*—although the suggestion is made that the 15th c. *mappe*, *mop*, is short for *mapple*, from *Mabel*, as a general name of a housemaid. There is a 17th c. *mob*, neglige dress, then disreputable woman; also an 18th c. *mob-cap*, a cloth cap, both of which are from L. *mappa*; *cp*. *mob*.

marabou.
See maravedi.

marathon.
This race (approximately 24 miles; but loosely applied to any long distance event) draws its name from the city of *Marathon*, about that far from Athens. When the Greeks defeated the Persians there, in 490 B.C., the runner Pheidippides brought back the news—so swiftly that after telling it he dropped dead. Browning, in his poem *Phedippides*, tells the story.

maravedi.
This Spanish coin (in gold, worth about $3.50; in copper, about one-third of a cent, and mentioned by Sir W. Scott and Sir W. S. Gilbert) was named from the ruling (Arabian) dynasty at Cordova (1087-1147) that coined it, the *Almoravides*, from Arab. *al Murabitin*, the Hermits, from *murābit*, hermit. The fine feathers milady used to wear, of the *marabou*, draw their name from the same source. The Arabs called the stork the hermit bird, from its appearance and its solitary ways.

marcel.
See Appendix II.

March.
See month.

mare.
See marshal.

marge, margin.
See mark.

marigold.
See primrose.

marinated (herring), marine, marital, maritime.
See lapis lazuli.

mark.
This word, OE. *mearc*, originally meant a boundary; then, a sign of a boundary; then, any sign, hence an impression. It is cognate with L. *margo*, *margin*—, whence Eng. *margin*, which has kept the basic meaning. For a time, in the 17th c., *margin* was given the fancier ending *margent*; *cp*. hold; hence also Eng. *marge*.

maroon.
The escaped slaves of the West Indies were called Sp. *cimarron*, wild. The Fr. (possibly mistaking this for *ces marrons*: *ces*, these) shortened it to *marron*. Since these fugitive slaves roamed the desert islands, the English applied the term, *maroon*, to men put ashore on such islands. The color *maroon* is from Fr. *marron*, from It. *marrone*, chestnut.

marron.
See castanet, maroon.

marry.
See lapis lazuli.

marsh.
See primrose.

marshal.
This man has risen in rank; originally he was a horse-tender (from Fr. *maréchal*, from OHG. *marah*, horse + *scalh*, servant). The feminine of *marah*, whence AS. *mearh*, was AS. *mere*, which

gives us *mare*. Nonetheless, the Teut. kings considered the *marshall* their chief household officer; his title was translated into LL. as count of the stable, *comes stabuli*, whence Eng. *constable*.

Bad dreams were attributed, in the middle ages, to several causes. There was, of course, the *nightmare*, that bore folk off on a hideous ride; also, AS. *mare* was a demon, from Sansk. *mara*, destroyer, from *mar*, to crush. Shakespeare, *King Lear* III,iv, speaks of "the *nightmare* and her nine foals." Women were especially troubled by an *incubus*, a male demon that sought to lie with them (L. *incubare, incubat—*, to lie on, whence Eng. *incubate*, to lie on eggs to hatch them; *incubation*, the hatching of a disease; *incubator*); there were laws covering the *incubus*, in the dark ages. The word is now extended to any heavy burden. Men were conversely troubled by a *succubus* (L. *succuba*, strumpet, from *sub, suc*, under + *cumbere*, from *cubare*, to lie. Whence also, Eng. *succumb*). Perhaps these were even worse than Freud!

We are told, incidentally, that there were more *feminine* than *masculine* witches—the word first referred to either sex, but from their preponderance became exclusively *feminine* — because *feminine* means lacking faith in God, from *fe* (It., from L. *fide*) faith, + *minus*, without [L. *femina* is actually related to *fellare*, to suckle, and *filius*, son, whence Eng. *filial*. *Masculus* is a diminutive of L. *mas*, male, whence OFr. *masle*, whence Fr. *mâle*, whence Eng. *male*. *Neuter* is L. *ne*, not + *uter* either, not either (gender); hence Eng. *neutral*, not of either side.]

martial, martinet.
See month: March.

martyr.
One suspected of witchcraft might be given the ordeal by fire, or the water-test: put her in, if she lives, it's proof the devil is helping her, therefore she must be killed. Death is witness to her innocence. Similarly, the death of the *martyr* is witness (Gr. *martys, martyr—*, witness) to the glory of the Lord.

Marxist.
See Appendix II.

Maryland.
See States.

masculine.
See lapis lazuli; marshal.

mash.
See knick-knack. *Mash* is a brewing term, akin to G. *Maisch*, crushed grapes; and to *mix*.

masochist.
See sadist.

mass.
This was originally a lump of dough, from Fr. *masse*, from L. *massa*, from Gr. *maza*, from *Heb. matzah*. The circular flat cake of the sacrament of Mithra was *mizd*; the cake in the rites of Osiris, *mest*. This sense may have influenced the religious meaning of *mass*, which is commonly traced through AS. *maesse* to L. *missa*, as used in *Ite, missa est*, that closes the service. (Why should the *mass* take its name from the words that announce it's over?) *See* mess, zymurgy.

Massachusetts.
See States.

master.
See mystery; month: May.

mastery.
See mystery.

masticate.
We use this word for chewing well; but its origin shows us that the subways did not first give vogue to the gum-chewer. For the word (LL. *masticare, masticat—*, to chew *mastic*) is from Gr. *mastiche, mastic*, a resin now used mainly for making varnish, but which was used as a chewing-gum in Greece and Turkey. But *see whip*.

mastiff.
This was originally, belike, "he who gets slapped". It is from OFr. *mastin*, first a house servant, then a house dog; from a LL. form *mansuetinus*, from *mansuescere, mansuet—*, to grow used to the hand. (Applied to the dog, the hand might be for petting.) The present form of *mastiff* is shaped by the influence of OFr. *mestif*, mongrel, from LL. *mixtivus*, from L. *mixere, mixt—*, *cp. ache*.

The inceptive root in *mansuescere* (L. *manu—*, hand, as in *manufacture*; L. *facere, fact—*, to make; *cp. affect, manoeuvre*), *suescere, suet—*, is also found in L. *desuescere, desuet—*, to grow out of using; and in L. *consuescere, consuet—*, to grow accustomed. There was, from the L. noun form, an early Eng. *consuetude*, which has lapsed into innocuous *desuetude*.

L. *suescere, suet—* is cognate with AS. *sidu*, custom; Gr. *ethos*, character; from Sansk. *svadha*, will, custom; and indeed anthropologists state that ethics is determined by custom.

mastodon.
See indenture.

mastoid.
This has nothing to do with the ear, but means shaped like a breast, from Gr. *mastos*, breast. The *mastoid process*, however, is a nipple-shaped bone in the skull. *Mastodynia* is a disease of the breast; *mastoiditis*, in the head.

masurium.
See element.

mat.
See volume. A floor *mat* is direct (OE. *matt*), from L. *matta*.

match.
See ache.

material, materiel.
See irrelevant, matter.

mathematics.
Many a drudging schoolboy will recognize that you must be disposed to learning if you are to master *mathematics*. The word itself warns those that read it: from Gr. *mathematikos*, disposed to learning, from *manthanein*, to learn. The early learning, being concerned chiefly with surveying (as after the Nile floods) and calculation of the calendar (*cp. scholar*), produced the limited sense of the word.

matinee.
See luncheon.

matins.
See bull.

matriculate.
See volume.

matrimony.
See morganatic.

matrix.
See volume.

matter.
This word, via Fr. *matière* from L. *materia*, stuff of which things are made, is perhaps thus to be traced to L. *mater*, mother, mother-stuff. Hence also, *matter*, the pus in a sore. Also the *material* of which things are made. This is via the L. adjective *materialis*. Since the mother-stuff is essential, we have the sense as in *material* witness, and it *matters* very much to me—though this is more often used in the negative. It doesn't *matter*.

In the early 19th c., the Fr. form *matériel* came into Eng. army talk, used of supplies, in contrast to *personnel*, manpower.

mattress.
In the east, the bed was on the floor. The "place where things are thrown down", then esp. where the bedstuffs were laid, is Arab *matrah*, from *tarha*, to throw. From this, via OFr. *materas*, comes our *mattress*. The more luxurious *sofa* is directly from Arab. *suffah*.

mature, matutinal.
See luncheon.

matzah.
See mass, zymurgy.

maudlin.
Mary Magdalen (of *Magdala*) having fallen at the feet of Jesus, wept, and repented, her name, *Magdalen*, is used as a general name for a repentant (woman) sinner. Since she is pictured as weeping, the Eng. corruption of her name, *maudlin*, has taken this sense.

maul.
See mail.

mausoleum.
The Egyptians have the reputation of building the most elaborate tombs, the pyramids; indeed, each Pharaoh's chief work was to build his own tomb. But in Halicarnassus, in the 4th c. B.C., Artemisia built such a magnificent tomb to her late husband, King *Mausolos*, that all elaborate tombs since have taken his name. (It crumbled in an earthquake, in 1375, having stood almost 1800 years.)

maverick.
It was unnecessary for *Samuel Maverick*, Texan rancher about 1840, to brand his calves, because they pastured on an island. From this practice, the

word applied to the unbranded calf was extended to politicians, esp. congressmen, that wear no party label.

maxim.
This is a shortening of L. *maxima propositio,* greatest statement, *i.e.*, general truth. For *maxim* gun, *see Appendix II.*

May.
See month.

mayonnaise.
See Appendix II.

mazda.
Men were so pleased with this improvement in lighting that they named it from the good principle (*mazda, Ormuzd*) in the ancient Persian religion, as in the *Avesta.*

mazurka.
See Appendix II.

mead.
See drink.

meal.
See immolate. The *meal* you enjoy eating is from AS *mael,* measure, point of time; *i.e.,* you eat at an appointed time.

mealy-mouthed.
This unpleasant characteristic was once quite the reverse. For *mealy-mouthed,* earlier *meal-mouthed,* is honey-mouthed. The Aryan word for honey is widespread: L. *mel;* Gr. *meli;* Goth. *milith.* This appears also in *mildew,* from AS. *meledeaw,* honey-dew — now reserved for a melon; but Coleridge ended Kubla Khan with the lines:

> For he on honey-dew hath fed,
> And drunk the milk of Paradise.

The term honey-dew, mildew, for decay is based partly on the appearance of the mould, and partly on folk euphemism: call the evil fairies the good folk, and they'll spare you.

Although *honey* was not an early word, OE. *hunig* (G. *Honig*) replacing Goth. *milith,* the *bee* was common Teut., AS. *beo.* Note that Swift's remark (in *Battle of the Books,* 1697, pub. 1704) that the *bee* gives us *honey* and *wax,* "thus furnishing mankind with the two noblest of things, which are sweetness and light", is developed by Matthew Arnold (in *Culture and Anarchy,* 1869) as a symbol of the contribution of the artist.

mean.
This is several words; but first some that look like it must be distinguished. *Demean* and *demeanor* are from Fr. *démener,* from *de,* down + *mener,* to lead, from L. *minari,* to threaten: the idea seems to be that if you threatened someone, he did as you wanted: the word was used of driving cattle. Thus from the same word, with prefix *a,* from *ad,* to, comes *amenable,* easily led. Similarly, *tractable* means easily drawn; *cp. distraction. Amenity,* however, is from Fr. *aménité,* from L. *amœnitas, amœnitat*—, pleasantness, calm, from *a,* without + *mœnia,* wall, rampart, *i.e.,* unthreatened. And *demesne* is a doublet of *domain,* from ME. *demein,* from OFr. *demeine,* from L. *dominium; see dome.*

Mean, meaning *medium,* also of *medium* value hence mediocre, is a doublet of *median,* from LL. *medianus,* from L. *medius,* middle, from Ayran root that gave AS. *midd,* whence Eng. *mid* and *middle. Mean,* common, is from OE. *gemaene,* of the many, a common Teut. word, related to L. *communis, common; cp. immunity.* To *mean,* to have *meaning,* is a common Ayran form: AS. *maenan;* OHG. *gimunt*—to have the *mind* on: AS. *gemynd;* L. *mens, ment*—, *mind;* whence *mental,* etc.; Sansk. *manas;* G. *Minne,* love; whence *Minnesinger,* singer of love; ON. *minni,* memory; Gr. *mnemon, mindful;* whence *mnemonic; cp. amnesty. Memory* is the mother of the muses.

meander.
There is a river, called the *Meander,* in Asia Minor, of which Ovid wrote: "The limpid *Meander* sports in the Phrygian fields; it flows backwards and forwards in its varying course and, meeting itself, beholds its waters that are to follow, until it fatigues its wandering current, now pointing to its source, and now to the open sea." Do you wonder that we speak of *meandering?*

measure.
See taxi.

Mecca.
See hegira.

meddle, median, mediate.
See immunity.

medicine.
See doctor.

medium.
One who comes in the middle, between you and the spirit world. Her success is less than *medium. See* immunity.

meerschaum.
This term for a light clay, used for tobacco pipes, is G. *Meerschaum,* seafoam (Eng. *mere* and *scum*). Being an odd word, it has developed a story. A certain German, Herr *Kummer,* made such pipes; in France, they were called *pipes de Kummer.* To the French, this sounded like *pipe d'écume de mer,* pipes of seafoam. This was then retranslated into the German. In fact, the French and the German translate an earlier Persian, *kaf-i-daryâ,* sea-foam.

megalithic.
See macrobian.

megaphone.
See microphone.

melancholic, melancholy, Melanchthon.
See complexion; element: bismuth.

Melba (toast).
See Appendix II.

mellifluous, mellow.
See amalgam.

melon.
See peach.

melt.
See omelette.

memory.
L. *memor,* mindful, developed the noun *memoria,* whence Eng. *memory* and Fr. *mémoire,* Eng. *memoir. Cp. amnesty.*

menagerie.
See chichevache.

Mendelian.
See Appendix II.

mental.
See mean, vehicle.

menthol.
See fee.

mentor.
This friend of Odysseus, *Mentor,* gets credit that's not his due: Pallas Athene, goddess of wisdom, assumed his form when she served as a guide to Telemachus, son of Odysseus, *q.v.*

menu.
See meticulous.

mercenary, mercer, mercerize, merchant.
See soldier.

mercurial.
See saturnine.

mercury.
See element; hermetical; Appendix II.

mercy.
This word is from L. *merces, merced—,* reward; *cp. soldier.* But in church Latin (The Lord have *mercy* on my soul!) it was used of the reward in heaven for those that helped persons that could not repay them on earth; by transfer it was then applied to the act in this world that was to win the Lord's favor hereafter.

mere.
See primrose. *Mere,* as an adjective (it's a *mere* trifle) was originally an intensifying word, from L. *merus,* pure, unmixed. Similarly, *quite,* as in *quite* so, means altogether: it is a doublet of *quit,* from L. *quietus,* discharged, set at peace (whence Eng. *quittance*); and the word *very* has almost lost its force: "I'm *very* glad to meet you" often seems less sincere than "I'm glad to meet you." *Very* meant truly, from ME. *verrai,* from OFr. *verai,* from LL. *verax, verac—,* whence Eng. *veracious,* from L. *verus,* true. Thus *verily* means truly. There was an old Eng. *veriloquous,* which meant, not talking very much, but speaking the truth.

meretricious.
See soldier.

meridian.
See posthumous. From the sense of noon, *meridian* came to mean the highest point of the sun's journey through the sky; thence, a great circle of the terrestrial globe.

meringue.
See Appendix II.

merit.
See soldier.

merry.
See lapis lazuli. *Merry England,* despite "God rest you *merry,* gentlemen" and other associations, draws the adjective from AS. *maera,* famous. A *merry Andrew,* clown, may be traced to the eccentricities of *merry* (famous) *Andrew Borde,* physician to Henry VIII of England.

mesa.
See mess.

meshuga.
See cider.

meso—, Mesopotamia.
See mess.

mess.
This first meant what was put on the table, as a *mess* of fish, a *mess* of pottage; thus *mess hall, officers' mess*—not from Sp. *mesa,* table, used in Eng. of a plateau, table-land, from L. *mensa;* nor from Gr. *mesŏs,* middle, from which the frequent Eng. prefix *meso—,* as in *mesozoic, Mesopotamia* (Gr. *potamos,* water; thus *hippopotamus,* water-horse) — but from OFr. *mettre, mes,* to send, to put (whence Eng. *message*), from L. *mittere, miss—,* to send, to put. From this source also come *mission; admit,* to send to, hence to let in and, figuratively, to acknowledge; *dismiss* (L. *dis,* away); *commit,* to put together (for safety), to entrust with a duty; *commissary; commission, q.v., premiss, premise* (L. *propositio praemissa*), that which is put before; *permit,* to send through, etc.

From the fact that things are often put down confusedly comes the other sense of *mess,* mix up. To *muss* is American for *mess,* though probably a mid 19th c. revival of an old Eng. variant, for around 1590 *muss* was a game in which small objects were thrown down and scrambled for . . . One should not make a *mess* of a *mission.*

message, messenger.
See mess, pass, trespass.

Messiah.
See criss-cross.

metabolism.
See parlor.

metal.
This is rather directly from Gr. *metallon,* mine, from Gr. *metallan,* to seek after, to explore. But this is probably a verb + the prefix *meta—,* used in many Gr. and Eng. words, with the senses of beside, across, after, beyond, and the like. Hence *metamorphosis* (Gr. *morphe,* shape); *metaphor* (Gr. *pherein,* to bear). *Metaphysics* indicated the (thirteen) books of Aristotle after those dealing with physics; their subject matter made it easy for this to shift its sense, as though the term meant (as it thus came to mean) beyond the physical.

metaphysics.
See metal.

metathesis.
See Spoonerism.

meteor.
The Gr. *meteora,* atmospheric phenomena, is from *meteoros,* raised up, from *meta—,* beyond (*cp. metal*), + *eor,* from *aeirein,* to lift; whence also *aerial; cp. debonair.*

Medieval natural history distinguished four types of such phenomena. *Aerial meteors* were winds. *Aqueous* (*cp. duke*) *meteors* were rain, snow, dew. *Luminous* (L. *lumen, lumini—,* light, cognate with L. *lux, luc—; cp. lamp*) *meteors* included the rainbow, the halo. And *igneous* (L. *ignis,* fire; hence *ignite;* LL. *ignis fatuus,* foolish fire, will o' the wisp) or fiery *meteors* were the lightning and the "shooting stars"—we reserve the name for these last; fragments that land on the earth are *meteorites.*

meteorite.
See meteor.

meticulous.
The person that is so afraid of going wrong that he pores over every detail of his work is well called *meticulous* (L. *meticulosus,* the ending *osus,* full of, the diminutive *ul,* added to *metus,* fear: full of little fears). *Timid, timidity* are from L. *timidus,* fearful, from *timor,* fear, from *timere,* to be afraid. (*Timorous* is as though from a L. *timorosus,* which does not exist.) *Timor* is traced to Sansk. *tamas,* darkness, from *tam,* to be breathless, to choke—which is a symptom of fear. To make

someone afraid is to *intimidate* him. Sansk. *tamas* also leads to L. *tenebrae,* darkness, whence *tenebrosus,* gloomy, whence Eng. *tenebrous;* akin to the Sansk. *tam* is Eng. *dim.*

Diminish, however, is from the older Eng. *minish* (L. *di, dis,* apart, with intensive force), from L. *minuta,* small, whence Fr. *menu,* a small portion; *minuet,* a dance with short steps, from *minuere, minut—,* to make small. The comparative of the adj. small, L. *minor, minus,* gives us directly a *minor,* and the *minus* sign. *Minute,* meaning tiny, was first in Eng. pronounced precisely like *minute,* a small measure of time or space. The meaning of *menu* may come, not from the size of the portion, but from the fact that the separate details of the meal are listed.

metropolis.
See police.

mew, mewl, mews, miaow, miaul.
See mute.

mho.
See Appendix II.

mica.
See isinglass.

Michigan.
See States.

microbe.
See microphone.

microcosm.
See macrobian.

microphone.
In the Gr. alphabet, the letter *o* occurs twice, with separate symbols: *omicron* and *omega*—which mean, respectively, *little o* and *big o,* like *Big Klaus* and *Little Klaus* in the tale. Thus *megaphone* means big talk (loud speaker); but *microphone* (a much more recent word) takes little talk and makes it big. This word was earlier (ca. 1890) *microaudiphone,* for hearing little sounds. There is also a patented instrument, *Magnavox,* which comes not from Gr. but from L. *magna,* great + *vox, voc—,* voice; *cp. entice.* A *micrometer* is for measuring small things (from *micro* + *meter,* measure). A *microbe* is a small particle of life (Gr. *bios,* life; whence *biology; cp. logistics*). There are many more. *Alpha* is the first leter, and *omega* the last, of the Gr. alphabet; hence, *from alpha to omega* means from start to finish, from soup to nuts—which you can get via the *microphone.*

mid.
See mean.

Midas.
See schlemihl.

middle.
See mean.

mid-Victorian.
See victoria.

midwife.
There is a spelling of this, *meedwife,* as though the woman were there for the *meed* or reward involved. It is much more properly the natural helpfulness of women in the hour of need: *midwife* is the *with-wife* (G. *mit*), ready to help. *Wife* is the feminine form, changed from the AS. *midwyrhta, with-wright,* a co-worker or assistant. The Romans had exactly the same feeling, whence L. *obstetrix,* the feminine ending on L. *obstitere, obstet—,* to stand by; whence our more formal *obstetrician*—who turns out to be just a *midwife* after all!

migrate.
See immunity.

mildew.
See mealy-mouthed.

mile.
This is a word direct (AS. *mīl*) from L. *milia,* plural of *mille,* a thousand (paces). The Roman *mile* was 1,618 yards; our own, 1,760. Break this down into paces, and you'll see the sense of the saying, "There were giants in those days"—until you bring the step back to normal by counting the Roman pace as the movement from one foot until that foot moves again.

Millennium (L. *mille* + *annus,* year), the thousandth year, was the time when the world was expected to come to an end. A *millepede* (*pes, ped—,* foot; *cp. pedagogue*) is a thousand-legger. *Million* and *milliard* are numbers coined from *mille.*

mill.
See immolate; dollar.

millennium, millepede.
See mile.

milliner.
In the 16th century much of the English finery was imported from Milan; especially bonnets, ribbons, gloves. A *Milaner,* whence Eng. *milliner,* was a dealer in such articles; then particularly a maker of hats.

million.
See mile, number.

millrace.
See racy.

mind.
See immunity; mean.

mingle.
See mongrel.

miniature.
This brings to mind a small picture, as though the word were related to L. *minor, minus,* less. But originally the word had nothing to do with the size; it is from It. *miniare, miniat—,* to paint with red lead, *minium.* The sound of the word altered the sense.

minister.
See month: May; mystery.

Minnesinger.
See mean.

Minnesota.
See States.

minority.
See month: May.

Minotaur.
See Europe.

mint.
See calamity, fee.

minuet, minute.
See meticulous.

mirror.
See emir.

mirth.
See lapis lazuli.

mischief.
See abuse.

miscreant.
Those that fashion words are often drawn into self-betrayal, or at least self-portraiture. If a man does not agree with you, he is obviously a wretch; thus the present sense of *miscreant,* from OFr. *mescreant,* present particple of *mescreire,* from L. *miscredere,* from *mis* (AS. *mis—,* whence Eng. *miss* confused with OFr. *mes,* from L. *minus*), away, awry + *credere, credit—,* believe, whence Eng. *credit.* The term, as Unbeliever, was first applied to the Saracens, then to rascals in general. *See agnostic.*

miser.
It is fit that we picture the *miser* as one wretched (L. *miser,* whence *miserable*) in the midst of plenty. The word probably took this meaning by joining an OE. *micher,* "a rich man that pretends to be very poor", from OE. *myche,* from OFr. *miche,* from L. *mica,* crumb; thus, a man that gives out bread not piecemeal but "crumbmeal".

miserable.
See miser.

miss.
See miscreant. *Miss,* short for *mistress,* is from OFr. *maistresse,* feminine of *maitre,* whence Eng. *master, mister,* from L. *magister,* from *magis* (old simple form of the comparative *maior,* replaced in classical L. by *magnus*); whence Eng. *magistrate; cp. month:* May. L. *maior,* superior, gives us both *major* and *mayor.*

missile, mission, missionary, missive.
See compromise, mess.

Mississippi.
See States.

Missouri.
See States.

mist.
See mistletoe.

mister.
See mystery.

mistletoe.
Why do we connect the *mistletoe* and Christmas? When we speak of a white Christmas, we must note that of course the sun is then obscured; Balder, the Norse sun-god, was killed with a twig of the *mistletoe.* The *toe* is from AS.

tan, twig, with the *n* dropped because later it was thought to mark the plural and thus be unnecessary (plural as in *children, oxen,* etc.). AS. *mistel* is a diminutive of *mist,* which is still Eng. for fog—but in G. *mist* means dung: the root is Teut. *migh,* to sprinkle, referring either to fine rain or to urine. (No direct connection with pessi*mist, q.v.*) The plant *mistletoe* is named, perhaps from the legend that it grew from bird-droppings, perhaps from the glue, or bird-lime, the berries contain: ODu. *mistel,* bird-lime.

mistress.
See mystery.

misuse.
See abuse; urn.

mix, mixo—, mixture.
See ache.

mnemonic.
"Except February, which, in fine
Has 28, in Leap Year, 29."
See amnesty.

mob.
In the late 17th c. it became fashionable to speak in fragments of words, much as now we speak of new projects by their initials. Thus *mob* is an abbreviation of L. *mobile vulgus,* the fickle throng. *Cp. chum.* Note that *vulgus.* first meaning the *common* (people); still, in *vulgar* fraction, was soon (by the supposedly educated) given its present sense, in *vulgar. Common* itself was likewise corrupted by those that did not vote in the House of *Commons.* The *Vulgate* bible (Jerome's version, 4th c.) was one made *common,* from L. *vulgare, vulgat—.* For *common,* see *community. Cp. map.*

mock.
This word comes via It. *moccare* from LL. form *muccare,* to wipe the nose; the gesture was taken as a sign of scorn. The verb is from LL. *muccus,* from L. *mucus,* Eng. *mucus;* the adjective appears in Eng. *mucous* membrane. Gr. forms are *mykton,* nose; *myxa,* slime; *cp. ache.* There is also Eng. *muck,* from *muk,* mire, manure, related to OTeut. *meuk,* soft. A man that (figuratively) pokes around in the slime is a *muckraker.* The libertine *rake,* by the way, is short for *rakehellion* or *rakehell,* perhaps by folk-etymology from ME. *rakel, reckless. Reck,* AS. *reccan* (+ —*los,* without), meaning to consider, is a variant of *reckon,* AS. *gerecenian,* to count, AS. *racu,* account; the word is related to the garden *rake* (AS. *raca;* common Teut.) in the basic sense of heaping, bringing together. If you *mock* the *muckraker,* there may be a *reckoning!*

mode, model, moderate, modest, modulate.
See accommodate.

mohair.
See cloth.

moire, moiré.
These words, borrowed from Fr., were taken into Fr. from Eng. *mohair,* earlier *mocayare; cp. cloth. Mohair* became Fr. *mouaire,* hence *moire;* the word was applied to a *mohair* cloth of a "watered" appearance. Then the Fr. developed a verb, *moirer,* to water cloth, the past participle of which, *moiré,* watered, became itself the name of a material.

moist.
The invitation to wet your lips is implicit in this word, from OFr. *moiste,* from L. *musteus,* juicy, *musty,* from L. *musteus,* new wine. The word, however, may come via medieval consideration of hot, cold, dry, and wet—indicating something that is none of these, but L. *mixtus, mixed,* whence OFr. *moiste,* whence Eng. *moist.*

molar.
See immolate.

molasses.
See amalgam.

mollify.
See omelette.

molybdenum.
See element.

moment, momentum.
See mute.

monarch, monastery.
See monk.

Monday.
See week.

monetary, money.
See fee.

monger.

This word has not suffered a lapse; from its earliest days it was a sign of contempt—but in early days the nobles held all traders in scorn. *Monger* is from AS. *mangian,* to trade; L. *mango,* a dealer. We use it in such compounds as *rumor-monger, war-monger.*

mongrel.

To be *among* persons is to be mixed with a crowd, from AS. *mang,* mixture, from *mengan,* to *mingle;* the AS. phrase corresponding to *among* is *on gemang. Mingle* is from the frequentative form of *mengan,* ME. *mengelen.* The product of a *mingling* is a *mongrel* (from AS. *mang* + a double diminutive, *er* + *el,* with a pejorative sense, as in *wastrel,* one that *wastes.* For *waste, cp. waist.*

monitory.

See fee.

monk.

Before the *monasteries* gathered them together (Gr. *monasterion,* from *monachein,* to live alone, from *monos,* alone) what was emphasized about the *monk* was that he dwelt apart, as an *anchorite. Anchoret* or *anchorite,* earlier *anachorete,* is from Fr., from Gr. *anachoretes,* from *ana,* back + *chorein,* to go: they went back to lonely places. The present spelling (with one *a* dropped) is through the influence of Eng. *anchor, anchoret,* the thought being, in popular etymology, that the first syllable was Eng. *an, ane, one,* alone. This is not the same as the word *anchor,* for holding a ship, which is L. *ancora* (the *h* is added, this time, by mistaken thought of the Gr. *ch, k*), from Gr. *ankyra,* from *ankos,* bend; the root is *ank,* whence Eng. noun *angle.* The verb *angle,* to fish, is the name for the object transferred to its use: from AS. *angel,* diminutive of AS. *anga, onga,* prick, goad; cognate with L. *uncus,* hook, from Gr. *ankos. See Anglo-Saxon.* (For *angel, see evangelist.*)

The Gr. *monos,* one, alone, becomes the prefix *mono—* in many Eng. words, *e.g., monarch* (Gr. *archon,* ruler, from *archein,* to rule); *monopoly* (Gr. *polein,* to sell); *monocle* (L. *oculus,* eye, whence *ocular, oculist*); *monogamy* (Gr. *gametes,* husband, *gamete,* wife, *gamos,* marriage, whence Eng. *gamic, gamete; bigamy,* two; *polygamy,* many); *monotheism* (Gr. *theos,* god; *atheism,* without; *polytheism*); this might grow *monotonous.*

Eng. *gammadion* (shaped like Gr. *gamma,* from Hebrew *gamal, camel, cp. dromedary*) in the 15th c. *fylfot,* is another name for *swastika,* a universally found symbol: *swastika,* from Sansk. *svastika,* from *svasti,* well, from *su,* good, + *as,* to be. The Eng. slang *gams,* legs, is from heraldry *gamb,* leg, from Fr. *gambe, jambe,* leg. A *gammon* of bacon is from OFr. *gambon,* whence Fr. *jambon,* from LL. *camba, gamba, ham,* from Gr. *kampe,* bend. *Gammon* and spinach, *gammon* meaning nonsense, *backgammon,* are from AS. *gamen, game,* sport (to make *game* of), a common Teut. word, from Goth. *gaman,* taking part, from *ga—,* together + *man, man.* The sense of *game,* able to endure, is from the spirit of the *game*-fowl, in cock-fighting. A *game* leg, however (earlier *gammy,* from OFr. *gambi,* bent), is another variation of *gamba,* leg. *Gambol* is from Fr. *gambade,* from It. *gambata,* from L. *gamba; gamble* is a combination of this and AS. *gamen.* A *gambit* in chess (sacrifice to gain a better position) is from OFr. *gambet,* from It. *gambetto,* a wrestler's trip, from L. *gamba.* The *viol da gamba* is the large one, played while held between the legs. But don't try to *gamble* (or *gambol*) with a *monk!* Also, *see pretzel.*

monkey.

Ape is common Teut., AS. *apa;* a name probably brought with the animal into Europe. But in the medieval beast tales, the various animals were given names. Best known of these tales is probably the *Romance of Renart* or *Renard* or *Reynard the Fox. Reynard* is a variant of OHG. *Reginhart,* strong in counsel. In these tales, the son of *Martin the Ape* was *Moneke* (possibly from an OHG. proper name; perhaps a diminutive of It. *monna,* female ape, of unknown origin). From the popularity of the tales, the name for the *monkey* persisted.

monkey-wrench.

See buck.

mono-, monocle, monogamy, monopoly, monotheism, monotonous.

See monk.

monster.

The original sense of this word was a divine portent, or warning (from Fr. *monstre,* from L. *monstrum,* from *monere,* to warn). But as misshapen creatures were accepted as lessons from God, the sense passed by this road to any marvel, but esp. one disproportioned, *monstrous,* beyond measure. But the word is influenced by and associated with L. *monstrare,* to show, which gives Eng. *demonstrate,* and (from Fr. *monstrance,* from LL. *monstrantia*) Eng. *monstrance,* the religious vessel in which the Host is exposed. *Muster,* which first meant to make a showing, then to gather as a show (of force), is OFr. *mostrer,* whence *moustrer·* (restored in Fr. to *montrer,* to show: *cp. insult*), from L. *monstrare.* Thus it is natural to see *monsters* at the circus freak show.

monstrance.

See monster.

Montana.

See States.

month.

This is a common Teut. word, AS. *monath,* from *moon,* from AS. *mona;* Gr. *mene,* whence L. *mens,* whence *Eng. menstrual,* etc.

January is the doorway (L. *janua,* door) of the year. The Roman gate-god, *Janus,* had two faces; one looked forth; the other, within. The guardian of the door is still called the *janitor. January* comes ultimately from the Aryan root, *ya,* to go.

February is the month of the feast of cleansing (L. *februa,* cleansing; akin to L. *fumus,* smoke, whence Eng. *fume;* to *fume* in anger is to have the brain clouded as with smoke; *fumatory; fumigate; fumade,* also *fair maid,* a smoked herring; the *fumarole* of a volcano; *fumidity; perfume*—L. *per,* through—from Gr. *thymos,* smoke, spirit, from Gr. *theos,* God, whence Eng. *theism, enthusiasm*— the God within one— etc., from Sansk. *dhuma,* smoke, whence Eng. *dust. Dust* thou art, to *dust* returnest . . .). During this period, Roman women sacrificed to *Juno Februa.*

March is the beginning of fair weather, when campaigns can start again; hence it is *Mars'* month (L. *Mars, Mart*—, god of war, whence Eng. *martial* and, via the name *Martin,* a *martinet* —perhaps from a *General Martinet* under Louis XIV of France). *March* was the first month of the Roman calendar.

April is the month when flowers come forth: L. *Aprilis,* from *aperire, apert*—, to open, whence Eng. *aperture,* from *apparere, apparit*—, to *appear; apparition,* from *ad,* to + *parere,* to be seen, to wear, whence *apparel, apparent.* There may also be some influence of Gr. *aphros,* foam, whence *Aphrodite, q.v.,* goddess of love, to whom the month was sacred. (*Apparel* may be from the idea of matching one's garments, from Fr. *à,* to + *pareil,* like, from LL. ? *apparicülare,* from L. *pariculum,* diminutive of *par,* equal. *Cp. auction.*)

May is the month of the greater god (*magnus,* great, *maior,* greater, whence Eng. *majority*), *deus maius,* Jupiter. *Major* and *majesty* are also from this source; from the doublet in L. *magister,* greater, come *magistrate* and, via OFr. *maistre, master.* Similarly from *minus,* less, come *minority* and *minister,* servant (of the Lord). *Cp. meticulous, miss.*

June is the month of the famous Roman gens (family), *Junius;* some say, the month of the *juniores,* the youth taken as soldiers of the state.

July is named (by Marc Antony) from the last Roman ruler before the Emperors, *Julius Caesar. Cp. shed.*

August is the month of the first Roman Emperor, *Augustus Caesar.* Refusing to have fewer days than his adopted father, *Julius,* he borrowed a day from February and gave August 31 days.

September is the original seventh month (L. *septem,* seven).

October is thus the eighth month;

November, the ninth;

December, the tenth.

The Julian (Roman) calendar in B. C. 46 established the year as 365¼ days, catching up the fraction every *leap year, q.v.* This is 11 minutes more than it takes the earth to travel around the sun, and by 1581 March 21 was late; it came 10 days after the vernal *equinox, q.v.* Therefore Pope Gregory XIII, in 1582, called the day after October 4 October 15; he changed the Roman (Old Style) calendar so that years ending —00 were not leap years unless divisible by 400. The Gregorian (New Style) calendar, with the year beginning on January 1, was not adopted in Great Britain until 1752.

mooch.

This word, revived in the cartoon *Minnie the Moocher,* is at least as old as the

15th century. From Fr. *moucher,* to blow the nose at (*cp. mock*); the verb was used in the sense of to pretend poverty; then (from beggars' ways) to slouch along, to loaf; hence, to play truant. It is probably connected with OFr. *muchier,* to hide, whence early Eng. *miche,* to lurk, to intend mischief. This sense probably remains in the words of Hamlet, when the dumbshow is played (*Hamlet,* III, ii, 158): "Marry, this is *miching* mallecho; it means mischief."

mood.
See wormwood.

moonstone.
See carnelian.

moot.
Some questions can be readily answered; some not at all. A ***moot*** question is one that it takes a town meeting to answer, from AS. ***mot, gemot,*** meeting; OSax. ***motian,*** to ***meet,*** whence AS. ***metan,*** whence Eng. ***meet.*** Out of your history classes may come memories of the old Saxon ***witenagemot,*** meeting of the wise men (AS. ***witt,*** sense, from AS. ***witan,*** to know, whence Eng. ***wit.*** The root is widespread: Goth. ***witan,*** L. *videre,* Sansk. *vid,* to perceive. Hence, one's mother ***wit,*** and the rest.).

mop.
See map.

moral, morale, morbid, morbific, morbus, mordant, more.
See remorse.

morganatic.
In feudal days, on the ***morning*** after marriage, it was the custom of the lord to give his wife a special gift—an estate, belike, or an umbrageous castle. But if he loved someone too far beneath him in rank to marry—his titles and possessions could not pass on to her children—he would mate with her in ***matrimonium ad morganaticum*** (L. ***matrimonium,*** marriage, whence ***matrimony,*** from ***mater, matr—,*** mother, ***cp. volume; morganaticum,*** pertaining to the *morning*: G. *morgen,* whence OE. *morwen,* whence Eng. ***morn, morning***): that is, she would receive the ***morning*** gift only. This was a ***morganatic*** marriage.

morgue.
See remorse.

Mormon.
See atone.

morn, morning.
See morganatic.

Morocco.
See cloth.

moron, morose, morphine, morphology.
See remorse. (Moron is perhaps the only word voted into the language. But note that *ampere,* from the Fr. scientist André *Ampère,* 1775-1836, was adopted at the international Electrical Congress held in Paris, 1881.)

morris (chair, dance).
See Appendix II.

morsel. mortal.
See remorse.

mortgage.
When an impoverished heir (eldest son of a noble) wished to borrow money, he would sign a ***pledge*** to pay when he came into the estate, that is, when his father died. This was called a ***mortgage,*** death *pledge.* For ***mors, mort—,*** death, *see remorse.* ***Gage,*** though French, is of Teut. origin, cognate with Goth. ***wadi,*** AS. *wedd, pledge,* as in ***wedding***: ***plighted*** troth; *cp. salary.* Also *see greengage.*

To *pledge* is via OFr. ***plegier*** from LL. *plevier,* from a Teut. verb, AS. ***pleon,*** to take a risk; G. ***pflegen,*** whence G. *Pflicht,* that which is ***pledged,*** duty; and Eng. ***plight,*** meaning ***pledged.*** If, however, you find yourself in a sorry ***plight,*** you have been "folded" improperly, or "worn at the folds"; this is from Fr. *plit,* condition (Eng. ***plait*** and ***pleat*** have kept the earlier sense) via OFr. ***pleit*** from L. *plicare, plicat—,* to fold (whence also *implicate,* to fold in; ***cp. plagiarism***); or L. *plectere, plect—,* to weave.

Moslem.
See Islam.

moss.
See alkali.

mother.
See woman.

motion, motive, motor, moult.
See mute.

mountebank.
See bank; somersault.

mouse.
See muscle.

moustache.
See whip.

move, movement.
See mute.

Mozart.
See complexion.

muck, muckraker, mucous, mucus.
See mock.

muff, muffle.
See camouflage.

mufti.
On the English stage, in the early 19th c., a number of plays pictured officers off duty wearing dressing gown and tasselled cap. This resembles the costume of a Mohammedan priest, Arab. *mufti;* whence a man wearing plain clothes, who on duty would be in uniform, is said to be in *mufti.*

mugwump.
This is a borrowing from Algonkin Indian *mugquomp,* chief. It was used by James G. Blaine, 1884, of those that bolted the party ticket, refusing to support him for the presidency, although enrolled members of his party. It has perhaps been best defined, recently in Congress (also attributed to Harold W. Dodds, President of Princeton University), as a man that sits on the political fence with his *mug* on one side and his *wump* on the other.

mulatto.
See mule.

mule.
This was first (L. *mulus*, cognate with Gr. *myklos,* ass) the offspring of a male ass and a mare. The offspring of a she-ass and a stallion was Eng. *hinny,* L. *hinnus,* Gr. *ginnos,* akin? to Gr. *gynes,* woman. Then Sp. and Port. *mulato,* from *mulo, mule,* was applied to any hybrid; hence, Eng. *mulatto.* Some, however, associate this word (and L. *mulier,* woman, whence Eng. *mulier, muliebrity*) with the black? Assyrian goddess *Mylitta.*

multifarious.
See infantry.

mum, mumble, mumbledy-peg.
See mute.

mumbo-jumbo.
In his *Travels in the Interior of Africa,* Mungo Park describes a custom by which noisy wives are quieted (for the civilized procedure, *see ducking-stool*). The Kaffirs summoned a spirit, who, after hideous howling, seized and beat the woman. Mungo Park calls this bogy *Mandingo;* the more widely used term is *Mumbo-jumbo.*

mummy.
See mute.

munch.
See cram.

Munchausen.
There was (perhaps) a *Baron Munchausen,* 1720-1795; there was certainly a German adventurer, Rudolph Erich Raspe, who, to keep himself alive in England (whither he had fled after thievery on the Continent), wrote, in 1785, the *Narrative of the Marvellous Travels of Baron Munchausen*—one of the endless series of travelliars.

mundane.
See vague.

municipal.
See immunity.

munition.
See avalanche.

murder.
Most early deaths were violent; *murder* meant just death, AS. *morthor,* common Teut. G. *Mord;* L. *mors, mort—; cp. remorse.*

muscle.
Have someone "make a *muscle*" and then relax his arm; to the imaginative it might seem a little mouse crawling back and forth. It did to the Romans; for *muscle* is from L. *musculum,* diminutive of *mus, mouse.*
This word came through the Fr.; much earlier, spelled *muscle, muxle,* and finally *mussel,* came the same word applied for similar reasons to the shellfish.
The African rodent *jerboa* is named from Arab. *yarbu,* loin muscle, because of its strength for jumping.

muse.
See amuse.

musk.
See salary.

muss.
See mess.

mussel.
See muscle.

Mussolini.
See cloth: muslin.

mustang.
See bronco.

muster.
See monster.

mutable.
See immunity.

mutation.
See mute.

mute.
This is a word that has doubled back: ME. *muet* is from LL. *mutettus,* diminutive of L. *mutus, mute;* then the ME. form was changed by association with the original Latin word, whence Eng. *mute.* The root is L. *mu,* a natural sound indicating a low murmur, akin to ME. *momme,* a low sound, hence silence, as in "Keep *mum!*" "*Mum's* the word!" The frequentative of *momme* was ME. *momelen;* whence *mumble. Mummy* is Fr. *momie,* from Arab. *mūmiyah,* embalmed body, from Egyp. *mum,* wax.

The game *mumbely-peg, mumbledy-peg,* used to be *mumble-the-peg;* from the penalty: pulling out by the teeth (*mumbling*) a peg driven into the ground.

Several unrelated words may be confused because of the same strong initial sound. *Mutilate* is from L. *mutilare,* to lop off, from *mutilus,* maimed, from Gr. *mytilos,* hornless. *Mutation* is from L. *mutare, mutat—,* to change; that which cannot be changed is *immutable;* that which is changed by agreement is *mutual* (L. *mutuus*). The Aryan root is *moi,* to change, cognate with *mov,* to *move,* whence L. *movere, mot—,* whence *move; motive* (that which impels or *moves* one); *motor* (the *moving* force); *motion,* a doublet of *movement,* as is also *moment,* from L. *momentum. Moment* earlier meant a cause of *movement.* When it became used for a small *movement* of time (the twinkling of an eye), the language borrowed directly from L. for *momentum.* Compounds include *commotion* (L. *com,* together); *promotion* (L. *pro,* forward); *locomotion* (L. *loco,* from a place, to a place), *locomotive; emotion* (L. *e,* out: this first meant migration; then a *moving* out of oneself, as in the slang phrases "Give out!" "*Emote!*"). Via. LL. *movita,* whence OFr. *meute,* comes early Eng. *mute,* a riot; whence *mutine, mutinous, mutiny.* From *mutare,* to change, via Fr. comes *mew,* used of changing feathers; the *mew* was thence the place where hawks were put at *moulting* time (*moult* is also from L. *mutare,* but through the Teut., AS. *mouten*); since this was usually near the stables, the word *mews* came to mean the cluster of stable-houses. To *mew* is also an echoic word, of the sound of a cat, also *miaow;* the baby's sound is slightly more pleasant, *miaul* or *mewl,* as in the first of the seven ages of man "*mewling* and puking in the nurse's arms" (*As You Like It,* II, vii, 145): God keep you with good capon lined!

mutilate, mutinous, mutiny, mutual.
See mute.

mutton.
In one of Sir Walter Scott's most popular books, *Ivanhoe* (1819), Wamba the jester delves into etymology for Gurth the swineherd. He points out that while the domestic animals are alive and must be tended, they are simple Saxon *calf* and *sheep, cow, pig, swine,* and the rest; but when they are dressed and ready to be served before the Norman conquerors, they are Milord Norman (French) *veal, pork, mutton, beef.* Had Wamba looked a bit further back, he'd have found several of the words common Aryan, for these animals were early domesticated, and their names are old.

Veal is via OFr. *viel* and *vedel* from L. *vitellus,* diminutive of *vitulus,* calf. *Vitulus* itself is a diminutive, not of *vita,* life (the lively little one: L. *vita;* Eng. *vital, vitality; cp. vitamin*) but—just the reverse!—of L. *vetus,* old (whence Eng. *veteran* and, via L. *inveterare, inveterat—,* to make or grow old, Eng. *inveterate*), related to *ve—,* the Aryan root for year: thus, first, a yearling. *See calf. Pork* is directly from Fr. *porc,* from L. *porcus,* whence also Eng. *porcine* and *porcupine,* from L. *porcus* + *spina,* thorn, whence also Eng. *spine.*

Lamb is common Teut., AS. *lamb. Sheep, ewe, ram,* are common Teut.: AS. *sceap;* AS. *ramm;* AS. *eowu,* Sansk, *avi.* The *pig* was ME. *pigge,* which first meant the young *swine; swine* is common Teut., originally *sowine,* the adjective from *sow,* AS. *sugu,* L. *sus.* The *beef* is from OFr. *beuf* (Fr. *boeuf*) from L. *bos, bov—;* from earlier Sansk. *go,* this is cognate with AS. *cu,* whence Eng. *cow, q.v.* And *mutton* is from Fr. *mouton,* but of Celtic origin.

From the most famous French farce, *Maitre Pierre Pathelin* (printed in Lyons in 1485, but probably written by one of the law-clerks (Basoche) of Paris, comes an expression that has become proverbial: *revenons à nos moutons;* let's get back to our *muttons.* A tailor has brought to the bar his dishonest shepherd, who has retained a lawyer that has defrauded the tailor of a suit; seeing the lawyer so confuses the tailor that he talks now of the stolen sheep, now of the stolen suit, until the judge (after crying endlessly *Revenons à nos moutons!*) finally bids the shepherd begone, and never appear before him again. The lawyer has told the shepherd that, to all the tailor's accusations, he should say just "Baa! Baa!"—intending to plead that the man, through association with the sheep, had become as innocent as they. Now, the lawyer asks the shepherd for his fee; the shepherd responds "Baa! Baa!" . . . Let's get back to our *muttons.*

muzzle.
See amuse, breach; *cp.* remorse.

myriad.
See myrmidon.

myrmidon.
The Gr. *Myrmidones* were the inhabitants of Thessaly, who followed Achilles to the Trojan War (*Iliad,* 11, 684). From their faithful obedience comes the sense of *myrmidon* as one that carries out any order, without scruples. Ovid suggests that the word is related to Gr. *myrmax,* ant; possibly it is also connected with Gr. *myrias, myriad—,* whence Eng. *myriad,* from Gr. *myrioi,* countless, ten thousand. That the same word should mean 'countless' and 'ten thousand' to the ancients should not astonish us, who speak of the countless stars we see at night, when all the naked eye can behold on the clearest night is just over one thousand stars.

mystery.
There is a three-fold mixture, but not a *mystery,* in the history of this word. The *mystery* play that brings the detective with all his sleuthing skill is from Gr. *mysterion,* a secret religious ceremony, from *myein,* to close (lips and eyes), to initiate. The medieval *mystery* play, dealing with the life of Jesus, and performed at first by the minor clergy, is from L. *ministerium,* the churchly office. Later it was acted by the apprentices of the guilds, the *mysteries,* as they were also called, because one sought *mastery* in them. "Every manuary trade is called a *mystery.*" This third *mystery,* mingling with the second, is from L. *magisterium.* The shift from *a* to *i* is also seen in *mister,* from *master; mistress,* from *mai(s)tresse; mistral,* from *maestral,* the *master*(wind). Thus *magister,* from L. *magis,* more, and *minister,* from L. *minus,* less, combine in *mystery. Cp. month: May.*

myxo—, myxoma.
See ache.

N

nab.
See knick-knack.

nacre.
See carnelian.

nadir.
See azimuth.

nag, nail.
See pylorus.

nainsook.
See cloth.

naive.
See neighbor.

naked.
Sometimes words get lost; perhaps this one found it had nothing on, and slipped away! The basic verb is gone; but the past participle remains in AS. *nacod;* Du. ***naakt;*** G. ***nackt;*** Goth. ***nagaths;*** Russ. ***nagoi;*** OFr. ***nocht;*** L. ***nudus;*** Sansk. *nagna.* From the L., also *nude.*

namby-pamby.
See niminy-piminy.

nankeen.
See cloth.

nap.
See knick-knack.

nape, napery, napkin.
See auction; *cp.* knick-knack.

narcissism, narcissus, narcotic.
See nuptials.

nasal.
See nasturtium.

nasturtium.
Taste the leaves of this flower, and you will understand the name. For it is from L. *nasus,* nose (AS. ***nosu, nasu,*** from L. *nasus,* from Sansk. ***nasa, nostrils.*** *Nostrils* are ***nose-thrills, nose-drills.*** Hence also ***nasal,*** from L. ***nasalis,*** of the nose) + ***tortium,*** twist. ***Cp.*** *torch.*

Columbine is the diminutive of L. *columba,* a dove. ***See*** also ***nuptials.*** The flower ***pink*** is not named from the color; but the color from the flower. To ***pink*** is to prick (as in sewing or fencing), to cut in at the edges, from Fr. ***piquer,*** whence Eng. ***pick,*** from AS. ***pycan,*** from L. ***picus, woodpecker:*** thus ***pick, peck,*** and ***pink*** are triplets. The flower is named from its cut-in petals. ***Pink*** also means the tip or point made by cutting; hence, the peak, as in ***the pink of perfection.*** But ***see pink.***

nation.
From L. ***nasci, nat—,*** to be born (***cp. neighbor***), ***nation*** first meant a group of persons born together. The element of race was prominent in early uses of the word; more recently, the political tie has been stronger.

native.
See neighbor.

natron.
See element: nitrogen.

nature.
From Fr. ***nature*** from L. ***natura,*** future form of L. ***nasci, nat—,*** to be born (***cp. neighbor***), ***nature*** first meant birth; then the character inherent in a person, his basic qualities. By extension, the basic qualities of anything—those that must be allowed for, as fundamental, perhaps unchangeable, as, an artist must know the ***nature*** of his materials: similarly, it's human ***nature!*** All these meanings had been acquired by the word in Latin; from the sense of a basic, pervasive quality, came the extension to ***nature*** as "the limit set to man"; hence, ***nature*** as the physical

aspect of the universe, and all the *natural* beauties of the field and sea and sky.

naughty.
See nausea.

nausea.
We have extended the meaning of this word, but it is very old, from Gr. *nausia,* from Gr. *naus,* ship, being first limited to sea sickness. From Gr. *naus, naut—,* we also have *nautical* (though of course not *naughty,* which means just worth *naught,* nothing, from *ne,* not + *aught,* anything. *Aught* is from *a,* one + *whit,* created thing, a doublet of *wight,* creature), and *nautilus,* a shell-fish supposed to swim as with a sail. The L. form, *naus,* whence *navis,* gives us *navy, navigate, naval,* and the rest. The *nave* of a church, from LL. *navem,* is from the frequent comparison of church and ship. The root is *na,* from earlier *sna,* from Sansk. *sna,* to bathe; *snu,* to flow. Perhaps *snake* is from this source; thus Sansk. *nag,* snake (*Kala Nag,* Black Snake, in Kipling's *Moti Guj, Mutineer,* and in other stories).

Church *nave,* however, is influenced by *nave,* the center or hub of a wheel, with its diminutive, *navel* or center of the body. This is a common Teut. word, AS. *nafu, nafa,* from Sansk. *nabhi, navel,* center, from *nabh,* to *burst* (the *navel* in earliest infancy is a projection, or 'bursting.' Similarily *burst,* an old Teut. word: AS. *berstan,* Icel. *bresta*—from the stem *brast,* intensive of *brak,* whence Eng. *break*—is related to AS. *breost,* Eng. *breast.* Chaucer uses *bresten,* to *burst.*).

Travel by air has recently, by analogy with *navigation,* been called *avigation,* from L. *avis,* bird; pilots are bird men.

nautical, nautilus, naval, nave, navel, navigate, navy.
See nausea.

Nazi.
See Dora.

Nebraska.
See States.

nebular, nebulous.
See cloud.

necromancy.
No spiritualist would accept this word as describing her activity; yet the black art, and black magic, are terms that suggest themselves—and suggested the LL. *nigromancy,* from *negro,* black,+ *mantia,* divination—for what is really from Gr. *necros,* a dead person, + *manteia,* divination, whence *mantis,* seer; *mania,* divine frenzy. Thus a *necropolis,* city of the dead (*cp. police*), is a formal word for a *cemetery. Cemetery* itself is a euphemism: he has gone to his last rest, from Gr. *koimeterion,* dormitory, from *koiman,* to put to sleep. The *mantis* (insect) is so named because its front legs seem to be arms joined in prayer. And *necromancy* is divination by raising the dead.

The popularity of divination may be suggested by a partial list of its varieties: *theomancy,* by oracles (god); *bibliomancy,* by the *Bible; psychomancy,* by spirits (the soul), *cristallomantia,* by images; *sciomancy,* by shadows; *aeromancy,* by shapes in the air; *chaomancy,* by clouds; *meteoromancy,* by meteors; *austromancy;* by the winds; *hieromancy,* by the entrails of sacrificed animals; *anthropomancy,* by human entrails; *ichthyomancy,* by fishes; *pyromancy,* by fire (ashes); *sideromancy,* by hot metal (Gr. *sideros,* iron; not L. *sidus, sider—,* star), *capnomancy,* by altar smoke; *myomancy,* by mice; *ornithomancy,* by flight of birds; *alectromancy,* by a cock picking up grains; *botanomancy,* by herbs; *hydromancy,* by water; *pegomancy,* by fountains; *rhabdomancy,* by a wand; *crithomancy,* by cake dough; *aleuromancy,* by meal; *halomancy,* by salt (Gr. *hals, halo—,* salt, whence *halogen,* salt-producing; *cp. racy*); *cleromancy,* by dice; *belomancy,* by arrows; *axinomancy,* by a balanced axe; *coscinomancy,* by a sieve; *dactyliomancy,* by a suspended ring; *geomancy,* by random dots on paper; *lithomancy,* by precious stones; *pessomancy,* by tossed pebbles; *psephomancy,* by pebbles drawn from a heap; *cataptromancy,* by mirrors; *tephramancy,* by writing in ashes; *foliomancy,* by reading tea-leaves (L. *folium,* leaf, whence *foliage, folio*); *oneiromancy,* by dreams (Gr. *oneiros,* a dream); *chiromancy,* by reading the hand; *onychomancy,* by nails reflecting the sun; *dactylomancy,* by finger rings (Gr. *dactylos,* finger); *arithmancy,* by numbers; *stichomancy,* by passages in books (L. *sortes Virgilianae,* the fate according to Virgil; turning at random to a page, as of the *Aeneid,* or putting down a finger at random); *onomancy,* by the letters of one's name; *gastromancy,* with *ven-*

triloquism (Gr. *gastor,* belly, whence *gastric;* L. *ventri—,* belly + *loqui,* to talk; *loquacious*); *gyromancy,* by spinning in a circle; *ceromancy,* by drops of molten wax.

necropolis.
See ambrosia, necromancy.

nectar, nectarine.
See ambrosia.

needle's eye.
See Prometheus.

nefarious.
When something is beyond words, it may be good, or bad, beyond our power of description. The odds are two to one on the bad. *Ineffable* is from L. *ineffabilis,* from *in,* not + *ef,* from *ex,* out + *fari,* to speak. This, of something good. But from the same source *fas, far—,* something spoken, came to be used of the oracles, hence divinely spoken, hence right; L. *nefas* was therefore wrong. *Nefarious* means, full of what should not be spoken, from *nefariosus,* from *ne,* not + *fari,* to speak + *osus,* full of. The third word is the good old Eng. *unspeakable, q.v.* (There is also *unutterable, q.v.,* but this is usually reserved for technical situations, without moral concern; it is therefore neutral in the odds above.) *See infantry.*

negative.
See runagate.

neglect, negligent.
See sacrifice.

negotiate.
See scholar.

neighbor.
The man next door, in the old days, was a farmer: *neighbor,* from *nēahgebūr, nigh boor. Boor* was a farmer; by contrast with polished city ways (thus *urbanity,* from L. *urbanus,* from *urbs,* city; also *rusticity,* from *rusticus,* from *rus, rur—,* country, whence Eng. *rural, rusticate; savage,* from Fr. *sauvage,* from L. *silvaticus,* from *silva,* the forest, the wilds, whence Eng. *sylvan; Pennsylvania,* Penn's woods. And *naive* is a doublet of *native,* from Fr. *naif, naive,* from L. *nativus,* from *nasci, nat—,* to be born, Eng. *natal*—whence also the *provincialism* of the *natives* of a large city.) it became a term of scorn. The same word in Dutch is *Boer,* whence the *Boer* War. Note, however, that *bond* also originally meant a farmer, a freeholder (AS. *bōnda,* ON. *bōndi,* from *būandi,* from *būa,* to dwell, to till, whence G. *Bauer,* peasant. This became tangled with the word *bond,* from *band,* derived from *bind* (AS. *binden,* a common Teut. word) and changed the meaning of *bondman, bondage.* From this *binden* comes the Du. *bond,* a confederation (as in South Africa) and the German *Bund. Churlish* is from *churl,* from OE. *ceorl,* also *carl,* meaning first a man of the common people. The fashioners of our words were not all democrats!

From the Du. and G. *Bauer,* farmer, came Du. *bouerij,* farm, whence our *bouerie, Bowery.* The *Bowery* in New City (as in the song: "I'll never go there any more!") was first a farm, then a farm road. These words are related to Eng. *bower,* from OE. *bur,* from Aryan *bhurom,* dwelling, from Aryan *bhur,* to dwell. The Eng. word, dropping out of general use, became poetic; thence was used of a dwelling amid the trees, an *arbour.* This *arbour* (though also spelled *arbor,* and changed as though it were that word) is not directly related to Eng. *arbor* as in *Arbor Day,* from Fr. *arbre,* tree, from L. *arbor* — the spelling changed back as though directly from the Latin. *Arbour* was earlier *erber* and *herber,* from L. *herba,* dried plant, whence Eng. *herb. Arbour* first meant an herb garden, often grown under trees, it came then to refer to the trees and, possibly influenced by *harbour,* a *bowery* retreat. This *bowery* is from Eng. *bower,* not G. *Bauer, above*).

nemesis.
The Greeks not only had a word for it; they usually had a god. *Nemesis* was the goddess of vengenance; originally, however, she meted out rewards as well as punishments. Humans being what they are, most deserved the sterner portion. Her name (like those of many of the olden gods) simply makes a person out of the idea: Gr. *nemesis,* just fate, from *nemein,* to measure what is due.

neodymium.
See element.

neologism.
See neophyte.

neon.
See element.

neophyte.
The use of *neophyte* in the Douai translation of the New Testament (1582) roused considerable protest at the time; the word did not become widely used until the past century. It is, however, found in the Gr. version of the *Bible* (I *Timothy,* iii, 6) as Gr. ***neophytos*** (in the *King James Version,* translated as novice). The word is, literally, newly planted, from Gr. ***neos, new,*** + ***phytenein,*** to plant; ***phyton,*** a plant. Eng. ***neo—*** is a frequent prefix, as in ***neologism,*** a new word, or the habit of using new expressions; ***neoplatonism,*** etc. Eng. ***phyt—*** and ***phyto—*** are even more frequent combining forms, in scientific relation to plants. *Neophyte,* of course, is figuratively used; first, one newly planted in the garden of the Lord; then, any beginner.

nepenthe.
See respite.

nepotism.
See simony.

nest.
This word, in exactly the same form, is found in several Teut. tongues. The L. cognate is *nidus,* which is used in Eng. also as a scientific term; ***nidification*** is nest-building; earlier Eng. ***nidary*** (***—ary*** from L. ***—arium*** as in ***aquarium,*** etc.) was a place for nesting. The Sansk. word was *nidd,* from *nizd;* for the word is formed from just what the birds do in it: *ni—,* down + *sed,* to sit. The root *ni—* is also common Teut., OHG. *nideri;* whence OE. *nithera;* whence Eng. *nether* as in the *nether* millstone. The root *sed—*is cognate with the common Teut. form, G. *sitzen;* AS. *sittan;* whence Eng. *sit; cp. strategy;* but it appears directly in L. *sedere,* whence *sedentary; cp. subsidy.*

A *nest-box* is one with a series of others inside, each fitting into the one larger as in a *nest.* A *nest-egg* was, first, a real or imitation egg left in the *nest* to stimulate laying; then, an amount left in the bank to gather more around it, or as a fund "for a rainy day."

nest-egg, nether.
See nest.

neuralgia.
See nostalgia.

neuter, neutral.
See marshal.

Nevada.
See sierra, States.

New Hampshire, New Jersey, New Mexico, New York.
See States.

newt.
See auction.

nexus.
This is directly from the L. *nexus,* knot, from *nectere, nex—,* to bind. To bind things together is to *connect* them; *connexion* was long preferred, and is still alternative, to ***connection.*** To bind something to another is to ***annex*** it; whence also *annexation.* Not to be confused with these is L. *nex, necis,* slaughter; with the intensive prefix ***per,*** through, thorough, this produced L. ***pernicies,*** destruction; and its adjective, ***perniciosus,*** gives us Eng. ***pernicious.*** The word is related to Gr. *nekros,* corpse (L. ***necare,*** to kill), whence *necromancy, q.v., cp. ambrosia.*

nibble.
See browse, knick-knack.

nibs.
See ***snob.*** ***Nib*** of a pen was earlier ***neb,*** from AS. ***nebb,*** beak. The word is cognate with ***snip,*** a small piece, ***nib;*** and *snap,* as one does with a beak; ***cp. knick-knack.***

nice.
This word first meant ignorant (OFr. *nice,* from L. *nescius,* ignorant, from *nescire,* from *ne,* not + *scire,* to know. The present participle, *sciens,* knowing, gives Eng. *science,* etc.). It has been suggested that the change in meaning is due to confusion with ME. *nesh,* delicate. But there is a natural psychological growth. A silent person might be ignorant, but might be shy; thus the word had both implications, came (as applied to females) to mean coy, reluctant, slow to show pleasure — then hard to please, exacting. From this came the sense of discriminating, able to judge delicately, to make *nice* distinctions. A person possessing this quality was a *nice* person; you liked her; hence the word was extended to include any pleasing, agreeable thing. *Cp. dainty.*

niche, nick.
See knick-knack.

nickel.
Goblins, gnomes, elves, and pixies were thanked for small favors and blamed for mishaps. Thus when the

miners found a shiny metal, they thought they were lucky; but when they were told it contained no copper, they blamed it on one of the most busy goblins, *Nicholas,* and called it ***nickel.*** As once its chief constituent, it became the name of the coin, U.S. half a dime. It is an abbreviation of G. *Kupfernickel, coppernickel; Nickel,* from *Niklaus,* whence *Nicholas.* He appears in happier guise as Saint Nicholas, Santa Claus; *cp. Blitzkrieg. Dime* is more prosaically from L. *decima (pars),* a tenth part; *cp. dollar. See element.*

nickname.
See auction.

nicotine.
We remember *tobacco's* coming to Europe through the story of Sir Walter Raleigh's servant, who saw Sir Walter smoking and doused him with a pail of water. The French memory is more potent; for the word ***nicotine*** comes from *Jacques Nicot,* who in 1560 introduced *tobacco* into France. Even the plant itself is named from him; it belongs to the species *Nicotiana.* The word ***tobacco*** is Sp. *tabaco,* large tube, the name the Spanish gave to the tube (pipe) through which the Indians smoked, or to the roll of *tobacco* leaves, like a large cigar—the name of the receptacle applied to what it holds. It may, however, be a native Brazilian word. ***Cigar, segar,*** is from Sp. *cigarro;* the Fr. diminutive is *cigarette;* the words are not American Indian, but their origin is unknown. It is suggested that the word is taken from *cigarro,* grasshopper, from the shape of the body.

nidification, nidus.
See nest.

nigh.
See neighbor.

night.
See week.

nightmare.
See marshal.

nihilist, nil.
See annihilate.

nimbus.
See cloud.

niminy-piminy.
This reduplication (*cp. scurry, patter*) imitates a somewhat more affected state than ***namby-pamby.*** The latter was coined by Henry Carey from *Ambrose* Philips, who wrote some feeble verses, about 1700, "to all ages and characters." Pope, in *The Guardian,* sheds some of his neatest irony on Philips.

nincompoop.
The suggestion that this word is a shortening, then corruption, of L. *non compos mentis,* with one's mind not composed, is probably misleading. An earlier form of the word was *nickumpoop;* this suggests a first part from the name *Nicodemus* (like *tomfool*), and a second part perhaps related to Du. *poep,* fool, whence Eng. slang *poop,* lummox. *Poop* had already been compounded with another shortening of *Nicodemus* in the early Eng. *poopnoddy,* also meaning fool. *Nicodemus* seems to have been a bit simple.

It is also suggested that ***ninny,*** in the same general sense, is a shortening of the name *Innocent*—an innocent being often a simpleton. But Sp. *niño,* It. *ninno,* both mean an inexperienced child; and seem to be related to the soothing sound: It. *ninna,* a lullaby, whence *ninnare,* to lull to sleep. Thus Gr. *nanna* and *nannas* were an aunt and an uncle; L. *nonna, nunna,* and *nonnus* were mother and father; Eng. *mama, mamma, dadda, daddy.* L. *nonnus* was used of a monk, Father; and from L. *nunna* we have ***nun.*** It does seem, however, that the word ***cretin,*** an idiot, is from the Swiss dialect word for *Christian*—either from an individual who bore that name, or because to the materialist anyone applying the *Christian* doctrine in this world would deserve the name.

nine.
See number.

ninepins, tenpins.
The *pins* here are bones, esp. legbones, which were first stood for the ball to roll at. Wood was introduced in the 14th c.; there is a statute of Edward IV of England (1332) forbidding "casting a bowle" (ball; but thence *bowling*) "at ninepins of wood, or nine shank-bones of an ox or a horse." The game is a very ancient one, rivalling dice, which first was quite literally rolling of bones. We still speak of a man as shaky on his *pins.*

In the 17th c. the name *skittles* came also to be applied; it is still used of a variant of the game. *Skittle* is a doublet of *shuttle,* earlier *shittle,* from AS. *scytel,* missile (Dan. *skyttel, shuttle;* ON. *skutill,* harpoon); related to AS. *scetan,* whence ME. *scheoten,* whence Eng. *shoot. "All beer and skittles"* refers to a good time without any troubles or grave concerns.

ninny.
See nincompoop.

nip, nipple.
See knick-knack.

nisei.
World War II has brought to attention the loyalty to the U. S. of the *nisei,* first generation of American born Japanese. Their fathers, first generation to come to the U. S., are *issei;* their sons, *sensei.* Japanese *sei* means generation; *is, ni, sen* are Japanese for one, two, three.

nitrogen.
See element, racy.

nob, nod.
See knick-knack.

node, nodose, nodule.
See noose.

noetic.
See anaesthetic.

nog, noggin.
See nugget.

nomocracy.
See number.

non sequitur.
See refrain.

nonce-word.
This is a word created *for the nanes;* earlier *for then anes* (*then* replacing the AS. dative, *than*: *for that once*); this was divided wrongly. Thus Jonson (in *Epicoene, or The Silent Woman,* 1609) says "A wife is a scurvy clogdogdo." No one has elsewhere used that descriptive term. C. Hodgson, in 1861 used aladdinize, meaning to transform as by magic, from the story of Aladdin with the wonderful lamp in *The Thousand and One Nights.* Such words carbuncle the N E D.

noncombatant.
See debate.

nondescript.
See shrine.

none, nones.
See bull.

nonentity.
See authentic.

noon.
See luncheon.

noose.
L. *nodus,* knot, has come into Eng. as a scientific term; its diminutive L. *nodulus* has given us Eng. *nodule,* also in scientific use; more generally used in Eng. *node,* knot. There are also *nodose* and *nodosity.* But via. Prov. and OFr. *nous* came Eng. *noose,* sometimes called *running noose; cp. lasso.* It's a knotty field; *cp. knot.*

norm.
L. *norma* was a carpenter's square; hence, pattern, rule. There is a southern constellation, *Norma,* the Rule. With the sense of rule or standard already acquired in Latin, it came into Eng. as *norm;* from this, a large number of words have grown: *normal, normality* (also, *abnormality;* L. *ab,* away from); *normalcy* ("America's present need is not heroics but healing; not nostrums but *normalcy*"—many think the form was coined in this speech by Warren G. Harding, while campaigning for the Presidency of the United States, in 1920; but the word was used at least as early as 1857; the N E D records also, in the year of my birth, a remark about "the mathematical *normalcy* of the female mind"). A *Normal* School is one, not that conforms to the standard, but that teaches the *norms* or rules of teaching.

normal, normalcy, normality.
See norm.

north.
See east.

North Carolina, North Dakota.
See States.

nostalgia.
There are two constant and opposing cries. One the poet has phrased:

I want to take the next train out,
No matter where it's going.

The other is as directly put in the words of any child: "I wanna go home!" Nostalgia is a literal translation of the latter feeling. It is from Gr. *nostos,* return home, + *algos,* pain (as also in *neuralgia,* nerve pain, etc.). Odysseus was an early sufferer.

nostril.
Nature has *drilled* two passages up our nose: ***nostril,*** from AS. ***nose thrill:*** ***thirl,*** narrow passage, Du. *drillen,* to pierce, to bore. It is by a pun on bore (torment) that the word came to be applied to the exercise of soldiers when they *drill.* All *drills* turn round and round, to bore.

nostrum.
Indian medicine men of the United States are in an old tradition; during the middle ages, vendors of panaceas and indulgences (bodily or spiritual cure-alls) often had acrobats and puppeteers to draw the crowd. But each held exclusive possession of the potent remedy; it was (with the editorial we!) ours: not known to anybody else. Hence, Eng. ***nostrum,*** from L. *noster, nostra, nostrum,* ours.

notch.
See knick-knack.

noumenon.
See focus.

nourish.
See tribulation.

November.
See month.

noxious.
See nuisance.

nubile.
See nuptials.

nucleus.
See plant.

nude.
See naked.

nugget.
Odd how words sometimes journey round! *Nugget* is probably diminutive of early *nug,* lump, a variant of *nog,* peg, stump. But this *nog* gives us *noggin,* a small drinking cup; and applying the name of the vessel to the contents gives us *nog,* a drink, as now in *eggnogg.* But we also find ***nugget*** spelled ***nigget*** and ***niggot*** (*e.g.,* in North's translation of *Plutarch's Lives*); which gives rise to the suggestion that via ***ningot*** (*an ingot*) it is from ***ingot.*** This was simply a metal poured in, from ***in*** + AS. *geotan,* to pour. (Just as ***ningot*** has stolen the ***n*** from ***an;*** ***cp. auction,*** so the Fr. word came from the Eng. but added the *l* of *le,* whence ***lingot.***)

nuisance.
This word, though still a pest, has lost considerable force. It was L. *necare, necat—,* to kill; Eng. *necation* is a nonce-word for killing. This became LL. *nocere, nox—,* to harm; L. *noxa,* harm; whence Eng. *noxious, obnoxious,* also *innocuous.* From the present participle, *nocens, nocent—,* comes the harmless *innocent.* From LL. *nocere* came OFr. *nuire, nuis—,* which has given us the noun Eng. *nuisance. Cp. nexus.*
Note that both in spelling and in derivation *innocuous* is not related to *inoculate,* which is from L. *inoculare, inoculat—,* to implant, from *in,* into + *oculus,* eye—then, from its appearance like an eye, bud. This meant first to insert a bud into a plant, in grafting; then it was used in medicine, of implanting the "bud" —germ or virus—of a disease so as to produce a mild case and thus render the patient immune.

null.
See anniversary.

number.
This word is via Fr. *nombre* from L. *numerus;* L. *numerare, numerat—,* to count; whence Eng. *enumerate,* to count out. The adjective gives us *numeral; numerical; numerous.* The root of L. *numerus* is in Gr. *nemein,* to give out for use; whence Gr. *nomos,* first a division, then things grown into use, then law, as in Eng. *nomocracy* (*cp. democracy*). Gr. *nomisma* was a counter, a coin in use; hence Eng. *numismatics.*

one.
This is common Teut., AS *an,* which gives us *a, an* and *one;* also *once.*

two.
This is from AS. *twa;* formerly AS. *twain* (the masculine) was used. In combinations it is *twi—;* also in *twice.*

three.
This is widespread Aryan, AS. *thri;*

L. *tres, tria;* Gr. *treis, tria;* Sansk. *tri.* Hence also *thrice.*

four.
This is also Aryan, AS. *feower;* L. *quattuor;* Sansk. *catur.* The *u* is dropped in *fortnight* (*fourteen night; cp. remnant*) and in *forty; cp. twenty.*

five.
This is another common Aryan root. AS. *fif;* OHG. *finf;* L. *quinque,* earlier *pinque;* Gr. *pente* (as in *pentagon*); Sansk. *pancha,* whence *punch; cp. drink.*

six.
This is closely from earlier forms: AS. *siex, sex;* L. *sex;* Gr. *hex* (*hexagon*); Sansk. *shash.*

seven.
Here again the word is found in all Aryan: AS. *seofan;* L. *septem;* Gr. *hepta* (*heptagon*); Sansk. *sapta.*

eight.
The English has varied a bit more here, from the Aryan background: AS. *eahta;* Du. *acht;* L. *octo;* Gr. *octo;* Sansk. *ashta.*

nine.
This is also Aryan; AS. *nigon;* L. *novem;* Gr. *ennea;* Sansk. *nava.*

ten.
Here again is a shift from the Aryan background: AS. *tien;* L. *decem;* Gr. *deka* (as in the *decalogue*); Sansk. *dasha.*

eleven.
This is common Teut., AS. *endlufen.* The first syllable is a form of *one;* the second is from the root of *left*: *one left* after ten.

twelve.
This is *two left* after ten; *see eleven.*

thirteen.
This is by metathesis from *three*. AS. *thriteen; —tyne, —tene,* is from *ten*: *three* and *ten.* Similarly *fourteen* through *nineteen.*

twenty.
This is AS. *twain, two,* + *—ty,* AS. *—tig,* from *ten*: *ten two* times.

hundred.
The Aryan word for 100 was *hund;* cognate with L. *centum;* Gr. *hekaton;* Sansk. *shatam;* added to this is *—red,* count; from L. *ratio,* to calculate, to figure; hence, to figure out, to reason; whence Eng. *ratio; rational; cp. rat.*

thousand.
This is common Teut., AS. *thusend,* which first meant a multitude. The first element is probably Aryan *tus,* force; Sansk. *tawas,* strong, the second part being akin to *hundred*: a strong *hundred.* It was used to translate L. *mille,* thousand, which itself was probably at first indefinite, like Gr. *myriad,* a multitude, ten thousand; *cp. myrmidon.*

million.
This is an augmentative, via Fr., through It. *millione,* from L. *mille,* thousand.

billion.
This was coined (L. *bi—,* two) in 16th c. France, to indicate the second power of a *million.* Thus *trillion,* etc. on to *googol, q.v.;* which makes quite a *number!*

numeral, numerical, numerous.
See number; *cp.* supercilious.

numismatics.
See number.

nun.
See nincompoop.

nuptials.
We use the plural, and so did the ancients, for the wedding rites: the adjective L. *nuptialis* is from *nuptiae,* wedding, from *nubere, nupt—,* to wed. Hence also our *nubile,* from L. *nubilis,* ready to wed. The L. word is cognate with Gr. *nymphe,* bride, whence the *nymphs,* the eternal brides of the streams and the forests—whence also, the Eng. scientific uses of the form *nymph—.*

Many of the Greek demigods draw their names from the personification of the original meaning. Thus also *Echo, e.g.*: she was in love with *Narcissus,* vainly; and she pined away until only her voice was left: but Gr. *echo* means sound, and the story grew from the meaning. Hence, such compounds as *echoism, echolalia. Narcissus,* looking in a pool, fell in love with his own image, grew numb with joy, fell into the pool and was drowned—but by the merciful gods changed into a flower, the *narcissus.* But Gr. *narkissos* is from *narke,* numb— which the flower was supposed to make one; it had *narcotic* effects, from Gr. *narkosis, narkot—*, numbness. Thus *narcotic* comes from the basic meaning of the flower, and *narcissism,* self-love, comes from the story that grew around it.

L. *nubere,* to wed, is from L. *nubes,* cloud, veil, and means thus the donning of the ceremonial bridal veil, a practice that— though the color has changed from Roman saffron to Christian white —has continued down the ages. *Cp. bridal.*

nur, nurl.
See knick-knack.

nutmeg.
See salary.

nutrition.
See tribulation.

nymph.
See nuptials.

O

obelisk.
Cleopatra's needle, we call the one in Central Park, New York: a diminutive figure for a colossal thrust of stone. But the Greeks did the very same thing, for Gr. *obeliskos* is the diminutive of *obelos,* which meant no more than a spit for roasting meat. The word *obelus* is now used for the dagger sign (†) in printing. The *obelisks* were erected in Egypt.

obelus.
See obelisk.

obese.
See indenture.

obituary.
The Romans were as careful to avoid direct reference to unpleasant things as any other people. Thus, as we say "gone west," deceased, they speak of one's going to meet (his ancestral shades): L: *obituarius,* the adjective ending, on *ob,* against, upon + *ire, it—,* to go. The pathway that one takes is thence one's *itinerary,* from L. *iter, itineri—,* journey, from *ire, it—.* To *reiterate* is to go over something again and again, though here related to L. *is,* that + the adverb ending, *—tem;* whence *item,* and L. *iterum,* again. A remark made by a judge "on the way," during the course of another opinion, is an *obiter dictum.*

object, objection, objective.
See subject.

oblation.
See suffer.

obligation, obligatory, oblige.
See behold.

oblique.
See onion.

obliterate.
This means simply to wipe off the letters, from L. *ob,* off + *litera, littera, letter,* from *linere, lit—,* to smear, since the *letters* were not carved but smeared on parchment. Hence, *literal.* The verb *literare, literat—,* to write, gives us *literati, literate, literature.* Since *letters* are marked in a line, the verb *linere,* to mark, may have influenced *line,* which is directly from the thread or cord with which one traces a *line,* from L. *linea,* string, from L. *linum,* from Gr. *linon,* flax, whence Eng. *linen. Cp. cloth.* By way of ME. *linage,* from Fr. *lignage,* from L. *lineaticum* comes Eng. *lineage. Lineare, lineat—,* to draw, depict, gives us *linear,* and (with the noun ending) *lineament. See oubliette.*

oblivion.
See oubliette.

obloquy.
See agnostic.

obnoxious.
See nuisance. (L. *ob,* in the way of; hence, exposed to).

obscene.
We speak of "filth"; so did the Romans: L. *ob,* upon + *caenum,* mud. The figure and the practice persist.

obscurity.
See chiaroscuro.

obsession, obsidian, obsidional.
See hospital.

obstacle.
See tank.

obstetrician.
See midwife.

obstetrics.
See tank.

obstinate.
See season.

obstruct.
See destroy.

obviate.
See vacuum.

obvious.
This is what meets you on the way, from L. *obvius,* from *ob,* against + *via,* way; *cp. trifle. Obviate* first meant to meet on the way; therefore, to clear out of the way before you reach your goal; *cp. prevent. See* vacuum.

occasion, occident.
See cheat.

October.
See month.

ocular, oculist.
See inveigle.

odd.
The development of this word has been *odd.* It was OHG. *ort,* point, angle. By the time this came to OE. as *odde,* it had already acquired the sense of the (*odd*) point of a triangle; then, figuratively, the *odd* man in a group (of three: the one whose word decided). From its connection with three, the sense was then extended (in Eng. only) to the other numbers between the even ones.
Note that OHG. *ort* is not the origin of Eng. *orts,* scraps of food; this is from OE. *ortys,* from an earlier *or,* negative, + *etan,* to *eat*: the part not eaten.

ode.
See paragraph.

odontology.
See indenture.

Odysseus.
This name serves as a symbol to the modern artist, who preaches full self-revelation, self-portrayal. For when *Odysseus* tried to hide his identity from the Cyclops, he said that his name was *No-Man* (Gr., *Odys*)—thus, inevitably when one tries to hide part of oneself, it is the divine, the *Zeus* in him, that falls away, and *no man* indeed that is left!

oecumenical.
See homo—.

of.
This is a most common form. OE. *aef, of,* away; OHG. *ab;* Sansk. *apa;* Gr. *apo;* L. *ab.* It was probably echoic in origin, akin to *huff* and the exclamation *Hup!* The emphatic form in Eng. is *off,* as in Be *off!*
The word *of* first meant away; then it was used to translate L. *ab, de, ex,* all meaning from. It was also used to translate Fr. *de,* from—but this also developed the meaning, belonging to, as: from New York, of New York. The word *de* became the common Romance preposition substituded for the old genitive (possessive) case; and Eng. *of* followed this course.
Huff refers to the quick in-and-out breathing, as when one is breathless; *Pouf!* and *puff* (also echoic) indicate expulsion of air. Thus *in a huff* means out of breath; esp., choked with anger. *Huff,* and *puff,* and blow the house down!

off.
See of.

offend, offensive.
See fence.

offer.
See suffer.

office.
See defeat.

offspring.
See attack.

ogre.
See Appendix II.

Ohio.
See States.

ohm.
See Appendix II.

—oid.
See kaleidoscope.

oil.
This word indicates that, however wide the sources of the *oils* in use today, the first source was the olive-tree. For *oil* is from AS. *ele,* from OFr. *oile,* from L. *oleum,* from Gr. *elaion, oil,* from *elaia,* olive-tree.

ointment.
See lotion.

O. K.

This symbol has probably more given sources than any other term. The favored seems to be Choktaw Indian *okeh,* it is so. Next comes the error due to bad spelling: *O. K.* marked on boxes to mean *All Correct;* this has been attributed to John Jacob Astor, and to President Andrew Jackson. There is also *Obadiah Kelly,* the early railroad clerk, who initialed all parcels he accepted. And—to skip a dozen or more theories —there is the ME. word *hoacky, horkey,* the last load of a harvest. It's *O. K.* with me!

Oklahoma.
See States.

old.
See world.

Old Bailey.
See villain.

oldster.
See young, youngster.

oleomargarine.

When this *Ersatz* product (G. *Ersatz,* substitute) was first introduced, in the mid 19th c., it was called *butterine.* From the *oil* (L. *oleum, oil, q.v.*) and the beady drops in the heating process (L. *margarine,* little pearl), about 1875 the manufacturers developed the more pleasing name *oleomargarine* (*g* sounded as in *go* and *get* it), which has survived.

The word *ersatz* was used as a military term in World War I; an *Ersatzbataillon* was a relief or replacement battalion. The English borrowed the word; when on leave in France, they might seek an "*ersatz* sweetheart."

In 1944, the U. S. National Association of *Margarine* Manufacturers voted that the *g* is soft.

omelette.

This is really an egg pancake. L. *lamina,* thin plate, has been taken directly into Eng. as a scientific term; it also gives us *laminable, laminated,* etc. Its diminutive was *lamelle,* also *lamette.* In OFr. *la lamette,* the thin plate (applied figuratively to the whipped and fried egg) became *l'amelette* (for similar transfers in Eng., *see auction*); whence Eng. *omelette.* The French, enjoying the food, suggest that it may be from Gr. *omelia,* from *oon,* egg + *meli,* honey; though a more prosaic eytmologist suggests Fr. *oeufs melés,* scrambled eggs.

Related to *lamelle* is the older *amel,* thin plate; with Fr. *en* (L. *in*), this gives us *enamel.* This in turn comes from (Fr. *émail*) OFr. *esmail;* OG. *smalt;* Gr. *meldein;* L. *mollis,* soft (whence Eng. *mollify*)—sources of Eng. *melt* and *smelt,* by which we produce *enamel.*

omen, ominous.
See auction.

omnivorous.
See sarcophagus.

one, once.
See number.

onion.

Those that have, with intended humor, transposed the saying "In *union* there is strength" to "In *onion* there is strength" in all probability did not know that in *onion* there is *union.* With the same vowel change as in *one,* from L. *unus, one, onion* is from L. *unio, union—, unity,* from *unus.* The idea is that the many many layers make but *one* sphere. The word *unio* was similarly applied to a large pearl. The *onion* has been used as a symbol, in that, far as you may peel, you never reach the core.

Scallion is the *Ascalon onion,* from *Ascalon,* Palestine. *Leek* is common Teut., AS. *leac,* whence *leactum,* vegetable garden. *Garlic* is from AS. *garleac,* spear *leek.*

The adjective from L. *unus* is *unicus,* single, whence Fr. *unique,* whence Eng. *unique.* The ending *—ique,* via the Fr., may be used in Eng. to suggest something fancy, as *physique* is opposed to a *physic* (both from Gr. *physike,* adjective, from *physis,* nature, from *phyein,* to produce). *Technique,* and *technical,* are from Gr. *technikos,* from *techne, art,* craft (*art* first meant anything made by man as opposed to nature; then, the skill in its making: the L. *ars, art—, art,* is a root meaning to fit together). *Romantic* (first, like *romance,* referring to the *Roman* tongue, Latin; then to the tales told in it, or their spirit) struggled for a while to hold the language against the Fr. form *romantique. Oblique,* on the other hand, had that ending in the Latin; *obliquus,* from *ob,* against + *leg, lic—,* bent.

only.
See alone.

onyx.
See carnelian.

opiate, opium.
See remorse.

opportune, opportunity.
See port.

optic, optician, optimist, option, opulent.
See pessimist.

oracle, oral.
See inexorable.

orange.
See peach.

oration, orator, oratorio, oratory.
See inexorable. (For *oration, orison, cp. win.*)

orchestra.
The *orchestra* that plays dance-music is closest to the original meaning of the word (Gr. *orcheisthai,* to dance). In the primitive Greek theatre, the still partly religious movement of the dancing chorus was performed in a great circular space, called the *orchestra.* In Roman times, and later, seats were placed here; hence the *orchestra* of the modern theatre. But the fore part of this section was reserved for the musicians; gradually the name of the place was transferred to those that used it, and *orchestra* (still applied to the main floor of a theatre) came to mean the band of musicians, instead of those that dance to their tunes.

orchid.
See test.

ordain, ordeal, order, ordinance, ordinary, ordination.
See augment, orient.

ordnance, ordonnance.
See augment.

Oregon.
See States.

organ.
In its various senses, this is via L. *organa,* from Gr. *organon,* an instrument, from *ergon,* work. The musical *organ* works (originally) with a bellows. From the source come *energy; organization; erg.* An *organism* is a group of *organs* functioning as a whole.

organism, organization.
See organ.

orient.
The mariner turns toward the north star; the Mohammedan, toward Mecca. If we want to *orient* ourselves we turn toward the rising sun (L. *oriri,* to rise, present participle *oriens, orient—*). Hence, the east. Related to this is L. *origo, origin—,* a beginning, whence Eng. *origin, original* (the beginning, therefore without earlier examples). Frequentative of *oriri* is L. *ordiri,* to begin, whence *ordo, ordin—,* whence Eng. *order, ordination,* and (L. *primus,* first, whence *prime*) *primordial.*

orifice.
See defeat.

origin, original.
See orient.

orison.
See win.

ornament, ornate.
See augment.

ornithology.
See tavern.

orotund.
See rote.

orthodox.
See paradox.

orthopedic.
See paradox; *cp.* pedagogue.

orts.
See odd.

oscillate.
In many parts of the world (including Rome), on feast days little dolls, puppets, balls, were hung up, to swing in the breeze. These were called *oscilla;* whence *oscillare, oscillat—,* to swing back and forth, whence Eng. *oscillate.*
This should be distinguished from the words from L. *os, or—,* mouth; *cp. inexorable.* Thus the frequentative verb form, L. *oscitare, oscitat—,* to gape, gives us Eng. *oscitant, yawning.* The diminutive, a little mouth, is L. *osculum,* whence the verb *osculare, osculat—,* and good Eng. *osculation.* Pope uses *osculable* as a nonce-word for a pretty girl; it should occur more often.

osculation.
See oscillate.

osmium, osmosis.
See element.

osseous, ossify, osteopath.
See ostracize (*-ous,* from L. *-osus,* full of; *—fy,* from LL. *ficare,* from L. *facere,* to make; *—path,* from Gr. *path—,* to suffer, to feel.) Gr. *pathos,* suffering, disease, gives us such words as *pathos, pathetic, sympathetic* (Gr. *sym—, syn—,* together), *antipathy* (L. *anti—,* against).

ostensible, ostentation.
See usher.

ostler.
See hospital.

ostracize.
If those around decide to leave an unpopular person as lonely as an *oyster* shut in its shell, they *ostracize* him. In ancient Athens, this was done by a vote, marked on pieces of tile, potsherd, or shell (Gr. *ostrakon,* burnt clay, shell). The word is closely related to Gr. *ostreon, oyster;* and *osteon,* bone, which gives us many Eng. words: *osseous, osteopath, ossify.* It is suggested that the word is related to Sansk. *as,* to throw, as bones were cast aside after eating.

otter.
This word illustrates the hazy ideas of olden times, in natural history. The L. *hydra,* water-snake (Gr. *hydr—,* water; *hydra* is still used of a water-monster; specifically, of the many-headed—hence Eng. *hydra-headed*—snake that held the marshes of Lerna, in Argolis; for each head struck off, two at once were formed; Hercules finally choked it to death) was Lith. *udra;* whence AS. and Eng. *otter.* The word is cognate with *water;* cp. *drink, wash.*

A *hybrid* is from quite different source: L. *hybrida, hibrida;* from Gr. *hybris,* unnatural violence (which seemed involved in the production): this first meant the offspring of a tame sow and wild boar; thence, any mixed breed.

ottoman.
With the western cult of the Oriental, toward the end of the 18th c., came notions of eastern luxury, of lounging in harems, of pillowed delights. The Arab. founder of a Turkish dynasty (ca. 1300) *Othman,* was pictured as bringing the lavish tastes of the Orient into Europe, and his name—in the form *ottoman*—became attached to a comfortable couch.

oubliette.
This delightful little dungeon, entered only through a trapdoor in the roof, whence a prisoner may be tossed a crumb of bread, is pleasantly named from the noun diminutive added to Fr. *oublier,* to forget, from LL. *oblitare,* from *oblivisci, oblit—,* whence Eng. *obliterate, oblivion.* For less lengthy and more enjoyable stays, we now call a place where no one can find us a *hideaway.*

ouija.
The famous board that gives all the answers is, its very name implies, a specialist in double-talk. It is no more than the effort of the spirit to make sure it is understood, no matter whether the listener be of the Teutonic or the Romance background. For *ouija* is a combination of Fr. *oui,* yes, and G. *ja,* yes: Yes, yes: in 27 languages it couldn't say no!

ounce.
See uncle.

out.
See unutterable.

outlandish.
See uncouth.

outrage.
Though one may be put out by an *outrage,* it is not related to *rage.* The ending is the noun form, as in *language, wreckage, dotage,* etc., from OFr. *—age,* from L. *—aticum,* forming an abstract noun from the neuter of the adjective. The stem is from Fr. *oute,* beyond, from L. *ultra*: that which is beyond decency, or beyond endurance. *Rage* is from Fr. *rage,* from LL. *rabies,* madness; which we use as the name of a disease, *rabies.* From this the verb L. *rabere, rabid—,* to be mad, gives us *rabid;* and possibly *rave,* though this comes via Fr. *rever,* to dream, whence also *reverie.*

ovary.
See pseudo—.

ovation.
When the Roman general returned

after a victory, he was met with shouts and rejoicing. *Ovare, ovat—*, to shout, whence *ovation.* The L. *ovare,* from *ouare,* is from Gr. *auein,* to call aloud, an imitative word, related to Sansk. *va,* to blow.

If the Senate was as well pleased as the people, it might vote the general a triumph. At the triumph, oxen were sacrificed, and roasted; at the lesser rejoicing, the *ovation,* sheep were sacrificed; whence the suggestion that the word might come from L. *ovis,* sheep.

over.
See overture.

overboard.
See board.

overdo.
See overture.

overflow.
See affluent.

overt.
See overture.

overture.
This comes at the beginning, not when things are *over*. *Over* is common Teut., AS. *ofer;* G. *ober, über;* cognate with Gr. *hyper,* in many English words, *hyper—, e.g. hyperbole* (Gr. *ballein,* to throw); L. *super,* also a frequent Eng. prefix, *super—, e.g. supersede* (L. *sedere,* to sit; *cp. subsidy.*) *Overture* is a late noun, from *overt,* open, from OFr. *ovrir, overt* (Fr. *ouvrir*), from L. *aperire, apert,* to open, whence Eng. *aperture.* Thus *aperture* and *overture* are doublets.

L. *aperire* was early confused with L. *operire,* to close; whence (*co,* together) Fr. *couvrir, couvert,* whence Eng. *couvert* or *cover* charge at night clubs; and *covert,* opposite of *overt.* L. *aperire* is probably *ab,* away + *perire,* cover; while *operire* is *ob,* up + *perire,* cover; the root *perire* is related to *parare,* to dress up, adorn, *prepare* (L. *pre,* before + *parare*). This gives us many Eng. words. In the sense of *prepare* for, hence ward off, it gives us *parry,* and through It. and Port. *para—* as a prefix, *parasol,* to ward off the sun (L. *sol,* sun, whence *solar; cp. trophy*), *parapet* (It. *petto,* breast: breast-high protection); *rampart* (earlier *rempart,* from *re-en-par*: to put up a defence again); and *parachute,* to ward off a fall. A *paratroop,* however, is not something that wards off a troop; but a *troop* that attacks from airplanes via *parachutes.* Fr. *parapluie,* to ward off rain, has been replaced in Eng. by *umbrella,* from It. *ombrella,* diminutive of *ombra,* from L. *umbra,* shade. From the past participle of L. *parare, parat—*, ready, hence waiting, displayed, came (through Sp. *parada*) the sense of a show, esp. as of a horse held in check; hence, *parade.*

The opposite of Gr. *hyper—*, over, is *hypo—*, under, whence also many Eng. words. *Hypocrite* was originally a secondary actor, who answered back. *Hypochondriac* (Gr. *chondros,* gristle: under the cartilages) was one whose nature was influenced by the soft part of the body, beneath the cartilage of the ribs, *i.e.,* by the liver, the seat of the melancholy; *cp. complexion.* The opposite of L. *super—*, above, *supra—*, beyond, and (through the Fr.) *sur— e.g. surtax,* is *sub—*, under; whence, also, many Eng. derivatives, *e.g. submarine,* under the sea. There are of course many compounds from Eng. *under, q.v., e.g., undermine;* but we must not *overdo!*

oviparous.
See shed.

owl.
See yokel.

Oxford.
See Bosphorus.

oxygen.
See element, racy.

oyster.
This has been a favorite food from early times, being Gr. *ostreon,* L. *ostreum,* possibly related to L. *os,* bone; *cp. ostracize.* Pistol says to Falstaff, in The Garter Inn (*Merry Wives of Windsor,* II,ii 2):

the world's mine *oyster,*
Which I with sword will open.

Sometimes "the *oyster*" is used in the sense of prize, or thing desired; from the story of the monkey, who, asked to judge to whom an *oyster* belonged, ate the succulency and gave each disputant a shell. Byron, in *Don Juan,* 1819, said "*oysters* are amatory food"; but Sheridan, in *The Critic,* 1779, had remarked: "An *oyster* may be crossed in love." But do not believe, as the children claim, that *a noisy noise annoys an oyster!*

ozone.
The bracing air of the seashore, rich in *ozone*, first had this constituent named (Fr., *ozone*) in 1840; from Gr. *ozein*, to smell, + —*one*. The suffix —*one* (Gr. *one*, daughter of) is used loosely as an ending for various chemical derivatives, *e.g.*, *acetone*.

P

pabulum.
See abbot.

pace.
See pass.

pachyderm.
See propaganda.

pacific.
See pay.

pacify, pact.
See defeat, propaganda.

paddock.
See parquet.

paean.
See pawn.

pagan.
Christianity spread more rapidly in the cities than in the outlying sections of the Roman Empire. Thus a countryman (L. *paganus,* villager, from *pagus,* district, from *pangere, pegi,* to fix, set: the country districts were marked off) according to Gibbons' *Decline and Fall,* was likely to be an unbeliever, a *pagan.* Similarly a *heathen* was first merely a dweller on the *heath,* wild open country. *Cp. neighbor.* (This story is true for *heathen,* but later research suggests a different story for *pagan.* It was used under the Cæsars to mean a civilian, as opposed to the *milites,* the soldiers: The Christians called themselves "the soldiers of the Lord," hence all others were *pagans*).

The city folk have by no means ceased scorning the country fellow, as the terms *bumpkin, rube* (from Reuben, a frequent farmer's name) and ninety-two more in *The American Thesaurus of Slang* attest. But the farmer today knows that the city dweller is equally inept in the country; hence the dude-ranch for the tenderfoot and his tribe. *Cp. police.*

page.
See propaganda.

pain.
See chary.

paint.
See arsenic.

painter.
This is three words. The animal, *painter,* is a corruption of *panther,* said to be from Gr. *panther,* from *pan,* all + *ther,* animal: partaking of features of every beast. (Gr. *ther,* whence L. *fer,* wild animal; *cp. treacle.*) *Panther* is more probably from Sansk. *pundarika,* leopard. The line for holding or towing a boat, *painter,* is probably ultimately from Sansk. *pankti,* line, from *pac,* to extend. But it has been traced to the first word, via OE. *panter,* noose, from OFr. *pantiere,* snare, from Gr. *pantheros,* catching every beast. There is, finally, the man that *paints,* from Fr. *peindre, peint,* from L. *pingere, pict—,* whence Eng. *picture, depict* (L. *de,* down). Thus "the *painter painted* a *painter*" might mean that a man that draws towed a wild animal.

pal.
See wig.

palace.
This is a home such as the Cæsars had, via Fr. *palais,* from L. *palatium,* from the *mons Palatinus, Palatine Hill* at Rome, where Augustus Cæsar, first of the Emperors, erected his stately home. It was fenced about, for *palatinus* is from L. *palus,* stake, enclosure, whence Eng. *pale, paling, impale. Beyond the pale* is outside the fence, thus not "one of our gang." The attendants of the *palace* were called It. *paladino,* whence Fr., whence Eng. *paladins,* esp. of the twelve peers of Charlemagne.

The *Palatine* hill has no relation to *Pallas* Athene. Her statue, bearing a spear (Gr. *pallan*, to brandish), is the *palladium*, defending the city. The *Parthenon* was erected in honor of this virgin goddess (Gr. *parthenos*, virgin; whence Eng. *parthenogenesis*, virgin birth; *cp. racy*). Eng. *Palladian* may mean, pertaining to *Pallas* Athene, or of the school of architecture of the Italian *Andrea Palladio* (1518-80).

Pole has two meanings, from separate sources. L. *palus*, whence AS. *pāl*, whence *pole*, hence a doublet of *pale*. The north *pole* and the south *pole*, however, are via Fr. *pôle*, from Gr. *polos*, axis. *Pale*, *pallid*, is from L. *pallere*, *pallid*, to turn *pale*; whence also *pallor*, inappropriate to a *palace*.

paladin, pale.
See palace.

palimpsest, palindrome.
See dromedary.

paling.
See palace.

pall.
See palliate.

palladium.
See element, palace.

palliate.
The simplest disguise is a *cloak* (L. *pallium*, *cloak*, whence Eng. *pall*; L. *palliare*, *palliatum*, to cloak) over the thing to be hidden. By a figure of speech, a *cloak* may be drawn over an offense, to *palliate* it. In early Eng. the word *cloke* was similarly used.

Cloak, *cloke*, is from OFr. *cloque*, from LL. *clocca*, bell, from the bell-shape of the early *cloak*. The word *clock* is from the same origin, as the early *"clocks"* were bells. (Up to the 4th c., church water-*clocks* did not ring bells, but clashed cymbals). The LL. *clocca* is probably of Teut. origin, AS. *clucga*; G. *Glocke*. The *clock* of a *stocking* is also named from its bell-shape. *Stocking* is from *stick*: that into which the foot is *stuck*; also, the *stocks*.

pallid, pallor.
See palace.

pall-mall.
See mail.

palm.
The original sense is the *palm* of the hand, from L. *palma*, from Gr. *palame*: AS. *folm*, whence Eng. *fumble* (influenced by an older *thumble*, from *thumb*, from AS. *thuma*; cognate with OPers. *tuma*, fat; L. *tumere*, *tumult—*, to swell, whence Eng. *tumor*, *tumult*). To *palm* off is from tricks of legerdemain, lightness of hand. The *palm* tree is named from the shape of its fronds; *palmetto* is a little *palm* tree; *palmyra* is from Port. *palmeira*, *palm* tree, not from *Palmyra* but from L. *palma*. *Palmistry* is from *palm* + *mystery*, *q.v.* The *Palmer* (one of *The Four P's* in Heywood's interlude, ca. 1543: *palmer*, *pardoner*, *potycary*, and *pedler*, who compete to see which can tell the biggest lie; the *Palmer* wins by saying he's never seen an impatient woman!) is one that bears a *palm*-branch as a sign that he has made the pilgrimage to the Holy Land.

palmer.
See chichevache, palm.

palooka.
See wig.

palpable.
See palpitate.

palpitate.
There are three Eng. verbs, *palp*, *palpate*, *palpitate*. The first two are from L. *palpare*, *palpat—*, to touch; *palpate* is used of a medical examination by feeling. The frequentative, to touch rapidly, hence to move back and forth quickly, is L. *palpitare*, *palpitat—*, hence Eng. *palpitate* and *palpitation* of the eyelids or the heart. Eng. *palpebra* is the anatomical term for eyelid; *palpus* is a zoological term for feeler. If it can be felt (hence, manifest) it is, as in *Hamlet*, a *palpable* hit.

pamper.
While this now refers to the spirit as well, its first use was of the body: *pamper* meant, to stuff with food: G. *pampen*; related to L. *pabulum*, from *pasci*, *past—*, to feed, also *pap*; *cp. abbot*. The It. form is *pamberato*, well fed, which suggests the telescoping of *pane*, bread, food, and *bere*, drink. Another suggested source for *pamper* is L. *pampinus*, tendril; Milton (*Paradise Lost*, V,214) speaks of the *pampered* boughs of fruit-trees. Perhaps we may speak of the hot-house products as *pampered* fruit.

It may, however, be the frequentative form of an earlier Eng. *pamp*, to stuff with food, from an earlier form *pimp*, *pamp*, *pomp*, to swell. Thus a *pimple* is a little swelling, often the result of "*pamping*". The *pomp* of a ceremony may have been influenced by this form, but *see pontiff*. The *pump* that brings water (with its Fr. form, *pompe*) is echoic of the sound of the plunger.

pamphlet.
The little *brochure* is stitched together, from Fr. *brocher*, to stitch; thus needlework cloth (*q.v.*) is, via Sp. *brocado*, Eng *brocade*. It is suggested that *pamphlet* has a similar derivation: from Fr. *par un filet*, (held) by a thread. For the more likely source, *see pan*.

pan.
The kitchen *pan* and the goat-foot god of the Greeks have little in common, in spite of Christopher Morley's quest of a divine *dishpantheism*. *Pan* (AS. *panne*; OHG. *pfanna*) is traced by some through LL. *panna* to L. *patina*, vessel — which may, through Fr. *patine*, give us Eng. *patina*, the coating on old metal. But by transfer from the contents to the container, *pan* may be from L. *panem*, bread. Thus *pannier* is a bread basket; *pantry*, a place for storing not *pans* but bread (Fr. *pain*, bread). The ancient Roman *sop* (AS. *sopp*, bread dipped in liquid; cognate with *sup* and *soup*) to the hungry populace was free *panem et circenses*, bread and circuses.

We have not yet scraped the *pan* (nor eaten the *pancake* or the *pandowdy*—an unpretentious but delicious apple pudding with molasses). The oriental "chewing-gum", of betel leaf and nut, is Eng. *pan*, from Hindu *pan*, Sansk. *parna*, feather, leaf (bird or tree plume). A *pandy* (corrupted to *paddy* and *paddywhack*) is Scots for a blow on the hand, from L. *pandere*, to hold out, extend, whence Eng. *expand*, *expansive*. In botany, a *panicle* is a cluster: L. *panicula*, diminutive of *panus*, an ear of millet, related to *panem*, bread. The *pancreas* is from *pan*, all + *kreas*, flesh: the sweetbread is all flesh. And *panic* was first an adjective, the *panic* terror induced by the god *Pan*. *Cp. congress.*

The god *Pan*, as god of nature, is connected with Gr. *pan*, *pant—*, all; perhaps with Sansk. *pavana*, wind, from *pu*, to purify: the cleansing wind. This has given rise to many English words. Among them is *banjo*, the Negro mispronunciation of *bandore*, from *Pandora*. This might have come into the Greek from the orient, where such instruments were played; but *Pandora* (*pan* + *dora*, from *doron*, gift) was the name of the first mortal woman, whom Vulcan, after fashioning her, brought to the other gods, and they gave her a box containing all their blessings. (You remember she opened it incautiously, and they all escaped, except hope, which was snug at the bottom.) *Pamphlet* is another roundabout word from this source: *pan* + *philus*, loved by all: a popular 12th c. little book, *Pamphilus, seu de Amore*, under its nickname, *pamphilet*, came to be used for all such leaflets. . . . Such words as *Pan-American*, *Pan-Germanic*, are obvious formations. Other words beginning in *pan* are discussed separately, below.

pan—, pant—, panto—.
There are three combining forms, all from Gr. *pas*; *pan*, *pant—*, all. The first is most frequent in words of general use, *pan-American*, *panathletic*. *Pant—*, before a vowel, and *panto—*, before a consonant, are used rather in scientific fields. Note that *pantechnicon* (*cp. onion*) was a 19th c. London term for a bazaar of general art merchandise, then a storehouse, then (short for *pantechnicon-van*) a *moving-van*. *Van* itself is short for *caravan*; from Pers. *karwan*, a company traveling together for safety; then, a covered wagon. *Pantopragmatic* is a humorous term for a universal busybody.

pancreas.
See pan.

pandemonium.
Milton in *Paradise Lost, I*, 756, coined this word for the name of the capital of Hell. By natural transfer, it came to mean fiendish noise and confusion. *Cp. pan.*

pander.
The usual ending *er*, one who, has probably changed this word, which is from Gr. *Pandaros*, the uncle of Cressida of Troy, who acted as go-between for Troilus who loved her. Boccaccio tells the story, but it is more fully presented by Chaucer. Hence the verb, to *pander* to one's appetites.

Pandora.
See pan.

pane.
This word is not from L. *pan* or Gr. *pan* (*Cp. pan*) but from Fr. *pan,* from L. *pannum,* cloth, piece of cloth; its diminutive, *panellum,* gives *panel.* Both words were applied to a bit of cloth stretched for various purposes, as to cover a window; hence, window *pane.* Both were also used of a piece of anything, in general; hence, *panel* of a wall, also used in a coal-mine. *Panel,* used of a strip of parchment, esp. that on which a sheriff wrote a list of names, gives us the jury *panel,* and the verb to *empanel, impanel,* a jury. *Panel,* from its use of the piece of cloth placed under the saddle to keep it from chafing, was later applied to the stuffed lining of the saddle, then to the saddle itself. The *paneled* wall and the window *pane* are thus both sprung from cloth. *Cp. pan.*

panegyric.
Speak only good of a man, in public. If you must, speak ill of him in private. (Too many interpret this as meaning, behind his back; its proper sense is, to him alone and for his betterment.) But the public practice of praise is perpetuated in the *panegyric,* which merely means a speech before the whole assembly: from Gr. *panegyris,* general assembly, from *pan,* all + *agora,* assembly.

panel.
See pane.

panic.
The vague fear of things unknown was by the Greeks attributed to *Pan, q.v.* Even on Wall Street, rumors and rush are the first signs of a *panic.*

panjandrum.
In 1755 a man named Macklin claimed he could repeat anything, after hearing it once. Samuel Foote at once rattled off: "And there were present the Picninnies, and the Joblillies, and the Garyulies, and the Grand *Panjandrum* himself, with the little round button at top." History does not record whether it was successfully repeated; but the word *Panjandrum* was repeated again and again, as the mock title of a man who deems himself the embodiment of all excellencies. *Cp. pan.*

pannier.
See pan.

panoply.
Mainly used today in a figurative sense, meaning full display of resplendent garb, *panoply* first meant in full armor (Gr. *pan* + *hoplites,* from *hoplite,* foot-soldier, from *hopla,* arms). *Cp. pan.*

pansy.
The flower (also earlier spelled *pensy, pensee*) is from Fr. *pensée,* thought, (from Fr. *penser,* from L. *pensare,* to think, frequentative of L. *pendere,* to weigh. *See aggravate.*). Ophelia (in *Hamlet,* IV, v) says: "There is pansies, that's for thoughts."

pant.
Did you ever awake from a nightmare, your eyes popping through the dark, your heart pumping wildly, your breath heaving in quick *pants?* Lucky, if not; but if so, you can appreciate that *pant,* to breathe heavily, is from Fr. *pantoisier,* from LL. *phantasiare,* to be oppressed with nightmare, from Gr. *phantasia,* nightmare; *cp. focus.* Coleridge, in Kubla Khan, says:

> And from this chasm, with ceaseless turmoil seething,
> As if this earth in fast thick pants were breathing,
> A mighty fountain momently was forced.

See pants.

pantaloon.
See pants.

pantechnicon.
See pan—.

panther.
See painter.

pantopragmatic.
See pan—.

pantry.
See pan.

pants.
This is an abbreviation of *pantaloons* (the diminutive of which is *pantalettes*). *Pantaloons* are part of the costume worn by the *pantaloon* (It. *pantalone,* from *San Pantaleone,* a favorite saint of the Venetians; the saint's name is from Gr. *panta,* all + *leone,* lion) in the medieval Italian mask, or *commedia dell' arte.* He was an old man, butt of the clown's jokes; hence, a *pantaloon* is linked by some with the slang *looney*: "Who's

looney now?" and *lunatic*—though these are from L. *luna,* the moon: moon-struck. Another diminutive of *pants* gives us *panties;* by imitation of this, the still more diminutive *scanties.*

papa, papacy, papal.
See abbot.

paper.
See bible.

papoose.
See abbot.

par.
See gossip; zipper.

para, para-.
This is three words, and at least three prefixes. *Cp.* periscope.

There is a *para,* a small Turkish coin, worth perhaps one tenth of a cent. *Para* is also a small weight in North Borneo; a measure of capacity in India. And, from the name of a port on the Amazon in Brazil, we have *para* rubber, and the *para* nut (Brazil nut).

As a prefix, *para—* is Gr., outside of, beyond, beside. It appears in *parallel* (Gr. *allelos,* one another); *paranoia* (Gr. *noos, nous,* mind); and hundreds of scientific terms. Through It. and Port. *para—* implies protection against, as in *parasol; see overture.* OFr. *par—,* by, through, gives us *paramour* (*amour,* love); *paramount* (OFr. *amont,* above, from L. *ad monten,* to the *mount*).

Still another source hides in *paraffin.* This word was coined in 1830, by the chemist Reichenback, from L. *parum,* barely + *affinis,* having *affinity* (whence Eng. *affinity,* from *ad,* to + *finis,* end: *i.e.,* adjoining), because its various types had little chemical *affinity, i.e.,* they resist forming compounds. (For *finite,* etc., *see finance.*)

parable, parabola.
See parlor.

parachute, parade.
See overture.

paradise.
The lost *paradise* was a garden, out of which (Gr. *para,* beyond, beside; also, via Port. against; *cp. overture*) the first of all humans were driven. This has affected the spelling; but the word comes through the Greek, from OPers. *pairidaeza,* from *pairi,* around (Gr. *peri—*) + *dez,* a heap, from *diz,* to form. Hence, a walled garden, as in modern Pers. *firdaus,* garden. The root *diz,* to form, is akin to AS. *dig,* to knead, whence Eng. *dough; cp. lady.*

paradox.
A *doxy* was a merry wench, from old Du. *docke,* doll. But Gr. *doxa* meant opinion. *Orthodox* (Gr. *orthos,* straight, right; also in *orthopedic,* foot-straightening). *Heterodox* (Gr. *heteros,* other; also in *heterogeneous,* from *genus, genera,* classes, *i.e.,* mixed). *Paradox* (*para—,* contrary, beyond). Hence there was both pride and pun in the man that remarked: "My *doxy* is *orthodoxy.*" *Cp. dogma.*

paraffin.
See para.

paragon.
A difficult thing to become—and as hard to trace. There are at least three suggestions. It may be made up of prepositions, from the Sp. expressions *para con migo,* in comparison with me; *para con el,* compared to him; etc. This traces it to three L. prepositions: Sp. *para,* from L. *pro* + *ad* (like Eng. *to* + *ward, toward*); Sp. *con,* from L. *cum,* with. If you don't like this, you may prefer the thought that it is from Gr. *parakonan,* to sharpen by rubbing, from *akone,* a whetstone. My own choice is theatrical: *paragon,* from *para,* beyond + *agon,* the dramatic conflict; *cp. agony.* Thus the *paragon* is outside the fight, beyond compare.

paragraph.
Early writing goes on without breaks between words or after sentences or *paragraphs.* When a break in the sense occurred, a mark was made under the first word of that line; this was called a *paragraph,* from Gr. *para,* beside + *graphos,* from *graphein,* to write. When the divisions were made, the term was transferred to the division.

Comma and *period* have had the opposite journey. A *comma* was a small section of a passage, from Gr. *comma,* from *koptein,* to cut. The longer passage was called a *period,* from Gr. *periodos,* from *peri,* around + *odos,* way: the course or circuit of a thought. Then the terms were applied to the marks setting off such passages. An *ode,* from Gr. *ode* (two syllables), from *aoide,* song, is from *aeidein,* to sing; but note that it was sung while the Greek dramatic chorus made its way across the stage. It usually consisted of three parts: the *strophe* (Gr. *strophos,* from *strephein,* to turn) as they came in, an independent *epode* as they stood, an *antistrophe* (*anti,* against) of the same meter as the *strophe* as they wended their way out. The *catastrophe* is the point in a drama (now, in life as well) in which the actions turn against the chief figure (Gr. *cata,* down, against: *catapult,* from *cata* + *pallein,* to hurl; *catalogue,* from *cata,* down + *legein,* to read; *catarrh,* from Gr. *catarrein,* to flow down)—which makes quite a *paragraph!*

parallel, paramount, paramour, paranoia.
See para.

parapet.
See overture.

parallel.
Dr. Samuel Johnson, walking in London, came upon a woman sweeping the street; she refused to stop so that he might pass. Drawing himself up, he roared: "Woman, thou art a *parallelogram!*" She was so dumbfounded that she stopped, and he walked on.

It has always been my thought he was lucky he did not call her by the solid figure, a *parallelepiped.* She might have fancied she understood the last two syllables.

One line beside another forms a *parallel,* from Gr. *parallelos,* from *para,* beside, against + *allelos,* one another. Add to this Gr. *gramme,* line, and you have *parallelogram.* The solid was earlier *parallelepipedon;* it has one *parallelogram,* its base, on the ground; the ending is Gr *epi,* upon + *pedon,* ground (*cp. ped-,* foot). Johnson's remark to the woman knocked the ground from under her broom.

paraphernalia.
In ancient times, when a woman married she often received, in addition to the dowry from her parents (which really she carried to her husband for marrying her) certain gifts from the husband which were her own. These were her *paraphernalia* (LL. plural of *paraphernalis,* from Gr. *parapherna,* from *para,* beyond + *pherna,* dowry, from *pherein,* to bear, whence L. *fer, cp. suffer*). From the comon tendency of the man, however, to treat all possessions, in the house as jointly owned, *i.e.,* as his own, the word came to mean just belongings.

paraphrase.
See periscope.

parasite.
In ancient Greece, the poor were admitted to the feasts after certain sacrifices; a *parasite* (Gr. *para,* beside + *sitos,* food) came in Roman times to be one that flattered for his meals, "sang for his supper". In the animal, and esp. the insect world, it also means one that feeds upon others. When such a relationship is mutually beneficial, as among the ants that keep cows, it is called *symbiosis* (Gr. *sym, syn,* together + *bios,* life).

parasol, paratroop.
See overture.

parboil.
See periscope.

parchment.
This word is not a document by which one reaches a goal, despite Fr. *perchemin,* through road; the Fr. is from LL. *pergamentum,* from *pergamena charta,* sheet from *Pergamum,* a city of Mysia in Asia Minor.

pardon.
See periscope.

paregoric.
What is now given to an ailing child was once the portion of an entire people. When the Greeks of the small city-states met, it was in the *agora,* marketplace; hence *agora* came to mean assembly. Most of the speeches there made (as still via radio today) were for the purpose of raising the morale of the people; so that the word for exhorting the public, Gr. *paregorein,* produced an adjective that meant comforting, soothing: Gr. *paregorikos.* We have properly applied this to a soothing syrup — though we are not so wise when we listen today!

pariah.
In medieval Europe, a leper had to beat two sticks together as he walked, as a warning to the public that one diseased was approaching. The *pariah* need not beat his drum. But the word is from the Tamil (Indian) *paraiyan,*

drummer, from *parai,* a large drum -- the beating of which at festivals was the duty of one of the lower castes of Indian. Most of the servants of the whites came from this caste, furnishing the outcast, or *pariah.*

parity.
See peep.

park.
See parquet.

parlance, parley, parliament.
See parlor.

parlor.
The name of a room often grew from its function. Thus the *boudoir, q.v.,* is the pouting room. The *salon* was originally the main living room, Fr. but of Teut. origin, from Goth. *saljan,* to dwell. A doublet is *saloon,* as used on ships, but elsewhere not for water. *Parlor* (from OFr. *parlour,* whence *parloir*) is the speaking room, from *parler,* to speak; LL. *parlatorium,* conference-hall. But this word has wider ramifications. For Fr. *parler* is from LL. *parabolare,* to make *parables,* from L. *parabola,* from Gr. *parabole,* from *paraballein,* to throw beside, to compare. The strict sense of this gives us the mathematical *parabola;* the figurative, the Biblical *parables.* Hence also *parley, parlance,* and the House of *Parliament,* from Fr. *parlement* (LL. *parliamentum*). *Parole* (first in the phrase *parole d'honneur,* word of honor) is from LL. *paraula,* from *parabola;* this took the place of L. *verbum,* word, in common *parlance,* because of the religious use of *verbum*: "in the beginning was the word." A *parlous* deed, however, is not one talked about, but due to the earlier pronunciation of *perilous. Peril* is from L. *periculum,* danger; the *per* is the root of *experiri, expert—,* to try out, whence Eng. *experiment,* which used often to involve danger. The present participle of this verb, *experiens, experient—,* gives us *experience;* the past participle gives us *expert.* Many a person in a *parlor* pretends to be *expert.*
The cannon (stone-thrower) of the ancients was called *ballista,* from Gr. *ballein,* to throw. Further words from this source are *embolism* (Gr. *em,* from *en,* in); *hyperbole* (Gr. *hyper,* beyond); *metabolism* (Gr. *metabole,* change; *meta,* elsewhere, after, etc. + *ballein*); *problem* (Gr. *pro,* forward: to put forward, to propose); *symbol, q.v.; see emblem.*

parlous, parole.
See parlor.

Parnassian.
See Dauphin.

parquet.
This was originally a small part of a *park,* then of a courtyard or a theatre, which had a wooden flooring; then, the flooring itself. The word is a diminutive of Fr. *parc, park*: *parquet.* Fr. *parc* was first a preserve for wild beasts, OE. *pearroc;* MHG. *pferrich,* enclosure, fence. From this, there is also an early Eng. *parrock,* which survives in the variant *paddock.*

parrot.
This bird, along with *Pierrot* (Fr. for sparrow) and the stormy *petrel,* takes its name from *Peter.* The first bird, because the apostle talked a lot; the last, because he walked on the waters. *Peter* itself is L. and Gr. for rock; whence the pun that founded the Catholic church: Jesus put his hand on *Peter,* and said "On this rock" shall I build. The same word is seen in *petrify,* to make into stone; and *petroleum,* from *petri—,* stone + *oleum,* oil. L. *petrus* and Syrian *Putras* suggest a connection with *buttress;* but *see butt.*
To *peter out* was first a U. S. mining term. Some suggest that it is from Fr. *péter,* to pass wind, from the echoic Fr. *pet,* as an expression of the miners' disappointment. It seems more likely to spring from the fact that the vein of ore has *petered,* turned into stone.
The domestic *pet* is perhaps a shortening of Fr. *petit; see pit.* To be *in a pet* was earlier to *take the pet,* to sulk at not being *petted;* and indeed a *petty* person is likely to be *pettish.* (Note that the expression *in petto* is via It. from L. *pectus, pector—,* breast; whence also Eng. *pectoral*—and has no relation to what goes on at *petting* parties.)

parry.
See overture.

parson.
This doublet of *person, q.v.,* became limited in the 11th c. to the *person* in charge of parish concerns. Note that at one time *person* and *parson* were pronounced alike (as *clerk* and *clark,* etc.).

parthenogenesis.
See palace.

Parthian (shot).
See Pyrrhic.

paschal.
See abbot, Easter.

pasquinade.
In 1501, before digging up antiques was common, a mutilated statue was unearthed in Rome (some say near the barbershop of one Pasqüin), and re-erected by Cardinal Caraffa. Annually on St. Mark's Day, anonymous verses (of religious or political satire) were hung upon it. It was supposed by some to represent a Roman named Pasquin. At any rate, the verses were "pasquined" (It. *pasquinata*), and each satire was called a *pasquinade. Cp. graffito.*

pass.
This word has come into Eng. by two routes from the same root. L. *passus,* step, *pace,* led to Fr. *pas,* Eng. *pass.* But the L. *passus* developed the LL. verb *passare,* whence Fr. *passer,* to *pass,* and the noun Fr. *pass*: partly from this Fr. noun and partly from the Eng. verb, to *pass* (from the Fr. verb), came the Eng. noun, *pass.* The meanings are also intertwined.

In general, the first *pass* meant a step (also, early, a section of a poem); in this sense, now obsolete, a more lasting variant is *pace.* It has survived in the sense of a way to go through, as in a narrow *pass;* a larger *pass* is a *passage, cp. trespass.*

The second journey gave us *pass* in the sense of the act of *passing,* as a *forward pass* in football; also the condition through which or to which a thing *passes,* as in such phrases as *it came to pass;* he found himself in a *sorry pass.* Hence, also, the quick *pass* of a magician, as with card tricks. *Permission to pass* has been shortened until *pass* means the permission; thus also *passport* and *password.*

The verb *pass* is the basic word for motion from one place to another.

There are a number of other forms from this source, which must not be confused with the *passion* flowering from L. *pati, pass—,* to suffer. Thus Eng. *impassible* means *passive* (unfeeling, or at least giving no signs of feeling), while Eng. *impassable* means that one cannot go by. *Passenger* is from Fr. *passager,* one going by (the *n* was added in ME., as in *messenger,* from *message,* from LL. form *missaticum,* from L. *mittere, miss—,* to send, whence also *mission* and *missioner* or *missionary; cp. compromise;* and also in *scavenger,* from ME. *scavager,* tax-collector, from *scavage,* originally a tax in London on foreign merchants, from a Du. *escauwer,* related to Eng. *show*: the same man was the London street commissioner). For *passive, cp. exact,* and references *passim*—though our word is *past.*

Paste and *pastry* (earlier *pasty*) are of course not related to *past* (a variant of *passed,* the regular *past* tense of *pass*); but from L. *pasta,* from Gr. *paste, pasta,* barley porridge, from Gr. *pastos,* sprinkled. *Paste* is still used of the dough mixed for making *pastry;* it is also applied to a mixture of flour and water used as an adhesive, and to similar substances, including "diamonds" made of *paste.*

passage, passenger.
See pass, trespass.

passive.
See exact.

Passover.
See Easter.

passport, password, paste.
See pass.

pastern.
See pester; abbot.

pasteurize.
See Appendix II.

pastor, pastoral.
See congress.

pastry.
See pass.

pasture.
See pester; abbot.

pathetic, pathology, pathos.
See apathy, osseous.

patient.
See exact.

patina.
See pan.

patois.
See slang.

patrician.
See pattern.

patriot.
See zipper.

patron, patronize, patronizing.
See pattern.

patten.
See blatherskite.

patter.
Pitter-patter is a double reduplicative form. It illustrates a fondness for repetition, as in *niminy-piminy, tittle-tattle, shilly-shally* (from *shall I?,* of a hesitant person), and a host more. *Cp. scurry.* But *patter* itself is a frequentative form of *pat,* which imitates the sound produced by the action.

But *patter,* in the sense of the salesman's glib, meaningless talk, has another origin. It is from L. *pater,* short for *pater-noster,* Our Father, the first words of the Lord's Prayer, and is drawn from the rapid reciting or mumbling of the words, as was frequent (says the Rev. A. Smythe Palmer, in *Folk-Etymology,* 1882) in "pre-Reformation times." Longfellow combines the two senses (*Midnight Mass for the Dying Year*):

> The hooded clouds, like friars,
> Tell their beads in drops of rain,
> And patter their doleful prayers.

pattern.
The father was the model of the family, the tribe, as the archetypal *pattern* is the Father in heaven, who made man in his image. The word shows this is in its background: *pattern,* from L. *patronus,* support, model, from *pater, patr-,* father. Thus also the fathers of the city, hence heads, the *patricians. Pattern* is thus a doublet of *patron.* It is well to *patronize* worth-while things; but don't—the wide failure to heed this advice developed the sense—don't be *patronizing.*

pause.
See pose.

pavilion.
Did you ever start to pitch a tent on a windy day, only to see the canvas go sweeping forth from you on two sides, like the wings of a giant butterfly? *Pavilion* (ME. *pavilon,* from Fr. *pavillon,* from L. *papilionem,* butterfly) was originally a tent; then, anything like a tent, such as a litter with a canopy, or a garden pleasure-house. It was also applied to a French gold coin of 1329, showing Philip VI of Valois under a canopy. It is now a fancy word for a semi-detached section of a building, as a hospital.

pawn.
As a security on a loan, etc., *pawn* is from Fr. *pan,* skirt of a gown; *cp. pane,* from L. *pannum,* cloth—a garment being the most common object to *pawn.* In Teut. tongues, a *d* or *t* grew on at the end (Du. *pand,* a pledge; G. *pfand;* AS. *pending,* whence *penny, pence*).

Pawn in chess is a doublet of *peon* (from L. *pedo, pedon—,* a foot-soldier; *cp. pedagogue*), which also through OFr. *peonier* gave us *pioneer*—who was originally the foot-soldier that went ahead to dig mines; then, anyone that goes ahead of a main body.

The flower *peony* is not related; its variant spelling *paeony* indicates its origin in L. *paeonia,* medicinal (it being supposed of helpful powers), from *Apollo Paian,* god of medicine (from Sansk. *pan,* ? to praise)—whence *paean,* a hymn in honor of Apollo. *See flower.*

pay.
One way of pacifying a person is to give him some money. To *pay* is precisely to *pacify,* from F. *payer,* from L. *pacare,* to appease, from *pax, pac—,* peace, whence *pacifist,* etc. *Cp. propaganda.* But the sailors have a different sort of *pay,* as in the expression "there's the devil to *pay*"—for the rest of that expression is—"and no pitch hot." To *pay* is to cover with pitch, from OFr. *empoier,* from Fr. *poix, pitch,* from Sp. *pegar,* from L. *picare,* to *pitch,* from *pix, pitch.* The "devil" may have been a sailor term for a seam hard to caulk; or may have been influenced by the idea of tarring and feathering persons not liked. *Pitch,* to heave, to throw, is not an early word, perhaps a variant form of *pick,* to *peek,* as it first meant to thrust in; *pitchfork. Pick* is from AS. *pycan,* from G. *picken,* to puncture, from Fr. *piquer,* from It. *piccare,* related to *picus,* woodpecker. *Tar* is an old Teut. word, AS. *teru,* related to *tree,* from AS. *treow,* Gr. *drus,* oak, from Sansk. *dru,* tree. This is probably related to OFr. *drui,* whence *druid,* whence Eng. *true.* It *pays* to be *true.*

pea.

"Pease porridge hot, *pease* porridge cold": thus begins the old nursery rhyme, from AS. *pise,* from L. *pisa,* from Gr. *pison.* The OFr. *peis,* whence Fr. *pois,* shows the final *s;* but English persons not acquainted with the subtleties of other tongues thought that sweet *pease* was a plural, and turned *pease* soup into *pea* soup. A *pea-jacket* is from Du. *pye,* coarse wool.

peace.

See propaganda.

peach.

When you look at, feel, taste, this delicious fruit, you can understand the expression "She's a *peach*!" The word came from the east, from Fr. *peche,* from OFr. *pesche,* from LL. *pessica,* from L. *Persicum* (*pomum*), the *Persian apple.* At first, indeed, and not only because of the garden of Eden, all *fruits* were *apples.* The Greeks had one general word, *melon* (later, *citron* included lemon and lime); the Romans had two: *malum* (from the Gr.) and *pomum* (whence Fr. *pomme*). Anglo-Saxon had *apple* and *berry.* Thus *quince* in AS. was *codapple,* whence *godapple;* as *potato* is still in Fr. *pomme de terre* and in G. *Erdapfel, earth-apple.* Pineapple was originally what it says, the *apple* (cone) of the pine; in the 18th c., because of the appearance, the name was transferred to what we now eat and drink.

Orange has lost an initial *n; cp. auction;* it is from Fr. *orange,* from Sp. *naranja,* from Arab. *nāranj,* from Sansk. *nāranga;* it was changed in L. from *arangia* to *aurangia,* the golden apple (L. *aurum,* gold); hence, the initial *o*: the fruit of gold. Sansk. *naranga* has been derived from *naga,* snake (Kipling uses the word, in his mongoose story) + *ranga,* bright color—recalling the *dragon-guarded* golden apples of the Hesperides.

Banana is from Sp., supposedly from Guinea, but Arab. *banana* means a finger: *banān,* the fingers and toes. *Cherry* is from ONFr. *cherise,* from L., from Gr. *kerasion* (*melon*) from *Cerasus* in Pontus—unless the place was named for the fruit: Gr. *keras,* horn (the bark is smooth as a horn). The *s* dropped, as from *pea, q.v. Pear* is from OFr. *piere,* from L. *pirum,* pear. *Grape* is from Fr. *grappe,* bunch (*grappe de raisins,* bunch of *grapes*); *raisin,* which we use only of the dried grape, is LL. *racimum,* from *racemum. Green gage* (plum) is *Sir William Gage,* who encouraged its growth in 18th c. England. *Damson* is the plum of *Damascus; cp. cloth. Quince* is a plural of *quine,* from ME. *quoyne,* from OFr. *coin,* from L. *cotoneum,* from *cydoneum,* from Gr. *kydonion* (*melon*), from *Cydonia,* in Crete. (This may, however, be a corruption of a Persian name for the fruit, + *melon.*) *Cantaloup* is from *Cantaloupo,* country seat of the Pope, near Rome, to which the melon was brought from Armenia.

Fruit is from L. *frui, fruct—,* to enjoy, whence Eng. *fruition;* L. *frux, frug—,* (Eng. *frugal*), profit; its plural, *fruges, fruits. Berry* is common Teut.; AS. *berie,* ON. *ber;* cognate with L. *per* in *juniper.* Also *see propaganda* (plum); *pommel* (pomegranate); *apricot.*

pear.

See peach.

pearl.

There are several guesses as to the origin of this word. Perhaps most likely is the surmise that it is named from its shape: L. *pirum, pear* (*cp. peach*), becoming LL. *perum;* its diminutive *perula* becoming Eng. *pearl.* L. *perna,* suggested under *carnelian, q.v.,* gets its meaning of shell-fish from the shape of the bivalve, from L. *perna,* ham. Also suggested is L. *pilula,* globule, diminutive of *pila,* ball: one of these forms led to Eng. *pill* ("always gild the philosophic *pill*"); by dissimilation *pilula* became *pirula,* some claim, whence Eng. *pearl.* At all events, the *pearl* comes from a bivalve.

peasant.

See hold.

peat.

The Fr. trace their word *petit,* small, to a Celtic root *pit,* pointed, small, akin to *pic,* point, whence *pick, q.v.,* and (directly from It.) *piccolo.* The Fr. *petit* was long used in Eng.; then spelled also *petty,* which form survived. The Celtic root, or an earlier Aryan, was also used in LL. *petia, pecia,* a bit; whence Eng. *piece.* As the word *peat* was applied first to the small pieces in which this substance was cut, for burning, and later to the turf or decomposed growth itself, this word is probably the origin of *peat. Cp. alkali.*

peccadillo.

See impeccable.

peck.
See pay; nasturtium. The *peck* measure seems allied to the other sense (Fr. *picotin,* peck; *picoter,* to peck). It was first applied to oats for horses (and, of course, sparrows: the Eng. expression "Keep your *pecker* up" is drawn from the tilt of the watchful bird).

pectoral.
See parrot.

peculate, peculiar, pecuniary.
See fee.

pedagogue.
A modern schoolmaster may not be quite a slave to his pupils; but the first *pedagogue* was a slave, who led his young master to school (Gr. *paidogogos,* from *pais, paid—,* boy + *agein,* to lead. Thus a *demagogue* leads the people—sometimes astray: from Gr. *demos,* the people, whence *democracy, q.v.* So also does an *agitator,* from L. *agere, agit—,* to stir, to lead, from Gr. *agein.* A *synagogue* is a place where persons—now, only Jews—are led together: Gr. *syn,* together.) It. *pedagogo* was shortened (by slang) into *pedant;* both these words show the scorn of the layman for those in spite of whom he learned (hence, Shaw's "Those that can, do; those that cannot, teach").

Confusion arises from the fact that the L. word for foot is *pes, ped—;* Gr. *pedon,* ground. Medicine uses the Gr. forms; thus *pediatrician* and *pediatry* deal with boys (children: grammatically as well as dramatically the male embraces the female); *podiatry* (Gr. *pous, pod—,* foot) deals with the *pedal* extremities. *Podagra* (Gr. *agra,* trap) is the medical name for gout. A *chiropodist* was first one that cared for the hands and feet (Gr. *chiro—, cheiro—,* from *cheir,* hand: *chiromancy,* divination by the hand; *cp. necromancy*). The word *chirurgeon* was long an Eng. word, from Gr. *cheirourgos,* from *cheir,* hand + *ergon,* work; via OFr. *surigien* it was gradually replaced by its easier-to-pronounce doublet, *surgeon.*

A fellow the soles of whose feet are facing yours when he is standing (some 8,000 miles away) is at the *antipodes.* G. *podion,* foot in the sense of base, gives us (in the L. form) *podium*—from which the Philharmonic is being delightfully conducted as I stay away and write; applied (in its plural, *podia*) to the imperial seat at theatre, it became OFr. *puie,* balcony, whence ME. *puwe,* whence Eng. *pew.*

The combinations from L. *ped—* are numerous; *e.g. pedometer, pedestrian. Impede* (L. *in* + *ped*) is to catch the foot in something; hence, to hinder. L. *expedire* is to get the foot out again (of a trap); hence, Eng. *expedite,* to speed up; *expedient,* that which helps the foot along, as with our *expeditionary* force. A *pedlar,* or *peddler,* however, although a person that goes about on foot, traces his descent through the AS. *ped,* basket; hence, a man that thus carries his wares.

The interlinkings can be carried further. Thus in Gr. *podagra* (Eng. *podagra,* gout) the *agra,* trap, catching, is related to Gr. *agein,* to bring, to lead, as in *pedagogue.* And Gr. *pous, podos,* foot (Gr. *peza,* ankle), is probably related to Gr. *pedilon,* sandal, *pedias, pediad—,* level, flat (Gr. *pedion,* plane, whence Eng. *pedion,* flat surface of a crystal), whence Gr. *pedon,* oarblade and its plural *peda,* rudder. This word, through It. *pedota,* helmsman, became It. *pilota* and Eng. *pilot,* a guide in a different field from the *pedagogue.*

pedigree.
Unless you draw from the spread of the roots, a family tree is more easily reckoned upside down. The usual lines for tracing ancestry are like a three-pronged rake, or the foot of a bird (Fr. *pié,* from *pied* + *de grue,* foot of a crane). In 15th c. England, this was spelled *pee-de-grew,* then *pedegru;* finally *pedigree.* Proud persons own *pedigreed* horses or dogs. *Cp. pedagogue.*

pedometer.
See ambulance; pedagogue.

peduncle.
See uncle.

peep.
See pipe. *Peep* and *peek,* to keep looking, are of unknown origin, though they first mean to keep bobbing up, perhaps as a bird. *Peer,* to look, was earlier *pire,* changed by the influence of the hope, in *peer,* to come into view, aphetic for *appear,* from L. *apparere; cp. month:* April. *Peer,* a noble, is from OFr. *per,* from L. *par,* equal (among those at court); hence, a jury of one's *peers.* Hence also *peerage* and, from the Fr. form, *parage,* Eng. *disparage.* This meant first (L. *dis,* away) to

marry away from one's equals, out of one's ranks; then, to treat slightingly, as society might the intruder; then, naturally, to vilify. Also L. *par,* whence Fr. *parité,* equality, whence Eng. *parity* and *disparity.* (*Disparate* is from L. *disparatus,* separate, from *dis,* away + *paratus,* ordered, ready; and *apparatus*—L. *ap, ad,* to, for—that which is prepared for a specific purpose.) *Cp. overture.*

Peeping Tom.
See boycott.

peer, peerage.
See peep.

pelican.
See penguin.

pellet.
See pelt.

pell-mell.
See mail.

pelt.
See camouflage. *Pelt* may be roundabout, from OFr. *peau,* skin, from MHG. *pelliz,* whence G. *pelz,* from OFr. *pelice,* a skin of fur, from L. *pellicea,* feminine of *pelliceus,* from *pellis,* skin.

Pelt, to strike by throwing, is perhaps from LL. *pultare, pulsare,* whence Eng. *pulsation,* iterative forms of L. *pellere, pulsum,* to drive, whence *impel, impulse,* and the *pellet* with which one is *pelted. Cp. Bursa, push.*

L. *pellere, puls—* gives us other compounds: *propel, propulsive* (L. *pro,* forward); *repel, repulsive* (L. *re,* back); *expel* (L. *ex,* out); *compel* (L. *com* as an intensive); also what beats, *pulsates,* inside us, our *pulse.*

There is a quite different Eng. *pulse,* which means a pottage, also the seeds of leguminous plants (*cp. legible*). This is from Gr. *poltos,* pottage, L. *puls, pult—.* The L. plural *pultes,* used of an application to reduce swelling made with such seeds, was mistaken for a singular form, whence Eng. *poultice.*

pen.
The early instrument for writing with ink was a feather (OE. *pen,* from OFr. *penne,* from It. *penna,* from L. *penna,* feather, from *pinna,* wing) with the quill pointed and split. The word just naturally grew into its present use. Eng. *pinna* is the broad upper, wing-like part of the ear; *pinnate* means feather-like, esp. as applied to leaves. *Pinnacle* (L. *pinnaculum,* diminutive of *pinna*) was a small wing-like projection, above the tower or turret of a building; hence, the top or peak of anything, the highest achievement. *Pinion* (from OFr. *pignon,* alternate form of *pennon*) is the end-part of the wing; then, as a verb, to cut this off; hence, to cripple, to bind. (Similarly, to seed may mean to take seeds out, as with seeded raisins, or to put seeds in, as with seeded rye bread.) From the feather worn as a plume comes *pennon,* a streamer; from a blending of this and *pendant* (Fr. *pendant,* hanging, from *pendre,* to hang, from L. *pendere; cp. aggravate*) comes *pennant,* esp. in the U. S. a flag awarded as an honor.

Pencil is of quite other origin (OFr. *pincel,* whence Fr. *pinceau,* from L. *penicillum,* diminutive of *penis,* tail, whence Eng. *penis*), and referred originally to the small artist's brush, that resembled a little tail.

Penicillium (of many sorts) is a fungus with branches like little *pencils;* from it is extracted the base of a medicine therefore called *penicillin.*

penal, penalty, penance.
See chary.

pencil.
See pen.

pendant.
See adipose, aggravate; pen.

pendulum.
See aggravate.

penguin.
Bird names travel farther than the birds. The albatross (*q.v.*) was first what we now call the *pelican,* then the black frigate-bird, before it was the white bird we know. The black-headed *penguin* gets its name from Welsh *pen gwyn,* white head—evidently by transfer from some other bird, after the original sense had been lost. (In the 16th c. it was applied to the great auk.) The *pelican* was first the woodpecker, from Gr. *pelekan,* from *pelekys,* ax (from the strength of its beak). *Grouse* was at one time applied to a bustard; the word is earlier *grewys,* from Fr. *grue,* from L. *grus,* crane. In aviation today, the word *pelican* is applied to a flying officer assigned solely to ground work.

penicillin.
See pen.

peninsula.
See island.

penitent, penitentiary.
See chary. The ending of *penitentiary* is L. *—arium,* a place; *cp. cellar.*

pennant, pennon.
See pen.

Pennsylvania.
See neighbor; States.

penny.
See dollar; pawn.

pension, pensive.
See adipose, aggravate.

pentagon.
See number.

penthouse.
I picture my friend enjoying the breeze, high in his *penthouse* on a towering city apartment building, while I swelter in the library telling him (he will know when he reads this!) that etymologically he's just sitting in an *appendix.* Just as the *appendix* (L. *ad,* to + *pendere,* to hang) is a little organ hanging onto the intestines, so the early houses had a roof hanging on to them, that thus formed a projecting shed, to shelter the domestic animals in bad weather. (Early churches had similar sloping structures; the word is influenced by Fr. *pente,* slope.) In the old days, when *the* and *a* and *an* were attached to their nouns (*cp. auction*), this was called *thappentice;* when the article was detached, it became *pentice, pentis.* Just as Gr. *krebs, crab,* whence OHG. *krebez,* whence OFr. *crevisse,* ME. *crevise, crevis* was by popular etymology (being in the water) changed into *crayfish,* so *pentis* (being part of a building) was altered into *penthouse* . . . and there my friend sits!

Crab is related to LG. *krabben,* to claw. *Crab* apple is apparently from Scan. *scrab* (? *scrub, q.v.*) apple; applied esp. to its sour, puckering quality. A *crabbed* person was a figure drawn first from the crosswise walk of the *crab,* then from the sour fruit, whence also slang *crabby* and an old *crab.* There are also a *crab* nut and a *crab* oil, corrupted from the South American *carap* tree. One should not be a *crab* in a *penthouse.*

penult.
This is short for *penultimate,* from L. *paene,* almost, next to, +*ultimare, ultimat—,* to come to an end; whence also Eng. *ultimatum;* from L. *ultimus,* final, superlative of L. *ulterior,* beyond, Eng. as in *ulterior* motives. (For Eng. *utmost, see unutterable.*) *Cp. island.*

The third syllable from the end of a word is the *antepenult* (L. *ante,* before; slang *ante* is an amount pledged or set aside before a play, as at cards; hence, *ante up* means to pay this money.) In many Greek words the accent falls on the *antepenult, e.g., Laocoon.*

peon, peony.
See pawn.

pepsin, peptic.
See dysentery.

per—.
See perish.

perambulate, perambulator.
See ambulance.

percussion.
See discuss.

peregrination.
See acorn, belfry.

peremptory.
See prompt.

perennial.
See anniversary.

perfect.
See defeat.

perfume.
See month: February.

perhaps.
See emporium.

peri.
See wig.

peri—.
See periscope.

peril, perilous.
See parlor.

period.
See paragraph.

peripatetic.
See Platonic.

periphrasis, periphrastic.
See periscope.

periscope.
The Gr. prefix *peri—* meant around; it is used in Eng. in many scientific words; also in a large number of more common words. Thus *periscope* is a device for seeing all around; for *scope, cp. dismal. Periphrasis* and *periphrastic* refer to roundabout speech; but note that Gr. *par—, para—, q.v.,* first meant beside, by extension also meant by, past, beyond; hence *periphrasis* and *paraphrase,* from Gr. *phrazein,* to declare; whence also Eng. *phrase.* Also the L. *per—,* thoroughly, comes via Fr. into Eng. *par—,* as in *parboil; pardon* (from LL. *perdonare,* to give wholly, to grant, remit, from L. *donare, donat—,* to give; whence *donation; cp. anecdote*).

perish.
The L. preposition *per,* used as a prefix, meant either through, or (as an intensive) through and through, thoroughly. It has the latter sense in *perish,* via Fr. *perir, periss—,* from L. *perire,* from *per* + *ire, it—* to go: to go completely. *Perish* the thought!

periwig.
See wig.

permeate.
See immunity.

permit.
See mess. *Allow* is a blend of two courses. OFr. *alouer* may spring either from L. *allauder,* from *al, ad,* to + *laudare,* to praise: or from L. *allocare,* from *al, ad,* to + *locare, locat—* (whence Eng. *locate, location*), to place. There were thus two early Eng. words, one meaning to praise, thence to approve, to accept as valid, to admit; the other meaning to assign as one's right (to *allocate*), to grant. The two senses gradually grew together.

permutation.
See immunity.

pernicious.
See nexus.

perplex.
This word as a verb occurs in Eng. mainly after the 16th c. Earlier it was an adjective, but also the form *perplexed* was used, from L. *perplexus,* from L. *per,* through, thoroughly, + *plectere, plex—,* to weave; *cp. complexion.*

persecute.
See pursue.

persiflage.
When a fellow meets a girl, he may indulge in airy *persiflage*—or he may just whistle. It amounts to the same thing, as the language recognizes. *Persiflage* is from Fr. *persifler* (*per,* intensive), from *siffler,* from L. *sibilare,* to whistle. Hence, also, *sibilant.*

person.
When we speak of someone as quite a *personage,* we do not recognize that his origin was sham. L. *persona* was a character in a play; whence the list of *dramatis personae,* characters in the drama. In ancient times, the great theatre spaces made it impossible to see facial changes; masks were therefore used, often with megaphonic mouthpieces. The mask was a *persona* (from L. *per,* through + *sonare,* to sound); then the term was used for the actor. Finally, just as we say "In that picture Claudette marries Clark Gable", identifying the character in the piece with the real *person* that *enacts* it, the word *person* came to be used for you and for Claudette. A *parson, q.v.,* is also a *person.*

perspire.
See inspiration.

persuade, persuasion.
See victoria.

perturbed.
See trouble.

peruke.
See wig.

peruse.
Originally this word had all the force of its origin, from L. *per,* completely, + Fr. *user,* to *use up,* from LL. *usare, usat—,* from L. *utere, us—; cp. usury.* The Fr. *user* still means to *use up,* which was the early sense in English. The verb gradually lost force; to it was attached the figurative sense of "to go through"

e.g., one's fortune; then, as the meaning lessened, to go through anything. Virtually the only meaning that is still in use is that of going through a book, *perusal*.

pervert.
See conversion.

pessimist.
The L. superlative of bad is *pessimus;* from this the nouns *pessimism* and *pessimist* were coined. Similarly, from the superlative of good, L. *optimus,* was fashioned *optimist.*

The comparative of bad, L. *peior,* formed *im,* in + *peiorare,* to make worse, whence Eng. *impair.*

Optimus is related to L. *ops,* power, wealth (two possessions that often go together) whence Eng. *opulent,* from Sansk. *apnas,* property. Close in form is Gr. *opsis,* sight, whence *opticos,* whence Eng. *optic, optician,* etc. An *autopsy* is just a seeing for yourself (*aut—*, from *auto—*, self). L. *optare,* to wish, gives us *optative; option; adopt* (*ad,* to). If a *pessimist* could *adopt opulence,* it might change his views.

pester.
This is so obviously linked with *pest,* the plague, that, of course, it means to plague one (from Fr. *empester*). Not so! This is another case of the sound changing the story . . . When animals were put out to *pasture* (from L. *pascere, past—*, to feed; whence *pastor; cp. congress*), they were tied about the *pastern* (part of horse's foot from fetlock to hoof), with LL. *pastorium,* whence It. *pastora,* whence *pastoja,* whence Fr. *pasture,* a tether. From this came the verb It. *impastojare,* whence Fr. *empestrer,* to shackle, to impede; thence, to annoy; from this, Eng. *pester.* A *pestered* person feels like a tied horse.

pestiferous.
See suffer.

pet, peter out, petrel, petrify, petroleum.
See parrot.

petticoat, pettifogger, petty.
See peat, pit.

phaeton.
See focus.

phagocyte.
See sarcophagus.

phantom.
See focus.

pharmacy.
See treacle.

phase, phenomenon.
See focus.

phil—.
See philander.

philander.
This trifling with the affections of women may come from the fact that *Philander* is a lover of men, from Gr. *philandros,* from *philos,* dear, from *philein,* to love, + *andr—*, man. The word is thus a doublet of *philanthrope, philanthropist;* it takes its special sense from the use of *Philander* as the name of a dallying lover in the medieval romances, as in Ariosto's *Orlando Furioso.* As a prefix, *phil—*, and *philo—*, make many Eng. words, *e.g.*: *Philadelphia* (*adelphos,* brother: city of brotherly love); *philology,* love of words; *philosophy,* love of wisdom; *philtre,* a love potion—and in such suffixes as *Anglophile,* lover of the English. *Andro—* and its twin *anthropo—* are also rich combining forms; *cp. sarcophagus.*

Certain animals, *e.g.* a small wallaby, are named *philander,* from having been first described (ca. 1700) by *Philander de Bruyn,* a Dutch naturalist.

The word *philandering* gained currency from the frequent use of the name: *Filandro,* loved (and ruined) by Gabrina in Ariosto's *Orlando Furioso,* 1516, 1532; *Philander* and Phyllis, in a 17th c. Eng. ballad; *Philander* in love with Erota, in John Fletcher's *Laws of Candy,* 1647; Congreve in *The Way of The World,* 1700; Steele in *The Tatler,* 1709. The practice, if not the name, is still current.

The *drosophila,* the fruit-fly often used in the study of heredity, is really the dew-lover: Gr. *drosos,* dew; whence also, the scientific term *drosometer,* that measures the deposited dew.

philippic.
See tribulation. The name *Philip* (Gr. *philippos*) means lover of horses; hence, the story of the son of *Philip* of Macedonia, Alexander the Great, and his steed Bucephalus. *To appeal from Philip drunk to Philip sober* was supposedly the course taken by a woman displeased with the decision *Philip* had made in her case.

Philippines.
See States.

philo-.
See philander.

philter, philtre.
See philander. (Gr. ***philtron,*** the suffix indicating the instrument).

phlegmatic.
See complexion.

phlox.
See flower.

phonograph.
See focus.

phosphorescent.
See affluent.

phosphorus.
See element, focus.

photogenic.
See photosynthesis.

photograph.
See focus.

photosynthesis.
Modern science has built many words from Greek and Latin roots. Thus Gr. ***phos, phot—,*** light (***cp. focus***) gives Eng. *photo*—as the beginning of many words such as *photo-electric. Synthesis* (Gr. putting together; *thesis* from Gr. ***tithenai,*** to put; *cp. Spoonerism;* for ***analysis, see psychoanalysis***) is combined with it to name the process of chemical combination effected by light, esp. as plants change the carbon dioxide and water of the air into carbohydrates: ***photosynthesis.***

Photogenic has an odd history. It was used from about 1840 to about 1870, instead of *photographic*. Technically, it has been used to mean producing light: *photo—,* light, + *genic,* bearing; *cp. racy.* In recent years, Hollywood scouts have used the word (possibly with faraway memory of *eugenic; eu—,* well, beautiful), and it has come into wide favor, applied to someone that ***photographs*** well.

phrase.
See periscope. (Gr. ***phrasis,*** speech, from *phrasein*).

phthisic.
Gr. *phtheirein* meant to destroy; with Gr. *zoon,* animal (*cp. plant*) it formed the rare Eng. word ***phthisozoics,*** the art of killing harmful beasts. Gr. ***phthinein,*** the reflexive form, meant to waste away; hence the noun Gr. ***phthisis,*** consumption, carried over directly into Eng.—unfortunately, much less rare. Note that it is pronounced *fthee'sis* or *thai'sis*. The related ***phthisic*** came into ME. spelled and sounded *tisik;* though the spelling has been restored to match the ancient Gr., the pronounciation set in middle English is retained.

physic, physique.
See onion.

physician.
See doctor.

phyt—, phyto—.
See neophyte.

piano.
See saxophone.

piazza.
See platypus.

piccolo.
See peat. (It. ***piccolo,*** small.)

pick.
See pay; nasturtium, pink.

Pickwickian.
In Charles Dickens' *Pickwick Papers,* 1836-7 (when the author was but 25), the Chairman calls upon Mr. Blotton to tell whether the term 'humbug,' which he had applied to Mr. Pickwick, was to be taken in its usual sense; Mr. Blotton replied that he had used the word *"in the Pickwickian sense."* This expression has since been used to take the sting out of an uncomplimentary remark. (Dickens took many of his names from real persons: *Pickwick* is a village in Wilts, England. Other names he invented to fit the character, following the tradition of the morality play: *Dotheboys Hall; Stryver.*)

picture.*
See arsenic, painter.

pie.
In most of its senses (***pie,*** a small Anglo-Indian coin, is from Hindī ***pa'i; pice,*** from Hindī ***paisa,*** one fourth of an anna, from Sansk. ***padi,*** quarter) ***pie*** comes from the bird, the ***magpie,*** from L. ***pica.*** (The ***mag*** is short for *Margaret,* as we speak of the *Jenny wren.*) The habits of the ***magpie,*** its

practice of gathering up odds and ends, are so well known that from its L. name Eng. *pica* is the medical term for a perverted desire to nibble at unpalatable things, such as chalk. While far from unpalatable (when home cooked . . . I trust you find it so, as well), the *pie* we eat is named from this same practice of mixing things together. A more logical use of the word is in connection with type; *pied* type. The *Pied Piper* is varicolored (the *magpie* is black and white; but the term *pied* is used now for streaks of any two colors, as the red and yellow costume of the court fool); note that *piebald* has no connection with lost hair, but means *balled* (streaked) like a *pie*.

Bald itself was also earlier *balled*, from Welsh *bal*, white-browed. The Elizabethans called a totally *bald* man a *pilgarlic* (*peeled garlic*). Garlic was deemed a cure for leprosy, hence associated with the disfigured.

Piepowder court was another early English term, for the summary courts established at fairs to handle vagrants, pickpockets and other petty nuisances. It is from OFr. *piepoudrous* (Fr. *pied poudreux*), dusty-foot, a term fitly used of the wayfarers and traveling salesmen of the time. *Cp. humble.*

piebald.
See pie.

piece.
See peat, pit. (*Piece* is directly from Fr. *pièce*.)

piepowder.
See pie.

piety.
See pittance.

pig.
See mutton.

pigeon.
Although this first meant a young bird, the second syllable was not influenced by Fr. *jeune*, young, as in Eng. *junior*. The present spelling, however, is from Fr. *pigeon;* the word was ME. *pyjon*, from OFr. *pyjoun*, a young bird, then esp. a young dove; from LL. *pipionem*, a chirping bird, from L. *pipire*, to *peep*, *q.v.*, an echoic word.

Several compounds are built on *pigeon*. Thus *pigeon-hearted* means timid; *pigeon-livered* meant gentle: both from the ways of the bird. A *pigeon pair* means twins of opposite sexes, or a boy and a girl in the family, from the usual brood of the bird. Some humans are *pigeon-breasted. Pigeons* are often raised in a series of nests set in holes side by side; hence, *pigeonhole*, of a series of compartments; to *pigeonhole* something is to file it for reference, or to get it out of the way.

pigeon-breasted; pigeon-hearted; pigeonhole; pigeon-livered.
See pigeon.

pigment.
See arsenic.

pigmy.
See pygmy.

pile.
This has many meanings, from several sources. The *pile*-driver puts in what began as a pointed stake, from AS. *pil*, dart, from L. *pilum*, javelin. A little ball, L. *pila*, is the source of the troubling *piles*. When things are *piled* up, they are from L. *pila*, pier; whence LL. *pilare*, whence OFr. *piler*, whence Eng. *pillar*. There are a few less common sources, in addition; for the *pile* of velvet, *see cloth*.

pilgarlic.
See pie.

pilgrim.
See belfry; saunter.

pill.
See pearl.

pillage.
See caterpillar.

pillar.
See pile.

pilosis.
See wig.

pimpernel.
Probably more persons know *The Scarlet Pimpernel* (1905) as a book (and motion picture, and the nickname of the hero) by Emma Magdalena Rosalia Maria Josefa Barbara, Baroness Orczy, than are aware that it is a flower. It takes its name from the two-winged shape—*bipinnate*—of the leaves; for *pimpernel* is from LL. *pipinella*, by dissimilation from *bipinella*, a diminutive of *bipinnula*, itself a

diminutive from *bipennis,* two winged, from L. *penna,* feather, wing; whence Eng. *pinnate, pennate; cp. pen.* Also *see scarlet.*

pimple.
See pamper.

pin.
See attack.

pinafore.
H. M. S. Pinafore (written in 1878) contained such satire of the Queen's Navy that, although Sullivan was knighted by the Queen, Gilbert did not receive the royal accolade until after Victoria's death.
But the Victorian (*q.v.*) tidiness began the century before. Imagine the Little Lady Fauntleroy of 1775 being warned "Don't spot your dress! Here's something to *pin afore* it"—and you have the origin of the *pinafore.*

pinchbeck.
See Appendix II.

pine.
See chary.. The tree is directly from AS. *pin,* L. *pinus.* The *pineapple* was originally the fruit (cone) of the *pine* tree; then any fruit of similar shape; from its shape we also have named the *pineal* gland. *Cp.* peach.

pinion.
See pen.

pink.
Several words have combined in this one. There is the imitation of the note of the chaffinch, or of water dripping: *pink pank.* Related to this, perhaps, is Du. *pinken,* to shut the eyes, to blink. From the half-shut eye comes the meaning of *pink,* small, surviving in *pinkie, pinkey,* little finger; also (G. *Pinke,* minnow) *pink,* a small fish, esp. a young salmon. The color may have influenced this meaning; the color was probably named from the flower (though *pink* is applied to the variety, whatever its color); possibly the flower was named from *pink eye,* little eye, as in Fr. *oeillet,* little eye. There is also Eng. *pink,* from Du. *pinke* and It. *pinco,* a sailing boat, esp. (Eng. *pinke* and *pinkey*) a narrow-sterned fishing boat.
The old Teut. word *picken,* to *pick* (Fr. *piquer,* prick; whence also Eng. *pique, piqué, piquant*) was nasalized in Low G. as *pinken,* to peck, to pierce. This was applied to making little holes in garments; hence, to adorn. Some have thought that the flower was named from this *pink,* in the sense of cutting in and out the edges; but the verb does not seem to have had this meaning until the 19th c., whereas the flower was named as early as the 16th. It was, indeed, very popular, and sometimes used as a general term for flower, as in the figurative expressions, the *pink* of courtesy, the *pink* of perfection. *Cp. nasturtium.*
A *pinker* is one that stabs (or works a *pinking* machine, for edging cloth); a *pinkster,* however, is a Whitsuntide occasion (frolic, feast), a corruption of Gr. *pentekoste, Pentecost,* Gr. fiftieth (day). And a *Pinkerton,* originally *Pinkerton man,* is a detective, generalized from the agency established in the U. S. in 1850 by *Allan Pinkerton.*

Pinkerton.
See pink.

pinna, pinnacle, pinnate.
See pen.

pioneer.
See pawn.

pious.
See pittance; supercilious.

pip.
See pit.

pipe.
This word first referred to the *piping* sound, and is imitative in origin—as also are L. *pipiare,* Fr. *pépier,* Eng. *peep,* and G. *Pfeifer,* whence Eng. *fife.* Then the noun came to have the general sense from the shape of the musical instrument; whence also the tube, as for inhaling tobacco.

pippin.
See pit.

piquant, pique, piqué.
See pink. *Piquant* is present participle; *piqué,* past.

pirate.
See private.

pit.
See pot. The *pit* of fruit is corrupted from *pip,* short for *pippin.* Until the 16th c. *pippin* meant a seed; then it was used for a seedling apple, which was naturally of good quality;

hence the slang "It's a *pippin!*" *Pippin* is from Fr. *pépin,* from Sp. *pepita,* seed, grain, perhaps from Fr. *petit,* small (particle), from the Celtic; whence It. *pezza,* Fr. *pièce;* Eng. *piece.* Hence also *petty;* and *petticoat,* from *petty* coat, first a coat men wore beneath a doublet; *pettifogger,* from *petty* + *fogger,* from the great mercantile family, *Fugger,* in Augsburg, 15th-16th c.; influenced by Du. *focker,* monopolist; *focken,* to cheat.

pitch.
See pay.

pithecanthrope.
This fellow exists also in the Gr. form *pithecanthropos,* and in the L. form *pithecanthropus.* In all cases it is a late formation, though for a very early form: the missing link. Though earlier said to exist (in the "Tertiary Period") the name was first definitely applied by Ernst Haeckel in 1868 to a creature supposedly halfway up the evolutionary scale from ape to man. The coinage is directly from Gr. *pithekos,* ape, + Gr. *anthropos,* man.
Some naturalists speak of *pithecanthropus erectus,* as the first creature unfeathered that stood upon two legs. The word has been put to learnedly jocular use, as in the *pithecanthropic* mummery, otherwise called monkey-business.

pittance.
An attempt (perhaps by the *pious*) has been made to derive this word from *picta,* a small coin issued by the counts of *Poitiers* (L. *Pictavensium*); whence OFr. *pite,* a French farthing, a mite. But LL. *pietantia,* which on to OIt. *pietanza* and Fr. *pitance* gave us the word, is from *pietas, piety.* The first use of *pittance* is as a charity bequest; thus, the present meaning comes from the usual size of gifts to charity. *Piety* and *pity* (Fr. *pitie*) are doublets, one expressing the feeling as within oneself; the other, the same feeling as it flows toward others. *Pious* is the same word, in its adjective form, from Fr. *pieux,* from LL. *piosus,* from L. *pius,* devout—the name of many popes.

pitter-patter.
See patter.

pituitary.
See garble.

pity.
See pittance.

place.
See platypus.

plagiarism.
This word existed first in the form of the agent, *plagiary,* referring both to the person and the act; Milton says: Borrowing without bettering is a *plagiarie.* But what we apply to literary property the Romans applied to personal; L. *plagiare, plagiat—,* to steal a free man, from *plagium,* kidnapping, a snaring, from *plaga,* a net. The root *plak,* to weave, is in Gr. *plekein;* Russ. *pleste,* to weave; L. *plectere, plicare,* whence Eng. *implicate,* to weave into; *cp. complexion.*

plane.
See plant, saxophone.

plan.
Although influenced by *plane* (Fr. *plan,* flat; *cp. saxophone*), this was earlier Fr. *plant,* and was first used for a ground-*plan* or outline, from L. *planta,* sole of the foot; *see plant.* Hence, a scheme.
Note that the expression *plain sailing* originally did not mean that the way ahead is simple and clear; it meant sailing by a *plane plan*: the earth shown as a *plane* surface instead of spherical. *Plane* was a fancy 17th c. alteration of *plain,* esp. in mathematics. May yours not often *"gang agley"!*

plane.
See plant.

planet.
Before the regular movement of *planets* about the sun was known, they seemed, to the ancients, stars wandering in the heavens. Hence the name. Gr. *planan,* to lead astray, in the passive form meant to wander; hence, Gr. *planetes asteres,* wandering stars. Thus Latin used *planetae* to mean *stellae errantes,* wandering stars (*cp. disaster; errand*); whence, by the usual trail through LL. and Fr., came our Eng. *planets.*
A *planetarium* (*cp. cell*) is a place where a model of the *planetary* system is displayed, with Venus and Mars and Neptune and the other gods now tamed to their solar orbit.

plangent.
See plant.

plank.
See plunge.

plant.
This word grew from the sole of your foot. When seeds or saplings were *planted,* they were tucked into the ground, then the soil stamped down by the farmer's feet: L. *planta,* sole of foot, hence *plant.* The Fr. *planter,* to *plant,* developed the figurative sense, to establish; whence a manufacturing *plant,* etc. *Animal* is anything that breathes, from L. *animal,* from *animus,* breath; Gr. *anemos,* wind, whence *anemone,* wind-flower. The breath of scandal, of ill-will, reveals an *animus;* if this is emphatic, L. *animosus,* full of breath, gives us *animosity*—which first meant high spirits, courage; then grew limited to bad spirits, hatred. A *nucleus,* kernel, is the diminutive of L. *nux, nuc—,* nut. *Protoplasm,* the basic substance of life, is from Gr. *protos,* first, from Gr. *pro,* before (*protozoa,* the first animal forms; Gr. *zoon,* animal, plural *zoa,* whence also *zoology,* the study of animals) + *plasma,* form, from *plassein,* to mold. Hence also *plastic;* and recently the Gr. word has been taken directly, in blood *plasma. Botany* is also from Gr., *botane,* from *boskein,* to graze, which, via L. whence It. *bosco,* whence ME. *busky, bushy,* gives us *bosky. Cp. flower; organism; vegetable.*

The *plantain* is thus named because its leaves suggest the sole of a foot. The banana-like fruit, *plantain,* is corrupted from a native West Indian name to Sp. *platano, plantano,* whence Eng. *plantain;* there is no resemblance to L. *platanus, plane* tree. The eastern *plane* tree (Gr. *platanos,* from *platys,* broad; *cp. vessel*) does have broad leaves.

A *plant,* slang for swindle, is something *planted,* i.e., hidden in a place.

plaque.
See plunge.

plash.
See knick-knack. An echoic word.

plasma, plastic.
See plant.

plate.
See element: platinum.

plateau.
See funny-bone

platform.
See plot.

platinum.
See element.

Platonic.
The early Greek philosophers had no schoolhouse. *Plato* taught in a park in Athens; *cp. academy.* Aristotle taught while walking about; hence he is called the *peripatetic* philosopher (Gr. *peri,* around + *patetikos,* from *patein,* to walk; *patos, path*). Aristotle's favorite walk was in a grove called the *Lyceum,* next to the temple of *Apollo Lykeios* (wolf-slayer ?, from Gr. *lykos,* wolf, whence Fr. *loup,* feminine *louve,* whence the *Louvre,* castle on a wolf-field)—whence our *lyceum.* Zeno taught in a portico or porch (Gr. *stoa,* porch) of the marketplace; hence, his ideas are called *stoic.* Associated with *Plato* is the *amor Platonicus, Platonic* love. *See* idea.

platypus.
See vessel.
Gr. *platys,* wide, combined in *plateia odos,* broad way, led to L. *platea;* thence by a LL. form *plattia* to Fr. and Eng. *place.* From the same LL. form came Sp and Eng. *plaza,* and It. and Eng. *piazza*—all three with variations due to the habits of the lands through which they have come.

plausible.
See explode.

plaza.
See platypus.

pleat, pledge.
See mortgage.

plenitude.
See police; foil.

plenty.
See police. It comes directly from L. *plenitas, plenitat—,* fulness, from *plenus,* full. *Cp. foil.*

plethora.
See police; foil.

plexus.
See complexion.

pliable, pliant.
See complexion.

plight.
See mortgage.

plop.
See plunge.

plot.
Here is entanglement. A *plot* of ground is from Fr. *pelote,* clod, diminutive of L. *pila,* ball. Influenced by OFr. *plat, plate,* flat, whence Eng. *plate* (and in the Sp. *plata* applied to metal *plate,* precious metal) it became *plat* of ground (which died) and *platform* (which destroyed the earlier *plotform*). Its first use as an intrigue is in the form *complot.* (The first syllable of many words has dropped, giving us such doublets as *fence* and *defence,* from L. *defendere,* to beat off; *sport* and *disport,* from OFr. *desporter,* to carry away, divert; whence Eng. *porter; cp. port; strain* and *distrain,* from OFr. *distreindre* and *estraindre,* from L. *stringere,* stretch, influenced by *sprain,* from OFr. *espreindere, espreign—,* from L. *exprimere, express—,* whence Eng. *express,* originally meaning to *press* out—which sense has been taken over by *strain; story* and *history,* from Gr. *historia,* from *histon, histor—,* learned, from root *eidenai,* to know. Perhaps related to L. *historia,* a tale, is L. *histrion,* performer in a play, whence Eng. *histrio* and *histrion,* actor, common words in the 16th and 17th c., now rare and usually contemptuous; also *histrionics,* now limited to stagey behavior.) It is suggested that *complot,* from OFr. *complote,* crowd, is also from OFr. *pelote,* ball, bunch; but it is more probably a shortening, *complictum,* of L. *complicitum,* from *complicare, complicat—,* to fold together, to intrigue. Hence one plotting with others is an *accomplice;* hence also *complicate; complex. Plots* usually are *complex.*

ploughshare.
See shed.

pluck.
This word, as a verb, spread wide over Europe, being borrowed by the Teut. tongues from a LL. form (It. *piluccare,* to *pluck*) from L. *pilus,* hair, whence Eng. *depilatory.* But through the farmlands it was applied to the *pluck* of a fowl, the viscera, the parts the farmer would thrust in his hand and *pluck* forth.

Various parts of the body, in folk physiology, are associated with different emotions. Thus the *Bible* speaks of the **bowels of compassion**; the factual basis of this may be noted in the more pithy expression, his bowels were loosed with fear. Thus the *pluck* came (esp. in 18th c. prize-fighting slang) to be considered the seat of courage, and gradually *pluck* acquired courage as its normal sense. Today, when one wishes to be forceful, one goes with folk physiology right back to the viscera, and exclaims That guy's got *guts!*

Guts (in the plural also in AS. *guttas*) was thought of as a channel; the word is from AS. *geotan,* to pour.

plum.
See propaganda.

plumb, plumbo—
See plunge.

plume.
See fleece.

plummet, plump.
See plunge.

plunder.
This is one of the few Eng. words taken directly from modern G. (ca. 1640). The G. noun *Plunder* meant rags; the verb *plunderen* was applied to carrying off everything, down to the very rags. A rather precise etymology for the present sense of *plunder!*

plunge.
With this word we *plunge* into a group of echoic words. The earliest is probably L. *plumbum,* lead (*plumbo—* is a combining form for chemical terms; the chemical symbol for lead is *Pb*), from the sound lead makes when thrown into water. This sound in Eng. is *plunk,* sometimes *kerplunk;* a lighter sound is *plop;* but in the same group are *bump, dump, thump, rump-a-tum-tump;* Shakespeare (*Hamlet* I,i, 65) has the ghost arrive "*jump* at this dead hour." *Plump* is the sound of something suddenly interrupted in motion; hence the adjective *plump,* meaning cut short, then applied to an arrowhead, blunt, rounded hence broad, hence pleasantly *plump.*

Fr. *plomb,* lead, had the diminutive *plombet, plomet,* ball of lead used on the end of a string to check the depth of water; hence, Eng. *plummet.* But this use of a *plumb-line* is older. L. *plumbicare* meant to heave the lead; directly this gives us the verb to *plumb* the depths; and via OFr. *plonquer, plongier, plunjer,* it gives us Eng. *plunge.*

To *plank* (sometimes *plunk*) a thing down may also be echoic; but it is at least influenced by the idea of putting it on the (*plank*) table. The *plank* of which the table is made is ME. *planke,* via Fr. and L. from Gr. *plax, plak—,* slab (of wood or marble), whence also Eng. *plaque;* and perhaps itself an echo of the sound this would make when cut or dropped.

plural, plurality, plus.
See foil.

plush.
See cloth; *cp.* remnant.

plutocracy.
See democracy; emblem.

pluvial.
See fleet.

P.M.
See posthumous.

pneumatic.
The Gr. *pneuma,* air, spirit, gives us several combining forms. (There is a less frequent form, *pneo—,* as in *pneodynamics, pneogastric,* from Gr. *pneein, pnein,* to blow.) *Pneumat—, pneumato—,* are used mainly in scientific terms; thus *pneumatic* means operating by air (as tires and pumps) or, rarely, related to the spirit, in religious use. *Pneumo—* is sometimes used in the same way, but is more often used in medicine, as a shorter form of *pneumono—*; both of these are from Fr. *pneumon,* lung, whence Eng. *pneumonia.*

The *dipnoan* fish are those (like the mudfish) doubly equipped (Gr. *di—* two): with lungs and gills.

pneumonia.
See pneumatic.

poach, pock, pocket.
See lobster.

poetaster.
See spinster.

poinsettia.
See Appendix II.

point.
See pungent.

poison.
See intoxicate.

pole.
See palace.

polecat.
Several guesses have been made as to the origin of this name for the skunk. *Pole* for *Polish;* though why wish it on them? Also *pool*-cat (Celtic *poll,* hole): the cat that hides in a hole; the trouble is that it doesn't. This is a case where your nose knows. *Polecat* is the *pul*-cat, from OFr. *pulent,* stinking: AS. *ful,* whence Eng. *foul;* L. *puter, putr—,* whence Eng. *putrid;* Sansk. *puy,* to stink, an imitative word, like *Pyew!* (The book in which I found this story has "No" next to it, in ink, in the margin; but persons should not write in library books! It is a much more appropriate source than the one now considered valid: *polecat,* from OFr. *pole,* whence Fr. *poule,* hen, whence Eng. *poult, poultry*—from its preying on the folk of the farmyard. *Poult* has a doublet, *pullet,* from L. *pulla,* hen, *pullus,* young animal.) But *see curfew; cp. poltroon.*

police.
Meaning, first, the regulation of order in a place, this word is from Gr. *polis, polit—,* city—from which come *politics* and its attendant train. Contrasting city-ways with country style gives us the sense of a *civil* tongue (L. *civis,* city, whence Eng. *civilian,* etc.) and *urbanity; cp. neighbor.* Thus *police* might be expected to yield *politeness* and *polish;* but no! *Polite* and *polish* are from Fr. *polir, poliss—,* from L. *polire, polit—,* from *po,* from *pro,* before + *lire,* from *linere,* to smear, whence Eng. *liniment.*

But *polis,* city, [which gives us such compounds as *metropolis* (Gr. *meter,* whence L. *mater,* mother), strictly, the chief cathedral city of a land; *cosmopolitan* (Gr. *cosmos, cosmet—,* order, the ordered universe, *kosmein,* to arrange, whence Eng. *cosmetics,* things to put one in order; *cosmic;* etc.)] was originally a crowd—only later, a crowd organized into a community—, whence Sansk. *puri,* town, from *pari,* from *par,* to fill, whence Gr. *ple* (Eng. *plenitude, plenty, plethora*), whence Gr. *pel,* full, whence *polis,* a crowd. *Cp. foil.* Thus from the earliest days, where there is a crowd you may expect the *police*. *Cp. pagan; gas.*

polish, polite.
See police.

polka.
See Appendix II.

poll.
This is a Teut. word (Du. *polle,* crown of the head), for head, as in the *poll-tax;* hence voting where they count the heads, at the *polls.* To *poll* is to trim the top (of person, hedge, tree); hence *pollard.* Pretty *Poll* is from *Polly, Molly, Mary*: *Polly* wants a cracker!

Some senses of *pole, q.v.,* intermingle with *poll,* e.g., *poleaxe,* earlier *pollax,* an ax at the head, but also on a *pole.*

Pollyanna.
This word has become general, from the young heroine of Eleanor H. Porter's story, *Pollyanna,* 1913. *Pollyanna* is the "glad child," who always sees the best in things.

polonaise.
See Appendix II.

polonium.
See element.

poltroon.
There are three stories given for this word, which earlier meant idle, slothful. Manifestly, the adolescent is lazy; hence the derivation from It. *poltro,* foal, from LL. *pullitrus,* diminutive of L. *pullus,* young animal, whence Eng. *pullet.* But, as the lazy are often found abed, it is also derived from *poltro,* a bed, from *polstro,* from G. *polster,* cushion, whence Eng. *bolster.* An idle fellow, dodging work, can easily be called a coward. There is, finally, a much more direct derivation. When recruiting sergeants simply went from house to house, rounded up any able bodied men, and conscripted them for service, one way of dodging draft was to show that your thumb was cut off (rupture, flat feet, etc. did not count in those unenlightened days!): L. *pollice truncus,* maimed of the thumb (L. *truncus, trunk,* whence *truncare, truncatus,* to cut off, whence Eng. *truncate*); from this expression we have *poltroon,* the coward that cuts off his thumb to avoid army service.

poly—.
See foil.

polygamy.
See monk.

polymorphous.
See remorse.

polytheism.
See monk.

pomade, pomegranate.
See pommel.

pommel.
The knob on a saddle gets its name from its shape, from OFr. *pomel,* from diminutive of L. *pomum,* apple. To hit someone with such a knob-shaped weapon is to *pommel* or *pummel* him. If the apple is full of seeds (L. *granatum,* seeded) it is a *pomegranate.* In Fr. *pomegrenade* was shortened to *grenade,* whence our fire-ball, *grenade,* and the military *grenadier.* An unguent supposedly made of apple-sauce, It. *pomatum,* gives us *pomade,* which in medicine has been reLatinized to *pomatum.* What we call a *potato,* from Sp. *patata,* from Haytian *batata,* is in Fr. *pomme de terre,* apple of the earth, and in G. *Erdapfel,* earth-apple.

The drink *grenadine* is from the fruit; the fabric *grenadine* is marked as with *grains* (L. *granatum,* with seeds or *grains;* whence Eng. *grain* and *granary*). The *garnet* ring you might wear takes its name from the color of the pulp of the fruit; *garnet* has shifted by metathesis from *grenat,* earlier *granat.* Which is far from applesauce.

pomp.
See pontiff.

pompadour.
See Appendix II.

pond.
See pound.

ponder, ponderous.
See aggravate.

pongee.
See cloth.

poniard.
See pygmy.

pontiff, pontifical.
Here is a word on which the folk-mythology worked early. *Pontiff* is

from L. *pontifex,* high priest (one of five), from *pons, pont—,* bridge + *facere, feci—,* to make. Thus Mommsen, in his *History of Rome,* I,178: "The five bridgebuilders (*pontifices*) derived their name from their function, as sacred as it was politically important, of conducting the building and demolition of the bridge over the Tiber." Milton, *Paradise Lost,X,*313, and Longfellow, *The Golden Legend,* V, use the word with similar reference to this meaning. Others, pointing out that L. *pont—* is from Gr. *patos,* Sansk. *patha, path,* way, remind us that the Romans were great road builders; as were the medieval clergy, esp. with roads for pilgrims to sacred shrines. All this makes it somewhat anticlimactic to remark that *pontifex* is originally a variation of *pompifex;* Oscan *ponte;* Umbrian *pontis,* from Gr. *pompe,* religious procession, from *pempein,* to send: one that directs the rituals. Hence *pomp* and ceremony. The change from *m* to *n* is frequent; it may be seen, *e.g.,* in *Pompeius,* whence *Pontius,* the man who wished a pilot to steer him to the truth—to which we have not yet built the bridge. Perhaps it is a bridge that must rest on faith; hence only the priest, the *pontifex,* may build! *Truth* is from AS. *getrīewe,* from *trēow,* faith. The trouble is that we are told *truth* is at the bottom of a well; but each one looking therein sees only his own image.

pope.
See abbot.

poplin.
See cloth.

porcine.
See mutton.

porcupine.
See mutton.

pork.
See aard-vark; mutton.

port.
The harbor or gate to a city is the avenue of much concern; thus, many words have sprung from L. *portus,* whence AS. *port,* harbor. In the sense of gate (L. *porta*) it survives in *porthole, sally-port,* and *portcullis* (Fr. *coulisse,* sliding, from *couler,* to flow). *Port* wine is Portuguese, from *o porto,* the harbor. Since the entrance to a city is the avenue of supply, L. *portare* means to bear; hence Fr. *porter,* to carry, whence Eng. *port* (as in *Port* arms!), *porter* (*porter,* the drink, is short for *porter's* ale; *porterhouse* is a tavern for *porters,* formed like alehouse; and *porterhouse* steak was a specialty of a well-known New York tavern of the 19th c.), *portly, deportment,* and the river *portage* (cognate with L. *port* is AS. and Eng. *ford,* a place where one can carry things across a stream. The automobile is named, of course, after Henry *Ford,* its manufacturer). *Cp. Bosphorus.*

If something is safely at the harbor (L. *ob + portunus*) it is *opportune,* and presents an *opportunity;* if it fails to arrive at the proper time, it is *inopportune.* Earlier, such failure was *importune, importunate* (Fr. *importun,* from L. *importunus,* unfit); from meaning untimely, these words came to mean troublesome, then insistent.

Import and *export* mean to carry in and out (of a harbor, or country); *important* is that which is worth bringing in, that which has weight, is of value; this sense is found also in the *import* of one's remarks. *Portunus* was the Roman god of harbors.

portcullis.
See cataract, port.

porter, porterhouse.
See port; plot.

pose.
When you *pose* you *pause*—etymologically also: from Fr. *poser,* from LL. *pausare.* A *poser* is a question or thought that makes you *pause.* Hence *compose,* to *pause* together; *propose,* to *pause* in behalf of; *expose*—this last word bids us *pause.*

There is a L. word *ponere, posit—,* to place, which gives us *compound, propound, expound.* But the middle ages found it convenient to *pause* when they placed something—and the first word above replaced the second, and tangled its meaning along. Thus *expose* is to place out (where all may view). *Proposal* is from the first source; but the two L. verbs fuse in *composition, exposition, proposition.* You *pause* when you place yourself in *position* for a *pose.* An *imposition* is a putting upon, either as a bishop lays on his hand or as a deceiver "puts one over on you," or—earlier—as a special punishment is put upon you. May you be spared two of the three! *Cp. posthumous.*

position.
See pose.

posology.
See dose.

posse.
When a criminal is at large, the whole force of the county may be roused for his capture. This, the word *posse* tells us; from L. *posse comitatus,* the force of the county. L. *posse, pot—,* (Eng. *potent; cp. husband*), from L. *potis,* powerful, + *esse,* to be. See any "Western" film. Hence also, *possible,* of that which has power to be.

possess.
See subsidy.

possible.
See posse.

post.
See posthumous.

posthumous.
Amateur gardeners are glad to purchase *humus,* good earth. And they have put an *h* into *posthumous,* as though it refers to the time after the ground has covered one. But a *posthumous* work is just the very very last, from L. *postumus,* the superlative of *post,* after. *Post* is, of course, a frequent prefix in Eng. *P.M.* is *post meridian,* after noon, from L. *merides,* from *medidies,* from *medi, mid* + *dies,* day. A soldier's *post* or station is LL. *postum,* from *positum,* from *ponere, posit—, cp. pose.* Hence also *position; deponent,* present participle of *deponere,* to place down; and the *post* that is placed in the ground. The *postman* was originally a fellow stationed (with horses) along a road, to pass on messages as the stick is passed in a relay race. The word was transferred from his place to his burden.

postliminy.
See limen.

postman.
See posthumous.

postscript.
See shrine.

pot.
This is a late AS. *potte,* from LL. *pottus.* Its origin seems to be a case of metonymy: contained becomes the container, the figure in "He's fond of the bottle." LL. *pottus* is from L. *potus,* drink, from *potare, potat—,* to drink, whence Eng. *potation;* also *potion; cp. intoxicate.* When we say someone has *gone to pot,* however, we do not mean that he is inebriate; this *pot* is from OE. *put,* from AS *pyt,* whence Eng. *pit;* used esp. of the *pit* of hell. Thus Gawin Douglas in his translation of the *Aeneid,* 1553, pictures folk

Deip in the sorouful grisle hellis pot.

A *potboiler* is a piece of writing that in one sense has *gone to pot. See intoxicate.*

potable.
See intoxicate.

potash, potassium.
See element.

potation.
See pot, intoxicate.

potato.
See pommel.

potboiler.
See catchpenny, pot.

potent, potentate, potential.
See husband. From the present participle, L. *potent—, potential* is that which is coming into power.

potion.
See intoxicate.

Potters' Field.
See acre.

potwalloper.
See wallop.

pouch.
See lobster.

poultice.
See pelt.

poultry.
See polecat.

pound.
See dollar.

Pound, an enclosure for animals, is a doublet of *pond,* an old Teut. word.

powder.
This has always been a fine dust. L. *pulvis, pulver—,* dust (whence also Eng. *pulverize*) by way of OFr. *puldre, poldre, poudre,* became Eng. *powder.* Thence also the early *piepowder court; cp. pie.*

power.
The L. *posse, potui,* to be able (*cp. posse; husband*) developed a LL. *potere.* Through the Romance shiftings this became *podeir,* thence OFr. *poeir,* whence (now as a noun from the verbal use) OE. *poeir, pouer,* and Eng. *power.* From the early sense of ability to do something, the meaning has been extended in various directions; as, numbers raised to the second *power; horse-power;* the *powers* among the orders of angel.

pox.
See lobster.

pragmatist.
See empiric.

praise.
See surprise.

praline.
See Appendix II.

pram.
See ambulance.

praseodymium.
See element.

pray, prayer.
See precarious. The bird of *prey* is via OFr. *preie,* from L. *praeda, prey,* whence also *predatory*—perhaps contracted from L. *praehendere,* to seize; *cp. surrender.*

preach.
See verdict.

precarious.
When you are angry at some one, you may heap *imprecations* upon him, from L. *im,* from *in,* against + *precari, precat—,* to pray. But if you are in doubt as to the outcome of a situation, you are likely to be full of *prayer* (L. *precari* + *—osus,* whence *—ous,* full of); hence your situation is *precarious* *Precious* has no relation to this; for it, *see carnelian.* A *deprecatory* tone is one that seeks to "*pray* down" something you do not wish to be blamed for. And *prayer* itself is via OFr. *preiere,* from L. *precari,* to *pray,* from L. *prex, prec—* *prayer.* The college term *Prexy* is, of course, a contraction of *President,* the one that sits before; *cp. subsidy.*

precept.
See disciple.

precinct.
The police districts of a city draw their name from the fact that they were measured around (L. *prae,* before + *cingere, cinct—,* to gird). But when you exclaim "That's a *cinch!*" you are drawing from the same source. Sp. *cincha* is the belt strap that holds on the horse's saddle, whence Eng. *cinch;* when this is tight the saddle is secure, *cinched.* The disease *shingles* (OFr. *cengle,* from L. *cingulum,* diminutive, from *cingere*) is so named because often its eruptions ring the body. The *shingles* on a roof—which give the pattern for a style of trimming women's hair—are ME. *shindle,* from L. *scindula,* diminutive, from *scindere, scidi, sciss—,* to split, whence Eng. *scission, scissors,* etc. *Cp. shed.*

precious.
See carnelian.

preclude.
See close.

precocious.
See apricot.

predatory.
See pray.

predetermination.
See determine.

predicament, predicate, predict.
See verdict.

predilection.
See sacrifice.

preempt.
See quaint, ransom; **drink.**

preen.
See propaganda.

prefect.
See defeat. (L. *pre—,* **before: to appoint before).**

prefer.
See suffer.

prefix.
See fix.

prehensile.
See surrender.

prelate.
See suffer.

preliminary.
See limen.

premise, premiss.
See mess.

premium.
See quaint.

prepare.
See overture.

preponderance.
See aggravate.

preposterous.
Originally this referred to things out of their proper order (L. *prae,* before + *poster,* after); the cart before the horse; but in these automobile days it is applied to anything that seems to deviate from the natural. The figure of speech *hysteron proteron* has exactly the same meaning: (Gr. *hysteron,* latter + *proteron,* former). When a salesman offers you a glowing picture of profits, so vivid you begin to see yourself spending what you have not yet made, his proposition is probably, in both senses, *preposterous.*

prerogative.
See quaint.

presbyter, Presbyterian.
See priest.

prescribe, prescription.
These words once referred to a title-page, or an introduction; they are from L. *pre—* before, + *scribere, script—,* to write; *cp. shrine.* Hence, of the words written down to be followed, as by a physician.

present, presentation, presentiment, presently.
See loafer, ascend.

preserve.
See family.

preside.
See subsidy.

press.
See command, *cp.* plot.

prestidigitator.
See prestige.

prestige.
A *prestidigitator* may not have much *prestige* among men of science; but they cannot be too *strict. Prestige* originally meant a conjurer's trick; thence, the power to dazzle, to charm; thence, the elevation due to the general admiration. As a conjurer's trick, it is from L. *praestigium,* delusion, from *praestigiae,* juggler's tricks, from *praestrigiae,* from *praestringere,* to bind before (to blindfold, therefore to hoodwink), from *prae,* before + *stringere, strict—* to bind, to draw. The early Eng. for conjurer was thus *prestigiator;* this became influenced by the technique, and from Fr. *preste,* from It., whence Eng. *presto* (*change-O*), with L. *digitator,* manipulator, from *digitus,* finger, whence Eng. *digit,* gives us *prestidigitator,* one who makes things disappear with his fingers (sometimes used of a sneak-thief).

We have wandered a bit from the narrow path, for "*strait* is the gate, and narrow is the way, which leadeth unto life" (*Matthew,* vii, 14). *Strait* and *strict* (L. *strictus,* narrow) are doublets, from L. *stringere, strict—,* to draw, to bind. This word has a numerous progeny. By another path (ME. *stranen,* from *streynen,* from OFr. *estraindre,* from *stringere*) comes *strain.* Hence *constrain* and *constrict* are doublets (L. *con,* from *cum,* together, *i.e.* to draw tight). So are *restrain* and *restrict,* to bind back. *Distrain* (L. *di,* from *dis,* apart) gives us also the noun *distress* (from OFr. *destrece,* from L. *district—*), which first meant the legal holding apart of goods, as a pledge for the redressing of a wrong; hence, the sorrow caused by such withholding. *District* is the territory held apart, under the jurisdiction of a feudal lord. The present participle of *stringere* is *stringens, stringent—;* whence Eng. *stringent.* By earlier Anglo-Saxon paths come other related forms. *String* is from AS. *streng;* L. *stringere,* to bind. G. *streng;* AS. *strong,* gives Eng. *strong.* But *see strike.*

Strain, in the sense of the *strain* of his speech, or he is of noble *strain,* is from ME. *streen,* from AS. *streon,* gain, from AS. *strienan,* to obtain, to beget. *Straight* comes by a slightly different path from the same basic meaning as *strait*: ME. *streicht, streght,* taut, the past participle of *strecchen,* whence Eng. *stretch,* from AS. *streccan,* to *stretch*: *stretched;* hence, the shortest distance between two points before Einstein.

Cord is from Gr. *chordon;* gut, hence string of musical instrument; also spelled *chord;* but *chord,* in music, does not deserve the *h,* added as though from the Gr.; it is from earlier *cord,* aphetic for *accord,* from Fr. *accorder,* from L. *corda,* harp-string (influenced by L. *cor, cord—,* heart, whence *cordial*), whence Eng. *concord, discord, accordian*: Thus *concord, e.g.* combines the notion of strings plucked together and of hearts that beat as one. *Twine* is from AS. *twin,* whence Eng. *twin, twain, twice,* from AS. *twa, two*: *two* strands twisted together; the idea of twisting dominates the verbs *twine* and *entwine.*

presto.
See prestige; *cp.* hocus-pocus.

presume, presumptuous.
See prompt.

pretend, pretentious.
See tennis.

pretext.
See text.

pretzel.
This word, via G. may be from LL. *bracellus,* bracelet. But it may more pleasantly have come from L. *pretiola,* a little reward—this being the sort of cake the monks gave, in the 16th c., to good children that had learned their prayers. The twist may thus represent the folded arms of the devout monk. Speaking of monks, there is another tale. *Antimony* is a LL. word; there is the doubtful suggestion that it is from Arab. *al-ithmid,* the name of the element. But folk-etymology traces the word (from Fr. *antimoine,* from LL. *antimonium,* against monks, monk's bane) to the man that found pigs grew fat on *antimony* mixed with grain, whereupon he fed it to some lean ascetic monks—who died of it. The Arab. word was corrupted in Gr. as *stimmid—,* L. *stibium;* whence the chemical symbol for the element is *Sb.* Also suggested is *anti-monos,* against being alone, as it usually occurs in combination. Such combinations turn etymology into a *pretzel!* But also ***see element.***

prevaricate.
A crook is one that has wandered from the straight path. *Prevaricate* (L. *praevaricari,* to walk crooked, from *prae,* before + *varicare,* to straddle, from *varus,* bent, knock-kneed) similarly grew from a literal to a figurative use. The same L. root gives us Eng. *varicose* (L. *varix, varic—,* the crooked and swollen vein). A man whose legs are crooked should at least keep a straight face.

prevent.
This word means, literally, come before (L. *prae,* before + *venire, vent—,* come). If a kindly person arrives before you, he gets things in pleasant readiness; hence the Common Prayer Book beseeches: *"Prevent* us, O Lord, in all our doings." In the more mundane stretches of our lives, he that comes before is likely to gather whatever is worth the taking, so that indeed latecomers are *prevented* from securing what they might desire. *Circumvent* (L. *circum,* around) has developed a similar implication. *Event,* however, that which *eventuates* (L. *e, ex,* out) has remained morally neutral, meaning merely that which comes out, the outcome. Thus also a *convention* (L. *cum,* together) is merely a coming together, hence an agreement (as we say "Let's get together on this;" a get-together); hence, something generally agreed upon, a general usage; whence, *conventionalism, conventionality,* etc. A *convent* (from Church L.) is a place to come together; in ME. it was *covent* (*cp.* Fr. *couvent*), which remains in *Covent* Garden, London. *Convenient* (from the present participle, *veniens, venient—*) has followed a more pleasant path: coming together, therefore agreeing, suitable, fit. An *invention* is a thing come upon. *Cp. speed.*

prey.
See pray.

price.
See surprise.

prick.
See attack.

pride.
See prude.

priest.
The Gr. *presbys,* old, had the comparative form *presbyteros,* elder. This word was applied to the elders of the community, then of the church community. By way of the L., and OE. *preost,* it became Eng. *priest;* but at the time of the Reformation, there was drawn more directly the term *presbyter,* and *Presbyterian*—a church in which the highest rank is the *presbyter* or elder. *Prester John* is of the same source, OFr. *prestre* from L. *presbyter.*

prig.
This word seems to be of cant origin; applied (perhaps from *prick,* from the piercing of pots to repair them) first, in the 16th c., to a tinker; thence to a wandering or petty thief. But it was soon used with much greater emphasis in religion; and it is suggested that it developed from a LL. *pregare* from L. *precare,* to pray (*cp. precarious*), as applied to those that put on airs of great religion; precisians in devotion. Thus a religious tract of 1684 speaks of the worldly *PR... IG...s* (meaning *p*roud and *ig*norant ones) as the cause of schism in the church.

prime.
When a book is called a *primer* (short *i*) it is usually a first reader, an elementary guide, in the field, from L. *prime,* first, whence Eng. *prime.* With the long *i,* however, it is one that dresses or trims the reader; this sense is more often applied to the *priming* of a gun; it is from earlier Eng. *prein,* from *proin,* which is the same word as *prune* (of trees). *Cp. propaganda. See orient.*

Note, however, that thus preparing or *priming* a gun, etc., is always something that must be done first; so that the two senses intertwine. From the L. adjective comes Eng. *primitive. Prime,* first in order, came therefore to be used of first in quality, as *prime* ribs of beef. Cp. *sirloin;* bull.

primordial.
See orient.

primrose.
This seems to be the *prime* (first) rose, early-budded through the snow. Thus Wordsworth, *The River Duddon*:

And gazing, saw the *Rose,* which from
the *prime*
Deserves its name.

It is, however, not connected with the *rose*—save by folk association, which changed the ending—being earlier *primerols,* from *primerole,* from Fr. *primverole,* from It. *primaverola,* diminutive of *primavera,* "the firstling of spring," from OFr. *verd,* green, from L. *virid*—. *Vera* is the goddess of spring. *Rose* is via L. *rosa,* from Gr. *rhodon,* whence Eng. *rhododendron,* rose-tooth tree; cp. *east*—probably of Oriental origin.

Similarly *rosemary* has no connection with either *Rose* or *Mary,* but is from LL. *rosmarinus,* sea-spray, from its growing along the coast. By a (false) association with L. *mas, mari,* male, whence *maritus,* husband, the *rosemary* was long worn at weddings. By a similarly natural interpretation of the sound, *marigold* was assumed to be the *golden* flower of the Virgin *Mary;* it is really a folk corruption of AS. *merscgealla,* from *mear, marsh,* whence Eng. *marsh, mere,* from L. *mare,* sea + *geallo,* gall.

print.
See command. The first sense was of a mark pressed in, as a *footprint;* this remains in the *printed* word.

prior, priority.
See ransom.

prison.
See surprise.

prisoners'-base.
See baseball.

privacy.
See private.

private.
This first meant without office or (of a soldier) rank, from L. *privatus,* bereaved, from *privare,* to *deprive,* from *privus,* single; whence also *privation,* and, by way of Fr. *privé,* Eng. *privy.* The shrub *privet,* earlier *prim* (*prime,* early-green) was changed because of its use to ensure *privacy.* In the 17th c., the English government issued "letters of marque" to owners of a "*private* man of war," authorizing them to attack enemy merchant vessels; by analogy

with volunteer, such a ship was called a *privateer;* then, its crew. The synonymous *pirate* is from L., from Gr. *peirates,* from *peiran,* to attempt, attack. When we speak of the *privileged* class, we mean the group that has its own special laws: *privilege* is from L. *privus* + *lex, legis, law; cp. legible.*

privation, privet, privilege, privy.
See private.

prize.
See surprise.

pro-ally.
See compromise. Thus we speak of the *pros* and *cons* of a matter. For *ally, see legible.*

problem.
In school, *problems* are things the teacher puts in your way; in real life, a *problem* is thrown in front of you, and you must work your way past. And the word is from Gr. *problema,* thing thrown before, from *pro,* before + *ballein,* to throw. *Cp. parlor,* where *problems* used to be discussed.

proceed, process.
See ancestor.

proclivity.
See climate.

procrustean (bed).
Between Athens and Sparta, just where a traveller might wish to spend the night, dwelt *Procrustes,* a giant with a keen sense of the fitness of things. He offered the passerby a bed; if the man was too short, *Procrustes* stretched him to fit; if too long, he lopped off the excess. The effort to fit any new situation into preconceived notions is *procrustean.*

proctor, procure.
See accurate.

production.
See duke.

profane.
That which was outside the temple (L. *pro,* before, outside, + *fanum,* temple; whence Eng. *fane*) was of course irreligious. Note, however, that the temple was first associated with rejoicing; the word *fane* (*cp. fanatic*) is from an earlier *fasnom,* related to *festum,* feast, whence Eng. *festival* and *festive.* Also related is L. *feria,* holiday, whence the county *fair.* The *fair* maidens were common Teut., Goth. *fagrs,* fit. The word first meant beautiful; it was then contrasted to foul, which first meant ugly; then both were used figuratively, as in *fair* play, foul play. Dark women being deemed sinister, even foul, the word *fair* took on its meaning of light.

This same *fair,* however, OE. *faegre,* through its cognate, G. *fegen,* to clean, to make fair, was used figuratively—clean sweep, clean up, etc.; from this came early Eng. *feague, feake,* to polish up; and the current slang, *fake.* A *faker* is not to be confused with the eastern *fakir, faquir,* from Arab. *faqir,* poor, applied by transfer from the beggar to the religious mendicant, not at all *profane.*

proffer.
See suffer.

proficient.
See prophet.

profile.
We think of this as a side view; it was first an outline drawing, as though one had traced a thread around—from L. *pro—,* forth, + *filare,* to spin, from *filum,* thread.

profit.
See prophet.

profound, profuse.
See futile.

progenitor.
See racy.

prognosis, prognosticate.
See prophet.

progress.
See issue.

prohibit.
See forbid.

project.
See subject.

proletarian, proletariat, proliferate, prolific, prolix.
See world.

Promethean.
See Atlas, and next entry.

Prometheus.

The well-known myth tells us that, for having shown man the secret of fire, *Prometheus* was fastened to a rock by the gods, with a vulture forever eating his forever renewed entrails. The name *Prometheus* means the provident (Gr. *promethes,* forethinking). But this is probably a Greek corruption, to make intelligible and give a story to Sansk. *pramantha,* the fire-drill (spindle that was whirled to set dry leaves and wood-crumbs afire). Note that one of the names of the devil is *Lucifer,* the light-bringer (L. *luci—,* light + *ferre,* to bring). Stories are woven about many things of old. Thus, the biblical remark, it is easier for a camel to go through a needle's eye than for a rich man to enter the kingdom of heaven, is explained in this manner: The shape of the small postern gate of the eastern walled city led to its being called "The Needle's Eye;" a camel can go through only by kneeling. This pretty parable seems to collapse when the Aramaic version reveals that the original word was not *camel,* but *rope.* But the folktales keep on growing.

promiscuous.

See ache, immunity.

promise.

See compromise.

promotion.

See mute.

prompt.

The L. *emere, empt—* first meant to take; as conditions grew more orderly, and the accepted method of taking was by purchase, it added the meaning, to buy. From it have come quite a number of words; *cp. quaint; ransom.* Something taken out, for instance, for others to go by, is *exemplary.* The manner or tone of one accustomed to taking (L. *per,* through, thoroughly, used as an intensive) is *peremptory.*

To take under one's wing, to take in charge (L. *sub,* under) was *sumere, sumpt—.* From the lavishness of those that used to take, e.g., the Roman circuses in charge, came L. *sumptus,* expense; *sumptuosus,* lavish (*cp. supercilious*); whence, Eng. *sumptuous.* But in turn L. *sumere* became the source of other forms. To take to oneself (L. *ad,* to) gave us Eng. *assume, assumption.* With L. *com, con,* together, altogether, we have to *consume, consumption* of food and the disease that takes you altogether, *consumption.* Soup that has "taken all the nourishment" from the meat is (directly from the Fr.) *consommé.* To take something first is to be *presumptuous;* to take it for granted ahead of time is to *presume.* To take back (an activity, hence, to start over) is to *resume*; hence a going back and giving the gist of a thing is to present (directly from the Fr.) a *résumé.* So generally did L. *sumere* become the term for taking, that there even developed a second prefix *sub,* under; hence, Eng. *subsume,* to take under (to include within another grouping, etc). Note that *sum, summit* (*cp. azimuth*); *consummate,* the highest altogether; *consummation,* are from L. *summus,* highest; not on this trail.

Back to the simple L. *emere,* to take, with the prefix *pro,* forth, ahead, we have *promere, prompt—;* hence, Eng. *prompt.* This was first a verb, to incite. That which went forth in good time was *prompt;* hence, also, the theatrical *promptbook,* so that, if an actor does not come forth at the right moment, you may *prompt* him. From the final *consumption,* no mortal is *exempt.*

propaganda.

One should always seek the source of *propaganda.* The word itself comes from *pro,* forth + *pago, pagere* (earlier *pacere, pangere*), *pact—,* to fasten, to plant; whence *propago,* a layer, a shoot. (From the simple form *pago, pagin—,* a fastening, we have Eng. *page, pagination.* The court *page* is from LL. *pagius,* perhaps from G. *pathicus,* sufferer, whence Eng. *pathic.*) Thus *propaganda* is the L. gerundive, that which should be planted or bound forth: first applied to grafting shoots (*cp. graft*); then by the Church in Rome, which in 1622 founded the *Congregatio de propaganda fidei,* for the *propagation* of the faith. Though *propaganda* may not work for *peace, peace* and *pact* are from the same source; also *appease, pacify; compact, impact,* all with the sense of binding—even *pachyderm* (Gr. *paxos,* firm, from Sansk. *pac,* bind + *derm,* hide; thus Eng. *epidermis*: Gr. *epi,* on, besides). The word *pay,* to clear a debt, is also from L. *pacare,* to appease, whence LL. *pacare,* to *pay, q.v.*

By another path, L. *propago, propagin—,* a shoot, whence It. *propaggine,* whence Fr. *provigner* (possibly influenced by Fr. *vigne, vine*), whence *progner,* to plant a shoot or sucker; this, from its allied task of cutting off the suckers, then the excess twigs, gives us OE. *proin, proine,* whence Eng. *prune*. Gascoigne, in *The Steele Glas,* 458, says that imps (*cp. graft*) "grow crookt, because they be not proynd". Birds *prune* (whence *preen*) themselves by plucking out feathers; hence, the ladies that *preen*—though it has also been suggested that this *preening* is from *proinen,* from OFr. *poroindre,* from *per* + *oindre,* from L. *ungere, unct—, to anoint,* whence Eng. *unguent, anointing* oil; *unction; unctuous* (L. *—osus,* full of, whence Eng. *—ous*: full of anointing oil, hence oily). *Anoint* is from OFr. *enoindre,* from L. *inungere,* from *in,* on + *ungere,* to pour oil.

Prune, the fruit, is not related to this word. We confuse *prunes* and *plums* today: *prune* is usually limited to the dried *plum,* but is also applied to the small purple *plum* (whence the color, and the cloth *prunella*) that is used for the drying: but *plum* and *prune* are the same word in origin, being doublets of Gr. *prounon, plum.* Stick in your thumb and pull out ***propaganda.*** ***See*** *curfew.*

propel.
See pelt.

propensity.
See aggravate.

prophet.
This is one that speaks ahead of the time, from Gr. *pro—* before, + *phetes,* speaker, from *phanai,* to speak. Through LL. *prophetia* and OFr. *prophecie* came Eng. *prophecy;* to *prophesy* was from the OFr. verb *prophesier.* Or else *prophet* was just one that spoke forth: Gr. *prophetes* came to mean interpreter.

One's *profit* (as when one was *prophetic* of the market) is via OFr. *profit* from L. *proficere, profect—,* to make ahead, make headway, advance, from L. *pro—* forward, + *facere,* to make. One who is doing well (from the present participle, *proficient—*) is Eng. ***proficient.*** *Cp. defeat.*

But one that (thinks he) knows in advance gives a *prognosis* (Gr. from *pro—* + *gignoskein,* to know; *cp. quaint, science*); via the L. verb *prognosticare, prognosticat—,* comes Eng. *prognosticate.*

prophylactic.
The L. prefix *pro—* is used to mean forward, before, in place of, or on the side of (as opposed to *con,* against). As a prefix in Gr., it meant before. From Gr. *phylassein,* to guard, a *prophylactic* is an advance guard; the word has been used since the 16th c. with special reference to guarding against disease. There is no relation to *lactic* acid, for which *see delight.*

propose, proposition, propound.
See pose.

proscribe.
See shrine.

prosecute.
See pursue.

prostitute.
See tank.

protagonist.
See agony.

protean, protein.
See remorse.

protest.
See test.

proto—.
The Gr. *protos,* first, gives us the frequent combining form, Eng. *prot—, proto—.* Thus *protoplasm* is the primordial life-stuff (Gr. *plasma,* moulded form; *cp. plant*); and the *protozoa* (Gr. *zoa,* animals) are the primitive forms of animal life. The neuter, Gr. *proton,* is used directly in Eng. as the basic unit of matter-forming electricity.

A *protocol* (Gr. *kolla,* glue; whence Eng. *colloid; cp. remorse*) was originally a leaf glued onto the case of a volume, with a summary or account of the manuscript; then, a record of the points made, esp. of an agreement at a conference; hence, the first draft of a document.

protoactinium.
See element.

protocol, proton, protoplasm, protozoa.
See proto—, plant, remorse.

proud.
See prude.

proverb.
The most important *word* in the Eng-

lish sentence is the *verb.* Hence *verb,* that once meant *word* (L. *verbum, word,* as in *Verbum sapienti satis est,* A word to the wise is sufficient), has come to mean the predicate term. A *proverb* was literally something *pro,* instead of, a word: an image, a figurative instead of a literal expression; hence, the Bible's "dark sayings", *Proverbs* i,6. From their popularity the *proverbs* came into everyone's mouth; hence, the word *proverb* came to mean a byword, a commonplace; now the word has gone back to a sort of middle ground, as a familiar but not despised expression of a general truth.

provide, provident.
See improvised.

provoke.
See entice.

prowess.
See prude.

proxy.
See accurate.

prude.
This is short for Fr. *prudefemme,* excellent woman. *Prude* is the feminine of *preux,* whence Fr. *preux d'homme,* whence *prud'homme. Proud* is the same word, from AS. *prūd,* from LL. *prodis,* from L. *prodesse,* to be valiant, whence Eng. *prowess,* from L. *pro,* forth + *esse,* to be. An excellent man showed *prowess;* an excellent woman was retiring; hence, a *prude. Pride* is from AS. *pryto,* from *prud.* But *see improvised.*

prudent.
See improvised.

prune.
See propaganda.

prussic.
See Appendix II.

psalm.
The song is named from the music (AS. *sealm,* from Gr. *psalmos,* twanging, from *psallein,* to twitch). The instrument thus twanged was Gr. *psalterion,* which gives us Eng. *psaltery* and *psalter,* the collection of songs from the harp once used with them. *Psalmody,* the art of singing sacred music, is from Gr. *psalmos* + *ode,* song. (*Ode* gives us Eng. *ode* and *tragedy; see buck.*)

pseudo—.
This combining form (before a vowel, sometimes *pseud—*) is from Gr. *pseudos,* falsehood; it applies to something that is **not what it seems to be. There are several** hundred such words in Eng., from *pseudapostle* (*apostle,* one sent with the message of the coming of the Lord, is Gr. *apostolos,* messenger, from *stellein,* to send) to *pseudovary* (*ovary* from L. *ovum,* Gr. *oon,* egg). Thus *pseudonym,* from *pseudo—* + *onyma,* name; the negative prefix *an—*gives us *anonymous.*

pseudonym.
See pseudo—.

psilo—.
This Gr. prefix is used in Eng. to mean bare, smooth, mere. Thus *psilopaedic* (Gr. *pais, paid—; cp. pedagogue*) is used of birds hatched bare, without down. A scornful term for a "mere *philosopher*", a shallow thinker, is *psilosopher.* There is of course no connection with *silo* (though the man's ideas may be as green as the fodder), from L. *sirus* from Gr. *siros,* a pit for corn; whence also *ensilage.*

psilosopher.
See psilo—.

psychoanalysis, psychanalysis.
(The second form, though the less frequent, is the more sensible. The *o* adds naught to the meaning, and interrupts the flow of the sound.)

Psyche, the soul, was loved by *Cupid* (L. *cupido,* desire, whence Eng. *cupidity*); he visited her only in the dark; a drop from her candle (when she sought to discover his identity) waked him, and he fled. To win him back, *Psyche* became the slave of his mother, *Venus* (*cp. win*). There is a symbol in all this; but the name is from Gr. *psyche, breath,* from *psychein,* to breathe. *Analysis* is from Gr. *ana—* + *lysis,* from *lyein,* to loosen.

The Gr. prefix *an—, ana—,* means up; back; again (before a vowel, Gr. *a—,* not, becomes *an—*). The same letters also form the suffix *—ana,* as in *Shakespeariana, Johnsoniana,* etc.; this may (like the literary *isms*) be used as a separate word. And as a separate word *ana* (from the Gr. adverb *ana,* again, which forms the prefix) is used in prescriptions to mean, repeat the amount. This gives you some idea of the complexity of *psychanalysis,* which was coined ca. 1896 by Dr. Sigmund

Freud, to name the method of treatment he used for mental cases when he turned from *hypnosis* (from Gr. *hypnos,* sleep).
Thus *anagram* (Gr. *gramma,* letter), the most famous *anagram* being of Pilate's question (*Bible, John* xviii,38): *Quid est veritas?—Vir est qui adest*: What is truth?—It is the man before you. Perhaps someone should psychanalyze Pilate.

pterodactyl.
See vogue.

ptomaine.
Even now quite dangerous, *ptomaine* poison formerly was sure death; you just watched the body fall down dead. The word says just that: It. *ptomaina,* from Gr. *ptoma,* corpse, is from *piptein,* to fall.

pucker.
When you *pucker* up your lips, you form them into a little pocket or pouch; *cp. lobster.*

pudding.
This is closely related to *sausage, cp. salary,* the first sense being intestine, then a black-pudding (from F. *boudin*) encased in the intestinal lining. The *g* was added as still in local dialects, *e.g., capting* for *captain, cp. achieve.* Pepys (*Diary,* July 16, 1667) speaks of "*wooling* knit stockings."

Puerto Rico.
See States.

puff.
See buff, of.

pugilist, pugnacious.
See pygmy.

pullet.
See polecat.

pulley.
Associated in sound with *pull,* this is really another case of an animal's giving its name to a contrivance for labor. *Cp. buck.* It is from L. *pullus,* colt, from Gr. *polos.* Similar uses are found in many languages, *e.g.,* Pers. *bakrah,* cow, clothes-horse, whence *bakarah, pulley. Cp. poltroon.*

pulsation, pulse.
See pelt.

pulverize.
See powder.

pummel.
See pommel.

pump.
See pamper.

punch.
See drink.

punctilio, punctual, punctuate, puncture.
See pungent.

pungent.
To *punctuate* is to mark off with little pricklings (from LL. *pungere, punct—,* to prick. Hence, of course, *puncture.* L. *punctum,* whence It. *punto,* whence Fr. *pointe,* whence Eng. *point*). A man that is easily pricked, that regards with utmost concern the fine points of courtesy, stands upon each *punctilio,* from It. *puntiglio,* diminutive of *punto.* A man that comes upon the prick of the hour, "jump" upon the *point,* like the ghost in Hamlet, is very *punctual.* And an odor pricking your nostrils (present participle of *pungere*) is *pungent.*

Punic faith.
See Dutch.

puny.
Little brother is often called *Bud*—because older brother tries to pronounce *brother* and produces *"budder"*, whence *Bud.* But as a consequence of his coming second, for many years he is, compared to the first born, a little fellow. Hence the change in meaning of *puny,* which first meant merely, born after, from Fr. *puisné,* from L. *post natus.*

pupil.
Let a schoolboy look closely into someone's eye; what will he see? The *pupil!* That's not a joke: the *pupil* of the eye was named from the face reflected in it. Among the baby words (*see abbot*) were L. *pupus,* boy, *pupa,* girl: imitative of the sounds of infancy, with the masculine and the feminine ending. Diminutives of these are *pupillus, pupilla,* which via Fr. *pupille* give us *pupil,* in both senses. Another Fr. diminutive, *poupette,* "a little baby, a plaything," gives us Eng. *puppet.* Another form of this is *puppy,* first any

plaything, then applied to the tiny dogs ladies like to carry. Thus, when someone calls a boy "a young *pup*", he is merely being etymological. (Gr. for girl, doll, and *pupil* of the eye is *kope*, whence perhaps the modern *kewpie* doll.)

puppet, puppy.
See pupil.

purchase.
Whenever a person wants something eagerly (L. *per;* Eng. *pure,* through and through—though the Fr. suggests that the prefix may be Fr. *pour,* for) one will *chase* for it indeed. Which is what *purchase* first meant (OFr. *chasser,* Picard *cachier,* whence Eng. *catch,* from LL. *captiare,* from *captare,* frequentative of *capere, capt—,* to take). To pursue; to acquire; then, to acquire in the customary manner, by *purchase.* Note that *chase, catch,* and *capture* are triplets; *cp. manœuvre.*

While *chase,* to hunt, comes via OFr *chasser, chase,* to engrave, is aphetic for OFr. *enchasser;* this first meant to enshrine, from *en,* in + *châsse,* shrine, from L. *capsa,* a receptacle (where holy relics were kept), from the same L. *capere.* From the same L. *capsa,* via Fr. *châsse,* comes the *chassis* of our automobile.

Chased from these verbs is, of course, not to be confused with *chaste,* from L. *castus,* pure. The emphasis on punishment rather than prayer is shown in the fact that this word has developed three verb forms, in which "to make pure" means, more and more strongly up the scale, to punish: directly from Eng. *chaste* we have *chasten.* The L. verb is *castigare, castigat—;* through OFr. *chastier* comes Eng. *chastise;* and directly from the L. the most vehement of the three, Eng. *castigate.* From L. *castus* probably was formed L. *castrare, castrat—,* to make pure, whence Eng. *castrate. Cp. casement; discuss.*

pure.
See curfew; *cp.* purchase.

puritan.
This word was originally a term of scorn, LL. *puritani,* those that would purge, being equivalent to the Gr. word for cathartic-givers. Applied to those that demanded still further *purification* of the established church of England, because of the association with *pure* (*cp. curfew*) it was accepted as a term of honor; hence, the *Puritans.*

purge.
See curfew.

purse.
See budget; Bursa.

pursue.
If you chase some one long enough, he may feel that you are *persecuting* him. He would not be far wrong: the two words are doublets; both first meant to follow through. *Pursue* is from OFr. *porsievre,* from *porsieure* (whence Fr. *poursuivre,* which is thus not from *pour,* for + *suivre,* follow) from L. *persequere,* popular form of *persequi, persecut—,* to follow through, from *per,* through, + *sequi, secut—,* to follow. *Cp. set.* It is clear that *persecute* comes directly from the L. form. From the simple verb come *sequel* and (present participle, L. *sequent—*) *sequence. Prosecute,* now with only legal application, means to follow in behalf of (the State)—though at first L. *pro* meant merely, forward. *Consequence,* and *consecutive* are from L. *con,* from *com,* together + *sequi. Consequential,* in the sense of important, refers simply to something that makes other things follow in its train. Thus words keep riding along.

pursy.
See Bursa.

purulent, pus.
See sorcerer.

push.
A number of Eng. words ending in *—sh* come from Fr. forms ending in *—ss*: brush; furnish. *Push* is from Fr. *pousser,* from L. *pulsare, pulsat—,* the frequentative of L. *pellers, puls—,* to drive. Hence our *pulse* beat. *Cp. pelt.*

pussyfoot.
Members of the cat family can draw in their claws and walk silently on the pads of their feet. To *pussyfoot* is therefore to walk stealthily—but with the idea that when least expected the claws may dart out. From its use as a nickname of the prohibitionist, W. E. Johnson (American, b. 1862), the term has been applied to all advocates of prohibition.

pustular, pustule.
See sorcerer.

putative, putrefy, putrescent.
See curfew.

putrid.
See curfew, polecat.

putty.
This was first a powder made of metal calcined in a *pot*; it was named from the container. Fr. *pot*, whence *potée, potful*, whence Eng. *putty*. The first type of *putty* was used for polishing glass; the present type, for holding glass in its frame. Also *see pot*.

pygmy (pigmy).
This fellow as big as one's fist (or so the Greeks thought, for the word is from *pygmaios*, dwarfish, from *pygme*, fist; also the length from elbow to knuckles) has ferocious connections. For Gr. *pygme* gave us L. *pugnus*, fist; this, the Romans used not so much for measuring as for shaking. They shook it at the rest of the world. Whence L. *pugnare*, to fight, whence Eng. *pugnacious* (full of fists); *pugilist*. A dagger held in the clenched hand is a *poniard*, via Fr. *poignard*, from *poing*, fist, from L. *pugnus*. To *impugn* is to fight against, from L. *impugnare*, from *pugnare*. Which helps to indicate why a *pygmy* has a hard lot.

pygophagous.
See sarcophagus.

pylorus.
Parts of the body often have names that indicate their shape, or their function. Thus, the ear *drum*, and *canals*. The *temple*, however, is not related to the building, but comes (via LL. diminutive *tempula*), from L. *tempus*, time—which gives us *temporal, temporary, contemporary*, etc. The "time" of the body can be taken by the pulse of the *temple*, *q.v.* It is also suggested as influenced by the same *tempus*, in the sense of seasonable: the seasonable spot to hit an enemy.

The opening from the *stomach* into the *intestine* is named from its post: *pylorus*, from Gr. *pyloros*, gatekeeper, from *pyle*, gate + *ouros*, watcher (as in *Arcturus*; *cp. arctic*). *Intestines*, from LL. *intestina*, from L. *intus*, within, simply means the insides. *Arm* is from Gr. *harmos*, cognate with *art*, anything made (hence, using the *arms*). *Artery* is from Gr. *arteria*, windpipe; since it was noticed that no blood is in them after death, it was assumed that the *arteries* carried *air*. *Belly* is from AS. *belig*, a bag, a bellows; Goth. *balgs*, a wineskin. Shakespeare knew "the fair round *belly*, with good capon lined." *Bowel* was named in reverse: from OFr. *bouel*, from L. *botellus*, pudding, diminutive of *botulus*, sausage, which was encased in the *bowel*-lining. *Clavicle*, collar-bone, locks up the chest: from *clavicula*, diminutive of L. *clavis*, key, from *claudere, claus—*, to close; whence Eng. *inclose; claustrophobia*, fear of *enclosure*; *cp. drink*. The *duodenum* is named for its length: the breadth *duodenum digitorum*, of twelve fingers. *Elbow* is from A.S. *el*, length of arm + *bow*, bend. *Finger* is the grasper, from ME. *feng*, prey, whence Eng. *fang*, from AS. *fangan*, to seize. *Hand* is a common Teut. word. The *instep* is earlier *instoop*, the in-bend of the foot. *Foot* is a general Aryan word: AS. *fot;* Gr. *pous, pod—*, *cp. pedagogue;* Sansk. *pāda*. *Jaws* are the *chaws*, the parts that *chew*, from AS. *céowan;* whence also the *chaw* of tobacco. The *jugular* vein is from L. *iugulum*, diminutive of *iugum*, yoke: it yokes the body and head. The *lungs* (ME. *lunge*, from Teut. *linght*, whence G. *licht*, Eng. *light*) are thus named for their *light* weight; in slaughtered animals, they are still called the *lights*. The *nail*, from AS. *naegel*, from Icel. *nagl;* whence also to *nag*, to scratch verbally; and, via AS. *gnagan*, to *gnaw*. *Stomach* is from OFr. *estomac*, from L. *stomachus*, *stomach*, which also meant liking, as in "I cannot *stomach* it," from Gr. *stomachos*, from *stoma*, mouth. *Stoma—* is a frequent Eng. combining form. *Thyroid* is from G. *thyreoeides*, shaped like a shield, from *thyreos*, shield. *Tonsils* is from L. *tonsilla*, a pointed stake. The *uvula* is a cluster (of grapes). The *vertebrae* are the turners, from *vertere*, *vert—*, to turn; *cp. advertise*. *Wrist* is also the turner, from AS. *wrest*, to turn; originally there were the *hand-wrist* and the *foot-wrist*, replaced by *ankle*, from AS. *ancleow;* Sanks. *anga*, limb + *claw*. From AS. *wrest* is also Eng. *wrest*. Here let us rest.

pyre.
This was first a hearth-fire (Gr. *pyra*) then the funeral pile. It is from Gr. *pur*, *pyr*, fire; *cp. curfew*. The Gr. *empyros*, fiery, from *en*, in + *pyr*, gives us the *empyrean*. A variety of glass that can withstand fire is called *pyrex*—perhaps

from *pyre* + L. *rex*, king; but *pyrexia* is the medical word for fever.

pyromaniac.
See curfew.

Pyrrhic (victory).
"Another such victory, and we are lost." Winning, but at too great cost, is the outcome of every war today; the expression comes from the defeat of the Romans, 281 B.C., by *Pyrrhus*, the king of Epirus in Greece. The expression *Parthian arrow*, or *Parthian shot*, is also ancient—from the practice of the soldiers of *Parthia* in western Asia, of shooting backwards from their horses while running away.

pyrrhonism.
See Appendix II.

pyx.
See box.

Q

quack.
See aboveboard.

quadrant.
See sext, square.

quaint.
An object that has been known for some time tends to seem a bit old-fashioned; if at the same time it is neat, well ordered, we call it *quaint.* For *quaint* comes from ME. *queint, coynt,* from OFr. *coint,* from L. *cognoscere, cognit—,* L. *co, con, cum,* together + *gnoscere,* to know, *cognate* with Eng. *know.* But it was influenced in its course through French, by *comptus,* from L. *comere, comptus,* to arrange, adorn, from *co* + *emptus,* to take (*Caveat emptor,* let the buyer beware!) With L. *ad,* to, are formed *acquaint, acquaintance;* as Burns puts it

John Anderson, my jo, John,
When we were first *acquent* . . .

Cognition is of the same origin, if we care to take *cognizance* of it.

L. *emere, emptus* gives us *preempt* (L. *pre, prae,* before) and *premium,* a taking before. The *comere, comptus* mentioned above give us *comb,* and *unkempt,* though *comb* is perhaps more plausibly traced to AS. *comb,* a crest; akin to Gr. *gamphos, comb; gamphe,* jaw, from Sansk. *gambha,* jaw, teeth, from *jabh,* to gape. An *example* is something taken out (so is a *sample,* which is its doublet); a person taken out is *exempt* (L. *exemere, exempt—*), not necessarily *quaint.*

Preempt is a back-formation from *preemption,* which first meant the (king's) right to take (buy) before others. He had other such *prerogatives, e.g., ius primae noctis,* the right of the first night. *Prerogative* is similarly from L. *pre,* before + *rogare, rogat—,* to ask; it applied in Roman times to the tribe or century (*prerogativa centuria; prerogativus tribus*) that (by lot) voted first. Asking is *rogation;* asking often (L. *inter,* between, at intervals) is *interrogation.*

With L. *ad,* we have the Eng. legal word *adrogate,* to ask for, to adopt; in the sense of adopting without right it comes as Eng. *arrogate* (L. *arrogare;* present participle *arrogant—; arrogat—*), whence also Eng. *arrogant.* To *abrogate* (L. *ab,* away) is to cancel. A *surrogate* (L. *sub,* under) is one asked to act as a *substitute.* Substitute is from L. *substituere, substitut—,* to appoint under, from *statuere, statut—,* to set up, to appoint, whence also Eng. *statute, cp tank. See prompt.*

quarantine.
This is direct from LL. *quarantina,* forty days, from L. *quaranta,* from *quadraginta,* forty. It was applied first, in all likelihood, to the forty day period of Lent; for which the term *quadragesima,* fortieth, has been substituted. Then it was applied to the forty day period in which a widow might remain in the home of her late husband, before relinquishing to the heir. Finally, it was applied to the forty days during which a ship from an infected port, or bearing infection, must wait before landing. (L. *quadraginta* is from *quadrus,* fourfold, from *quater,* from *quattuor,* four + *—ginta,* from *dakanta,* tenth, from *decem,* ten.)

quarry.
The retriever may be proud of the game it fetches for its huntsman master; but circus training shows that what the animal wants most is the bit of food, its reward. "Get that, and you'll get this!" And the word for the reward has been transferred to what the animal must bring, to earn it. *Quarry* may be explained along three roads, which do not roam from this remuneration.

It is explained as from OFr. *curée,* from *corée,* from LL. *corata,* the pluck, from L. *cor,* the heart—the entrails being thrown to the dogs. It may be earlier *quirre,* from OFr. *cuirée,* from L. *curare,* to clean, to eviscerate (*curare* gives us *cure*). The earliest explanation (end of the 12th c.) traces *cuirée* to OFr. *cuir,* leather, hide, from L. *corium,* because the parts for the dogs were spread on the killed beast's hide. The dogs doubtless did not care!

quarter.
The American coin shows the original meaning: *one-quarter* (fourth) of a dollar, from Fr. *quartier,* from L. *quartarius,* fourth part, from *quartus,* fourth, from *quattuor,* four. A *quart* is one-fourth a *gallon.* (*Gallon* is ME. for container, from LL. *galléta,* container, bowl.) The other meanings of *quarter* developed later; thus, towns were divided into four parts (north, east, south, west) called Fr. *quartiers,* whence Eng. *quarters.* To find *quarters,* or (in war time) to give one no *quarter,* relates to lodgings in a *quarter* of the town. OE. *quartern,* a place of confinement, prison, may be here pertinent—to give no *quarter* is to kill instead of holding captive; and this *quarter* may be related to L. *carcer,* prison, whence Eng. *incarcerate;* or to AS. *cweartern,* prison, from *cweart,* lament + *ern,* house: a wailing-house; *e.g.,* any concentration camp.

quash.
See knick-knack. *Quash* is from L. *quassare,* frequentative of *quatere, quass—,* to break. *See* also *discuss.*

quean, queen.
See banshee.

quest, question.
See exquisite.

queue.
See cue.

quiescent, quiet.
See coy; acquit.

quince.
See peach.

quintessence.
The Dionne *quintuplets* come in a set of five, from L. *quintuplus,* from *quintus,* five. Similarly, L. *triplus,* by three, gives us *triplet.* The rarest distillation of a perfume is called the *quintessence,* as though five times distilled. The word, however, was first used to mean the fifth essence, or element ,of which the universe is made. The first four are earth, air, fire, and water. The fifth, added by the Pythagoreans, was the ether, rarest and most pervasive of all, and the substance of the heavenly bodies.

quintuplet.
See quintessence.

quire.
See exquisite.

quisling.
This word is one of the most quickly adopted of recent additions to the language; in fact, it is well-nigh universal (outside of Germany and Japan). It is simply the name of *Major Vidkun Quisling,* who headed the Norwegian Nazi party, and took charge of Norway when the Germans invaded, April, 1940—used as a common noun to mean such a betrayer.

quit.
See acquit.

quite.
See mere.

quixotic.
Miguel Cervantes wrote a novel, *The History of Don Quixote de la Mancha* (the first part in 1605; second part, 1615), of a visionary and idealistic knight, whose name has given the word *quixotic* to our language. The name itself was satiric, from Sp. *quixote,* later *quijote* (L. *coxa,* hip) whence Eng. *cuisse,* armor for the front of the thigh: thus the hero was called *Sir Thighpiece.*

quoin.
See coin.

quorum.
This word is L. *quorum,* of whom, genitive plural of *qui,* who. It is retained from the old commission appointing a person as one of a body (esp. justices of the peace): *quorum vos . . . unum esse volumus,* of whom we desire that you be one (*duos, two, etc.*). At first the man himself (each man thus especially named) was called a *quorum;* then the whole company as it functioned; then (early 17th c.) the word was used of the number necessary for valid functioning.

R

rabid, rabies.
See outrage.

racketeer.
The suffix indicating agent, *—er,* when spelled *—eer,* usually implies disrepute, as in *profiteer;* so also does *-ster; cp. spinster.*
In the disorderly streets of 17th c. England, pickpockets used to start a disturbance (a *racket*) in order to concenter the attention of their victims. (A statute was passed in 1697, forbidding the throwing of squibbs, rockets, and other distracting devices.) Hence the dishonest implications of the word *racket.*

racy.
This means, marked by its *race,* containing the savor of its source. *Race* comes from three trails. *Race,* a trial of speed, is common Teut., AS. *raes,* a swift course, from Sansk. *rish,* to flow; this sense remains in *millrace. Race,* lineage, seen in It. *razza,* is from OHG. *reiza,* a stroke, line, as it marks the direct line of descent. This is probably also influenced by the third *race,* a root (Shakespeare, *Winter's Tale,* IV,iii,50, speaks of a *"race* of ginger"), from OFr. *rais,* from L. *radicem,* from *radix, radic—,* root, whence Eng. *radical; cp. rascal.*
Similarly, *generous* means, full of the spirit of the *gens* or *genus* (from OFr. *genereux, generous,* from L. *generosus,* from L. *genus, gener—,* breed, *kin,* whence Eng. *genus.* By way of Goth. *kuni, kin* and *kind* (originally pronounced with a short *i;* Hamlet's first words are the pun "A little more than *kin* and less than *kind"—kind* being first the attitude proper toward one's *kin*) are of the same source. From the Ayran root *gan,* to beget, Sansk. *jan,* to beget, springs a most fertile tribe, by the way of Gr. *genos,* race, from *gignomai,* I am born, whence L. *gignere, gent—,* whence *genere, generat—,* to beget: *general,* referring to all the tribe, then, the representative, the leader, its superlative, It. *generalissimo; genius,* the spirit, or the guardian spirit, of the tribe; *gentle,* of the race; *gentile,* of the race, then in the Vulgate *Bible,* of the race talked about, *i.e.,* not one's own race, therefore, pagan; and, by other paths, *genteel* and *jaunty* (from Fr. *gentil*); *degenerate,* to fall from the race (standard); *regenerate,* to bring up to it again; *indigenous* (Gr. *endon,* within), native; *progenitor,* one who sends the tribe forth, a founding father; *heterogeneous,* of other *genus; homogeneous,* of the same *genus; hydrogen, generating* water, *cp. drink; oxygen* (Gr. *oxys,* sour); *nitrogen* (Gr. *nitron* whence Eng. *nitre,* from Heb. *nether*). Try to be *congenial* (L. *con, com,* together): friendly as birds of a feather. *Cp. cyanide.*

radar.
This takes its name from the initial letters telling what it does: *r*adio *d*etecting *a*nd *r*ange-finding. *See Dora.*

radical, radish.
See rascal.

radium, radius.
See element; X-ray.

radon.
See element.

ragamuffin.
See tatterdemalion.

rage.
See outrage.

raglan.
See Appendix II.

raisin.
See peach.

rajah.
See island.

rake.
See mock.

ram.
See mutton.

rampart.
See overture.

ranch, rank.
See harangue.

rankle.
When something *rankles*, do you think of a fabulous monster as the cause of your ills? The word was originally a noun, meaning a festering sore. By way of OFr. *raoncle*, it is traced to OFr. *draoncle*, from LL. *dracunculus*, an ulcer, literally a little *dragon*, diminutive of L. *draco, draconis*, from Gr. *drakon*. There was a very severe ruler of Greece, the archon *Draco*, 621 B. C. from whom (in association with the monster) we have the adj. *draconic*. (Gr. *drakon, dragon*, is from *drakein*, to see: apparently the monster was the ancient variety of pink elephant!) The soldier called the *dragoon* derives his name from the instrument he used to carry, a *dragoon* (*dragon*), so-called from the fact that it would dart fire. From *dragon arum* to *dragonwort*, the term is used frequently for names of plants, insects, and fishes.
Dragoman, an interpreter or guide in the near east, comes from Old Arabic *targumān*, interpreter, from Chaldee *targēm*; from this the *Targum*, an Aramaic interpretation of the Bible. The old word for *dragon*, however, suggested the title for a recent thriller play, *Dracula*.
(Some authorities, challenging that dropping of the *d* to produce *rankle*, declare that the word is from OFr. *raoncle*, from L. *ranunculus*—diminutive of L. *rana*, frog—which is also the name of a plant, the plant supposedly used by beggars to rub on their arms and faces to produce pitiable sores, or *rankles*.)

ransom.
This is a doublet of *redemption*, the one physical; the other, spiritual. L. *emere*, to buy + *re*, thus *redemere, redempt—*; whence *redemeed, redemption*; via OFr. *reanson*, whence ME. *raunson*, gave us Eng. *ransom*. For *preempt*, *see quaint*. As times change, now we use the term *priority*, from LL. *prioritas*, from L. and Eng. *prior*, from L. *pri, pre*, before. *See prompt*.

rap.
Rat-a-tat-tat. This is imitative of the sound; the verb (from ME. *rappen*) was formed from the noun. But if you say you "don't care (give) a *rap*," you are referring to an Irish counterfeit coin of the 18th c. (In Germany also, a bad penny was called a *rap*, from *rabe*, raven—instead of an eagle.) When you don't care a *fig*, it is not the delicious fruit you'd give, but It. *fico*, a snap of the fingers. (The fruit is from Prov. *figa*, from L. *ficus, fig*.)
Rapt, ravished, is a mixture; from ME. *rapen*, from *hrapen*, to act quickly (whence Eng. *rapid*) and L. *rapere, rapt—*, to snatch, to seize; whence Eng. *rape*, and *rapture*, which first meant a seizure (caught in the spell of beauty).

rape (turnip).
See alcohol.

rape, rapid.
See rap.

rapier.
See rascal.

rapture.
This is from the adj. *rapt*, carried off (L. *rapere, rapt—*, to snatch). Used often of being carried off to heaven, it came to mean carried away by joy. Less happy derivatives are *rape* and *rapine*. *Ravish*, which has both senses, is from the same L. word, by way of Fr. *ravir, raviss—*, which also gives us a *ravishing* beauty. From L. *rapina*, whence OFr. *raviner*, to *ravage* (another form, a doublet, from *ravir*), comes *raven*, not the bird, which is common Teut.; OE. *hraefn*, to pillage; this old verb survives in the adj. *ravenous*. The violent rush of the plunderers was also applied to the tumultuous rush of flood waters; then, to the *ravine* or mountain gorge worn by such a torrent. Thus there is reason for *rapture* at such sights as the Grand Canyon. *See rap*.

rarefaction.
See defeat.

rascal.
This word has lost some of its intensity, for it once meant the scrapings of society (OFr. *rascaille*, from LL. *rasciare*, from L. *radere, ras—*, whence

raze; razor; erase, to scrape out. This is not connected with OHG. *raspon,* to *rasp;* OHG. *hrespan,* to rake together; whence *rasp, raspberry,* and ? *rapier.*). This L. *radere, ras—,* gives us *rash,* an eruption. *Rash,* headstrong, is old Teut., from Sansk. *rick,* to attack, from *ri,* rise. There is also an early Eng. *rash,* to tug or tear; this is from OFr. *eracer,* from L. *eradicare,* from *exradicare,* to take out by the root, from the L. root word *radix* (in mathematics), *radical* (in mathematics and politics: one that goes to the roots of the matter), and *radish,* an edible root. A *rascal* often has a close shave.

rash, rasp, raspberry.
See rascal.

rat.
This animal came with the migration of the other savages from the east. Its name was taken from the Teut. into LL. *ratus;* AS. *raet,* ME. *raton* (a diminutive), Eng. *rat* (full sized). From the notion that *rats* desert a sinking ship (Shakespeare has Prospero say, in *The Tempest* I, ii, 147-8, of the ship in which he and Miranda were marooned: "the very *rats* Instinctively have quit it") the word was applied to those that desert or betray a cause; hence, a scoundrel: by a pun, specifically in Ireland to those (in 1921-22) that favored *rat*ification of the treaty with England. [*Ratify* is via Fr. *ratifier* from LL. *ratificare, ratificat—,* to make valid, from L. *ratus,* accepted, + *facere,* to make. L. *ratus* was the past participle of *reri, rat—,* to think, to calculate; whence also *pro rata; rate,* agreed amount, proportion, hence degree of speed etc.; and *ration; cp. number.* To *rate,* scold (also *berate*: *be—* is an Eng. intensive prefix; it is also a privative prefix, as in *behead;* also, it makes a transitive verb of other words, as *bemoan, befoul;* and it is used to express derision, as in fool, *befool; bedeck, cp. deck; bedizened, cp. distaff*) is aphetic for ME. *arate,* to blame; via OFr. *areter* (Chaucer says that if you find any error in his verse, you should *"aret* it to Adam Scrivener") from L. *reputare, reputat—* (*repute* was used also for *impute*) whence also *reputation; see character.*]

The *rat* a woman may use to pad her hair is from the usual color and shape and scorn of the object. The exclamation *Rat!,* nonsense, is a minced pronunciation of *Rot!* These are respectively shortened from *drat* (*Drat it!*) and *drot,* which last is aphetic for *God rot it!* And *rot* is common Teut., AS. *rotian*—another reason for abandoning a ship.

rate, ratify.
See rat.

ratio, rational.
See number.

ratskeller.
See read.

rave.
See outrage.

ray.
See X-ray.

raze, razor.
See graze; rascal.

read.
The "three r's" carry one a step beyond literacy: *reading and 'riting and 'rithmetic.* (For the last, *see algebra.*)

Read is common Teut., AS. *raedan,* which first meant to make out, whence Eng. *riddle* (either the puzzle or the solving: *Riddle me this!*) Then it meant counsel, OE. *rede,* G. *rat,* whence *Rathaus,* council - house, town - hall; *Ratskeller,* town-hall cellar, drinking hall. Not only after drinking, much one *reads* remains a *riddle!*

Writing is practically confined to the English. The early word, AS. *writan,* to scratch on bark, was common Teut., but when it came to *write,* most languages have turned to the L. *scribe*: G. *schreiben,* Fr. *écrire,* from L. *scribere; see shrine.* (*Scribere* also first meant to dig in, rather than to mark on the surface.)

ready.
See turmeric.

realm.
This was originally a kingdom; then, any region. It may have come from a LL. *regalimen,* a noun form from L. *regalis, regal* (*cp. royal*) from L. *rex, reg—,* king. Or from the same source, more roundabout: it was earlier Eng. *reame,* OFr. *reeme,* from LL. *regimen,* rule; there was an OFr. form *real, regal;* this then influenced the spelling and sound of *reeme, reaume,* and changed it to *realm.* But *see regimen.*

ream.
Paper-making came into Europe with the Arabs, via Morocco into Spain. The bundle of sheets, Arab *rizmah,*

whence Sp. *resma,* whence OFr. *rayme,* became Eng. *ream.*

rebate.
See bazooka.

rebel.
See avulsion.

rebuff.
See buff.

rebus.
A *rebus* is a word game in which the words are represented by things. The Latin for 'by things' is *rebus.* In medieval carnivals, the Paris basochiens (law students) wrote satires *de rebus quas geruntur,* on current events; to avoid persecution, they masked these with pictures. The practice has become a mild form of game.

recalcitrant.
The bucking bronco that kicks back is *recalcitrant* (L. *re,* back + *calcitrare,* to kick, from *calx, calci—,* heel). But an *intractable* (L. *in* + *tractabilis,* from *tractare,* to handle, frequentative of *trahere, tract—,* to draw) person is also *recalcitrant.* (L. *calx, calci—* also means lime; *see calculate.*)

Tract, space, is from L. *tractus,* a stretching out, originally it was used as a stretch of time; *tract,* a document, is short for *tractate,* from *tractare,* to handle, to deal with: *tractatus,* dealt with (in speech or writing). A *track* (OFr. *trac*) is the mark left when something is drawn along. A *contract* is something drawn together (L. *con, com*), hence, an agreement. To *detract* is to draw from; hence to lessen; to *subtract,* to draw under. To *distract* is to draw away from; if we continue, the reader may grow *recalcitrant.*

recede.
See recess, recessional, ancestor.

receipt, receive, reception.
See recipe.

recipe.
This is directly from L., being the imperative of the word *recipere,* to *receive,* set down by physicians at the head of a prescription. *Recipere* is from *re,* again, back + *capere, capt—,* to take; *cp. manœuvre.* A doublet of *recipe,* via OFr. *receite,* from ME. *receite,* is *receipt.* This has by learned restoration (L. *recipere, recept—*) inserted the *p;* from similar sources *conceit* (originally an idea, a taking together) gives us *concept; deceit* (L. *de,* from) has as its doublet the longer form *deception.* Similarly we have *conception* and *reception.* The verbs *receive, deceive, conceive,* are all via OFr.—*receivre, deceivre, conceivre* — from the L. forms.

reckless, reckon.
See mock.

recline.
See climate.

recluse.
See close.

recognition, recognize.
See scourge.

recommend.
See command.

recondite.
Several trails lead twistingly, even in Latin, from this *recondite* source. The simple word is L. *dare, dat—,* to give; *see date.* The prefix *con, com,* together, produced *condere, condit—,* to put together. But things can be put together in various ways.

The word was applied to cities; it then meant to establish, to found; this sense has not come into English, but lingers historically in the way the Romans reckoned dates: 1000 *a.u.c., ab urbe condita,* from the founding of the city (Rome was founded 753 B.C.). To put things together also means to store them, hence to preserve them; in connection with food, this came to mean the preserving process, to pickle. This sense came into early Eng. in the verb *condite,* to pickle, and is preserved in the noun *condiment.* But if you store things, lay them up, you may also be safeguarding, or even hiding them; and *condere* came to mean to hide. L. *conditus* thus meant secret; with the prefix L. *re—,* back, we have Eng. *recondite.* Hence also L. *abscondere* (L. *ab, abs,* away, + *con, com,* together, + *dare,* to put: to put away together) meant to disappear, to make invisible; then, to depart from a place; hence Eng. *abscond; cp. askance.*

reconnoitre.
See scourge.

record.

The primitive way of keeping *records* was apparently to keep them in mind, or to learn them by heart (OFr. *recorder,* from L. *recordari,* from *re,* again + *cor, cord—,* heart.) From the sense, to memorize, the word came to mean, to recite, to tell; then to set down, esp. in some permanent form. The phonograph *record* is one such form. From the setting down, the word came to be used of things (worthy to be) set down, as when a runner breaks a *record.*

To keep *tally* (from OFr. *tallier,* whence Fr. *tailler,* to cut) indicates the old system of taking a double-notched stick and cutting it in half, so that each of two persons would have the same *record,* as a check. The Fr. *tallier* is from LL. *taliare,* from *talis,* like: from the two equal parts. (Similarly, the idea of payment in kind—an eye for an eye—is in *retaliate,* from L. *re,* back + *talis,* like.) Hence also, via Fr., Eng. *tailor.*

A doublet of *retaliate* is *retail,* which came much later, via Fr. *retailler,* to cut up, and meant to deal in such small items that the records would be kept by the *tally* method. A dealer in large quantities, in the *gross* (LL. *grossus,* large, hence also coarse, which first meant large, as opposed to fine), was OFr. *grossier,* whence Eng. *grocer.* The English company of *Grocers* dealt wholesale in spices and other foreign produce; thence, the word was applied, as a polite term, to any food-dealer.

recount.

See calculate.

recreation.

See inn.

rectify, rectitude.

See royal.

recto.

See conversion.

rectum.

See royal.

red.

This color has been associated with blood down the ages. In English, about the 13th c., appear associations with "*red* revenge" and violence. By the 17th c. the *red* flag is a signal for battle; it is thus listed in Chambers' *Encyclopedia* in the mid-18th c. In national flags, the color *red* is still explained as representing the blood of the people. It became specifically associaed with revolution, along this trail, through the *bonnet rouge, red* cap, of the Jacobins of the French Revolution, and the *red* shirt of the followers of Garibaldi in mid-19th c. Italy. The term *red,* meaning revolutionary or radical, grew more widespread, of course, after the Russian Revolution in this century. By a figurative shading of the tone, those that talked rather than practiced radicalism were referred to as *parlor pinks. Cp. left.*

The word *red* is common Teut., AS. *read;* cognate with L. *ruber, ruddy,* L. *rufus,* red, L. *rubigo,* rust. *Orange* has a long trail from Sank. *naranga; cp. peach. See yellow.* For *green, see grass. Blue* is also common Teut., AS. *blaw;* cognate with L. *flavus, yellow* (not the only case of mixing colors). *Indigo* was *indico* in the 16th c., direct from the Spanish: *Indian* (cloth thus dyed). *Violet* is from Fr. *violette,* diminutive of OFr. *viole, viola* (the flower); cognate with Gr. *ion; cp. iodine.* For *pink, see nasturtium.*

The nobles of Castile, Spain, first used the term *blue blood* (*sangre azul;* Eng. *sanguinary, cp. complexion*) to indicate that they were free from the "darker" blood of the Moor and the Jew.

To see red, to be roused to anger, is partly from the association of *red* with violence, and partly from the practice of waving a *red* cape to rouse the bull in the Spanish bullfight—although the bull is color-blind.

Red tape was applied to official delay in the 18th c. England, where the dispatch cases (*dispatch, q.v.,* means haste) had their *red tape* untied with slow and ceremonious detachment.

redeem, redemption.

See ransom.

redingote.

This word has double-crossed the Channel. Borrowed (in the 19th c.) by the French, from Eng. *riding-coat* (which it tries to pronounce), it was taken back by the English as the name of the French style.

reduction.

See duke.

reduplicated words.

Chit-chat, ding-dong, etc. *See* scurry.

refection.
See defeat.

refer.
See suffer.

refine.
See finance.

reflect.
See accent.

reformation.
See formula. (L. *re,* back, again).

refraction.
See discuss.

refractory.
See refrain; *cp.* discuss.

refrain.
When the captain of the good ship Pinafore bade the sailor: *"Refrain,* audacious tar, your suit from pressing", he little knew what a hornet's nest of words he had knocked from the beams. *See audacious; see tar.* The *suit* is from Fr. *suite,* from the LL. form *sequere, sequit—* from L. *sequi, secut—,* to follow (L. *non sequitur,* it does not follow, is used in Eng. as the identification of a logical fallacy.) To *execute* (L. *ex,* out, + *sequi, secut—*) is to follow out, as the *executive* branch of the government supposedly follows out the instructions of the legislative. In the remarks:

"What do you think of his *execution?"*
"I favor it."—

the first speaker has in mind the way the man follows out his project (playing, etc.); the second, the way the mourners follow him out.

If things follow appropriately, they *suit;* hence also the *suit* (*set, q.v.*) of clothes, or cards, or of rooms (for which the Fr. *suite* is also used in English). To *sue* is via OFr. *suer, suivre,* from the same *sequere,* used mainly legally; hence the *suitor* at court, but also for the lady's hand, as the audacious tar. For other forms from this source, see *pursue.*

The *refrain* one sings breaks back upon the music; it is via Fr. *refrain* from OFr. *refraindre,* from L. *re,* back, + *frangere, fract—;* which more directly has given us *refraction, refractory; cp. discuss.* But to *refrain,* to hold back (as the audacious tar is bid) is via OFr. *refrein—* from L. *refrenare,* to hold in check, from *re,* back, + *frenum,* bridle. This is perhaps related to L. *frendere,* to gnash the teeth, as one may well be inclined to do.

Yet more. When, in 1901, condemned murderers were first set in the *electric* chair, by analogy with *execution* there was coined the word *electrocution.* This has no immediate relation with *circumlocution* (L. *circum,* around; *see agnostic*) nor to the *interlocutor* (L. *inter,* between), the "middle speaker" at the minstrel show, who passed the jokes to the end-men. This joke pacemaker is now called the *emcee* (*M.C., M*aster of *C*eremonies); the current stage term for his butt is *stooge,* perhaps from earlier *stodge,* a dull person (whence also *stodgy*), from the early verb *stodge,* to walk heavily, to stick in the mud.

refreshment.
See inn.

refuge, refugee.
See devil.

refund.
See futile.

regal, regale, regalia.
See royal.

regenerate.
See racy.

regent.
See alert; royal.

regicide.
See shed.

regimen.
This line of conduct is from L. *regere,* to rule; *cp. alert.* It may have come via a LL. form *regalimen,* from L. *regalis, regal;* it is, however, closely allied to Eng. *realm,* which was earlier *reame* from L. *regimen,* rule, the *l* entering through the influence of ME. *real,* royal, from *regalis.*

Both Eng. words first meant governing, rule; thence *regimen* kept the sense of a course of conduct, esp. the rules for health. *See* realm.

regiment.
See royal.

rehabilitate.
See ability. (L. *re,* back, again).

rehearse.
See hearse.

reimburse.
See Bursa.

reiterate.
See obituary.

reject.
See subject.

rejoice.
See joy.

relax.
See talc.

relevant.
See irrelevant.

relief.
This word is via Fr., from L. *relevare,* to raise, from *levis,* light. The literal sense remains in sculpture, high *relief* and bas (low) *relief.* A person that is lifted up is *relieved.* The present participle of L. *relevare, relevans, relevant—,* helping, therefore significant, gives Eng. *relevant,* also *irrelevant,* though not incompetent and immaterial. "For this *relief,* much thanks."

religious.
See sacrifice.

remain.
See remnant.

remand.
See command.

remnant.
This marks a laziness that has recently gone into reverse. It is from Fr. *remanant,* present participle of *remanoir,* from L. *remanere, remanent—,* to remain, to hold back, from *re,* back + *manere, mans—,* to keep, to hold, from *manus,* hand, whence Eng. *manual; cp. manœuvre.* A *mansion* was first a place that held soldiers overnight, on their marches; it also is shortened in Fr. *maison,* house. Other such contractions are *enmity* (from *enimity,* from *in* + *amity,* from L. *amicus,* friend, whence Eng. *amical, amicable; inimical*); *fortnight* (from *fortennight,* from *fourteen night*); *plush* (from *pelushe,* from LL. *pilucca,* from *pilus,* hair; *cp. wig*); *dirge* (from *dirige,* from the antiphon in the Office for the Dead, beginning *Dirige, Domine, Deus meus, in conspectu Tuo viam meam,* Guide, O Lord my God, my life into Thy vision. Eng. *requiem* is from the introit of the same mass: *Requiem aeternam dona eis, Domine,* Grant them eternal rest, O Lord).
Nowadays, despite *libary* and *Febuary,* it seems easier to add a letter: *atheletic, slippery ellum*: in a century or so these may be the correct forms, over which philologists will speculate.

remorse.
Dan Michel of Northgate, Canterbury, about 1340 gave to his translation of a French *moral* work the title *Ayenbite* (Againbite) *of Inwit,* otherwise, *remorse* of *conscience.* L. *con,* from *com,* with + *science,* from *scientia,* knowledge, matches *in* + *wit,* wisdom. L. *re,* again + *morsus,* from *mordere, mors—,* to bite, has prevailed in the Eng. *remorse,* which keeps gnawing inside one. The present participle of the Fr. *mordre,* to bite, gives us Eng. *mordant*—though in music the word is taken via It., from L., whence Eng. *mordent.* A pleasant word from the same source is *morsel* (OFr. *morcel,* whence Fr. *morceau,* from diminutive of *mors,* bite). There may be an earlier connection of L. *mors,* bite, with L. *mors, mort—,* death, whence Eng. *mortal, immortal,* and the flower (via Fr.) *immortelle,* everlasting. From L. *mori,* to die, came L. *morbus,* disease, as in Eng. *cholera morbus;* the adjective L. *morbidus* gave us Eng. *morbid,* also (L.—*ficus,* from *facere,* to make, to cause) *morbific.* The *morgue* is apparently not from L. *mors,* death; originally it was a room in which new (live) prisoners were inspected by the police so as never to be forgotten; it is probably via Fr. *morgue,* face, by extension from its meaning of haughty demeanor (used in Eng. in this sense by Matthew Arnold), from Languedoc *morgo,* pride. *Mors,* death, and *mors,* bite, may be related to L. *mos, mor—,* custom (that which bites in); this gives us *moral* (a coinage of Cicero to translate the Gr. *ethicos, ethical*); and *morale* (by error from the Fr.); also *morose,* which at first meant fastidious, as a stickler for the customary, the proper thing; then (by excess of this) unsocial, gloomy, sour. Thus an *immoral* act was originally just one to which folk were unaccustomed; *cp. uncouth.* These words are probably not related to Gr. *moros,* stupid, which gave the 16th and 17th c. a word we could well revive, Eng. *morology,* foolish talk; and later *moron,* which was adopt-

ed in 1910 by the American Association for the Study of the Feeble-Minded. (*Moron* is the fool in Moliere's *La Princesse d'Elide,* 1664.) The word gave rise to the following reflection:

See the happy moron,
He doesn't give a damn.
I wish I were a moron.
My God! Perhaps I am!

Half-foolish, half-wise (Gr. *soph—,* wisdom) we have the college *sophomore.* But *see sophisticated.*

There is also a Gr. word *morphe,* form, used as a frequent combining form in Eng.: *morphology; amorphous* without definite form; *polymorphous,* assuming many forms, like the amœba and the old-man-of-the-sea, *Proteus,* whence Eng. *protean;* etc. *Protein* is via G. *Proteinstoffe,* first material, from Gr. *protos,* first, found in many Eng. words, *e.g. protocol,* from Late Gr. *protocollon,* fly leaf—pasted in with a summary of the mss.—, from Gr. *kolla,* glue, whence Eng. *collagen, collenchyma, colletic,* and other scientific words; *collodion,* from Gr. *collodes,* glue-like, *colloid; collotype;* and that form of modern art made by gluing objects onto the canvas, *collage. Cp.* plant. For a long time glue was mainly fish-glue, which is, directly from the Gr., Eng. *ichthyocolla.* Since this glue was extracted from the bladder, isinglass (*q.v.*: Du. *huisenblas,* sturgeon's bladder; *blas, blad,* Eng. *bladder*) was also called *ichthyocolla. Ichthy—* and *ichthyo—* are Eng. combining forms, as in *ichthyology,* the study of fishes; *ichthyolatry,* worship of a fish-god; *e.g.,* Dagon; *ichthyophagist,* fish-eater, *cp. sarcophagus. Ichthus,* fish, is a Christian symbol, being spelled by the initial letters of *I*esus *Ch*ristos, *Th*eou *U*ios, *S*oter: Jesus Christ, God's son, Saviour.). Ovid called the god of sleep *Morpheus,* whence *morphine.* But a per-that suffers from *remorse* does not sleep easily, or easy. The Gr. *opos,* vegetable juice, had a diminutive, *opion,* which was applied to poppy juice, and gives us *opium,* whence *opiate.*

On entering the Roman circus, the gladiators cried toward the Imperial box: *Te morituri salutamus,* We who are about to die salute thee. In this, Eng. and L. are well contrasted: our analytical tongue, dividing an idea into its several parts; the Roman synthetic language, building into a unit the various elements of an idea: for the one L. word, *morituri,* five Eng., *who are about to die.*

More is a common Teut. word, OE. *ma.* But now no *more.*

remunerate.
See immunity.

render, rendition.
See surrender. *Rent* is from a LL. *rendita,* from the same source: that which is given in return. To *rend* something to pieces is OE. *rendan,* found in OFrisian, but not in the other Teut. tongues.

renegade.
See runagate.

Renovated.
See grass.

repair, reparation.
See zipper.

repast.
This originally referred to a light meal eaten between meals; eating again, from OFr. *repast* from *repaitre,* from L. *re,* again, + *pascere, past—,* to feed; *cp. pester, abbot.*

repatriation.
See zipper.

repel.
See pelt.

repent.
See chary.

replete.
See foil.

replica, reply.
See complexion.

reprehensible.
See surprise.

repress.
See command.

reprimand.
See command.

reprisal.
See surprise.

reputation.
See character.

requiem.
See remnant.

resent.
This word first meant something like what we now convey by *react*: to feel back (from Fr. *ressentir,* from L. *re,* back + *sentire, sens—,* to feel, whence Eng. *sense, sensation*). By the natural flow of human nature, it came to refer to things "felt bad". Similarly, *retaliate; cp. record.* Early preachers used to speak of *"resenting* God's favours"—just as the early prayer asks the Lord to *prevent* us in all our doings. *Cp. loafer, prevent.*

resentment.
See ascend, resent.

reside.
See subsidy.

resign.
The literal sense of this word dominates in the verb, from L. *re—,* back, + *signare, signat—,* to *sign;* whence also *signature; assignation* (a *signing to*). The first meaning was to relinquish, to give up; but the word was used in religion, of giving oneself up to God; hence, the person that is *resigned* to his fate. Both senses persist in *resignation.*

resignation.
See resign.

resilient.
See somersault.

resist.
See tank.

respect.
See auction, scourge, respite.

respiration.
See inspiration.

respite.
When the sad lover (in Poe's *The Raven*) cried for *"respite* and *nepenthe",* it was a feeling much stronger than *respect* that moved him. The words, however, are doublets, from L. *respicere, respect—,* to look back, look again, regard. Since you look twice at something that deserves attention, *respect* and *respectful* took their present sense (at times, with a little fear). From L. *respect—* via OFr. *respit* was a more roundabout journey. The first sense was time allowed for further examination of a matter; then, any postponement, esp. of something undesired.

Nepenthe, a drug mentioned in the Fourth Book of the *Odyssey,* is from Gr. *ne,* not, + *penthos,* sorrow. *Cp. repent.*

respond.
See spouse.

rest.
See tank.

restaurant.
See inn.

restitution.
See tank.

restoration, restore.
See inn.

restrain, restrict.
See prestige.

result.
See somersault.

resume, résumé.
See prompt.

resurrect.
This word is from L. *resurgere, resurrect—,* to rise again, from *surgere, surrect—,* to rise, from *sur,* above + *gerere,* to act (whence, via Fr. *sourdre,* comes *source*). *Resurge* is a doublet of *resurrect.* During the 18th and early 19th c., when the efforts of the doctors to understand the human frame were meeting conservative opposition, a *Resurrection man* was one that raised from the grave the bodies used for anatomical study. (Dickens presents one in Jeremy Cruncher, in *A Tale of Two Cities.*) Such a man had, of course, to be *resourceful,* full of ways of rising again and again.

resurrection.
See sorcerer.

retail.
See record.

retaliate.
See resent.

retire.
See tire.

retort.
See torch.

retract.
See distraction.

retrench.

The *truncheon* may be a large club, but it is from Fr. *troncon,* diminutive of Fr. *tronc,* from L. *truncus,* trunk; *cp. poltroon.* Via LL. *trincare* from *truncare,* to cut, we have OFr. *trencher,* whence Eng. *trencher,* platter on which meats were cut; the *trencherman,* first the cook that served the cut meats, then the man that helped himself to them; the present participle *trenchant* (a cutting remark), and the *trench* that was first a path cut through the woods, but survives in the narrow excavation, the *trench*—replaced in warfare by the current "foxhole". If persons dig themselves in securely, they *intrench* themselves in a position; but to *retrench* goes back to the original meaning, to cut down . . . And probably from the action of the *truncheon* (via OFr. *troncher, troncer*) comes good Eng. *trounce.*

retribution.
See tribulation.

revamp.
See vamp.

reveal.
See cloth: voile.

réveillé, revel, revelation, revelly.
See avulsion.

revenge.
See vengeance.

reverie.
See outrage.

revert.
See conversion.

review, revise.
See improvised.

revive, revivify.
See victoria.

revolution, revolve, revolver.
See volume.

revue.
See improvised.

revulsion.
See avulsion.

reward.
See lady.

rhenium.
See element.

rhinestone.

This is a stone from the river *Rhine,* Germany (Fr. *caillou du Rhin, Rhine* pebble). There is an Eng. *rhine,* pronounced *reen,* from AS. *ryne,* OE. *rune,* also Eng. *run,* meaning drain. The good Russian hemp known as *rhine,* or *rine* hemp, was G. *rein Hanf,* clean hemp. The Gr. *ris, rin—,* nose, gives us Eng. *rhinal* and many scientific words with the prefix *rhino.* Thus the *rhinoceros* is from Gr. *rino* + *ceras,* horn. Since about 1660 *rhino* has been slang for money, and *rhinocerical* has meant rich, probably from the size and fat of the creature (*i.e.,* well provided).

rhino, rhinoceros.
See rhinestone.

rhizo-.
See licorice.

Rhode Island.
See States.

rhodium.
See element.

rhododendron.
See primrose.

rhymester.
See spinster.

riddle.
See read.

ride.
See deride, riding.

ridiculous.
See deride.

riding.

On horseback, or of a ship that *rides* at anchor, this is a common Teut. word; AS. *rīdan.* Of a section of a country: while the Romans divided their cities into *quarters* (whence the Latin Quarter, *q.v.*), the English divided their countryside into *thirds,* from AS. *thrithing,* whence *triding.* (Similarly a group of ten households was a *tithing,* from AS. *teotha,* tenth, whence Eng. *tithe.*) But when the words came to be separated, *Northriding, Southriding* — which had been contracted from *Norththrithing,* etc.—took the *th* along with the *Nor* and the *Sou,* leaving *Riding* as the word for the district.

right.
See left.

rigmarole.
Two traditions, not clearly separable, intertwine in this word. It is a corruption of OE. *ragman-roll;* but not in the current sense of *ragman.* For a *ragman* seems to have been an officer who made the feudal allegiance lists (the tax lists); it is thus applied in the *ragman-roll* of Edward I of England, in 1296. But (in ways not known but perhaps understood) *ragman* was also an old name for the devil (so used in *Piers Plowman,* C. xix, 122). In this sense it was also applied to a coward (Icel. *ragr,* coward + *mannr, man* . . . Like OE. *bad,* Eng. *bad, ragar* first meant effeminate; *baedling,* effeminate man, whence Eng. *bantling,* but *see bank* for another suggestion). With these two paths crossing, *rigmarole* came to mean a long piece of nonsense, as though the devil were wagging your tongue.

rile, Riley (the life of).
See island.

ring.
See harangue.

rip.
See zipper.

riparian.
See world.

risibility.
See deride.

rival.
Those living on opposite banks of a stream (even those on the same side, if it has annual changes, like the Nile) are likely to be *rivals;* hence the suggestion that *rival* is from L. *rivalis,* of the stream, from *rivus,* stream. Via Fr. *rivière* this gives us *river;* and a *rivet* (Fr. *rive,* bank of stream) is that which fixes the border (as in the Egyptian surveys after the floods); Fr. *rive* is from L. *ripa,* Eng. *riparian; cp. world.* We even derive *derive* from this source: from Fr. *dériver,* to lead water away from the stream, from L. *derivare, derivat—,* whence Eng. *derivation.* To *arrive,* of course, is to reach the shore (L. *ad,* to), which is at least the mariner's destination. For roundabout journeying, etymology has few *rivals.*

river, rivet.
See rival.

roam.
All roads lead to *Rome* — and all travelers get there. While Christians were on pilgrimage to the Holy Land, long before the Grand Tour took Englishmen to *Rome,* wealthy travelers from the Orient came to the eternal city. Its religious hold brought many pious, later. Thus It. *romeo* (without *Juliet*), Sp. *romero,* OFr. *romier,* all meant a pilgrim to *Rome.* Hence, Eng. *roam.* (This derivation is denied by the scholars of the NED, who offer no other suggestion.)

rob.
See bereave.

robin.
This word (OFr. diminutive of *Robert,* from OHG. *Hrodeberht,* glory-bright) is attached to many ideas, like *dicky* and *jack.* The *round robin* arose in the British navy. If a discontented crew framed a petition, the captain had the right to hang the top signer as a mutineer. In 1612, on the brig *Catherine* at Gibraltar, the sailors hit upon the idea of signing their names in a circle (like spokes), taking the base of a statuette of a robin (?) to make the central circle; hence, *round robin.*

robot.
This word came into our language from the play by Karl Capek, *R.U.R.,* 1921 (*Rossum's Universal Robots*: mechanical men). The word is Czech, from *robota,* work, from OSlav. *rob,* slave, whence Russ. *rab.*

rodent.
See graze. Rodent is the present participle of *rodere. Cp. bed.*
From *rodere, ros—,* to gnaw, come also Eng. *corrode, corrosion* (L. *cor, com,* altogether), and *erosion* (L. *e, ex,* out). The *rodeo,* however, is from Mexican Sp. *rodear,* to go around, from L. *rotare, rotat—* (whence also Eng. *rotation; cp. rote*); its first meaning was the round-up of cattle.

rodeo.
See rodent.

rodomontade.
See Appendix II.

rogation.
See quaint.

roil.
See island.

roll.
See calculate; **rote.**

Roman (calendar).
See month.

romance, romantic.
See onion.

rondeau, rondel.
See rote.

room.
See rummage.

roorback.
This word (sometimes spelled *roorbach)* for a false report or rumor might well be given currency again. It comes from a book, *Travels of Baron Roorbach,* 1844, attacking James K. Polk, candidate for the presidency of the United States.

rooster.
See coquette.

roquefort.
See Appendix II.

rosary.
The L. *rosarium,* rose-garden, was applied figuratively to a book of devotion, a garden of roses for the Lord. Then it was used of a book of prayers, then of the beads by which the prayers are counted. *See bead.* For *anthology, see Athens. Thesaurus* is directly from Gr. *thesauros,* treasure, *q.v.*

rose, rosemary.
See primrose.

Rosetta Stone.
See hieroglyphics.

rostrum.
This word for a platform is L. *rostrum,* beak, from *rodere, rost—,* to gnaw— but not from the Mussolini jaws of the speakers. The prows of ancient ships were prolonged with decorations in the shape of beaks; and the platform in the Roman **Forum was** decorated with such beaks, taken from the Antiates in 338 B.C.

rot.
See rat.

Rotary (Club).
The first of these organizations, mainly of business men, but for community and international betterment, met in Chicago in 1905; its name rises from the fact that meetings were held in *rotation* at the members' homes. *See rote.*

rotation.
See rodent, rote.

rote.
To learn by *rote* was for some time thought to mean learning by music, as now the factory folk work. (*Rote* was the name of an olden musical instrument, a sort of harp; the word was also applied to a sort of fiddle, from OHG. *hrota.*) This *rote* is of quite different origin. L. *rumpere, ruptus,* to break (*eruption,* a breaking forth; *corruption*: *cor, cum,* altogether broken; *rumpus;* etc., *cp. bank*) in the phrase *via rupta,* broken way, meant a road, *e.g.,* a road cleared through a forest. Note that if an army is broken, *rupta,* it is put to *rout. L. rumpere, rupt—,* whence Fr. *rompre, rot,* whence *route,* a road; also, the diminutive *rotine,* whence *routine,* a beaten path. Another spelling of *route* is *rut*—many roads were at first mere cart tracks. Hence we have here not doublets but quadruplets: *route, rout, rote,* and *rut.*
What *rolls* on a *route* is L. *rota,* a wheel, whence *rotundus, round,* whence Eng. *rotund, round.* (*Orotund* is coined from *ore rotundo,* with round mouth.) Hence also diminutive *rotula,* kneecap; *rotation,* the *Rotary* clubs. A *roué* is a man that has been "wheeled:" broken on the wheel (punishment for criminals); it was applied to the companions of the Duke of Orleans during his Regency of France, 1715-23, as men that should have been thus treated. *Roll* and *roulette* are OFr. *rouler* from *roler* from LL. *rotulare,* to revolve, from L. *rotula,* a little wheel. The verse forms, *round, rondeau, roundel, roundelay* (from OFr. *rondelet,* a little *rondel—,* influenced by *lay,* song, from AS. *lāc,* sport, whence Eng. *lark*—not the bird!—from Goth *laiks,* dance) are variations from this source, all implying words that return like a wheel. *See* crowd.

rotula, rotund, roué, roulette, round, roundel, roundelay, rout, route, routine.
See rote.

rove, rover.
See bereave.

royal.
The L. words for king, *rex, regis* and kingly, *regalis,* came in OFr. to be *roi* and *roial.* From this through the Normans came Eng. *royal* and *royalty. Royalty* was also applied to jurisdiction granted by the king, esp. to mineral products; then to the sums acquired by virtue of such rights; then to similar sums from the sale of books, etc.

Directly from L. the same words were adopted in Eng. Thus we have *regal; regent,* present participle of the verb *regere, regens, regent—, regi, rectum,* to rule, to make straight—since what the king did was right—and a right line was a straight one: as in right angle—we have Eng. *rectitude, rector, rectify, erect,* etc. Also, in anatomy, *rectus* is applied to various muscles with straight fibres, and the final, straight section of the large intestine is the *rectum. Regalia* are the trappings of a king; *regale,* to entertain in kingly fashion—though this has been traced through Eng. *gala* to AS. *gal,* gay; Goth. *gailjan,* to cheer. The L. noun *regimen,* from the same verb, is used directly in Eng. Originally it meant the act of governing, rule; then it was extended to the system of rules, or procedure. Similarly, from LL., *regiment,* the fact or the method of rule, was extended to the military force that ensured the rule. To straighten together (L. *corrigere,* from *com + regere*) is to *correct.* You cannot *correct* the *incorrigible.* Straight down (*de + regere*) is *direct,* whence also *direction.* A *directory* is a book of rules; then a list of persons; in the Fr. *directoire* it was the group of men *directing* the Revoution from 1795 to 1799; hence, a style of dress popular in that period. *See alert.*

royalty.
See royal.

rubber.
The word *rub* is common Teut., its source unknown. When *caoutchouc* (a native Caribbean word) was introduced, Joseph Priestley (who discovered[1] oxygen, 1774) noticed that it *rubbed* out pencil marks; hence, our most useful *rubber.*

rubidium.
See element.

rubric.
The *ruby* was named from its color: from OFr. *rubi,* from LL. *rubinus,* from L. *ruber,* red. As directions along the sides of church books were written, then printed, in red, by transfer of the color to the thing colored, we have *rubric.*

ruby.
See rubric.

rum.
See drink.

ruminant, ruminate.
See knick-knack.

rummage.
Originally, as sometimes now; *room* meant space. It is common Teut., Goth. *rum;* G. *Raum* as in *Lebensraum,* space to live in. In OFr. it was *rum* or *run,* whence Eng. *run,* part of a ship's hold. What goes into a ship's hold was the *rummage;* from the confusion in which cargo lay on the wharf came the present *rummage* around, and *rummage* sale.

While *run* is found in AS. *rinnan, yrnan,* it is not common, though elsewhere in Teut.; we probably took it from ON. *rinna, renna;* up in the north cold, folk have to keep moving fast.

rumor.
See drink.

rumpus.
See rote.

run.
See rummage.

runagate.
This contemptuous word for a good-for-nothing has a double story. It seems obviously from *run + agate. Agate* is still used, to refer to improper goings on, from *a,* on + *gate,* path, way, manner; this is more frequently spelled *gait.* It is from ON. *gata. Gate,* an opening, a door, is from AS. *geat;* ON. *gat.* Both are common Teut. words.

Actually, however, *runagate* is a corruption, because of the thoughts above, of the word *renegade*—which was first used by the Spaniards of Christians that, when captured by the Moslems, adopted the religion of their conquerors, from L. *re,* back + *negare, negat—* (whence Eng. *negative*), to deny, from *neg,* not + the verbal ending.

rupture.
See bank.

rural.
See neighbor.

Russia.
See Viking.

rustic, rusticate.
See neighbor

rut.
See rote.

ruthenium.
See element.

S

sabbatical.
Through Fr. *sabbat* and LL. *sabbaticus,* this is from Heb. *shabath,* to rest. *See jubilee.*

sabotage.
This term, derived from Fr. *sabot,* shoe, (from Turk. *shabata,* galosh) does not mean to throw a shoe, instead of a monkey wrench, into the machinery. It is the old peasant type of shoe, which became a slang word meaning an inferior tool or workman; hence Fr. *saboter,* to work badly. With the rise of trade union activity, it took on the sense of deliberately bad work. It is suggested, however, that the current use springs from peasants' trampling their landlords' crops.
Savate, a doublet of *sabot,* old shoe, is now used in Fr. and Eng. for the kick allowed in certain types of boxing.

sack.
See drink.

sacrament, sacred.
See sacrifice.

sacrifice.
To *sacrifice* was, originally, not to give up, but to make something holy, from L. *sacer,* holy + *facere,* to make. Hence also *sacred* and (L. *sacramentum*) *sacrament,* sacred oath. (The *sacrum* in anatomy, is the *os sacrum,* the *sacred* bone, at the base of the spine.) Since that which is made holy is given over to the gods, from the human point of view it is given up; hence the meaning of yielding one thing to gain another, as a *sacrifice* hit in baseball. A *sacrilegious* person is one that steals *sacred* things, from L. *sacer* + *legere,* to gather, to pick; *cp. legible.*
Through its compounds (*legere, lect—* becomes—*ligere, —lect-*) this source is extremely fruitful; do *see legible!*
One who chooses among various things (L. *dis, di—*) usually *delights* in them, finds them *delectable* (for this path, *see delight*); he will therefore stay attentive to them; hence, be *diligent.* Otherwise (L. *nec—,* not) he will be *negligent,* and *neglect* them. Once he has found them pleasant, he will thereafter (L. *pre,* before) have a *predilection* for them. And if he returns to them again and again (L. *re—,* again) in loving care, he will be L. *religens,* careful, devoted; with the ending L. *—osus,* full of: full of devoted care, we have Eng. *religious.* Thus the literate and the *religious* spring from one fount!

sacrilegious.
See sacrifice.

sacristan.
See sext.

sacrum.
See sacrifice.

sad.
See satisfy.

sadist.
The *Marquis* (so he called himself; really Count, Comte) *de Sade* (1740-1814) wrote books, and is supposed to have lived a life, marked by an excessive delight in inflicting pain. From him *sadism* and the *sadist* have taken their name. (*Saddest* also describes the victims.) The opposite perversion, an excessive delight in receiving pain, is called *masochism.* The *masochist* derives his name from *Leopold von Sacher-Masoch* (1835-95), whose books picture this. A *sadistic* person and a *masochistic* one would be mated like Jack Spratt and his Jill.

saffron.
See salary.

saga.
See acre.

sagacious.
This word and *sage,* meaning much the same, are of different origin. *Sage* is via Fr. *sage,* from L. *sapius, sabius,* wise, whence Eng. *sapient. Sagacious* is from L. *sagax, sagac—,* quickwitted, from *sagire,* to perceive. Similarly *trifle, q.v.,* and *trivial* are come by different paths; and *scullery* and *scullion, q.v.*

sage.
See flower; sagacious.

St. Vitus' dance.
See guy.

salaam.
See Islam; *cp.* so-long.

salad.
See alcohol.

salary.
The expression to earn's one *salt* had deep meaning, in the days before refrigeration, when *salt* was the chief means of keeping meat from showing decay. L. *salarium,* salt-money, was the figurative word for what we (now literally) call *salary.* Things preserved with *salt* (L. *sal*) were L. *salsa,* whence Eng. *sauce, saucy.* This led to LL. *salsicia,* whence OFr. *saussiche,* whence ME. *sausige,* whence Eng. *sausage.* L. *salsarium,* dish for sauce, via F. *saucière,* became Eng. *saucer. Spice* is OFr.*épice,* from *espece,* from L. *species, species,* kind, from *specere, spect—,* to behold (whence *specific; specimen; special,* aphetic for *especial,* from *e,* from *ex,* from + *specialis,* apart from the type; *cp. speculate*). There were four "kinds" in the early shops: *cinnamon, clove, nutmeg, saffron.* (*Cinnamon* is from Heb. *qinnamon. Clove* is from F. *clou,* from L. *clavus,* nail; from the shape of the bud. *Nutmeg* is a corruption of OFr. ? *nux* + *muge,* from LL. *nux muscata,* musky nut, from LL. *muscus, musk. Saffron* is from Arab. *za'farān.*)
Both *spicy* and *saucy* are used of ideas and manners; the latter, influenced not only by taste but by the figurative use of *Attic salt,* dry wit (as opposed to *acetum Italicum, Italian vinegar,* a less bright and more insolent wit.)
If you receive an *emolument,* its origin is in the profit of the ancient miller: from L. *emolere,* to grind out. *Wages* are pledges, originally declarations (that one would pay); hence, to *wage* war, from OFr. *wage,* from Goth. *wadi,* pledge, whence LL. *vadium,* whence Eng. *wed,* which first meant to pledge marriage.

salient, sally.
See somersault.

salon, saloon.
See parlor.

salt.
See salary.

saltation, saltatory, saltpetre.
See somersault.

salutary, salute, salvation, salve.
See salver.

salver.
This word for a dish indicates the dangers of eating in the middle ages. There might be poison at any meal; hence, a portion of each course was placed on a dish and then eaten by a *salver* (L. *salvare, salvat—,* whence Eng. *save, salvation,* and from the noun *salus, salut—, salute,* a wishing good health; *salutary,* etc.) whose death might *save* the diners. The word was transferred from the man to the dish. A *salve* is similarly something that helps *save* you.

samaritan.
See Appendix II.

samarium.
See element.

samovar.
This is a self-boiler, Russ. *samo—,* self (cognate with Eng. *same*) + *varit',* to boil.

sample.
See quaint.

Samson.
See Achilles tendon.

sandblind.
This mistake produced several other forms. *Blind* is common Teut. The *sand* is from AS. *sam—,* half, cognate with L. *semi—.* Folk-change to the more familiar *sand* has led to Shakespeare's use of the terms *gravel-blind* and *stone-blind.* Also, we speak of *throwing sand in one's eyes;* and when children fall asleep at night, it is the

Sandman that carries them to the Land of Nod.

sandwich.
John Montague, *Earl of Sandwich* (d. 1792) was a great gambler; you couldn't drag him away from the gaming tables, even for food. Once, when he stayed twenty-four hours without break, meat was brought to him, between two slices of (toasted) bread. Thus, at 5 a.m., August 6, 1762, appeared the first specimen of what is today the most frequent form of food, the *sandwich.*
Long before the name, however, the practice flourished. It is part of the Jewish Passover meal, the earliest recorded instance being when Hillel (ca. 100 B.C.) took bitter herb and unleavened bread, and ate them together. Thus the *sandwich* is a symbol of man's triumph over life's ills.

sangrail.
This is the *holy grail,* LL. *sanctus gradalis,* from L. *sacer,*, *cp. sacrifice;* and L. *crater* (*q.v.*), bowl. According to one story, the *Holy Grail* is the dish that held the paschal lamb (of the Passover service; *cp. Easter*) of which Christ and the apostles were partaking at the Last Supper. According to another legend, it is the cup from which they drank the wine, which Christ said contained the blood of the New Testament. It is added that Joseph of Arimathaea kept the cup, and in it caught some of the blood of Jesus at the cross (hence the spelling *sangreal,* as though F. *sang real,* true blood). Lost, the *sangrail* became the quest of the Knights of the Round Table; only he that is pure in heart, *sans peur et sans reproche* (without fear and without reproach) may attain it—as did Sir Galahad. Lowell puts it to further symbolic use in *The Vision of Sir Launfal,* 1848, where the *sangrail* becomes the purity itself, of thought and conduct, within the individual. Still referring to the blood of the Christ was the earlier spelling (Fr. 15th c., *sang roial*), *sangroyal,* royal blood. A *Galahad* is often applied to a person deemed faultless.

sanguine.
See complexion.

Sanskrit.
In contrast to the mainly spoken vernaculars, *Sanskrit,* the earliest written language of our speech group, seemed well ordered, refined. *Sanskrit* is from Sansk. *samskrta,* perfect, from *sam—,* together (Gr. *sym—;* Eng. *same*) + *krta,* made, from *kr,* to do (Eng. *create*). The vernaculars were called *Prakrit,* from Sansk. *prākrta,* unrefined.

sap.
A word is enough for the wise; that's why English has some four hundred thousand. The phrase was L. *verbum sap*—abbreviated from *verbum sapientibus satis est,* a word (*q.v.*) to the wise is enough. L. *sapere,* to taste, hence learn, has the present participle *sapiens,* as in Eng. *homo sapiens,* the highest order of primates. Hence also Eng. *sapid* and *insipid* (L. *in,* not, + *sapidus*).
The *sap* of a plant-stalk is common Teut., but probably from L. *sapa,* boiled juice, from *sapere.* The word *sap* also came to mean soft (as of stalks that contained *sap*); hence *sapskull, saphead,* a simpleton, shortened to *sap;* also *sappy,* in both senses. A *sapper,* soldier that dug mines, used a Fr. *sappe,* spade, earlier Eng. *zappe,* from It. *zappa.* A tree beginning to spread its *sap* is a *sapling.*

sapid, sapling, sapper, sappy.
See sap.

sapphire.
See carnelian.

Saracen.
See sirocco. The origin of this name is open to conjecture; St. Jerome traced the name to *Sara,* wife of Abraham in the Bible.

sarcophagus.
The ancient Greeks buried bodies in coffins (or pits) made of a kind of limestone, which supposedly consumed them. They called this coffin a *sarcophagus* (from Gr. *sarx, sarc—,* flesh + *phagein,* to eat). Though we no longer use that stone, we have kept the word. The root *phag,* to eat, is elsewhere used: *phagocyte* (Gr. *cytos,* receptacle; used in Eng. compounds to mean cell); *anthropophagi,* cannibals (Gr. *anthropos,* man, whence Eng. *anthropology, anthropomorphic,* man-shaped; *anthropoid,* manlike); the early Scots were referred to as *pygophagous* (ham-eating; *cp. calibre*). In poverty-stricken parts of the U. S., even today, *geophagy* (Gr. *ge, geo—,* earth, whence *geography,* writing about the earth) is practiced. The L. *vorare,* to swallow, correspondingly gives us a number of Eng. words: *voracious, devour; omnivorous* (L. *om-*

nis, all, whence Eng. *omnibus*, for all, whence *bus*, etc.)'; *herbivorous* (L. *herbis*, grass, whence Eng. *herb*); *carnivorous* (L. *carnis*, flesh, whence Eng. *carnal; carnage*, from It. *carnaggio*, with augmentative ending, a devil's feast of flesh; *carnation*, the flesh-colored flower, later corrupted to *coronation*, because used in chaplets: Spenser in the April eclogue of the *Shepher's Calendar* says:

Bring *coronations*, and sops in wine,
Worne of Paramoures;

incarnation, the Lord's coming in the flesh; *cp. carnival*). Thus we return to *sarcophagus*, which was also used (to the 17th c.) of flesh-eaters. *Sarcasm* is from Gr. *sarcasmos*, from *sarkazein*, to speak bitterly, literally, to tear flesh. But *mordant* (Fr. *mordre*, to bite, *mordant*, biting, from L. *mordere, mors—*, whence *morsel; see remorse*) has no connection with *mausoleum, q.v.* A *morsel* is akin to Eng. *bit*, a piece *bitten* off.

sard.
See carnelian.

sardine.
See Appendix II.

sardonic.
If you feel the impulse to grin *sardonically*, beware! The L. *herba sardonia*, plant of *Sardinia*, was poisonous, and twisted the face into a contorted grin during the death-throes.

sardonyx.
See carnelian.

sark.
See berserk.

sash.
See casement.

sassafras.
This mild-seeming tree is literally a stonebreaker (that is, the ancients used it for stone in the bladder). Our form of the word, via Sp. and applied to an American tree, is probably influenced by the Indian name; but it is from earlier *sassifragia*, from *saxifraga herba*, stone breaking plant, from *saxum*, stone + *frangere, fract—*, to break. The more direct *saxifrage* is also an Eng. word; but it is suggested that the name may result from the plants' sprouting in the clefts of rocks, as though they had broken through. The purple goat's-beard, the *salsify*, is from It. *sassefrica*, from *saxum* + *fricare*, to rub. Note that *frangere* gives us *fraction*, etc.; *cp. discuss;* and *fricare* leads to *friction; cp. afraid.*

Satan.
In Heb. *satan* (emphatic form, *satana;* whence Gr. and early Eng. *Satanas*) meant adversary, from the verb *satan*, to plot against. In the *Old Testament* of the *Bible*, the word refers to human adversaries; when it refers to the (fallen) angelic tempter, it is always The Adversary. This is usually translated *diabolus* (*see devil*) in the *Vulgate;* but in the *New Testament* Greek the usual form is *Satanas*, which is used also in the *Vulgate* and in Eng. by Wyclif. The word is now used for the supreme spirit of evil.

satchel.
This was originally a small *sack;* L. *saccus, sack* (*cp. drink*) having the diminutive *saccellus*, which became OFr. *sachel* and Eng. *satchel.*

sate, satiate, satire.
See satisfy.

satisfaction.
See defeat.

satisfy.
This word has a simple story; but compound relatives. It is from OFr. *satisfier*, from L. *satisfacere*, from *satis*, enough + *facere*, to make. If you have ample you are *satiate.* But if you are *sated*, you are likely to be a bit *sad.* At least, *sad* originally meant having enough (AS. *saed, sated*, a common Teut. word), and the Eng. *sate* is an earlier *sade* changed through association with L. *sat, satis.*

A *satire*, now an attack, was originally a poetic mixture. The word is of figurative growth: L. *satura lanx*, full dish (*satura*, from *sat*, enough) was applied to the literary work, then shortened to the first term: *satura*, whence *satire.* The same *sat*, whence *satura*, full, whence *saturare, saturat—*, gives us Eng. *saturate.* To reach the *saturation* point may be to *sate* rather than to *satisfy.*

saturate.
See satisfy.

Saturday.
See week.

Saturn, Saturnian.
See season.

saturnine.
Astrology, from the supposed influence of the planets, gave meaning to Eng. *saturnine, jovial, mercurial*—the last is influenced by the constant flow of "quicksilver."

sauce, saucer, saucy.
See salary.

saunter.
We are told that the joy of life is in the striving; for no worthy goal is ever attained—since it but becomes a way-station toward the next. Then, some ask, why hurry? This seems to have been the attitude of the *pilgrims* (*pilgrim*, from OE. *pelegrim*, from OFr. *pelegrin, pelerin*, from It. *pellegrino*, from *peregrino*, from L. *peregrinus*, foreigner, from *pereger*, traveler, from *per*, through + *ager*, country, cognate with Eng. *acre*: *agriculture*), for the speed of their journey to the Holy Land is shown in the word we now have, from the French for Holy Land: *Sainte terre*, whence *saunter*. That they were no more hurried on horse we learn from Chaucer's *Canterbury Tales;* from the gait of such travelers came the *Canterbury gallop*, shortened to *canter*. (The stories they told have no connection with *cant;* though in the sense of hypocrisy, it comes from *cantare*, frequentative of *canere*, to sing (Eng. *chant, incantation*, etc., *cp. incentive*) as applied to the whining plea of the beggar, who indeed sometimes posed as a pilgrim—much as young men sell subscriptions "to pay their way through college." And there was a preacher, *Andrew Cant*, d. 1663, whose wide unpopularity may have helped give the word its bad meaning.

sausage.
See salary.

savage.
See neighbor.

savate.
See sabotage.

save.
See salver.

saw-buck.
See buck.

saxophone.
Most musical instruments (except those electrically operated: the *theremin*, named for its inventor, gives sound as the hand merely moves toward it or away) were invented long ago, and gradually improved. Thus the *piano* (short for *pianoforte*, from It. *piano e forte*, soft and strong), is a development of the *spinet* (invented by *Giovanni Spinetti* of Venice, ca. 1664) and the harpsichord. But the *saxhorn* was one of a group of trumpet-like instruments invented just the past century by the Belgian Charles Joseph *Sax* (1791-1865) and improved by his son (Antoine Joseph) Adolphe. One of this group, seldom used for the orchestra, is the popular band instrument called the *saxophone*.

Piano is from L. *planus*, soft, low, flat, whence *plane* and its doublet *plain*, flat, hence clear; whence also *explain*, to flatten out, to make clear, and *explanation*. *Plain*, meaning the same as *complain* (L. *com*, from *cum*, together, used as an intensive) is from Fr. *plaindre*, from L. *plangere* (*plag*), *plactus*, to strike, to beat (the breast), hence to lament. The present participle of *plangere* is *plangens, plangent—*, whence *plangent*, as of waves striking the shore. *Forte* is from L. *fors, fort—*, strong, which also gives us *fort, fortify* (+ *ficare, facere*, to make), *fortitude*, and *fortalice* (from OFr. *fortelece*) with its doublet that has replaced it, *fortress*. The suffix *—phone* means voiced, sounding; *cp. focus*.

Note that *plain sailing* did not first mean clear going, but going by *plane* chart, on which the route was mapped as though the earth were a *plane* instead of a sphere.

scab, scabies.
See shave.

scale.
See echelon.

scallion.
See onion.

scalp.
See tuft.

scamp.
A *loafer* seems at first to have been

a fellow that runs around the countryside, from G. *Landlaufer,* from *Land* + *laufen,* to run; the pace has slowed down of late. A *scamp* was also a fellow that ran off along the highways, leaving his sober work on the fields to *scamper* off, from Fr. *escamper,* from L. *ex,* out of + *campus,* field; *cp. camp; see loafer.*

scan.
See echelon.

scandal.
This used to be, not something you caused yourself, but something others got you into. (Anyone involved will say that it still is!) It is from Gr. *skandalon,* a snare; thence (from the other's point of view), a stumbling-block; thence the present meaning, a stumbling-block to social success. *Cp. echelon; see slander.*

scandium.
See element.

scanties.
See pants.

scapegoat.
This is the *escape goat* (*Bible, Leviticus* xvi, 10) upon which the sins of the people are laid, and which is then let go into the wilderness. (The Heb. *Azazel,* given in the Revised Version as a proper name, with *"dismissal"* in the margin, is rendered L. *caper emissarius* in the Vulgate; this is translated by Tindale as *scapegoat.*) A similar practice is found in various parts of the world; the Christ is of course the divine *scapegoat,* taking upon Himself the sins of all the world.

scare.
See harum-scarum.

scarf.
This was first a purse hung from the neck (Fr. *escarpe, escrepe*); in time the purse became merely an ornament, and the importance shifted from the bag to the band. The cognate Eng. *scrip* (from *escrepe*) was used in Shakespeare's day for wallet. Both words are of Teut. origin, ON. *skreppa.* They seem unrelated to It. *scarpa,* wall, whence Fr. *escarp* and Eng. *scarp* and *escarpment.* (The shift of *p* to *f* is listed in *Grimm's Law,* in the Preface.) *Scrip,* paper money, is short for *subscription* (the receipt being used for currency); cp. *shrine.*

scarlet.
This was originally not a color, but a cloth; a rich cloth in blue, green, brown but most frequently in the "royal purple", which color then took the name from the cloth. Hence it is sometimes applied to things that present this color, as *the Scarlet Lancers; the scarlet pimpernel; the scarlet woman* (*figuratively*); *scarlet fever.* The word itself is aphetic from OFr. *escarlate;* which probably came with the Crusaders, from Pers. *siqalat, suqlat,* a rich cloth—which also came into early Eng. as *ciclatoun,* a rich, usually golden, cloth.

scavenger.
See pass.

scene.
See shed.

sceptic.
See scourge.

scheme.
See hectic.

schism, schismatic, schizophrenia.
See shed.

schlemihl.
This word, for a clumsy or stupid person, is drawn from the name of the hero of *The Wonderful Story of Peter Schlemihl,* 1814, by Adelbert von Chamisso. *Schlemihl* was a man without a shadow, having sold his to the devil for the never-empty purse of Fortunatus; but he gained no more from his bargain than *Midas*—whose wish was granted that everything he touch turn to gold; hence he could not eat nor drink—and became the symbol of greed overreaching. Apollo gave *Midas* the ears of an ass, which shows he was an early variety of *schlemihl.*

scholar.
Scholars smile (if I can testify) when they think of the origin of the word. It is from Gr. *scholazein,* to have *leisure* (via Gr. *schole,* leisure, whence Eng. *school*). Leisure implies time for discussion, but also the discussion of academic—*i.e.,* of immaterial—concerns. Similarly the ancient Jews said that nests and the ripening of womanhood are the essential things;

geometry and the calculation of the calendar are the sweetmeats of learning. By an opposite growth business *negotiations* take away one's *leisure*: *negotiate* is from L. *negotiare,* to deal, from *nec,* not + *otium,* ease. For leisure, *see immunity.*

Though whales travel in *schools,* it is not to learn. Theirs is a Du. *school,* AS. *scolu,* crowd. But this has been intertwined with *shoal,* earlier *shald,* from AS. *sceald,* shallow—partly because numbers of fish are usually observed where it is *shallow. Shallow* itself seems to be a late doublet of *shoal.* It should not be necessary to observe that a *scholar* should not be *shallow.*

school.
See scholar.

sciagraphy, sciamachy.
See science.

science.
This word is the present participle, *sciens, scient—,* of L. *scire, scit—,* to know. *Cognition* is lumping your knowledge (L. *cog,* from *com,* together + *gnoscere*); *recognition* is gathering it into yourself again (L. *re,* again). *Cognizance* is a re-Latinized form, from ME. *conisaunce,* from OFr. *conusance,* from *conoistre,* from L. *cognoscere, cognit—;* and the *cognoscenti* are the same via It. *conoscente. Cp. quaint.* One that knows but a little is a *sciolist,* from LL. *sciolus,* diminutive of L. *scius,* from *scire.* Note that the prefix *scio—, scia—,* may be from Gr. *skia,* shadow; as in *sciagraphy,* shadow-writing; *sciamachy* (Gr. *machia,* battle). Gr. *skia,* shadow, cloud, is akin to Eng. *sky; cp. shed.* The word *scientist* was coined by William Whewell of Cambridge, in 1840.

scintilla.
See scintillate.

scintillate.
Tinsel is a word that has undergone both metathesis and aphesis. (See list at front of book.) For *tinsel* is aphetic for Fr. *étincelle,* sparkling goods (from the idea of goods with sparkles put on, came the sense of showy, then tawdry), from OFr. *estinceller,* to be decked out with sparkles. And this is from LL. form *stincillare,* by metathesis from L. *scintillare, scintillat—* to sparkle, from L. *scintilla,* a spark. This comes directly into Eng. when we say there isn't a *scintilla* of evidence against him; and the verb has come over in Eng. *scintillate* (pronounced with the *c* silent, so that if you sin till late, no one will see); it is for all to behold that you *scintillate.*

sciolist.
See science.

scion.
See graft.

scissiparous.
See shed.

scissors.
See shed; precinct.

sconce.
See askance.

scone.
***See* bun.**

scope.
See dismal.

score.
"What's the *score?*" is a question the answer to which depends; but a *score* is always twenty. The shepherd, telling the tale of his sheep (*see tally*) could count on his fingers and toes; then he'd make a notch (*score,* cognate with *shear*) on a stick, and begin again. Thus to figure would be, to keep *score.*

scotch.
See hopscotch.

scour.
See hussar, scourge.

scourge.
If you rub very hard, you may remove the skin; to "take the hide off" someone is to *scourge* him, via OFr. *escorgier,* from L. *excoriare, excoriat—,* (whence also Eng. *excoriate*), from L. *corium,* hide. Note that *corium* (used in Eng. physiology of the true skin under the epidermis) has physical but not etymological connection with *core,* center, heart, a ME. word probably from Fr. *cœur,* from L. *cor, cord—,* heart; whence also *cordial; cp. prestige.*

To *scour* first meant to purge or cleanse, from OFr. *escurer* from L. *ex,* out, completely, + *curare,* to care for, to *cure.* Then it became limited to the most frequent way of cleansing. To *scour* the countryside is to go over it thoroughly, as in search of something—though this sense may be from earlier Eng. *scour,* a rush, from ON. *skur,* storm; and perhaps was influenced by ME. *discoure,* discover, used to mean to *reconnoitre,* to *scout.*

Scouts apparently went forth by night; a *reconnaissance* was made by day. For *scout* (which first meant not the person but the act) is from OFr. *escoute,* listening, from *escouter,* to listen, from L. *auscultare, auscultat—,* whence also Eng. *auscultation,* from L. *aus—,* from *auris,* ear; Eng. *aural* (to *scout* an idea is from ON. *skuta,* to taunt, possibly influenced by It. *scuotere,* from L. *excutere,* to shake off); whereas *reconnoitre* is from OFr. *reconnoitre* (Fr. *reconnaitre*) from L. *recognoscere, recognit—,* to inspect, from L. *re,* again, + *cognoscere, cognit—,* to know. Thus *recognizance, recognition,* and *reconnaissance* are from the same source; also *recognize,* which in the 16th and 17th c. was *recognosce.*

A *spy* was also at first not the watcher but the watching, for which we use *espial.* It is short for *espy,* from OFr. *espier;* It. *spiare;* but also OHG. *spehon,* to look; L. *specere, spect—,* to look, whence also *inspect, disrespect. Cp. auction; speculate.* The cognate Gr. word is *skeptesthai,* to look; hence a *sceptic* (*skeptic*) is one that keeps on looking, is never satisfied. A *cynic,* of course, is a dog; *cp. canary.*

scout.
See scourge, shout.

scratch.
See knick-knack.

scrawl.
We speak of making hen-tracks on paper; the thought is in the word *scrawl,* which first was an intensive of *crawl.* As a noun it was used of a small crab (OFr. *escrouelle,* fresh-water shrimp). For a time the word was used as a synonym of sprawl; then it was applied figuratively to sprawly handwriting. *Cp. penthouse.*

scribble, scribe.
See shrine.

scrimmage.
See skirmish.

scrip.
See scarf.

script.
See shrine.

scroll.
See volume.

scrub.
This word, as in *scrub oak,* and *scrub* trees near the timber line, is a variant of *shrub,* common Teut., AS. *scrybb.* To *scrub* comes from the use of the twigs for the purpose. Thus *broom* was first the name of a plant, and *brush* was what was cut off (*underbrush*) when hedges or trees were trimmed. AS. *brom,* whence *broom,* had the diminutive AS *braemel,* later *braemble,* whence Eng. *bramble* bush—to scratch them in again.

scrunch.
See knick-knack.

scruple.
This was first "a little sharp stone falling into a man's shoe," from L. *scrupulum,* diminutive of *scrupus,* stone, from Sansk. *kshur,* to cut, whence Gr. *skuron,* stone chippings. Sometimes (as with Shylock in *The Merchant of Venice*) it was a stone used as a small weight; hence, from both these sources, something that had to be regarded. Thus *scrupulous,* attentive to small particulars.

scrupulous.
See scruple.

scrutiny.
See inscrutable.

scuffle.
See drivel.

scull, scullery.
See scullion.

scullion.
This fellow that works in the *scullery* got here by a different journey. *Scullery* is not the place where dishes (OE. *sculls,* from Fr. *escuelles*) are washed, but it is a washroom, from OE. *squylerey, swillery* OE. *swyll* (hence Eng. *swill,* to wash down, to guzzle), *squill,* to wash; Dan. *skylle.* The *scullion,* on the other hand, comes from Fr. *escouillon,* sweeper, from L. *scopa,* broom. *Skillet,* however, is earlier *skullet,* from

Fr. *escuellette,* diminutive of *escuelle,* dish, from L. *scutella.* Don't break the dishes!

The *scull,* oar, was named (in the 14th c.) perhaps from the dishlike shape of the blade. The same shape probably gave us our *skull,* for which the AS. term was headpan. (Note that OFr. *escuelle* is from L. *scutella,* diminutive of L. *scutum,* shield; *cp. equable.* And that *escouillon,* sweeper, may have been influenced by Fr. *souiller, to soil, cp. dirt.*).

scum.
See shed.

scurf, scurvy.
See shave.

scurrilous.
See scurry.

scurry.
There are many reduplicated words in English; Henry B. Wheatley has compiled a dictionary of them. He finds three main sorts. (1) Those in which the second part changes the first letter: *namby-pamby, hodge-podge, hanky-panky, hocus-pocus. Tiny;* but *teeny-weeny.* (Nearly half of these begin with *h;* some may belong in class 3.) (2) Those in which the vowel changes. About three-fourths of these change an *i* to an *o*: *sing-song.* (3) Those, not nearly so many, that add a letter: *arsey-varsey.* There are two other types: (4) those in which each half is a real word: *rag-tag, clap-trap, big-wig;* and (5) echoic words: *boo-hoo, bow-wow, clickety-clack, ding-dong, flip-flap.*

In most of these combinations the second part is the main form: *bibble-babble, criss-cross, dilly-dally, pitter-patter; cp. patter.* In a few, the first is the important member: *handy-pandy, rowdy-dowdy, royster-doyster.* Very rarely, the duplicating half becomes more important than the original part; it may even survive alone. *Hurry* is such a word, being formed as a variant, *hurry-whurry,* from *hurr,* from *whurr,* itself an imitative word. Thus *hurry* gets its meaning from the sound of things moving swiftly along. Then *hurry,* in its turn, formed a duplication, *hurry-scurry,* from which the reduplicative *scurry* has been taken as a separate word. *Scurrilous* is from L. *scurra,* buffoon, whose ways and words were often coarse.

scutellum, scutulum, scutum.
See equable.

scuttle.
This word, which now means to open a hole in a ship, first meant to close one. It is from Du. *schutten,* to shut, from OFr. *escoutille,* a hatch; AS. *scyttel,* a bar. Applied first to the cover, the word was transferred to the hole (hatchway), which often let in water during heavy seas; thence, to the present meaning. The *scuttle* that holds coal is from AS. *scutel,* from L. *scutella; see scullion.*

se—.
See separate.

seal.
See sign.

season.
This is a good *season* to confess that etymology is seldom more than a guess. When nobody can make a more plausible suggestion, the proffered one stands —though occasionally all efforts bog down into a "source unknown". The word *season, e.g.,* is commonly traced, through Fr. *saison,* to LL. *sation—,* seed time, from L. *serere, sat—,* to sow (related to *sat,* enough: *see satisfy*) But the earliest found uses of the word *season* apply it in general, not just to planting time. Hence some prefer to trace it to a LL. *sation—,* by dissimilation from L. *statio, station—*from which does come the It. word for season, *stagione.* You reads your volume and you takes your choice. More clearly related to *sat,* sow, is the golden age before the gods began to fight, the *Saturnian* period, ruled by *Saturn,* father of Jupiter (*cp. jovial*) and god of agriculture.

L. *statio, station—,* from *stare, status,* to stand, from Gr. *statos,* whence *histanai,* to cause to stand, gives us many Eng. words. *Status, state, static; statue,* that which stands; *stature,* one's standing; *statute* (L. *statuere, statutum,* to stand up, establish). From It. *stato, state,* comes *statista,* Eng. *statist,* politician; by way of 18th c. German this gives us the noun *statistics,* which first meant the study of the supplies etc. of a *state.* What stands out about one is one's *estate,* which first meant one's condition. *—stat* is a combining form, as in *thermostat,* a device for keeping heat constant (Gr. *thermos,* heat, whence *thermometer; Thermos* bottle). ***Constitute, constituent*** (from the present participle), ***institution,*** etc. are combinations from *statuere.* When all things stand away from a person, he is ***destitute*** (L. *destituere,* from *de* + *statuere*). Closely allied are such words as ***destine, destiny, destination*** (L. *destinare,* to make fast) and *obstinate* (L. *obstinare, obstinat—,* to stand against). A good ***destination*** is always in ***season.*** *Cp. stationery, tank.*

secant.

See knick-knack.

secede.
See ancestor.

secluded.
See close.

secret.
See secretary.

secretary.
When we speak of a private *secretary,* we are going back to the first sense of the word: L. *secretarius* is from *secretum, secret.* This noun is formed from the past participle of *secernere, secret—,* to sift apart; whence also *secretion. See garble.*

secretion.
See secretary.

sect, section.
See set.

secure.
See accurate.

sedan.
In the early 17th c. a popular mode of travel was in a closed seat on two poles, with a bearer in front and another behind. In 1634 Sir Sanders Duncombe secured a monopoly for such conveyances in London. He called them *sedan* chairs (? It., from L. *sedere,* sit. Cognate is AS. *sittan,* whence Eng. sit).
Automobile manufacturers borrowed the word to describe a car with one door (on each side) leading to one inner compartment. Similarly ***limousine*** is a closed car; earlier, a closed carriage, from the hood worn by the people of the province of *Limousin,* France. *Cp. taxi.*

sedate, sedentary, sediment.
See subsidy.

sedition, seduce.
See separate.

seersucker.
See cloth.

segment.
See sext.

segregate.
See absolute.

selenite.
See carnelian.

selenium.
See element.

seltzer.
See drink.

semen.
See semi—.

semi—.
This prefix, L. *semi—,* half, in part, somewhat, is very widespread. It exists as OHG. *sami—;* Sansk. *sami—;* Gr. *hemi—,* as in ***hemisphere;*** OE. *san—, cp. sandblind.* L. also has the form *demi—,* which is from L. *dimidium,* half, from *di—,* (Gr. *di—, dis,* twice; also L. *bi—* as in ***biennial***) + *medium,* whence also Eng. *medium, q.v.*
The earliest word from this form in Eng. was ***semicircular,*** about 1450. Since then, compounds have multiplied, until we even have, in music, a *semidemisemiquaver.* Play it if you can!
Note that ***seminary*** is not related; but from L. ***seminarium,*** seed-plot, from L. *semen, semin—,* seed, whence also Eng. ***semen, seminal.*** A ***seminary*** was first a literal garden; then, figuratively, a place where the young are bred, or an art or science is cultivated. To *disseminate* is to scatter seeds.

semiannual.
See anniversary.

seminal, seminary.
See semi—.

semper (fidelis, paratus).
See sempiternal.

sempiternal.
This word pours snow on Everest: it adds L. ***semper,*** always, to L. ***aeternalis,*** forever, from *aeviternus,* from *aevum,* age.
Semper is used in several Latin phrases now current. *Sic semper tyrannis,* thus always to tyrants, was made the motto of Virginia in 1779

(perhaps from the instances in Patrick Henry's best known speech); it was sadly misused at the death of Lincoln. *Semper paratus,* always prepared, is the motto of the U. S. Coast Guard; *semper fidelis,* always faithful, that of the U. S. Marines.

Other words in these mottoes give us Eng. words, *e.g., tyrant; fidelity; apparatus* (L. *ap, ad,* to, + *paratus,* ready, past participle of *parare,* to make ready, whence also Eng. *prepare*: L. *pre,* before; *cp. zipper*).

sempstress.
See spinster.

sensation, sense, sensible, sensitive, sensual, sensuous, sentence, sententious, sentiment.
See ascend, resent.

sentinel.
This word, derived by some from OFr. *sentinelle,* sentry-box (as from It. *sentina,* latrine, from the resemblance) is originally not an army but a navy term. For *sentina* meant both latrine and the hold of a ship, where the bilge-water gathered, and LL. *sentinator* was the one that pumped water from the ship's hold. Thus the *sentinel* was the man that was on constant watch for the water in the hold; hence, a man on watch. *Sentry* is from the same word, corrupted by a fancied origin in Fr. *sentier,* beat, path, from OFr. *sente,* from L. *semita,* path.

sentry.
See sentinel.

separate.
The L. *se* meant by oneself; it became a preposition, L. *se, sed,* meaning apart, away. This in turn became a prefix, from which a number of words were formed that have come into English; *e.g., secure, cp. accurate; secede, cp. ancestor; segregate, cp. absolute; secluded, cp. close.*

L. *seducere, seduct—,* from *se* + *ducere, duct—, cp. duke,* gives us *seduce,* to lead astray, *seductive, seduction.* A going away (L. *ire, it—,* to go; *cp. obituary*) is *sedition.* And with L. *parare, parat—,* to dress up, to arrange; *cp. overture*) we have *separate,* to arrange apart.

September.
See month.

septic.
See creosote.

sequel, sequence.
See pursue, *cp.* set.

sequin.
This word is from It. *zecchino,* little coin, from *zecca,* the mint, from Arab. *sikka, die* for casting coins. Thus, when "the *die* is cast" (the expression's first famous use was by Julius Cæsar, as he crossed the Rubicon), the figure may be drawn from two sources: earlier, the numbered cube (*die,* plural *dice*) which when tossed decides one's fortune; or the stamp (*die,* plural *dies*) which when hardened fixes the design. In either *case* (*q.v.*) the *die* is via OFr. *de* from L. *datum,* given (whence also Eng. *data*); the word was transferred from the fate to the cube that determined it.

Originally a coin, *sequin* is used in dressmaking of a small round *spangle. Spangle* is probably an Eng. diminutive of MDu. *spange,* a clasp, a glittering ornament. To *spangle* is to adorn with gleaming spots, as in the *star-spangled* banner. Long may it wave!

To *die,* our common lot, is from the Scand., ON. *deyja.* It is not AS., which used the word *steorfan,* whence *starve* (*q.v.*), a most frequent way of *dying.* The origin of *dye,* to color cloth, (OE. *deag*) is unknown, but the spellings *dye* and *die* were long used, in both senses, interchangeably. The man who colors cloth says We *dye* to live.

sequoia.
This large, long-living variety of tree was named in honor of a Cherokee Indian, *Sequoiah,* who invented the syllabary system for writing down his native tongue.

seraglio.
The women of Turkey are locked up every night—as indeed most persons in cities are. A woman of the Sultan's palace was Turk. *sarayli,* from *saray,* a palace. The Italians combined this Turkish word with the idea of being locked up (as western palaces were not in the middle ages), from L. *serrare,* to lock, from *sera,* bolt, and produced It. *serraglio,* whence Eng. *seraglio,* the women's quarters.

This L. *sera* is connected with L. *serere,* to join, whence Eng. *series,* things joined. It should not be confused with L. *serra,* saw, whence L. *serrare, serrat—,* to saw, whence Eng. *serrate; serra,* a sawfish or a mountain range—though we more often use the Sp. *sierra, q.v.* From L. *serrare,* to lock, however, are the *serried* ranks of soldiers now seldom seen in war.

The *harem* is from Arab. *haram*, prohibited, hence a sanctuary, then the women in it. In Persia and India the women's part of the house is called the *zenana*, from *zan*, woman, cognate with Gr. *gyne; cp. banshee.*

serenade.
See world.

serendipity.
This happy faculty of finding what one did not seek was named by Horace Walpole from the fairy tale *The Three Princes of Serendip* (*Serendip* is the former name of Ceylon.) Thus Saul set forth to find his father's asses, and found a kingdom. *Serendipity* is the treasure of every artist.

serene.
See world.

series, serrate, serried.
See seraglio.

servant, serve, service.
See family.

sesame.
This is a grain, from Gr. *sesame*, from Arab. *simsim;* common in the orient. The meaning, magic key, is derived from the tale of *Ali Baba and the Forty Thieves*, in the *Thousand and One Nights* (*Arabian Nights*), wherein the cave of the robbers opens only when someone pronounces "Open *Sesame!*" Little did the tellers of those tales fancy that one day electricity would make their magic true!

sesquicentennial.
See anniversary.

sesquipedalian.
Sesqui— is prefix to a number of words; it is short for L. *semis*, half + *—que*, and: a half more, one and a half. In his *Ars Poetica* (line 97) Horace coins the word L. *sesquipedalis* (L. *ped*, foot; *cp. pedagogue*), whence Eng. *sesquipedalian*, of "foot and a half long" words and those prone to use them.

session.
See subsidy.

set.
The verb, to put in a place, is the causal of *sit*, which is common Teut. AS. *sittan, settan; cp. fell.* As in a full *set* of teeth, it is not from the verb (*i.e.*, things *set* in order, *set* together) but a triplet of *suit*, *q.v.* (of cards, of clothes), and *suite* (of rooms): from It. *setta*, from L. *secta*, from which *secuta*, following from *sequi, secut—*, whence Eng. *sequel, consecutive* (L. *con*, from *cum*, together), *sect* (that follows one opinion, though here influenced by *secare, sect—*, to cut, as a *schism*, from Gr. *schisma*, cleft, from *schizein*, to split; *cp. shed; pursue.* Thus *secare* gives us *section.*) *Cp. sext.*

seven.
See number.

sewer.
A *succulent* steak is a juicy one, from L. *sucus*, sap, whence AS. *sūcan*, to *suck*. It has been suggested that *sewer* is aphetic for LL. *exsuccus*, draining the juice. But the real origin may be observed in the OFr. form, *esseveur*, a channel for the overflow water from a fishpond. *Sewer* is from LL. *exaquare*, to drain, from L. *ex*, out + *aqua*, water. What goes through the *sewer* is the *sewage*.

sex.
See sext.

sext.
See bull. A *sextant* is a *sixth* part of a circle, or an instrument with a graduated arc of that size, for measuring angles and altitudes, esp. to get one's bearings at sea. (Thus a *quadrant* is a quarter-circle, or an instrument of that arc, from L. *quadrans, quadrant—*, fourth.) A *sexton*, however, is via OFr. *segrestein*, from LL. *sacristanus*, from L. *sacer, sacr—*, holy; whence also Eng. *sacristan*, who lives in a *sextry*. *Sex—* in combinations refers to *six*, L. *sex; sixth*, L. *sextus;* but the *sex* that combines (or that distinguishes male from female) is from L. *sexus*, cognate with L. *secare, sect—*, to divide. This gives us also *sexual; disect; insect, q.v.; section* and via OFr. *secion* Eng. *scion; secant, cp. knick-knack; sect*, but *see set; segment* (L. *segmentum*, earlier *secamentum*); *vivisection* (L. *vivus*, alive, as also in *viva voce*, with the live *voice*, orally; *viviparous, cp. viper*), and more.

sextant, sexton, sextry.
See sext.

shade, shadow, Shah.
See shed.

shale.
See echelon.

shallow.
See scholar.

shampoo.
Or a rub-down? Gentle fingertip pressure is the correct style, the word indicates; it is from Hind. ***shampo,*** to press.

shank.
See luncheon.

shanty.
See incentive.

share.
See shed.

shark.
Reversing the usual transfer, the fish is named from the man. (There is a L. ***carcharus,*** shark, but the other influence seems older in English.) *Shark* is from G. *Schurke,* rascal, esp. a greedy parasite (whence sailors applied the word to the fish)—apparently coined from the idea of clutching, scratching, from Du. *schurken,* to scratch. *Shark* has a doublet, *shirk,* which first meant living on others, hence, dodging work. The change of vowel occurs also in *pall mall, cp. mail; Derby; clark* (surviving as a name) and *clerk. Clerk* is from AS. *clerc,* from *cleric,* from Gr. *clericos,* belonging to the clergy, from *cleros,* a portion. This idea was applied to priests by Christian writers, because "the Lord is their inheritance." *Clerk* draws its business application from the literacy of the *clergy.* Thus Lucien Benda's book *La Trahison des clercs,* 1927, means betrayal neither by *clergy* nor by *clerks,* but by the learned class . . . *Treason* is from OFr. *traïson,* from L. *tradition—,* from *tradere, tradit—,* to deliver, betray, whence *traditor,* whence *traitor,* from *trans,* across + *dare,* to give. Also handed across is *treason's* doublet, *tradition. Cp. college.*

shave.
This daily practice of any man that's not a barbarian (*q.v.*) is common Teut., OE. *sceafan,* from OHG. *scaban,* akin to L. *scabere,* to scratch, whence Eng. *scabies.* Eng. *scab* is OE. *sceabb,* influenced by, and probably from, the same root. Early Du. *schabbe* was used figuratively, to mean a slut; hence, *scab,* a *scurvy* fellow—whence the use, first in the U.S., of *scab* in labor disputes. *Scurvy* is the adjective from *scurf,* from OE. *sceorfan,* to gnaw, *scearfian,* to cut to shreds—stronger members of the *shaving* family.

shear, shears.
See shed.

sheep.
See mutton.

sherbet, sherry.
See drink.

shed.
Anglo-Saxon, Latin, and Greek are all tangled in this word. It comes from AS. *sceaden,* to divide, sprinkle (divide finely); as in *shedding* blood; *watershed.* From the same word, via OE. *sceran,* to cut, come *shear* and *shears;* also *ploughshare;* and *share,* a portion or part divided. The AS. words are cognate with L. *scindere, sciss,* from Gr. *schizein,* to split, to cut. Mingling with this came L. *cidere, cis—,* from *caedere, caes,* which originally meant to strike, to slay—whence L. *homicidium,* whence *homicide* (L. *homo,* man), and in modern times coined on this model *fratricide* (L. *frater, fratr—* brother, whence *fraternity*); *regicide* (L. *regis,* of the king); *suicide* (L. *sui,* of one's self). From the usual method of killing, *caedere* came to mean to cut, giving us (from OFr. *cisoires,* from L. *cisorium*) *scissors;* also, *incision, incisors* (teeth that cut in), *incisive.* By way of OFr. *chisel* (Fr. *ciseau*) we have Eng. *chisel.* From L. *caedimentum,* a cutting, whence *caementum,* whence *cementum,* comes Eng. *cement,* its earliest form being chips of stone. From the fancied connection of *caes—,* the past of *caedere,* with *Julius Caesar,* we have *Caesarean* birth, birth by *incision* (From the fact that Augustus and the other successors of Julius adopted the name *Caesar* came the titles *Kaiser* and *Czar* or *Tsar.* Persian *Shah,* however, is not from eastern scorning of the Roman rule, but from an old Persian word allied to Sansk. *ksatra,* dominion.) The L. *sciss—* also gives us the scientific term *scissiparous,* giving forth by splitting. (Thus also, *viviparous,* bringing forth alive, as some snakes and all humans; and *oviparous,* bringing forth in an egg, as other snakes and all birds, *cp. viper.*) This is also called, from the Gr.,

schizogenesis. There are many Eng. combinations with the prefix *schizo—*, *e.g.*, *schizophrenia*, split or dual personality. From the Gr. noun *schisma*, cleft, we have *schism*, *schismatic*.

But the word *shed*, in the sense of a lean-to (originally just a roof on poles, or outthrust from a building) for protection against rain or sun, is from ME. *schade*, from OE. *sceadu*, *scead*. From this we have *shade* (of which the spelling *shed* in this sense is a variation); and from its oblique case, *sceadwe*, comes the word *shadow*. An earlier form of *shade* is OE. *schudde*, cognate with G. *Schuts*, protection; but *shutter* (on the window) is from AE. *scyttan*, to *shut*. In hot weather, one may wish to *shed* one's clothes, and get beneath a *shed*, in the *shade*.

The trail goes farther, to the Sansk. root *ska*, to *cover*. Hence the foot-*cover*, AS. *sceo*, whence *shoe;* the earth-*cover* AS. *scua*, whence *sky* (which first meant cloud); the stage *cover*, Gr. *skene*, whence *scene;* and the stagnant *cover*, OHG. *scum;* OFr. *escume;* G. *Schaum*, as in *Meerschaum*, *q.v.*, whence Eng. *scum*. To *skim* is to remove the *scum* (as also, to pit, to seed, etc.—though to seed works both ways: seeded raisins and seeded rye bread). Which *covers* quite a lot of territory! But *see overture*.

shibboleth.
When the Israelites of Gilead wished to detect the Ephraimites (*Judges*, XII, 6), they chose a sound the latter could not make: *sh*, and asked them to pronounce the word *shibboleth* (picked at random; it means river, possibly chosen because of the nearby Jordan.) Milton uses *shibboleth* (*Samson Agonistes*, 288) as a test password.

shilling.
See dollar.

shilly-shally.
See patter.

shimmey, shimmy.
These are of course variations of Fr. and Eng. *chemise*, from LL. *camisia*, which is probably of Gaulish origin. The expression "to shake a *shimmy*," meaning to dance in a lively fashion, was shortened to *shimmy*, meaning to dance. Not all gall is divided into three parts.

shingle, shingles.
See precinct.

ship.
The earliest water-wagons were hollowed logs. Gr. *skaphein*, to hollow, is cognate with the common Teut., OHG. *scif*, AS. *scip*, G. *Schiff;* whence Eng. *ship*, its doublet *skiff*, and the *skipper* that takes them in charge.
See shipshape.

shipshape.
This was earlier *shipshapen*, meaning *shaped* (neatly and compactly) as things should be in a *ship*. But the use of the word was helped by its reduplicated form; *see knick-knack*.

The *—shape*, more frequently *—ship* (*hardship*, *horsemanship*, *lordship*), from OTeut. form *—scip*, from *skap*, to create, indicates a condition (*authorship*), a rank (*professorship*) or the qualities that go with it (*craftsmanship*) or the privileges and prizes (both senses remain, in *scholarship*). The suffix *—hood* (earlier *—head*, as in *godhead*, *maidenhead*) is more limited to a state of being, or condition; it is ME *—hod*, OE *—had*, G. *—heit;* Gothic *haiduz*, manner: *likelihood*, *girlhood*, *godhood*, *maidenhood*. The first suffix has no relation to what sails the sea, nor the second to what crowns the body.

shirk.
See shark.

shirt.
See skirt.

shoal.
See scholar.

shoe.
See shed.

shoot.
See ninepins, shout.

short.
See skirt.

shoulder.
See bow.

shout.
When the early English shot at their enemies, they probably also howled their scorn, an early mocking battle-cry. Hence ME. *scheoten*, *shoot* (*cp. ninepins*) gave us also the form *scout*, to deride. (For *boy scout*, *see scourge*.) This mocking

call, taking the louder form of a battle-cry, hence any loud cry, continued this sense in the variant *shout*.

shove, shovel.
See drivel.

show.
This word was common West G., OE. *sceawian.* Its first sense was to look at, then to look out for, hence to provide. This sense remains in its cognates; the OTeut. root *skau—* being probably akin to Gr. *skopos,* from *skeptesthai,* to look out, whence Eng. *skeptic, see scourge,* and *scope, see dismal.* Cognates without the *s* are Sansk. *kavi,* seer; L. *cavere,* to look out, whence Eng. *caveat,* warning; *cp. quaint.* About 1200 the word took on causative force, to cause to see, to display, from which stem the present meanings.

shrapnel.
See Appendix II.

shrine.
Throughout the middle ages, all things connected with writing were linked with the clergy (*cp. stationery*). A *shrine* was first a coffer where writing materials and (always expensive) manuscripts were kept, from AS. *scrin,* from L. *scrinium,* from *scribere, script—,* to write. Being secure, they were then used for sacred relics of martyrs and saints; thence, the present meaning.
The verb is fertile in Eng. compounds, in most of which the prefix makes the meaning clear: *conscript,* written together (as on the public rolls); *prescription; describe; manuscript* (L. *manu,* by hand); *scribe, script, scribble; ascribe, proscribe; transcribe; nondescript* (that cannot be written down); *postscript, inscription; subscription.*

shrink.
See shrive.

shrive.
The L. *scribere, script—,* to write (*q.v.*) is a potent verb. It has driven out the native term in most Teut. tongues, save English; but here it appears in *scribe, script,* and bobs up in unexpected places; *cp. shrine.* Thus the medieval writings most familiar to the common people were the recorded judgments, penalties imposed; hence OHG. *scriban,* to write, became OE. *scrifan,* to decree, to impose penance. By transfer from the punishment to the absolution then granted, we reach the Eng. *shrive.* Sometimes (as in Coleridge's *The Ancient Mariner,* vii) this is spelled *shrieve.*
Shrivel is not a diminutive of *shrive,* but akin to Sw. *skryvla,* to wrinkle—which may, however, be a variant of Sw. *skrynka,* to wrinkle, akin to OE. *scrincan,* whence Eng. *shrink.*

shrivel.
See shrive.

shrub.
See scrub.

shuffle, shuffle-board.
See drivel.

shut, shutter.
See shed.

shuttle.
See ninepins.

Siamese (twins).
This word, which of course meant relating to *Siam,* took on a special meaning when in 1814 two *Siamese* boys, Chang and Eng, were born united at the waist. They lived for sixty years, and gave their appellation to all of the sort that have succeeded them.

sibilant.
See persiflage.

sibling.
See gossip.

sic.
This word, L. for thus, is used (in parenthesis) to indicate that something which seems wrong is to be taken just as printed: the error was in the original passage, or the item is strange but true. *See* also *sempiternal.*

sick, sickle.
See sock.

sideburns.
This variety of whiskers was favored by *General Burnside,* during the War between the States. They were called *burnsides,* but, as they were on the sides only, and not the chin, it is easy to see how his name was turned around, to make them *sideburns.* *Cp.* vandyke.

sidereal.
See consider.

siege.
See subsidy.

sierra.
Saw-tooth chains of mountains earn this name, from Sp. *sierra,* from L. *serra,* saw. If they are quite high they might even be *Sierra Nevada,* from Sp. *nevada,* snowy. *Cp. seraglio.*

siesta.
See luncheon.

sigil.
See sign.

sign, signal, signature.
See resign. The L. verb is from L. *signum, sign.* Hence L. *insignis,* marked out (the *in* is intensive); whence L. *insignia,* Fr. *enseigne,* Eng. *ensign.* This meant a watchword, a *signal* (from L. *signalis,* marked); then a *sign* over an inn (in this sense, Eng. *sign* is aphetic for *ensign*); a banner, then the officer that bears the standard, our *ensign. Cp. jesse.*
The diminutive of L. *signum* was *sigillum;* whence Eng. *sigil* and, via OFr. *seel,* Eng. *seal.* Since the *seal* (sign) of a man was used to close a document, we have *sealing* wax, and the verb to *seal,* to close. The mammal *seal* is common Teut., OE. *seol.*

silhouette.
Etienne de Silhouette, d. 1767, was known as the most niggardly Controller-General of France. Why, he wouldn't even have full paintings made for his home, just outline drawings! In scorn of his petty economies, the folk called these black portraits *silhouettes.*

silicon.
See element.

silk.
See cloth.

silly.
Many have said that to call such fields as economics science, is *silly.* But others have noted that a history of economics might be written in terms of the word *silly.* It was OE. *seely* (still used in the original sense, in some sections of the British Isles) G. *saelig,* blessed—the Germans (Jews) may still refer to a dead person as *e.g.* "My mother *selig*".. With the Norman Conquest, the victorious Normans had nothing to do but hunt and play; they were blessed, *seely.* Thus gradually the word came to mean idle; Coleridge speaks of "the *silly* buckets on the deck" of the Ancient Mariner's ship, when the long drought gave them nothing to do. But the growth of democracy gave dignity to labor; and the growth of industry gave labor to all—hence, one that was idle must be a little foolish: *silly.* Though it was formerly held that the foolish were "touched by God"—*touched* sometimes means a bit foolish—this touching was different from that which originally made a man *silly*—I mean blessed.

silo.
See psilo—.

silver.
This word is widespread Teut., OE. *siolfor.* Its Aryan forms are lost; the Romance word is seen in Eng. *argent, q.v.;* but there are Slavic cognates, e.g., Russ. *serebro;* Pol. *srebro.* From the brightness of the metal, the word is used in naming many plants, fishes, etc.
See element.

similar, simile.
See assimilate.

simon pure.
This is not from the innocent honesty of *Simple Simon;* but the name of a Quaker in the play *A Bold Stroke For a Wife,* 1717, by Susannah Centlivre. Colonel Feignwell wins Miss Lovely by pretending to be *Simon Pure;* the actual Quaker, after many annoyances, proves that he is the real *Simon Pure.* Hence, anything genuine.

simony.
This word marks a wide medieval abuse, the buying of church positions. It takes its name from the proposal of *Simon* (*Bible, Acts* viii, 18) that he purchase the power of blessing. The practice of the Popes, of finding good posts for their relatives, has given us another word, *nepotism,* from It. *nepote,* from L. *nepos, nepot—,* nephew (which may be a euphemism for son). In politics, both practices proceed today.

simple, simpleton, simplicity.
See complexion.

simulate, simultaneous.
See assimilate.

sin.
See impeccable.

sincere.
There are four stories as to the origin of this word. (1) It is L. *sin,* from *sym,* together, wholly + *cernere,* to sift; wholly sifted, separated out, disinterested. (2) It is from L. *sin,* from *sine,* without + the unknown root of. Eng. *caries,* decay; L. *sincerus,* without decay, pure. (3) and (4) both trace the word to L. *sine,* without + *cera,* wax. (3) says it is therefore pure honey; hence anything pure. (This reminds us of Swift and Arnold, finding in the hive the source of man's two greatest needs: honey and wax, hence sweetness and light.) (4) finds a more practical origin; defective pottery had the cracks closed with wax, then rubbed to prevent their being noticed: "without wax" therefore meant whole, unimpaired, or pure. The rest is pure guess work. *Sinecure,* L. *sine,* without + *cura,* care, is more roundabout than this etymology implies. It was first applied to a priest without a church: he had *beneficium sine cura,* a benefice without *cure* (of souls).

sine.
See brassiere.

sinecure.
See sincere.

sinister.
See dexterity.

sinuous, sinus.
See brassiere.

sir, sire.
See yeoman.

siren.
Today, when *sirens* sound, they are warnings of danger. When first presented, in the twelfth book of the *Odyssey,* they were the danger. They were (Gr. *Seiren*) the damsels with the dulcet tones that sang to lure the sailors to the rocks. Odysseus had his men put wax in their ears, while they tied him to a mast, so that he is the only mortal that has heard the *sirens* sing, and lived. According to one version, they are part woman, part bird. *See answer.*

sirloin.
This term for the upper or choice part of the loin of beef (Fr. *sur,* over + *longe,* from L. *lumbus,* side) was by folk etymology associated with a place of honor. Thus we are told that not Charles II, but before him Henry VIII, knighted it. From this association, the double *sirloin* is called a *baron* of beef.

sirocco.
Sometimes called the *siroc,* this hot wind across the Mediterranean draws its name from Arab. *sharq,* east, (from which it blows), from *sharaqua,* to rise. Similarly the *Saracen* (*q.v.*) came from the east.

Sisyphean.
See atlas.

sit.
See strategy; *cp.* nest.

six.
See number.

skate.
See blatherskite.

skeleton.
In ancient times—although in battle men might be widely carved—and in the middle ages—although criminals might be drawn and quartered—*anatomy* (*q.v.*) was unknown. Thus the only way in which a full *skeleton* was to be seen was through death in the desert, say, and the body's drying until only the bones were left. This fact remains in the word itself; for Gr. *skeleton* means dried up, from *skellein,* to dry up. This may, indeed, have been in the mind of those that first called at a long-winded speaker: *"Dry up!"*

skeptic.
See scourge.

skiff.
See ship.

skillet.
See scullion.

skim.
See shed.

skin.
This word is from ON. *skinn,* from OHG *scindan,* to flay, to peel.

The verb, however, early meant both to grow a *skin* and to strip off the *skin.* Shakespeare says (*Hamlet* III,iv, 147): "It will but *skin* and film the ulcerous place"; in this sense it is akin to *skim, scum; cp. shed.* From the sense of stripping the *skin* come the meanings, first of taking all one's money at gaming, then, of cheating. Other uses are in *skin-deep;* a *skinflint*, one so pinching that he'd take the *skin* off a stone.

skipper.
See ship.

skirmish.
Whether the man or the meaning came first is hard to say; but *Scaramouch* in the Italian *commedia dell' arte* is always starting fights: It. *scaramuccia,* a skirmish, whence Fr. *escarmouche,* whence Eng. *scarmoch,* whence *skirmish.* Also corrupted, esp. in football slang, to *scrummage,* whence *scrimmage.*

skirt.
The garment men wear under their jackets, the *shirt*, is from AS. *scyrte,* from the adjective AS. *sceort, short.* Eng. *short* is from this word, but probably via a LL. *excurtus* from L. *curtus,* short; *cp. cutlet.* And through ON. *skyrta* we have Eng. *skirt;* the European women (until about the 19th c.) wore no drawers; the short *shirt,* gradually lengthened, grew into a separate garment, the *skirt.* The word is sometimes transferred (in slang, but from the 16th c.) from the garment to the person that wears it.

skittles.
See ninepins.

skull.
See scullion.

sky.
See shed; science.

skylark.
The *lark* (earlier *laverock,* common Teut., AS. *lawerce;* G. *Lerche*) soars while singing, hence *skylark.* A *lark,* gay time, until about 1800 was *lake,* sport, from ME. *laik,* play; AS. *lac,* contest; Goth. *laiks,* dance. As sailors used to romp with one another up the rigging, they too added the heavens to their *skylarking.* That's a bird of another wing.

slack.
This word is common Teut., OE. *slaec,* OHG. *slach.* It meant, originally, lacking in energy, *relaxed* (without the *s*—*cp. slow, show*—it is cognate with L. *laxus,* loose). The verb *slacken* has a doublet, *slake,* which basically means to lose energy, to diminish, but is most frequently applied to diminishing one's appetite or thirst.

slake.
See slack.

slander.
This was first used, from the *Bible,* in the sense of being a stumbling-block to someone, causing him to fall; hence, to discredit; and then, to defame. It is a doublet of *scandal, q.v.,* from earlier *sklawnder,* from OFr. *esclandre, escandle,* from L. *scandalus,* trap.

slang.
This word, from Du. *slang,* snake, was used in the early 19th c. to mean chain, fetters. Thence applied to the criminals, it was further transferred to their talk, *slang.* Unfortunately for this devious explanation, the word was used to refer to language before it was used to mean chains! NED lists it as "origin unknown." The same is often true of its instances, which are the meteors of speech.

Similarly the origins of *argot* and *patois* are (to the English) unknown, though *patois* is referred to *pat,* imitating rapid speech; *cp. patter.* The French as usual are more fertile in suggestions. They trace *argot* to It. *gargo;* or perhaps to L. *argutari,* to dispute; L. *argutus,* tricky; *cp. argue.* The It. *gargo* is from *gergo,* from Gr. *hiero,* sacred: *lingua gerga,* sacred language, known only to the initiate; from this same source, with the softening of the vowel, we have *jargon.* (The English say merely that *jargon* imitates the sound of chattering birds; from the same imitative root as *garble* and *gurgle.*) And *patois* the French derive from earlier *patrois,* from L. *patrius* (*sermo*), native talk, *i.e.,* local dialect. It all makes what some call a colorful *slanguage.*

slap.
See spank.

slat.
See slate.

slate.
This word has come via the French, but was probably taken into the Romance tongues from the West German. The stem *slaitan,* to break open, to burst something, was the causative form of AS. *slitan,* to split (intransitive), whence Eng. *slit.* (OHG. *slizan,* to *slit,* gave OFr.

esclice, a splinter; whence, Eng. *slice.*) AS. *slifan,* to split, gave us Eng. *sliver.*

Slaitan went into OFr. as *esclater,* to burst out; whence we observe persons behaving with *éclat.* This gave two noun forms, OFr. *esclate* and *esclat,* both meaning a piece split off; from these we have Eng. *slate* and *slat. Slate,* applied to the stone that easily splits into flat slabs, was transferred to the color; to a tablet for writing on, made of such stone; and to a record, as, a *clean slate.*

slave.
See free.

sleazy.
See cloth. From the flimsiness of the material comes the meaning of the adjective.

sleeveless.
It should be noted that the *sleeve* was once a separate article of clothing, from G. *Schleife,* ribbon, favor. A *sleeveless* errand, one that proves futile, is explained in four ways. There is the dry etymological suggestion that it is a corruption of *thieveless* (no relation to robbers) or *thewless,* from AS. *theon,* to profit + *less,* without. This might have shifted from *thieveless* to *sieveless* (as *thow-thistle* became *sow-thistle;* as *loves* and *loveth* alternate, etc.); then by association develop into *sleeveless*... If not the origin, the development is explained by the three more suggestions. (1) It means a herald's errand: the herald's tabard (outer cloak bearing the lord's arms) was *sleeveless,* and he was usually sent upon a formal demand that was spurned. (2) It was a fool's errand: the court fool's costume had one *sleeveless* arm; and it was the custom, on April Fool's Day, to send persons on "some errand"—as Congreve puts it, in 1689—"that is to no purpose." (Similarly today, persons may be given the 'phone number of the Aquarium, and told to ask for Mr. Fish, etc.) More pleasantly (3) it was the errand of an unlucky knight; those that were favored went forth with their lady's *sleeve* upon their arm; if a knight went *sleeveless,* he seemed fated to return forlorn.

sleight of hand.
See yeast.

sleuth.
The word *slow* is common Teut., OE. *slaw,* dull. A number of words traveling northward through Europe acquired an *s* (*cp. show*); hence this may be cognate with L. *laevus,* Gr. *laios,* left—the left hand being associated with clumsiness and bad luck; *cp. dexterity.* The noun form was OE. *slaewth,* whence early Eng. *sleuth;* but also ME. *slawth,* whence Eng. *sloth.*

There is quite a different *sleuth,* from ON. *sloth,* track, trail. A dog used for trailing was a *sleuth-hound;* this has been shortened to just the *sleuth,* whence our modern detective.

slice.
See slate.

slime.
See life.

slip.
There are several early forms that come together in this word. Among the rare ones is OE. *slip,* slime, as on fish; this survives in the *cowslip.* More common is MLG. *slippe,* a cut, a *slip* in the sense of a twig or shoot used for grafting; hence, other things small, as a *slip* of paper, a *slip* of a lad. Most common in current use is *slip* from OHG. *slipf,* a sliding, hence an error. This gives us the *slip* in which a ship slides for landing or repairs; a *slipknot* or leash for dogs; a *slip* of the pen; the *slip* betwixt cup and lip; and the various things that *slip* over: early, the neck-hole in a shirt; then, the *slip* women wear, the *pillow-slip,* and to give someone *the slip.* And that which you *slip* on your foot is a *slipper.*

slipper.
See slip.

slit, sliver.
See slate.

slogan, slughorn.
See bugle.

sloth.
See sleuth. The animal gets its name from its habits.

slow.
See sleuth.

sluice.
See close.

sly.
See yeast.

smack.
See clasp, smoke.

small.
See grit.

smaragdus.
See carnelian.

smash.
See clasp, knick-knack.

smell.
No one knows where this comes from.

smelt.
The fish is common, AS. *smelt.* For the process, *see* omelette.

smock.
See smoke.

smoke.
This is a common Teut. word, AS. *smoca;* Gr. *smuchein,* to burn slowly. To *smoke* out, in the sense of discovering, may have been influenced by the process of burning a fire at the base of a hollow tree to *smoke* out the animal (or bees) therein; but this sense is originally from AS. *smeagan,* to examine, from *smeccan,* to taste, whence G. *Schmack;* Eng. *smack,* a hearty pressure of the lips; then, a blow. Where there is *smoke* there may be fire, but there is concealment; whence the modern *smoke-screen,* and the ancient *smuggling; smuggle,* Du. *smokkelen.* Therefore, in the *smoke* you can only creep; and the primitive Saxon kitchen-bedroom was probably *smoky* o' cold nights. Whence the garment into which you creep, *smock,* from AS. *smoc; smugan,* to creep. But not everyone—just the better dressed, wore a *smock;* hence *smug,* which first meant neat; then, self-satisfied at one's neatness.

smug, smuggle.
See smoke.

snafu.
See Dora.

snail.
See thief.

snake.
See nausea. More directly, snake is from AS. *snaca,* from OHG. *snahhan,* to crawl.

snap.
See knick-knack; nibs.

snarl, snatch.
See knick-knack.

sneak.
See thief.

sneer.
This word is imitative in origin; applied first to animals, it meant to snort, to twitch the nose. In humans, this is accepted as a sign of scorn.

sneeze.
This word was originally a misprint; the form was OE. *fnese;* but as the *fn* combination grew out of use in English, the initial *f* was mistaken for the long form of *s.* OE. *fneosan* meant to snort; *cp. sneer.* It grew into ME. *fnese;* then a form *nese, neeze,* developed; when the initial *s* appeared, the sound of *sneeze* seemed appropriate, and this word remained in favor. But related to *neeze* was ON. *hnjosa,* snort; probably both forms are echoic; and it may have been thought that (as with *plash, splash; mash, smash; cp. knick-knack*) the intensive form of *neeze* was *sneeze.* The effects of sound are not to be *sneezed* at.

sniff, sniffle.
See snuff.

snip.
See knick-knack.

snob.
A *snob* would feel less important if he knew what he really was: the word arose in the 18th c., as slang for a cobbler's apprentice. In 19th c. Cambridge, an upper classman was a *nob,* from *nob, knob,* head, hence important; a Freshman was a *nib* or *nibs*: *his nibs* is a person that things himself important; and the townsmen (nonstudents) were *snobs.* De Quincey uses *snobs* of "scabs" during a strike. *Snob* is, quite appropriately, related to *snub*—which first meant to cut short; hence, a *snub* nose.

There is another, quite different tale. In the 17th c., when commoners were admitted to Cambridge University, they had to put, next their names, *sine nobilitate,* without nobility; this was abbreviated *sine nob.;* then *s. nob,* whence *snob.* Naturally, many of them were more royalist than the king, haughtier than the nobles; hence the condescension of the *snob.* The important thing is, not to select your derivation, but not to be one. *Cp. knick-knack.*

snub.
See snob.

snuff.
This word may be basically echoic, akin to *sniff;* hence also *snuffle* and *sniffle,* frequentatives. A *snuff* was a short quick breath; hence, the powdered tobacco *snuffed* up; hence, a pinch of *snuff*—by transfer (?) the pinch that puts out a candle, and the glow of a candle-end. Hence, to *snuff out* in the figurative senses.

so.
See alone.

soap.
Cleanliness is next to godliness; but L. *sapo, soap,* has no relation to L. *sap—,* wisdom; *cp. sap.* The Romans and Oriental peoples used unguents and perfumes; *soap* is a Teutonic contribution, AS. *sape. Softsoap* is a semiliquid variety; hence, to *softsoap* a person is to grease him over with smooth words, flattery. A *soap opera* is a radio play (usually of inferior quality) presented during the daytime for housewives, sponsored by manufacturers of *soap* or other household commodities.

soap opera.
See soap.

soak.
See sock.

sober.
See intoxicate.

social, socialist, society, sociology.
See sock.

sock.
You may follow someone because you admire him, or because you are hunting him (*cp. pursue*). An admiring follower may become a companion; thus L. *sequi, secut—,* to follow, led to the noun *socius,* companion. The adjective from this, L. *socialis,* gives us *social* (whence *sociology* and the Marxians all); the noun, L. *societas,* led to Eng. *society.* To join with someone (L. *as* from *ad,* to) is to *associate;* to break such a bond (L. *dis,* apart) is to *dissociate.*

L. *socius* must not be confused with L. *soccus,* though both mark a *social* occasion: L. *soccus,* a light shoe (as worn by the Roman comic actors) whence OE. *socc,* slipper, whence Eng. *sock.* "If Jonson's learned *sock* be on" (Milton, *L'Allegro,* 1634) refers to comedy. *Sock,* in the slang sense, to beat, is one of a series. When you urge a dog to *sick* 'im, the verb imitates the sound you make; a form of *Seek* him! (common Teut., AS. *secan*). One step stronger is to *sock* 'im; the next stage, to *soak* 'im one! If you are *sick,* the word is common Teut., AS. *seoc.* (*Sickle* is a diminutive, from L. *secula,* from *secare,* to cut.) To *soak,* to *steep,* is from OE. *socian,* to *suck* in, a weak form of OE. *sucan,* whence Eng. *suck;* L. *sugere, suct—,* to *suck;* whence Eng. *suction.* A little one that *sucks* is a *suckling;* from this by backformation comes the verb, *suckle. Sugar* may have been influenced by L. *sugere;* it is via OFr. *sucre,* from *zuchre,* from LL. *zuccarum,* from Arab. *sukkar.* The verb to *steep* is from OE. *steap,* from OTeut. *staupom,* a vessel for water. The adjective *steep* is also from OE. *steap,* from OTeut. *staup, stup;* from this comes the OE. weak verb *stupian,* to lower, to bow, whence Eng. *stoop.* One will *stoop* to put on (or dodge) a *sock.*

Socratic irony.
See braggadochio.

soda.
See drink, element.

sodium.
See element.

softsoap.
See soap.

soil.
See dirt.

sojourn.
This word first meant to stay for a short time; but, as guests linger, the meaning spread. It is from OFr. *sujurner* or *sorjorner,* from LL. *subdiurnare* or *superdiurnare,* from L. *sub,* under, or *super,* over + *diurnum, day.* Either way, it meant to stay a short time. *Cp. jury.*

solace.
See insolent.

solar.
See overture.

solarium.
See cell.

soldier.
The *soldier* was a common figure in early England; there are over a score of different spellings of the word. But he was also a *mercenary;* for the word is (It. *soldato,* paid) from *solde, soude,* pay; Fr. *sou,* from It. *soldo.* The *mercenary* was perhaps better paid; at any rate, he has a more high-sounding word for the same occupation: from LL. *mercenarius,* from *merces, merced—,* reward. The basic meaning of *merces* is something traded (fighting, for the gold); hence also L. *merx, merc—,* goods for trade, whence Eng. *mercer* and, via the present participle (L. *mercatans*) of L. *mercatari,* to trade, whence OFr. *marcheant,* also our Eng. *merchant.* Thus also L. *mereri, merit—,* to earn, to work for hire, gives us on the one hand *merit* (earned), and on the other, through L. *meretrix, meretric—,* one that gives herself for pay; hence Eng. *meretricious.* (The best service cannot be bought.) This is related to L. *emere, empt—,* to buy; *see ransom.* Note that to *mercerize* cloth is from *John Mercer,* a dyer, who patented the process in 1850. Brave as the soldier of today may be on the battlefield, and ready as he is to offer himself for dangerous tasks, so far as camp work is concerned the soldier's favorite slogan is, "Don't volunteer!"—whence the meaning of *to soldier* on the job. *See mercy.*

solecism.
See insolent.

soliloquy.
See agnostic.

so-long.
This expression of farewell may be a corruption of *salaam,* from Arab. *salām,* peace; *cp. Islam.* But, noting such expressions as the Fr. *à bientôt,* to our soon meeting, we may consider it influenced by the thought that "it will seem *so long* until we meet again." A professor, asked for a rating before the due date, said to the student: "You've waited so long, so long, *so-long!*"

solstice.
See overture.

solution, solve.
See absolute.

somersault.
Although this word is sometimes spelled *summerset* (and although *summer* is from OE. *sumor,* from MLG. *somer;* Sansk. *sama,* half year) there is no relation between the overturning spring and the later season. *Somersault* is a corruption of OFr. *sombresaut,* from *soubresault,* from L. *super,* over, + *saltus,* leap, from *saltare, salt—,* frequentative of *salire,* to leap. *See insult.* Note that *saltimbank* from Fr. *saltimbanque,* from It. *saltimbanco,* leap on bench, has counterpart in *mountebank; cp. bank.* And the dance *saltarello,* the *saltigrade* spider (L. *saltus* + *gradere,* to advance) *saltation,* the *saltatory* exercise, have no relation to *saltpetre* (Gr. *petr—,* rock; *cp. parrot*) and table *salt,* for which *see salary.*

The Roman equestrian performer (or vaulter) was L. *desultor,* leaper down. From this came the use of the adjective, L. *desultorius,* jumping about, fluctuating, wavering; thence it came to mean unmethodical and became Eng. *desultory.*

A leap is thus a *sally* (through the Fr. *saillir,* to rush forth, to jut out). The present participle of L. *salire* is L. and Eng. *salient,* though the meaning comes from the Fr. use. Something that leaps back (L. *re—,* back) is *resilient,* directly from the present participle of L. *resilire, resilient—, result—.* And that which has leapt back, the consequence of an action, is the *result.*

son.
Son and *daughter* are both widespread words, as one might expect. *Son* is basically from Aryan *sunu,* from Sansk. *su,* to beget: one sown, brought forth. As he is to become master, that suffices. *Daughter,* however, is ultimately from Sansk. *duhitri,* from *duh,* from *dhugh,* to milk (Eng. *dugs*): the milker of the family.

sonant, sonata.
See absurd.

songstress.
See spinster.

sop.
See pan.

sophism, sophist.
See sophisticated.

sophisticated.
This word has journeyed considerably from its source, Gr. *sophos,* wise, *sophia,*

wisdom. The verb Gr. *sophizesthai*, to become wise, developed the meaning to work out, to devise, to find a way. This change came through the influence of the *sophists*, the wise men; for they taught eloquence, rhetoric (as Socrates was accused) not for the purposes of finding out the truth, but to win an argument, even showing how to "make the worse seem the better reason." Hence *sophism* came to mean clever, subtle, but false reasoning. (From *sophism* came the personal noun *sophumer*, an early Eng. word for one that reasons falsely; later, *sophomore*—which folk etymology links with *moron; cp. remorse.*) Now *sophism* is used of a false argument, while false but specious reasoning in general is called *sophistry*.

The verb *sophisticate* (LL. *sophisticare, sophisticat-*, to devise) came to be used, in the middle ages, of mixtures devised by the alchemists; hence, of things removed from their natural or simple condition (as with the *sophisticated* person, no longer *unsophisticated*); hence, it was first applied in Eng. to impure mixtures, adulterate (*cp. world*), impure. Something of this remains as an implication.

Sophy, aside from its use as a (female), name, has been used in Eng. to mean a wise man, or wisdom in general. But there is also a *sophy*, meaning the ruler of Persia (esp. of the dynasty from 1500 to 1736, founded by Ismail *Safi*); this is Pers. *safi*, from Arab. *safi-ud-din*, pure of religion. This is not to be confused with *sufi*, an ascetic mystic, from Arab. *sufi*, man of wool (the cloth he wore), from *suf*, wool. But a *sophist* tries to pull the wool over your eyes.

sophistry.
See sophisticated.

sophomore.
See remorse, but also sophisticated.

sophy.
See sophisticated.

soporific.
See defeat.

sorcerer.
The L. *sors, sort-* meant one's fate, one's lot or portion in life; hence, the kind of life in store for one. It gradually (LL. *sorta;* OFr. *sorte*) became the general word for kind; whence Eng. *sort*: men *of this sort; this sort of* material. *Out of sorts* means not feeling the kind of way one usually does. From this noun came the verb to *sort*, to arrange by kind; this meaning is influenced by (and the word may also have developed as aphetic from) Fr. *assortir*, from L. *ad*, to, + *sorte;* hence Eng. *assort, assorted.*

One who attempted to arrange someone's lot was LL. *sortiarius*, OFr. *sorcier*, early Eng. *sorcer;* then (partly by back-formation from *sorcery*) the current *sorcerer*.

The practice of drawing lots is sometimes called Eng. *sortition*. There is also a Fr. *sortir*, to go out (perhaps related to this L. *sorta;* but more probably, like Sp. *surtir*, to spring out, from a LL. form *surctire*, from L. *surgere, surrect-*, to spring up; whence Eng. *surge; insurrection*, a rising against; *resurrection*, a rising again: L. *surgere* is from *sur, super*, upward, + *urgere*, to impel; whence Eng. *urge, urgent*), whence Fr. and Eng. *sortie*. But *see resurrect.*

Though some persons' lot may be *sordid*, this word is of other origin; a rare L. *sordes* (plural only), filth, and the verb *sordere*, to be dirty; hence, Eng. *sordid*, which first meant dirty, then repellent because of filth; then, squalid. *Sordid* was also early used of the *purulent* discharge of a sore—in early times, likely to be a dirty mess indeed. Note that the word here is *purulent*, from L. *pus, pur-*, the fluid secreted in *suppuration* (L. *sub*, under + *purare, purat-*, to form *pus*); the small rounded elevation beneath which the *pus* gathers is the diminutive L. *pustula*, Eng. *pustule;* hence, *pustulant, pustular, pustulate, pustulous*, refer to the formation of *pustules*. To relate this *pus, pur-*, with *purity* (*cp. curfew*) would call for a *sorcerer*.

sordid.
See sorcerer.

sore, sorrow.
See sorry.

sorry.
I'm *sorry*, but this word has no relation (save by attachment of meaning) with *sorrow*. *Sorry* is the AS. adjective *sar, sore*, with the adjective ending added: AS. *sarig*, whence *sorry*. *Sorrow* is a common Teut. word, from AS. *sorh*, from *sorg;* Du. *zorg*, G. *Sorge*, care. *Frau Sorge, Dame Care*, was an all too common visitor to medieval households.

sort, sortie.
See sorcerer.

soteriology.
See creosote.

soul.
This is very common Teut., OE. *sawol, sawl.* Its ultimate origin is undetermined.

south.
See east.

South Carolina, South Dakota.
See States.

soviet.
This word is directly from Russ. *sovjet,* council, from *so,* together (as L. *co*) + Slav root *vjet,* to speak (Russ. *otvjet,* answer; *privjet,* greeting). It is akin to Serbo-Croat. *savjet.* The Bulgarian national assembly is the *sobranje,* from *so,* together + *ber,* to gather, cognate with Eng. *bear,* L. *fer,* Gr. *pherein,* Sansk. *bhr.* Hence, the *Union of Socialist Soviet Republics,* the *USSR.*

sow.
See mutton.

soy, soya.
See legible.

spaghetti.
See macaroni.

span.
See spoon.

spangle.
See sequin.

spaniel.
See Appendix II.

spank.
This seems an echoic word, from the sound of a swift blow, a *slap* or *smack*—both also echoic; *cp. clasp.* But the sense of swift motion carries over into a *spanking* breeze; hence the *spanker* on a sailboat. From the sense of lively, dashing, came the general application in the sense of excellent, well-done, with an implication of showiness (Dan. *spanke,* to strut). *Cp. bounce.*

spar, sparable, spare.
See affluent.

spark, sparkle.
See attack.

sparse.
See affluent.

speak.
See unspeakable.

spear.
See affluent.

speck, speckle.
See swivel.

special, species, specific, specimen.
See salary.

spectacle, spectator, spectre, spectrum.
See speculate.

speculate.
Spectacle is from L. *spectaculum,* from *spectare,* look, frequentative of *specere, spect—,* to behold; whence also *spectator, spectre,* an appearance; *spectrum,* that which is seen, the range of light. *Cp. salary; fee.* From L. *specere* came L. *speculum,* mirror, whence Eng. *specular;* and L. *specula,* watchtower. This gave the L. verb *speculari, speculat—,* to watch from a distance, to spy—hence, to guess what that distant whirl of dust and speck might really be, whence Eng. *speculate.*

speech.
See ache, unspeakable.

speed.
This word moved in the opposite direction from *prevent, q.v.* It first meant success, good fortune (OE. *sped, spaed,* from *spowan,* from OHG. *spuon,* to prosper). The olden wish, when one started a journey, was *Godspeed!* But since, in most cases, in order to prosper one had to "get there firstest with the mostest," the word changed its meaning. And the wish changed to *"Good speed"*—as the watch cries to the hurrying horsemen in Browning's "How They Brought the Good News from Ghent to Aix"—though he never makes quite clear what the good news is.

spell, spelling.
See goodbye.

spend.
See expend.

sperm.
This is another word for seed (*cp. semi-*), Gr. *sperma* being the noun from Gr. *sperein,* to sow.

sphere.
See trophy.

sphinx.
From the Egyptian figure (human head and breast; body of a lion) perhaps grew the legend of the riddle of the *Sphinx,* the monster that harassed Thebes until Œdipus solved the riddle; hence, any person or thing with a seemingly insoluble mystery.
The riddle: What is it that goes on four feet in the morning, two feet at noon, and three feet in the evening? The answer: Man, for he crawls in the morning of his life, walks erect in the noon of his power, and uses a crutch in the evening of his age.

spice.
See salary.

spick.
See spoon.

spider.
See spinster.

spike.
See spoon.

spinach.
See Appendix II.

spinal.
See spinach, in *Appendix II.*

spindle.
See swivel.

spine.
See mutton, spinach.

spinet.
See saxophone.

spinster.
Obviously, one that spins. But it is the suffix that has the story. Originally, it was feminine only, and was applied in occupations once carried on by women—since taken over by men, and the words lost, though some of them are preserved as names, *e.g., Baxter,* from *bakester,* of which the masculine gives the name *Baker.* As men did the work, some of the words had a second feminine suffix added, to indicate women: *sempster,* whence *sempsteress,* whence *sempstress; songster, songsteress,* whence *songstress.* Applied to men, the suffix usually indicates inferiority (*rhymster*) or other bad traits (*punster, gangster, trickster*); this is even more apparent in the LL. form of the suffix (which is originally the combination of Sansk. *—as— —tar*); *poetaster.* (*Minister, magistrate,* are formed with the Sansk. comparative suffixes *—yans— —tara; cp. month*: May.)
Spinning being the frequent occupation of an unmarried woman, in the 17th c. *spinster* came to be appended to feminine names as the legal indication of celibacy; hence, an old maid. From AS. *spinner, to spin,* via the noun form *spinthra* to OE. *spithra,* came also the *spinning* insect, the *spider.*
Note that the suffix *—ist* is also frequently applied to indicate scorn, as in *communist, fascist, nudist, plagiarist* (earlier *plagiary*), and even, when first used, *chemist.*

spiral, spire.
See trophy.

spirit, spiritual, spiritualist, spirituous.
See trophy.

spit, spital, spittle.
See hospital. Several meanings of *spit* are of different origin. The slender, pointed rod, such as meat is thrust on for roasting, is direct from OE. *spitu,* MDu. *spit,* rod. Hence also, a scornful term for a sword; also, a narrow projection of land into the water. There is also a *spit* (OE. *spittan*) meaning to dig, or to dig up, with a spade; as a noun, the depth of a spade-thrust; or the amount of earth a spade will lift, a spadeful. A *"spittin'* image" of some one is a corruption of "the very *spit* and image of", an exact likeness down to the minutest detail.

splash.
See clasp, knick-knack.

sponge.
"To throw up the *sponge"* means to surrender. At a prizefight, the helpers or seconds have wet *sponges* with which they lave their battler between rounds. If he is being too severely pummeled (in the days before the referee called the fight over for such reasons) the second might throw the *sponge* into the ring, as a sign that his fighter is beaten.
The word *sponge* is by dissimilation from Gr. *sphoggos, spoggos, sponge.* The L. cognate is *fungus,* which was also applied to the *spongy* land-growth we too call *fungus.* There is a legal

term, Eng. *fungible*—of quite other origin. It is from L. *fungibilis*, but has borrowed the sense of the verbal expression, L. *fungi vice*, to act in place of. From this L. *fungi, funct—*, to act, to perform, we have the word *function*: what a thing ought to perform—colloquially used ("I attended an important *function* the other night") as though it meant performance. When his life's performance is over, a man is *defunct;* though we trust that he did not conclude the performance by throwing up the *sponge!*

spoon.
This is from AS. *spon,* a chip of wood, a thin piece, common Teut. From the openness and shallowness, the word *spoony* was used in the 18th c. to mean a fool; then someone foolishly fond (*q.v.*); hence, to *spoon* in the sense of to make love.

The same word appears in the phrase *spick and span* (for *spick and span new*): *spick* is *spike,* nail (L. *spica,* ear of corn; Sw. *spik,* nail); and *span,* from ME. *span-new;* new as a chip. *Span,* a stretch, is common Teut., AS. *spann.*

Spoonerism.
Many persons, when excited or embarrassed, transpose the initial letters of words. A preacher-offender, the *Rev. W. A. Spooner,* d. 1930, gave his name to the failing (which is sometimes deliberate, for humor, as with the man that remarked that after a week-end the park is full of *b*eery *w*enches. "Is the *b*ean *d*izzy?" "*M*ardon me, *P*adam, this *pie* is occup*ued*. Allow me to *s*ew you to another *sh*eet.") Long before this gentleman, the transposition had a technical name: *metathesis,* from Gr. *metatithenai,* to tranpose, from *meta,* across, + *tithenai,* to put. *Theme,* from this root, is a doublet of *thesis*. An *hypothesis* is a suggested basis, a putting under, literally a *supposition* (from L. *sup,* from *sub,* under, + *ponere, posit—*, to place; *cp. pose.*) A *theorem* or *theory,* however, is something examined into, from Gr. *theoria,* a viewing (*theorema* is a late formation), from *theoros,* from *thearos,* spectator, from *theasthai,* to behold—whence also that place for beholding things, the *theatre* (where there may be heard many a *Spoonerism!*).

sport.
See plot.

spot.
See blot.

spouse.
There is something final in this word, like the *fiat* (Let it be done!) of an emperor, or the *imprimatur* (Let it be printed!) of a pope. For this word means Spoken!, from OFr. *spose,* from L. *spondere, spons—*, to speak, to pledge; whence Fr. *épouser,* whence Eng. *espouse,* to speak out. From the present tense, with other prefixes, we have *respond,* to speak back; *correspond,* to speak back together. A *corespondent* is a later, legal, form of the same word, boding ill for the *spouse*. To be *despondent* is to pledge away—after which one usually is! Literally, it is from L. *despondere animum,* to yield ones' spirit. To *sponsor* is to speak for.

sprain.
See plot.

spring, sprinkle.
See attack.

spruce.
See Appendix II.

sputum.
See blot.

spy.
See scourge.

square.
Most persons know that a *square* is a four-sided figure (with equal sides and angles); but the word itself says as much: from OFr. *esquarre,* from LL. form *exquadra,* out of four. Hence, *quadrant,* a *quarter* section; and indeed *quarter*, *q.v.* But the most noticeable aspect of a *square* is the right angle, and the earliest use of *square* in Eng. is as an instrument for marking right angles; also called (from the shape of the instrument) a *T-square;* also a *try-square*. From the laying out of a *square,* in geometry, as along the sides of a right triangle, come the principles that led to the use of *square* to mean a number multiplied by itself; conversely, to extract the *square root*. From the attitude involved —fighting *on the square* meant face to face—*on the square* came to mean straightforward, honest.

squash.
See absquatulate, knick-knack.

squat.
See absquatulate.

squid.
This is the end of a chain of imitative words. It is from *squit* a dialect form of *squirt,* which was earlier *swirt.* All imitate the swish of motion or sound.

squire.
See equable.

squirrel.
This is from OFr. *escureul,* from a L. diminutive of *sciurus,* from Gr. *skiouros.* It is pleasant, thinking of the animal, to note that this is perhaps from Gr. *skia,* shadow + *oura,* tail: the animal that makes a shade with its tail.

squirt.
See squid.

stab.
See tank.

stable.
See vestibule.

staff.
See distaff.

stage, stagnant, stagnate, staid.
See tank.

stalactite.
The Gr. *stalassein, stalakt-,* to drip, had the noun form Gr. *stalagma,* a drop. Hence Gr. *stalaktos,* dripping, produced the modern L. *stalactites,* whence Eng. *stalactite,* for the upper icicle of a cavern drip; and modern L. *stalagmites* gave us Eng. *stalagmite* for the mound formed by the drops. Perhaps related was L. *stagnum,* a pool; whence Eng. *stagnate; see tank.*

stalagmite.
See stalactite.

stalk.
See talc.

stall, stallion, stamen, stammer.
See tank.

stamp.
See clam.

stampede.
See clam.

stance.
See state.

stanch, stanchion.
See tank.

stand, standard, stanza.
See state; tank.

star.
See disaster.
The *star* may (as opposed to the wandering planets, *q.v.*) be the light that *stays* in its *station*; *see tank.*

starboard.
See board.

starch, stare.
See stark.

stark.
This was a common ME. word, meaning strong. There was an earlier word, AS. *staer,* rigid, whence Eng. *stare,* to look fixedly, which grew confused with *stark* (hence, Eng. *starch*) and changed AS. *staerblind* into Eng. *stark-blind.* But *stark,* strong, is sometimes used with intensifying force, *e.g., stark* mad. *Stark naked,* however, is another confusion, it being earlier ME. *start-naked,* from AS. *steort,* tail.

start, startle.
See commence.

starve.
This word first meant to die, from AS *steorfan,* to die; G. *sterben.* In early days, the phrase *to starve of hunger* was so common that the last two words were deemed unnecessary and dropped off. (*Starvation* is the only Eng. word in which the L. suffix *—ation—,* the act of, has been added to an Anglo-Saxon stem.) *Cp. sequin.*

state.
See season. The present participle of *stare, stans, stant—,* gives us *stand, stance, circumstance* (L. *circum,* around); *stand* is also common Teut.; Sansk. *stha.* A *stanza* is a group of lines *standing* as a unit. *Cp. tank.*
From the political sense of *state* came the use for formal references: an apartment of *state,* one used only on ceremonial occasions; the important dead are allowed for a time to lie *in state.* Thus ca. 1650 the captain's room (or one set aside for royalty or government representatives

traveling) on a ship was called the *stateroom;* but note also that on early U. S. steamboats (ca. 1835) the cabins were named after the various *states* of the Union.

stateroom.
See state.

States (United we stand). *See* state.

Alabama.
An Indian tribe of the Creek Confederacy. *Alibamu* is Choctaw, I clear the thicket.

(Alaska.
Al-ay-es-ka, Eskimo for great country.)

Arizona.
Perhaps from Sp. *Arida zona,* dry belt; more probably from Indian *ari zonac,* small spring.

Arkansas.
Algonkin Indian name for the Quapaw tribe.

California.
The Sp. name of an earthly paradise, in an early 16th c. romance of chivalry, *Las Serges de Esplandian.* Folk etymology tells that Catalan missionaries in 1769, however, called the land hot as a furnace, *calor de forni.*

Colorado.
The colored country (Sp.).

(Columbia, District of.
Named in 1791, by the Federal Commissioners who established the capital district, in honor of *Christopher Columbus.*)

Connecticut.
Indian *Quonecktacut,* river of pines.

Delaware.
Lord De la Warr, governor of Virginia, came into Delaware Bay in 1610.

Florida.
Sp. flowery: said to have been named on the Feast of Flowers (Easter) by Ponce de Leon in 1513.

Georgia.
From *King George II* of England. (George III lost it.)

(Hawaii.
Native *Owhyhe,* place where, in 1779, Captain Cook was killed.)

Idaho.
Indian, *Eda hoe,* light on the mountain.

Illinois.
Indian ??, the river of men.

Indiana.
The state of the Indians.

Iowa.
Name of a Sioux tribe: *Alaouez,* sleepy ones. Their own name for themselves was *Pahoja,* gray snow.

Kansas.
Name of a Sioux tribe, folk of the south wind.

Kentucky.
Iroquois *Ken-tah-ten,* land of tomorrow.

Louisiana.
Named (by Robert de la Salle, who in 1682 came down the Mississippi) for *King Louis XVI* of France.

Maine.
From *Maine,* province in France, owned by *Queen Henrietta Maria,* wife of King Charles I of England.

Maryland.
Named after the wife of Charles I, above.

Massachusetts.
Algonkin *Massadchu-es-et,* small place at big hills.

Michigan.
Indian tribe and place: *michi gama,* great water.

Minnesota.
Sioux Indian, sky-blue water.

Mississippi.
Indian *maesi sipu,* fish river.

Missouri.
Name of a Sioux tribe.

Montana.
Sp. mountainous.

Nebraska.
Omaha Indian, wide river.

Nevada.
Sp. snow clad.

New Hampshire.
From County of *Hampshire,* England.

New Jersey.
From the Island of *Jersey.* Patent was granted in 1664 by the Duke of York to Lord John Berkley and Sir John Carteret; Carteret had been administrator of the island.

New Mexico.
Aztec *mexitli,* title of their war god.

New York.
From *Duke of York,* who in 1664 was granted the patent by his brother, King Charles II of England.

North Carolina.
From *Charles I of England* (L. *Carolus*), who in 1629 granted the patent to Sir Robert Heath. Called *Carolana* until 1662-3, when Charles II granted a new patent.

North Dakota.
Sioux Indian, alliance.

Ohio.
Iroquois Indian, great.

Oklahoma.
Choctaw Indian, red folk.

Oregon.
The most probable sources of this name are: *origanum,* the wild sage; *oregones,* Sp. for big-eared; *oyer-un-gen,* Shoshone Indian, place of plenty; *aura agua,* Sp. for golden water; *Wauregan,* Algonkin Indian, beautiful water.

Pennsylvania.
L. *Pennsilvania,* Penn's Woods, from *Admiral William Penn,* whose son, the Friend William Penn, was granted a charter (1681) by Charles II.

(Philippines.
Sp. *islas Filipinas,* islands of *Philip,* colonized from Mexico, named for King *Philip* II of Spain.)

(Puerto Rico.
Sp., rich port.)

Rhode Island.
Originally called Providence Plantation. The name *Isles of Rhodes* was chosen by the General Court in 1644.

South Carolina.
See North Carolina.

South Dakota.
See North Dakota.

Tennessee.
Called *Frankland* (from Franklin) from 1784 to 1788. *Tennese* was Cherokee Indian for the chief town and the river.

Texas.
Indian *Tejas,* allies.

Utah.
From the Indian tribe, the *Utes.*

Vermont.
Fr., green mountain.

Virginia.
Named by Sir Walter Raleigh (1584) for *"the virgin queen,"* Elizabeth of England.

Washington.
Originally *Columbia,* changed to avoid confusion with the District. Named after *George Washington.*

West Virginia.
See Virginia.

Wisconsin.
Indian, meeting of the rivers. The spelling was decided by Congress; earlier forms were *Ouiscousin, Misconsing, Ouisconching.*

Wyoming.
Indian, hills and valleys. From *Wyoming Valley* in Pennsylvania, widely known through Campbell's poem, *Gertrude of Wyoming.*

static.
See tank.

station.
See season.

stationery.
You have been told to discriminate between *stationary* and *stationery.* The second is longer in the language; other-

wise, they are the same word. Certain men were allowed to set up a permanent stall near the church, for the sale of clerical goods; as opposed to the itinerant peddlers, they were *stationers.* (from L. *station—; see season*). Since the clergy alone could write, and since much of their work involved writing, the *stationery* store came gradually to specialize in writing materials (in England, they were licensed to sell books, in the University towns). Now cigars and lollypops have been added. The later *stationary* has preserved the literal meaning.

statistics.
See season.

stature, status, statute.
See tank; element (at end).

stave.
See distaff.

steadfast.
See tank; *cp.* bed.

steal, stealth.
See talc.

steed, steel.
See tank; *cp.* bed.

steep.
See sock.

steer.
See stern.

stellar, stellify, stellio.
See disaster.

stentorian.
From earliest times the role of the herald has been to stand in front of the army and dictate terms to the enemy. A herald with the voice of fifty men was *Stentor,* in the Iliad; hence, loud tones are *stentorian.* Today the radio is the still, small voice (except in my neighbor's set) heard round the world.

step.
See clam; tank; stoop.

stereotype.
See stern.

sterile.
See tank.

sterling.
The first makers of money in England, who established a reputation for the purity of their coinage, were the *Ostomanni,* or *Easterlings,* from North Germany. From them, the *sterling* silver penny. It is also suggested, however, that *sterling* is the AS. diminutive of *star* (*cp. gossip*), with which some of the early Norman coins are marked. A pound *sterling* was first sixteen ounces of *sterling* pennies.

Crown and *angel* are other coins named from their designs; *kopeck* is Russ. *kopejka,* diminutive of *kopyo,* lance, which the Tsar carries on the coin. A *florin* was named either from *Florence,* or from the lily (It. *fiora,* from L. *florem, flower*). *Coin* (doublet of *coign,* corner) is from L. *cuneus,* wedge, from Gr. *conos,* a peg, a *cone; cp. coin. See dollar.*

stern.
The adjective, meaning severe, is from AS. *styrne* (which should make the spelling *sturn*); G. *starr,* stiff; Gr. *stereos,* rigid, whence Eng. *stereotype.* The results of printing from a solid plate of type metal gave *stereotyped* its meaning of endlessly unchanging. The rear of a ship (which Skeat thinks changed the spelling of the adjective) is from ON. *stjorn,* steering, from *styra, steer.* But the adjective is more probably spelled by analogy with earlier *austern,* whence *austere,* from Gr. *austeros,* drying (the tongue) from *auein,* to dry. *St. Luke,* XIX, 21, "I dread thee: for thou art an *austerne* man." As the dry wind came from the south, this may be related to L. *auster, austr—,* south; *cp. aurora.*

There is also a Gr. *sternon,* chest, that gives us the prefix *stern—, sterno—,* and the *sternum.*

stew.
This seems closer to hot water than to hot air; yet its first meaning seems to have been a hot air bath, AS. *stofa.* But the two are allied, as hot air is likely to contain steam. The AS. is probably from LL. *extufare,* to steam out, from Gr. *typhos, vapor,* whence Eng. *typhus* and *typhoid,* from Gr. *typhein,* to smoke. From AS. *stofa* also comes *stove,* which doublet of *stew* (the *w* used to sound like *v* or *f*) also meant a hot air bath; later, the oven that produced it. From bathing in hot vapor came the *stew* that one eats; from the

ill repute of the old steam-baths came the sense of *stew*, a brothel. This *stew* perhaps came via OFr. *estuve*, a hot bath; there is also an OFr. *estui* (Fr. *étui*, case, from ? AS. *stowigan*, from *stow*, place), which gave Eng. *stew*, a tub for keeping fish fresh until cooking time. *Steward* is quite unrelated; *cp.* *lady*.

steward.
See lady.

stibium.
See element: **antimony.**

stick, stigma.
See ache, attack.

still.
See instil.

stilus.
See style.

stimulant, stimulate.
See stimulus.

stimulus.
See style. L. *stimulus*, goad, was borrowed in Renaissance medical books, for something that quickens body activity. From the L. noun came the verb *stimulare, stimulant-* (present participle), *stimulat-*, to prick, to urge ahead; whence Eng. *stimulant, stimulate.*

sting.
See attack; humbug.

stink.
See tank.

stipend, stipple.
See stubble.

stipulate.
Today, lawyers exchange documents, signed and sealed; in ancient Rome, the parties to an agreement broke a straw (L. *stipula*, straw, whence *stipulari, stipulat—*, to come to terms) to seal an oral agreement. Without swallowing a camel's back, each was then expected to prove no man of straw. The L. *stipula* is a diminutive, probably of *stirps*, stem, which forms the verb *ex(s)tipare, extirpat—*, to pluck out by the stem (roots and all), from which comes Eng. *extirpate.*

Though rarely since the 17th c., *stirp* is used to mean race, or a line of descent; *stirps* (plural *stirpes*) is still used in law and biology. The breeding of newer, better species or types (as Ayrshire cattle and golden bantam corn) was called *stirpiculture* before *eugenics* replaced it, in the mid 19th c. (For *eugenics, see evangelist; racy.*)

stitch.
See ache, etiquette.

stocking, stocks.
See palliate.

stodgy.
See refrain.

Stoic.
See Platonic.

stolid.
See tank.

stoma, stomach.
See pylorus.

stone.
See carnelian.

stooge.
See refrain.

stoop.
See sock. The *stoop* of a house is from Du. *stoep*, related to the common Teut. word, OE. *staepan*, whence Eng. *step.*

stop.
See tank.

store; storey; **story.**
See attic; plot. *Cp.* tank.

stow.
See tank.

straggle.
There is an early *strake* (from the OTeut. form *strak*, whence also *strakjan*, OE. *streccan*, and Eng. *stretch*), which got tangled with OE. *strica*, Eng. *streak* —until the *streak* superseded the other form. But in the meantime *strake* had probably developed a frequentative, *strackle*, to *stretch* back and forth, which is preserved in the form *straggle*, to go up and down without order; then, to stray. There is also an early *strackle-brain* (as we say *scatterbrained*); but this may have been influenced by the aphetic *stract*, from *distract; cp. distraction.*

straight.
See prestige.

strain.
See prestige; *cp.* plot.

strait.
See prestige.

strange.
See uncouth.

strangle.
This word has lost an *e* which the French added. It is via OFr. *estrangler* from L. *strangulare, strangulat-*, to choke (whence also Eng. *strangulation*), from Gr. *straggale*, halter, *straggos*, twisted. The source is thus the twisted rope with which the act was earliest performed.

strangulation.
See strangle.

strapping.
See bounce. *Strap* is a weaker form of *strop*, imitative in origin. The word is found in LL., *struppus, stroppus, strap.*

strategy.
They tell of the Chinese general who, sending his advance guard through a wooded section where the enemy might lay an *ambush*, ordered each man to take a stone, and hurl it into the trees: if birds flew away, there were no men hidden there, and the army could proceed. The guard threw the stones; the birds flew away; the army marched—and was *ambushed*. For the opposing general, hiding his men in the trees, had ordered each to catch a bird, to release when the approaching force threw stones. Each of these tricks was a *strategem*; the general plan by which a general leads his forces to victory is his *strategy*, from Gr. *strategos*, general, from *stratos*, army + *agein*, to lead.

Ambush is from OFr. *embusche*, from *embuscher*, to hide in the *bushes*. *Ambuscade* is the same word via It. or Sp.: Fr. *embuscade*, from Sp. *emboscada*, from *emboscar*, to hide in the bushes. There was an early Eng. *emboss*, to plunge into the woods. The change in the first syllable was influenced by Eng. *embage*, from L. *ambages*, from *ambo*, around, + *agere*, to do. There was an early Fr. *bauche*, shop, whence Fr. *debaucher*, to lure from the shop, to corrupt, whence Eng. *debauch*. Eng. *debouch* is from Fr. *de*, from, + *bouche*, mouth; hence, to come into the open. *Bush* is a ME. word not found in AS.; G. *Busch;* LL. *boscus*, from It. *bosco*, whence Eng. *bosky*, also *busky*.

Insidious is from Fr., from L. *insidius*, from *insidiae*, ambush, from *insidere*, to lie in wait, literally, to sit against, from L. *in*, against + *sedere*, to *sit*. Related to this are *sit*, common Teut., AS. *sittan; site; situation*. *Cp. subsidy*. But don't rely on armchair *strategists!*

stratosphere, stratum.
See trophy.

straw.
See destroy.

streak.
See straggle, strike.

stretch.
See prestige, straggle.

strew.
See destroy.

strict.
See prestige.

stricture, strigil.
See strike.

strike.
This is a strong verb, widespread Teut., the Aryan root, *streigh-, strig;* OE. *strican, strac; strike, struck*. The weak form OE. *strik* gives us Eng. *streak* (*cp. straggle*) and early Eng. *strickle;* another form, *straik*, gives us Eng. *stroke*. The root is found also in L. *stringere, strict-* to brush lightly, which via the adjective *strigilis* (LL. *strigulum*, currycomb) gives us Eng. *strigil*. This is a different word from the same form, L. *stringere, strict-*, to bind, whence Eng. *stringent; cp. prestige*. Thus *stricture* may mean a tightening, as in medicine, or a touching lightly, as in a passing remark (now, influenced by the other sense, always an adverse comment). L. *stringere*, to stroke lightly, developed also the sense of stripping leaves from a branch; this may have influenced the thought in *strike sail, strike the colors*.

Most of the eighty-eight major meanings of the verb *strike* in N E D follow clearly from the three main senses: to go forward, as to *strike* across the field; to mark, as to *strike* off the list; and to hit, to *strike* a blow. Thus, from the last comes the sense of making a vigorous movement, as though *striking* a blow, as a swimmer *strikes out* for the shore, or a batter *strikes* until he is *struck out*. To *strike work* (shortened, to *strike*, as workers in protest) developed figuratively, as the slang expression to *knock off* for a few days, from *knock, strike*. (*Knock*, AS. *cnocian*, is probably echoic; *cp. knick-knack*). Similarly, to *strike off* may mean to produce something quickly (*strike off* a sonnet); but it may mean to catch the features of something precisely, the same as to *hit off*. (*Hit* is from ON. *hitta*, to meet with, to *hit* upon; but the Eng. developed the sense of "meeting with" in the form of a blow. To *strike it off* is the same as to *make a hit* with someone.) Always *strike home!*

strike-breaker.
See whippersnapper.

string, stringent.
See prestige.

stroke.
See strike.

strong.
See prestige.

strontium.
See element.

strophe.
See paragraph; apostrophe.

struck.
See strike.

structure.
See destroy.

stub.
See stubble.

stubble.
The form *tip* was an early word for point; it first appeared in Eng. in the combination *tiptoe*. It also was used as a verb, to touch lightly; a harder touch was a *tap;* both words are probably imitative. The phrase *tit for tat* was earlier *tip for tap*.

Carry the point down a little and you have *stip*, an early Aryan form for stalk; thus L. *stirps*, stem; diminutive *stipula*, straw, whence Eng. *stipulate, q.v.* Also L. *stipes*, trunk, has come into Eng. both as *stipes* and as *stipe*, botanical terms, along with the diminutives Eng. *stipula, stipella*. But (as straws to beggars) L. *stips* also came to mean alms, then a small sum; thus L. *stips* + *pendere*, to weigh, gave L. *stipendium*, money payment, whence Eng. *stipend*, and perhaps a *tip*.

Rapidly sounded *p.p.p.p.* seems to imitate a quick pricking (hence from Du. *stip*, point, came *stippen*, to prick or mark with a point; whence, the frequentative *stippelen*, Eng. *stipple*). But the interruption has more of a *b* sound; hence what is left when the *stip* (*tip*) is cut is the *stub*. And *stub* (Gr. *stupos, stump*—*stump* and *stub*, early, had the same senses) meant what was left when a tree, *e.g.*, was cut down, against which you might *stub* your toe; then, anything short and thick, as a *stub* of a man; the *stub* of a pencil. The frequentative of *stub* is *stubble*, the short ends that remain when stalks of grain are cut.

stump.
See tank.

stump.
See stubble. There is an OHG. *stumpf*, cut, blunted; but for the further history of the word, etymologists are *stumped*. A *stump-speaker* is one that goes about speaking—originally, in the U. S.—on the *stumps* of large trees; then he was replaced by the soap-box orator; the first recorded use of this sense of *stump* dates from the year 1775. If you have ever walked through a pine forest, imagine the trees cut down, then a farmer trying to plough the new field full of the *stumps*, and you'll understand why this country gave birth to the expression "I'm *stumped!*"

stupendous.
The L. *stupere* (its present participle *stupens, stupend*—) means to strike senseless; it lost force through being used in hyperbole, as we say "You could have knocked me down with a feather!" and the like—though something of the original power lingers in *stupor*. That which struck one dumb was *stupendous*. The person struck dumb is *stupid;* apparently, he remains so. The technical words *stupe* and *stupeous*, however, are from L. *stupa*, tow, flannel.

stupid.
See stupendous; *cp.* tank.

stupor.
See stupendous.

sty.
For pigs, this is common Teut., AS. *stig;* a *steward* is AS. *stigweard*, warden of the *sty; cp. lady*. It is from AS.

stigan, rise, from the raised fence. For *sty* on the eye, *see stymie.*

Stygian, Styx.
See lethargy.

style.
All the uses of this word go back to L. *stilus,* a stake, then an instrument for pricking marks on waxed tablets. He that manipulated the instrument well had a *stilus exercitatus,* a practiced *style;* he that handled it poorly had a *stilus rudis,* a rough *style*: thus the word referred to the handwriting. The words Eng. *style, stilus,* and (incorrectly) *stylus* are used in technical senses for pointed instruments or parts of bodies; but even in classical times the word had come to mean the manner of writing, then of doing, things. Hence, the accustomed or current manner: to be in *style, stylish.*

The root of L. *stilus* is *sti-,* to prick. From this comes Gr. *stylos,* pillar; whence, St. Simon *Stylites* and any other *stylite,* who sat or stood on a pillar to prove his devotion. Thus *stylistic* means relating to literary *style;* but *stylitic* means relating to ascetics, esp. those that dwelled from pillar to post. *Stylo-* is a combining form, from Gr. *stylos,* pillar, in scientific terms, e.g., *stylomastoid, styloid* process. And probably from the same root is *stimulus,* a prick or goad to action.

stylistic, stylite, stylitic.
See style.

stymie.
Every golf player knows, and hopes to avoid, a *stymie*: another ball cuts his off from view of the hole. Golf is an old game, and this is probably from an old word; a *stymie* was one that could not see well, from *styme* (esp. a Scots word), a glimpse, a tiny bit, used mainly in the phrase *not see a styme.* This word dropped from the language; but the game of golf goes on.

AS. *styme* is a noun from AS. *stigan,* to rise; hence also AS. *stigend, styan,* and the diminutive *styany,* the little swelling on the eye. This word was misunderstood as *sty-on-eye;* hence our present *sty.*

suasion, suave.
See victoria.

sub—.
See overture.

subject.
This *subject* of conversation or *object* of consideration (it was first in logic and grammar that the two were opposed) is from L. *subicere, subject-,* from *sub,* under, + *jacere,* to throw. L. *ob* means in the way of. L. *jacere, jact-,* to throw, is a most fruitful source of English words. *Objection* is the act of throwing something in the way; *subjective,* from the grammatical sense, means concerned with the *subject,* hence with the first person, oneself; *objective,* from similar usage, means with personal emotions removed—but also literally, as a passive form, it means that which lies in the way, hence the *objective* or goal. With other prefixes we have *abject; adjective; dejected* (*see wasp*); *eject; injection; interjection,* something thrown between; *reject; project; trajectory,* the path of something thrown across. By way of Fr. *jeter,* to throw, from the same L. source, comes the *jet* of a fountain and (by transference from the throwing forth to its source) the *gas jet.*

To *float* on the water is from AS. *flotian,* but influenced by Fr. *flotter,* from L. *fluctuare, fluctuat-,* to wave (whence Eng. *fluctuate; cp. affluent*) from L. *fluctus,* wave. From Fr. *flotter* comes *flotsam,* goods found *floating* on the ocean; this is usually contrasted with *jetsam,* goods cast ashore by the waters; but originally *jetsam* was the noun from *jettison,* which means to cast overboard so as to lighten a ship in peril.

The frequentative of L. *conicere, conject-,* to throw together, was *conjectare,* to cast; from this came Eng. *conject* and *conjecture,* which first meant to cast together the signs and omens in order to forecast; hence—as belief in such procedure waned—to guess. I guess that's enough on this *subject.*

subjective.
See subject.

subjugate.
The olden sign of conquest, of *subjugation,* from L. *subjugare, subjugat—,* from *sub,* under + *jugum,* yoke, was to cross three spears and have the foe crawl under. This cross is the form of a *yoke,* for driving oxen; and for both purposes the word is old and widespread: AS. *geoc;* Goth. *jok;* L. *jugum;* Sansk, *juga.* Through L. *jungere, junct—,* to join, come *junction* and *juncture;* via Fr. *joindre* come *join, joint,* and *jointure* (first, holding property together, as man and wife). A

conjunction; subjunctive; the grammarian is interested in *joinings,* as well as the lawyer. *Con,* from *com,* together, also gives us *conjugal* bliss.

The Gr. *zeugma,* a *yoking,* from Gr. *zeugnynai,* to *yoke,* gives us the Eng. figure of speech, *zeugma.*

In northern Europe, crawling under the yoke gave place to running the *gauntlet*—which was, however, not so much a sign of submission as of punishment. Some say this is from Fr. *gantelet,* diminutive of *gant,* glove, with which the person is struck; the word is sometimes spelled *gantlet.* It is more probably from ME. *gantlope,* from Sw. *gatelop,* from *gate,* way + *lopp,* run—whence Eng. *lope; elope* (*e,* from, away); *interloper,* first a ship that ran between (trespassed on) the privileges of the English chartered companies. The knightly way to present a challenge or defi, was to strike across the face with one's glove, or fling it on the ground; this is, of course, to throw down the *gauntlet. Cp. lobster.*

Conjunctivitis is a swelling (*—itis,* swelling, as in *tonsilitis, appendicitis,* etc.) of the *membrane conjunctiva,* the *conjoining membrane,* that links together the eyelids and the eyeball. *Cp. yokel.*

subjunctive.
See subjugate.

sublimation, sublime, subliminal.
See limen.

submarine.
See overture.

subscribe.
See shrine. From the literal sense, to write under (as when one signs a petition or an order) came the two uses, as when one *subscribes* to a magazine, or when one *subscribes* to the principles of democracy. In a more commercial field, *underwrite* has taken the same sort of shift; from signing one's name under something, comes the sense of guaranteeing. *Cp. under-*.

subside, subsidy.
Subsidy is a thing *sitting* nearby until needed: from L. *sub,* under + *sidere,* from *sedere, sess—,* to sit. It was applied first to the Roman military reserves, which waited (kneeling) in the background until called into action. *Subside* is from the same source. From the simple verb (present participle, *sedent—*) come *sedentary;* and *sediment,* the part that sits on the bottom. From *sedare, sedat—,* to set (the casual of *sedere*), we have *sedate, settled.* A *session* is merely a sitting; to *supersede* is to sit above, hence replace. (In olden classes, seats were assigned by quality of work, best first: if you surpassed someone, you at once *superseded* him.) To *possess* is from *possidere, possess—,* to sit in power, from *posse* + *sedere; cp. posse.* The king and the judge sit before all others present; from their official duties comes the shift in meaning (L. L. *pre,* from *prae,* before—either in time or in place) of *preside. See strategy*—which reminds us that from L. *sedem* via LL. *sedicum* comes Fr. *siège,* whence Eng. *siege.* Both of these are really aphetic for *assiege* (L. *as,* from *ad,* to), to sit down to. Similarly *besiege* is ME. *bi—, by,* near, + *segen,* from *siège,* to sit down by . . . whether it be a town or a maiden.

To sit at a job is to be *assiduous;* hence also *assiduity.* To sit back, hence to stay, is to *reside;* and that which stays is the *residuum* or (via Fr.) *residue,* from L. *residuum* from *residere; re,* back.

substance.
See tank.

subsume.
See prompt.

subtle.
This word survives in the figurative sense only; it is drawn from weaving (L. *subtilis,* from *sub,* under + *texlis, telis,* from *texere, textum*: *see text*). Meaning of fine or delicate *texture,* it was applied to ideas the interweaving of which could not be discerned.

Subtle and *subtlety* have doublets, *subtile, subtility,* which with other forms are retained in scientific use.

subtract.
See distraction.

succeed, success.
See ancestor.

succubus.
See marshal.

succulent.
See sewer.

succumb.
See marshal.

such.
See alone.

suck, suckle, suckling, suction.
See sock, sewer.

sue.
See refrain, suit.

suffer.
"Suffer the little children to come unto me." The two meanings of this word, to allow, and to feel pain, are separated in *sufferance* and *suffering;* they are joined in the origin of the word, L. *ferre, lat—,* from Gr. *pherein,* to bear. Bear itself means both to carry and to "bear up", to *endure. Endure* is from Fr. *endurer,* from L. *indurare, in* with intensive force + *durus,* hard. The physical application remains in *durable.* The physical remains also in most of the compounds of this very *fertile* stem (*fertile,* bearing; *fertilize*). The present form gives us *conference* (L. *con,* from *com,* together), a bringing together; *defer* (L. *de,* down, to bring down, to submit); *infer; prefer* (L. *pre,* before); *proffer,* (L. *pro,* toward); *refer; transfer; differ, indifferent* (L. *dis,* apart); *interfere, q.v.,* to bring between; *offer* (L. *ob* + *ferre,* to bring toward). *Coffer,* however, is from Fr. *coffre,* from L. *cophinus,* from Gr. *kophinos,* basket, which, via OFr. *cofin,* gives also Eng. *coffin.*

From the past form, *lat—,* come other words. The *ablative* case was primarily used to indicate direction from (L. *ab,* from + *latus,* borne). Thus also *ablatitious; superlative* (borne beyond); *translation* (borne across); *oblation* (borne toward). A *prelate* is one brought before, given preference, hence one (a churchman) of high rank. A person whose deeds are borne aside is *dilatory;* thence also, via OFr. *delaier,* Eng. *delay;* and if *latus,* borne away, be related to *latus,* wide, also Eng. *dilate* (L. *dilatare,* to widen).

As a suffix, *—fer,* bearing, is frequent, often with *—ous* (from L.*—osus,* full of): *lucifer, cp. atlas; carboniferous; vociferous* (*voci—,* voice). I'd better stop, or this will seem *pestiferous.*

suffice, sufficient.
See defeat.

suffix.
See fix.

sufi.
See sophisticated.

sugar.
See candy; *cp.* sock,

suicide.
See shed.

suit.
See set; pursue. If something *suits* you, you follow it. If you follow something (legally) you *sue* for it; if you follow something thoroughly (L. *per,* through) you *pursue* it.

suit, suite.
See refrain.

sulfanilamide.
This drug (NH_2 C_6 H_4 SO_2 NH_2) is named from its sources: *sulf*uric + *anil*ine + *am*monia, + the ending *—ide.*

sulfur, sulphur.
See element.

sully.
See dirt.

sum.
See azimuth.

summer.
See somersault.

summit.
See azimuth.

sumptuous.
See prompt.

sundae.
There is rivalry between states as to the origin of this delicacy. In Evanston, Ill., sodas were forbidden on the Sabbath; hence *Sunday sodas* were given without the soda-water: icecream and syrup. In Wisconsin, when the habit grew of asking for syrup on icecream, since it was more expensive, the stores would sell it for 5c on *Sunday* only. In either event, partly to make the name fancy, and partly because pious folk objected to the use of the holy name, the spelling was changed to *sundae.* Have a good one!

Sunday.
See week.

sunder.
See sundry.

sundry.

The verb to *sunder* is from OE. *sundrian,* from earlier *asundrian.* This is formed from the adjective *sunder* (used only as a combining form, e.g., OE. *sundorspraec,* private speech; or in the phrases *on sunder, in sunder;* from these, *onsunder, osunder,* developed *asunder*), separate, apart, private. There further developed the form OHG. *sunderig,* separate-like, which was shortened to *sundrig,* thence Eng. *sundry*—which first was used of things of different sorts, or belonging to different persons; hence, distinct, then with reference merely to the fact that there are several items involved, *sundries.*

super-.

See overture.

supercilious.

Have you noticed that slight lifting of the eyebrow, which indicates that something is unworthy of attention? That look of disdain? (*Disdain,* from Fr. *desdeign,* from LL. *dedignari,* from *de,* from + *dignari,* to be worthy, from *dignus,* worthy. Hence also Eng. *deign;* L. *dignitas,* whence *dignity; indignant,* angry because of unworthy treatment; etc.) *Cilium* (plural *cilia*) is L. for eyelash; whence Eng. *cilia* and *ciliary.* L. *super,* above, added to this, gives us L. *supercilium,* eyebrow. The suffix *—ous* [L. *osus,* full of, as in Eng. *bellicose* (L. *bellum,* war); *courageous, pious,* etc.] properly pictures a disdainful person as full of eyebrow: *supercilious.*

superintend.

See tennis.

superior.

See azimuth.

superlative.

See suffer.

supersede.

See overture; subsidy.

superstition.

See tank.

supple, supplement, suppliant, supplication, supply.

See application.

supposition.

See Spoonerism.

suppuration.

See sorcerer.

supra—.

See overture.

surd.

See absurd.

surfeit.

See defeat.

surge.

See sorcerer.

surgeon.

See pedagogue.

surname.

This word has shifted spelling and meaning. It has at times been spelled *sirname,* as though the family name (only nobles had family names, through the middle ages); then *sirename,* as though the name of one's *sire,* father; hence, the family name. But Bishop Nicholson, in his *Exposition of the Catechism,* 1661, speaks of every Christian bearing two names; the one of nature, which is the name of his house, family, or kindred, and this he brings into the world with him; the other of grace, of favour, being his *surname,* that is over and above added unto him (L. *sur,* on, above). The Bishop's derivation is right, but his definition is wrong. The Christian or baptismal (first) name, is all most persons had; gradually, as a *surname,* a man's occupation (Baker) or birthplace (London) or fatherhood (John*son;* *Mc*Coy; Aarono*vich;* Bron*sky*) was added. In some parts of Europe, this occurred en masse, by law, in the 19th c.; county clerks assigned names, and your friendship or your purse accounted for such names as *Dun(g)hill* or *Rosegarden.*

surprise.

The L. *prachendere,* to take before, hence to grasp, to seize, to hold, became a source of new compounds; *see surrender.* In LL. it was shortened to *prendere, prensi;* this became Fr. *prendre, pris,* to take. The feminine of Fr. *pris* was *prise,* thing taken; this gives us the Eng. *prize* of war; also (to get a hold on) to *prize* up a board. (The *prize* that is a reward, however, is a doublet of *price,* OFr. *pris* from L. *pretium,* reward; another doublet, via LL. *pretiare* and OFr. *preisier,* is Eng. *praise;* perhaps these are related to *prayer; cp. precarious.*)

From the L. *praehendere* comes not only the *prize* but the *prison* via *prehens—, prens—*, and the noun form *prension—*. An *apprentice* is a young man taken to learn; a man who undertakes something— literally, takes something between (his own hands)—is an *entrepreneur;* this is directly from the French, which gives us also *enterprise*. A thing that ought to be taken back is *reprehensible;* and when you take it back (an eye for an eye) you achieve *reprisal.*

There were early Eng. nouns *susprise* and *supprise*, from L. *sub*, under; both of these have succumbed to *surprise*, from L. *super, sur*, over. To *surprise* was first to overtake, to catch up to, to catch in the act; finally, it has come to indicate the emotion appropriate to such sudden *surprisal*, and has become equivalent to astonish (*q.v.*). The change was taking place in the time of the American lexicographer Noah Webster (1758-1843; *An American Dictionary of the English Language*, 1828), whose wife, so runs the legend, caught him kissing the parlormaid. Quoth Mrs. Webster: "Why Noah, I'm *surprised!*" "Madame," Noah drew himself up to respond, "*You* are astonished; *I* am *surprised!*"

surrender.

Render unto Caesar the things that are Caesar's; this means, literally, give back, from Fr. *rendre*, from L. *reddere*, from *re*, back + *dare*, to give. A *rendition* is a giving back of a passage. *Surrender* would seem to be a "giving back under" (or over: *sur* might be from L. *sub*, under or L. *super*, over): but it is possibly from *se rendre*, to give oneself up.

The *n* in *render* (Fr. *rendre*) slipped in through analogy with its antonym, *prendre*, to take, from L. *praehendere, praehens—*, to grasp, to hold before, whence Eng. *prehensile*. To *apprehend* is thus to take to (oneself) before, from *ad* + *prae* + *hendere*: hence, either to understand, or to *anticipate* (L. *ante*, before + *capere*, to take) in the sense of hanging upon the event, worrying, being *apprehensive*. Similarly *comprehend*, to take together, may mean to understand or to include; the second sense is dominant in *comprehensive*. *See surprise.*

surrogate.

See quaint.

surround.

This word (like *abound*) is from L. *undare*, to well, to flow, whence Eng. *undulate*. L. *super*, above + *undare*, meant to overflow, to *abound*. *Cp. abundance*. A *surrounding* wave was one that flowed all over an object. Milton (who uses the word seven times, and almost the first in English) employed it always to mean an encircling wave; this sense has survived.

surtax.

See overture.

swarm.

See answer.

swastika.

See monk.

sway.

See victoria.

swear.

See answer.

sweet.

This word is common Teut., OE. *swete*, from earlier *swot, swad;* Sansk. *svadus, sweet;* L. *suavis*, from *svadvis*, whence Eng. *suave; suasion*, making things sweet; *cp. victoria*. Also cognate is Gr. *hedys*, sweet; thus *hedesthai*, to rejoice; *hedone*, pleasure; whence Eng. *hedonism*. *Sweet* is used to form many names of flowers, and other pleasant combinations; almost all the world has a *sweet tooth.*

sweetbread.

See inspiration.

sweetheart.

See heart.

swell.

This was a common Teut. verb, OE. *swellan, swollen*; its various meanings rise from the basic sense of increasing in size. The noun was used figuratively in the 18th c., as of one puffed up with pride; also in the phrase *to cut a swell*, to dress up in the height of style, to parade as a gentleman, a *swell;* hence, from those taken in by such behavior, the approving "That's *swell!*"

swerve.

See victoria.

swift.

See swivel.

swine.

See mutton.

swivel.

There was an early Eng. *swive,* from OE. *swifan,* to move quickly (whence Eng. *swift*), to move about. The second sense developed the form *swivel,* that which moves about, now used in combinations such as *swivel-gun, swivel-chair.*

The endings *—el, —le,* may indicate operatives; or they may be frequentative or diminutive. As operative: *swivel; spindle* from *spin.* As diminutive: *darkle* from *dark.* (*Dark* is from OE. *deorc,* not found in the other Teut. tongues. *Dark* as a verb was gradually replaced by *darken,* to make *dark.* There was an early adverb *darkling;* when *—ly* replaced *—ling* as the adverb ending, this was felt to be the participle of a verb; hence by back-formation came to *darkle.* Note that *—ling* is also used as a diminutive: *duckling; cp. gossip.*) As frequentative: *fondle,* from *fonnen, fonned,* to be foolish; *cp. fond.* In some cases, the ending is both frequentative and diminutive in force. Thus to *sparkle* means to give forth a lot of little *sparks; cp. attack.* And to *crackle* is to form a lot of little *cracks,* as on a surface or (echoic of the sound) as a *crackling* fire; *cp. crunch.* Similarly *speckle* from *speck* (AS. *specca,* also not in the other Teut. tongues). Also *see drivel.*

sybarite.

See Appendix II.

sycophant.

When a fellow wants to get a good mark, he may polish up an apple and place it on teacher's desk; his classmates call such a lad an *apple-shiner.* Less complimentary localities use the term *bootlicker.* The Greeks had a name for it: *fig-shower. Sycophant* is from Gr. *sykon,* fig + *phanein, phant—,* to show; *cp. focus.* This was the fellow that informed the officers in charge when (1) the figs in the sacred groves were being taken, or (2) when the Smyrna fig-dealers were dodging the tariff. Liddell and Scott, however, in their *Greek Lexicon,* say all this is a mere figment. An early Eng. word for the same fellow was *lickspittle.*

sylph.

This word was coined by Paracelsus, in the 16th c., to indicate the spirits of the air that embraced chaste mortals. It is perhaps fashioned after *nymph* (Gr. *nymphe,* bride) and L. *sylvanus,* of the woodlands, *cp. Pennsylvania;* perhaps influenced also by Gr. *silphe,* the grub that turns into a butterfly.

sylvan.

See neighbor. The *y* is in imitation of the Gr. *hyle,* wood, matter; used in Eng. compounds, *e.g. hylozoic; hylophagous* (as the beetle; *cp. sarcophagus*), *hylobate,* a wood-walker.

sym—.

See syndicalism.

symbiosis.

See parasite.

symbol.

This was originally a token, in the form of an object broken in twain, so that identity could be proved by having the two parts match (as in James Branch Cabell's *The Cream of the Jest*). Thus the *symbol* became a sign. This story hides within the word, from Gr. *symbolos,* from *symballein,* from *sym,* together + *ballein,* to put, to throw.

symmetry.

See syndicalism.

sympathetic.

See osseous.

symphonic.

See syndicalism.

symposium.

This gathering for mutual discussion has changed little from the ancient Greek days of Plato's *Symposium;* but originally it was a gayer affair, as the word implies (Gr. *sym,* together + *posis,* drinking, from *pinein,* to drink). A *Symposium* of the livelier sort is that of Trimalchio in Petronius' *Satyricon* (1st c. A.D.). *Cp. intoxicate.*

symptom.

See syndicalism.

syn—.

See syndicalism.

synagogue.

See pedagogue.

syncopation.

There is a medical word, *syncope,* heart failure, from Gr. *syn—,* together, + *kop—,* stem of *koptein,* to strike off. Hence *syncope* means a cutting off together of all body functions. But the verb *syncopare, syncopat*—was applied in grammar with the sense of cutting together, blending: contracting a word by omitting a letter or more in the middle, as *o'er* for *over*. In prosody, this was extended to apply to shifting stress, beginning with a stress where normally an unaccented sound would occur; this use is found also in music, when a note begins on a normally unaccented part of the bar and is held into the normally accented part—one of the devices used in jazz, *q.v.*

syncope.
See syncopation.

syndicalism.
The Gr. prefix *syn*—, together, is found in many Eng. words (before *m* and *p*, it is often *sym*—, as in *sympathy; symmetry*, measuring together; *symphonic*, sounding together; *symptom*, originally the disease, from Gr. *symptoma*, mischance, from *sympiptein*, to fall together, to happen to: Gr. *ptoma*, fall, mischance, dead body, *cp. ptomaine*).
The Gr. *syndic*—*syn* + *dike*, judgment —was a civil magistrate; hence LL. *syndicare, syndicat*—, to judge, then to come together for executing judgment and gradually for other purposes, until we have the *syndicates* of today. While *syndicate* was usualy used of capitalists, in France the term *chambre syndical*, meeting room, was applied to the places where laborers came together, in the early days of the trade union movement, then to the groups themselves; hence, *syndicalism*.

syndicate.
See syndicalism.

synopsis.
When you take a view of a thing as a whole, seeing it all together, you make a *synopsis;* from Gr. *syn*—, together, + *opsis*, view; *cp. pessimist*. Hence the *synoptic* Gospels (the first three, of Matthew, Mark, and Luke) look together over the one story of Jesus.

synoptic.
See synopsis.

synthesis.
See photosynthesis.

syphilis.
This disease, which has recently come from hidden corners into the light of public attention, was first given wide notice in 1530. The Italian Girolamo Fracastoro wrote a poem, *Syphilis sive Morbus Gallicus* (*Syphilis, or the Gallic Disease; cp. Dutch*), in which the name represented both a shepherd and the disease that attacked him. The word itself is from Gr. *sym*, together + *philos*, love.

syrup.
See drink.

system.
See tank.

systole.
See diabetes.

syzygy.
This triplet of *y's* is a disguised use of the prefix Gr. *syn*—, together—the *n* disappearing before the *z*. It is from Gr. *syzygia*, a yoking together, from *syn* + *zyg*— from *zeugnynai*, to yoke. *Syzygy* has the same basic meaning, whether used in astronomy, anatomy, biology, prosody, mathematics, or theology.
From the same root comes the figure of speech *zeugma* (She slipped on a kimono and the top step), and the mineral *zeuxite*. The mineral was found (1814) in the *Huel Unity* mine in Cornwall; T. Thomson translated *"unity"* into Greek, *zeuxis*, yoking—and called the stone *zeuxite*.

T

tabby (cat).
See cloth. But there is also suggested *tibbie,* a pet name from Tibalt, Tybalt, Theobald (bold in God), name of the cat in the medieval beast epic. Thus Chapter 10 of Caxton's *Reynard the Fox* (from Fr. *renard,* fox) is entitled: "How the kynge sent Tybert the catte for the foxe." And in Shakespeare's *Romeo and Juliet,* III, when *Tybald* asks "What wouldst thou have of me?" Mercutio taunts him: "Good king of the cats, nothing but one of your nine lives."

tabernacle, table, tablet.
See inn.

taboo, tabu.
We borrow this word from the South Seas. In Tongan it is *tabu;* but it also appears as *kapu, tambu, tapu.* The idea that things are forbidden, or must be hidden, is preserved in such practices as putting a spot of ashes on the forehead of a beautiful child, so that the devil won't carry her away; and in the many stories of forbidden sights, from Gr. *Psyche, Pandora's box, Lady Godiva, Beauty and the Beast,* up to *Bluebeard's* room. The hiding of names is also widespread; it survives in the fairy-tales of *Tom-Tit Tot* and *Rumpelstiltschen. Cp. boycott; totem.*

tabula rasa.
See inn. .

tack.
See tag.

tact.
See taste.

tactics.
The Gr. phrase *ta taktika* means matters of arrangement, from *tassein, takt—,* to set in order. It is akin, through L. *tangere, tact—,* to touch, to Eng. *tact; cp. taste.*

tadpole.
See toad.

tag.
The *tag* in *rag, tag, and bobtail,* is from a Scandinavian stem meaning point or thorn (Norw. *tagg, tack;* Fris. *take,* thorn); thence, also, *tack,* which is influenced by OFr. *taque,* from *tache,* aphetic for *attach.* This is a doublet of *attack, q.v.*

The game of touch, *tag,* is perhaps ultimately from L. *tangere, tact—,* to touch; *cp. taste. Fens,* that keeps you safe in the game, is from *fend,* to ward off, aphetic for *defend* from L. *defendere, defens—,* to strike back. But note that in the early game (before posts and bases were substituted) you were safe when you touched iron—which historically was believed to ward off witches. In Lincolnshire the chaser (the one that's *"it"*) was called *Horney, i. e.,* the devil.

Stories have similar origin in folk beliefs. Thus we are told that *Little Red Riding Hood* is a myth of the night (French call twilight the time *entre chien et loup,* between dog and wolf: day, when the dog roams with his master; and night, when the wolf prowls): the Red cloak is the sun; she is devoured by the wolf at night; and in the basic versions, the huntsman rips the beast open and she comes forth whole again. Similar legends of dawn and birth may be found in many lands. The Melanesian hero with red obsidian rips Dawn out of the belly of Night. The Gr. story of *Kronos,* time, and the Heb. tale of *Jonah,* have points of resemblance.

In the *Edda,* there is a story very similar to that of *Jack and Jill,* but clearly referring to the tides, as the moon waxes and wanes. *Cp. taboo; totem.*

tailor.
See record.

taint.
See attain.

talc, talcum.
This was used by the Arabs for mica, and borrowed as *talc* or *talcum* in the European tongues. As oil of *talc*, or *talcum* powder, substances bearing this name were the bases of cosmetics. The Arabs derive their term from Persian *talk*.

To *talk* adds a frequentative —*k* to Eng. *tale* (*cp. tally*), which is common Teut., AS. *talu*, for both speech and number; AS. *tellan*, to list in order, hence Eng. *tell* (to count, and to recount in the sense of relating). Other words with this frequentative ending are *lurk* (also *lurch*, to prowl; to *lurch* when the sea rolls is via Fr. *lacher*, to let go, from LL. form *laxiare*, from *laxus*, loose; whence Eng. *lax*, *relax*) from *lower; stalk*, AS. *stealcian*, from *steal*, AS. *stelan*, whence also *stealth;* and *walk*, *q.v.* from *wallow*.

The *talesmen* of the jury, for a trial by one's peers, were originally drawn from "such persons as might be standing around," L. *tales de circumstantibus*. The good luck *talisman* is via Sp. *talisman* from Arab. *tilsam;* but this was from Gr. *telesma*, payment, fulfilment, used of the religious rites; from *telein*, to bring to pass, from *telos*, goal—whence *teleology*. A goal is usually far off, and Gr. *tel*—, *tele*— afar, is frequent as a prefix, from *telaesthesia*, perception of things far off, (more commonly *telepathy*: Gr. *patheia*, feeling), to *telson*, the last segment of the abdomen in shellfish.
Cp. focus.

tale.
See talc.

talent.
Originally but now only historically, this was L. *talentum*, a sum of money, a balance, a weight; from Gr. *talanton*, of the same meaning. But the *Bible*, *St. Matthew*, xxv, 14-46, tells of the man that gave his goods unto his servants: "And unto one he gave five *talents*, to another two, and to another one; to every man according to his several ability"—and from this parable came the present meaning, a man of no small *talent*.

talesmen, talisman.
See talc.

talk.
See talc.

tally.
See record.

tame.
See diamond.

tamp, tamper.
See tattoo.

tandem.
The usual way of harnessing horses is side by side. College students will have their little jokes: when they saw a pair of horses harnessed one before the other, lengthwise, they called them harnessed *tandem*, lengthwise (L. *tandem*, at length), twisting the word for time into use for space.

tangent, tango.
See taste.

tank.
Earlier Eng. for this word was *stank* (from OFr. *estang*, whence *étang*, from L. *stagnum*, a pool, *i. e.*, *standing* as opposed to running water, from present participle *stans*, *stant*—, of *stare*, *stat*—, to *stand*, *stay*, *cp. season*), a pool. A *tank* was a large cistern, esp. one carrying water in a wagon; hence, our present army *tanks*: to preserve secrecy, the parts of the first of these engines of war were labeled as for *tanks*: the name stuck. Akin to the sense of standing water are *stagnant* and *stagnate*. In the sense of *stay*, support, we have *stanchion;* in the sense of *stay*, stop, we have *stanch*. *Stand* is from the same root, from Sansk. *stha*, to *stand*. With its variants, this is one of the richest sources we have: *stap*, to make *stand; star*, to *stand* fast; *stak*, to fix, *stick; stabh*, to *stop*. These give too many words for detailed consideration; a few may be listed (NED will break them up, but in most of them the relation is clear.): *standard, understand, withstand; stable, establish, stage, staid, stamen; arrest; contrast; obstacle; obstetrics; rest; statue; armistice; interstice; destitute; prostitute; restitution; superstition; circumstance, constant, extant, distant, instantaneous, stanza, substance; assist, resist, consist; stolid; sterile; stop; stupid; static; ecstasy; system; step; stab; stump; stammer; steadfast; stood; steer; steel; stow; story*. A *stall* is a *stand* in a *stable;* a *stallion*, a horse for breeding, too spirited for harness, was a horse kept in a *stall*.

Stank, the past of *stink,* is from another source: from AS. *stincan, stanc, stonc,* to smell, to rise as vapor; Goth. *stiggkwan,* to strike (the nostrils).

Tankard is also from another source, being (in Eng.) some 200 years older than *tank;* it is from OFr. *tanquard* by metathesis, from ? L. *cantharus,* from Gr. *kantharos,* a large pot.

tankard.
See tank.

tantalize.
See atlas.

tantalum.
See element.

tap.
See stubble, tattoo.

tape.
See taper.

taper.
The pith of the *papyrus* was used for candle wicks; hence (by dissimilation: *paper* becomes *taper*) the *taper* we use. *Cp. bible.* From its gradual diminishing downwards comes the sense of the verb to *taper.* The *tapir* is from a Central American native name, *tapira;* from the same language (Tupi) comes *tapioca,* from *tipi,* dregs, + *og,* to squeeze. Sp. *tapia* means wall of mud, used also in English. The word *tape* may be from the long strip of pith, the *taper.*

tapioca, tapir.
See taper.

tar.
See pay.

tarantella, tarantula.
See Appendix II.

target.
This is the diminutive of *targe,* a shield, and was used of the small round shield, as opposed to the long oval one that hid the whole body. Eng. *targe* is related to OHG. *zarga,* border, but probably through the Fr. from Arab. *al darqah,* shield. From the shape of the objects set up for shooting practice, the word spread to anything aimed at. Yet it is likely that when politicians make a man a *target* for their abuse, they are also using him as a shield for their own offences.

tariff.
"Millions for defence, but not one cent for *tribute!*" The Americans were the first nation that refused to pay the Mediterranean pirates to let their vessels pass unmolested. For many years, other peoples had been paying; and since many of the pirate ships had headquarters in *Tarifa,* North Africa, the payment of blackmail was called *tariff.* (Same persons think it still is!) *Tribute* is from L. *tribuere, tribut—,* to give, to assign, from *tribus,* branch, tribe; *see tribulation.*

Arab. *ta'rif* means explanation, from *'arafa,* to make known. Its first Eng. meaning was an arithmetic table; hence, a schedule of rates. (The derivation from the city is by folk etymology.)

tarpaulin.
This was first an awning—so used by Captain John Smith. The *tar* was used for waterproofing. The *paulin* is a form of ME *palyoun,* canopy, a folk corruption of *pavilion, q.v.*

tart.
See torch.

tartan, tartar.
See tatterdemalion.

task.
See deck, taxi.

taste.
To *taste* was first to handle, to *test, q.v.,* by the touch; then esp. the touch of tongue and palate (from OFr. *taster,* whence Fr. *tâter,* from LL. *taxare, taxt—,* to handle, intensive of L. *tangere, tact—,* to touch—whence Eng. *tact,* which first meant the sense of touch, feeling, then discrimination, power to feel differences. The present participle of *tangere, tangens, tangent—,* gives us the mathematical term *tangent:* the first person present tense, *tango,* I touch, gives us a dance.) *Taste* often deals with *intangibles,* that cannot be touched; yet it is not true that there can be no arguing about *taste* (*De gustibus non disputandum:* Eng. *gusto; dispute*). *See deck.*

tatterdemalion.
Did you ever catch a *tartar?* He's not easy to handle; in fact, he was once just a *Tatar,* one of an Oriental tribe; but in the early 13th c. Genghis Khan and his *Tartars* swept like the fiends of

hell over Asia and Eastern Europe, wherefore the Romans changed the name to *Tartar,* after their *Tartarus* (Gr., *Tartaros*), hell. Note that *Hades* (also *Ades,* from Gr. *Haides* or *Aides*) is the God of the dead, also the entire underground world: both the *Elysian Fields* of the blessed and the *Tartarus* of the damned. After the oriental hordes had lapsed to wandering *"gypsies"* (for *gypsy, see gyp*) the word *Tartar* came to be used of such wanderers, than was corrupted to *tatterdemalion,* with the fanciful ending as in *rapscallion, curmudgeon, ragamuffin.*

Tatar itself is a word like barbarian, *q.v.* It is Chinese *ta-ta,* meaning a person of outlandish speech. *Hottentot* is a similar coinage of the South African Dutch, to indicate the (to the European) choppy way of native talk.

Tartar, in chemistry, is from Gr. *tartaron,* probably from Arab. *durdi,* tartar; Pers. *durd,* sediment. The cloth *tartan* is via OFr. *tartarin,* from LL. *tartarinum,* a material imported through *Tartary.* There is also a material *tarlatan,* earlier *tarnatane,* perhaps related. The *tartan,* the *swift* Mediterranean boat, is from It. *tartana,* perhaps from Arab. *tarīdah,* chaser. And *tatter,* which of course influenced *tatterdemalion* (Capt. John Smith called the *Tartars tattertimallions*), is Teut.; Icel. *toturr,* rag.

tattoo.

This is at least two words. When drums beat *tattoo,* at bedtime: earlier *taptoo,* from Du. *taptoe,* from *tap,* a faucet + *toe,* to shut: this was the signal for the taverns to close. A variation of this *tap* is *tamp* (Fr. *tamponner,* to plug), and *tampion.* But the word is doubtless also preserved by *tap,* to strike, of imitative origin.

The designs created by injecting pigments beneath the skin (of clear-skinned persons) or by inflicting scars (among dark-skinned), the *tattoo* marks, are of east island origin: Maori, *ta,* to scar; Tahitian *tatu,* pricking.

Tamper is either from *tamp,* above—one who *tamps,* esp. *taps* the charge, and fills the hole, for blasting; or a variation of *temper,* meaning first, to mix clay, then to meddle. *Temper* (AS. *temprian,* from Fr. *temperer,* from L. *temperare,* to apportion, moderate, regulate, *temperi,* seasonably, from *tempus, tempori—,* time) in all its range of meanings (to *temper* steel; a bad *temper*) begins with the idea of softening or regulating, as time itself might: *temper* the wind to the shorn lamb (which is not the *Bible,* but Laurence Sterne). Hence, *distemper* implies unregulated, immoderate, mixed—the last gives it its sense, in painting. *Cp. complexion.*

taunt.

See tit for tat.

taut.

See duke.

tavern.

See inn. (No etymological connection with *Avernus,* descent to which is easy: *Aeneid,* VI, 126. *Avernus,* from Gr. *aornus,* from *a,* without + *ornis,* bird; whence *ornithology*: the fumes from this lake in Campania were supposed to kill all birds flying over it; they also led to its being taken as the entrance to hell . . . The *tavern* has also been taken as the entrance to hell.)

tawdry.

St. Audrey (*Etheldreda* from AS. *Aethelthryth,* patron saint of Ely) died of a tumor of the throat, which she deemed a punishment for her early love of necklaces. *St. Audrey's lace* was a necklace, such as was sold on her fair day (Oct. 17). The term was extended to include other objects bought at this, and at other fairs; and from the general quality of such articles, the word, now *tawdry,* took its present meaning.

tax.

See taxi.

taxi.

Most men that call for a *taxi* have little thought of the roundabout way they are going. The word is a shortening of *taximetercabriolet. Cabriolet* (Fr., a little *cabriole*) is a two-wheeled carriage, named from the bouncing or leaping motion it often had (Sp. *cabra,* from L. *caper, capr—,* goat. From this source we have *caper; capricious;* the It. musical term *capriccio; caprice,* a sudden bounding, an impulse; and the island of *Capri*: *see canary.*). *Tax* (L. *taxare,* to censure, to charge) was early used of something required from persons, property, etc., for the support of a government; often this was imposed in the form of labor: that is, it was a *task*— which, like Fr. *tâche,* is another form of the word *tax.*

—*meter*, of course, means measure; and the little carriage that bounces like a goat, equipped with an instrument to measure the charge for its use, is now named by the four letter word, *taxi*. *Cp. sedan*. But *see deck*.

tea.
See drink.

teach.
The first meaning of this word (still basic) is to show; it is akin to OE. *tacn*, whence Eng. *token*, and to G. *zeigen*, to show. There is an early Eng. verb to *tee*, to show; *cp. team*. OE. *taeccan*, whence *teach*, is related to Sansk. *dic*—, whence L. *dicere*, to say, as in Eng. *indicate; cp. verdict, destroy*.

team.
There are three sources of Eng. *tee*. Two of these have lapsed from use; *tee*, to show, from OE. *teon* from *tihan;* cp. *teach;* and *tee*, from the same OE. *teon* (thus confused) but from earlier *teohan*, to draw—this form remains in G. *ziehen*, but died out in Eng. in the 15th c. It survives in the word *team*. The third *tee*, as in curling and golf, though there is an earlier *teaz*, is probably from the name of the letter T, later used as the name of a mark (as we now say X marks the spot).
Team is from earlier forms *teuh*—, *tug*— (whence Eng. *tug*, as also in *tugboat*), cognate with L. *duc—; cp. duke*. The first meaning was to lead or bring forth; it was applied to childbirth; then to the brood or litter. From this the sense extended to any closely associated group, as a *team* of horses, the twenty-mule *team*, the baseball *team*, and the spirit of *team-play*.

tease.
See heckle.

technical, technique.
See onion.

tee.
See team.

teetotal.
"Dicky Turner", of Preston, England, ca. 1830, claimed to have invented this word, is thus memorialized on his gravestone. Unfortunately for the claim, the word is older than he. In prohibition drives, some promise temperance; some, *total* abstinence. Since many of these drink *tea* instead of liquor, *teetotaler* suggests itself as a playful coining. Weekley suggests that the form may have been influenced by the game of *teetotum*. This was first called *totum*: spinning a top with a letter on each side: *T, totum; A, aufer; D, depone; N, nihil;* later the Latin was replaced by Eng.: *T*, take-all, *H*, half, *P*, put down, *N*, nothing. Since *T* won, the game came to be called *teetotum*, (now sometimes *Put and Take*), which might easily have contributed to *teetotal*.

tegument.
See deck.

tel—, tele—.
See talc.

telaesthesia.
See talc.

telegraph, telephone.
See focus.

teleology, telepathy.
See talc.

telescope.
See dismal.

tell.
See talc.

tellurium.
See element.

telson.
See talc.

temper.
See tattoo.

temperature, tempest.
See complexion.

temple.
For the *temple* in the head, *see pylorus*. The *temple* grew up around the arch-shaped section of the sky an augur would mark off with his hand—the part of the sky which he would observe for the omens (L. *templum*, Sansk. *temp* ? cognate with *tend*—, to stretch, whence *tendency, contend*, etc., *cp. tennis*. From this we have L. *tenuis*, thin —G. *dünn*, whence *thin; dehnen*, to stretch—which may also have influenced the *temple* of the body, the *thin* part).
When the augur watched the *temple* of the sky, he *contemplated* (L. *con-*

templari, contemplat—) the proper course.

temporal, temporary.
See pylorus.

temptation.
See tennis.

ten.
See number.

tenacious.
See lieutenant.

tenant.
See abstain.

tend.
See tennis.

tendency.
See temple; tennis.

tendentious, tender, tendon, tendril.
See tennis.

tenebrous.
See meticulous.

tenement, tenet.
See tennis.

Tennessee.
See States.

tennis.
This popular game (favorite in Elizabethan days as well: remember that the Dauphin, in Shakespeare's *Henry V*, shows his scorn of Henry by sending him a tun of *tennis balls*) may take its name from the warning (that used to be) called by the server: (ME. *tenetz!* whence *tennes;* modern Fr. *tenez!* Take!). But this verb is one of the most widespread in the formation of English words; only a glimpse can here be given.

L. *tenere, tent—,* in combinations *tinere,* means to hold. Related are L. *tendere, tendens, tensi—, tent—,* to keep holding, to stretch, from Gr. *tenein,* from *tenon,* confused with the preceding in forming words (*e.g., tendon*); L. *tenuis,* thin, whence Eng. *tenuous;* L. *tender—,* whence Fr. *tendre,* whence Eng. *tender,* delicate. Legal *tender* is that which is held forth (aphetic for *attender*); *tenure,* the right to hold; *tenement,* originally the fact of holding, then land held, or any immovable property, esp. a building. A belief held is a *tenet.* A projection to hold is a *tenon,* forming a joint. The meaning that is held throughout a document or a speech is its *tenor;* which is also, originally, the voice that carries or holds the main melody (in medieval *canto firmo*). *Tend* is aphetic for *attend,* to stretch toward; whence also, *tendentious,* and the *tendril* of a vine. *Tense* and *tension* imply stretched, as on *tenterhooks* (the *tenter* was a frame for stretching cloth, held by hooks; then the word was used figuratively). Another stretching of cloth (for shelter) gives us *tent. Tensor* refers both to the stretching of muscles and to an aspect of stress in higher mathematics—which many have found quite a strain. *Temptation* is from *temptare, temptat—,* to handle, to test, intensive of *tendere,* changed from *n* to *mp* through thought ? of the timely opportunity (L. *tempus,* time). *Content* is from L. *continere,* to hold together, which also gives us *continent,* meaning both a large body of land, and self-*contained; contentment, contain* and (through Fr. *continuer*) *continue.* (*Contention* and *contentious,* quarrelsome, come from L. *content—,* from *contendere,* to stretch or strain, *contend* . . . *Pretend,* to stretch forth, to hold before—as a defense—as a claim, then with emphasis on its falsity; also, *pretentious.*) *Intentional* means with the mind directed toward it, therefore purposeful. *Intend, superintend, intense, intensify,* are but a few more of the words, from L. *tenere, tent—* and L. *tendere, tent—.* Note, however, that *tentative* comes from LL. *tentare,* from L. *temptare,* to *tempt,* try, feel—which gives us also *tentacle,* a little feeler. Also *tense,* referring to verbs, is from OFr. *tens,* modern Fr. *temps,* from L. *tempus,* time.

Tennis may be sprung from OFr. *tenies* (plural of *tenie,* from L. *tœnia,* band), the string—now net—over which the ball is played. Hence LL. *tenieludium;* L. *ludium,* play, game, whence Eng. *interlude,* a play between courses or acts. Philip E. Hitti, in his fascinating history, *The Arabs,* suggests that *tennis* is rather from *Tinnis,* a city of the Egyptian Delta, noted in the middle ages for its linen, from which the best *tennis* balls were made. Finally, *taunt* is from OE. *tenten,* to try, from L. *tentare,* influenced by OF. *tancer,* to chide.

For other formations, *see attempt.*

tenon, tenor.
See tennis.

tenpins.
See ninepins.

tense, tension, tensor, tent, tentacle, tentative, tenterhooks, tenuous, tenure.
See tennis.

terbium.
See element.

terce, tercel.
See tierce.

tergiversation.
This word, now used of roundabout talk to dodge an issue, used to mean to desert a cause. It is from L. *tergiversare, tergiversat—,* from *tergum,* back + *versare, versat—,* to turn: to turn one's back on. In scientific use, *tergum* is Eng. also; and *terg—* is a combining form; as also *dors—,* from L. *dorsum,* back; whence Eng. *dorsal.* To *endorse* is to sign on the back—though this was restored from earlier Eng. *endoss,* via Fr. *en* + *dos,* back, from the L. *dorsum.*

term.
See determine.

termagant.
This word for a scolding woman was before that a roaring rascal in early English drama—the limitation in sex being due to men's opinion of women. Still earlier, *Termagant* was a supposed Saracen god, linked with Mahound . . . note how that last syllable indicates the Christian scorn of Mahomet, Mohammed. But the word wandered through even earlier transmogrifications. It is from OFr. *Tervagant,* from It. *Trivigante,* linked with Diana of the crossways (*trivia; cp. trifle*). And confused in its trail is It. *termigisto,* boaster, "The child of the earthquake and the thunder", from *trismegistus,* the thrice great. Many of the early medieval pseudoscientific texts are attributed to *Hermes Trismegistus.* The best way to get rid of a *termagant* is not to tell her this story, but to run. (More seriously, the shift of sex is probably due to the long eastern robe the character wore, which to western eyes seemed feminine.)

terminal, termination, terminology, terminus.
See determine.

termite.
This creature was known to the ancients, as in LL. *termes,* earlier *tarmes,* a wood-worm, from L. *terere, trit,* to rub, from Gr. *teirein,* to rub, to bore. The plural of *termes* was *termites* (three syllables) ; in Fr. this came to be considered the plural of a two-syllable word, *termite* —thus formed by the error. L. *terere* developed a frequentative *terebrare, terebrat—* ,to bore, which gives us some scientific terms: *terebra, terebration,* and the genus of the *terebratula.* Eng. *attrition* is from L. *ad,* to, + *trit—.* Another frequentative developed, L. *triturare, triturat—,* to thresh; whence Eng. *trituration; cp. tribulation, terse.*

terrestrial.
See terrier.

terrible.
See terse.

terrier.
This dog is really one concerned with *terrestrial* affairs, from Fr. *terre,* from L. *terra,* earth. It was used to hunt the badger, and unearthed its prey. *Territory* is also traced to this source; but may be from *terrere, territ—,* to frighten: grounds from which one is warned to keep away. *Cp. terse.* A soup *tureen* is earlier *tereen,* from Fr. *terrine,* earthen: an earthenware pot.

territory.
See terrier.

terror.
See terse.

terse.
The slang expression "He gave me the brush-off" is preserved in the word *terse,* which first meant polished, wiped, from L. *tergere, ters—,* to wipe. A *detergent* is something that wipes off. To *deter,* however, comes from L. *deterrere,* to frighten away; whence also (L. *terrere,* to frighten; L. *terror,* fear) Eng. *terror* and *terrible;* from L. *terror* + *facere,* to make, comes *terrify.* This L. verb is cognate with *trepidare, trepidat—,* to be excited; whence Eng. *trepidation,* and (+ *in,* not) *intrepid.*

The difference made by a little extra pressure is shown in the history of L.

terere, trit—, to rub (instead of to wipe); this gives us *trite*: things rubbed so much their freshness is worn; also *attrition.* L. *detrimentum,* whence Eng. *detriment,* wearing away; what is left is the *detritus.* Only one of this group has moved to a tenderer mood: *contrite,* which first meant rubbed together, bruised, crushed; but then was applied to those crushed by their sense of sin, therefore repentant. *Cp. tribulation.*

test.
Putting a matter to a *test* may be done in various ways; the most important in the middle ages was of course to put metals into a pot, to see whether one had succeeded in making gold. *Test* is from OE. *teste,* from OFr. *test,* whence Fr. *tête,* head, applied both to the skull and to a potsherd (which the skull might resemble); but the basic source is L. *testa,* brick, then any piece of dried earth (as a pot, pottery), from *tersta,* from *tersa,* dry ground, whence *terra,* earth. The root for dry, *tars,* gives Ir. *tir,* land, L. *torrere,* to parch, whence *torrid* and *torrent, q.v.*

To *attest* (L. *ad,* to), *contest* (L. *con,* against), *protest* (L. *pro,* forth), however, are related to *testify* (L. *ficare,* from *facere,* make); *testis,* a witness, (also and earlier a *testicle* . . . the L. diminutive of *testis* is *testiculus* . . . from the early practice of placing the hand on the seat of manliness when swearing: the *King James Bible* calls it hand on the thigh). *Detest* was originally to call down the gods to witness against some one (L. *de,* down); this was later interpreted as showing that one disliked the person. When a man dies without a witness to what he desires, he dies *intestate. Testator* and *testament* are from the same source; the L. adjective *testimonialis,* relating to a witness, gives Eng. *testimony* and *testimonial. Testy,* however, takes us back to the top of the body: heady, headstrong.

The Gr. word for *testicle* was *orchis, orchid—;* whence (from the shape of its *tuber*) milady's favorite flower. Thus the *orchid;* but also *orchidectomy* or *orchiotomy,* the technical term, for *castration,* which was applied esp. to eastern slaves, to keep the women pure (L. *castrare, castrat—,* from *castus,* pure; *cp. purchase*). Keeping the race pure (Port. *casta, race;* feminine of *casto, chaste,* from L. *castus*) developed the Indian *caste* system—to which we apply the term used by the Portuguese. But this is difficult to *test!*

testament, testator, testimonial, testimony, testify.
See test.

Texas.
See States.

text.
From L. *texere, textum,* to weave, *textum* came to mean the tissue or web of which a thing was woven. Applied to a book, it meant the words themselves; in LL., the Gospel; then, a passage used as the basis, the *text* of the day's sermon.

Seeking to discern the meaning of a word from those around it is to judge by the *context* (L. *con, com,* together). A *pretext* (L. *prae,* before) was at first just a curtain; then, something put before to conceal the truth—like the smoke screen, borrowed from modern war in figurative use.

The *texture* of anything is that of which it is woven, or the quality of the weave. *Cp. subtle; see toilet.*

thallium.
See element.

Thames (set on fire),
See incinerator.

thatch.
See deck.

theatre.
See Spoonerism.

theism.
See month: February.

theistic.
See theology.

theme.
See Spoonerism.

theology.
This is the science (*cp. logistics*) of religion, from Gr. *theos,* god. Hence also *theistic* and *atheist* (Gr. *a,* without). The word shifted to L. *deus,* whence Eng. *deist*—which has no negative form.

Aristotle divided theoretical philosophy into three branches: mathematics, physics, *theology.* The Greeks (Stoics) distinguished three sorts of *theology,* mythical, natural, and civil (dealing with ceremonies); the Christian division was into dogmatic theology (as received and delivered by the Church), natural (in accord with reason and nature), and pastoral (in relation to the needs of men).

theorem, theory.
See Spoonerism.

theremin.
See saxophone.

thermometer, thermostat.
See season.

thermostat.
See element (at end).

thesaurus.
See treasure.

thesis.
See Spoonerism, decay.

thespian.
According to Gr. lore, the first actor was *Thespis,* who in the 6th c. B. C. traveled about in a cart, and who introduced the protagonist (*cp. agony*) to give response to the religious chorus of the ancient festivals.

thief.
This common Teut. word for *stealing* is (like *steal, stealth; cp. talc*: when a feeling *steals* over you there is of course no robbery) basically connected with unnoticed action: OE. *thiof*, Du. *dief*, OHG. *diup*, are related to the older stem *teup*, as in Lithuanian *tupeti*, to crouch. Hence, too, the *sneakthief; sneak* from? AS. *snican*, to crawl, as does the *snail* (AS. *snaegel*, diminutive of AS. *snaca*, which first meant worm, but gives us Eng. *snake, q.v.*).

thimble.
This word is (via AS. *thymel* from AS. *thuma, thumb*) from *thumb*; the *le* indicates the instrument, as also in *handle*, from *hand; cp. palm.* The early *thimble* was leather; ON. *thumall* was the *thumb* of a glove. The well-known guessing game of the pea under one of three *thimbles* is called *thimblerig; rig* meaning first to equip, to fit out, then to trick. *Cp. swivel.*

Perhaps the ending is the same in *throttle*, meaning to take by the *throat* (AS. *throte;* the root meant to swell); the noun *throttle* looks like a diminutive of *throat,* but appeared a century and a half after the verb. *Cp. assassin.*

thin.
See temple.

thing.
The topics discussed at a deliberative assembly range from soup to nuts, cabbages to kings, aal to zymurgy. Hence it is that *thing,* the AS. word for deliberative assembly, applied next to the matters discussed at such an assembly, came to be one of the most general words in the language, to include any and every *thing*.

thirteen.
See number.

thither.
See weather.

thong.
See Bursa. *Thong* is from AS. *thwang,* strap, akin to G. *zwingen,* to bind.

thorium.
See element.

thorough, thoroughfare.
See dollar.

thousand.
See number.

thrash.
See limen.

thrasonical.
See Appendix II.

three.
See number.

threshold.
See limen.

thrice.
See number.

throat.
See thimble.

throng.
The period of turmoil in the German Romantic movement was called the *Sturm und Drang*, storm and pressure. G. *Drang* is the same word as Eng. *throng,* a press of persons, a crowd, *q.v.*

throttle.
See thimble.

through.
See dollar.

throw.
This word first meant to twist or turn; the old Teut. root *thrae* was still earlier *tre—, ter—,* akin to L. *ter—,* to bore; *see termite.* It was applied to twisting silk into thread; perhaps from a step in this process (more probably, from the twist of the wrist in throwing something) it came to its present meaning, as when a ball is thrown, or the blame for an action.

thug.
The violence in this word is honestly (if one may here use that term!) come by: *thug* is from *Hind. thaga,* to deceive. In India, until its suppression by the British in 1830, *thuggery* was well organized, with some religious overtones; its chief practice consisted in going innocently along with an intended victim until the set time for strangling him, whereupon he was silently dispatched. The Hind. term *p'hansigar,* strangler, was supplanted by the euphemistic *thag,* a cheat. Their life is pictured in *Confessions of a Thug,* by Meadows Taylor, d. 1876.

thulium.
See element.

thumb.
See palm, thimble.

thumping.
See bounce.

thunder.
See torch.

Thursday.
See week.

thyroid.
See pylorus.

thyrsus.
See torch.

tiara.
See tire.

tibia.
See bloomers.

tick, ticket.
See etiquette.

ticket-scalper.
See tuft.

tickle.
See cat-o'-nine-tails.

tide, tidings.
See tidy.

tidy.
Time and *tide* wait for no man. This might be mere duplication, as with many early phrases, *e. g., might and main,* for the first meaning of *tide* is simply *time*: *Yuletide, eventide;* hence, the *tidings,* happenings. Thus *tidy* meant *timely,* seasonable; hence, in proper appearance. Low *tide* and high *tide,* originally meaning low and high time, were applied to the sea in LG. *tide* and Du. *tijde.*

tie.
See duke.

tier.
See tire.

tierce.
The L. *tertius,* third, come into OFr. as *terce* and *tierce.* From its often being a third (?) to milady and her knight, the male falcon, a pet, was called little third one: *tercel, tercelet, tiercel, tierclet;* also *tercel-gentle.*

Tierce came to be used of a number of things: the third (of the eight) parries or thrusts in fencing; a sequence of cards in gaming; a third of a pipe (42 gallons) in measuring wine; a musical interval or note; a division of a shield, in heraldry; the third hour of the canonical day, *cp. bull.*

timber.
See lumber.

time.
Although this word comes from a root *ti,* to stretch, it was quite early used not merely of *time* but of the fit *time,* hence, of good *time,* prosperity. The early word for everyday *time* was tide; *cp. tidy.* As tide took on its more limited application to the shifting waters, back into the more general sense came *time.* All in good *time.*

timid.
See meticulous.

timocracy.
This word got confused quite early. Aristotle used *time* to mean value; hence *timocracy* (*cp. democracy*) means government by those holding things of value, i.e., property suffrage. But Plato accepted *time* as meaning a synonym of value, worth, honor; hence, government by these imbued with love of honor.
L. *timor* means fear; whence, Eng. *timorous* (*—ous* from L. *—osus,* full of; *cp. supercilious*). A *timoneer* (as *The Gondoliers* in Gilbert's play) is a helmsman, from Fr. *timon,* from L. *temon—,* pole. The word *timon* was used in English, 14th to 16th c., for rudder. But *Timon of Athens* (as in Shakespeare's play) was a notorious misanthrope; whence the word *timon* is used of such a man.

timorous.
See meticulous, timocracy.

timothy.
See Appendix II.

tin.
See element.

tincture.
See attain.

tinfoil.
See foil.

tinsel.
See scintillate.

tint.
See attain.

tip.
This word has several meanings, with origins more or less obscure; connected with *tap* and with *top.* In the sense of a sum of money given for good service, other languages are more specific, *e. g.,* Fr. *pourboire,* for drink. It is suggested that our word is formed from the practice, in early 18th c. London coffee-houses, of having a box in which persons in a hurry would drop a small coin, to gain immediate attention. The box was labeled *To Insure Promptness;* then just with the initials, *T. I. P. See stubble.*

tirade.
See tire.

tire.
There are several senses of this word: to weary; to dress; the hoop or rubber that encircles a wheel (originally, bound it together); to tear a prey, as a vulture does; a train (so used only by Spenser). The first and third of these survive; the second continues in the theatrical *tiring* room, and the compound *attire* (L. *ad,* to + *tire, tiere,* OFr. for row; OFr. *a tire* means in order, from OHG. *ziari,* from G. *zier,* ornament. This is perhaps from L. from Gr. *tiara,* whence Eng. *tiara,* from Pers. *tajwar,* crowned, from *taj,* crest, crown. *Taj* is now used of the cone-shaped cap the dervishes wear.). Eng. *tier* is a doublet of *tire.*
The original sense seems to have been crest; then crown; hence, a circlet, such as women make in adorning their hair; Jezebel "*tired* her head." From this came the meaning to adorn, to dress, to put in order. The automobile *tire* is a reborrowing from the idea of encircling.
Two of the senses are of different origin. *Tire,* to tear a prey, is from AS. *tirigan,* to vex. *Tire,* to exhaust, is from AS. *teorian;* this and the verb before are both from AS. *teran,* to *tear,* hence, to wear out. *Tier,* in the sense of rank or row (from the several rows of circles in hair adornment), is intertwined with AS. *teran,* to produce; Fr. *tirer,* to draw (It. *tirare*), whence *tirade,* a draught, or something long-drawn, esp. a scolding. Put on a *tiara* for your next *tirade;* and then *retire* (draw back)!

tit for tat.
See stubble. Note, however, the Fr. phrase *tant pour tant,* so much for so much—which doubtless helped fashion the Eng. form of the expression; and which, with its sense of paying back, gave us Eng. *taunt,* which first meant a sharp or clever rejoinder.

titanic.
See atlas.

titanium.
See element.

Titian.
See Vandyke.

titillate.
See cat-o'-nine-tails.

toad.
This word has few known relations; but the *toad* was long considered poisonous, and avoided. From OE. *tadige,* it survives also in Eng. *tadpole* (of which the *pole* is probably *poll,* head: at first the little one seems all head).
Medieval traveling medicine-men used to have an assistant who'd swallow a *toad* (or seem to), so that the master could display his healing powers; these helpers were called *toad-eaters;* then the term came to mean a flattering follower, which sense continues, though the word has been shortened to *toady.*

toady
See toad.

toast.
This is parched (not burnt) bread, from OFr. *toster,* from L. *torrere, tost—; cp. torrent.* In the middle ages, drinks often had sopped in them a piece of spiced and *toasted* bread; it is assumed that from this comes the habit of drinking a *toast. The Tatler* (No. 24, June 4, 1709) tells that the use of the word arose when a celebrated beauty of the time of Charles II was in the Cross Bath; one of her admirers took a glass of the water in which she stood, and drank her health to the company. Another present said he liked not the liquor, but would have the *toast* (*i. e.,* the lady sopped in it). Thereafter, when men drank to the one they delighted to honor, it was called a *toast.* But *toast* is probably from *toss,* to drink at a draught; a hard drinker was called a *toss-pot.* A *toper,* similarly, is from Sp. *topar,* to knock; It. *topa!* clink glasses. What is now called the *M. C.* (*Master of Ceremonies*) is still in more formal terms the *toastmaster.*

tobacco.
See nicotine.

toccata, tocsin.
See touch.

toilet.
This is the Fr. *toilette,* diminutive of *toile,* cloth, woven material, from L. *tela; texere, text—,* to weave, whence Eng. *text, texture.* Thus *in the toils* means caught in the net. In front of the glass wherein the French admired their beautifiction, stood a small table, covered with a cloth; the word for the cloth gradually was transferred to the table, then to the entire process of preparing oneself there. Hence, our *toilet.*

token.
See teach.

tome.
See anatomy.

tongue.
We use the word *tongue* to mean *language;* but at first *language* meant the same thing: via Fr. *langage* it comes from Fr. *langue,* OFr. *lengue,* from L. *lingua, tongue;* whence also *linguistics.* But there is also an etymological relationship; for *lingua* is for earlier *dingua,* akin to the root *dig—, dic—,* to speak; *cp. verdict;* and *tongue* is from a cognate OTeut. form *tungon.*
The spelling of *tongue* is a learned error; from OE. *tunge* we should have the spelling *tung,* as in *lung;* to keep the *g* hard before *e,* the letter *u* might be inserted; but the final *e* was already silent; but out of a dozen spellings (*tonge, tunge, tounge, toong,* etc.) what survived is on everyone's *tongue.*

tonsil.
See pylorus.

tonsilitis.
See subjugate.

tonsillectome, tonsillectomy.
See anatomy.

tooth.
See indenture.

toothsome.
See awry.

top.
This is a common Teut. word, AS. *top,* ON. *toppr,* tuft of hair. Apparently the *topknot* was a favorite excrescence of primitives on several continents; whence the Chinese pigtail and the Indian *scalping.* (*Scalp* first meant skull; it is short for *scallop,* a shell-shaped vessel.) The spinning *top* is from Du. *top,* G. *Topf,* pot, the hollow kind that hums as it spins. To sleep like a *top,* however, has no relation to the end of the spinning, but is from Fr. *taupe,* mole—a quite appropriate figure.

topaz.
See carnelian.

toper.
See toast.

topic, topography.
See evangelist.

torch.
Twisted tow, lighted on a stick, gave a fairly lengthy if unsteady illumination. Hence the *torch* (Fr. *torche,* from OIt. *torchio,* from LL. *torculum,* a little twist, from *torquere, tort—,* to twist). Similarly *torchon* (from the Fr.), a duster or dishcloth, is from *torcher,* to wipe, from *torche,* a bunch of twisted straw.

Many words spring from this source. *Torture* (Fr., from L. *tortura*) was usually applied by twisting the limbs or body. *Tortuous* and *torsion* come directly; roundabout—perhaps from the shape of the feet, perhaps by later assimilation—comes *tortoise.* To *extort* (L. *ex,* out) is to twist out of a person; to *distort* (L. *dis,* away) and to *contort* (L. *con, com,* together) indicate different ways of misshaping; the first is now used of ideas, the second, of the features. A *retort* is a remark twisted right back; physically, a glass with the neck bent back (LL. *retorta*). By way of a LL. *torquementum* comes *tormentum,* whence Eng. *torment,* a stone-hurling engine of war that worked by *torsion;* hence, a similarly operated instrument of *torture;* from the machine the word was applied to its consequence—just as *torture* may refer to the operation or the resultant anguish. *Tornado,* the whirling storm, is by way of the Sp. *tornar,* to turn; but it may be from, or influenced by, Sp. *tronada,* thunderstorm, from Sp. *tronar,* to *thunder,* from L. *tonare;* akin to AS. *Thor,* whence *Thursday; Thor's Day;* Eng. *thunder,* from AS. *thunor;* ON. *thorr,* whence *Thor;* ultimately Sansk. *tan,* an imitative word, to resound. The legal *tort* is likewise from *tortus,* twisted; also the edible *torta,* later *tart,* the dough being twisted together. The *torso,* however, should not be twisted; it is from L. *thyrsus,* from Gr. *thyrsos,* stalk, stem, staff. *Thyrsus* is the staff borne in the revels of Dionysus. Which well might extinguish a *torch!*

toreador.
See Europe. (Sp. *torear,* from Sp. *toro,* bull, from L. *taurus*).

torment, tornado.
See torch.

torrent.
The roaring, boiling rush of a swollen stream may indicate the origin of the word (L. *torrere,* to burn; present participle *torrens, torrent—,* boiling). Hence we may also have a very *torrent* of words. The adj. from this verb (L. *torridus*) gives us the name for the ***torrid* zone.** Note also that in Scotland, though now of a milder flow, the word for stream is *burn.*

torrid.
See torrent.

torsion, tort, tortoise, tortuous, torture.
See torch.

tory.
This term for a conservative originally meant a hunter (Ir. *toraighe,* pursuer, from *toir,* to pursue). It was applied to the 17th c. dispossessed Irish, who lived by plundering the English in Ireland. Then it was applied to any Irish Royalist or Papist; later, to the English that opposed the exclusion of James (a Catholic) from the throne. In 1689 it became the name of one of the two great political parties of England, which grew from the Cavalier anti-exclusionists. In the early 19th c. the term Conservative replaced it, but (without the capital T) it remains a term for a dyed-in-the-wool conservative. The 17th c. Scots that marched on Edinburgh were called Whiggamores; this, shortened to Whig, was applied to the Exclusionists. It became the name of the other English political party, but has never become a common noun, being displaced by liberal; *cp. liberty.*

tortoise.
See turtle.

total, totalitarian.
See tout.

totem.
This word is from Algonkin *aoutom,* sign of the tribe—the *t* being the last sound of the possessive: "our tribal charm." The *totem-pole* is usually crowned with the tribal forebear. This North American Indian word, bringing not disaster but victory, is thus the opposite of the South Seas word *taboo,*

q.v. Usually the *totem* was an animal (from which the tribe may claim descent, as the Greeks from the gods; thus there were animal gods); we see relics of this belief widespread in the stories of animals friendly to men: throughout the *Arabian Nights; Puss In Boots; The Frog Prince.* Snakes helped the "father of medicine", Aesculapius, whom angry Zeus slew by lightning; and those to whom the *Bible* is not a holy book may deem similarly helpful the snake that taught man to eat of the tree of knowledge. The Mohammedan admits ten animals into Paradise: Jonah's whale; Solomon's ant; the ram Abraham sacrificed instead of his son Isaac; Belkis' cuckoo; the prophet Saleh's camel; Balaam's ass; Moses' ox; the dog of the Seven Sleepers; Noah's dove; Mohammed's ass.

touch.
When you knock on a door, the sound resembles *toc, toc.* From this came It. *toccare* (Sp. and Port. *tocar*) OFr. *tuchier,* whence Fr. *toucher,* and all the meanings of our Eng. *touch.* The music term *toccata* is from the same word; while *tocsin* (Prov. *tocasenh*) is the same *toc* + L. *signum,* a *sign,* alarm, bell. *Toco,* slang for corporal punishment, certainly implies a *touch!* For the meaning *touched,* foolish, *see silly. Cp. win.*

touchy.
This word is not related to *touch, q.v.,* although influenced by its spelling and meaning. It was earlier *tetchy,* from OFr. *entechié,* conditioned, from *teche,* characteristic. The Fr. word developed a pejorative implication, of bad condition; hence Fr. *tache,* blemish. This meaning in the Eng. word has been almost overpowered by the suggestion of sensitivity, from *touch.*

tournament, tourney.
See attorney.

tousle.
See heckle.

tout.
The racetrack *tout* is not one that knows everything: Fr. *tout,* all, from L. *totus, totalis,* whence Eng. *total* and *totalitarian.* He was first a spy (ME. *tuten,* from AS. *totian,* to peep, to watch for). He watched all the horses before a race; hence, he could advise, then solicit bets etc.

tow.
See duke, win.

town.
See villain.

Towser.
See heckle.

toxic, toxin.
See intoxicate.

trace, track.
See train.

tract.
See distraction.

tractable.
See mean.

tractate, tractor.
See distraction.

tradition.
See shark.

tragedy.
See buck.

trail.
See train.

train.
From L. *trahere, tract—,* to draw, comes a group of related words; *cp. distraction.* Thus L. *tractus,* a drawing, a succession of moving things, passed through It. *tracciare* and Fr. *tracer* to Eng. *trace.* Possibly from the cognate Teut. forms, via. OHG. *trek,* a pulling, or a line drawn—but probably more directly from Fr. *trac*—comes Eng. *track.* (Note that we also speak of a *trek,* from the Du. *trekken,* to draw, to journey by ox-team). A LL. diminutive of L. *traha,* draw-sledge, was *tragula;* whence via OFr. *traille,* Eng. *trail.* And a different diminutive from the same L. was OFr. *trahine,* whence our Eng. *train.*

Train first meant delay, dragging along; then was applied to something dragged along, as a bird's plumage, or the *train* of a dress; then to a group of persons or vehicles moving one after the other, as later to a railway *train;* and figuratively, as to a flood that brings a fire in its *train.* One *train,* now unfortunately obsolete, was a succession of coated dates, figs, raisins and almonds strung on a thread. But from drawing things out, one after the other (so that by the process one may become adept) we have the various forms of *training* . . . Perhaps another form of the basic root remains in the girls that go *traipsing* around (earlier *trape* and *trapes*, now *traipse*).

traipse.
See train.

traitor.
See shark.

trajectory.
See subject.

trammel.
Used now mainly as a verb, this word was first a noun, meaning a net; hence, anything that tangles or hinders. It is a common word, applied both in snaring birds and in netting fishes, from It. *tramaglio*, from LL. *tremacula*, from *ter, tri*, thrice + *macula*, spot. There are two suggestions: that the net was made of three layers of cloth; or (more plausibly) that there were three "spots", or bright pieces of cloth, tied on to attract the fishes. L. *macula* is seen in Eng. *immaculate; cp. mail.*

tramp, trample.
See cram.

trance.
This was once a much more dreadful word. L. *transire*, from *trans*, across + *ire*, to go—whence Eng. *transition, transitive, transitory*—was used of the crossing from life to death: OFr. *transe*, deathly anxiety. Its compound, *entrance*, to hold in a *trance*, has become more pleasant still. It must not be confused with the n. *entrance*, which is from Fr. *entrer*, from L. *in* (*t*), into + *ire*, to go in, to *enter*.
Several other words have undergone similar melioration. *Enchant* is, by way of Fr. *enchanter* (L. *in*, against + *cantare*, to chant, from *canere*, to sing), originally of the same evil intent as an *incantation*. *Charm* (Fr. *charme*, from L. *carmen*, song, from *canmen*, from *canere*, to sing) was also originally an *incantation;* we still have *charms* against evils—chief among them a beauteous lady's *charm! Enthrall* (*thrall*, from ON. *thraell;* OHG. *dregil*, servant, runner; AS. *thraegan*, to run) meant literally to enslave. A *bewitching* creature, now admired, might in earlier days have been burned at the stake. (*Witch*, from AS. *wicca*, is cognate with G. *weihs*, holy, from *weihen*, to consecrate; and with L. *victima*, sacrificial creature, from *vincere, vict—*, to conquer; hence, *victor, victim; victory* •••—).

transcribe.
See shrine.

transfer.
See suffer.

transfusion.
See futile.

transgress.
See issue, trespass.

transition, transitive, transitory.
See trance.

translation.
See suffer.

transmutation.
See immunity.

transpire.
See inspiration.

trapeze, trapezoid.
See kaleidoscope.

treacle.
The Eng. word *deer* (originally any wild animal; *King Lear* III,iv,144, has "rats, and mice, and such small deer") is old, with widespread cognates: OHG. *tior*, whence G. *tier;* L. *fera;* Gr. *ther*, game, whence *therion*, wild animal. From the L. *fera*, wild animal, come *ferocious* and (via OFr. *fers, fiers*) *fierce*.
The Gr. *theriaka pharmaka*, medicines against wild beasts (Eng. *pharmacy*, etc.) was shortened to L. *theriaca*, whence OFr. *triacle*. As these antidotes were usually syrups, the word came to mean any syrup; esp., in Eng. *treacle*, the syrup drained in the process of making sugar, sometimes now used figuratively of oversweet or of slow and sticky things. (*Pharmakon*, plural *pharmaka*, drug, is probably from Gr. *pharein, pherein*, to bear: bringing help; *cp. focus.*) Also *see beast*.

treason.
See shark.

treasure.
That which you *treasure*, you seek to preserve. The root of this word is Aryan, *dha*, to place. It appears in Gr.

as *thesauros,* whence L. *thesaurus* (whence the Eng. doublet, *thesaurus,* as in Roget's standard work), whence It. *tesoro,* whence Fr. *tresor,* whence Eng. *treasure. Treasury,* by the way, is a shortening of earlier *treasurery.*

tree.
See pay.

trek.
See train.

tremble, tremendous, tremor.
See delirium.

trench, trenchant, trencher, trencherman.
See retrench.

trepidation.
See terse.

trespass.
This word is via OFr. *trepasser* from LL. *transpassare,* from *trans,* across, + *passare, passat—,* to *pass,* from L. *passus,* step, from L. *pandere, pass—,* to stretch. A *passage* (same in Fr.) was first the act of going by, then also the place along which one went, thus short for *passageway; cp. pass.*

The different tongues have differently handled the L. word *transpassare.* Thus in Fr. *trépasser* means to *pass across* into the next world; whereas in Eng. to *trespass* is to *transgress,* to *pass across* the bounds of permitted behavior. (This may be a natural consequence of Catholic France' concern for the next world, and Puritan England's worry about the present world. Note—*cp. issue*—that *transgress* has taken the same course, as though we were indeed a sin-conscious people!)

trial.
See try. (OFr. noun form, *trial, triel,* from *trier*).

triangle, tribal, tribe.
See tribulation.

tribulation.
The Romans ground out their corn with a heavy roller, mentioned in Vergil's *Georgics* among agricultural instruments: the *tribulum,* diminutive noun, from *tritere, trit—,* to rub, from Gr. *tribein,* to rub. Being ground under and pressed out made an excellent metaphor to express the trials and *tribulations* of the early Christians. In the literal sense, we have the word *trituration;* from the same source, *attrition; nutrition* is from another source, L. *nutrire, nutrit—,* to *nourish* (*nourish* is via Fr. *nourrir, nourris—,* from L. *nutrire*). A thing rubbed down by constant use is *trite; cp. terse.* A *diatribe* is a rubbing through (Gr. *dia,* through, as in *diaphanous,* showing through; *cp. focus*) or a wearing through, applied by the Greeks to the wearing through of time in endless talk. From the frequent lengthy *philippics* (first, by Demosthenes against *Philip of Macedon*), *diatribe* came to mean a violent attack.

The origin of *tribe,* L. *tribus,* is unknown. It is probably not from many persons "rubbing shoulders" (Gr. *tribos,* rubbing). The L. prefix *tri—,* three (as in *triangle,* L. *angulus,* corner) has been suggested, + a root of the L. verb to be, *fu—* (Gr. *fyle*); the word was applied to the three groups of early Romans. Hence, the protector of the "commons" group was L. *tribunis,* whence Eng. *tribune* and *tribunal.* The money assigned (to the *tribe,* or for the *tribe* to pay) was *tribute;* hence, *tributary.* Hence also *attribute,* to assign to; *contribute,* to pay together (L. *con,* from *com,* together); *distribute* (L. *dis,* away, apart); and *retribution,* paying back (L. *re,* back). *Retribution,* indeed, often brings on *tribulation. See termite.*

tribunal, tribune, tributary, tribute.
See tribulation.

trickster.
See spinster.

trident.
See indenture.

trifle.
This word, which first meant a false story (ME. *trufle,* from OFr. *trufe,* tall tale) came to its present meaning by association with the unrelated *trivial* (L. *tri,* three + *via,* way, road. Crossroads being a place where news is exchanged, and most news being unimportant gossip, the adj. from L. *trivium,* a junction of roads, came to its sense today; although Brewer suggests *trivial* is from *trit—,* rubbed, worn; *cp. tribulation*). *Trifle* is probably the same word as *truffle* (OFr. *trufe,* from L. *tubera,* plural of *tuber,* a swelling, whence diminutive *tubercle,* whence *tuberculosis.* This is cognate with L. *tu-*

mere, to swell, which gives us a number of Eng. words: *tumult,* the swell of sound; *tumulus,* a little swell of ground; *tumescent, tumid, tumor.*)

From L. *via,* way, come not only the Eng. direction *via,* but *viaduct,* and *viaticum,* which provides the way either in this world, or to the next.

triplet.
See quintessence.

triskele, triskelion.
See fylfot.

trite.
See terse.

trituration.
See tribulation.

triumph.
See trump.

trivial.
See trifle.

trochaic.
See troche.

troche.
Here is another word (*cp. apostrophe*) that comes by two paths and two pronunciations from one source, back into one word. The lozenge (pronounced as one syllable in England) is from Fr. *trochisque,* from Gr. *trochiskos,* globule, diminutive of *trochos,* wheel, from *trechein,* to run. The *trochaic* meter is from the same root, but via the Gr. adjective *trochaikos,* which properly leaves two syllables in Eng. There is also the "pick-and-run" bird, the *trochilus,* fabled to clean the crocodile's teeth. *See* helicopter.

trochilus.
See troche.

trope.
See trophy.

trophy.
A *trophy* was originally a monument erected where an enemy was turned back. Gr. *trepein,* to turn, whence *trope,* turning, defeat, whence *tropaion,* putting to flight, whence L. *trophaeum,* whence Fr. *trophée.* As soldiers carried home mementos taken from the stricken foe, the term enlarged its meaning.

A *trope,* figure of speech, is a turning of a word from its literal sense. The *tropic* region is that in which the sun turns after the *solstice* (L. *solstitium,* from *sol,* sun + *sistere,* to stand).

The Gr. *helios,* sun, gives us the *heliotrope,* flower that turns to the sun. Gr. *trepein,* to turn, should be distinguished from Gr. *trephein,* to nourish; in Eng. this exists in scientific compounds of *troph—,* e.g. *trophoblast;* and with the negative (Gr. *a—,* not) in *atrophy,* to waste away. The poison *atropine* (used in the *tropics* as a preventive of malaria, esp. by the United Nations in World War II when quinine was unobtainable) is named from the flower *atropa* (the deadly nightside), turning from the light (L. *a—,* away); though perhaps to be traced to *Atropos,* one of the three Fates, the Unturning, the Inflexible One.

Those interested in aviation will note that one range of the *atmosphere* (Gr. *atmos,* vapor) is the *troposphere,* where there are convective (turning) disturbances; it is below the *stratosphere* (L. *sternere, strat—,* to spread; whence Eng. *stratum,* layer) which appears almost as one layer, since the temperature scarcely changes with the height. *Sphere* is via Fr. from Gr. *sphaira,* ball; Gr. *speira,* winding, gives us Eng. *spiral;* but the church *spire* is a later sense (from the shape) of AS. *spir,* long blade of grass, related to *spar* and *spear,* for which *see affluent.* To *aspire,* however, was first to breathe upon (much the same as *inspire, inspiration, q.v.*) then to breathe toward, seek to reach, from L. *ad,* to + *spirare, spirat—,* to breathe—whence also the *spirit,* L. *spiritus,* originally the breath of life or animating principle in each of us. The various meanings of *spirit* follow from this, as the evil *spirit* that directs a person, the *spirits* summoned by a *spiritualist.* Hence also the use as the basic principle or essence of anything; as the four *spirits* of the medieval alchemists. These were quicksilver (mercury), orpiment (yellow arsenic), sal ammoniac, and brimstone (sulphur). Hence, too, *spirits* of turpentine, and animal *spirits* more exuberant with alcoholic *spirits.* Note that *spiritual* is reserved for more ethereal aspects; *spirituous* (*cp. supercilious*) for the more earthy.

tropic, troposphere.
See trophy.

trouble.
When things get all whirled around,

"all balled up", you're in *trouble,* from OFr. *torbler,* from LL. *turbulare,* frequentative of *turbare,* to twist about, to whirl (whence *turbulent; turbine; disturb*: L. *dis,* apart), from *turba,* whirl, disorder, mob. *Cp. torch; butt.* To be *perturbed* (L. *per,* through) is to be thoroughly twisted. Then you're in *trouble* indeed!

trounce.
See retrench.

trousers.
See bloomers.

trudgen.
See Appendix II.

true.
See pay.

truffle.
See trifle.

trump, trumpery, trumpet.
There is seldom a connection between the *trump* of doom and the *trump* in cards. The former is short for *trumpet,* from OHG. *trumba,* an imitative word, like *drum* and *rhumba.* The latter is short for *triumph,* from L. *triumphus,* from Gr. *thriambos,* hymn to Bacchus; the card game was called *triomphe* in French. However honest the English, it is interesting that from Fr. *trompe* came *tromper,* to cheat, whence *tromperie,* cheating; whence Eng. *trumpery;* also, from *to trump,* to go one better, the sense of *to trump up,* to devise a cheat.

truncate, trunk.
See poltroon, branch.

truth.
See pontiff.

try.
The form of this word suggests a Romance origin, but its source is unknown. One guess is a LL. *tritare,* to thresh, to grind out, from L. *terere, trit,* to rub; *cp. tribulation.* Another would trace it to Fr. *tirer,* to draw, in the sense of drawing out, testing.
The first use of *try* in Eng. was in the sense of distinguishing among things; then, to separate the good from the bad, as metal from ore—hence, to purify by fire. Thence, to search out, to *try out,* to discover the truth of a matter. From this it is but a step to putting a man on *trial;* this sense developed in England by 1300. Since tests and *trials* are often arduous, there came the sense as in "If at first you don't succeed . . . " and then to *try* your patience.

Tsar.
See shed.

T-square.
See square.

tuberculosis.
See tuberose.

tuberose.
This once was three syllables; mistaken association with the *rose* changed the sound. The word is from L. *tuber,* swelling, + *osus,* full of; usually this changes in Eng. to *—ous,* as in *courageous; cp. supercilious;* but the name of the flower comes directly from L. *tuberosa* (feminine of *tuberosus*). There is also an Eng. *tuberous; tuber* is likewise used as an Eng. word, for the potato, the dahlia bulb, and the like.
The diminutive of *tuber* is L. *tuberculum,* whence Eng. *tubercle;* and a person full of little *tubers* has *tuberculosis. Cp. primrose.*
The *dahlia* was named after Anders *Dahl,* an 18th c. Swedish botanist, pupil of Linnaeus.

tuck.
See win.

Tuesday.
See week.

tuffet.
See tuft.

tuft.
This word is from OFr. *touffe,* a bunch of small things, leaves, feathers, hair. The *t* is an Eng. addition, as with *graph, graft; draff, draft,* etc.
Until about 1880, *tuft* was applied to the gold tassel worn by titled undergraduates at Oxford and Cambridge; hence, a *tuft-hunter* is one seeking to win the favor of a celebrity (somewhat as the American Indians sought *scalps.* To *scalp* the market is to take almost one's very life; i.e., to buy cheap and sell dear; hence, the theatrical *ticket-scalper.*).
Little Miss Muffet sat on a diminutive *tuft,* a *tuffet.*
Scalp is a contraction of *scallop,* shell-shaped bowl, hence skull, from AS. *scealu,*

cup, whence also Eng. *scale; cp. echelon.* The transfer of meaning came with the translation of the 68th *Psalm* (21): "But God shall wound the head of his enemies, and the *hairy scalp* of such an one that goeth on still in his trespasses."

tug.
See duke, team, win.

tumor, tumult.
See palm, trifle.

tungsten.
See element.

turbine.
See trouble.

turbot.
See butt.

turbulence.
See butter.

turbulent.
See trouble.

tureen.
See terrier.

turkey.
What we now call by this name is native to the new world. The *guinea-fowl,* known to the ancient Greeks as *meleagris* (this is still the technical name of the American genus) was brought into Europe through *Turkey,* hence called the *turkey* or the *turkey-cock.* The American bird was thought to be a species of this bird; when the difference was discovered, the word *guinea-fowl* (so called because brought by the Portuguese from *Guinea* in Africa) was kept for the old-world bird, and the *turkey* was transferred to the Thanksgiving table.

turmeric.
This root (of an East Indian, or by extension other, plant) or the powder made thereof, deserves its name. With the final letter changed to *c* by analogy with more familiar words, it is from Fr. *terre merite,* worthy earth. Properly applied, it is the chief ingredient in a flavorous *curry.* The dish *curry* is from Tamil *kari,* sauce; and indeed in many dishes the most important element is the sauce.

To *curry* a horse is from OFr. *correier,* earlier *conreder,* from LL. *con,* together + *redare,* to put in order; but the root *red—* is Teut.; it is seen also in *array* (L. *ad,* to, for a purpose), and through Goth. *garaiths* gave AS. *geraede,* whence Eng. *ready.* To *curry favor* is folk etymology; the original expression was to *curry favel. Favel* (from OFr. *fauvel,* from a Teut. stem *falwo—,* whence Eng. *fallow,* the color—*fallow* land is influenced by this, from the color of earth turned up and left to lie; but is from AS. *fealg,* a harrow; MHG. *valgen,* to dig) was used as the name of a horse, esp. of one in medieval allegory as a type of cunning hypocrisy. Note that *fawn,* as a color, is short for *fawn-color;* the word (from OFr. *faon, feon,* from a LL. form *fetonem,* is from L. *fetus,* incorrectly *foetus,* offspring) first meant the young of any animal, then (as deer changed from meaning animals in general to a special kind) the young of the deer. And *to fawn* (just as *fetus* is related to *felix, felic—,* happy; whence *felicity* and *felicitations*) is related to AS. *fahnian,* to rejoice, a variant of *faegnian,* from *faegn,* glad, whence Eng. *fain.* Cubs seem always happy, playful creatures. The sense of *fawning, to curry favor,* is from the way in which animals wag the tail, and lick the hand of their beloved master . . . Absent thee from *felicity* awhile.

turn.
This word, though early in Eng., is not Teut. but Romance. The noun is via OFr. *tourn, torn,* from L. *tornus,* from Gr. *tornos,* a turning-lathe. The verb appeared in Eng. by the 7th c., OE. *tyrnan* and *turnian,* from L. *tornare,* to turn. We often speak of *twisting* and *turning;* the ideas are related, so are the Latin words: the root is *tor—; see torch.*

Eng. *twist* is akin to Eng. *twine; cp. prestige.* The stem, however, had two courses: Du. *twisten,* to disagree; Icel. *tvistra,* to scatter; and Flemish *twisten,* to twine. Thus the Eng. *twist* first meant to divide—but one always divides the hairs into separate groups before entwining them in a braid; hence the word was very soon used of *twisting* things together. From this, the more general use arose, of wringing or *twisting* out of shape; figuratively, e.g., *twisting* a phrase from its original meaning.

The N E D lists 41 separate meanings of the noun *turn;* and 80 major meanings (some with 25 or 26 subdivisions) of the verb. They all spin from the original sense of rotary movement. You gave me such a *turn!* e.g., implies the spinning head from sudden shock; a clever *turn,* in the sense of trick, comes from the literal *turn* of the wrestler seeking a throw. Other special meanings *turn* upon the same basic sense.

There is a vegetable called the *neep,* from OE. *naep* from L. *napus;* when pulled from the ground (like a beet), it looks as though it had been spun; hence, it is most commonly called the *turnip.*

See attorney.

turncoat.

A *turntail* is one that gives you the view of his back side, *i.e.,* runs away. A *turncoat* is one that readily changes his alliance. The story is told, among others, of a Duke of Saxony with holdings between France and Spain, and of Emmanuel, an early Duke of Savoy between France and Italy, that he had a coat made with the colors of one country on one side and those of the other on the other, so that he might wear, outside, the color of the country he wished at the moment to favor.

turnip.

See turn. One large *variety,* brought to England from *Sweden* about 1780, was called the *Swedish turnip;* now the *swede.*

turntail.

See turncoat.

turtle.

When the voice of the *turtle* is heard in the land, it is springtime; and you hear the cooing of the *turtle-dove.* The word is from AS. *turtla,* masculine, *turtle,* feminine, a diminutive or dissimilated form of L. *turtur*—which *turtur* was once used in Eng. also—an echoic word from the sound of the cooing. Eng. *turturring* has been used of the sound.

The word *turtle* (as also *dove*) is frequently applied to persons as a term of endearment, the bird being long used as a symbol of constancy and devotion. Perhaps because they also were frequently found in pairs (but also from the sound) the *tortoises* (earlier *tortose, tortuce,* from Fr. *tortue,* from LL. *tortuca;* possibly from the twisted legs; *cp. torch;* but perhaps from a native name) were given by sailors the now more common name of *turtle.* If we omit the word *dove,* today we think first of the *sea-turtle. Dove* (perhaps from *dive,* from the nature of its flight) is not found in early Eng. or AS., but is common Teut. *Dive* is from OE. *dufan,* to duck. or OE. *dyfan,* to dip, related to OE. *dyppan* whence *dip* and *deep.* Sometimes this gets too *deep!*

Because of the dialect *turkle,* variation of *turtle,* it is suggested that the word is influenced by the long, tough neck the *turtle* has in common with the *turkey.*

tussle.

See heckle.

tuxedo.

When you wear a tuxedo, you really are a wolf. The word is from Algonkin *p'tuksit,* round-footed, applied in scorn to the *Wolf Tribe* of the Delaware Indians, in Orange County, New York. After them were named *Tuxedo Lake* and *Tuxedo Park;* taken by the Lorillard family in settlement of a bad debt, in the early 19th c., this became a pleasure resort for the wealthy. In the 1880's, the *Tuxedo Club* was established; from this, the tailless dinner jacket (worn first by Griswold Lorillard) wears its name.

twain.

See number.

tweed.

See cloth.

tweedledum and tweedledee.

See crater.

twelve, twenty.

See number.

twice.

See number, prestige.

twig.

See branch.

twill.

See cloth.

twin, twine.

See prestige.

twist.

See turn.

twitter.

See chatter.

two.

See number, prestige.

tycoon.

This word, popularized by *Time* magazine for a business magnate (L. *magnus,* great) is Jap. *taikun,* from Chin. *ta,* great + *kiun,* prince.

Typhoon has a double story. There is the Chin. *ta,* great + *fung,* from *feng,* wind. But there is also the Arab. *tufan,* hurricane, from Gr. *typhon,* whirlwind. *Typhon,* a giant and father of the winds, was buried by the gods under Mt. Etna; *cp. atlas.*

These two (the Gr. coming through the Arab. via Urdu) merged in the present *typhoon,* which might blow many things together. The god of the winds, among the Romans (*Aeneid,* I,52) was *Aeolus,* from whom the *Aeolian* harp.

type.

This widely used word first meant that which was struck, from Gr. *typtein,* to strike. But very early, Gr. *typos* was used of that which was "struck off", a representation of an object; hence a symbol or general representation of a class or group. Hence, of course, the later application to the printed characters and to the figures from which they are struck, as on the *typewriter* and in all the concerns of *typography* (Gr. *graphein,* to write). The earlier meaning has continued, along with the newer applications; and the earlier sense alone is seen in such forms as *typical* and *typify.*

typhoon.

See tycoon.

typhus.

This word, from Gr. *typhos,* smoke, vapor, vanity, conceit, was used in early Eng. from LL. *typhus,* to mean pride. Dropped in the 17th c., it was revived (or taken afresh from the Gr.) at the end of the 18th c. to mean a fever that clouded the mind. The more familiar *typhoid* fever simply means, like *typhus;* it was long supposed to be a form of the other disease; but it is now more accurately called *enteric* fever—*enteric,* from Gr. *enterikos,* from *enteron,* intestine, "inner"; *cp. dysentery.*

typical.

See type.

tyrant.

See hold, sempiternal.

tyre, Tyrian.

The word *tyre* has more senses than letters. Used interchangeably with the *tire* of a wheel, in the 15th and 16th c., it was revived in that sense, in England, for the automobile *tire.* It was the name of a Syrian snake, *tyre,* from which was drawn an extract of supposedly great medicinal power, *tryacle*—perhaps confused with *treacle, q.v.* From the reptile, "an adder full of scales," the word *tyre* was applied to a scaly leprosy. More pleasantly, from *Tyre,* a Phoenician city, the word *tyre* was applied to a cloth there made, also to a wine. As an adjective, *Tyrian* dye; this was so valued for its royal purple that the word *Tyrian* alone came to be used for the color. There is a mineral called *Tyrite,* but from the Norse god *Tyr.* Before you *tire, see tire.*

U

ubiquitous.

The L. *ibi* meant there, *ubi* meant where. The enclitic —*que,* which usually meant and, here has an intensive force: "and here and here and here"; so that *ubique* meant everywhere. The noun L. *ubiquitas* gives us Eng. *ubiquity*. The adjective was *ubiquitarius,* which produced the early Eng. *ubiquitary;* but this was emphasized by the ending L. —*osus,* full of, Eng. —*ous; cp. supercilious;* so that now such things are *ubiquitous.*

ugly.

A pious soul may call someone "*ugly* as sin"; a superstitious one need not say "*ugly* as a goblin", for the word itself says that: *ugly* is from *oughlic,* from AS. *ough,* goblin + *lic,* like. It is closely allied with ON. *uggr,* fear; also with *ugh,* the instinctive expulsion of disgust.

ulterior, ultimatum.

See penult.

ultraism, ultramarine.

See lapis lazuli.

ultraviolet.

See under.

umber.

See umbrage.

umbrage.

We are told that once Alexander the Great stood before Diogenes—you remember, the man that lived in a barrel, and carried a lamp by daylight, seeking an honest man. Alexander told Diogenes he might have whatever he desired; the sage apparently took *umbrage* at the remark, for he asked the great monarch to step out of his light. L. *umbra,* shadow; hence, shadow of suspicion, etc. From it we also have the color *umber;* and poets have spoken of *umbrageous* groves.

umbrella.

See overture.

umpire.

See auction.

uncle.

L. *avus,* ancestor, was used specifically of the grandfather; thence L. *atavus,* short for *quatavus,* was the fourth (L. *quattuor,* four) back from the grandfather, the great-great-great grandfather. This became the general word for remote ancestry; hence, Eng. *atavism,* throwback.

A diminutive of *avus* was *avunculus,* applied first to a mother's brother. This through Prov. *avoncle, aoncle,* became OFr. *oncle* and Eng. *uncle*—now applied to a mother's or a father's brother or brother-in-law, and loosely to elderly men and the pawnbroker. The last use may be from the L. *uncus,* hook, with which the pawnbroker put up the articles; but is more probably a euphemistic explanation of the new supply of money: "I got it from my *uncle.*" Also *see Dutch; Uncle Sam.*

The diminutive L. —*unculus,* Eng. —*uncle,* survives in *homunculus* (L. *homo,* man; the adjective *humanus* gives us *human, humanity*) and *carbuncle* (L. *carbo*—, coal; *cp. ajar*); a red stone; then, a reddish pimple. Similarly Eng. *anthrax,* from Gr. *anthrax, anthrac*—, coal, meant a ruddy boil, then a fever with that sort of eruption; while Eng. *anthracite* still means hard coal. There are other such words, as *peduncle* (L. *pes, ped*—, foot). More directly than the relative, there comes from the L. his manner, which (esp. when he's being *Dutch*) may be truly *avuncular.* In the word *uncle* itself, only the diminutive remains.

From L. *uncus,* hook, through the adjective L. *uncinus,* comes Eng. *uncinate,* used in biology. The L. *uncia,* meaning one-twelfth of a pound or of a foot, produced more common Eng. words. St. Jerome used it (*unciales litterae*) to describe the large, round, separate letter of early classical manuscripts; hence, Eng. *uncial.* But by way of AS. *ynce, ince,* it gives us Eng. *inch,* one-twelfth of a foot; and more directly it gives us Eng. *ounce,* one-twelfth of a pound (Troy). The same L. *uncia,* meaning the animal the *ounce,* is probably from the native Asiatic name, Pers. *yuz.*

Uncle Sam.
See Yankee.

uncouth.
The tendency to laugh at, to despise (or fear) things unfamiliar, is one of the most deep-rooted in mankind. It has shaped the meaning of many words (*cp. pagan; remorse*).

Thus, anything unknown was deemed rude, *uncouth,* from AS. *uncuth,* unknown, from *un,* not + *cunnan, cuth,* to know. Similarly, *outlandish* first meant merely foreign, from AS. *utland,* out land; and *strange* is from OFr. *estrange,* from L. *extraneus,* from *extra,* outside. Without the emotional implications, the same word gives us *extraneous.* In much the same way, *lewd* reached its present meaning from the original sense of ignorant, unlettered, from AS. *laewede,* layman, probably from L. *laicus,* not a cleric. And a *wanton* is one untaught, from ME. *wantowen,* from *wan,* not + *towen,* trained, from *teon,* to draw out, to educate. (Thus the archaic Eng. *wanhope* means despair. *Cp. win.*)

Possibly related to AS. *wan,* lacking, is AS. *wann,* lacking color; this first meant black (absence of color), then pale; hence, Eng. *wan.*

unction, unctuous.
See lotion, propaganda.

under.
See overture. AS. *under* meant both beneath (L. *infra,* whence the *infernal* regions, Dante's *Inferno; inferior*) and among, between (L. *inter,* whence *intercede*: *cedere, cess,* to go; *international; interest*: from *interesse; sum, esse,* to be, + *inter*: to be concerned). The L. forms are cognate with the common Teut. word: G. *unter;* Du. *onder;* ON. *undir.* The L. *infra dig* is short for *infra dignitate,* beneath one's *dignity.* Light ranges from *infrared* to *ultraviolet.*

under—.
This very common Eng. prefix has several linked senses. First, physical position below: *undercurrent; undermine,* now also figuratively. Thence, rank below: *under-secretary.* Thence, inferior or deficient status: *underfed; underdog; underclothed* (the first sense remains in *underclothes*); *under-exposed.* With some words (after the 16th c.), it means less than: *underbid, undersell.* In some cases, a secondary sense developed, as though the prefix implied "*under* one's charge": *undertake.* An *undertaker* was one that attempted a project; in the 18th c. a producer of plays was an *undertaker;* from the association of early stores with the church (*cp. stationery*) came the present meaning—not found in the verb.

Note that some words have different senses (developed only by use) according as another word follows, or is prefixed: *understand, stand under; overtake, take over; overlook, look over; upset, set up,* the noun *setup.* Usually the form with the prefix is less literal.

undermine.
See overture.

underskinker.
See luncheon.

understand.
See tank.

undertaker.
See under—.

undulation.
See wash.

uneasy.
See ease.

ungainly.
See again.

unguent.
See lotion; *cp.* propaganda.

union, unique, unity.
See onion.

universe, university.
See college.

unkempt.
See quaint.

unleavened.
See yeast.

unless.
Even our humble connectives have

their stories. The first part of this one was changed by false analogy with *un,* not. It was originally *on less that,* meaning that *on any less basis,* the action given later would have occurred. Thus, "I'll go *unless* I am sick" means, on any less event than illness, I shall go.

unsophisticated.
See. sophisticated.

unspeakable.
See nefarious. *Speak* is common Teut., AS. *specan,* from *sprecan. Speech* is the noun, AS. *spaec,* from *spraec.*

unutterable.
See nefarious. *Utter,* to give *out* (sound) is from the adjective *utter,* meaning *outer,* from AS. *uttera,* comparative of *ut, out.* The superlative survives in *utmost.*

Upanishad.
It is interesting to note that this name of a Sanskrit treatise on God and the basic problems of life suggests the *Bible's Twenty-third Psalm*: to lie down in green pastures, and perhaps Walt Whitman's "loaf, and invite your soul". It is Sansk. *upa,* near, + *ni-shad,* to sit down, lie down.

uranium.
The Gr. *ouranos,* heaven, was also the name of the god of heaven, *Ouranos* (L. *Uranus*), husband of *Gaea* (heaven and earth: Gr. *ge,* earth, whence Eng. *geometry; cp. sarcophagus*). Urania was the Muse of astronomy. The planets have been given names of classical deities; on March 13, 1781 William Herschel in England noted the first planet to be discovered with the telescope; it was ultimately called *Uranus.* When a new element was discovered (Klaproth, 1789) in pitchblende, it was called *uranium.* It is the last of the elements, number 92 in the atomic system, as *Uranus* was (then) the most remote of the planets. Calculations showed the astronomers that further gravitational pulls were being exerted on the planet; these and *uranoscopy* revealed Neptune in 1846; and, in 1930, Pluto.
See element.

urbanity.
See neighbor.

urchin.
See graft.

urge, urgent.
See sorcerer.

urine.
This word was originally of more general use, from L. *urinare,* to wet, to pass water. The passive form *urinari* meant to be wet, to dive; until the 18th c. *urinator* was used in Eng. to mean diver. Even longer, one meaning of *urinal* was a phial for solutions (in alchemy); the common meaning, however, had also developed in the Latin.

urn.
This may be named from the material, or from the usual contents. It is from L. *urna,* from *urere, ust—,* to burn: baked clay, pottery; but the name grew attached to the particular type of *urn* in which were kept the ashes of the dead. The past form remains in Eng. *combustible, combustion,* burning together.
L. *urere, ust—,* should not be confused with the more *useful* L. *uti, us—;* from this comes *usual, use* and (in addition to the words listed under *usury, q.v.*) *abuse; disabuse,* to cease being *abused,* to wake to the awareness of *misuse; usage.* Eng. *usurp* is from Fr. *usurper,* from L. *usurpare,* a telescope of *usu* + *rapere,* to seize *for use* (or *by use*: possession being nine points of the law).

usage.
See urn.

use.
See usury.

usher.
The *usher* was originally a doorman; then one that stood near the door to show you to your seat; hence, the present use. Earlier Eng. forms were *huisher* and *husher;* the word is from Fr. *huissier,* from Fr. *huis,* door, from LL. *ustium* from L. *ostium,* door. An *ostiary* is still a church-term for a doorkeeper. (The *Ostian* Way led to the harbor of ancient Rome). The word is related to L. *os, or—,* mouth; *cp. inexorable;* but should not be confused with the words from Gr. *osteon,* bone; *cp. ostracize.*
Note also that *ostensible* (though related to showing) is from a different source: L. *ob—.* in the way (*cp. obvious,* with the same sense-growth) + *tendere, tent—* to stretch (*cp. tennis*): something held out to view, as the bathing beauties at *Ostend.* L. *obstendere, ostendere,* developed a frequentative, *ostentare, ostentat—,* to keep showing, whence Eng. *ostentation.*

usual
See urn.

usurp.
See urn.

usury.
The shift in sense is slight, from *using* to *using up.* Thus from L. *utere, us—*, come the *use* that is custom, and *utility;* and the *utensile* (via the adjective from the present participle, L. *utens*); but also *usury,* from L. *usura* (a future tense), the profit from the *use,* for the wear and tear. *Utility* has no original opposition to *futility; see futile;* nor is it (??) related to *uterus,* via L. *uterus,* from Gr. *hystera,* whence Eng. *hysteria, q.v. Fertile* is the adjective form from L. *ferre,* to bear; and that which stays *unfertile* is *sterile,* from L. *sterilis,* from Gr. *steiros,* from Sansk. *stari,* barren cow; Goth. *stairo,* barren woman. (In early days, the cow was more important.) *See urn.*

Utah.
See States.

uterus.
See hysteria, usury.

utility.
See usury.

utmost.
See unutterable.

utopia, utopian.
See evangelist.

uvula.
See pylorus.

V

vacant, vacate, vacation.
See vessel.

vaccinate.
See bachelor.

vacuum.
See vessel. In LL. *vacuum* was popularly replaced by a form *vocitum, voitum,* which through OFr. *vuide, voide,* became Eng. *void.* Thus *vacuum* and *void* are doublets.

The OFr. *esvuider,* to empty out, produced Eng. *avoid,* which first meant to make empty, to make *void.* The adjective *devoid* (from OFr *desvuidier,* later *devider,* whence ? Eng. *divide; see widow, improvised*) has kept the meaning of empty; but by confusion with Fr. *eviter,* to evade (*see wade*), *avoid* shifted to its present meanting. The Fr. *eviter,* from L. *e,* out, + *vitare,* to flee, is represented in Eng. only by the negative adjective *inevitable.* L. *vitare* is probably an intensive of L. *viare, viat—,* to go, from *via,* way. From this comes Eng. *obviate,* to meet on the way; hence, to take care of, dispose of; and L. *obvius,* Eng. *obvious,* what gets in your way, therefore must be seen. Hence also *deviate,* to turn from the way, and *devious,* like this discussion.

vade-mecum.
See wade.

vagabond, vagary, vagrant.
See vague.

vagina.
See vanilla.

vague.
If your mind wanders, things present will be rather *vague;* and *vague* comes from L. *vagus,* wandering. The verb L. *vagari, vagat—,* to wander, gives us Eng. *vagary* and (L. *di, dis,* away) *divagation;* via L. *vagabundus,* in one form *vagamundus* (L. *mundus,* world, whence Eng. *mundane*), Eng. *vagabond.* There is also a form *wagabond,* possibly influenced by the other word, *wander. Wander,* though not in OHG., is elsewhere common Teut., AS. *wandrian,* a frequentative related to OE. *wendan,* whence Eng. *wend. Vagrant* comes by a slightly different path, it seems; from ME. *vagaraunt* from OFr. *waucrant, walcrant,* the present participle of OFr. *walcrer,* to *walk* (*q.v.*)—which *wandered* into the Fr. from the northern tongues. The interrelations of the whole group are rather *vague.*

vain.
This word (from L. *vanus,* empty) and its noun *vanity* (L. *vanitas, vanitat—*) have gone through the same progression of meanings. By the time the word had reached English, the sense had already shifted from empty to (therefore) idle, useless; something of both meanings deepens the cry (*Ecclesiastes* i,2): *Vanity* of *vanities,* saith the Preacher, *vanity* of *vanities;* all is *vanity.* Applied to a person, it clearly must mean foolish, stupid; *cp. silly.* But those without sense are given to complacent self-esteem; hence *Vanity Fair* is frequented by those that are *vain;* and it is *in vain* (idly, to no purpose) that one may seek to lesson them (alas, or lessen them!).

vair.
See incinerator.

valedictory.
See verdict.

valentine.
Won't you be my *Valentine?* On the day of the martyrdom of *St. Valentine,* February 14, it was the playful fashion to pick one's sweetheart for the ensuing year; a delightful habit now lapsed to the sending of pretty or facetious cards. The practice is supposed to have attached itself to that date, as the approximate time of the pairing of birds. But it has also attached itself to the saint. The word is probably a shifting of OFr. *galantine,* a lover, a *gallant,*

from Fr. *galant,* whence Eng. *gallant;* Rabelais speaks of *Viardiere le noble valentin,* meaning *gallant,* from Fr. *galer,* to have a good time, from OHG. *geil,* wanton, whence AS. *gal,* whence Eng. *gala.* It was esp. natural that there should be a shift from *galantine,* for that word had come to mean a fish sauce, from OFr. *galatine,* possibly related to Gr. *gala,* milk; *cp. delight.*

valet.
See varlet.

valid.
See infirmary.

Valkvrie, Walkyrie.
The *Valkyriur* or *Valkyries* were the twelve maidens, servants of *Woden* (whence *Wednesday; cp. week*) or Odin; they bore to Valhalla the warriors who died in battle. The word is from ON. *valkyrja,* from *valr,* slain in battle + *kyrja,* chooser, from *kur,* a stem of *kjosa,* to choose. The *Walkyrie,* the Eng. form (applied early as a translation of the Roman Furies) is earlier *waelcyrie*: *cyrie* from *cur,* a stem of *ceosan,* whence Eng. *choose.*

valor.
See infirmary.

value.
See verdict.

vamoose, vamose.
This word came into our language simply enough, being borrowed along the Mexican border from Sp. *vamos,* let's go. *See vanish.*

vamp.
This is a contraction of ME. *vampey,* from OFr. *avanpié,* from *avant pied,* fore part of foot, applied to that part of the shoe. To *vamp,* also *revamp,* (L. *re,* again) thence means to cobble, to patch up; this sense is applied to a musical accompaniment. Similarly *van* is a shortening of *vanguard,* from Fr. *avantgarde.* In slang use, *vamp* is short for *vampire,* from the Magyar *vampir,* also in Russ. and other Slav. languages. *Cobble,* to mend clumsily, is from *cobble,* lump, stone, diminutive of *cob,* knob, rounded top, from AS. *copp,* akin to *cap,* from AS. *caeppe,* hood, from LL. *cappa,* from ? *capitulare,* head-dress; *cp. achieve.*
From the sense of patching, making something do, *vamp* is used in music of an improvised prelude or accompaniment.

vampire.
See vamp.

van.
See vamp; pan—.

vanadium.
See element.

vandal.
See Dutch.

vandyke (beard).
Sir Anthony Van Dyck, the Flemish painter (1599-1641) dressed his figures in collars with a deeply cut edge; his men wore beards of the same cut. From the English way of spelling his name the fashion in beards, short and pointed, is labelled. The Italian painter Tiziano Vecellio (died 1576) painted a model with "bright golden auburn" hair—which we have extended to red, and—Anglicizing his name, too—call *Titian.*
The full *beard* is common Teut., esp. in names: G. *-bart;* ON. *-barthr;* cognate with L. *barba, cp. barbarian.* Just a touch on the chin is called a *goatee,* as it resembles the beard of the *he-goat.* (The *-ee* is usually a passive or a diminutive ending, as in *bootee,* also *bootie, employee, divorcee, settee.*) A tuft under the lower lip is an *imperial* (*cp. empire*), from the fact that one adorned Napoleon III (1808-73). The hair past both ears along the cheeks is referred to as *burnsides,* from General Ambrose Everett *Burnside* (1824-81), commander of the Army of the Potomac during the War Between the States; sometimes, from their location, these spreads are called *sideburns.* For *moustache* and *whiskers, see whip.*

vanilla.
Now its chief rival, *vanilla* was originally used in England to scent *chocolate*: Mexican *chocolatl,* from *cacao,* the *cacao-tree,* from which the paste was made, whence *cocoa.* This is not related to *cocoanut,* which is Port. *coco,* bugbear, ugly-face, originally skull, from L. *concha,* skull, shell, whence Eng. *conch q.v.*: the *coconut, cocoanut* is so called from the resemblance of its shell-markings to an ugly face. From *conch* (pronounced *conk*), skull, comes the slang *conk,* to hit on the head. The same L. *concha* was applied to a small boat, a *cock*boat; whence, by transfer to land-carriage, Fr. *coche,* whence Eng. *coach, q.v.* *Vanilla* is from Fr. *vanille,*

from Sp. *vainilla,* pod, diminutive of *vaina,* scabbard, sheath, from L. *vagina,* which is also an Eng. scientific term.

vanish.
When things vanish into thin air, they leave an empty space, a *vacuum* (L. *vacuus,* empty, whence L. *vacare, vacat—,* present participle *vacant—,* whence *vacant, vacate, vacation*). The earlier word for empty was L. *vanus; cp. vain;* whence the inceptive *evanescere,* to begin to empty out, whence Eng. *evanescent* and via OFr. *esvanir, esvaniss—,* Eng. *evanish* and its more familiar aphetic form, *vanish.* The Eng. *vamoose, q.v.,* is from Sp. *ir, yendo* (*L. iendum*) *voy,* an irregular verb from L. *ire, it—,* to go; *cp. obituary.*

vapid.
See wade.

variegated.
See variety.

variety.
The spice of life calls for *varied* sensations (L. *varius,* changing, *variegated,* speckled). But the speckled face is marked with *varioles,* as in *variola,* small-pox (LL. *variola,* diminutive of *varius;* the Sp. *viruela* suggests the influence of L. *virulent-,* from *virus,* poison; whence Eng. *virus* and *virulent*). One may *vary* his diet in *various* ways—but do not mispronounce (or overwork) the *vermiform* appendix (from L. *vermis, worm;* whence also *vermin*).

variole, various.
See variety.

varlet.
A *vassal* of the feudal days was originally a growing youth, the type that would be chosen as a servant (Ir. *fas,* growth; Eng. *wax;* possibly *wax hale,* grow healthy, whence Eng. *wassail, q.v.;* though ME. *waes hael,* be healthy, is also suggested).

The diminutive of *vassal,* an old Celtic word, was *vassalet,* whence *vaslet;* whence came doublets meaning servant, footman: *valet,* and *varlet.* One has kept the original meaning; the other shows us the reputation such fellows had.

Wax, in both its senses, is an old Teut. word. The bees*wax* is perhaps related to L. *viscum,* birdlime, mistletoe, *q.v.*—whence *viscid, viscous. Cp. vegetable.*

varsity.
See college.

vary.
See variety.

vas, vase.
See vessel.

vaseline.
For new articles and processes, new words are constantly coined. Many of these are mongrels, part from one language, part from another. Thus Robert A. Chesebrough, about 1870, coined *vaseline,* from G. *Wasser* + Gr. *elaion,* olive oil.

vassal.
See varlet; *cp.* bachelor.

vast.
See waist.

Vatican.
The residence of the Pope is on the *Vatican Hill* in Rome. The hill draws its name from pagan days, however, when it was the site of the temple of the seer, from L. *vaticus,* the adjective from L. *vates,* prophet. Thus to *vaticinate* is to foretell; and a *vaticide* (*cp. shed*) is one that kills a prophet.

vaudeville.
In the 15th c. Olivier Basselin composed satirical drinking songs. They were called, after the place where he lived and sang, *Val* (valley, plural Fr. *Vaux*) *de Vire,* Normandy, *vaux de Vire.* In the 18th c. such songs were inserted in farces; brought from *Vire* to the city (Fr. *ville*), the word was corrupted to (*comédies avec*) *vaudevilles;* by the 19th c. the farces themselves were simply *vaudevilles;* Scribe wrote them by the hundreds. Americans borrowed the term for what the English call Variety.

veal.
See mutton.

vector.
See vehicle.

vegetable.
This word had difficulty growing fixed in the language; Shakespeare (*Pericles,* III,ii,36) uses *vegetive;* Jonson (*The Alchemist,* I,i,40), *vegetal.* It is via Fr. *vegetable,* able to live, from L. *vegetabilis,* from *vegetare,* to enliven,

from *vegere, vegetus,* to arouse. This is akin to *vigere,* to flourish, whence *vigorous,* and *vigilis,* wakeful, whence *vigil, vigilant.* The common root is *wag,* to be lively, strong, whence Goth. *wakan,* to *wake;* whence possibly also *wax; cp. varlet.* To *vegetate* means to behave like a *vegetable,* to grow by lying in the sun, etc. A recently coined word (used of a Chinese sect, in 1895: after *unitarian,* etc.) is *vegetarian,* who may or may not be *vigorous. Cp. plant.*

vegetarian, vegetate.
See vegetable.

vehemence, vehement.
See vehicle.

vehicle.
Before this was used of a carriage, it was applied to any substance, such as a liquid, used as the bearer of another substance, dissolved in it. The word is from L. *vehiculum,* the diminutive noun form from *vehere,* to carry. To *inveigh* against something is to be carried away against it (L. *in,* against); earlier forms in English were *invey, invehe.* The present participle, *vehemens, vehement—,* seems naturally to give us *vehemence, vehement;* but the suggestion is also made that these are from L. *ve, vehe,* prefix meaning lacking, + *mens, ment—,* mind (whence also *mental*). Certainly a *vehement* person tends to lack control of his mind. Thus *vehemence* leads to *violence.* This is from L. *violare, violat—,* whence Eng. *violation:* from L. *vis, vi—,* force. This should be distinguished from L. *videre, vis—,* to see; whence *visual; evident; visage; cp. improvised. Visa* and *visé* are the past participles (the first, from L. *carta visa;* the second, from Fr. *viser*), meaning seen, inspected; hence approved.
The L. *vehere, vexi, vectum,* also is the source of Eng. *invective, convex* (to lead together), *vector* analysis. The L. *vexare, vexat—,* to shake, by way of Fr. *vexer,* gives us *vex;* directly from the L. comes considerable *vexation.*

veil, velours, velvet.
See cloth.

venal, vend.
A *venal* person is one that can be bought, from L. *venum,* goods for sale. To *vend* is from L. *venum* + *dare,* to give; *cp. date.*
This must be distinguished from *venial,* from L. *venialis,* the adjective from *venia,* pardon.

venerable, venerate, venereal.
See win.

vengeance.
To *vindicate* oneself may not seem the same as to *avenge* a wrong; and while *avenge* may carry some sense of just retribution (*cp. tribulation*), it is now used almost interchangeably with *revenge.* But (with prefixes, L. *a, ad,* to, for; *re,* back) the three are from the same source, also in Eng. *venge:* from Fr. *venger,* OFr. *vengier,* from L. *vindicare, vindicat—.* The adjectives, *vengeful* and *vindictive,* (earlier *vindicative*) show the relations more closely. L. *vindicare* itself is from L. *vim* (accusative of *vis,* force; whence Eng. *vim*) + *dicere,* to say: to speak with power; *cp. verdict.* Thus although *Vengeance* is mine, saith the Lord, the human has built into his words the practice of extracting an eye for an eye.

venial.
See venal.

venison.
See win.

vent, ventilate.
See dollar.

ventriloquism.
See necromancy.

venture.
See dollar.

Venus.
See win. (She usually does win!)

veracious.
See mere.

verandah.
See attic.

verdict.
Truth being (as Pilate knew) something no one man can determine, it is left nowadays to the finding of twelve, who deliver their *verdict,* from OE. *verdit,* from OFr. *verdit,* from L. *veredictum,* from *vere,* truly + *dictum,* saying, from *dicere, dict—,* to speak—, whence Eng. *diction, dictionary. Dictate* is from L. *dictare, dictat—,* to tell what to say, to command, frequentative of *dicere.* There is a third L. form, *dicare, dicat—,* to proclaim. (Note that Old French had lost both *e* and *c;* the *c* was put back into Eng. *verdict* by analogy with *benediction*—L. *bene,* well—

malediction—L. *male*, ill—*contradiction*—L. *contra*, against— all of them later arrivals in English, not by way of Old French).

These three Latin forms are most fruitful sources of English words; the meanings of some can be gathered from the prefix. The L. *addicere, addict*—, was a legal term, meaning to deliver by sentence of the court; an *addict* is thus bound to or given over to (figuratively, to a habit). *Abdicate* (L. *ab*, away + *dicare, dicat*—,); *dictaphone*, which is a recent (1907) irregular coinage, from *dictate* + —*phone*, talk, as in *telephone*; *cp. focus*; *dedicate* (L. *de*, in regard to); *indicate*. *Adjudicate*; *judge* is from OFr. *jugier*, from L. *judicare*, to proclaim the law: L. *jus*, law; *cp. just*. *Valedictory*: L. *vale*, be well, fare well, from L. *valere*, to have worth; via Fr. *valoir*, past participle *valu, value*, comes Eng. *value*. *Edict; predict; predicate; preach* is from Fr. *precher*, from L. *praedicare*, to proclaim before (the public). Also from L. *valere*, via It. *valore* comes Eng. *valor*, which first mean worth by virtue of rank (14th through 16th c.), but by the 15th c. had also come to mean worth due to manliness; thence, courage.

Predicament is from L. *predicamentum*, used to translate Aristotle's Gr. *kategoria, category*, from *kategorein*, to speak publicly against (Gr. *cat*—, *cata*—, *cath*—, down, against; *cp. paragraph*: + *agora*, the public forum); Aristotle speaks of the ten *categories*: all the ways in which one can speak of a subject; hence, *predicament* meant first, a *category* or class; then a state of being (as in a certain class); then, by the slide process (*see* list in preface) an unfortunate state of being. A *condition* (from ME. *condicion*, from L. *condicion*—, from *condicere*, to state together) was first a state of affairs demanded as prerequisite for something else—you do this and I'll do that—hence, the *condition* of its existence; then, its manner or state of being. The L. past participle, used without change in Eng. *dictum*, by way of It. *detto, ditto*, said, mentioned before, became Eng. *ditto*. But silence is golden.

verdigris, verdure.
See vernacular.

verge.
See conversion.

vermicelli.
See macaroni.

vermiform.
See variety.

vermilion.
See macaroni.

vermin.
See variety.

Vermont.
See States.

vermouth.
See wormwood; *cp.* drink.

vernacular.
History shows us that often the habits, the language, of a conquered people impose themselves upon the conquerors. Thus after a time the Saxon serfs gave the basic words of the language to their Norman masters. The L. *verna*, servant, esp. a slave born in one's house, gave L. *vernaculus*, domestic; whence our *vernacular*. *Vernal* is, of course, of quite other origin, L. *vernalis*, of the green season, from *ver*, spring; whence (via L. *viridis*, green), springs *verdure*. *Verdigris* is OFr. *vert de Grece*, Greek green, though the reason for the association with Greece is unknown—as one might expect, it was at times spelt *verdigrease*.

vernal.
See vernacular; month.

versatile, verse, versed, verso.
See conversion.

versus.
See advertise; conversion.

vertebra.
See pylorus; *cp.* conversion.

vertex, vertical, vertiginous, vertigo.
See conversion.

very.
See mere.

vesper.
See argosy.

vespers.
See bull.

vessel.
This word has changed the size of its meaning a few times. It is via OFr. *vesseal, veselle* from L. *vascellum,* small *vase,* diminutive of *vas,* something hollowed. The word *vas,* plural *vasa,* whence Eng. *vase,* is itself used in Eng. of a hollow organ inside the body; whereas *vessel* is now used of the larger sorts of ship (hollowed bodies). It still refers, also, to hollowed articles for holding liquids.

The plural of the L., *vascella,* developed in Fr. into a collective noun; thus there are two Fr. words: *vaisseau,* referring to both dishes and ships, and *vaiselle,* for which we use Eng. *plate,* emphasizing the flat ones (Gr. *platys,* broad, as in *platypus,* flatfooted) rather than the hollowed.

The root *vas—* is close to *vag—,* to wander, *cp. vague,* and *vac—,* to be empty (L. *vacuum*), whence not only what nature abhors but also, via the verb *vacare, vacat—,* present participle *vacant—,* to empty, our Eng. *vacant, vacate,* and (leaving one's place empty for a while) *vacation.* For *vassal, cp. varlet.* Also *see waif.*

Figuratively, instead of the weaker sex, we may speak of the weaker *vessel*—and with more pertinence, for this limits the quality to the body (*vessel,* container), without any idea of the will, of who wears the breeches, *q.v.* More than Shakespeare (*Henry V,* IV,iv,71) know that "the empty *vessel* makes the greatest sound."

vest, vesta, vestal.
See invest.

vestibule.
The suggestion has been made that this is a place for throwing off one's *vestments* (*—bule,* from Gr. *boulein,* to throw). The L. *vestibulum,* entry, porch, is more probably from *ve—,* apart (Sanks. *vi—,* apart; *dvi,* two) + *stabulum,* an abode, whence Eng. *stable*: hence, an anteroom apart from the dwelling.

vestige, vestigium.
See investigate.

vestiment, vestment.
See invest.

veteran.
See mutton.

veterinary.
This expert was first called in, not for milady's pet poodle or caged canary, but as a "horse-doctor", to care for animals needed on the farm. The word is L. *veterinarius,* from *veterina animalia,* beasts of burden, animals old enough to work; *see mutton.*

veto.
When the office of the Roman tribune (*cp. tribulation*) was established, in the name of, and for the sake of, the people, he was given power to cancel certain bills of the Senate or edicts of the magistrates. The tribune carried out this function by formally saying: *Veto,* I forbid. *Veto* is the first person singular, present active of L. *vetare,* to forbid.

vex, vexation.
See vehicle.

via, viaduct, viaticum.
See duke, voyage.

vibration.
See whip.

vicar, vicarious, vice, vice-president, viceroy.
See lieutenant.

vicinity.
See Viking.

vicious.
See lieutenant.

victim, victor.
See trance, victoria.

victoria, Victorian.
The L. *vincere, vici, vict—,* to conquer, gives us in Eng. both the *victor* and the *victim.* Hence *invincible,* that cannot be conquered; *cp. trance.* The L. noun *victoria, victory,* is sometimes used as a shout of triumph: Cry *victoria!* and as a name, esp. of the Queen of England, *Victoria* (1837—1901). After her, various articles have been named, from a carriage (named *victoria* by the French, in her honor) to a plum, a cloth, a pigeon. From the characteristics of the Queen and her period, a measure of complacency, conservatism, belief in progress, and other middle-class attributes come to mind when we say *Victorian.* Their greater smugness and prudery is *mid-Victorian* (though it should be noted that the period contains its own contradictions, *e.g.,* W. S. Gilbert).

To *convince* someone is to overcome his objections; to *convict* him (though for a time used in the same way) has come to mean to overcome the arguments in his behalf. Thus *convict* was first an adjective, from the L. past participle; then a noun; then a verb, from L. *convincere, convict—*. To *convince,* to lead one to believe, is often misused for to *persuade,* to lead to one to act, from L. *per,* through, used as an intensive, + *suadere, suasi—,* to lead someone to like a thing, to make it sweet. Hence also *persuasion*. From the simple form comes moral *suasion;* the word is related to L. *suavis,* sweet, *q.v.*, gentle; whence Eng. *suave*. To *sway* is from LG. *swajen,* Du. *zwaaien,* to shake, to totter; also Du. *zwerven* meant to move irregularly, to totter, to turn aside; hence Eng. *swerve*. To fall under the *sway* of something means to be moved to and fro by it; hence, imperial *sway*: *Victoria!*

There may be some relation, either between *vita,* life, or *victor,* conqueror, and L. *victus,* sustenance; whence the LL. *victualis*. This by a roundabout journey (OFr. *victaile, vitaile, vitale;* whence early Eng. *vitaile, vitayle*—some sixty different spellings are recorded—*vittel, vittle;* then the Eng. spelling was brought closer to the L. original, but the pronunciation has been kept like the older forms: *vittle*) gives us Eng. *victual*. Often used in the plural, as *Victuals* for *victory!*

L. *vita,* life, whence Eng. *vital* and *vitality,* is related to the verb *vivere, vit—,* to live. This gives us a number of Eng. words: *vivid,* lively; *vivacious; vivarium; viva voce,* with the living voice; and combinations such as *vivisection; cp. set*. With L. *re,* back, we have *revive* and *revivify*. From LL. *vivanda, vivenda,* things needed for life, comes the Fr. and Eng. *vivandière;* and, through the Fr., *viands*. *Vivat,* may he (it) live, is sometimes used for applause, sometimes in the Latin as a battlecry, as in *Vivat justitia, ruat coelum,* Let justice live, though the heavens fall!

victory, victual.
See victoria.

Vienna.
See dollar.

view.
See improvised.

vigia, vigil, vigilance, vigilant, vigor, vigorous.
See alert; vegetable.

Viking.
The raids of the *Vikings* went far and wide, starting from the bays and creeks of their native Norway (ON. *vīk,* bay). While they seldom settled in any one place, they made many camps, as did the Romans.

Their name may thus have come from AS. *wīc,* camp, from L. *vicus,* village, of the same street, whence Fr. *voisinage,* whence Eng. *vicinage;* from L. *vicinitat—,* neighborhood, whence Eng. *vicinity*. *Cp. villain.* But (as the Manchus in China, the Franks in Gaul; whence, France; *cp. free*) they stayed for some centuries as conquerors to the east; the Finns called Sweden *Ruotsi,* its inhabitants, *Rus;* hence, the name *Russia*.

Whether the first part of the name comes from ON. *vik* or from AS. *wic,* the *—ing* was an early masculine ending, meaning a man of . . . It remains with diminutive or scornful effect, as in *darling, q.v.*, hireling.

village.
See villain.

villain.
This word illustrates the influence of of social attitudes upon meanings. L. *villa* (? a diminutive of *vicus,* hamlet) meant a farm with all its buildings; then, influenced by the It. form, a mansion, a *villa*. A collection of such buildings (from the L. adj. *villaticum*) grew into a *village*. A song of farm and country life is a *villanelle,* which became one of the fixed forms of Fr. verse. A dweller on the farm was a *villein* or *villain*. These two spellings have been preserved: the first has kept its original sense, a peasant farmer under the feudal system; the second, expressing the city dweller's contempt for the country lout, came to mean one base-born and low-minded; then, any one naturally given to evil. In this sense there also developed the adj. *villainous,* and the n. *villainy* (until the 19th c. usually spelled *villany*). In Fr. *ville* has come to mean city (by a growth similar to that of Eng. *town*: AS. *tūn,* enclosure, *tynan,* to fence—Du. *tuin,* garden; G. *Zaun,* hedge, *q.v.*—became a homestead, then a larger cluster of houses); and in this sense *ville* is

used as the suffix to many Eng. place-names: Nash*ville;* Glovers*ville,* where gauntlets and mittens are made; Potts*ville,* where the mighty Casey swung his bat in vain. *Cp. agony.*

L. *vicus,* hamlet, Gr. *oikos,* house, are akin to AS. *wic,* settlement. Thus, Eng. *bailiwick* is the settlement or district controlled by a *bailiff*: LL. *baiulivus,* man in charge of a fort: L. *ballium,* castle-wall, whence London's Old *Bailey;* as also from L. *baiulare,* to bear, from *baiulus,* porter, we derive *bail, q.v. Ballium* is perhaps corrupted from, or influenced by, L. *vallum, wall,* rampart. And originally an *interval* (L. *inter,* between) is a space between ramparts.

villanelle, villein.
See villain.

vim, vindicate, vindictive.
See vengeance.

vine.
See propaganda.

vinegar, vintage.
See drink.

viol, viola.
Various such forms are from root *vid,* whence LL. *vidula,* whence Eng. *fiddle,* from L. *fides,* string of a lute. *Violin* is from It. diminutive *violino;* the augmentative is It. *violone,* which again has a diminutive, *violoncello.* The great *viol* is a *viol da gamba; cp. monk.* These, and the L. *viola,* the *violet* flower (*cp. red*) have no relation to L. *violare, violat—,* to misuse, outrage, whence Eng. *violate, inviolate, violation, violence.*

violate, violation, violence.
See vehicle, viol.

violet.
See red.

violin, violoncello.
See viol.

viper.
This rather common snake was early noticed as breeding not by egg, but bringing its young forth alive. The name states that fact: *viper* is short for L. *vivipera,* from *vivus,* alive + *parere,* to appear, to bring forth. Hence, also, *viviparous; cp. shed.* The fable of the *viper,* nourished and kept warm at a human breast, biting the person that reared it, has led to the application of the term to a spiteful or malignant person.

virago, virescent, virgin, virginal.
See virtue.

Virginia.
See States; virtue.

virginium.
See element.

viridine, virile.
See virtue.

virtue.
There were giants—at least, heroes—in those days! Sansk. *vira,* hero, whence Gr. *heros, hero,* man, and L. *vir,* hero, man; *virilis,* manly, whence Eng. *virile.* The quality of manliness was *virtus, virtut—,* whence Fr. *vertu,* whence ME. *vertu;* the *i* was restored to bring it nearer the L., in Eng. *virtue.* In Renaissance Italy, *virtu* was used esp. of excellence, *virtue,* in the fine arts; one that possessed this was a *virtuoso.* The L. *viridis,* green (hence, flourishing), whence *virescent, viridarium, viridian,* etc., may be related to this; as is *virago,* a manly woman. *Virgin* (L. *virgo, virgin—*) is probably not; from it also come *virginal,* the old musical instrument (variety of spinet; *see saxophone*), as played by young girls; and *Virginia,* named after the *"Virgin* Queen" Elizabeth of England.

virtuoso.
See virtue.

virulent, virus.
See variety.

visa.
See vehicle.

visage.
See improvised, vehicle.

viscid, viscous.
See varlet.

viscount.
See lieutenant.

visé.
See vehicle.

visible, vision, visit, visual.
See improvised.

visual.
See vehicle.

vital, vitality.
See mutton, victoria; cp. vitamin.

vitamin, vitamine.
Mankind has been subsisting on *vitamins* for some centuries; but their existence (like M. Jourdain's prose) has just been discovered. The word was coined by Vladimir Funk, in 1910, from L. *vita,* life + *amine,* from *ammonia,* from *sal ammoniac,* from Gr. *ammoniakon,* from the spring at the temple of *Jupiter Ammon. See ammonia.*

vitiate.
See lieutenant.

vitreous, vitrification, vitrify.
See vitriol; cp. defeat.

vitriol.
This word has had its meaning several times refracted. From L. *vitrum,* glass, the diminutive *vitriolum,* Eng. *vitriol,* was applied to a sulphate of any of several metals, esp. powdered and used for medicine: they looked like glass. Then the terms *elixir of vitriol, spirits of vitriol* and *oil of vitriol* were used for liquid compounds or solutions; the last, esp., for concentrated sulphuric acid. Gradually *vitriol* alone was used in this sense; and, from the potency of the acid, for very strong feeling or speech; hence *vitriolic.* More directly L. *vitrum.* glass gives Eng. *vitreous, vitrify,* and more.

viva voce.
See sext, victoria.

vivacious, vivandiere, vivarium.
See victoria.

vivify.
See defeat.

viviparous.
See viper; *cp.* shed.

vivisection.
See sext.

vocable, vocabulary, vocal, vocation.
See entice.

vociferous.
See suffer.

vodka.
See drink.

vogue.
This word came to mean power, or sway, from the sway, motion, course of a ship, or (more probably) from the sway or stroking of the oar, from Fr. *voguer,* from It. *vogare,* to row (Sp. *boga,* rowing; *en boga,* in the vogue). OHG. *waga,* a wave, whence Eng. *wag.* AS. *wagian,* to rock, is a weak verb from the strong verb *wegan,* past participle *wagen,* to bear, to weigh; whence both *weigh* and *wagon, waggon.* (*Wag* in the sense of jesting fellow is probably an allusion to the fate of such a heedless one: *wag-halter,* gallows-bird, one that will *wag* in a halter.) From the same root via AS. *wecg,* piece of metal, comes *wedge,* from its primary use, for moving, *i.e.,* splitting, trees. The *wing* (or *wagger*) of a bird is Scand. in origin: Icel. *vaengr,* Goth. *wagjan,* to *wag,* shake. AS. for *wing* is *feder,* whence G. *feder,* whence Eng. *feather;* related to L. *petna,* whence *penna,* whence *pennant; cp. pen,* and Gr. *petron,* whence *pteron, pteryg—. Ptero—* and *pterygo—* are Eng. combining forms, as in *pterodactyl,* with *wings* on his fingers.

voice.
See entice.

void.
See vacuum.

voile.
See cloth.

volatile.
See volley.

volcano.
The armorer of the Greek gods had his forge within the bowels of Etna, the *volcano* in Sicily (more turbulent, recently, with fires on its surface). From his name, *Vulcan,* comes *volcano.* More directly, and recently (ca. 1825), *vulcanize* was coined; although in the 1590's a blacksmith was called a *vulcanist.*

volition.
See valley.

volley.
This term for bullets flying through the air is via Fr. *volée* from L. *volat—,* from *volare,* to fly. This gives us also *volant, volatile.* There is a frequentative form, *volitare, volitat—,* flitting, which

has Eng. forms such as *volitant, volitate.* Since we seek to fly toward that which we desire, there may be some relation between *volare* and L. *volo, volens,* infinitive *velle,* to wish, to will; whence Eng. *volition;* via the L. noun *voluntas, voluntat—,* come Eng. *voluntary, volunteer.*

Just as that which is chosen (L. *opt—*) seems to be the best (L. *optimus; cp. pessimist*), so that which is desired becomes the *voluptuous* (which may be compounded of L. *vol,* to will and L. *opt,* to choose; L. *voluptas, voluptat—,* pleasure, has its source in *volo,* I wish); hence *voluptuary,* and more.

volt.
See Appendix II.

voluble.
See volume.

volume.
This word springs from the early shape of books, which were of parchment rolled on a stick, or two sticks for easy unrolling, as still with the holy book of the orthodox Jews. *Volume* is Fr., from L. *volumen,* a coil or roll, from *volvere,* to roll. (*Scroll* is from the material: OE. *scrowle,* from *scrow,* list, from OFr. *écrou,* from L. *scrobis,* trench, thence membrane of the uterus, used in making parchment. Note that *matriculate* is thus related, not to the *Alma Mater,* gracious mother: one's own college; but to LL. *matricula,* list of members, diminutive of *matrix, matric—,* womb [hence, Eng. *matrix,* place of origin; basic mould: shortened in printing to *mat*:] membrane of the uterus, used in making parchment. In classical L. *matrix* meant gravid animal, from *mater,* mother.)

L. *volvere, volut—,* to roll, gives many Eng. words. *Voluble, volute; involve, revolve, devolve; revolver,* on which the cartridge case rolls back; *revolution,* a rolling back; *convolution,* etc. *Cp. walk.*

voluntary, volunteer.
See volley.

voluptuous.
See volley.

volute.
See volume.

voracious.
See sarcophagus.

vortex, vorticist.
See conversion.

votary.
See vote.

vote.
When the ancients *devoted* themselves to a thing—or *devoted* a thing to a god—they made a *vow* concerning it: L. *de,* in regard to, + *vovere, vot—,* to *vow. Vow* itself is via OFr. *vou* from the same L. *votum;* hence *vow* and *vote* are doublets; the *vote* registers the determination. (In some uses, *vow* is aphetic for *avow,* which is a doublet of *avouch,* which in turn has the aphetic form *vouch,* to *vouch* for. There are from OFr. *avochier, avouer,* from L. *advocare, advocat—,* to call to, for, in behalf of; whence also *advocate.*) The word *vote* meant first a solemn pledge; then an ardent wish; then a formal manner of making one's wish or intention known: thus the modern sense. And to *devote* oneself (to a religious life) is to become a *votary.*

vouch, vow.
See vote.

voyage.
The L. *viaticum* meant provision for a journey; it is used in Eng. in the same sense, but esp. of the Eucharist administered to a dying man, as his best provision for the journey to the next world. The same L. *viaticum* became It. *viaggio,* OFr. *veiage, vayage;* whence Eng. *voyage* —transferred from the wherewithal to the trip. The L. word is from L. *via,* way; the ablative case of this, *via,* by way of, is used in Eng.; from it also comes *viaduct; cp. duke.* The word is also Fr., as in *Bon Voyage!*

vulcanize.
See volcano.

vulgar.
See immunity; *cp.* mob.
Also from L. *vulgare, vulgat—,* to make public, comes L. *textus vulgatus,* shortened in Eng. to the *Vulgate* (text of the *Bible*), usually applied to the L. version of St. Jerome, completed in 405 A.D.

Vulgate.
See vulgar.

vulpine.
There is a comedy of Ben Jonson called *Volpone, or The Fox* (1605). *Vol-*

pone is the name of the chief character; but it is also the fox: we have Eng. *vulpine,* from L. *vulpinus,* foxlike, foxy; from L. *vulpes,* fox, *q.v.* (The word for wolf reverses the consonants. We have Eng. *louvre,* an 18th c. dance, from the Fr. *Louvre* at Paris; the building was named from the wolf-field, *louve,* wolf, feminine, *loup,* masculine; L. *lupus*). *Wolf* itself is spelled in many early ways; among these, such forms as OE *wulphes* suggest a relation with both L. *lupus* and L. *vulpes.*

W

Waac, Wac.
See Dora.

wade.
This is common Teut., but in the sense of going through things on land. It is related to L. *vadere,* to proceed. But L. *vadum* means ford; and by the 13th c. *wade* had come to be used of walking in water. Burton (1658) says that *—ford* has been added to place-names because of the *vadosity* of the water there. (G. *w* is pronounced like Eng. *v;* L. *v* is pronounced like Eng. *w.*)

Some senses of *fade* have been influenced by L. *vadere,* and spelled *vade*, Eng. *invade* and *evade* are from the same L. word; as is also the *vade-mecum,* go with me. *Fade* is, via Fr. *fader,* from Fr. *fade,* insipid, colorless, from L. *vapidus,* stale, whence likewise Eng. *vapid. Cp. vacuum.*

wafer, waffle.
See gopher.

waft.
See waif.

wag.
See vogue.

wage, wages.
See salary.

waggon, wagon.
See vogue.

waif.
This in early Eng. meant lost (or stolen but unclaimed) property that is turned over to the lord of the manor. Some trace it via OFr. *gaif* to L. *vacuus,* unowned, empty; and by the same token find the source of Eng. *waive* in OFr. *gaiver,* from L. *vacuare.* It seems more probably that these words are of Scand. origin, meaning something loose or wandering, flapping, and related to *wave,* from AS. *wafian,* to brandish (also to *weave,* from AS. *wefan,* to move to and fro). Thus *waive* meant first to outlaw, to abandon, thus to cause to become a *waif.* To *waver* is a frequentative of to *wave.* The ocean *wave* did not appear (as a word) until the 16th c.; earlier it was ME. *wawe,* from AS. *waeg.* This *wave* is related to *waft,* old Du. *wahten,* to *watch* (AS. *wacian,* whence to *watch*) : the first meaning of *waft* was to convoy ships; then perhaps signalling directions from ship to ship; hence the present meaning. *Cp. vessel.*

wain.
This is a doublet of *waggon,* AS. *waegn; see vogue.*

waist.
There are confusions as well as protrusions here. This word was earlier spelled *wast,* and is the same as *waste*— not, however, as many wish and as some (*e.g.* Archdeacon Charles I. Smith, *Common Words,* 1865) suggest, as "that part of the figure which *wastes* in the sense of diminishes"; but precisely the opposite; the word is from AS. *waest,* whence *waxan,* to grow, whence Eng. *wax, cp. varlet.*

The modern Eng. *waste* is from another source, going far back, as it is both common Teut., AS. *weste,* G. *wuste,* whence *Wüste,* wilderness and L. *vastare,* to waste, whence Eng. *devastate*, to lay *waste,* from *vastus, vast,* desolate; whence Eng. *vast.* Our current form seems to have come along the Latin route, rather than direct from Anglo-Saxon, which would have produced a different spelling, *weest;* there were two forms in ME.: *wast,* from the Fr., from L. and *weste,* from the AS.; the second died out; in G., it was the Teut. form that survived. The first Quarto *Hamlet* (I,ii,198) says "In the dead *vast* and middle of the night"; the other early editions have *"waste".*

waive.
See waif.

wake.
See ache, vegetable.

walk.
The sailor's gait (or the horseman's) is closest to this word, which first meant to roll, from AS. *wealcan,* to roll; L. *valgus,* bent, bandy-legged, also *volvere, volut—,* to roll, *cp.* *volume;* Eng. *wallow.* To roll over, and press, cloth, was the next sense the word had; what we call to full; the early *walker* was a fuller—both words survive as proper names; we find in Percy's *Reliques*:

She cursed the weaver and the *walker,*
The cloth that they had wrought.

From the sense to stamp about, came gradually the present meaning.

walkie-talkie.
See whippersnapper.

Walkyrie.
The Eng. form of *Valkyrie, q.v.*

wallop.
To *gallop* a horse, you may have to *wallop* him; *wallop* is merely a doublet (with the causal sense) of *gallop, q.v.* The word was also used of the rapid bubbling of water as it boils; hence a *potwalloper* is one that boils water, a cook (not a dish-washer).

wallow.
See walk.

walnut.
See Dutch.

wan.
See uncouth.

wander.
See vague.

wane, want.
See win.

wanton.
See uncouth; *cp.* win.

war.
See warrior; *cp.* carouse.

ward, warden.
See lady; *cp.* warrior.

warm.
This is common Teut., OE. *wearm,* related to Sansk. *gharma (ghwarma),* heat, Gr. *thermos (cp. season),* L. *formus,* warm. This L. word seems to have no direct descendants in Eng. There are three other L. stems beginning *form—.* L. *forma,* shape, is quite productive: *form, formal, formality; uniform* (L. *unus,* one: of one *form;* hence also the *uniform* that is worn by all of a group or army); *formulate,* from *formula* a diminutive (in L., of *forma*); and other words ending in *—form,* as *cruciform,* in the *form* of a cross. There is also L. *formica,* ant. This gives us *formic* acid, secured from a fluid emitted by ants; *formication,* the feeling of ants creeping over one's flesh (not to be confused with *fornication,* from L. *fornicare, fornicat—,* from *fornix. fornic—,* an arch, as in *fornicated* leaves; then a vaulted chamber, then a brothel); *formaldehyde* (*form*ic *al*cohol *dehyd*rodgenatum, abbreviated); and other scientific terms connected with the ant. There is, finally, L. *formido,* dread; *formidare, formidat—,* to be afraid of; whence Eng. *formidable,* used when things look as though they may grow hot for you. The island of *Formosa* is the shapely isle; it is also rather *warm. See formula.*

warn.
See garnish.

warp, warped.
See ballot, wasp.

warranty.
See warrior.

warren.
This word first meant land enclosed for breeding and guarding game. It is from OFr. *warenne,* but originally from the Teut.; *see warrior.*

warrior.
In the frequent battles of north Europe, words as well as blows were exchanged. Thus *war* is a common Teut. word, ME. *werre,* from OHG. *werra,* strife. This came into Fr. as *guerre,* whence It. and Sp. *guerra.* [The letter *w* was not in L. or early Romance; hence the doublets *guard* and *ward, guardian* and *warden* (AS. *weardian*); *guile* and *wile* (AS. *wil*); *guarantee* and *warranty* (OHG. *werento,* from *weren,* to protect).] The Fr. developed a verb *guerreier,* to make war; whence *guerroyeur,* one that makes war; these

were reborrowed into ME. *warreyour,* whence Eng. *warrior. See garret.*

wash.

This appears to have been a widespread practice: the word is common Teut. (save that it's not found in Gothic); there are over a hundred early forms of the word. It is from an old Teut. root form *waskan, watskan,* akin to *wat—, water,* which is also common Teut., AS. *waeter,* G. *Wasser; cp. drink.*

Water is also widespread, and in various forms. One variant, *waet—,* has come into Eng. as *wet.* Another, *ud—,* seen in Old Prussian *undo,* L. *unda,* wave (whence Eng. *undulation,* etc.), is also seen in Sansk. *udan,* Gr. *hydor* (whence Eng. *hydraulic, hydrogen; cp. drink, racy*), *hydra, water*snake; *otter, q.v.*

Also cp. *Washington, Appendix III.*

Washington.

See States.

wasp.

This creature is named from the house it builds: OE. *waesp, waefs,* from root *webh,* to *weave;* whence also Eng. *web.* The *warp* (AS. *weorpen,* to throw) is that over which the *woof* is thrown; hence also Eng. *warped,* bent. (Similarly Fr. *déjeté* means *warped,* from *déjeter,* to throw down, though it has come into Eng. in the other sense, as *dejected,* from the Fr. from the L. *deicere, deject—,* from L. *de* + *jacere,* to throw; whence also the L. frequentative *jactare, jactat—,* to throw forth, which gives us Eng. *jactation,* boasting—and the double frequentative L. *jactitare, jactitat—* whence Eng. *jactitation,* which means both boasting and restless throwing about of the body, as in sleepless nights. *See subject.* From L. *jacere,* to throw, comes also the diminutive *jaculum,* a dart, whence L. *jaculari, jaculat—,* to dart, and Eng. *ejaculation,* that darts out.) The *weft* is also from *webh—,* to weave; AS. *wefta.* The *woof* is from an earlier ME. *oof,* a thread, altered by the influence of the other words; but there was also ME. *owef,* from *o,* on + *wefan,* to *weave.* Thus the words are *interwoven;* and *cp. wax.* *Waspish,* applied to persons, is from the prompt sting of the *wasp* when troubled, though sometimes used instead of *wasp-waisted,* from the very small waist of the *wasp.*

wassail.

Although applied to the spiced ale offered on Twelfth Night and Christmas Eve, this word is not related to *ale,* which was a common Teut. word; *cp. bridal.* The words on handing someone a drink were AS. *Wes heil,* be healthy. ON. *heil,* AS. *hal,* gives us Eng. *hale.* The form *wes* is the imperative of AS. *wesan,* to be — whence Eng. *was* and *were.* The answer, on accepting the cup, was *Drink hail!* But *see varlet.*

waste.

See waist.

watch.

See ache.

water.

See drink; *cp.* wash.

watershed.

See shed.

watt.

See Appendix II.

wave, waver.

See waif.

wax.

In the sense of grow, this is common Teut., and widespread, being related via OTeut. to a root *waxs,* Indogermanic *aweks, auks;* Sansk. *uks,* to grow; whence Gr. *auxein,* L. *augere, auxi, auct—,* whence Eng. *augment; cp. auction.*

In the sense of what is in the beehive, *cp. wasp.* (Perhaps the two words are one, *wax* being what *waxes* (*i.e.,* grows) in the honeycomb. But it is at least influenced by, if not sprung from (via OE. *weax*) the Indogermanic root *weg,* to weave. *Cp. wasp;* but also *see varlet.*

wayward.

See away.

weak.

See wicked.

wealth.

This word, alas, shows the commercial tendency of society. It first meant well-being, from *weal,* from AS. *wela,* whence *well,* as still in the affairs of the *commonweal,* or *commonwealth.* A similar form is *health,* from AS. *hāl,* whence *hale;* whence also *heal* and (AS. *halig*) *holy.* *Whole* is another form of the same word, as in *wholesome;* the *w* was added about the 15th c.

When the English pray for their ruler "in *health* and *wealth* long to live", they mean in *health* and happiness. But the measure of happiness came more and more to be the money that the poor thought might purchase it; hence, the present meaning of the word *wealth*.

wean.
See win.

weather.
As might be expected, this is a widespread form (though not found in Gothic; *cp. world*): OE. *weder;* not with the *th* until the 15th c. It seems to come from an Indogermanic root *we,* to blow, + *dhro—;* note that in Russian *vedru* is used of fair weather; in Lithuanian, *vydra* is a storm. That seems to blow both hot and cold; let's hope that friends often get together! But alas, not all things *weather* well, as the same word took another form, Eng. *wither.*

The word *whether* was first a pronoun; it is a combination of Eng. *who* + an ending like *either. Who* is from AS. *hwa; whether,* from AS. *hwaether.* In the same way, *whither* is *who* + a form like *hither* (itself from *he* + *there; thither* is from *that* + *there*). *Either* is more complicated: *ay* + *gewhether,* each of two, became *aeghwaether;* this, shortened to AS. *aegther,* became Eng. *either.* In any *weather.*

weave, web.
See ballot, waif; *cp.* wasp.

wed.
See salary.

wedge.
See vogue.

wedlock.
Wedlock is a padlock (*Proverbial Observations,* 1742). This word, the last syllable of which suggests the "till death us depart" of the marriage ceremony, is actually from AS. *wedlac,* from *wed,* a pledge + *lac,* gift: the gift given to cement an engagement. A bachelor was often listed on medieval registers as (L.) *solutus,* loose, unchained.

Wednesday.
See week.

week.
A common Teut. word. AS. *wicu,* from *wice,* service; G. *Wechsel,* change; L. *vicem,* change; *cp. lieutenant.*

Sunday—the day of the sun.

Monday—the day of the moon.

Tuesday—the day of Tiw: Teut. god of war, hence replacing the Roman *Martis dies,* day of Mars; Fr. *mardi.* The word *Tiw* is cognate with *L. deus,* god, and Gr. *Zeus.*

Wednesday—Wodin's day: king of the Norse gods.

Thursday—Thor's day: the thunderer. (*Cp. torch.*)

Friday—the day of Friya or Frigga, Norse goddess of love, wife of Wodin. (*Cp. free.*)

Saturday—the day of Saturn, Roman god of agriculture. (*Cp. satisfy.*)

day—common Teut., AS. *daeg.* First meant the hours of sunlight; the entire period of twenty-four hours was *night,* the basic Aryan word: AS. *niht;* Gr. *nykt—;* Sansk. *nakta.*

ween.
See win.

weft.
See ballot, wasp.

weigh.
See vogue.

welcome.
This seems clearly a combination of *well* and *come,* as in Fr. *bien venu;* in L. *bene venias*: the adverb *well* and the imperative or the past participle of the verb *come.* (*Come* is common Teut., AS. *cuman;* summer is *icumen* in.) The second part of this derivation is partly right; but the whole word has been adjusted to the thought above, from OE. *wilcuma,* from *wil,* as Eng. *will,* desire, + *cuma,* guest, *comer.* One you desire as a guest is of course *well come, welcome.*

well.
See wealth, will; *cp.* welcome.

wellington (boot).
See Appendix II.

welsh.
See Dutch.

wench.
The merry *wench* we think of today is wholly feminine; formerly the word referred to one of either sex — but a weakling; hence the gradual restriction to the weaker sex. OE. *wenchel* is from AS. *wencel,* weakling, from *wincian,* to bend, to waver, from Sansk. *vank,* to

bend. The final *el* was supposed a diminutive and dropped; similarly *thrush* was formed from *throstle;* and *date, q.v.,* (the fruit) and *almond, q.v.,* lost their final *l.*

wend.
See vague.

werewolf, werwolf.
See wormwood. In the middle ages, an ugly, dwarfish, or otherwise deformed child might be a sign that the real child had been rapt away, and this bratling left in its place, as by the fairies, or changed into a man-wolf, a *werwolf.*

west.
See east.

West Virginia.
See States.

wet.
See wet blanket; wash.

wet blanket.
This term rises from the olden practice, when there was a fire, of dropping a *blanket* into a pool of water, then throwing it over the flames. From this, it came to be used figuratively of one that puts a *damper* on anything, esp., that destroys the fun of an occasion.
Wet is AS. *waet,* related to *water.* To *damp* is to choke (whence the *dampers* of a piano and a furnace); the first meaning of the noun *damp* was a poisonous vapor, as in coal mines; the sense of moist comes from Du. *damp,* vapor; G. *Dampf,* steam. *Cp. dump.* For *blanket, see black.*

whack, whacky.
See Dora.

whatnot.
That old remark that mother left her topknot in the *whatnot* has little meaning to the dweller in the streamlined steam-heated apartment of today. There is no room for that commodious container of knick-knacks, the *whatnot.* The word was first two words, at the end of a list: threatened my life, my reputation, my fortune, my home, my happiness—*what not?* Then combined, it was used of an odd assortment or an odd person; finally, of a set of shelves to hold such oddities as one might collect in an idle lifetime.

wheat.
See black.

wheedle.
In her provocative book, *Shakespeare's Imagery,* 1935, Caroline Spurgeon points out that whenever the idea of a flatterer occurs in the plays, it brings along references to a dog or spaniel, fawning and licking: candy, sugar or sweets, melting or thawing — and that any of these images can start the chain. Thus Julius Caesar checks the prostrate Metellus Cimber:

> Be not fond,
> To think that Caesar bears such rebel blood
> That will be *thaw'd* from the true quality
> With that which *melteth* fools, I mean, *sweet* words,
> *Low-cròoked* court'sies and base *spaniel-fawning* . . . (III,i,39)

And Hamlet says to Horatio (III,ii,64):

> Why should the poor be flatter'd?
> Nò, let the *candied tongue lick* absurd pomp,
> And *crook* the pregnant hinges of the knee
> Where thrift may follow *fawning.*

Such associations point to a deep-felt connection; it is rooted in the language. *Wheedle* is from G. *wedeln,* to wag the tail; whence G. *anwedeln,* to *fawn* on. (The same double sense is in the Gr. *sainein.*) *Fawn* is more simply from AS. *fahnian,* to rejoice, to *fawn;* an AS. doublet of *faegnian,* from *faegan,* glad, whence Eng. *fain.* But *adulation* again has the double sense, from L. *adulari,* to flatter, to wag the tail. The association is probably from the habit, down the ages, of having dogs at dinner tables, wagging their tails, begging or teasing their masters to pass them some food.

wheel.
There was no equivalent for this in American Indian, as they lacked the object: one of the first great inventions. (On the other hand, it seems that they invented the idea *zero,* before the Arabs, from whom we borrowed it; *cp. cipher.*) The opening sound was at first guttural, being akin to Gr. *cyklos, cycle,* wheel; Sansk. *cakra—,* also circle and *wheel;* our word is from OE. *hwegol,* from an OTeut. form *chwegula;* the basic meaning being to turn. Thus L. *colus* is the distaff of spinning; L. *colere* means to till the soil; *colere, cult—,* whence Eng.

cultivate; cp. colonel. We are "what makes the *wheels* go round".

whether.
See weather.

Whig.
See tory.

whim.
See whimsy.

whimper.
See whip.

whimsy.
This seems to be a later formation, along with *whim,* from the reduplicated *whim-wham* (*cp. scurry*). This itself is probably imitative of the sense of lightness and flitting-aboutness; similarly we have *flim-flam,* whence *flimsy.* There is an ON. *hvima,* to let the eyes wander; but the *whimsical* person is just as likely to fix his gaze.

whine.
There was a seldom used OE. *hwinan,* the sound of an arrow in the air; the word *whine* is imitative, as is the weaker *whinny.* The humane horses of the last journey of Gulliver's Travels are called the *Houyhnhnms.*

whinny.
See whine.

whip.
This is another of the many imitative words: of sudden movement. The *h* does not appear in its early forms, and the word is probably related to L. *vibrare, vibrat—,* whence Eng. *vibration*: the L. stem *vib—* being also imitative. From the idea of speed, or a sudden blow, or the *whip* with which the blow is dealt, various other senses have developed, *e.g.,* the party *whip,* the man that keeps members of a political party obedient to the leader. Also *see bounce.*

Other imitative words are *whimper* (frequentative of an earlier *whimp*), *whirr, whirl, whiz, whist, whistle, whisper; cp. whine, scurry.* The game *whist* is named from the silence (*Whist!*) that used to be maintained during the play. *Whisk,* whence *whisker,* a brush (also first without the *h*: Eng. *wisk* from OHG. *wisc,* wisp of hay, dish-cloth, from the quick movement therewith) led to men's *whiskers,* first used humorously of what we now call the *moustache*: the brushers. The humorous word became the regular one, now generally attached to the cheeks. *Moustache,* earlier *mustachio* (from It. *mostaccio,* but later modified by Fr. *moustache*) comes from farther Gr. *mystax,* from *mastax,* jaw—which gave its name to the early chewing-gum. *See* masticate; vandyke.

whippersnapper.
A frequent manner of forming a noun of agent, the one that performs an act, is to add *r* or *er* to the verb naming that act, *e.g., baker, teacher.* The suffix may be attached to the second part of a compound expression, as *strike-breaker, merry-maker, go-getter.* Occasionally it is omitted from such expressions, as when a boy is called a *cut-up.* On the other hand, by what the N E D calls a "jingling extension", it may be added to both parts, as when current slang speaks of a *messer-upper* or a *mower-downer.* That this is by no means merely a recent practice is indicated by the existence (since 1674) of *whippersnapper,* an insignificant fellow that makes noises to attract attention.

Rarely, there is an analogous coinage for the instrument used by the agent, as in *walkie-talkie,* the portable radio receiving and transmitting set used in World War II.

whippet.
See whip.

whirl.
See whip.

whirr.
See scurry.

whisk, whiskers.
See whip.

whisky.
See drink.

whisper.
See whip.

whist, whistle.
See whip.

whit.
See nausea.

white.
See black.

whither.
See weather.

Whitsunday.

This is commonly the seventh Sunday after Easter, on which the white baptismal robes were worn by the newly baptized. For the word is simply *White Sunday*. The shortening, however, disguised the origin, so that the word has been divided; and there are a *whitsun* ale, a *whitsun* week (also a *whit* week) and even a *whitsun Sunday*. Scotland uses the word, quite apart from the religious sense, as the end of a term: *Whitsun Day*.

To *baptize* is directly from Gr. *baptizein*, to immerse, frequentative of *baptein*, to dip, which every *Baptist* knows.

whiz.

See whip.

who.

See weather.

whole, wholesome.

This word first meant unharmed, unwounded; hence, all there. It is common Teut., existing in many forms, among them *hale*, which has also survived, keeping the original sense. (The *w* was added in the 15th c., by analogy with many other words; *hoard, hood, hore* are among those that also added a *w*, but only the last of these retained it. *Whore* was AS. *hor, adultery;* the OTeut. root was *choron—*. related to OIrish *cara*, friend; L. *carus*, dear, whence L. *caritas, caritat—*, love, whence Eng. *charity*.) Its sense of *healthy* led to its use, in various languages, as a salutation, as in *hail; wassail, q.v.* Another old form led to our Eng. *heal* (the early verb *whole* meant to make *whole*, to *heal*).

To *hale* someone to court is from Fr. *haler*, to pull; later we drew it from the same Fr. word in the form *haul* (though the Fr. is probably from OHG. *halon, holon*, whence G. *holen*, to fetch).

See wealth.

whoop, whooping-cough.

See cough.

whop, whopper.

See bounce.

wick.

See wicked.

wicked.

We may think of the *wicked* as strong evil-doers; but they are feeble in their resistance to sin. The word is from ME. *wikke*, feeble; it is thus a doublet of *weak*, from AS. *wāc*. Hence the call for correction instead of punishment.

There are, however, other suggestions. There is also AS. *wicca, wizard*, feminine *wicce, witch;* so that *wicked* might mean *bewitched*. And Henry Bett advances the idea that *wicked* (and *wick*, the live part of a candle) are doublets of *quick*: *wicked* meaning lively; hence, wayward. *Quick* is from AS. *cwic*, living, as in *quicksilver* and "touched to the *quick*", *i.e.*, through the epidermis to the raw, live flesh. From living it, also, came to mean lively; but no moral implication grew attached.

widow.

Since marriage has made of two one, a *widow* is a woman that has been emptied of herself. The OE. *widewe* is from the Indo-European root *widh—*, to be empty; as in Sansk. *vidh*, to lack, *vidhava*, widow; L. *viduus*. bereft, *vidua*, widow. Eng. *divide*, from L. *dividere*, may have this source; but *see improvised*. From the L. we have Eng. *viduage*, widowhood; *vidual*, and *viduity;* the *individual* is, of course, that which cannot be *divided*. The *widow-bird* (though sometimes by influence of its African habitat called *whidah-bird*) is named from the black feathers, as though in mourning (the black feathers are on the male!).

Wien (Vienna).

See dollar.

wife.

See woman; *cp.* husband.

Originally *wife* mean the same as *woman;* then it was used of a *woman* of low rank or employment, as in *fishwife;* often with old, as in *old wives' tale*. Then, as country folk today say *my woman* (sometimes, *the old woman*) when they mean *my wife*, so peasants of the 8th and 9th c. began to say *my wife* when they meant the *woman* of their house, and the word came to its present meaning.

wig.

Like the man that needs one, this word has lost its top: it is aphetic for *periwig*, the *peri* being mistaken for a prefix (as not in Gilbert and Sullivan's *The Peer and the Peri*, where the *peri* is the lower half of the hero. This *peri* is from Pers. *pari, peri*, originally a malevolent spirit. . . The comic opera pair, after their successes with titles beginning with *P*: *Pirates, Patience, Pinafore*, before abandoning the lucky letter doubled it as subtitle to *Iolanthe, or the Peer and the Peri.*) The adornment for the bald was earlier *periwike,* and is a doublet of *peruke,* from It. *perucca,* from Sp. *peluca,* from Sardinian *pilucca,* from L. *pilus,* hair, whence Eng. *pilo—,* hairy, as in Eng. *pilosis. Toupee,* first the *topknot* of the *periwig,* is from AS. *top,* from ON. *toppr,* tuft of hair.

The slang *palooka* may have some memory of this term; though it is a comic-strip coinage, perhaps from *pal* with telescopic suggestions of *lunatic* (*looney*) and *loco,* and the dialect *"lookū' here",* etc. The colloquial *pal* is via Eng. Gypsy from Turk. Gypsy *pral, phral,* comrade, brother — cognate with Sansk. *bhrātri,* Eng. *brother,* and L. *frater; cp. shed.*

wight.
See nausea.

wild goose chase.
This was at first (16th c.) a name for what children now call "follow master" or "follow the leader": a game, often on horseback, in which others had to pursue whatever course the leader took, as the flock follow the leader in a flight of wild geese. Since, in this game, the leader took a most erratic course, with dodgings about and shifts to make following difficult, the term came to be used for an erratic course; then for a pursuit unlikely to overtake the thing hunted (as one is unlikely to catch a *wild goose*).

wile.
See warrior.

will.
This is a very widespread word: OE. *willan,* past *wolde;* OHG. *wellen, well* (and in Eng. what you wish is—we trust—but etymologically anyway, *well* for you); L. *velle, volui,* whence Eng. *voluntary, cp. volley*); Sansk. *varati,* wishes. The NED has almost twenty-six columns devoted to the word *will.*

willy-nilly.
Most reduplicative words (*cp. patter; scurry*) seem formed for the pleasure or the emphasis of the double sound. There is a more basic reason for *willy-nilly.* AS. *willan,* to desire, is a common Teut. stem; its negative was *nyllan.* Thus, what one must do whether he will or he won't, he does *will he, nill he, willy-nilly.* (For *nil, see annihilate.*) *Willy-nilly* served as well for *will I* or *will ye;* but must not be confused with the Australian tornado, known to the natives as a *willy-willy.*

win.
At first win meant merely to struggle (AS. *winnan,* to strive after); but since stories are usually told by, or about, the *winner,* it came to mean to struggle successfully. But the story goes farther back, to a common Teut. *wan,* to desire, and therefore (later) to strive; this is from Sansk. *van,* to ask. From the Sansk. comes L. *venus, veneris,* to desire: whence of course *Venus,* goddess of Love, but also in her train *venereal,* relating to love, but esp. to diseases attributed to sex. L. *venerare,* to love, to honor, whence Eng. *venerate, venerable. Venery,* which means indulging in Venus' delight, also means hunting, from OFr. *vener,* from L. *venari,* to hunt, also from the basic sense, to desire. The L. noun *venation* gives us *venison,* which first meant any flesh from the hunt; thus *benediction, benison; oration, orison.*

There is a longer trail in the AS. *Wyn,* joy, gives us *winsome,* which at first meant propitious (helping to *win*), then fair. Teut. *wan,* whence *wana,* use, *wanyan,* to accustom: this works by two paths. Directly in AS. *won,* to be used to, whence ME. *wonen;* its past participle is *wont,* whence Eng. *wont,* as in the phrase "It was his *wont* to rise early." By way of OHG. it became *wenjan, wennan,* whence Eng. *wean,* to accustom: the process was to accustom the babe to bread instead of breast. The same *wan,* to struggle, grew into AS. *wén,* to strive after, hence to expect; whence Eng. *ween.*

Want is from another source, for its first meaning was not to desire, but to lack, thence to need, desire. Icel. *vant,* neuter of *vanr,* lacking, is its origin, whence AS. *wanian,* to decrease, whence Eng. *wane. Wan* is also used as a prefix (Du. *wanhoop,* lack-hope, despair): thus Eng. *wanton,* from ME. *wantouen,* from *wantowen, cp. uncouth*—from AS. *wan,* lacking + *towen,* from *togen,* past participle of *teon,* to draw, to bring up. The verb gives us both *tow* and *tug. Tug, tuck* (to draw together) and *touch* (to come together) are triplets. AS. *togen* is cognate with L. *ducere, duct—,* draw; whence *conduct; education;* etc.; *cp. aqueduct.*

wince, winch.
See lobster.

windfall.
We usually think of apples, but this word was first applied to trees. On many of the old English estates, the timber might not be felled by the nobles, it belonged to the King; but the trees blown down by storms were exempt from this royal holding; hence, an unexpected piece of good fortune was a *windfall.*

window.
The earlier spelling, *windore* and *windor* suggest that this is *wind-door,* an opening for ventilation. It was earlier still regarded as a peep-hole: the first AS. terms were *egthyrl* (eye-drill) and *eagdura* (eye-door). Our word is really from ME. *wind-oge,* from Icel. *vindauga,* from *vindr,* wind + *auga,* eye: thus combining the two values of air and vision.

wine.
See drink.

wing.
See vogue.

wink.
See lobster.

winsome.
See win.

winter.
In the torrid zone, the year is divided into the dry and the rainy season; but one season in the temperate zones is similarly named. For *winter* is from a nasalized form of the Indo-European *wed—, ud—,* to be wet, related to water; *cp. wash.*
Autumn is from L. *autumnus,* perhaps from *auctumnus,* the time of increase, from *augere, auct—; cp. auction.* For *spring, see attack; see somersault* for *summer.*

Wisconsin.
See States.

wiseacre.
See acre.

wit.
See moot.

witch.
See trance; *cp.* wicked.

witchhazel.
The *hazel* is a common Teut. word; the *witch* is a folk addition, as the wood of the tree was supposed to have the power of counteracting the spells of *witches.* That syllable, however, is a corruption of OE. *wick,* from *wicken,* whence *quick,* alive: probably so named because it is a twig of the *witchhazel* that responds as though living when the diviner holds it over ground whereunder water runs. *Witchhazel* is the wood used in divining rods. *Cp. trance. Divine* is from L. *divinus,* pertaining to the gods, from *divus, deus, god;* directly from Fr. *deviner,* to predict, to foresee as do the gods.

wither.
See weather.

withstand.
See tank.

wizard.
See wicked.

wold.
See gallop.

woman.
The creature was produced from the rib of man; the origin of the word is more disputable. Samuel Purchas, *Microcosmus,* 1619, indicates one theory: she is "a house builded for generation and gestation, whence our language calls her woman, womb-man." And indeed, Sansk. *vama* means both udder and woman, and is a distant source of our word *womb;* Heb. *racham* means a woman and the womb; OE. *moder* means womb, and gives Eng. *mother.* Eng. *quean* (now reserved for a *woman* in disrepute) is related to Gr. *gune, gyne,* woman, whence *gynecology,* and L. *cunnus,* which Horace uses to mean a girl. . . . Others attach their experience to the first syllable; thus G. Gascoigne, *The Steele Glas,* 1576, says "They be so sure even *woe* to *man* indeed": *woman,* from woe-man. Actually, an *f* has dropped from the word: *woman* is from AS. *wif-mann,* the *wife* or female of the *man* kind. (The *f* has similarly dropped in *leman,* from OE. *leofman,* a *lief,* or preferred, person, a sweetheart. The change from *i* to *o—wifman,* whence *woman*—is seen also in *I will* and *I will not, I won't.*) *Wif* is itself from AS. *wifan,* to join, to weave, and refers (probably) not to the *wife's* being

linked to her husband, but to the usual occupation of the female department of the household. Baking and weaving; weaving is preserved in *woman;* baking, in *lady, q.v. See wife.*

wont.
See win.

woodchuck.
See coquette. (One could never have asked: "How much wood would a *we-jack* chuck?")

woof.
See wasp.

word.
In the beginning was the *word*: Sansk. *vratam* meant command, law. From this came L. *verbum* (*see sap.*), *word,* and the widespread Teut. forms, *e.g.*, Eng. *word.*

world.
The world may seem very *old;* but for human concerns it is at least *man-old*: from OHG. *wer,* man + AS. *ald, eald, old;* AS. *yldo,* an age: before the Teut. languages were separated these two were combined to mean the age of man, the course of man's life, of man's experience, etc.—a chain of senses that culminated in the present sense of the place in which man finds himself. *Old* is itself quite *old,* AS. *ald* being related to Goth. *alan;* L. *alere, alt—,* to nourish. Thus L. *altus* means nourished, therefore tall, high, deep, whence *altitude, alto;* and *ex* (as an intensive: standing out) + *altus* gives us *exalt.* From AS. *eald* comes *elder,* a doublet of *older;* also **alderman,** from AS. *ealdorman,* from *ealdor,* parent, head of family.

On the L. side of the growth *alere* gives us *alumnus,* nurseling, foster-son; feminine *alumna. Pro,* forth + *alere,* whence *proles,* offspring, whence *proletarius*: this term was applied in Rome to the lowest class of citizens, who could not own property, who were regarded as serving only by bearing offspring for the state, whence *proletarian, proletariat,* who now in the U.S.S.R. supposedly are the state. *Prolific* is *proles* + *ficare,* from *facere,* to make; *proliferate,* from *proles* + *ferre,* to bring. Also from *alere,* to nourish, come *aliment,* nourishment, *alimentary* canal; *cp. alimony.*

The inceptive form of *alere,* to *nourish,* is *alescere,* to grow; with L. *ad,* to, whence *adolescere, adult—,* whence the growing *adolescent* and the grown *adult.* (*Adulterate* has quite a different source: *ad,* to + *alter,* other, different: to change to something different, to *alter;* hence, to corrupt.) With L. *co, com,* together, we have the inceptive forms *coalesce,* and *coalition.*

While *prolific* is from this source, the synonym *prolix* is from *prolixus,* past participle of *proliquere,* from *pro,* forth + *liquere,* to flow, to be *liquid.* Hence also *liquor.* L. *liquidus,* of flowing water, thence came to mean clear; hence, *liquidate,* to clear off an account. The base is Sansk. *li,* to melt, *liquefy;* related to *ri,* to drip, ooze, distil; whence L. *ripa* (LL. *riva*) bank, whence Eng. *riparian* rights, and L. *rivus,* whence Fr. *rivière,* whence Eng. *river.* Note that *elixir* is not related: it is from Arab. *el, al,* the, + *iksir,* philosopher's stone, from Gr. *xerion,* a drying powder, from *xeros,* dry, whence L. *serenus* (originally of the clear sky: *sera,* evening, whence Fr. *soir,* Eng. *serenade*), *serene.* Which seems to carry us a good way around the *world!*

worm.
See wormwood.

wormwood.
The suggestion of sackcloth and ashes comes from the bitterness of the herb thus named, and that taste probably twisted the word. It is from AS. *wermod,* also G. *Wermuth,* from *wer,* man (as in *werwolf*: OS. *wer;* L. *vir*) + *muth, mood,* which first meant courage, strength. The herb was early used as an aphrodisiac, and is still mixed in drinks, whence *vermouth.*

Eng. *worm* is from OE. *wyrm* (used also of serpent or dragon, as in *Beowulf*), cognate with L. *vermin; cp. variety.*

worship.
This has no relation to the vessel in *warship* (nor to the first syllable of my name, *Shipley,* which is shortened from *sheep lea*): the second part, *—ship, q.v.,* means state, condition. The first part was AS. *weorth,* value. The word was first a noun, indicating high *worth,* preserved in the expression Your *Worship,* of one deserving veneration. Thence the verb. From the financial aspect usually attached to thoughts of value comes the query How much is he *worth?* Other things are more *worth* while.

worsted.
See cloth.

worth.
See worship.

wrap.
See develop.

wrath, wreath.
See awry.

wreath, wreathe.
See writhe.

wrest.
See pylorus.

wriggle, wring.
See awry.

wrist.
See pylorus.

write.
See read.

writhe.
Like all words beginning with *wr* (most with *w*, for that matter) this is not Romance, but common Teut., OE. *writhan*, to twist. A weak form of the same verb gives us *wreathe*. The word *wreath* referred first to anything twisted, as a band or fillet, a ring, then esp. one on the brow of a noble or champion; hence, of flowers. It is of course used figuratively of clouds, smoke, snow, and other convolutions. *Cp. awry.*

wrong.
See awry.

Wyoming.
See States.

X

X ray.

The L. *radius* was the spoke of a wheel. Hence, when folks began to speak of *radiation,* they were simply applying to light the idea that its beams seem to travel forth as spokes from a wheel. Hence (via Fr. *rai*) Eng. *ray.* The element Mme Curie and her husband isolated was named *radium* because it seems to give forth *rays* without any loss. We speak in Eng. of the *radius* of a circle, directly from the L. word. When W. C. Röntgen, Professor at Würzburg, discovered (1895) a *ray* the nature of which he could not determine, he borrowed from algebra the letter used to designate an unknown item, and called it the *X ray.*

xenon.

See element.

This "stranger in the air" has company of other words from Gr. *xenos,* guest, stranger, foreigner. There are a number in natural history, from *xenia* and *xenacanthine* to *xenurine.* Some tribes practice *xenogamy,* marriage only outside the tribe. Too many persons, forgetting pioneer and proper ways, have lost the sense of a stranger as guest, and must be cured of *xenophobia.*

xylophone.

Although some of the bars are now made of metal or plastics, this is indeed the voice of the wood; from Gr. *xylon,* wood, + *phone,* voice. The prefix *xylo*— is used in many Eng. scientific words, *e.g., xylochrome, xylopolist;* also *xylene, xylyl,* and the like.

Y

yacht.

This word is from Du. *jagt,* earlier *jacht,* from *jagten,* to speed, to hunt, from OG. *gahi,* quick, lively — whence Eng. *gay;* akin to G. *gehen,* AS. *gan, gangan,* ME. *gon,* whence Eng. *go, gone;* also *gang.* The *yacht* was a speedy boat with which the privateers (*cp. private*) hunted. More recently, millionaires' sons would get their *gang* and have a *gay* time on a *yacht.*

Yankee.

John Bull, the Englishman, was first named, 1712, in the title of a series of political pamphlets by John Arbuthnot, in which *Nicholas Frog* is the Dutchman, and *Lewis Baboon,* the Frenchman. Du. *Jan,* diminutive *Janke,* in the New World became *Yankee,* the name the Du. colonists had for the English. It was taken as a flag in *Yankee Doodle.* (However, the Flanders nickname for the Dutch was *Jan Kees,* Johnny Cheese.) *Gringo* is the term the Mexicans gave the American (English). It may be from Sp. *griego,* Greek (as in "It's Greek to me.") ; but it is commonly supposed to be from the opening words of a song by Burns, popular with the soldiers in the Mexican War:

Green grow the rashes O
The happiest hours that ere I spent
Were spent among the lasses O.

Soldier themes vary little down the ages.

The origin of *Uncle Sam,* for the United States, is unknown. The most common story is that the term spread from *"Uncle Sam" Wilson,* a U. S. inspector of meat at Troy, New York, after the Revolution.

yaw.

See gaga.

ye.

This was the primitive form of the first person plural pronoun, in the Aryan tongues: AS. *ge;* OHG. *ir;* Gr. *hym—;* Sans. *yuyam.* The dative and accusative form was AS. *eow,* Eng. *you.* The genitive of *ye* was AS. *eower,* G. *eurer,* Eng. *your.*

The word *ye* in such archaistic absurdities as *Ye Olde Curiosity Shoppe* is actually *the,* and should be pronounced as such. The first letter is not *y,* but "thorn" (more like a *p,* or a *y* with a line closing the top), the AS. symbol for *th.* Ignorance and the desire to be "fancy" often go together.

yeast.

This common Teut. form (AS. *gist*) goes back to Sansk. *yasyati,* to boil or bubble. It has no relation to the east, despite its rising. Without it we have *unleavened* bread; *cp. matzah.* The *leaven,* however, is related to the *levant,* the east. It is via Fr. *levain* from L. *levamen,* that which raises, from L. *levare, levans, levant—* (present participle), *levat—,* to raise. The frequentative of L. *levare* is *levitare, levitat—,* to lift; whence Eng. *levitation.* Hence also, via Fr. *lever,* to raise, comes the Eng. *lever,* with which (given the fulcrum) one might raise the world. The L. adjective *levis* (with a short *e*) means light; with a long *e,* it means smooth; hence Eng. *levigate,* to smooth, to make into a smooth fine powder. *Levity* is lightness; the physical sense is obsolete; there remains only the sense of lightness of thought or purpose. Although light, the stem seems unrelated to *leven, levin,* Eng. poetical word for lightning. It has no relation, either, to the Jewish *levirate* marriage (this word is from L. *levir,* brother-in-law), as shown in the Biblical story of Ruth and Naomi; nor with the *Levitical* proceedings of the Jews, from the tribe of *Levi,* assistants to the priests.

For slight of hand, however, we sometimes use the Fr. term *legerdemain,* light of hand: Fr. *léger* from a LL. form *leviarius,* from L. *levis,* light. The earlier Eng. form was not *slight* but *sleight* (as we again spell the term: *sleight of hand*), from ON. *slaegth* from *slaegr, sly* . . . which sometimes seems to make things rise more effectively than *yeast.*

yellow.

This word (from AS. *geolw—;* note G. *gelb,* yellow and G. *geld,* gold; cognate with L. *helvus;* Gr. *chloros,* whence Eng. *chlorine, chlorophyll,* from *chloros* + *phyllon,* leaf) is interesting for its associations. *Yellow* is the color of the medieval fool (who carried on his stick, or bauble, the symbols of fertility); it was at first the color of love. Malvolio (Shakespeare, *Twelfth Night*) shows his love by putting on yellow hose. But Gr. *chloros* (from *chlon,* a young shoot) meant both light yellow and light green; gradually yellow was used for lust and green for love. The medieval German women of pleasure wore *yellow* as a sign; in Russia the "*yellow* ticket" was their passport. G. *gel* meant both; from it come G. *geil,* lustful and G. *gelb,* yellow. Eng. *gull,* yellow, survives in the sense of fool. At the banquet of the Lord Mayor of London, in November, the fool used to be summoned to leap into a huge bowl of custard.

Gooseberry is corrupt for *groose,* earlier *grozell berry,* from Fr. *groseille,* from G. *kraus,* curly. But the corruption suggests the association of *goose* with simpleton; and the green of the berry (as also in *greenhorn*), the unripeness of the fool. Hence a favorite early English desert was *gooseberry fool,* a plate of gooseberries covered with custard. Striking with the fool's bauble is linked with hazing and the rites of initiating (*i.e.,* creating one of the tribe or society), and may be traced to old totem practices of fertilization. *Cp. cat-o'-nine-tails.*

yeoman.

The *yeoman* of the Guard probably did good work, for his reputation has made the expression "he did *yeoman* service" apply to excellent performance. The word itself was originally *young man;* the *young men* being used as pages or servants. *Cp. young.* Thus the G. *Junker* was also G. *Jung Herr,* young Sir. The G. *Herr,* now used like Eng. *Mister* (from *master,* from L. *magister; cp. mystery*) was, also like Eng. *Mister,* once a more important title; it is from G. *hehr, noble.* Note (despite the association with G. *Jung,* young) that the noble was often in olden times the patriarch: G. *hehr* is related to Eng. *hoar,* white-haired; just as *sir,* a shortening of Eng. *sire,* is via Fr. *sieur* from L. *senior,* elder: the Elders of the city were the magistrates.

The *Junker* is thus not related to *junk,* which has two other sources. The boat is from Port. *junco;* but (it was not applied first to the Chinese ships) we are not sure whether it is borrowed from the Javanese *djong,* or directly from the Port. *junco,* reed, of which its sails were fashioned; *cp. junket.* The *junk* that you find in a *junk-shop* was originally also from the sea; the *junk-shop* itself was a sailors' supply store. Perhaps from the Port. *junco,* reed, rushes, the word *junk* was used, until the mid-18th c., of worn-out ship's cable; then, pieces of old cable used for patch work; then, any old pieces, hence the current sense.

yodel.

See Yule.

yoke.

See yokel; subjugate.

yokel.

"Ain't he the wise old *owl!*" says the song; but for more years the solemn blinking bird has been the symbol of stupidity. *Yokel,* which some have connected with *yoke* (a common Aryan word: AS. *geoc;* L. *jugum, jungere, junct—,* to join, whence *junction, conjunction; cp. subjugate.* Sansk. *yuga*), as implying a farm boy, a rustic, is probably linked with Shetland *yuggle,* owl; Dan. *ugle,* AS. *ule, owl.* Thus early Eng. *guff, goff,* from OE. *gofish,* stupid, whence Eng. slang *goof,* is from It. *gofo,* from *guffo, owl,* possibly from Pers. *kuf, owl.* Similarly our slang, *plumb loco* is good Sp. *loco,* stupid, from It. *locco,* a fool, from *alocco,* an *owl,* from L. *ulucus, owl.*

you.

See ye.

young.

This common Teut. form is traced to an Indo-European root *juwnkos,* whence L. *juvencus; see youth. Gaudeamus,* or *gaudy night,* has become the Eng. term for a party, esp. a college revel (L. *gaudere,* to rejoice, whence also Eng. *gaudy,* showy), from the first words of the song:

Gaudeamus igitur
Juvenes dum sumus . . .
"Then let us rejoice while we are young."

Junker is sometimes spelled *Younker; cp. yeoman.* And flippancy or immaturity (*cp. spinster*) is in the *youngster, q.v.* The village of *Yonkers* was first *Yonkers Kill, Yunge Herr* creek.

youngster.
This word, with its contemptuous ending (*cp. spinster*), is really corrupted from a title of pride among the Germans: from *Junker,* from *jungherr,* from *jung, young* + *herr,* sir, lord. The earlier Eng. form, still used of animals, is *youngling.* By analogy with *youngster,* the familiar *oldster* has been coined.
See young.

your.
See ye.

youth.
This word, like *young, q.v.,* is common Teut., AS. *geong, young;* AS. *geogoth youth.* The nasal sound drops in the transfer from adjective to noun, as also in Du *jong, jeugd* and G. *jung, Jugend.* It has kept out of L. *juvenis, youthful* (whence Eng. *juvenile*) and the L. noun *juventus;* from the Sansk. *yuvan.* L. *juvencus* means bullock. Perhaps from the idea of the young fellow's being a helper to the adult, the L. *adjuvare* (*ad,* to) means to help. Its frequentative is *adjutare,* to assist; the present participle of this, *adjutant—,* helping, gives us Eng. *adjutant.* In the 17th c., the word used was *adjuvant.*

ytterbium.
See element.

yttrium.
See element.

Yule.
It is suggested that this is related to *wheel,* from the turning of the sun at the year's end; but it is more directly connected with the festivities at that time, when primitive folk were reassured that nights were receding and the time of eternal darkness was not yet come. *December* and *January* were once called the *former Yule* and the *after Yule,* from ME. *yollen,* to cry aloud, from AS. *gylan,* to make merry, whence G. *jodeln,* whence Eng. *yodel.* Also Icel. *jol, Yule,* via OFr. *jolif,* gives us Eng. *jolly.* Hence we make merry at *Yuletide*—although Queen Victoria's husband was the first to develop the practice of a green Christmas tree (instead of a burning *Yule* log) for the celebration.
Pleasant seeming may hide grimmer fact; Satan may lurk behind apparently innocent pranks. Thus OFr. *jolif* (Fr. *jolie,* pretty, gay) is traced through LL. *diabolivus* to L. *diabolus,* devil, q.v.

Z

zany.
There is an old saying that the Lord takes especial care of his fools. (It is probably as true as that drunkards escape accident.) Yet it has etymological sanction in the *zany*, the buffoon of the medieval comedy. For *zany* is from *Zanni*, from It. *Giovanni*, from Heb. *Yohannan*—which name means The Lord showeth mercy, from *Yo*, for *Jehovah* + *hanan*, to show mercy.

zenana.
See seraglio.

zenith.
See azimuth.

zenophobia.
See Dutch. The better spelling is *xenophobia; see xenon.*

zephyr.
See cipher.

Zeppelin.
See blimp.

zero.
See cipher.

zest.
We speak of something as adding *zest* to a situation. Originally, it was the *zest* that made something piquant—especially a drink—for the *zest* was a piece of orange or lemon peel put in, from Fr. *zeste*, skin on fruit segment. The word was transferred from the object to its effect.
The Fr. *zeste*, membrane that divides the segments of a nut or fruit, is from L. *scistus*, from L. *scindere, sciss—*, to cut; *cp. shed.*

zeugma.
See subjugate.

zinc.
See element.

Zionist.
Every man has a hill to climb—and bears his own cross. But the hill of the *Zionists* antedates the Christian climbing. The Heb. *tsiyon* means hill; but the word is applied esp. to the hill at Jerusalem on which the city of David was built, which is thence looked upon as the center of the Jewish faith. The movement *Zionism*, for the reestablishment of the Jewish homeland in Palestine, was founded in 1896 by *Theodor Herzl.*

zipper.
This word, coined in the 1930's to name a convenient fastening device, is of imitative origin. It is from *zip*, which represents the sound of cloth *ripping*, or an insect or a bullet in flight. The *zipper* moves quickly, but is supposed to prevent the *rip*. *Rip* is Low G. in origin, Frisian *rippe*, to tear; Flem. *rippen*, to pull off roughly; it has no connection with *riparian* (*see world*) though it may demand *repair*. *Repair* is from Fr. *reparer*, from L. *reparare, reparat—*, to restore; whence *reparations*, from L. *parare*, to *prepare; see overture*. Note, however, that Eng. *par* (L. *par*, equal) and Eng. *peer* (the House of *Peers*) are Fr. *pair;* to *repair* may thus be to make equal again. *Cp. peep.*
To *repair* to a place is from OFr. *repairier* from LL. *repatriare*, to go back (L. *re*, back) to one's fatherland, L. *patria* from Gr. *patris*. Hence also *expatriate* and *repatriation;* and (Gr. *patriotes*) *patriot.*

zircon.
See carnelian.

zirconium.
See element.

zodiac.
This circle of heavenly signs through the seasons was of gradual growth. The

ancient Accadians spoke of the Furrow of Heaven, ploughed by the heavenly Directing Bull (our *Taurus,* from L. *taurus,* bull); from ca. 4000 to ca. 1700 B.C., this was the first of the signs. And then there were six; all animals, hence Aristotle called it the circle of the *Zodion* (Gr. little animal, diminutive of *zoon,* animal, neuter of *zoos,* living, from *zon,* life, from *zaein,* to live). *Libra,* the scales, was the first non-living sign added.

zoology.
See plant.

zymograph.
See graffito.

zymurgy.
This word refers to the process or the art of fermenting (as in making wine), from Gr. *zyme,* leaven (*cp. graffito*) + *ourgia, ergia,* working, whence also *energy.* Thus *zym—, zymo—,* are used to form various compounds, *e.g., zymogen, zymosis.* An *Azymite* is one that uses unleavened bread in the eucharist, hence a name (applied by the Greek Catholics) for the Roman Catholics. And an *azyme* (Gr. *a,* not) is a piece of the unleavened bread used by the Jews during the Passover festival, called by them *matzah,* plural *matzoth,* from Heb. *matzah,* to press dry. Where the *King James Bible* (*I Corinthians,* v, 7) says "purge out therefore the old leaven, that ye may be a new lump, as ye are unleavened. For even Christ our passover is sacrificed for us:" the older Eng. version (Wyclif) says "as ye are *azymes.*"

APPENDIX I.

Doublets.

(*After a set of words, indicates that they are discussed in the main list.)

Doublets are words that have arrived in our language by different routes from the same source. The following are some of the most common. They can all be traced in the N E D, if you like the hunting; their presence here suggests the richness of the language, and the varying stories of words—some of these, from the same source, have taken quite different meanings.

abbreviate—abridge.*
acute—cute—ague.*
adamant—diamond.*
adjutant—aid.
aggravate—aggrieve.*
aim—esteem—estimate.
allocate—allow.
alloy—ally.*
an—one.
antic—antique.
appreciate—appraise—apprize.
aptitude—attitude.*
army—armada.*
asphodel—daffodill.
assemble—assimilate.
astound—astonish—stun.
attach—attack.*

band—bond.*
banjo—mandolin.*
bark—barge.
beaker—pitcher.
beam—boom.*
belly—bellows.*
benison—benediction.*
blame—blaspheme.*
block—plug.
book—buck (wheat)—beech.*
boulevard—bulwark.
brother—friar.

cad—cadet.*
cadence—chance.
cage—cave.*
calumny—challenge.*
cancel—chancel.*
cant—chant.*
captain—chieftain.*
cavalry—chivalry.*
cell—hall.
channel—canal.*
charge—cargo.
chariot—cart.
chattel—cattle—capital.*
check (in chess)—shah.* (*Checkmate* is Pers. *shah mat,* the king is dead.)
costume—custom.*
crate—hurdle.

daft—deft.
dainty—dignity.

danger—dominion.*
dauphin—dolphin.
deck—thatch.
defeat—defect.
depot—deposit.
devilish—diabolical.*
diaper—jasper.
disc—discus—dish—dais—desk.*
ditto—dictum.

employ—imply—implicate.*
ensign—insignia.
etiquette—ticket.*
extraneous—strange.*

fabric—forge.
fact—feat.
faculty—facility.
fashion—faction.
feeble—foible.
flame—phlegm.
flask—fiasco.*
flour—flower.*
fungus—sponge.*

genteel—gentle—gentile—jaunty.*
glamour—grammar.*
guarantee—warranty.*

hale—whole.*

inch—ounce.*
isolation—insulation.*

jay—gay.

kennel—channel—canal.*
kin—genus.*

lace—lasso.*
listen—lurk.
lobby—lodge.
locust—lobster.*

manœuvre—manure.*

monetary—monitory.*
monster—muster.*
musket—mosquito.

naive—native.*

onion—union.*

paddock—park.
parable—parabola—parole—parley—palaver.*
parson—person.*
particle—parcel.
patron—pattern.
piazza—place—plaza.*
poignant—pungent.
poison—potion.*
poor—pauper.
pope—papa.*
praise—price.

quiet—quit—quite—coy.*

raid—road.
ransom—redemption.*
ratio—ration—reason.
respect—respite.*
restrain—restrict.*
rover—robber.

saliva—slime.
scandal—slander.*
scourge—excoriate.*
scout—auscultate.*
secure—sure.
sergeant—servant.
sovereign—soprano.
stack—stake—steak—stock.
supervisor—surveyor.

tamper—temper.*
triumph—trump.*
tulip—turban.
two—deuce.*

utter—outer.

valet—varlet.*
vast—waste.*
veneer—furnish.
verb—word.*

whirl—warble.

yelp—yap.

zero—cipher.*
(and hundreds more).

APPENDIX II.

Words From Names.

(*After a word, indicates that it is discussed in the main list.)

Many names, without change or slightly modified, have come to be used as common nouns, to designate an object or action associated with the person or place. Some of these have had a vogue and passed [*e.g.*, *Lillian Russell*, half a cantaloup with ice cream in its hollow, from the American actress of the early 20th c.; *Fletcherize*, to chew thoroughly, from *Dr. Horace Fletcher*, who prescribed thirty-two chews per bite; *Hooverize*, to use food economically, from *Herbert Hoover*, Quaker food administrator of the U. S. in World War I, later president; *Oslerize*, to kill, or urge the killing of, all men over forty, from *Dr.* (*Sir*) *Wm. Osler*, d. 1919]; others have become a more enduring part of the language. Only a few such words are listed below, with the source. *See* also *cloth*.

Adonis*:
Beautiful Greek youth, *Adonis*, loved by Aphrodite.

agaric:
Agaria, town in Sarmatia.

agate*:
Achates, river in Sicily.

alexandrine:
Medieval French poem about *Alexander* the Great.

Alice blue:
Alice Roosevelt Longworth. Many colors and flowers, esp. roses and dahlias, have been named after persons.

America:
Amerigo Vespucci, Italian explorer and mapmaker; also Columbia, Colombia, Columbus: *Christopher Columbus*, Italian explorer.

ammonia*:
Jupiter Ammon, Roman god.

ampere:
A. M. Ampère, French physicist.

Ananias:
Ananias, stricken *dead* (*Bible, Acts* v) for lying about what he got for a piece of land, to cheat the church of its share. His wife, Sapphira, who shared his guilt, shared his fate. Theodore Roosevelt, President of the U. S., 1901-1909, often spoke of men as members of the Ananias Club.

Annie Oakley:
Expert rifle shot, with Buffalo Bill's circus, *Annie Oakley* used to shoot playing cards; hence, the name was applied to punched free tickets.

aphrodisiac*:
Aphrodite, Greek goddess of love; *cp. erotic*.

areopagus:
Gr. *areis pagos*, the hill of *Ares* (god of War), where the Athenian high court met.

argosy*:
Ragusa, in Dalmatia.

Argus-eyed:
Demigod of 100 eyes, *Argus*, whom jealous Juno set to watch Io—as with most jealous ones, in vain. After his death, *Argus'* eyes were set in the peacock's tail.

arras:
A fabric, then a hanging made thereof (through one such, Hamlet slew Polonius), from the chief place of manufacture, the town *Arras* in Artois.

artesian well:
First bored, 18th c., at *Artois*, France.

astrachan:
Astrakhan, Russia.

Atlantic*:
See atlas.

atlas*:
Giant *Atlas*, punished by the gods.

babbitt:
The businessman in *Babbitt*, by Sinclair Lewis, 1922. Also, babbittry.

bacchanals*:
Bacchus, god of wine and revelry.

bakelite:
Leo H. Baekeland, 1863-1944.

bartlett (pear):
Enoch Bartlett, Massachusetts.

battology*:
Battos, a stammerer in Herodotus; *see abate* in main list.

bayonet:
Bayonne, France.

begonia:
Flower introduced into England from Jamaica ca. 1775, named after *Michel Begon* (1638-1712) Fr. governor of Santo Domingo.

bellarmine*:
Cardinal Bellarmine, 16th c.

bergamask:
See end of this Appendix.

bison:
Gr. *bison,* from *biston, Bistonia,* Thrace.

blanket*:
Thomas Blanket, set up loom in Bristol, 1340. Also influenced by Fr. *blanch,* white.

bloomers*:
Mrs. Amelia Bloomer, American, ca. 1850.

bobby:
Sir Robert (Bobby) Peel, London chief of police; hence, also, *peeler.*

bohemian:
Bohemia, eastern Europe, supposed origin of the Gypsies. Popularized in Henri Murger's *La Vie de Bohème,* 1877.

bowdlerize*:
Thomas Bowdler; 1818 edition of Shakespeare.

bowie:
Col. James Bowie, d. 1836.

boycott*:
Capt. Boycott, Irish land agent.

braille:
Louis Braille, 1834.

brie:
Brie, ancient section of France.

Bright's disease:
Dr. Richard Bright, London, described kidney diseases, 1827.

bronze*:
Brundisium, Italy.

brougham:
Lord Brougham, ca. 1850.

Brownian movement:
Dr. Robert Brown, ca. 1870.

brummagem*:
Birmingham, England.

bunsen (burner):
R. W. Bunsen, Heidelberg, ca. 1890.

Caesarean*:
Julius Caesar.

camellia:
G. J. Camelli, Jesuit priest, d. 1706.

camembert:
Camembert, town in Normandy.

cantaloup*:
Cantalupo, Italy.

cardigan:
Earl of Cardigan, fought in Crimean War, 1855.

caryatid:
Gr. *karyatid,* priestess of Artemis at *Caryae,* Laconia, Greece.

Cassandra:
Cassandra, true prophetess no one believed, in the *Iliad.*

cereal*
Ceres, Roman goddess of grain and harvest.

chalcedony:
(Mentioned in the *Bible*: *Rev.* xxi, 19) from ? *Chalcedon* in Asia Minor. Also found as *charcedonia,* as though from Gr. *Karchedon,* Carthage.

cherrystone clams:
Cheriton, Virginia, on Chesapeake Bay.

Chippendale:
Thomas Chippendale, England, 1775.

coach*:
Fr. *coche,* from Gr. *Kutsche,* from Hung. *kocsi,* from *Kocs,* Hungary.

Colombia, Columbia:
See America.

cologne*:
Cologne, Germany.

colophony:
Colophon, town in Lydia. Gr. *colophon* means summit, end; hence, the use in printing.

colt:
Samuel Colt, 19th c. American.

copper*:
Cyprus.

coulomb:
Fr. physicist, *C. A. de Coulomb,* d. 1806.

cravat:
Fr. *cravate,* Croat; Croatian *Hervat,* man of *Croatia,* Austria.

cupidity*:
Cupid, young Roman god of desire; *cp. erotic.*

currant:
Corinth, Greece.

daguerreotype:
L. J. M. Daguerre, 19th c. French.

dances:
See end of this list.

dauphin (Fr. dolphin)*:
Dauphiné, province of France. Similarly, the English Prince of Wales.

derby*:
Lord Derby, began the races in 1780; the hat was worn there.

diesel (engine):
Rudolf Diesel, German, 1858-1913; engine developed in the Krupp factory, 1893-7.

diddle:
Jeremy Diddler, in James Kenney's farce *Raising the Wind,* 1803.

doily:
Doyley, 18th c. London linen draper; but (H. Betts points out) the *d'Oily* family held the manor of Fish Hill for giving the king "a tablecloth of three shillings in price."

dollar*:
From silver mined in *Joachimsthal,* Germany.

dumdum bullet:
First used by the British Bengal Artillery at *Dumdum,* near Calcutta.

Duncan Phyfe:
New York cabinet maker, *Duncan Phyfe.*

Dundreary (whiskers):
Lord Dundreary, in Tom Taylor's farce, *Our American Cousin,* 1859.

echo*:
Nymph *Echo,* in Greek mythology.

epicurean:
Epicurus, Greek philosopher, 341-270 B.C.

ermine:
Armenia; the animal (not from Armenia) was named from the fur.

erotic:
Eros, Greek god of love, corresponding to Roman Cupid.

euhemerism:
Sicilian critic, *Euhemerus,* ca. 315 B. C., who gave human interpretations to the Greek myths.

euphuism*:
Euphues, book in two parts, by John Lyly, 1579-1580.

fabian:
Quintus Fabius Maximus, called *Cunctator* (Delayer) because his avoidance of direct battle foiled Hannibal in the Second Punic War, 317 B.C. Hence, also, English *Fabian Society,* founded 1884, of Socialists, opposed to change by violence.

Fahrenheit:
G. D. Fahrenheit, German, 1686-1736.

faience:
Faenza, Italy.

Fallopian (tube):
Fallopius of Modena, d. 1562.

farad:
Michael Faraday, English scientist, 1791-1867.

Ferris (wheel):
G. W. G. Ferris, 19th c. American.

fez:
Fez, Morocco.

forsythia:
William Forsyth brought it from China, ca. 1800.

frankfurter*:
Frankfort, Germany. *See dollar* in main list.

frieze*:
(Cloth) *Friesland,* Holland; (architecture) *Phrygia.*

galvanize:
Luigi Galvani, It. physiologist, 1737-98.

gamboge:
From *Cambodia.*

gardenia:
Dr. Alexander Garden; came from Scotland to South Carolina, studied the flora of the Blue Ridge Mountains.

gargantuan*:
Gargantua, book by François Rabelais, 1534.

gasconnade:
Gascogne, Gascony, France.

gauss:
Karl K. Gauss, German mathematician, d. 1855.

gavotte:
See end of this Appendix.

gibus:
M. Gibus, French hatmaker, ca. 1850.

Gilbertian:
The master of comic opera, *Wm. Schwenk Gilbert,* 1836-1911; at his best when paired with the musician, Arthur Sullivan.

gladstone (bag):
W. E. Gladstone, English, 1808-98.

Gobelin:
Gobelin family of dyers and tapestry weavers, 18th c. France.

gongorism:
Gongora, Spanish author, 1561-1627.

Gordian knot*:
Gordius, Phrygian workman who became king by being first to enter the temple of Jupiter at *Gordium* after an oracle had said whoever first entered was to be made king. His son, Midas, gave to the temple the chariot *Gordius* had driven; and another oracle prophesied that whoever would untie its knot would conquer Asia. Alexander succeeded—with his sword.

gothite:
The poet (and scientist) *Goethe,* German, 1749-1832.

greengage:
Sir William Gage, English, ca. 1760.

Gregorian (calendar*; chant):
Pope Gregory XIII, 1582.

guillotine.
A Fr. physician, Joseph I. *Guillotin,* in 1789 suggested the use of this device, at first called *Madame Guillotin.*

hamburger*:
Hamburg, Germany. *See dollar* in main list.

havelock:
General Henry Havelock, against the Indian mutiny (U. S.), 1857.

Heaviside layer:
O. Heaviside, 20th c. British physicist.

hector*:
Hector, prince of Troy.

helot:
Helos, town in Laconia, conquered by Sparta.

henry:
Joseph Henry, American physicist, 1797-1878, discovered how to produce induced electric current.

hermetically*:
Hermes, Greek messenger of the gods.

hiddenite:
W. E. Hidden, New York.

Hitlerism:
Adolph Hitler, German Nazi* leader, 20th c.

Hobson's choice:
Thomas Hobson, 17th c. London stableman, made every person hiring horses take the next in order.

hyacinth* (also jacinth):
Young Spartan, *Hyacinth,* changed by Apollo into the flower.

indigo*:
Sp. *Indico,* L. *Indicum,* of *India.*

iris*, iridium:
Iris, Greek messenger of the gods, changed by jealous Juno into the rainbow.

jacinth:
See hyacinth.

Jack Ketch:
Jack Ketch, the hangman during the reign of James II of England.

Jack Tar:
Dickens' term for a sailor, from *tarpaulin,* or their hats of *tarred* cloth. *Tar* was used for sailor as early as the 17th c.

jeremiad:
Jeremiah, Hebrew prophet, 629-586 B.C.

jobation:
Job, Hebrew 8th c. B.C.; model of patience.

Jonah*:
Jonah, character (and book) of the *Bible.*

joule:
James P. Joule, English physicist, 1818-89.

jovial*:
Jove, Jupiter (Heb. *Jahveh?*), Roman god.

Julian calendar*:
Julius Caesar; also, *July. August* is from *Augustus Caesar.*

laconic*:
Laconia, Lacedaemonia, Greece.

lambert:
Johann H. Lambert, German physicist.

landau:
Landau, town in Bavaria.

Laputan, Laputian:
From the visionary inhabitants of *Laputa,* the flying island in Jonathan Swift's *Gulliver's Travels,* 1726.

lavaliere:
Louise de la Lavalière, mistress of Louis XIV of France.

lazar:
Lazarus, beggar in the Bible.

leather-stocking:
The five *Leather-Stocking Tales* of the U. S. Indian frontier, written by James Fenimore Cooper from 1823 to 1841. The best known is *The Last of the Mohicans,* 1826.

Leninism:
Nicolai Lenin, first leader of Soviet Russia.

Leyden jar:
Invented, 1745-6, at *Leyden,* Holland.

lilliputian*:
From the tiny folk of *Lilliput,* in *Gulliver's Travels. Cp. Laputan.*

limousine*:
Limousin, ancient province of France.

loganberry:
American named *Logan* produced this hybrid.

Lothario*:
The gay *Lothario,* in Rowe's drama *The Fair Penitent,* 1704.

lyceum*:
Lykeion, garden in Athens.

lynch*:
James Lynch of Virginia?

macadamize:
John L. McAdam, Scottish engineer, 1755-1836.

machiavellian*:
Niccolo Machiavelli, of Florence, 1469-1527.

mackinaw:
Mackinaw Island, between Lake Huron and Lake Michigan, North America.

mackintosh:
Charles Mackintosh, invented the material; English, 1766-1843.

magnet:
Magnesia, whence also *magnetism, magneto.*

magnolia:
Pierre Magnol, Fr. professor of medicine, d. 1715. *Cp. nasturtium,* in main list.

malapropism:
Mrs. Malaprop, in Sheridan's comedy *The Rivals,* 1775.

Malpighian tubes:
Marcell Malpighi, Italian anatomist, 1628-94.

manil(l)a:
Manila, capital of the Philippines.

mansard roof:
François Mansard, French architect, 1598-1662.

marcel:
French hairdresser, *Marcel Grateau,* 19th c.

martinet*:
French army drillmaster, *General Martinet,* under Louis XIV.

Marxist:
Karl Marx, 19th c. socialist.

maudlin*:
Mary Magdalen, in the *Bible.*

mausoleum*:
Mausolus, ancient King of Caria.

maxim (gun):
Hiram S. Maxim, American, 19th c.

mayonnaise:
Port Mahon, Minorca.

mazurka:
See end of this Appendix.

McIntosh (apple):
John McIntosh, Canadian.

Melba toast:
Mme. Melba, opera singer. Nellie *Melba,* stage name of Helen Porter Mitchell, Australian, 1861?-1931. *Melba* is taken from **Melbourne, Australia.**

Mendelian:
Abbot Gregor Mendel, Austrian botanist, 1822-84.

mentor*:
Mentor, teacher of Telemachus, in the *Odyssey.*

Mercator projection:
Gerhard Mercator, Flemish geographer, 1512-94.

mercerize*:
John Mercer, English calico printer; process patented 1850.

mercurial, mercury:
Mercury, Roman god; *cp. hermetically,* in main list.

meringue:
Mehringen, Germany?

mesmerism:
F. A. Mesmer, Viennese, ca. 1775.

mho:
See ohm, of which it is the converse.

milliner*:
Milan.

mnemonic:
from *Mnemosyne,* mother of the Muses; their father was Zeus. ***Mnemosyne*** **is** Greek for memory.

morphine*:
Morpheus, Roman god of sleep.

morris (chair; dance):
The chair is from William *Morris,* Eng. poet and social reformer, 1834-96. For the dance, *see end of this Appendix.*

Morse code:
Samuel F. B. Morse, 19th c. American.

negus:
Col. Francis Negus, under George III of England.

nicotine*:
Jean Nicot, French, 1560.

Nestor:
Nestor, ancient king of Pylos, Greece.

Occam's razor (principle of parsimony):
William of Occam, English philosopher, d. ca. 1349.

odyssey:
From the journey of *Odysseus.*

ogre (first used in Perrault's Contes, Fairy Tales, 1697):
Orcus, Roman god of Tartarus, whence It. *Orco,* whence *orge,* whence *ogre.*

ohm:
G. S. Ohm, 19th c. German physicist.

Olympian:
Olympus, Greek mountain, abode of the gods.

panama (hat):
Panama, Central America.

panic*:
Pan, Greek god of nature (Gr. *pan,* all).

parchment*:
Pergamum, Asia Minor.

Parthian (glance, shot):
Parthia, ancient west-Asian kingdom.

pasteurize:
Louis Pasteur, French scientist, d. 1895.

peach*:
Persicum, Persian.

peeler:
See bobby.

peony*:
Apollo Paion, Greek god of healing.

percheron:
Le Perche, Normandy.

philippic*:
Demosthenes' orations, in ancient Athens, against *Philip of Macedon,* 382-336 B.C.

pinchbeck:
Christopher Pinchbeck, maker of musical clocks, London, d. 1732. (The meaning of the first syllable helped keep the term in vogue.)

Platonic*:
Plato, Greek philosopher, d. 387 B.C.

Plimsoll (line, mark):
S. Plimsoll, helped pass the British Merchant Shipping Act of 1876.

poinsettia:
Joel R. Poinsett of South Carolina.

polka, polonaise.
See end of this Appendix.

pompadour:
La Marquise de Pompadour, mistress of Louis XV of France.

praline:
Marshall Praslin du Plessis, whose chef created this delicious confection.

Prince Albert:
Prince Albert, husband of Queen Victoria, 19th c. England.

procrustean*:
The Greek giant, *Procrustes.*

protean*:
Proteus, son of Neptune (Roman god of the sea), refused to use his gift of prophecy; to avoid plaguy questions he kept changing his shape. Similarly, in *The Arabian Nights,* the old-man-of-the-sea.

prussic (acid):
Prussia; cp. spruce.

Ptolemaic system:
Ptolemy, Alexandrian geographer, ca. 130 A.D.

Pullman:
George M. Pullman, 19th c. American.

pyrrhic* victory:
Pyrrhus, king of Epirus, after defeating the Romans at Asculum in Apuleia, cried: "One more such victory and we are lost!"

pyrrhonism:
Pyrrho, Greek sceptic philosopher, 4th c. B.C.

quisling*:
Major Vidkun Quisling, head of the Norwegian Nazi party; took charge of Norway on German invasion, April, 1940.

quixotic*:
Don Quixote, in book of same name by Miguel de Cervantes Saavedra, 1605.

raglan:
Lord Raglan, British general, died of cholera during the Crimean campaign of 1855.

rhinestone*:
The river *Rhine.*

rodomontade:
Rodomonte, boastful king of Algiers, in *Orlando* romances.

Roentgen ray:
W. K. Roentgen, 19th c. German physicist.

roquefort:
Roquefort, town in France.

Rosetta Stone*:
Rosetta, Egypt.

Rosicrucian:
Translates into Latin last name of *Christian Rosenkreuz,* supposed to have founded the Society in 15th c. Germany.

Salic (law):
LL. *Salicus, Salian* Frank, from *Sala* River, Fr. *Saale.*

Sally Lunn:
18th c. pastrycook, *Sally Lunn,* of Bath, England.

samaritan:
Samaria, Palestine (*Luke* x,33).

sandwich*:
John Montagu, Earl of *Sandwich,* 1718-92.

sardine, sardonic*, sardonyx*:
Sardinia, Gr. *Sardo.*

satire*:
Satyr, Greek demigod, in form half man, half goat.

saxophone*:
Antoine J. Sax.

Scrooge:
A miserly, mean old fellow, always ready to "put the screws on"; in Dickens' *Christmas Carol,* Scrooge reforms when chastened by the ghost of his wiser former partner. Dickens (and Balzac in France) jotted down odd names encountered in life, for apt use in stories.

Seidlitz (powder, water):
Seidlitz, village in Bohemia, near a mineral spring.

sequoia*:
Sequoya, Indian who invented the Cherokee syllabary.

shanghai:
Shanghai, seaport in China.

Sheraton:
Thomas Sheraton, English cabinet-maker, ca. 1800.

shrapnel:
Lt. Henry Shrapnel, English; invented 1784.

silhouette*:
Etienne de Silhouette, director of the French treasury; 1757.

simony*:
Simon Magus, Samaritan sorcerer who wanted to buy the power of the Holy Ghost.

sisyphean*:
Sisyphus. See Atlas, in main list.

socratic*:
Socrates, Athenian philosopher (reported in Plato's Dialogues), d. 400 B.C.

solecism*:
Soloi, Cilicia.

spaniel:
OFr. *espagneul,* Spanish; Fr. *Espagne,* Spain.

Spencer:
Earl Spencer, English, under George III.

spinach:
Hispania, Spain, a doublet of *Spanish.* (Popeye doubtless sailed the *Spanish Main.*)
From L. *hispanicum olus, Spanish* herb; though some derive it from L. *spina,* thorn (hence, a thorn-like process, and Eng. *spine* and *spinal* column. A *spineless* person is one (figuratively) without backbone.

spruce (adjective):
Earlier, *pruce,* the fashion of *Prussia.*

Stalinism:
Joseph Stalin, Soviet leader after N. Lenin, 20th c.

stentorian*:
Stentor, loud-voiced herald in the *Iliad.*

Steve Brodie ("do a Brodie"):
Steve Brodie leapt from Brooklyn Bridge unharmed.

sybarite:
Sybaris, in southern Italy, noted for its luxurious ways.

tabasco:
Tabasco, Mexico.

tangerine:
Tangier, Morocco.

tarantella, tarantula:
See end of this Appendix.

thrasonical:
Thraso, the braggart in *The Eunuch* (161 B.C.) by the Roman playwright Terence. The name is from Gr. *thrasys,* bold.

timothy:
Timothy Hanson, carried the grass seed from New York to Carolina, ca. 1720.

titanic:
Titan. See Atlas, in main list.

tobacco*:
Tabago, island of the Antilles. But *see* main list.

Trotskyite:
Follower of *Leon Trotsky,* leader of the world-revolutionary section of the followers of Lenin, 20th c.

trudgen:
John Trudgen, fast swimmer, before spread of the Australian crawl.

Vandyke*:
English form of name of *Anthony Van Dyck,* Flemish painter, 1599-1641.

vaudeville*:
Vaux de Vire, valleys of Vire, Normandy.

venery:
Venus, Roman goddess of love; *cp. aphrodisiac. See win,* in main list.

Victoria*:
Queen Victoria, first Empress of the British Empire, 19th c.

volcano*:
Vulcan, blacksmith of the Roman gods, husband of Venus.

volt:
Alessandro Volta, 19th c. Italian physicist.

vulcanize:
See volcano.

watt:
James Watt, 19th c. Scottish inventor.

Wedgewood ware:
Josiah Wedgewood, English potter, 1730-95.

Wellington (boot):
Arthur, 1st duke of *Wellington,* Eng. general 1769-1852.

Winchester rifle:
Oliver F. Winchester, 19th c. American.

wulfenite:
F. X. von Wulfen, Austrian mineralogist.

Xant(h)ippe:
Xanthippe, shrewish wife of the Greek philosopher Socrates, 469-399 B.C.

Zeppelin*:
Ferdinand, Count von Zeppelin, German, d. 1917.

Dances are often named from the place of their origin: the *morris dance* is *Moorish; mazurka* means women of *Mazuria; polka* and *Polonaise* (Fr.) mean woman of *Poland; tarantella* and *tarantula* are from *Taranto,* Italy. The *gavotte,* Prov. *gavoto,* is from *Gapotte, Gap,* town in France. The *bergamask* is a rustic dance from *Bergamo,* in the state of Venice.

Many terms in botany, physiology, medicine, and other sciences take their names —*e.g., Eustachian* tube, *Eustachian* valve, from *Bartolommeo Eustachio,* Italian anatomist, 1524?-74—from the man that discovered or described the object or operation.

APPENDIX III

Given Names, Their Sources and Meanings.

The language or language group from which the name originally came is indicated in full, or with the following abbreviations: Celt. . . . Celtic; Gr. . . . Greek; Heb. . . . Hebrew; L. . . . Latin; Teut. . . . Teutonic.

Many names were originally place names; they may be construed as meaning "one that lies in, or near . . .", *e.g., Bradley*: (one that lives by or on) the broad meadow.

Quite often, a name that is a family name becomes a forename, especially through the practice of preserving the mother's family name by giving it to the first-born son; this may be either the first given name, or the middle name with a first name that the person later discards. Thus if a *Mary Addison* marries a *Henry Jones,* they may call their son *Addison Jones;* thus *Burgess Meredith; Nunnally Johnson; Robinson Jeffers; Bernard Shaw.* The British statesman (*Leonard Spencer*) *Winston Churchill* should not be confused with the American novelist, *Winston Churchill.*

There are more first names commonly used for boys than for girls; but invention is much freer with names of girls, especially when chosen anew for actresses or models. Fancy here ploughs three fields:

1) Variations of common names, e.g. *Paula, Paulette, Paulie, Paulina, Pauline, Pola, Polie, Polyna; Lilias; Charlcie, Charlice, Sharleen, Sharline; Mari.*
2) Words from other sources, e.g. *Alpha; Candy; Sable; Ginger.*
3) Far-fetched or invented names, sometimes with the aid of numerology or other portents, e.g. *Cypriennе; Saba; Aza; Malka.*

Of course, most names are chosen today because they are part of the family tradition, or for euphony or other reasons, quite without regard to their original sense.

A

AARON: Heb. He who is exalted.
ABBOTT: Heb. Father.
ABDALLAH: Pers. (Arabic, *Abdullah*). Son of God.
ABELARD: Teut. Noble bold.
ABIAH, ABIJAH: Heb. Father of the son.
ABNER: Heb. My father is a lamp.
ABRAHAM: Heb. Father of a host.
ABRAM: shortened from *Abraham.*
ABSALOM: Heb. Father is peace.
ACHILLES: Gr. Silent, valorous.
ACKLEY, ACKERLEY: Teut. Oak meadow.
ADAIR: Celt. Ford by the oaks.
ADALBERT: Teut. Noble bright.
ADAM: Heb. Man.
ADDISON: Teut. Son of Adam.
ADELBERT: variant of *Adalbert.*
ADELMO: Teut. Nobler.
ADELPHO: Gr. Brother.
ADOLF, ADOLFO, ADOLPH: Teut. Noble wolf.
ADON: Heb. Lord.
ADRIAN: L. Black-earth.
AENEAS: Gr. Praiseworthy.
AGAR: Heb. Stranger.
AHERN: Celt. Lord of horses.
AIDAN: L. Helper.
AINSLEY, AINSLIE: Celt. One's own meadow.
ALAIN, ALAN: Celt. Speedy. *See Allan.*
ALARIC: Teut. Ruler.
ALASTAIR: Gr. Unforgetting.
ABBY: Teut. Fair Harbor.
ABIGAIL: Heb. My father is joy.
ABRA: Egyptian. Charm.
ACACIA: Gr. Innocent.
ADA, ADAH: Heb. Ornament.
ADELAIDE, ADELE, ADELLE: Teut. Noble maid.
ADELINA, ADELINE: Teut. Little noble one.
ADESSA: L. She is here.
ADNA: Heb. Delight.
ADONICA: L. Sweet.
ADORA: L. Adorned.
ADOSINDA: Teut. Of great power.
ADRIA, ADRIENNE: Gr. Bold.
AGALIA: Gr. Never quiet.
AGATHA, AGATHE: Gr. Good.
AGLAIA: Gr. Brightness.
AGNA, AGNES: Gr. Lamb.
AHOLA: Heb. Tent.
AIDA: Italian. Leader.
AILEEN: variant of *Helen.*
AIMEE: French form of *Amy.*
ALAMEDA: Indian. Grove.
ALANE: Celt. Cheerful.
ALANNA: Celt. Harmonious.
ALATHEA: Gr. Truth.
ALBERTA, ALBERTINE: Teut. Nobly bright.
ALCYON, ALCYONE: Gr. Calm.
ALDA: Teut. Rich.
ALDABELLA, ALDABELLE: Teut. + L. Rich and beautiful.

ALBERT: short for *Adalbert*.
ALBIN: L. Fair.
ALBION: Celt. White cliff.
ALCOTT: Teut. Old cottage.
ALDEN: Teut. Old town.
ALDO: Teut. Experienced.
ALEXANDER: Gr. Aid to men.
ALEXIS: Gr. short for *Alexander*.
ALFONSO: Italian form of *Alphonse*.
ALFRED: Teut. Elf counsel.
ALGERON: Celt. Bearded.
ALLAIN, ALLAN, ALLEN: L. Cheerful. (*See Alain*).
ALLISON: Teut. Holy fame.
ALONSO: variant of *Alphonse*.
ALOYSIUS: L. Grace.
ALPHEUS: Heb. Successor.
ALPHONSE, ALPHONSO: Teut. Battle keen.
ALPIN: L. Lofty.
ALTAIR: Arabic. Soaring eagle.
ALTON: Teut. Old village.
ALVA, ALVAH: L. White.
ALVIN: Teut. Noble friend.
AMADEUS: L. Lover of God.
AMBLER: L. Easy-going.
AMBROSE: Gr. Immortal.
AMIEL: Heb. Busy with the Lord
AMOS: Heb. Burden bearer.
ANASTASIUS: Gr. One that will rise again.
ANATOLE: Gr. Sunrise.
ANDRE: French form of *Andrew*.
ANDREW: Gr. Manly.
ANGELO: Gr. Angelic; messenger.
ANGUS: Celt. Of great virtue.
ANSELM: Teut. Warrior of God.
ANSON: Teut. Born of God.
ANTHONY: L. Flourishing.
ANTON, ANTONIO: forms of *Anthony*.
ARCHIBALD: Teut. Very valiant.
AREND, ARENT: Teut. Eagle power.
ARGYLE: L. White clay.
ARIEL: Heb. Lion of God; L. of the air.
ARISTIDE, ARISTIDES: Gr. Son of the best.
ARKWRIGHT: Teut. Carpenter.
ARMAND: Teut. Leader of a host.
ARMIN: Teut. Firm.
ARMITAGE: Teut. Truce.
ARMOUR: L. Weapon.
ARMSTRONG: Teut. Strong-armed.
ARNO: Teut. Eagle.
ALETHEA: variant of *Alathea*.
ALEXANDRA, ALEXIA: Gr. Helper of men.
ALFREDA: Teut. Elf-counselled.
ALICE, ALICIA: Teut. Noble.
ALINE: Teut. High-born.
ALISON, ALISOUN: variants of *Alice*.
ALISTAIR, ALISTE: Teut. Turned aside.
ALLEGRA: L. Lively.
ALLISON: form of *Alison*.
ALMA: L. Kindly.
ALMEDHA: Celt. Fair of form.
ALMERIA: Arabic. Princess.
ALMIRA, ALMYRAH: L. At whom we wonder.
ALOHA: Hawaiian. Love.
ALONZA: short for *Alphonsa*.
ALOYS, ALOYSIA: Teut. Famous maid of war.
ALPHONSA, ALPHONSINA, ALPHONSINE: Teut. Eager to fight.
ALTHA, ALTHAIA: form of *Althea*.
ALTHEA: Gr. Healing (variant of *Alathea?*).
ALVINA: L. Little lively one.
ALWIN: Teut. Friend of the elves.
ALYS, ALYSIA, ALYSON: forms of *Alice*, etc.
AMABEL, AMABELLE: L. Lovable, beautiful.
AMANDA: L. Worthy of love.
AMARA: Sanskrit. Immortal.
AMARANTH, AMARANTHA: Gr. Everlasting flower.
AMARYLLIS: Gr. Rippling.
AMBROSIA: Gr. Food of the gods; deathless.
AMELIA: form of *Emilia*.
AMINTA: Gr. Protectress.
AMY: L. Beloved (see *Aimée*).
ANASTASIA: Gr. Risen again
ANATOLA: Gr. Sunrise.
ANDREA: Gr. Manly.
ANEMONE: Gr. Breath; wind-flower.
ANGELA: Gr. Messenger; angelic.
ANGELICA, ANGELINA, ANGELINE, ANGELIQUE: Gr. Little angel.
ANITA: Spanish for Little *Ann*.
ANN, ANNA, ANNE, ANNIE: Gr. French, and English forms of *Hannah*.
ANNABEL: L. Beautiful Ann.
ANNETTE: French for Little *Ann*.
ANTHA, ANTHEA: Gr. Flower.
ANTOINETTE, ANTONIA: L. Graceful.
APRIL: L. Blooming.
ARABELLA: L. Fair refuge.
ARAMINTA: L. Altar of the warning goddess.
ARBUTUS: L. Fair flower.
ARDEL, ARDELIA, ARDELLA, ARDELLE: L. Industrious.
ARETHUSA: Gr. Chaste.
ARGENTA, ARGYRA: L. Silvery.
ARIADNE: Gr. Sweet singer.

Arnold: Teut. Eagle strength.
Arthur: Teut. Eagle of Thor.
Arvad: Heb. Healer.
Asher: Heb. Fortunate.
Ashley: Teut. Ash grove.
Athanasius: Gr. Immortal.
Athol: Teut. High-born.
Atwater: Teut. By the river.
Atwell: Teut. By the spring.
Atwood: Teut. By the forest.
Aubrey: Teut. Fair-haired leader.
August, Augustine, Augustus: L. Imperial.
Aurelius: L. Golden.
Austin: short for *Augustine*.
Averil, Averill, Avery: Teut. Courageous.
Axel: Teut. Heaven reward.
Aylmer: Teut. Noble fame.
Aylwin: Teut. Noble friend.

Ariana: L. + Heb. Altar of grace.
Arietta, Ariette: L. Little song.
Arista: G. Best.
Arleen, Arlene, Arline: variants of *Eileen*.
Arnoldine: Teut. Strength like an eagle's.
Artemis, Artemisia: Gr. Flawless one.
Aspasia: Gr. Welcome.
Astrid: Teut. Love's desire.
Atalie: Heb. Innocent.
Audrey: Teut. Noble helper.
Augusta: L. Imperial.
Aura: Gr. Halo, breath.
Aurelia: L. Golden.
Aurora: L. Dawn.
Averil, Averill: Teut. Fearless.
Avis: L. Bird.
Ayesha: Persian. Happy.
Azalea: Gr. The flower.

B

Bailey: Celt. Bailiff.
Bainbridge: Teut. Short bridge.
Baldwin: Teut. Royal friend.
Balfour: Celt. Pasture.
Bannin[illegible] [illegible]ut. Announcing.
Bannis[illegible] [illegible]r. Pomegranate.
Barbou[illegible] [illegible]ut. Barber.
Barclay [illegible]iant of Berkeley.
Barnaba[illegible] Barnaby: Heb. Son of consolation.
Barnard: Teut. Bold bear.
Barry: variant of *Henry?* Celt. Good shot.
Barrymore: American, after the stage family.
Bartholomew: Heb. Born of furrows.
Barton: Teut. Homestead.
Baruch: Heb. Blessed.
Basil: Gr. Kingly.
Baxter: Teut. Baker.
Bayard: Teut. Wise.
Beauford: French. Fine Food.
Beaufort: French. Fair and strong.
Beaumont: French. Fair height.
Beauregard: French. Fair view.
Bellamy: L. Fair friend.
Belmont: L. Fair height.
Ben: Heb. Son; Celt. peak.
Benedict: L. Blessed.
Benjamin: Heb. Son of my right hand (favorite son).
Benito: Italian for *Benedict*.
Berkeley: Teut. Birch grove.
Bentley: Teut. Winding meadow.
Benvenuto: L. Welcome.
Bernard: variant of *Barnard*.
Berthold: Teut: Bright bold.

Babette, Barbara: Gr. Little stranger.

Bathilda: Teut. Bottle maid. *See Hilda, Mathilda.*

Bathsheba: Heb. Daughter of the vow.

Batista: Gr. Baptized.

Beata: L. Blessed.

Beatrice, Beatrix: L. Making blessed.

Becky: short for *Rebecca*.

Begonia: from the flower (which was named after a man).

Belinda: L. graceful.

Bella, Belle: French. Beautiful.

Bernadette, Bernadine: Teut. Little bear.

Berenice, Bernice: Gr. Bringer of victory.

Bertha, Berta, Bertina: Teut. Bright.

Beryl: Gr. Foreseeing.

Bess, Bessie, Betsy, Bettina, Betty: forms of *Elizabeth*.

Bertram: Teut. Bright raven.
Bertrand: French form of *Bertram.*
Beverly: Teut. Beaver meadow.
Bevis: Teut. Bow.
Bill: short for *William.*
Bion: Gr. Lively.
Bishop: Teut. Watcher.
Bjorn: Teut. bear.
Blair: Teut. Plainsman.
Blake: Teut. Dark.
Blakely: Teut. Bleak meadow.
Boaz: Heb. speed.
Bob: Short for *Robert.*
Boniface: L. Fortunate.
Booth: Teut. Open shop.
Boris: Russian. Fight.
Bosworth: Teut. Dairy farm.
Boyd: Celt. Blonde.
Bradfield: Teut. Broad field.
Bradley: Teut. Broad meadow.
Bradshaw: Teut. Broad forest.
Bradstreet: Teut. Broad way.
Brendan: Teut. Flaming.
Bret, Brett: Teut. A Breton.
Brian: Celt. Strong.
Brigham: Teut. Town by the bridge.
Brock: Teut. Badger.
Broderick: Teut. Plague of the king.
Brook, Brooks: Teut. Little stream(s).
Bruce: Celt. Ruler.
Bruno: Teut. Dark.
Bryant: form of *Brian.*
Bud: short for *Brother.*
Buck: variant of *Huck; Hank; Henry.*
Burgess: Teut. Freeman.
Byron: Teut. Clear vision.
Burke: Teut. Stronghold.

Beulah: Heb. Married.

Beverly: Teut. Beaver meadow.

Bianca: Italian form of *Blanche.*

Biddy: short for *Bridget.*

Billee, Billie: feminine forms of *William.*

Blanche: L. White; pure.

Blossom: Teut. Flower in bloom.

Boadicea: Celt. Victorious.

Bonita: Italian. Little good one.

Bonnibelle: L. Good and beautiful.

Bonnie: L. Little good one.

Brenda: Teut. Flaming sword.

Brenna: Celt. Dark.

Bridget: Celt. Fiery dart.

Brunhilda: Teut. Brown maid of battle.

C

Cadwallader: Celt. Strategist.
Caesar: L. Ruler; hairy.
Caleb: Heb. Faithful as a dog.
Calvin: L. Bald.
Cameron: Celt. Crooked nose.
Campbell: Celt. Crooked mouth.
Canute: variant of *Knut.*
Carew: Celt. Castle moat.
Carl: Teut. Manly.
Carleton: Teut. Country town.
Carlisle, Carlyle: Teut. Country tower.
Carrol, Carroll: variant of *Carl.*
Carter: Celt. Driver.
Carvel: Teut. Song.
Carver: Teut. Sculptor.
Cary: Teut. Walnut.
Casey: Celt. Brave.
Casimir: Slavic. High prince.
Caspar, Casper: Persian. Horseman.
Cecil: L. Blind.

Calixta, Calixte: Gr. Of great beauty.
Calla: Gr. Beautiful.
Callidora: Gr. Gift of beauty.
Calliope: Gr. Beautiful sounding.
Callista: Gr. Of great beauty.
Camilla, Camille, Camellia: L. Temple maiden.
Canace: L .Daughter of the wind.
Candace: L. Glowing.
Candida: L. Shining white.
Canella: L. Fragrant tree.
Cara: L. Dear.
Carla: Teut. Manly.
Carlotta: Spanish. Little manly one.
Carmel, Carmela: Heb. Vineyard.
Carmen: L. Charming one; song.
Carmencita: L. Little charming one.
Carmine: Heb. Vineyard.
Carol, Carola, Caroline, Carolyn, Carrie: forms of *Carla.*

CEDRIC: Teut. General.
CHAD: short for Chadwick.
CHADWICK: Teut. Village haven.
CHALMERS: Teut. Steward.
CHANDLER: Teut. Candle-maker.
CHAMPION: L. Winner in the field.
CHARLES: Teut. Strong.
CHAUNCEY: Teut. Chancellor.
CHESTER: L. Camp.
CHRISTIAN: Gr. Follower of *Christ.*
CHRISTOPHER: Gr. *Christ*-bearer.
CICERO: L. Farmer.
CLARE, CLARENCE: L. Illustrious.
CLARK: Teut. Scholar.
CLAUDE, CLAUDIUS: L. Lame.
CLAUS: Gr. Victory.
CLAYTON: Teut. Clay village.
CLEMENT: L. Merciful.
CLIFFORD: Teut. Ford at the cliff.
CLINTON: Teut. Hill town.
CLIVE: Teut. Cliff.
CLYDE: Gr. Strong.
COLBY: Teut. Near the mine.
COLE: Teut. short for collier, coalman.
COLIN: Gr. Triumph.
CONAN, CONANT: Celt. Wisdom.
CONRAD: Teut. Wise counsel.
CONSTANT, CONSTANTINE: L. Steadfast.
CONWAY: Celt. Wise.
COOPER: Teut. Barrel binder.
CORBET, CORBIN: L. Raven.
CORDELL: L. Rope.
COREY: Teut. Chosen.
CORLISS: modern. From the American inventor.
CORNELIUS: L. Crowned.
COSMO: Gr. Orderly.
COWAN: Teut. Mason.
CRAIG: Celt. Crag.
CRISPIN: L. Curly haired.
CUTHBERT: Teut. Famous bright.
CYRANO: L. Warrior.
CYRIACK: Gr. Lordly.
CYRIL: Teut. Slpendor.
CYRUS: Persian. The sun.

CASSANDRA: Gr. Winning love.
CASSIA: Gr. The tree.
CATHERINE: variant of Katherine.
CECILIA: L. Blind.
CELESTE: L. Heavenly.
CELESTINA, CELESTINE: L. Little heavenly one.
CELIA, CELINE: short for *Celestine.*
CHANDA: Sanskrit. Spirit that destroys evil.
CHAREMON: Gr. Dear to the spirit.
CHARICIA, CHARIS, CHARISSA: Gr. Beloved.
CHARITY: Gr. Love.
CHARLENE, CHARLOTTA, CHARLOTTE: Teut. Little strong one.
CHARMA, CHARMION: Gr. Delight.
CHERIE, CHERRY, CHERYL: French and coined forms of *Charis.*
CHLOE: Gr. Fresh.
CHLORIS: Gr. Green goddess of flowers.
CHRISTABEL, CHRISTABELLA, CHRISTABELLE: Gr. Beautiful baptized one.
CHRISTINE: Gr. Little follower of the Lord.
CICELY: variant of *Celia.*
CLAIRE: French form of *Clara.*
CLARA, CLARE: L. Illustrious.
CLARIBEL: L. Illustrious and beautiful.
CLARICE, CLARISSA: L. Famous.
CLAUDETTE: L. Little lame one.
CLAUDIA, CLAUDINE: L. Lame.
CLEMENCE, CLEMENTINA, CLEMENTINE: L. Merciful.
CLEONICE: Gr. Glorious victory.
CLEOPATRA: Gr. Glory of her land.
CLIO: Gr. Glorious; Muse of history.
CLORINDA, CLORINDE: Persian. Famous.
CLOTILDE: Teut. Famous in battle.
COLETTE: Gr. Little winner.
COLLEEN: Irish. Little maiden.
COLUMBINE: L. Dove.
CONSTANCE, CONSTANTIA: L. Steadfast.
CONSUELA, CONSUELO: L. Advice.
CORA: Gr. Maiden.
CORAL: Gr. Coral.
CORALIE, CORALINE: Gr. Like the coral.
CORDELIA: Celt. Jewel of the sea.
CORINNA, CORINNE: Gr. Little maiden.
CORNELIA: L. Crowned.
COSETTA, COSETTE: short for Nicolette.
CRYSTAL: Gr. Clear.
CYNTHIA: Gr. Goddess of the moon.
CYRILLA: Gr. Imperious.

D

Dagobert: Teut. Sword bearer.
Dale: Teut. Valley.
Damon: Gr. Conquering.
Daniel: Heb. God is my judge.
Darius: Persian. Ruler.
Darwin: Teut: Brave friend.
Daryl: Teut. Dear little one.
David: Heb. Beloved.
Dean: L. short for deacon.
Delmar: L. Of the sea.
Demetrius: Gr. Sacred to the earth.
Denis, Dennis, Denys: French forms of *Dion.*
Derrick: Teut. Ruler.
Desmond: L. Potent in the world.
Devereux: French. Dutiful.
Dewey: L. Like the dew (usually, after *Admiral Dewey,* battle of Manila, Spanish-American War of 1898).
Dexter: L. right-hand; clever.
Diccon, Dick: short for *Richard.*
Dietrich: Teut. Ruler.
Dion: Gr. short for *Dionysos,* god of revelry.
Dominic, Dominick: L. Belonging to the Lord; Sunday.
Donald: Celt. Proud chief.
Doran, Doremus: Gr. A gift; we shall give.
Douglas: Celt. Dark.
Doyle: Celt. Dark stranger.
Dudley: Celt. Fair field.
Duff: Celt. Dark.
Duncan: Celt. Dark haired.
Dunstan: Celt. Dark stone.
Durand, Durant: L. Enduring.
Duval: L. From the valley.
Dwight: Teut. Wisefellow.

Dagmar: Teut. Glory of the day.
Daisy: Teut. Eye of the day (the flower).
Dale: Teut. Valley.
Damita: L. Little lady.
Daphne: Gr. Laurel tree (sign of triumph).
Dara: Heb. Pearl of wisdom.
Darlene, Darline, Daryl: Teut. Dear little one.
Dawn, Dawna: Teut. Sunrise.
Deborah: Heb. Bee; industry.
Deirdre: Celt. Sorrow.
Delia; Gr. Chaste.
Delilah: Heb. Delicate.
Delinda: Teut. Gentle.
Dell, Della: Teut. Valley (or, short for *Adelle*).
Delora, Deloris: forms of *Dolores.*
Delphine: Gr. Little dolphin.
Demeter; Gr. Goddess of harvest.
Denise: Gr. Serving *Dionysos.*
Desiree: L. Beloved.
Devi: Hindustani. Goddess.
Diana, Diane: L. Goddess of the moon (also *Cynthia*).
Dianthe: Gr. Divine flower.
Dinah: Heb. Vindicated.
Dolce: L. variant of *Dulcy.*
Dolly: (short for *Dorothea?*) Little doll.
Dolores: L. Sorrows (the seven sorrows of *Mary*).
Dominica: L. Belonging to the Lord; Sunday.
Donna: L. Lady.
Donnabel, Donnabella: L. Beautiful lady.
Dora: short for *Dorothea.*
Dorcas: Gr. Gazelle.
Dorinda: Gr. Little gift.
Doris: Gr. Sea maiden.
Dorle: L. Little golden one.
Dorothea, Dorothy: Gr. Gift of God.
Douce: French. Sweet.
Drusilla: Gr. Eyes of dew.
Dulce: L. Sweet.
Dulcibella, Dulcibelle: L. Sweet and beautiful.
Dulcinea, Dulcy: L. Sweet little one.

E

Earl: Teut. Noble.
Eben, Ebenezer: Heb. Stone of strength.
Edel, Edelbert: Teut. Noble bright.
Edgar: Teut. Fair protector.
Edmond, Edmund: Teut. Blessed peace.
Edward: Teut. Guard of goods.

Edith: Teut. Bright gift.
Edna: variant of *Adna.*
Edwina: Teut. Prosperous friend.
Effie: short for *Euphemia.*
Eileen: Irish form of *Helen.*
Eireen: form of *Irene.*

EDWIN: Teut. Prosperous friend.

EGBERT: Teut. Sword bright.

EGMONT: Teut. Powerful protector.

EINAR: Teut. Battle chief.

ELBERT: Teut. Fame bright (short for *Edelbert?*).

ELI, ELIA, ELIAS, ELIJAH: Heb. The Lord is God.

ELIOT, ELLIOTT: Celt. Hunter.

ELLIS: variant of Elias.

ELMAR, ELMER: Teut. Right.

EMANUEL: Heb. God is within us.

EMERSON: Teut. Nobly born.

EMERY: Teut. Leader at work.

EMIL: L. Follows the good.

EMMANUEL: Heb. form of *Emanuel.*

EMMET: Teut. Industrious.

ENNIS: Gr. Praiseworthy.

ENOCH: Heb. Dedicated.

ENRICO: Italian form of *Henry.*

EPHRIAM: Heb. Fruitful.

ERASMUS: L. Lovable.

ERIC: Teut. Heroic.

ERNEST: Teut. Zealous.

ERROL: L. Wanderer.

ERWIN: Teut. Triumphant lord.

ETHAN: Heb. Strength.

ETHELBERT: Teut. Noble bright.

ETTORE: Italian form of *Hector.*

EUCLID: Gr. Well famed.

EUGENE: Gr. Well born.

EUSTACE: Gr. Well put together.

EVAN: Celt. Young fighter.

EVERARD, EVEREST, EVERETT: Teut. Always bold. (*Everest* is the earth's highest mountain).

EZEKIEL: Heb. The Lord is my strength.

EZRA: Heb. Helper.

ELAINE: Celt. form of *Helen.*

ELBERTA: Teut. Lofty fame.

ELEANOR, ELINOR: variants of *Helen.*

ELFINA: Teut. Little wise one.

ELFRIDA: Teut. Wise peaceful.

ELISABETH: variant of *Elizabeth.*

ELISE: short for *Elizabeth.*

ELIZA, ELIZABETH: Heb. God is my oath.

ELLA: L. Little one (or, short for *Helen*).

FLLEN, ELLINE: variant of *Helen*

ELOISE: Teut. Holy famous.

ELSA, ELSIE: Teut. Good cheer (or, forms of *Alice* or *Elizabeth*).

EMMYLOU: Compound of *Emma* and *Louise.*

ELVIRA: L. Manliness.

EMANUELA: Heb. God is within us.

EMILIA, EMILY: Gr. Busy.

EMMA: Teut. Nurse.

ENA: Gr. purity.

ENID: Celt. Soul.

ERICA: Teut. Heroic.

ERNA: Teut. Modest.

ERNESTINE: Teut. Little zealous one.

ESMERALDA, ESMERELDA: Spanish. The greatly admired one.

ESTELLE: L. Star, variant of *Stella.*

ESTHER: Persian. Star.

ETHEL: Teut. Noble.

ETTA: head of the hearth.

EUDOCIA, EUDOCIE: forms of *Eudosia.*

EUDORA: Gr. Beautiful gift.

EUDOSIA, EUDOXIA: Gr. Well thought of.

EUGENIA, EUGENIE: Gr. Well born.

EULALIE: Gr. Fair-spoken.

EUNICE: Gr. Fair winner.

EUPHEMIA: Gr. Well spoken of.

EUPHRASIA, EUPHRASIE: Gr. Rejoicing.

EUSTACIA: Gr. Well standing.

EVA: form of *Eve.*

EVADNE: Gr. Sweet singer.

EVALINA, EVALINE: little *Eva.*

EVANTHE: Gr. fair flower.

EVE: Heb. Life.

EVANGELINE: Gr. Little bearer of good tidings.

EVELINA, EVELYN: Celt. Little pleasant one: little *Eve.*

F

FABIAN: L. Farmer; delayer.

FAIRFAX: Teut. Light-haired.

FEDERICO: Italian form of *Frederick.*

FELIX: L. Happy.

FERDINAND: Teut. Peace bold.

FERGUS: Celt. Fierce chief.

FAITH: English form of L. *fide,* trust.

FRANCHETTE: diminutive of *Frances.*

FANNIE, FANNY: forms of *Frances.*

FAUSTINA: L. Little lucky one.

FAWN, FAWNIA: Teut. Young deer.

FAY: Spanish form of *Faith;* English form of *Fairy.*

FEDORA: form of *Theodora.*

FELICE, FELICIA: L. Happy one.

Fielding: Teut. Lad of the fields.
Fingal: Celt. White stranger.
Finley: Celt. Sunshine.
Fiorello: L. Little flower.
Fisk: Teut. Faith.
Fitz: (Fr. *fils*, son). Son of-.
Fletcher: Teut. Arrowsmith.
Florian: L. Flourishing.
Floyd: Celt. Brown.
Francis: Teut. Free.
Frank: short for *Francis*.
Franklin: Teut. Freeholder.
Fraser, Frasier, Frazer: L. curly-haired.
Fred, Frederick: Teut. Peaceful ruler.
Fremont: Teut. Peaceful guard.
Fritz: Teut. Peaceful lord (form of *Frederick?*).

Felipa: variant of *Filippa*.
Fern: Teut. The plant is a symbol of sincerity.
Fidelia: L. Faithful.
Fifi, Fifine: Heb. Addition.
Filippa: Gr. Lover of horses.
Flavia: L. Flaxen-haired.
Flora: L. Flower.
Florabel: L. Flower of beauty.
Florella: L. Little flower.
Florence: L. Flowering.
Floretta: L. Little flower.
Florinda: L. Flowering.
Frances, Francesca: Teut. Free.
Francine: Teut. Little free one.
Freda: form of *Frieda*.
Frederica: Teut. Peaceful ruler.
Freya: Teut. Beloved.
Frieda: Teut. Peaceful.
Fritzie: form of *Frederica?*
Fulvia: L. Golden.

G

Gabriel: Heb. Strength of God.
Gaillard, Gailliard: Teut. Lively one.
Gamaliel: Heb. Reward of God.
Gardiner, Gardner: Teut. Keeper of a garden.
Garibaldi: Italian.
Garret: Teut. Honored.
Garrick: Teut. Fighter king.
Garrison, Garry: Teut. Protection.
Garry: See above. Also, short for Garibaldi.
Garth: Teut. Garden.
Garvey: Teut. Spearsman.
Gary: Teut. form of *Garvy*.
Gavin: Celt. Battle-hawk; smith.
Gawain: Celt. form of *Gavin*.
Gaylord: Teut. Lively master.
Gaynor: Teut. Lively head.
Geoffrey: Teut. Happy in peace.
George: Gr. Farmer.
Gerald, Gerard: Teut. Bold spearsman.
Gerhard, Gerhart: Teut. Gold warrior.
Gervais: Teut. Warlike.
Gideon: Heb. Of the hill.
Gifford: Teut. Kindly.
Gil, Gilbert: Teut. Bright servant.
Giles: Gr. Shield.
Gilford: Teut. Wide ford.
Giordano: Italian, from the River *Jordan*, q.v.
Giovanni: Italian for *John*.
Glenn, Glynn: Celt. Valley.
Godfrey: Teut. God's peace.
Godwin: Teut. Friend of God.
Gordon: Celt. Upright man.
Graham: Celt. Stern-faced.

Gabriella, Gabrielle: Heb. God is my strength.

Gail: short for *Abigail*.

Galatea: Gr. milk-white.

Gay: L. Merry.

Genevieve: Celt. Sea foam.

Georgette, Georgia, Georgiana, Georgina: Gr. Farmer; girl of the fields.

Geraldine: Teut. Little one with the bold spear.

Gerda: Teut. Girdled.

Gertrude: Teut. Bold in truth.

Gilberta, Gilbertine: Teut. Bright servant.

Gillian: English form of *Julia*.

Gina: L. Little one (Japanese, Silvery).

Gladys: Celt. Lame.

Glen, Glenn, Glenna, Glenyss: Celt. Mountain dale.

Gloria, Gloriana: L. Fame.

Godiva: Teut. Gift of God.

GRANT: French, great.
GRANTLAND: Teut. Deeded land.
GRANVILLE: French. Great city.
GRATIAN: L. Thankful.
GRATTAN: Teut. Fenced land.
GRAYSON: Teut. Son of *Gray*.
GREGG: Teut. Increase.
GREGORY: Gr. Watchful.
GRENVILLE: form of Granville.
GRIFFITH: Celt. Faithful.
GRISWOLD: Teut. Grey woods.
GROSVENOR: L. Great hunter.
GROVER: Teut. Woodsman.
GUIDO: Italian. Guide.
GURTH: Teut. Girded (with a sword).
GUS, GUSTAVE: Teut. Staff of the good.
GUY: French, short for Italian *Guido*, leader.

GOLDA, GOLDIE, GOLDINE, GOLDY: Teut. Golden one.

GRACE, GRATIA: L. Grace, thanksgiving.

GRETA, GRETCHEN, GRETEL: German shortenings of *Margaret*.

GRISEL, GRISELDA: Teut. Grey-eyed one.

GUINEVERE: Celt. Fair.

GUNHILD: Teut. Brave fighter.

GUSSIE, GUSTY, GUSTAVA: feminine of *Gustave*.

GWENDOLINE, GWENDOLYN, GWENNA: Celt. White-browed.

H

HAAKON: Norse. Spearsman.
HALBERT: Teut. Bright stone.
HALDANE, HALDEN: Teut. Valley home.
HAMILTON: Teut. Hill town.
HAMLET: Teut. Village.
HAMNET: Teut. Bright home.
HANK: Teut. short for *Henry*.
HANLEY: Teut. Wide meadow.
HANS: Teut. short for *Johannes, John*.
HARDY: Teut. Enduring.
HAROLD: Teut. General (*Hereweald*, army leader; *see Walter*).
HARPER: Teut. Player on the harp.
HARRISON: son of *Henry*.
HARRY: variant of *Harold* or *Henry*.
HARVEY: Teut. Noble warrior.
HAVELOCK: Teut. Surety (name of English general in India).
HAYDEN, HAYDON: Teut. Hill with ledge.
HAYWOOD: Teut. Hedged woods.
HECTOR: Gr. Support.
HEINRICH: Teut. form of *Henry*.
HENRY: Teut. Home lord.
HERBERT: Teut. Army bright.
HERCULES (Heracles): Gr. Glory of *Hera;* chosen one.
HERMAN: Teut. Army man.
HEZEKIAH: Heb. Strength of God.
HEYWOOD: form of *Haywood*.
HILARY: L. Merry.
HILDEBRAND: Teut. War sword.
HIRAM: Heb. Lofty.
HOBART: form of *Hubert*.
HOLMES: Teut. Meadow.
HOMER: Gr. Hostage.
HORACE, HORATIO: L. Keen-eyed.
HOWARD: Teut. Castle guard.
HOWELL: Celt. Lordly.
HUBERT: Teut. Bright *Hugh*.

HADASSAH: Assyrian. Star.

HAGAR: Heb. Timid one.

HAIDEE: Gr. Modest.

HALIMA: Gr. Sea moss.

HANNAH: Heb. Grace.

HARRIET, HATTIE: Teut. Head of the hearth.

HAZEL: Heb. Behold the Lord.

HEATHER: Teut. The flower of the heath.

HEBE: Gr. Youth.

HEDDA, HEDWIG, HEDY: Teut. Lady guard.

HELEN: Gr. Dawn-bright.

HELGA: Norse. Holy.

HELMA: Teut. Rudder; guide.

HELOISE: Teut. variant of *Eloise*.

HENRIETTA, HENRIETTE: Teut. Little head of the hearth (*see Harriet*)!

HEPHZIBAH: Heb. She is my delight.

HERMA: Teut. Beloved.

HERMIONE: Gr. High-born maiden.

HERMOSA: L. Beautiful.

HESTER, HETTY: variants of *Esther*.

HILARIA: L. Jolly.

HILDA: short for *Mathilda*.

HILDEGARD, HILDEGARDE: Teut. Guardian in battle.

HILGA: variant of *Helga*.

HOLLY: Teut. The plant.

HONORIA: L. Honorable.

HOPE: Teut. Expectation.

Huck: Teut. variant of *Henry.*
Hugh, Hugo: Teut. Lofty.
Humbert: Teut. Giant bright.
Humphrey: Teut. Home peace.
Hortense, Hortensia: L. Gardener.
Huldah: Heb. Weasel: sprightly.
Hyacinth: Gr. The flower.
Hypatia: Gr. Excellent one.

I

Iago: Italian variant of *Jacopo, Jacob.*
Ian: Celt. variant of *John.*
Ichabod: Heb. Inglorious.
Ignatius: Gr. Fiery.
Immanuel: Heb. With God's help. (Form of *Emanuel?*)
Ingram: Teut. Raven.
Ira: Heb. Watchful.
Irwin: variant of *Erwin.*
Isaac: Heb. Laughter.
Isadore: Gr. Gift of *Isis.*
Isaiah: Heb. Salvation of the Lord.
Isidor: form of *Isadore.*
Israel: Heb. Triumphant in the Lord.
Ivan: Russian variant of *John.*
Ianthe: Gr. Violet.
Ida: Gr. Happy.
Ilga: varinat of *Helga.*
Ilona, Ilone: Gr. Radiant.
Imogen, Imogene: Gr. Born of love.
Ina: L. Little one.
Inez: Gr. Maiden.
Inola: L. Like a bell (bells were first used in churches in *Nolà*, Italy; 5th c.).
Irene: Gr. Peace bearer.
Iris: Gr. Rainbow.
Irita: Gr. Little *Iris.*
Irma: Teut. Noble maid.
Isabel: Spanish form of *Elizabeth.*
Isadora: Gr. Equal gift.
Iseult, Isolde: Celt. Fair.
Ivy: Teut. The plant.

J

Jacinto: Gr. Clad in purple (as is a king).
Jack: variant of *Jacob* or *John.*
Jacob: Heb. Supplanter.
Jacques: French form of *Jacob;* hence, the *Jacobins.*
James: English form of *Jacob.*
Jan: Dutch form of *John.*
Jason: Gr. Healer.
Jasper: Persian. Lord of the treasure.
Jay: L. short for *Jacobus;* Teut. lively.
Jeffrey: variant of *Geoffrey.*
Jeremiah, Jeremy, Jerry: Heb. Uplifted by the Lord.
Jerome: Gr. Holy.
Jesse: Heb. Wealthy.
Jim, Jimmy: short for *James.*
Joab: Heb. The Lord is father.
Joachim, Joaquin: Heb. The Lord will judge.
Job: Heb. Persecuted; patient.
Joel: Heb. The Lord is God.
John: Heb. The Lord is gracious.
Jonah, Jonas: Heb. Dove.
Jonathan: Heb. Gift of the Lord.
Jordan: Heb. descendant; Fr. variant of of *jardin,* garden.
Joseph: Heb. He shall increase.
Joshua: Heb. The Lord is salvation.
Jacobina: Heb. Little supplanter.
Jacqueline: French form of *Jacobina.*
Jamesina: English form of *Jacobina.*
Jane, Janet, Janice: forms of the feminine of *John.*
Jasmine: Gr. The flower.
Jean, Jeanne, Jeannette, Jennie, Jenny: forms of the feminine of *John.*
Jemima: Heb. Dove.
Jennifer: Celt. White wave.
Jessamine, Jessamy: forms of *Jasmine.*
Jessica, Jessie: Heb. Wealthy.
Jewel: L. Thing of joy.
Jill: short for *Julia.*
Joan, Joanna: other forms of the feminine of *John.*
Jocelyn: L. Lively.
Johanna: feminine of *John.*
Josephine: feminine of *Joseph.*
Joy: L. Gladness.
Joyce: L. Merry.
Juana, Juanita: Spanish feminine forms of *John.*

JOSIAH: Heb. The Lord supports.
JOYCE: L. Merry.
JUAN: Spanish form of *John.*
JUDAH, JUDE: Heb. Praised.
JULES, JULIAN, JULIUS: L. Light-bearded.
JUSTIN: L. Upright.

JUDITH, JUDY: Heb. Praise unto the Lord.

JULIA, JULIANA, JULIET: L. Soft-haired.

JUNE: L. Young.

JUSTINA, JUSTINE: L. Upright.

K

KARL: German form of *Carl.*
KASPAR: German form of *Laspar.*
KAY: Gr. Rejoicing.
KEAN, KEANE, KEENAN, KEENE: Celt. Sharp.
KEITH: Celt. Windy.
KELVIN, KELWIN: Teut. Fighting friend. (*See Calvin.*)
KEMP: Teut. Champion.
KENDALL: Celt. Valley chief.
KENELM: Teut. Royal helm.
KENNETH: Celt. Handsome.
KENT: Celt. Chief; Teut. Known.
KENYON: Celt. White-haired.
KING: Teut. Ruler.
KIRK: Celt. Church.
KIT: short for *Christopher.*
KNUT: Danish. Club.
KURT: Teut. Laconic.

KAMA: Sanskrit. Desire.

KAREN: Gr. Pure.

KARLA: variant of *Carla.*

KATE, KATHERINA, KATHERINE, KATHLEEN, KATHRINE, KATHRYN: forms from Gr., pure one.

KAY: Gr. Rejoicing.

KENDRA, KENNA: Teut. Knowing.

KITTY: form of *Katherine.*

KOMALA: Sanskrit. Charming.

L

LAMBERT: Teut. Brave lamb.

LANCELOT: Teut. Warrior.

LANDERS, LANDIS: Teut. Son of the plains.

LARRY: short for *Laurence.*

LATHAM: Teut. Low village.

LAURENCE, LAWRENCE: L. Victor.

LAZARUS: Heb. God's help.

LEANDER: Gr. Renowned.

LEE, LEIGH: Teut. Meadow.

LEMUEL: Heb. Devoted to the Lord.

LENNOX: Celt. Quiet stream.

LEO, LEON: L. Lion.

LEONARD: Teut. Bold as a lion.

LEONIDAS: Gr. Lionlike.

LEOPOLD: Teut. Bold and beloved.

LEROY: French. The king.

LESLIE: Teut. Dell.

LESTER: Teut. Meadow camp (*Leicester*).

LEVI: Heb. United.

LEWIS: Teut. Famed fighter.

LADORNA: L. Adorned.
LAKSHME: Sanskrit. Slender.
LALA: Slavic. Flower.
LALAGE: Gr. Vivacious.
LAURA, LAUREL, LAURETTE: L. The tree (sign of triumph).
LAVERNE: L. Spring.
LAVINIA: L. Cleansed.
LEAH: Heb. Languid.
LEALA: Teut. Faithful.
LEATRICE: variant of *Beatrice.*
LEDA: L. Slim.
LEILA: Arabic. Dark beauty.
LELA: variant of *Leala* or *Leila.*
LENA: short for *Helena.*
LENORA, LENORE: short for *Eleanore.*
LEONA: L. Lioness.
LEONORA, LEONORE: forms of *Eleanore.*
LESLIE: Teut. Dell.
LETITIA, LETTICE, LETTY: L. Gladness.
LIBBY: form of *Elizabeth.*
LIDA: variant of *Ludmilla.*
LILIAN, LILLIAN, LILY: L. The flower (sign of purity).
LINA: short for *Carolina.*

LINCOLN: Celt. Deep stream (usually, after *Abraham Lincoln*).
LINDLEY: Teut. Meadow with lindens.
LIONEL: L. Lion club.
LLEWELLYN: Celt. Lightning.
LLOYD: Celt. Brown.
LOCKWOOD: Teut. Enclosed forest.
LORENZ, LORENZO: forms of *Laurence*.
LOUIS: French form of *Lewis*.
LOVEL, LOVELL, LOVETT: Teut. Young wolf.
LOWELL: Teut. Low spring (name of American poet).
LOYALL: L. Faithful.
LUCIAN, LUCIUS: L. Light.
LUDLOW: Teut. Humble man.
LUDWIG: Teut. form of *Lewis*.
LUKE: Greek form of *Lucius*.
LUTHER: Teut. Famed Fighter.
LYDDELL, LYDELL: Gr. Lydian.
LYLE: Teut. variant of *little*.
LYMAN: Teut. Manly.
LYNN: Celt. Lake.

LINDA: short for *Belinda*.
LINNET: Celt. Shapely.
LISA, LISETTE, LIZETTE, LIZZIE: short for *Elizabeth*.
LOIS: Gr. Desired (or short for *Aloys*).
LOLA: Teut. Manly.
LORA, LORETTE: variants of *Laura*.
LORNA: Teut. Lonely.
LORRAINE: L. Sad.
LOTTA, LOTTIE: short for *Charlotte*.
LOTUS: Gr. The flower.
LOUELLA: Little *Louise*.
LOUISA, LOUISE: French forms of Teut. Famed fighter.
LUCASTA: L. Bright and pure.
LUCIA, LUCILE, LUCILLE, LUCINDA: L. Bright.
LUCRETIA: L. Lucky one.
LUCY: L. Bright.
LUDMILLA: Slavic. Love of the people.
LYDA, LYDIA: Gr. from *Lydia*.
LYNELLE: form of *Linnet*.
LYNN: Celt. Lake.

M

MADDOCK, MADDOX: Celt. Power.

MAGNUS: L. Great.

MAHON: Celt. Chief.

MALCOLM: Celt. Servant of *St. Columba*.

MANUEL: Heb. God with us.

MARC: Heb. Bitter; Marc, Marcius, Marcus: L. Warlike.

MARK: L. Bright (but *see Marc*).

MARSHALL: Teut. Leader.

MARTIN: L. Warlike.

MARVIN: Celt. High hills.

MASON: Teut. Stone worker.

MATTHIAS, MATTHEW: Heb. Gift of the Lord.

MAURICE: L. Dark (Moorish).

MAURY: Gr. Twilight.

MAX, MAXIM, MAXIMILIAN: L. Of the greatest.

MABEL: (short for *Amabel?*) Celt. Merry.
MADELEINE, MADELINE, MADELON: variants of *Magdalen*.
MADGE: short for *Margaret*.
MAE: variant of *May*.
MAG, MAGGIE: forms of *Margaret*.
MAGDALEN, MAGDALENA, MAGDALENE: Heb. Watchtower.
MAGNA: L. Great.
MAISIE: Scots form of *Mary*.
MALVINA: Celt. Handmaid.
MANLY: Teut. Manlike.
MANUELA: Heb. God with us.
MARCELLA, MARCELLE: Little *Marcia*.
MARCIA: L. Warlike.
MARGARET, MARGARITA, MARGIT, MARGOT, MARGUERITA, MARGUERITE: Gr. Pearl.
MARIA, MARIE, MARIETTA, MARIETTE: form of *Mary*.
MARIAN, MARIANNA, MARIANNE: telescoped from *Mary* and *Ann*.
MARIGOLD: The flower.
MARILYN, MARION: Little *Mary*.
MARJORIE: variant of *Margaret*.
MARLENE: Like unto *Mary*.
MARSHA: variant of *Marcia*.
MARTHA: Heb. Sorrowful.
MARY, MARYA: Heb. (Greek form of *Miriam*); but Heb. *Marah* means bitter. A most common name from its use in the Bible.
MATHILDA, MATILDA: Teut. Mighty in battle. *See Bathilda*.

MAXWELL: Teut. Big spring; Celt. fair son.

MAYNARD: Teut. Mighty.

MELVILLE, MELVIN: Teut. Chief.

MEREDITH: Celt. Sea guardian.

MERLE: L. Thrush.

MERLIN: Celt. Hill by the sea.

MERRILL: Gr. Fragrant.

MERTON; form of *Martin.*

MERVIN, MERVYN: Celt. Raven of the sea.

MEYER: Teut. Dairyman.

MICHAEL: Heb. Who is like unto the Lord?

MILES: L. Soldier.

MILLARD: Teut. Grinder.

MILTON: Teut. Mill town.

MITCHELL: Teut. form of *Michael.*

MONROE: Celt. Mount on the *River Roe,* Ireland: Red swamp.

MONTAGUE: French. Of the precipice.

MONTE: L. From the mountain.

MORGAN: Celt. Dweller by the sea.

MORRIS: English form of *Maurice.*

MORTIMER: L. Bitter place by the sea.

MORTON: Celt. Big hill.

MOSES: Egyptian? Because of his history taken to mean drawn from the water.

MURRAY: Celt. Great body of water.

MYRON: Gr. Bearing incense (myrrh).

MAUD, MAUDE: variant of *Magdalen.*

MAUREEN, MAURY, MAURYA: Celt. forms of *Mary.*

MAXINE: L. Little great one.

MAY: L. from the month, time of blossoming.

MAYBELLE: a variant of Mabel, but suggesting the beauty of spring.

MEG, MEGAN, MEGGIE: forms of *Magna.*

MELANIE: Gr. Dark one.

MELBA: L. Honeyed one.

MELIANTHE: Gr. Sweet flower.

MELICENT: Gr. Honey-sweet.

MELINDA: Gr. Honeylike.

MELISSA: Gr. Honeybee.

MELVINA: Gr. Sweet little one.

MERLE, MERLINE, MERNA: L. Thrush. (*Merna* may be a variant of *Myrna.*)

MERYL: Gr. Incense.

META: Gr. Beyond.

MICHAELA: Heb. Divine.

MICKEY, MICKIE: short for *Michaela.*

MIGNONNE, MIGNONETTE: L. Dainty little one.

MILDRED: Teut. Gentle adviser.

MILICENT, MILLIE, MILLY: forms of *Melicent.*

MIMI: Teut. strong fighter.

MINA: L. Little one (or short for *Wilhelmina*).

MINERVA: L. The goddess of wisdom.

MINNIE: Teut. Beloved (or short for *Wilhelmina*).

MIRA, MIRANDA: L. Worthy of wonder.

MIRIAM: Heb. Rebellion (*see Mary*).

MOIRA: Gr. Fate.

MOLLY: variant of *Mary.*

MONA, MONICA: Gr. Alone.

MORNA: Celt. Beloved.

MURIEL: Gr. Incense.

MYNA, MYRNA: Gr. Sorrowful.

MYRTLE: Gr. The plant (symbol of beauty).

N

NAHUM: Heb. Comforter.

NAPOLEON: Gr. Lion of the new city.

NATHAN, NATHANIEL: Heb. Gift of God.

NEHEMIAH: Heb. The Lord comforteth.

NEIL: Celt. Champion.

NELSON: Celt. Son of *Neil.*

NESTOR: Gr. One that remembers.

NADA, NADINE: Slavic. Hope.

NAIDONA: Gr. House of God.

NAN, NANCY, NANETTE: variants of *Ann.*

NANINE: G. Little one.

NAOMI: Heb. Pleasant to behold.

NARCISSA, NARCISSE: Gr. Beauty.

NATALIE, NATHALIA, NATHALIE: L. Little one born (on Christ's birthday).

NELL, NELLIE, NELLY: variants of *Helen.*

NETTIE, NETTY: Teut. Neat.

NICOLE, NICOLETTE, NICOLLE: Gr. Conqueror.

NEVILLE: L. New city.
NEWELL: L. Kernel; Teut. new spring.
NEWTON: Teut. New town (name of English scientist).
NICHOLAS: Gr. Conqueror.
NIGEL: L. Dark.
NIMROD: Heb. Fiery rod; great hunter.
NOAH: Heb. Rest.
NOEL: French. Christmas.
NORMAN: Teut. North man.

NINA, NINETTE: Spanish and French diminutives: little one.
NOEL: French. Christmas.
NOLA: Celt. White shouldered.
NONA: L. Ninth.
NORA, NORAH: short for *Honoria* or *Leonora.*
NORINE, NORITA: diminutives of *Nora.*
NORMA: L. Model.
NUBIA: L. Cloud.
NYDIA: L. Nestling.

O

OAKLEY: Teut. Oak meadow.
OBADIAH: Heb. Devoted to the Lord.
OCTAVIUS: L. Eighth.
OGDEN: Teut. Dell of oaks.
OLAF: Teut. Champion.
OLIVER: L. Bearer of the olive branch.
OMAR, OMER: Arabic. Better.
ORIN: Celt. White.
ORLANDO: Italian form of *Roland.*
ORRICK: Teut. Golden king.
ORSINO, ORSON: L. Little bear.
ORTON: Teut. Fruitful.
ORVILLE: French. Golden city.
OSBORN: Teut. Divine bear.
OSCAR: Celt. Leaping warrior.
OSMOND, OSMUND: Teut. Whom the gods favor.
OSRIC: Teut. Divine power.
OSWALD: Teut. Divine ruler.
OTIS: Gr. Keen of hearing.
OTTO: Teut. Mountain.
OWEN: Celt. High-born.

OCTAVIA: L. Eighth.

ODELETTE, ODETTE: Gr. Little song.

OLGA: Teut. Holy.

OLIVE, OLIVIA: L. The tree (sign of peace).

OPAL: Gr. The jewel (sign of hope).

OPHELIA: Gr. Helper.

ORABELLE: L. Pious beauty.

ORDELLA: Teut. Wise counsel.

ORETTA: L. short for *Honoretta* little honored one.

OUIDA: coined name of the novelist; pet name for *Louise.*

P

PABLO: Spanish form of *Paul.*

PADDY: short for *Patrick.*

PAOLO: Portuguese form of *Paul.*

PARKER: Teut. Guard of the park.

PATRICK: L. Noble.

PAUL: L. Little.

PEDRO: Spanish form of *Peter.*

PERCIVAL: Celt. Guard of the Grail.

PERCY: Celt. Keen-eyed.

PERRIN, PERRY: Teut. form of *Peter.*

PETER: Gr. Rock.

PHELAN: Celt. Wolf.

PHILBERT: Teut. Outstanding.

PAMELA: Gr. Sweet one.
PANSY: L. Thoughtful; the flower.
PANTHEA: Gr. God in everything.
PATIENCE: L. The virtue.
PATRICIA: L. High-born.
PAULA, PAULINE: L. Little.
PEARL: L. The jewel (symbol of health).
PEGGY: form of *Margaret.*
PENELOPE: Gr. Weaver.
PEONY: Gr. The flower.
PERDITA: L. Little lost one.
PERPETUA: L. Everlasting.
PHILIPPA: Gr. form of *Filippa.*
PHILOMEL: Gr. Lover of music (the nightingale).
PHILOMENA: Gr. Little lover.
PHOEBE: Gr. The moon.

PHILIP: Gr. Lover of horses (applied to the son of Alexander the Great).

PHINEAS: Teut. Open-faced.

PIERRE: French form of Peter.

PRENTICE, PRENTISS: Teut. Learner (short for *apprentice*).

PRIMUS: L. First.

PUTNAM: Teut. short for Puttenham, watering town.

PHYLLIDA, PHYLLIS: Gr. Fresh as spring.

PILAR: L. Tall, strong.

POLLY: variant of *Molly*.

POPPY: L. The flower.

PORTIA: L. Leader to safety.

PRIMROSE: L. Early blossoming.

PRISCILLA: L. Old-fashioned.

PRUDENCE: L. The virtue.

PRUNELLA: L. The plant.

PSYCHE: Gr. Soul.

Q

QUENTIN, QUINN, QUINTUS: L. Fifth.

QUILLER: Teut. Fledgling.

QUEENA, QUEENIE: Teut. Ruler.

R

RALPH: English form of *Randolph*.

RANDALL: Scots form of *Randolph*.

RANDOLPH: Teut. Guarded by the wolf.

RAPHAEL: Heb. The Lord healeth.

RAYMOND: Teut. Quiet protector.

REGINALD: Teut. Powerful judge.

REGULUS: L. Little king.

REINHOLD: Teut. Unconquerable.

RENATO: L. Reborn.

RENE: French form of *Renato*.

REUBEN: Heb. Behold, a son!

REX: L. King.

REXFORD: Teut. King's ford.

REYNOLD: variant of *Reginald*.

RHYS: Celt. Chieftain.

RICHARD: Teut. Bold fighter.

RIDGELEY: Teut. Ridge meadow.

ROBERT, ROBIN: Teut. Fame-bright.

RODERICK: Teut. Famous powerful.

RODMAN: Teut. Surveyor; guide.

RODNEY: Teut. Famous in counsel.

RODOLPH: variant of *Randolph*.

ROGER: Teut. Famous spear.

ROLAND: Teut. Glory of the land.

ROLF: variant of Randolph.

ROMEO: L. Good man of *Rome*.

RONALD: variant of *Reginald*.

ROSCOE: Teut. Swift steed.

ROSS: Teut. Steed.

ROY: L. King.

ROYAL, ROYALL, ROYCE: L. Kingly.

RUDOLPH: variant of *Randolph*.

RUFUS: L. Red.

RUPERT: variant of *Robert*.

RUSSELL: Teut. Red-haired.

RACHEL: Heb. Lamb of God.

RADHA: Hindustani. Flower of heaven.

RAGNA, RAYNA: variants of *Regina*.

REBA, REBECCA, REBEKKAH: Heb. Snare (of beauty).

REGINA, REINE: L. Queen.

RENATA, RENEE: L. Born again.

RHODA: Gr. Rose.

RITA: short for *Marguerita*.

ROANNA: Teut. Famed grace.

ROBERTA: Teut. Fame-bright.

ROLANDA: Teut. Fame of the land.

ROMANZA: L. Romance.

ROSABEL: L. Beautiful rose.

ROSALIE, ROSALIND, ROSALINDA, ROSALINDE, ROSELYN: L. Fair as a rose.

ROSAMOND, ROSAMUND: Teut. Famous guard.

ROSE: Teut. Famous (The Teut. *hros*, famous—from which we get Eng. *hero*—was later associated with the flower).

ROSELLE, ROSETTA: L. Little rose.

ROSEMARY: L. Rose of the sea; the flower is a symbol of remembrance. The name may also be a compound of *Rose* and *Mary*.

ROSINA, ROSITA, ROSLYN: diminutive forms of *Rose*.

ROWENA: Celt. White skirt.

ROXANA, ROXANE: Persian. Dawn.

RUBY: L. Red.

RUTH: Heb. Mercy.

S

Salvador, Salvatore: L. Saviour.
Samson: Heb. Like the sun.
Samuel: Heb. Heard of the Lord.
Saul: Heb. Asked of the Lord.
Sawyer: Celt. Woodcutter.
Schuyler: Teut. Learned.
Scott: Celt. Northman; tattooed.
Sebastian: Gr. Majestic.
Selig: Teut. Blessed.
Sewell: L. and Teut. Drain spring.
Seymour: French, from *St. Maur* (the holy Moor).
Shawn: Celt. variant of *John*.
Sheldon: Teut. Shield bearer.
Sherwood: Teut. Clearing in the forest.
Shirley: Teut. County meadow.
Sidney: French, from *St. Denis* (*see Denis*)
Siegfried: Teut. Peace conquers.
Sigismund, Sigmund: Teut. Victor.
Silas: L. Woodsman.
Silvanus: L. Of the woodland.
Silvester: L. Forester.
Simeon: Heb. Hearkening.
Simon: Gr. form of *Simeon*.
Sinclair: French, from *St. Clair* (*see Clara*).
Sitwell: Teut. Favorable place.
Snowden: Teut. Snowy hill.
Solomon: Heb. Peaceful.
Spencer: Teut. Steward.
Stacy: L. Steady.
Stanislaus: Gr. Praise of the state.
Stanley: short for *Stanislaus;* Teut. stony meadow?
Stanton: Teut. Stony town.
Stanwood: Teut. Stony woodland.
Stephen: Gr. Fitly crowned.
Sterling: Teut. Little star; true.
Stewart: Teut. One in charge.
Strother, Struther, Struthers: Teut. Stream(s).
Stuart: French form of *Stewart*.
Sumner: L. Summoner.
Sven: Danish. Youth (swain).
Sylvester: variant of *Silvester*.

Sabina: L. Little holy one.
Sada, Sadie, Sadja, Sadye, Sally: variants of *Sarah*.
Salome: Heb. Peaceful.
Sandra: short for *Alexandra* or *Cassandra*.
Sapphira: Heb. Beautiful.
Sara, Sarah: Heb. High-born.
Satya: Sanskrit. Sincere.
Selena, Selina: Gr. Like the moon.
Selma: Celt. Fair.
Serafina, Serafine, Seraphine: Heb. Afire with love of God.
Sharlene: little Shirley.
Sheila: Celt. form of *Cecilia*.
Shirley: Teut. County meadow.
Sibyl: Gr. Prophetess.
Sidonia, Sidonie: Phoenician. Enchantress (or feminine of *Sidney?*).
Sigrid: Teut. Winning wisdom.
Silvia: L. Forest maid.
Sonia, Sonya: short for *Sophronia*.
Sophia, Sophie: Gr. Wisdom.
Sophronia: Gr. Wise-thinking.
Stella: L. Star.
Stephanie: Gr. Fitly crowned.
Susan, Susanne, Susette: Heb. Lily.
Sybil: variant of *Sibyl*.
Sydney: feminine variant of *Sidney*.
Sylvia: variant of *Silvia*.

T

Talbot: Teut. Hunter; bloodhound.
Taylor: Teut. Tailor.
Ted, Teddy: short for *Theodore*.
Terence, Terry: L. Tender.
Thaddeus: Heb. Praise.
Thatcher: Teut. Roof-maker.

Tabitha: Heb. Gazelle.
Tallulah: American Indian (Cherokee). Name of a river, probably imitative of a frog's call.
Tamar: Heb. Palm tree.
Teresa, Terese: variant of *Theresa*.

Thayer: Teut. Animal (German *Thier*).
Theobold: Teut. Strong for the people.
Theodore: Gr. Gift of God.
Theron: Gr. Animal.
Thomas: Heb. Twin.
Thorne: Teut. Thorn.
Thorpe: Teut. Village.
Thurston: Teut. Stone of *Thor.*
Timothy: Gr. One that honors the Lord.
Tobias: Heb. Goodness of God.
Tom, Tommy: short for *Thomas.*
Tracy: L. Leader.
Travers: L. Across.
Tremont: L. Three-hilled.
Trent: L. Thirty.
Trevor: Celt. Prudent.
Tristram: Celt. A blusterer. (Name later given to hunters; then—from French *triste,* sad—associated with sadness).
Tybal, Tybalt: forms of *Theobald.*

Thalia: Gr. Flourishing.
Thecla: Gr. Glory of God.
Thelma: Gr. Nurseling.
Theodora, Theodosia: Gr. Gift of God.
Theresa, Therese: Gr. Bearing the harvest.
Thomasena, Thomasina, Thomasine: Heb. Little twin.
Thora: Teut. Devoted to *Thor,* god of battle and thunder.
Thyra: Teut. Devoted to *Tyr,* son of *Thor,* god of victory.
Tilda, Tildy, Tillie: variants of *Matilda.*
Tina: L. Little one.
Tracy: short for *Theresa.*
Trilby: Teut. Near the well.
Trixine, Trixy: short for *Beatrix.*
Truda, Trudy: short for *Gertrude.*

U

Udolph: Teut. Fortunate noble.
Ulric, Ulrich: Teut. Noble lord.
Ulysses: Gr. Wrathful.
Uriah: Heb. Light of God.

Uda: Teut. Rich.
Ulrica: Teut. Noble lady.
Una: L. Unique; one.
Undine: L. Little one of the waves.
Ursula: L. Little bear.

V

Valentine: L. Little strong one.
Valery: L. Potent ruler.
Vaughan, Vaughn: Celt. Small.
Vern, Vernon: Celt. Green country.
Victor: L. Conqueror.
Vincent: L. Conquering.
Virgil: L. Flourishing.
Vladimir: Slavic. Glory of princes.

Valance: L. Powerful.
Valerie: L. Healthy.
Vanessa: Gr. Butterfly.
Vashni: Heb. Strong.
Vashti: Persian. Star.
Vanya: Russian variant of *Yvonne* (*Ivan*).
Venus: L. Goddess of love.
Vera: L. Truth.
Verna, Verne: L. Springlike.
Verona, Veronica: L. Image of truth (perhaps a variant of *Berenice*).
Victoire, Victoria, Victorine: L. Conqueror.
Vida: L. Empty.
Villetta: L. Of the village.
Viola, Violet: L. The flower (sign of modesty).
Virginia: L. Chaste.
Vita: L. Life.
Vivian, Vivienne: L. Lively.
Volante: L. Flying.

W

WALCOTT: Teut. Stone cottage.
WALDEMAR: Teut. Famed power.
WALDEN: Teut. Powerful.
WALDO: short for *Waldemar.*
WALLACE: Celt. Stranger.
WALT, WALTER: Teut. Leader of the army (*Wealdhere; see Harold*).
WARD: Teut. Guardian.
WARING: Teut. Watchful.
WARNER: Teut. Protector.
WARREN: Teut. Park.
WARRICK: Teut. Fighting king.
WASHINGTON: Teut. Town by the sea. The *Wash* is a bay on the east coast of England. *Washed* by the waves; hence, *awash*. (usually, after George Washington.)
WAYNE: Teut. Waggon.
WEBSTER: Teut. Weaver.
WENDELL: Teut. Wanderer.
WESLEY, WESTLEY: Teut. Western meadow.
WHITNEY: Teut. White island.
WILBUR: Teut. Wild boar.
WILFRED: Teut. Lover of peace.
WILLARD: Teut. Of strong will.
WILLIAM: Teut. Protector.
WILLIS: Teut. Shield.
WILLOUGHBY: Teut. Near the willows (name of English explorer, died 1551).
WILMAR, WILMER: Teut. famed resolve.
WINSTON: Teut. Friendly town.
WINTHROP: Teut. Friendly village.
WOLVERTON: Teut. Town of good peace.
WOODROW, WOODRUFF: Teut. Forester.
WRIGHT: Teut. Worker.
WYNDHAM: Teut. Windy village.
WYNNE: Teut. Gain.
WALTA: Teut. feminine of *Walt.*
WANDA: Teut. Shepherdess.
WEDA: variant of *Ouida.*
WENDA, WENDLA: Teut. Wanderer.
WILHELMINA: Teut. Little guard of the host.
WINIFRED: Teut. Peacemaker.

X

XAVIER: Arabic. Glorious.
XERXES: Persian. Lion king.
XENIA: Gr. Hospitality.

Y

YARDLEY: Teut. Meadow yard.
YVAIN, YWAIN: Celt. Young warrior.
YARMILLA, YARMILLE: Teut. Boisterous.
YOLANDA, YOLANDE: Teut. Fairest.
YSEULTE, YSOLDE, YSOLT: variants of *Iseult.*
YVETTE: Teut. Little vine.
YVONNE: Celt. feminine variation of *John.*

Z

Zachary: Heb. The Lord hath remembered.
Zebediah: Heb. The Lord hath given.
Zeno, Zenos: Gr. Gift of *Zeus*.
Zadah, Zaidee: Arabic. Prospering.
Zaneta: Heb. Grace of God.
Zara, Zarah: Arabic. Sunrise.
Zenobia: Arabic. Her father's pride.
Zoe: Gr. Life.
Zora, Zorina: Slavic. Dawn.
Zuleika: Arabic. Brilliant and fair.